A TEXTBOOK OF
APPLIED ENTOMOLOGY

VOLUME-I

A TEXTBOOK OF APPLIED ENTOMOLOGY

VOLUME–I
CONCEPTS IN PEST MANAGEMENT

(LATE) K.P. SRIVASTAVA
Former Professor and Head
Department of Zoology
Banaras Hindu University,
Varanasi, India

(LATE) G.S. DHALIWAL
Former Professor of Ecology
Department of Entomology
Punjab Agricultural University,
Ludhiana, India

GURSHARAN SINGH
Former Professor of Entomology
&
Dean of Postgraduate Studies
Punjab Agricultural University, Ludhiana, India

KALYANI PUBLISHERS
LUDHIANA - NEW DELHI - NOIDA (U.P.) - HYDERABAD
CHENNAI - KOLKATA - CUTTACK - GUWAHATI - KOCHI - BENGALURU

KALYANI PUBLISHERS

Head Office

B-1/1292, Rajinder Nagar, **Ludhiana**-141 008 • Ph : 0161-2760031, 2745756
E-mail : kalyanibooks@yahoo.co.in **Website :** www.kalyanipublishers.co.in

Administration Office

4779/23, Ansari Road, Daryaganj, **New Delhi**-110 002 • Ph : 011-23271469, 23274393
E-mail : kalyani_delhi@yahoo.co.in, kalyani_delhi@kalyanipublishers.in

Works

B-16, Sector-8, **NOIDA** (U.P.)

Branches

1, Mahalakshmi Street, T. Nagar, **Chennai**-600 017 • Ph : 044-24344684
Gopabandhu Lane, Behind Govt. Bus Stand, Badambadi, **Cuttack**-753 012 (Odisha) • Ph : 0671-2311391
4-3-65/2/A, Behind HVS Public School, Raghunath Bagh
Sultan Bazar, **Hyderabad**-500 095 • Ph : 040-24750368
10/2B, Ramanath Mazumdar Street, **Kolkata**-700 009 • Ph : 033-22416024
Arunalaya, 1st Floor, Saraswati Road, Pan Bazar, **Guwahati**-781 001 • Ph : 0361-2731274
Koratti Parambil House, Convent Road, **Kochi**-682 035 • Ph : 0484-2367189
No. 24 & 25, 1st Floor, Hameed Shah Complex, Cubbonpet Main Road, **Bengaluru**-560 002

16 + 420 = 436 Pages 20" x 30" 54.5 Formes

KPP Q 32316 1

S-37892 1

Reprinted, 2023

Datalink Computer
(A-ENT-20)

ISBN 978-81-272-6164-1

PRINTED IN INDIA
At Process World India, C-90, Sec-63, NOIDA

PREFACE

FOURTH EDITION

Publication of "*A Textbook of Applied Entomology*" in two volumes authored by Prof. K.P. Srivastava filled a gap in the discipline of applied Entomology by providing a sort of ready reckoner for the students and teachers. The first volume appeared in 1988 and the second one in 1993. Both the volumes were revised in 1996 to update the information on various emerging areas. Another revision of the book followed in the year 2010 by Dr G.S. Dhaliwal who introduced several new chapters in the Volume-I for the benefit of the readers which was well received. The simple, lucid and easy-to-understand language used in these volumes found a great favour among the users. The well-meaning illustrations and documentation of relevant data in the tables helped the students to comprehend the subject in an objective way. The book had dominated the scene of Entomology in India for over two decades. While the Volume-1 dealt with general concepts in pest management; the Volume –II was focused on recommendations for the field control of insect pests of different crops employing various techniques of pest management. The first volume, in hand, was compiled in fifteen chapters dealing with principles of pest management, physical, mechanical, cultural, legal, biological and chemical control of insects pests. Novel approaches of insects control were discussed in the chapters on biorational pesticides apart from separate chapters on biotechnological approaches and genetic control.

Though the basic concepts of applied entomology remains unchanged, but the scientific developments in the area of novel and innovative approaches of insect pest management demanded an updation through revision of the Volume, of course after a period of about ten years. Though, Dr G. S. Dhaliwal was keen to revise this volume of the book but due to his untimely death the task could not be undertaken. Dr K P Srivastava had already expired in the year 2002. When the publisher contacted me to do this job, I could not think of a better opportunity to contribute to the entomological knowledge relating to management of insect pests.

Maintaining basic format of the book as per Prof. Srivastava's and Prof. Dhaliwal's vision, several chapters in the volume have been revised/updated, and recent information included wherever available. Latest information in the area of Insect Growth Regulators has been incorporated in the relevant chapter highlighting status of these compounds in the Indian and global context. The rarely dealt topic relating to behavioural response of insects to the applied insecticides has been added in the chapter dealing with the behaviour modifying chemicals. The chapter on genetic control has been strengthened by incorporating latest knowledge relating to control of Mexican fruit fly by employing Sterile Insect Technique. Old information concerning pesticides for the control of insect pests has been substituted with the latest one available from the Directorate of Plant Protection, Quarantine and Storage, Government of India. Table depicting the latest status of transgenic crops in India and abroad, providing resistance to various pests, has been added in the relevant chapter.

I express my gratitude to families of Prof. Srivastava and Prof. Dhaliwal for imposing confidence in me to undertake the revision of the book. I am also grateful to Mr Raj Kumar, Kalyani Publishers, for his keen interest and enthusiasm to bring out the revised version of the book at the earliest possible. My thanks are due to Col. V.M. Joneja, Datalink Computer, Jalandhar, for his painstaking efforts to typeset the matter and the illustrations. It is hoped that the revised book would provide updated information to all the stakeholders including students and teachers working in the area of applied entomology.

2021

Gursharan Singh

PREFACE

THIRD EDITION

Prof. K.P. Srivastava's *A Textbook of Applied Entomology* was published in two volmes; the first volume appeared in 1988 and the second one in 1993. Both the volumes were revised in 1996 to update the information on various emerging areas. These volumes found a great favour among students and teachers in view of the thorough coverage of the subject matter in concise manner, use of easy-to-understand language and well-meaning illustrations. The book had dominated the scene of Entomology in India for over a decade. However, the book needed another revision in view of the change in pest, pesticide and pest management scenario at the national and global level. Prof. Srivastava was very keen to revise the book, but he expired on October 10, 2002 after a brief illness and hence, the task could not be undertaken. When Prof. Srivastava's family and the publisher contacted me to do this job. I could not think of a better opportunity to pay my humble tribute to this great teacher, scientist and above all, a human being.

While maintaining the basic format of the book as per Prof. Srivastava's vision, all the chapters in both the volumes have been thoroughly revised, and recent information included wherever available. In volume I, the chapter on Applied Control : General Methods has been expanded and developed into three independent chapters, viz. Physical, Mechanical and Legal Control; Cultural Control and Host Plant Resistance. In adition, two new chapters, viz. Biotechnological Approaches, and Integrated Pest Management : Progress and Perspectives, have been included. In volume II also, two new chapters, viz. Pests of Spices, and Insects in Relation to Plant Diseases, have been added. In addition, all the scientific names of the insects and their placement have been checked and the changes incorporated wherever required.

Some of the topics which do not form a part of the approved syllabus have been excluded. The descriptions of several new pests have been included, the banned and withdrawn pesticides have been taken out and the latest recommendations for management of pests have been added. Many of the illustrations have been redrawn, a few excluded and some new ones have been added. The information on current status of apiculture, sericulture and lac culture in India, has also been incorporated. The bibliography has been given a new outlook by including leading publications that had appeared in the last decade.

I express may gratitude to Prof. Srivastava's family, viz. Mrs Surya Lata Srivastava (wife) and Mrs Shobhana Srivastava (daughter), for imposing confidence in me to undertake the revision of the book. I am also grateful to Mr Raj Kumar, Kalyani Publishers, for his keen interest and enthusiasm to bring out the revised version of the book. I am also thankful to Col. V.M. Joneja, Datalink Computer, Jalandhar, for his painstaking efforts to typeset the matter and the illustrations. My sincere thanks are also due to Dr Vikas Jindal, Assitance Entomologist and Ms Bharathi Mohindru, Assitant Professor of Plant Protection, Punjab Agricultural University, Ludhiana for their consistent help throughout the revision of the book. I hope the book would meet the requirements of the students and teachers in applied entomology, and their valuable suggestions would be most appreciated.

G.S. Dhaliwal

PREFACE

FIRST EDITION

Insect pest control techniques have changed a great deal since the first inorganic insecticide was scientifically employed in 1867 or the first synthetic organic insecticide, DDT was discovered in 1939. The strategy now is to replace insecticidal by the non-insecticidal techniques which have come up in large numbers over the years. Nevertheless, in our and other developing countries, insecticides still dominate the scene of insect pest control with disastrous effects on our environment. There could be many reasons for this state of affairs, but one that stands out clear in my mind, is the outdated syllabi on Applied Entomology preserved by our universities, where the agricultural scientists, who ultimately man the pest control programmes of the country, are being turned out. It is, therefore, time that our unversities reorient thier syllabi to include the recent advances in insect pest control methods and strategies. The present book can come handy to help bring about this change.

While giving a course in Applied Entomology to the postgraduate students of my Department, I encountered three difficulties : firstly, no book indigenous or foreign, gave all the topics on the subject in a single volume, secondtly, most books available on the subject, have devoted bulk of their space to insect taxonomy and anatomy, applied aspect inadvertently, getting an inadequate treatment, and thirdly, the currently available books written for Indian students, have either completely ignored the modern methods of insect pest control or have dealt them in a sketchy manner. This book attempts to overcome these shortcomings and thus, lightens the work of the teachers and students, who seek to obtain an up-to-date and concise material in a single volume. This, in my opinion, is one important plus point of this book. Other qualities, I leave to the discerning readers to discover for themselves.

I take this opportunity to thank my colleague Professor M.S. Kanungo, FNA, for his help in the preparation of Chapter 10 of this book and Prof. Lallan Rai of the Institute of Agricultural Sciences, Benaras Hindu University, for many useful suggestions. I have special thanks to offer to my several research scholars for their help in many ways. Grateful acknowledgement are also made to several authors and publishers who have graciously, lent their illustrations for this book. Their names have been mentioned at appropriate places. My acknowledgements will remain incomplete if I do not mention Mr. Raj Kumar of the Kalyani Publishers, whose interest and enthusiasm in putting the work into print has been admirable. However, the ultimate responsibility for any slip or error will remain mine and I shall greatly appreciate if the same are brought to my notice by my kind readers.

K.P. Srivastava

CONTENTS

PART–I

INTRODUCTION

- Insects, Pests and Pest Management

INSECTS, PESTS AND PEST MANAGEMENT

INTRODUCTION

Insects are one of the most versatile and fascinating groups among all the animals. They have dominated the earth and excel all other animals in both diversity and magnitude. There are atleast three times as many species of insects as of all other animals combined. They are the most ubiquitous of all animals and are virtually found wherever life can exist. There are insects living in the Himalayas, at freezing temperatures in the inhospitable wastes of Antarctica, on the burning dunes of deserts, in hot water (60°C) springs and burrowed far underground. A few species occur in salt water, and quite a number of them occur in fresh water, but insects are essentially a terrestrial group. In size, they vary from microscopic beetles which can easily pass through the eye of a needle, to large moths, with wing span of more than 32 cm.

Insects have also found many successful ways of surviving than the other organisms that share the planet with them. Some caterpillars have large imitation eyes on their sides that hoodwink would-be predators. Other insects assume the appearance of sticks or leaves or bird droppings as camouflage. First termites, and later, some wasps and bees and all the ants came to live in family groups, most individuals losing their reproductive capacity to the advantage of the colony as a whole. Some insects are capable to laying eggs even before sexual maturity and due to their very short life span, the offsprings are produced more frequently. In time, insects became skilled architects, paper-makers, spinners of webs, agriculturists, potters, herders and even undertakers. They learned to enslave other insects, to make war and to manage nurseries. Thus, nature has provided wonderful attributes to the insects and they have received wide attention from scientists, naturalists, nutritionists, forensic experts, aesthetes and the farmers.

Despite their remarkable diversity of form and habits, insects posses several common features by which, the group as a whole can be distinguished. The insects are tracheate arthropods in which the body is typically divided into three parts, namely head, thorax and abdomen; they usually posses two pairs of wings and three pairs of legs. With few exceptions, the eggs are laid and the young form may be quite different from the adult, most insects undergo some degree of metamorphosis.

ORIGIN OF INSECTS

According to various estimates, the insects came into existence 350-500 million years ago. The earliest known fossil insect is *Rhyniella praecursor*, a collembolan from the Devonian period of Scotland. The available evidence indicates that it might have fed on plant juice obtained through punctured wounds. By the end of Carboniferous period, all the modern groups of insects, including Ephemeroptera, Orthoptera, ancestral Hemiptera and Mecoptera were well-developed. In the Peruvian period, 19 orders of insects were in existence. The Endopterygota (Neuroptera, Mecoptera, Trichoptera and Coleoptera) were well-developed by then. By the early Jurassic period, with the addition of Dermaptera, Phasmida and Thysanoptera and the loss of extinct orders, the fauna was essentially a modern one, with the presence of existing families of several orders, such as Odonata, Orthoptera, Diptera and Hymenoptera. The most prominent groups that emerged during the Mesozoic were the Hymenoptera, Cecidomyiidae (Diptera) and Lepidoptera.

The evolution of land plants seems to have been closely followed by the evolution of insects. The first land plants evolved in the Devonian, and the first undoubtedly phytophagous insects are known from the Carboniferous. The first record of winged insects almost coincided with the record of tall forest trees in the upper Carboniferous period. Thereafter, modern orders of phytophagous insects appeared steadily throughout the fossil record. The last to appear were the Lepidoptera, coincident with the rise of angiosperms in the Cretaceous. Several other important groups evolved after the appearance of the angiosperms and a number of primitive insects became instinct.

The abundance of angiosperms, with their diversified plant surface characteristics, architecture and chemical factors, provided the three factors, needed for insect proliferation, *i.e.* food, shelter and oviposition sites. These factors offered an ideal habitat for insects, which consequently diversified themselves in the ecosystem. Reciprocal adaptation and counter adaptation between plants and insect phytophages has been an important mechanism, driving

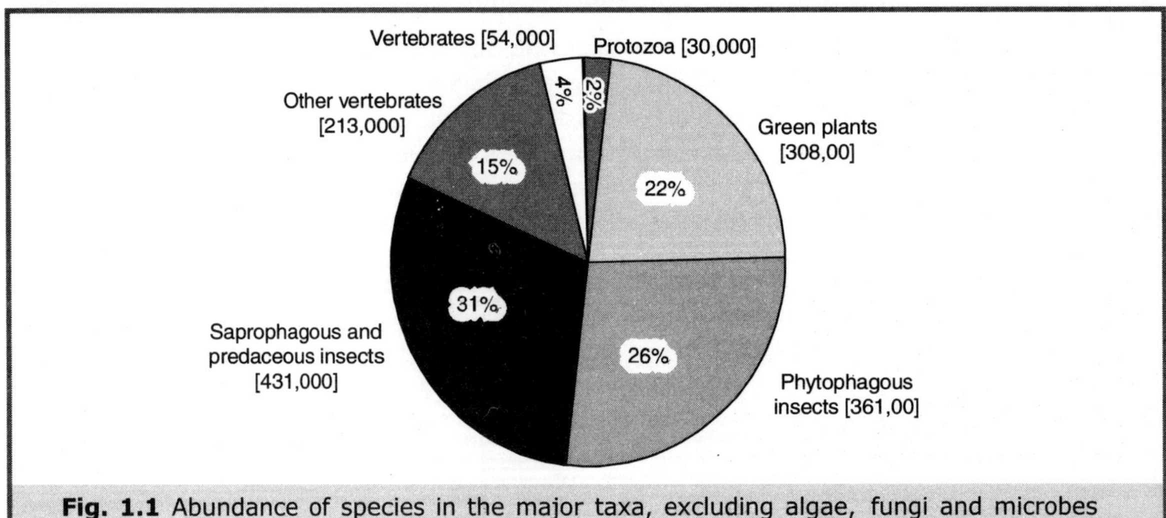

Fig. 1.1 Abundance of species in the major taxa, excluding algae, fungi and microbes (After Strong *et al.*, 1984).

a steady increase in plant and insect diversity over a broad sweep of fossil record. Presently, for every species of green plant, there is roughly a species of phytophagous insect (Fig. 1.1). Most insect orders are not phytophagous (20 of 29), but over half of insect species are phytophagous.

DOMINANCE OF INSECTS

Today, the insects constitute the largest class not only of the animal kingdom, but also of the whole living world of all the 1.7 million species described, approximately 45,000 are vertebrates, 2,50,000 are plants and 9,50,000 (56%) are insects. According to recent estimates, the total number of insect species is considerably larger than was previously thought and may range from 4 to 10 million. Of the estimated number of species in the world, about 64 per cent are thought to be insects (Fig. 1.2). Over a period of several hundred million years, insects as a class, have acquired many distinctive structural, developmental, physiological and behavioural perfections, which have enabled them to occupy this dominant position.

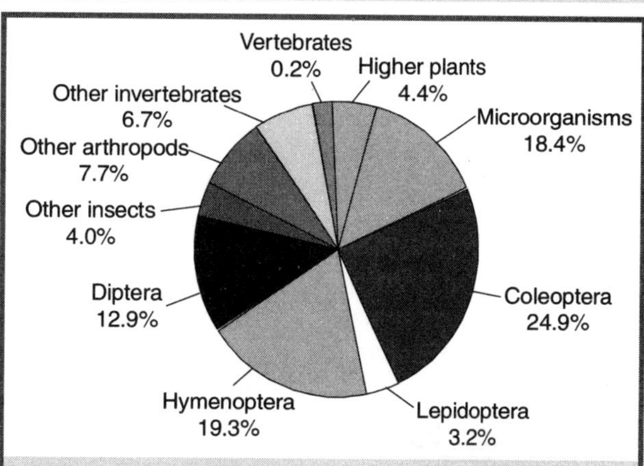

Fig. 1.2 Estimated proportions of species of insects and other groups of organisms of the global total (After Groombridge, 1992)

Exoskeleton

The hard, chitinous exoskeleton provides area for muscle attachment, protects muscles and internal organs from mechanical injury and prevents desiccation of the body. The exoskeleton has also turned the appendages into good tools for digging, preying, oviposition, etc. In addition, it provides protective colouration with the help of which insects can camouflage or create fear in their enemies by warning colouration. Lastly, the exoskeleton maintains the shape of the body much more efficiently than the endoskeleton.

Small Size

During the evolutionary course, the insects have developed a large number of smaller individuals than a smaller number of larger individuals. This step immensely increases the chances of survival of the species. Smaller individuals are able to survive on small quantity of food and can take refuge in small niches against the exigencies of climate as well as biotic stress factors. For example, more insects can be accommodated in a limited space, so that the competition or struggle for existence is less marked. Moreover, larger number of individuals increase the chances of variability and mutation. The muscular strength of insects is phenomenal due to their smaller size. A flea with a body length of about 12 mm can jump a horizontal length of more than 30 cm and a height up to 20 cm. An ant can carry a grain much heavier than its own body.

Quicker Speciation

The possession of chitinous exoskeleton and the aerial mode of life have probably been the largest contributors to so much speciation in insects. Due to mechanical rigidity of the exoskeleton, even minute variations in the external genitalia lead to reproductive isolation and consequent fixation of the species. The acquisition of wings has helped insects to lead life under much diverse ecological habitats which has provided the trigger for variations. The vast increase in the number of species has immensely increased the economic potentialities of the insects as a class.

Hexapod Locomotion

Insects share the jointed nature of legs with other arthropods but the number of such legs has reached an ideal stage of evolution in insects. During locomotion, the insect body rests on a tripod, while the other three legs move forward. The tripod mode provides stability as well as easy manoeuvrability to insect locomotion.

Differentiation of Body

Differentiation of body into head, rigid thorax and legless abdomen is a particularly favourable arrangement for terrestrial arthropods. The mobility of the head (in contrast to Arachnida) may have facilitated the development of various types of mouth parts (and hence varied feeding habits) and also better orientation during flight and landing. The consolidation of thorax offers rigid attachment for the legs and yet flexible base for the insertion of wings. Functions of digestion, excretion and reproduction have been regulated to usually distensible and flexible abdomen.

Functional Wings

The power of flight greatly increases the chances of survival and dispersal of insects. Functional wings increase the feeding and breeding range, and provide a new means of eluding natural enemies. Sturdy wings of locusts and some butterflies enable them to undertake intercontinental migration. The structural perfection of these wings can be gauged from the fact that a hive bee can fly at 9 km per h, a hoverfly at

12 km, a hawk moth 17 km and a butterfly up to 90 km.

Tracheal Respiration

Tracheal system supplies oxygen directly to each and every cell of the body. It has been made possible by invagination of a relatively enormous surface area permeable to both oxygen and water. In this system, water loss, so critical to small terrestrial animals, can be greatly reduced because contact with the external environment is only via the spiracles.

Developmental Characteristics

The full life history of the holometabolous insects consists of four well-defined stages : the egg, the larva, the pupa and the adult. Two of these stages, mainly feeding larval stage and reproductive adult stage, are so different from each other not only in structural details but also in requirements of food and habitat that competition between the parent and the offspring for food or shelter is eliminated. Further, by the interpolation between the larval and adult stages of a quiescent stage of pupa with great resistance and practically no food requirement, the two active stages are best fitted into different seasons optimum for them. Complete metamorphosis has enabled insects to combine the advantages of two different ways of life and at the same time avoid many of the disadvantages of both. The voracious feeding and digesting ability of larvae have enabled insects to be prolific reproducers.

Reproduction

Insects are prolific breeders. On an average, they produce 100-150 eggs per female, but there are some, like the honey bee which produces 2000-3000 eggs per day and the queen termite, which lays 60 eggs per second. A single pair of house flies is capable of producing 191, 010, 000, 000, 000, 000, 000 individuals during a period of just five months. The progeny of a single cabbage aphid would weigh 822 million tons after 10 generations. If all her descendents survive,, in one year a chain of these aphids would be long enough to encircle the earth. However, survival rate of insects is very low (2 per 20,000 larvae in case of house fly) in nature due to large number of natural enemies and vagaries of weather. Nevertheless, insects produce a large number of progeny by adopting all methods of reproduction nature has invented, *i.e.* parthenogenesis, polyembryony, paedogenesis, hermaphroditism and viviparity, by producing several broods a year, and having short-life cycles so as to be able to reproduce quickly. Reproduction not only enables insects to survive their numerous natural enemies, but also to compete successfully, with animals more advanced than themselves (including man) for the resources available on the earth.

Chemical Communication

Small size of insects limits their ability to locate food, sexual partner and avoid danger through visual and tactile stimuli. But a dazzling variety of insect behaviour is elicited in response to minute amounts of chemicals emanating from their conspecifics, other animals, plants and even dead organic matter. Pheromones are utilized by insects for sexual attraction, alarm, aggregation, caste determination and a variety of other functions. On the other hand, allelochemicals provide information regarding host plants, prey, natural enemies, suitability of a habitat for food and oviposition, etc. The sensitivity of insects to communication chemicals can be judged from the fact that their antennal receptors have been shown to respond to even a single molecule of the sex pheromone.

Physiological Adaptations

Terrestrial insects face an acute shortage of water, and excretion in the form of ammonia and urea requires enormous quantity of water for elimination from the body. These insects have developed the ability to excrete in the form of uric acid which is insoluble in water and eliminated in the solid form. This mode of excretion helps to conserve water in terrestrial insects. Diapause is another enormously valuable adaptation to fluctuating environmental conditions. Physiological changes occurring prior to onset of diapause are useful for tiding over unfavourable climatic conditions. Inspite of the presence of a large number of repellents, antifeedants, toxicants, development disruptors and metabolic inhibitors in plants, insects are able to survive and multiply on these plants. This is due to different escape and detoxification mechanisms developed by insects. Surprisingly, even plants (*Chrysanthemum, Derris, Nicotiana, Azadirachta, Melia,* etc.) containing highly toxic chemicals are utilized as host plants by various insect species. Insects even utilize some of the toxic secondary plant substances as cues for identification of their host plants. The versatile behavioural and metabolic pathways of insects have helped them in survival, multiplication and speciation.

Parental Care

Parental care is an indication of higher evolution. In no other invertebrate, this trait is as greatly developed as in insects particularly, in social insects—ants, bees, wasps and termites—

which take good care of their brood. In some insects (Hydrophilid beetles), the females carry their eggs on their backs until they hatch and in some others (giant water bug, *Belostoma*), the males do this job. Female sand-wasp, *Ammophila* paralyses caterpillars by its sting to oviposit on its body, so that the larvae on hatching get a ready food. Dermapterans guard their eggs until they hatch, and cockroaches carry them in the protective oothecae. Some parasitic insects attach their eggs to the body of the host itself, *e.g.* water boatman, *Ramphocorixa* does this to crayfish. European beetle, *Clythra* deposits its eggs on foliage and covers them with their excrement, so that they appear as small bracts or buds. Ants mistaking them for bits of vegetable refuge pick them up and carry them to their nests where the larvae hatch and live as guests (inquilines). Botfly, *Dermatobia hominis*, visits marshy places, where mosquitoes are emerging from their pupae. It seizes an emerging mosquito, quickly deposits 10-12 eggs on the abdomen and legs, and releases its hold. Mosquitoes carry the eggs to man, whose body warmth hatches them and the young maggots dig into the flesh of the victim (their host). Parasitic hymenopterans have adopted a unique method called phoresy, whereby they attach themselves to the body of their host to reach its nest to oviposit their own eggs on the newly laid eggs of the host itself. Obviously, all these devices are various ways of parental care which ensure survival of the progeny.

BIODIVERSITY OF INSECTS

The insects are considered to be the most diverse group among all the animals on this planet. With the numerical advantage gained during evolution spanning 250-500 million years, insects have adapted themselves to various ecological niches and are, therefore, found everywhere. They also perform a disproportionate number of functional roles, viz. herbivory, predation, parasitism, decomposition, pollination, etc. The insects have developed varied type of associations with plants; some insects are flower pollinators and others are herbivorous. The association between flowering plants and their pollinators is probably the most spectacular and classical example of mutualism in the living world. Approximately, two-thirds of all flowering plants are pollinated by insects and in return, plants provide food in the form of nectar and pollen to insects.

All the species of insects (Class Insecta) have been classified into 29 orders under two sub-classes, viz. Ametabola and Metabola (Table 1.1).

Table 1.1 An outline of classification of insects

	Subclass and Order	Examples	Economic importance
	Subclass I. Ametabola (Apterygota) Adults wingless (primitive condition), no metamorphosis, moulting even in adults.		
	Orders		
1.	Thysanura	Three-pronged bristle tails, silverfish	Pests in the kitchen, damage books, paper, starched clothes
2.	Diplura	Two-pronged bristle tails	Few only briefly attack
3.	Protura	Proturans	germinating seeds and few
4.	Collembola	Spring tails	feed on leaves of lucerne and clovers in particular

	Subclass and Order	Examples	Economic importance
	Subclass II. Metabola (Pterygota) Adults usually winged (may be secondarily wingless), metamorphosis occurs, do not moult as adults except mayflies). **Division A : Hemimetabola (Exopterygota)** Metamorphosis incomplete, no true pupal stage, wings develop externally in nymphal stages.		
	Orders		
5.	Ephemeroptera	Mayflies	—
6.	Odonata	Dragonflies	—
7.	Plecoptera	Stoneflies	—
8.	Grylloblattodea	Mole crickets	—
9.	Orthoptera	Crickets, grasshoppers, locusts	Major pests of plants
10.	Phasmida	Stick insects, leaf insects	Minor pests of plants
11.	Dermaptera	Earwigs	—
12.	Embioptera	Web-spinners	Pests of edibles (cockroaches),
13.	Dictyoptera	Cockroaches, mantids	predators (mantids)
14.	Isoptera	Termites	Pests of timber, roots
15.	Zoraptera	Zorapterans	—
16.	Psocoptera	Psocids, booklice	—
17.	Mallophaga	Biting lice, bird lice	Parasites of vertebrates (birds in particular)
18.	Siphuculata	Sucking lice	Parasites of some vertebrates
19.	Hemiptera	Plant bugs, leafhoppers, scale insects, aphids, cicadas	Major pests of plants
20.	Thysanoptera	Thrips	Minor pests of plants
	Division B :Holometabola (Endopterygota) Metamorphosis complete, pupal stage present, wings develop internally in pupal stage.		
	Orders		
21.	Neuroptera	Lacewings, antlions	Minor pests of plants
22.	Coleoptera	Beetles	Major pests of plants
23.	Strepsiptera	Stylopids	—
24.	Mecoptera	Scorpion flies	—
25.	Siphonaptera	Fleas	Parasites of some vertebrates
26.	Diptera	Flies	Major parasites of man and animals, minor pests of plants
27.	Lepidoptera	Butterflies, moths	Major pests of plants
28.	Trichoptera	Caddis flies	—
29.	Hymenoptera	Ants, bees, wasps, sawflies	Largely beneficial insects (pollinators, honey givers, entomogenous), some minor pests of plants (sawflies).

The most diverse order of insects based on the actually described species is the Coleoptera (3,49,000 species) followed by Lepidoptera (1,19,000), Diptera (1,10,000) and Hymenoptera (95,000) (Table 1.2). However, taking the total of undescribed and described species into consideration, the number of Lepidoptera fall much below Hymenoptera and Diptera. Nearly half of all existing insect species feed on living plants. The prominent among the herbivores are the Lepidoptera, Hemiptera, Orthoptera and some small orders such as Thysanoptera and Phasmida. A substantial proportion of the herbivorous insects belongs to Coleoptera, Hymenoptera and Diptera, all three of which also include numerous species with predatory and parasitic habits (Schoonhoven *et al.*, 2006).

Table 1.2 Number of herbivorous species in various insect orders

S.No.	Insect Order	Total number of species	Herbiborous species Number	%
1.	Coleoptera	3,49,000	1,22,000	35.0
2.	Lepidoptera	1,19,000	1,19,000	100.0
3.	Diptera	1,10,000	35,700	32.5
4.	Hymenoptera	95,000	10,500	11.1
5.	Hemiptera	59,000	53,000	89.8
6.	Orthoptera	20,000	19,900	99.5
7.	Thysanoptera	5,000	4,500	90.0
8.	Phasmida	2,000	2,000	100.0

Source : Schoonhoven *et al.* (2006)

Insect biodiversity in India is restricted to about 52,000 species. These constitute about 6 per cent of the world insect fauna. About 155.5 insect species are found for every million hectare of land in India, while these estimates vary with countries, viz. 9.5 in USA, 91.4 in UK and 97.2 in South Africa. There are about 2.83 insect species for every flowering plant species in India. This ratio is low when compared with other countries, viz. 4.45 in USA, 14.9 in UK and 10.9 in South Africa. The low insect to plant ratio in India is largely due to comparatively higher plant biodiversity in the country. Insects of agricultural importance are

Table 1.3 Biodiversity of insects of agricultural importance in India

S.No.	Insect order	Total number of species	Endemic species	Extent of edemism (%)
1.	Coleoptera	15,289	5,198	34
2.	Diptera	6,093	2,135	35
3.	Hemiptera	5,216	2,421	46
4.	Hymenoptera	4,264	2,920	68
5.	Isoptera	310	145	47
6.	Lepidoptera	15,000	1,500	10
7.	Mantoidea	4,264	2,920	68
8.	Neuroptera	315	256	81
9.	Odonata	494	115	23
10.	Orthoptera	900	330	37

Source : Dhaliwal *et al.* (2007)

found in high endemism in India (Table 1.3). Except for Lepidoptera, the endemism of insects in various orders in India is very high. Even in Lepidoptera, where endemism is only 10 per cent, the economic importance of lepidopterans in terms of their damage to crops and role in pollination is very high (Dhaliwal *et al.*, 2007).

ORIGIN OF PESTS

A pest is any organism whose population increases to the extent that it starts causing annoyance, inconvenience or injury to man, his animals, plants and material possessions. A pest may be an insect, mite, nematode, bird, rodent, fungus, bacterium, virus, weed or any other organism.

The general evolutionary processes of nature provide situations for an organism to assume the status of a pest. It may not be possible for man to direct the evolutionary processes, but the ecological events can be modified to his advantage. About 10,000 years ago, before man started living in communities and began to organize agriculture, the vegetation on earth and the animals it supported, presumably, lived more or less in a natural balance. The supposition may be supported by the fact that the perennial forests today, untouched by man's influence, exhibit a balanced ecosystem. It can be said that the plants and the animals in a stable ecosystem live and die fitting in the energy cycle like cogs of a wheel and no one species increases in numbers out of proportion to cause a threat to the others.

However, to provide more food to the increasing population, man had to cut down forests and clear the savannas to bring more land under cultivation. In this process, he might have disturbed the balance of nature with the result that original fauna receded to whatever natural vegetation was left. On cultivated lands, a faunal vacuum was created, as new niches were formed in the newly established agroecosystems. Perhaps, the herbivora that survived were those which could do well on the crops grown or on the original vegetation that persisted.

Introduction of a New Pest

When an insect gets introduced into a new favourable habitat without its natural enemies, it gets established as a pest and becomes more abundant. The woolly aphid became a serious pest of apple in the Niligiris, as there was no natural enemy of the pest to exercise natural control over its multiplication. The cassava mealy bug, *Phenacoccus manihoti* was accidently introduced into Africa. The absence of natural enemies resulted in the spread of the mealy bug across Africa, where major outbreak and devastating losses caused food shortage. The other examples of introduced insects becoming pests are San Jose scale and cottony cushion scale of citrus into India, gypsy moth and European corn borer into North America, rice water weevil in Japan and Korea, and insect pests of *Eucalyptus* into New Zealand and South Africa.

Introduction of New Crops and Strains

Many pest problems are new-encounter situations, where the crop has been introduced into an area and pests that have not evolved with the crop, attack the introduced crop. For example, the rice delphacid, *Tagosodes orizicolus*, a native of South America, has become a severe pest after the introduction of rice into South and Central America. Mostly, improved strains of crop plants are susceptible to pests, whereas the local coarse varieties are resistant to pest attack. Sometimes, minor insects assume the status of major pests with the introduction of new varieties or strains of crops. The improved Cambodia cotton strains are highly susceptible to the spotted bollworm, *Earias* spp. and the stem weevil, *Pempherulus affinis* than the *desi* cotton strains. Similarly, cotton jassid was not so serious problem on the indigenous cotton, *Gossypium arboreum* in India. However, with the introduction of American cotton,

G. hirsutum in the beginning of the century, this insect became a dominant pest of cotton. The hybrid sorghum (CSH1) and cumbu (HB1), introduced for large scale cultivation, were severely attacked by stem fly, stem borer and gall midge than the local varieties. The growing of cabbage crop in the plains of Madurai district of Tamil Nadu as a new venture resulted in the windespread incidence of the green semilooper, *Trichoplusia ni*. Similarly, introduction of sunflower in Punjab for large scale cultivation resulted in increase in the incidence of *Helicoverpa armigera*.

Change in Habitat

The change in the habitat of the species or in the activities of man may increase the severity of several insect pests. For example, increased urbanization in India has provided conditions conducive to breeding of *Culex quinquefasciatus*, and filariasis has thereby spread to new areas. The destruction of forest over wide areas for cultivation affects several of the weather conditions, viz. temperature, diurnal variations, humidity, rainfall, wind velocity, etc., in that locality and thus, set conditions favourable for some insects to develop enormously and assume pest status. The insects feeding on trees and plants in the forest are driven to neighbouring areas where they may infest the cultivated crops and become new pests.

Crop Intensification

Intensification involves (*i*) an increase in the number of crops grown per year, (*ii*) planting of large, contiguous fields instead of small isolated fields, (*iii*) a change from polycropping to monocropping, (*iv*) an increase in the use of agricultural chemicals, and (*v*) planting of high yielding varieties responsive to fertilizers. There is ample evidence that cropping intensification has been responsible for changes in insect pest populations. Pest responses to environmental changes are dynamic and a change that is detrimental to one species may offer new opportunities to another, leading the changes in species composition and abundance. Cropping intensification may result in insect-resistant crop cultivars becoming susceptible to pests through the development of resistance-breaking biotypes or strains. Biotypes are known to develop among 40 insect pests, among which biotypes of gall midge and brown planthopper have posed serious problems in India. Pesticides are causing harm, especially in developing countires, where pest populations are becoming resistant and natural enemies are destroyed. Natural enemy destruction has led to the resurgence of pest populations and outbreaks of secondary pests. For example, pyrethroids kill parasitoids and predators and thus encourage certain pests like aphids, scales, mealy bugs, planthoppers and spider mites to multiply to enormous proportions.

CATEGORIES OF PESTS

The pest status of a species is determined by a number of criteria, viz. increase in the number of insects, change in the type of damage, more pronounced damage due to conducive climatic conditions, changes in the methods of cultivation or harvesting, and fluctuations in the market value of the crop. Insect infestations are sometimes referred to as epidemic or endemic. When the infestation occurs in a severe form in a region or locality at a particular season or time, it is known as ***epidemic***. If the infestation is a regular feature and confined mostly to a particular area or locality, it is referred to as ***endemic***. Two major classes of pest outbreaks have been identified, viz. eruptive and gradient. The ***eruptive outbreak*** spreads out from local epicentres to cover large areas. The eruptive outbreak is self-perpetuating, *i.e.* once initiated, positive feedback processes operating at high population densities maintain the outbreak. On the other hand, ***gradient outbreak*** does not spread from local epicentres to cover large areas. It is not self-driven and is entirely dependent on external environmental or internal genetic conditions. This type of outbreak arises and subsides, as its driving forces change in time and space. Insect pests are classified in several ways and the following terms are generally applied.

Regular pests. The insects which are closely associated with a crop and occur most frequently are called regular or key pests. The thrips on chillies and cardamom, aphid on cotton, fruit borer on brinjal, and shoot and capsule borer on castor are examples of regular pests.

Occasional pests. Occasional or sporadic pests are those, whose populations remain low and insignificant. They assume pest status occasionally in certain years due to favourable climatic conditions or depletion of natural enemies. Examples include locusts, grasshoppers, hairy caterpillars, crickets and cutworms.

Potential pests. These pests normally cause negligible damage, but may become highly destructive resulting from some disturbance in the environment and the consequent increase in their population, *e.g.* armyworm on wheat and tobacco caterpiller on cotton.

Major pests. Major pests are those which occur quite frequently on a crop in severe form and repeated control measures are necessary to avoid economic damage. Examples include brown planthopper and gall midge on rice, whitefly and scale insect on sugarcane, and American bollworm and whitefly on cotton.

Minor pests. The populations of these pests generally remain low and these do not cause any economic damage. These pests are easily amenable to available control measures. Examples include grey weevil, thrips and mites on cotton, hispa and root weevil on rice and mealy bugs, thrips and mites on sugarcane.

INSECT INJURIES IN PLANTS

Insect injury in plants is caused almost entirely by their feeding activity with the exception of a few insects like the cicadas, which injure plants through their egg laying behaviour. The nature of plant injury is, therefore, determined by the type of mouthparts the pests possess and their feeding behaviour (Table 1.4). Some of the insect pest species are host specific and they feed on plants of a single species and are termed as ***monophagous***. Many lepidopteran larvae, hemipterans and coleopterans fit into this category. Others attack plant species belonging to the same family and are known as ***oligophagous***. For example, cabbage butterfly (*Pieris brassicae*) and Colorado potato beetle (*Leptinotarsa decemlineata*), feed on a number of plant species, all belonging to the same plant family, Brassicaceae and Solanaceae, respectively. Others are capable of feeding on plant species belonging to several diverse families and are called ***polyphagous***. For example, green peach aphid (*Myzus persicae*), has been recorded to feed on members of more than 50 plant families. Insects inflict injury to plants either directly or indirectly in their attempts to secure food and almost all the portions, viz. roots, stem, bark, shoots, leaves, buds, flowers and fruits of plants are damaged.

Direct Effects of Feeding

Direct effects of feeding are a result of feeding by chewing insects, piercing and sucking insects, internal feeders, subterranean insects and stored product insects.

Table 1.4 Type of insect injuries caused in plants

S. No. Type of mouthports	Feeding behaviour	Types of injury	Pest groups
1. Biting and chewing	Remove portions from leaves, stems, flow-ers, fruits or roots.	1. Holes or notches in leaves and tissues or whole leaves consu-med.	Larvae of most Lepido-ptera, larvae of some Coleoptera and Ortho-ptera.
		2. Surface feeders producing windows.	Early instars of some Lepidoptera.
		3. Stems chewed at ground level.	Cutworms (Lepidoptera).
		4. Stems, shoots or branches bored.	Some Coleoptera and Lepidoptera larvae.
		5. Seeds consumed.	Some Lepidoptera larvae (*e.g.* pea moth).
		6. Fruits tunnelled inter-nally.	Some Lepidotera larvae (*e.g.*, codling moth, pomegranate butterfly).
		7. Roots damaged.	Some Coleoptera larvae, termites.
		8. Surface of tubers chewed or tunnelled.	Larvae of some Coleoptera and Lepido-ptera (*e.g.*, potato moth).
2. True pier-cing and sucking	Feed on plant sap, may damage conduc-ting vessels, inject toxic saliva into plants; excrete honey-dew.	Weakening of plant; stun-ting, distortion, necrosis, growth of sooty mould on honey-dew, may produce specks on leaf surface.	Hemiptera of all kinds. Thysanoptera (thrips) and mites. Larvae of Diptera.
3. Superficial piercing and sucking	Pierce cells only to remove contents; att-ack mostly foliage and flowers.	Minute white flecks on attacked parts which may get bleached or bronzed and die prematurely.	
4. Rasping	Shred plant tissues; ingest sap and macerate tissues; bore or tunnel into attacked parts.	Ragged wounds in roots or stems; mines in leaves, tunnels in tap roots or bulbs.	

Chewing insects. The insects possessing biting type of mouthparts chew off external plant parts, grind them up and swallow. They cause damage by various ways: (*i*) Feed on the leaves and defoliate the plants, *e.g.* castor semilooper, red hairy caterpillar and slug caterpillar. (*ii*) Feed on the growing points of plants, *e.g.* grapevine flea beetle. (*iii*) Make small holes in the leaves, *e.g.* flea beetle. (*iv*) Notch the edge of the leaves, *e.g.* ash weevils, *Myllocerus* spp. and rice grasshopper. (*v*) Riddle leaves with large holes of irregular shape and size, *e.g.* cabbage semilooper. (*vi*) Feed on a layer of surface tissue of leaf *e.g.* diamondback moth. (*vii*) Roll up leaves and feed within, *e.g.* cotton leaf roller. (*viii*) Feed on bark of plants or trees, *e.g.* bark caterpillar. (*ix*) Cut the stem of tender plants at the time of germination, *e.g.* cotton surface weevil *Attactogaster finitimus*. (*x*) Nibble and cut off earheads, *i.e.* rice grasshoppers. (*xi*) Feed on buds and flowers, *e.g. Maruca testulalis* on red gram. (*xii*) Eat partially on the grains and give chalky appearance, *e.g. Helicoverpa armigera* on sorghum.

Piercing and sucking insects. These insects remain outside, pierce through the epidermis and suck the sap. Many sucking insects inject their salivary secretions into the plant tissue and the toxins therein accelerate the damage. Different kinds of symptoms of damage are caused as a result of feeding by these insects : (*i*) A general chlorosis is caused by feeding on the leaves of plants, resulting in ultimate withering and drying of the affected portions, *e.g.* groundnut aphid, *Aphis craccivora.* (*ii*) Faint yellow speckling of leaves may be produced, *e.g.* castor whitefly. (*iii*) Silvering or whitening of leaf surface may be caused, *e.g.* thrips on onion, groundnut, etc. (*iv*) Hopperburn or necrotic brown lesion, *e.g.* brown planthopper on rice. (*v*) Crinkling or curling of leaves, *i.e.* aphids, thrips and leafhoppers. (*vi*) Proliferation of tissue around the site of feeding, *e.g.* whitefly, *Bemisia tabaci.* (*vii*) Distortion of foliage and clustering of terminal shoorts, *e.g.* croton mealy bug. (*viii*) Premature shedding of developing fruits or drying of shoots, *e.g.* mealy bugs and scales. (*ix*) Premature fall of fruits, *e.g.* fruit sucking moths.

Internal feeders. The internal feeders cause damage by remaining within the plant tissues during a part or all of their destructive stages. This is accomplished by the adults thrusting their eggs into the tissue or by the larvae, eating their way after hatching from the eggs. There are various categories of internal feeders like leaf miners, gall insects, borers and worms or weevils.

Leaf miners. The larvae are usually small in size, live in between the two epidermal layers of the leaves and feed on the food material inside, *e.g.* citrus leaf miner, mango leaf miner, etc.

Gall insects. Some insects in their immature and/or adult stages form special deformities known as galls, which provide shelter and food to the insect. Due to the formation of the galls, growth of the plant may be impaired and setting of fruits, grains and seeds may be adversely affected, *e.g.* paddy gall fly and blossom mango midge.

Borers. The larvae feed on the wood or pith of the plant or part of the plant, which may generally be large enough to contain the body of the pest, *e.g.* rice stem borer and maize borer.

Worms. They are the borers in flower buds and fruits including bolls, nuts and seeds, *e.g.* jasmine budworm, brinjal fruit borer and coton pink bollworm.

Subterranean insects. These insects live in the soil and feed on the roots of plants and trees by chewing or boring or sucking or forming the galls. Many soil insects are host specific and most of them damage the crops in their larval stage. The larvae may feed externally on the roots or bore into the root, while some sucking insects suck the sap from the roots. Though the damage caused to the root may vary, depending upon the species and crop affected, generally the attacked plants show stunting, discolouration, withering and death of the plants. Examples of root feeders include whitegrub (*Holotrichia* spp.), cutworms, flea beetles, chafers and root aphids.

Stored product insects. The stored product insects attack the produce in three ways : (*i*) It may be a continuation of a field attack, *e.g.* potato tuber moth and sweet potato weevil. (*ii*) The eggs may be laid in the field itself and damage may occur in storage, *e.g.* bruchid beetle. (*iii*) The infestation may continue from the material stored earlier and carried over to fresh material stored later in godown, *e.g.* rice weevil and flour moth.

Indirect Effects of Feeding

There are several indirect effects of feeding by insects, which may affect the quality and/or quantity of the produce. (*i*) Due to heavy incidence by insect pests, the final produce may exhibit loss of quality by reducing nutritional value or marketability, *e.g.* cabbage riddled with shot holes by the semilooper, *Trichoplusia ni* and brinjal fruits bored by larvae of *Leucinodes orbonalis*. (*ii*) Heavy incidence of some pests may cause hindrance in the harvest of the crop, *i.e.* cotton bolls damaged by bollworms, and cabbage heavily infested with aphids. (*iii*) The insects are responsible for the spread of many plant diseases caused by bacteria, fungi and viruses. Many plant viruses are exclusively dependent upon their insect vectors for dissemination.

Injury by Other Means

There are several other means by which insects inflict injury to crops : (*i*) A few species are known to cause injury to plants by their act of oviposition. For example, the cicada splits the wood severely on twigs of one year old growth for egg laying, which results in drying of the plant beyond that point. The cow bugs inject their eggs in rows into the tissue of tender stem and thus cause injury. (*ii*) Sometimes parts of plants are removed by insects for the construction of their nests. For example, the leafcutter, *Megachile anthracina* removes neat circular pieces of foliage from plants like rose, redgram, etc. Similarly, tropical leaf-cutting ants are known to strip off leaves from plants and trees and carry them to their nests. (*iii*) Ants and some other insects may carry injurious insects such as aphids and mealy bugs, to the crop plants. They feed on the honey-dew, excreted by these insects.

CHANGING STATUS OF INSECT PESTS

Rapid increase of population during the last century has necessitated intensification of agriculture through the introduction of high yielding varieties, expansion of irrigation facilities and application of increased amounts of agrochemicals. Besides, the cultural practices like spacing, croprotation, sowing times and tillage methods were also modified to achieve maximum productivity per unit time from the available land. While undoubtedly contributing to higher yields, this technology package has also resulted in severe outbreaks of insect pests. Following the introduction of high yielding varieties (HYVs) and associated technology, there has been a tremendous increase in the number of insect pests damaging various crops, viz. pigeonpea (250), rice (225), sugarcane (215), cotton (170), etc. Many minor insects have started assuming serious proportions, whereas several pests have spread to new areas.

The incidence of brown planthopper, yellow stem borer and leaf folder has increased manifold with the cultivation of modern high yielding varities of rice. Gall midge, originally being confined to monsoon season, has, of late, become a pest in summer season also. The spread of rice cultivation into the non-traditional north-western states like Punjab and Haryana, has brought up the problem of whitebacked planthopper. The continuous cropping of maize in northern parts of India has led to the emergence of shoot fly, *Atherigona* spp., as important pest in spring sown maize. *Pyrilla perpusilla*, a serious pest of sugarcane has developed a perference for hybrids of maize and sorghum. Sorghum midge, earhead bug and aphids are gaining importance in many sorghum growing regions. There are also reports of invasion of sugarcane woolly aphid, *Ceratovacuna lanigera* in several parts of India.

Severe outbreaks of whitefly and American bollworm have been observed on cotton during the last decade. American bollworm appeared in serious form in parts of Andhra Pradesh and Tamil Nadu during 1987-88, where it caused about 66 per cent loss in yield of seed cotton. The pest caused severe losses to cotton crop in Haryana, Punjab and Rajasthan during 1990. However, after the introduction of Bt cotton, the severity of *Helicoverpa armigera* has considerably declined, but the incidence of mealy bug, *Phenacoccus solenopsis* has considerably increased.

A number of polyphagous pests have also attained serious status. Most dreaded of these is *H. armigera,* which has been recorded on more than 180 cultivated and uncultivated plant species, of which chickpea, pigeonpea, cotton, tomato and tobacco are considered to be the key source crops. Similarly, *Spodoptera litura* has been recorded on more than 115 species of cultivated plants in India. The serpentine leaf miner, *Liriomyza trifolii,* has started appearing in serious proportions on several field and vegetable crops.

Insect pest problems in agriculture are probably as old as agriculture itself. However, under subsistence agriculture, the pest numbers were generally low as the productivity was poor. The insect pests were kept under check by cultural and mechanical practices developed by farmers largely through trial and error. However, the green revolution technology has resulted in severe outbreaks of insect pests in agricultural crops.

High Yielding Varieties

When altering the genetic make up of the crop plant to increase yield with little or no attention to pest attack, natural resistance may be lost or greatly reduced. Efforts to breed plants more palatable to human taste by elimination of such factors as bitterness and hairiness may also result in development of more susceptible varieties. Moreover, the fields planted to modern varieties, which are short and heavy tiller-ing, develop a distinctly different microclimate conducive for proliferation of insect pests.

Monoculture

In agriculture, the natural plant community is removed, destroyed and usually replaced by a single crop species. Larger the area that is planted to a single crop, the greater the potential for pest problems. Generally, same crops are maintained in a given area year after year and this helps in survival and multiplication of the pest throughout the year. Large scale monoculturing of cotton, paddy, sugarcane and vegetable crops in India in contiguous blocks has resulted in rapid increase in number and intensity of pest attacks.

Nutrients

Altering the nutrient level in the soil affects the concentration of nutrients in the host plant, which, in return, influence the pests that are feeding on the plant. The HYVs are nitrogen responsive and require extensive use of nitro-genous fertilizers to provide maximum yield. High levels of nitrogenous fertilizers significantly increase the incidence of most insect pests. Increase in soil moisture level due to frequent irrigations also helps in build up of insect pests.

Pesticides

The advent of synthetic organic pesticides during 1940s enabled us to gain an upper hand in the struggle against insect pests. However, the large scale indiscriminate use and abuse of these insecticides has resulted in increased attacks of insect pests on many crops. This may be due to development of insecticide resistance, resurgence of insect pests or outbreaks of secondary pests. The insecticides may kill natural enemies of target pest or potential pest. They may also alter crop physiology to make the plant more susceptible to attack by insects or they may even directly stimulate reproduction of surviving in-sects.

Cultural Practices

New agronomic recommendations like closer spacings, sowing times, rotations, harvesting procedures, etc. are essentially meant for exploiting the full genetic potential of high yielding varieties, but are simultaneously favourable to most of the insect pests. In cultivated fields, crop plant densities are carefully controlled to obtain the maximum population possible for optimal growth resulting in maximum economic yield. The new plant spacings often result in an ecological situation that encourages pest outbreaks.

ASSESSMENT OF PEST POPULATIONS

Pest population studies are helpful in pinpointing the factors that bring about numerical changes in the natural population and also in understanding the functioning of the life system of the pest species.

Pest population studies are of two types :

(*i*) **Extensive studies.** These studies are spread over a large area and are needed to understand the distribution pattern of a population, to predict the damage it is likely to cause, to initiate control measures and to relate changes in the population to certain climatic or edaphic factors. A particular area is observed once or at the most a few times during the season and counts are made of a particular developmental stage of the pest.

(*ii*) **Intensive studies.** These studies involve repeated observations in a given area when it is desired to determine the contribution of various age intervals to the overall rate of change in the population or the dispersal of species. In this case, the number of successive developmental stages are counted, and life-tables and budgets are prepared for determing the key factor(s).

Measurements taken to estimate pest population density fall into three categories, viz. absolute estimates, relative estimates and population indices.

Absolute Estimates

The total number of insects per unit area (1 ha, 1 m row length, 1 m2 quadrat, etc.) is the absolute estimation. The numbers per unit of the habitat (per plant, shoot or leaf) indicate the density of population. The estimates of absolute population and population density are used for preparing life-tables, study of population dynamics of field populations and to calculate oviposition and mortality rates.

The following methods are commonly employed for estimating absolute population:

(*i*) **Quadrat method.** Small areas or quadrats are chosen at random from a large area which contains the population. A large number of quadrats are required for over-dispersed population than that in the randomly distributed population. Stratified sampling is followed in the case of aggregated distribution, i.e. the population is divided into different strata and varying number of samples is taken from each stratum. From a quadrat, the insects may be counted or collected directly as in the case of fairly immobile but relatively large insects such as cutworms, caterpillars and grasshoppers. In case of tissue borers such as sugarcane borers, maize borer, etc., the estimation is done by first removing the infested plants from the quadrats and then counting them after splitting open the plant parts.

(*ii*) **Capture, marking, release and recapture technique.** This technique is generally used for estimating the population of flying insects. The losses or gains in a population over a period can be determined with the help of this method. The estimate of density fluctuations and the death rate can also be made for making comparisons between different forms of pests under varying environmental conditions. The different types of markers used are paints and dyes, labels, mutilation, radioisotopes, etc. For effective application of capture-recapture technique in population estimation, the following assumptions have to be met :

- The marking of individuals does not lead to changes in their behaviour or longevity and the marks do not get lost easily.
- The marked individuals, after being released, become completely mixed up with the unmarked individuals of the population.
- The population is sampled randomly with respect to its mark status.
- The method of marking should be such that it should distinguish between different dates of capture.
- The population under study must be reasonably stable and not subject to rapid fluctuations in numbers.

Relative Estimates

In relative population estimates, the samples usually represent an unknown constant proportion of the population. A given amount of labour and equipment is utilised to yield much more data than is possible for absolute estimates. Such estimates are useful in making comparisons in space or time. These are useful for studying the activity patterns of a species or for determining the constitution of a polymorphic population. The relative estimates are influenced by a number of factors like variation in

(*a*) behaviour of an insect with change in age, (*b*) level of activity of the pest as influenced by its diurnal cycle, (*c*) responsiveness of sexes to trap stimuli, and (*d*) efficiency of the trap or the searching method, besides the pest population.

The methods employed for relative estimates include the catch per unit time or effort and the use of various types of traps.

(*i*) **Net sweepings.** Various types of collection nets are available for use in different habitats and the sweep net is the most widely used for sampling insects from vegetation. A sweep consists of a half circle or 180° swing with a hoop of an insect net held in a vertical plane. Only those individuals on the top of the vegetation and those that do not fall off or fly away on the approach of the collector can be caught with the sweep net. The efficiency of catch with a sweep net will be influenced by changes in the habitat, species, weather and vertical distribution of the pest species. The number of sweeps necessary to obtain a mean that is within 25 per cent of the true value will depend upon the pest species, its spatial distribution and the diurnal periodicity. Usually, 10 sweeps may be sufficient to assess the general population of any species and the population is reported in terms of number per 100 sweeps.

(*ii*) **Line-transect method.** If one walks in a straight line at a constant speed through a habitat, the number of individuals can be counted. This technique is used for quantitative comparisons both between different species, and between different occupiers of habitats. This technique was originally employed by botanists for estimating the population of plants, but could not be easily used in animals owing to their mobility from place to place. However, the data based on number of encounters have been used for estimating the absolute population of locusts and grasshoppers.

(*iii*) **Use of traps. In** this case, it is the insects rather than the observer that would make the action leading to their enumeration. Traps are of two types, viz. ***interception traps*** (that catch the insects randomly) and ***attraction traps*** (which attract the insects in some way). Various types of interception traps are flight traps, aquatic traps, pitfall, light and other visual traps. The flight traps that combine interception and attraction include sticky traps and water traps. The traps that attract the insects by some natural stimulus or substitute include the shelter traps, trap crops, bait traps, chemical attractants and pheromones.

Population Indices

Population indices do not count insects at all, but rather they are measures of insect products or effects. Under field conditions, it is not possible to estimate the absolute population in most of the cases. It, therefore, becomes necessary to establish a relationship between absolute estimates and population indices or the relative estimates so that the latter two types of estimates could be converted to absolute terms by using certain correction factors.

(*i*) **Insect products. In** some cases, a species that is difficult to sample creates products directly that are easily sampled by absolute methods. The insect product most often sampled is frass or excrement of lepidopteran defoliators. The rate at which frass is produced can be estimated from the amount falling into a box or funnel placed under the trees. The size and shape of the frass pellets is rather constant for a given species and instar; this allows one to identify the species and age composition of defoliators.

(*ii*) **Plant damage.** The amount of damage caused by insects to crop plants is a function of the pest density, the characteristic feeding or oviposition behaviour of the species and the biological characteristics of the plants. Different methods have to be adopted for measuring damage by direct and indirect pests.

(*a*) ***Direct pests. These*** pests attack the produce directly, destroying a significant part of its value. Bollworms on cotton and fruit borers in fruit and vegetable crops are examples of such pests. The damage by direct pests is sampled on the basis of absolute or relative numbers of damaged unit, e.g. number of damaged bolls per plant, apples per tree, pods per meter row length, etc.

(*b*) ***Indirect pests. Damage*** by indirect pests may be measured by estimating the extent of defoliation in case of defoliating pests like lepidopteran caterpillars, leaf beetles, grasshoppers, etc.

Many devices like planimeters, photoplanimeters, leaf area meters, etc. are now available for quantifying the extent of defoliation. In case of sap-sucking insects like aphids, jassids, white flies, etc. damage may be estimated by change in coloration of the leaves, plant vigour and size. For root feeders, damage to root system may be evaluated by percentage of nodes below the soil surface having injury, force needed to pull a plant from the soil, etc.

For a correct and scientific understanding of a pest population, it is of fundamental importance to develop sound methods of population estimation. This involves two considerations. First, the life stage (egg, larva, pupa or adult) at which counting can be made most advantageously, and secondly, the actual process of counting. The ideal approach to population estimation would be to count all the individuals. However, with most of the pest species it is not possible to count them over an area large enough to be of use in a practical study and hence some method of sampling becomes necessary. For devising a satisfactory and successful sampling programme, consideration has to be given to the nature of the sample, mode of sampling, the size and number of samples. The precision of a pest population estimate based on a given sampling technique would depend upon both the properties of the population in terms of its density and degree of aggregation, and upon the charactersitics of the sampling plan, i.e. the number and size of samples.

LOSSES CAUSED BY PESTS

The food plants of the world are damaged by more than 10,000 species of insects, 30,000 species of weeds, 1,00,000 diseases (caused by fungi, viruses, bacteria and other microorganisms) and 1000 species of nematodes. The loss suffered by a crop is a function of the pest and the crop plants. Crop loss is reduction in quantity and/or quality of yield and is measured as the difference between actual yield and attainable yield due to the effects of one or more pests. The assessment of crop losses due to pests is helpful in prediction of crop production and planning for higher production in the future.

Types of Losses

The losses due to pests can be categorised in many ways, depending upon the significance of pests and their management.

Direct losses. These relate to the decrease in productivity (quantitative) or intrinsic value/ acceptability of the produce (qualitative). Direct quantitative losses include killing of flowers, buds, twigs of whole plant due to infestation by pests like locusts and grasshoppers, bollworms, fruit borers, root borers, etc. The examples of direct qualitative losses include light infestations of fruits by scales, puncturing of normal fruits immediately before harvest owing to feeding or ovipositional activity. Damage by the pests to the fruit trees from blooming to harvesting periods results in quantitative losses in the earlier phase and qualitative losses in the latter phase.

Indirect losses. These are primarily of economic interest, *i.e.* decreased purchasing power of farmers due to reduced production. These will lead to decrease in related activities, reduced productivity of agro-based industries and forced acceptance of less desirable substitute products.

Actual losses. These include the total value of losses, both direct and indirect, cost of control measures along with the amount spent on researches for developing pest control technology and also the expenditure incurred for diffusing pest control knowledge among farmers.

Potential losses. The potential losses refer to the losses likely to be sustained without the adoption of crop protection measures.

Avoidable losses. It is that proportion of crop losses which can be saved by proper use of currently available crop protection technology.

Unavoidable losses. It is that proportion of crop losses which cannot be prevented by use of currently available crop protection technology.

Estimation of Crop Losses

The estimation of crop loss due to pests is critical to pest management. The evaluation of pest damage is useful in pest management in the following ways :

- Defining the economic status of a given pest species.
- Establishing economic injury levels and economic threshold.
- Estimating the effectiveness of pest control measures.
- Evaluating crop varieties for their reaction to insect pests.
- Helping in deciding the allocations for research and extension in plant protection, and
- Helping in assigning priorities on the basis of relative importance of different pests.

A brief overview of the techniques adopted for the assessment of crop losses caused by insect pests has been given below :

Mechanical protection. The crop is grown under enclosure of cotton cloth or wire gauze in order to keep the pests away from the crop. The yield under such enclosures is compared with that obtained from the infested crop under similar conditions. This technique has been used with various modifications for estimating the losses caused by jassid and whitefly in cotton. The barriers may be substituted for cages in the case of non-flying insects. The limitation in case of enclosures is that the plants generally become weak and pale due to changes in micro-environment. This technique cannot be employed on large scale because it is time consuming and impracticable under field conditions.

Chemical protection. The crop is protected from pest damage through the application of pesticides. The yield of the treated crop is compared with that of the one which has been subjected to normal infestation. This technique has been extensively used and can be employed on a large scale in farmers' fields. It should, however, be ensured that treated and untreated fields/plots should be as similar as possible in respect of soil type, variety, fertilization and cultural practices. The major shortcoming in this approach is that the crop treated with chemicals may be physiologically affected and hence may give either more or less yield.

Comparison of yield in different fields. The yield is calculated per unit area in different fields carrying different degrees of pest infestation. The correlation between crop yield and degree of infestation is worked out to estimate the loss in yield. This technique can be used for estimating crop loss due to different pests over a larger area. The yield in different fields may, however, be influenced by soil heterogeneity.

Comparison of yield of individual plants. In this case, the individual plants from the same field are examined for the incidence of pests and their yield is determined individually. The average yield of healthy plants is compared with that of plants showing different degrees of infestation and the loss in yield is estimated. The same data can also be used for working out a correlation between yield and infestation on the basis of individual plants. This technique has been used with various modifications in maize borer, sugarcane borers and aphids. In this method, soil heterogeneity factor is considerably reduced as compared to the previous method, where comparison is made among different fields. However, the fact that different plants show varying degrees of infestation is itself an indication that plants differ from one another in some unidentified factor(s) due to which they exhibit different degrees of infestation. This factor may be genetic, physiological or it may be mere soil heterogeneity in the same field. Moreover, this method is also time consuming and involves lot of labour.

Damage caused by individual insect. Preliminary information is obtained from studies on biology of the pest species. The details regarding the amount of damage caused by different ages or stages of the insect pest are worked out and the amount of loss is calculated. This technique is quite convenient in case of leaf-feeding insects. However, it is difficult to use this technique over a large area since it is time consuming.

Manipulation of natural enemies. The pest is controlled by introducing parasitoids/ predators into the field and the yield of such a crop is compared with that on which no such measures have been adopted. This technique has, however, not been widely used. This method is feasible only on small plots and not applicable on a field scale.

Simulation of damage. In this case, pest injury is simulated by removing or injuring leaves or other parts of the plant. The simulated damage may, however, not always be equivalent to the damage caused by an insect. Insects may inject long-acting toxins rather than producing injury instantly. Feeding on margins of leaves may not be equivalent to tissue removal from the centre of the leaves. Insect feeding is usually extended over a period of time and it is rather difficult to incorporate the concept of rate of injury in simulation studies. Furthermore, the period of leaf removed may be important, as for example the age, quality and position of the leaf on the plant. In addition, time of simulating damage with respect to the stage of plant growth is also critical. Simulated studies have been conducted on spotted bollworms on cotton in India.

Extent of Losses

Pests have reduced the productivity of crops since the dawn of agriculture and farmers have been looking for ways of protecting their crops from these organisms. Although crop protection aims to avoid or prevent crop losses or to reduce them to an economically acceptable level, the availability of quantitative data on the effect of various categories of pests is very limited. The generation of experimental data is time-consuming and laborious, losses vary from growth season to growth season due to variation in pest incidence and severity, and estimates of loss data for various crops are fraught with problems. The assessment of crop losses is needed for demonstrating where future action is needed and for decision making by farmers as well as at the government level.

The first attempt to estimate crop losses due to pests at global level was made during 1964-65, when the losses due to insect pests were put at 10.8 per cent. Since then, the production technology has undergone a tremendous change and the global losses due to animal pests, diseases and weeds during 1988-90, were estimated to be 15.6, 13.3 and 13.2 per cent, respectively. The total losses due to all categories of pests were estimated at 42.1 per cent. The introduction of gene technology has added a new dimension to pest management. Since the early 1990s, the production systems have changed significantly, especially in crops like maize, soybean and cotton in which the advent of transgenic varieties has modified the strategies for pest management in some major production regions. Therefore, estimates were again made during

2001-03, according to which the total losses due to all categories of pests were calculated as 32.1 per cent The losses due to animal pests, diseases and weeds were estimated at 10.8, 12.5 and 8.8 per cent, respectively (Table 1.5). As reported in the year 2014, arthropods alone destroy an estimated 18–26 % of annual crop production worldwide, at a value of more than $ 470 billion.

Extensive surveys carried out in India during early 1960s, revealed that fruits, cotton, rice and sugarcane suffered 25, 18, 10 and 10 per cent yield losses, respectively. The losses in other crops were quite low. However, during the early 2000s, the losses increased considerably due

Table 1.5 Global losses due to animal pests (arthropods, nematodes, rodents, birds, slugs and snails), weeds, pathogens (fungi, bacteria) and viruses in six major crops

Crop	Crop losses (%)				
	Animal pests	Weeds	Pathogens	Viruses	Total
Wheat	7.9	7.7	10.2	2.4	28.2
Rice	15.1	10.2	10.8	1.4	37.5
Maize	9.6	10.5	8.5	2.7	31.3
Potatoes	10.9	8.3	14.5	6.6	40.3
Soybeans	8.8	7.5	8.9	1.2	26.4
Cotton	12.3	8.6	7.2	0.7	28.8
Average	**10.8**	**8.8**	**10.0**	**2.5**	**32.1**

Source : Oerke (2006)

to intensification of agriculture. The highest losses were reported in cotton (50%), followed by sorghum and millets (30%), rice (25%), maize (25%) and oilseeds (25%) (Table 1.6). The monetary value of annual yield losses in the important agricultural crops has been estimated to be ₹ 689 billion. In addition, losses to the tune of about ₹ 61 billion occur during storage. Thus, there is an annual loss of about ₹ 750 billion due to field and storage pests in India. It is imperative to contain these colossal losses by following various pest management tactics in such a way that the pests are contained without the ecological harm to the environment.

Table 1.6 Crop losses due to insect pests under traditional and modern agriculture in India

Crop	Losses (%)			Monetary value
	Traditional agriculture (early 1960s) (1)	Modern agriculture (early 2000s) (2)	Change in loss (2–1)	(million Rs) of loss in 2000s
Cotton	18.0	50.0	+ 32.0	2,87,600
Groundnut	5.0	15.0	+ 10.0	16,080
Maize	5.0	25.0	+ 20.0	21,340
Other oiiseeds	5.0	25.0	+ 20. 0	53,700
Pulses	5.0	15.0	+ 10.0	33,600
Rice	10.0	25.0	+ 15.0	1,64,300
Sorghum and millets	3.5	30.0	+ 26.5	42,680
Sugarcane	10.0	20.0	+ 10.0	46,540
Wheat	3.0	5.0	+ 2.0	23,560
Average/Total	**7.2**	**23.3**	**+ 16.1**	**6,89,400**

Source : Dhaliwal and Koul (2010)

PEST MANAGEMENT

Insect pests have been associated with crop plants ever since the evolution of agriculture about 10,000 years ago. The population of pests under natural conditions was regulated by extremes of climate, prevalence of a number of natural enemies and diseases. During ancient times, humans had to live with and tolerate the ravages of insect pests, but gradually learned to improve their condition through trial and error experiences. Over the centuries, farmers developed a number of mechanical, physical, cultural and biological control measures to minimize the damage caused by phytophagous insects. Synthetic organic insecticides developed during the mid-twentieth century, initially provided spectacular control of these insects and resulted in the abandonment of traditional pest management practices. This was followed by the development of insect resistant varieties, biorational approaches, genetic control measures and more recently the biotechnological approaches (Fig. 1.3). The significance of achieving sustainable food production through the use of ecofriendly pest management techniques is being realized more and more in the recent past.

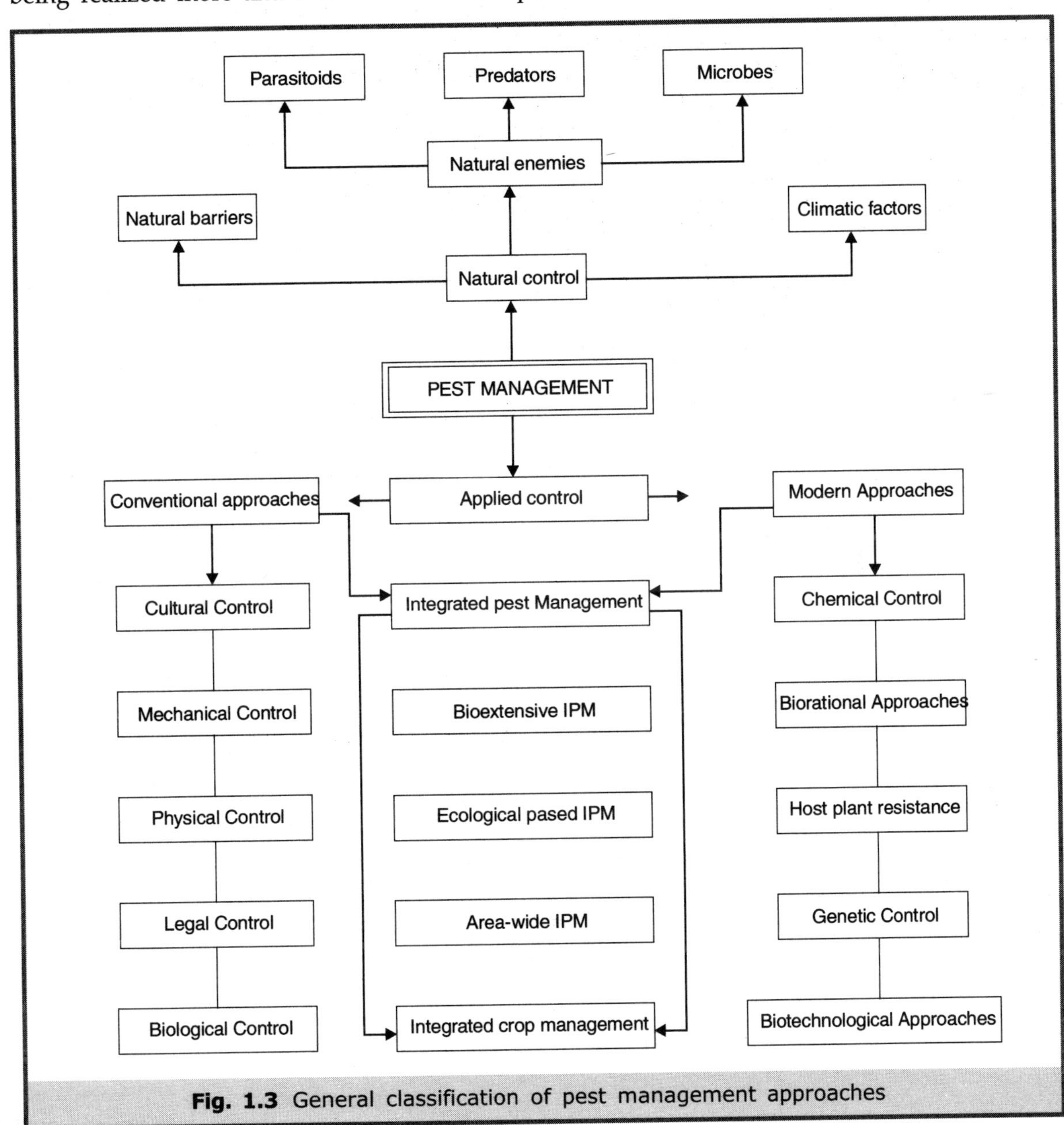

Fig. 1.3 General classification of pest management approaches

Natural Control

In this case, the control of insect pests goes on in nature without the intervention of man. The natural factors that keep a check on the pest populations are climatic factors, natural barriers, natural enemies and diseases.

Climatic factors. Temperature, humidity and day length (photoperiod) directly affect the populations of both the pests and their host plants. The seasonal development of phytophagous insects is closely correlated to the development of their host plants. This correlation is exploited by man to control pests to some extent. Climate also restricts the dispersal of pests to particular localities or else they would spread for and wide.

Natural barriers. Natural topographic barriers like mountain ranges, large bodies of water (seas, oceans) and deserts prevent pest migration from one favourable area to another. But for these barriers, the pests would perhaps have been able to counter the adverse effects of climate and kept on breeding by migrating to climatically favourable areas as soon as the weather conditions in their native place turned unfavourable. Apart from checking insect migration, these barriers affect the climate itself and so the ability of the pests to live in changed weather conditions. For instance, insects living in the moist windward side of a mountain will be quite different and incapable of living on the dry leeward side even if they had the opportunity to migrate. Similarly, insects living near large bodies of water get so adapted to humid conditions that they cannot live in drier conditions. For the same reason, soil types also limit the distribution and multiplication of soil insects.

Natural enemies. There is not a single group of vertebrates, starting from fishes up to mammals, which do not feed on insects. These animals keep insect populations under check to a great extent. Amongst insects themselves are a large number of entomophagous species that either capture and devour other insect species (predators) or lay their eggs in or on the body of other insects (parasites) to enable their progeny to get a ready supply of food on emergence.

Diseases. Like all living beings, insects are also attacked by microbes, referred to as entomogenous pathogens that produce fatal diseases in them and thus keep a check on their populations. These pathogens belong to viruses, rickettsiae, bacteria, protozoans, nematodes and fungi.

Applied Control

In this case, man's intervention is involved to devise and implement suitable pest control measures. Applied control can further be divided into two broad categories, viz. conventional approaches and modern approaches.

Conventional approaches. Conventional approaches are those which have been evolved by hit and trial, and subsequently refined to achieve desirable pest control.

Cultural Control. Cultural control includes the well-established agricultural practices that make habitats less suitable for pests. The methods used may either directly affect a pest, stimulate an increase in the density of a pest's natural enemies or make the plant on which a pest feeds to escape the attack. These practices are more useful as prophylactic rather than as curative measures. Nevertheless, these practices are economical, convenient and without any hazards.

Mechanical control. Mechanical control involves the use of manual devices and machines to contain the pests. Mechanical control measures give immediate tangible results and are generally popular and convincing to the farmers, even though these are time-consuming, laborious and are often applied, when much damage has already been done.

Physical control. Physical control involves the manipulation of temperature, humidity and radiant energy for suppression of pests. These methods are particularly useful for destroying stored grain pests. Due to their limited applicability, physical control methods have not gained prominence.

Legal control. Legal control aims to prevent or control pest damage through legislation. It includes the setting up of quarantine station, systems for monitoring pest populations, and mechanisms for the certification of pest free plants and animals.

Biological control. Biological control is the regulation of pest populations by bioagents, *i.e.* parasitoids, predaceous insects and microorganisms. Biological control is relatively cheap, ecofriendly and long-lasting. However, bioagents are generally slow in action and take long time to establish and provide an effective pest control.

Modern approaches. Modern approaches are those, which have been invented by man with specific target groups of pests and subsequently improved to achieve sustainable pest control in an ecologically benign manner.

Chemical control. Chemical control involves the use of various insecticides and other chemicals either to kill or repel the insect pests. The inorganics and botanicals had dominated pest control in traditional agriculture. The advent of DDT and subsequently several other organic insecticides revolutionized the chemical pest control. However, the misuse and overuse of these insecticides have caused several environmental problems like pollution, insecticide resistance and insect resurgence. Nevertheless, pesticides have played a pivotal role in increasing the world food supply.

Biorational approaches. Biorational approaches include natural or synthetic compounds that effectively control insect pests, but are less toxic to non-target organisms (such as humans, animals and natural enemies) and the environment. Most of the biorational pesticides are preferred to conventional pesticides because of their specificity to target pests, efficacy at low rates and non-persistence in the environment. Such compounds include insect growth regulators (IGRs) and various semio-chemicals; now commercial formulations of many of these are available for eco-friendly control of insect pests.

Host plant resistance. Host plant resistance refers to the development of plant varieties, capable of resisting the attack by pests. The advantages of using resistant varieties include greater crop yield, relatively low cost of development, and absence of adverse environmental effects. However, the length of time to develop resistant variety is quite long, ordinarily 10-15 years with crop plants and even longer with trees. Moreover, the development of insect biotypes capable of damaging resistant varieties is a bottleneck of this approach.

Genetic control. Genetic control includes methods that render pests less capable of reproduction, for example, the sterile insect release method (SIRM), use of chemoterilants and sterility resulting from mating incompatibility or abnormal gametogenesis. SIRM has been successfully used against several pests. In spite of its being specific, permanency of effect and non-polluting, SIRM has its limited applicability.

Biotechnological approaches. Biotechnology involves the utilization of biological agents such as microorganisms, cells of higher plants or animals or their cellular constituents for the isolation of useful products related to human welfare. In pest management, it is the use of genetically modified organisms in the production of crops or animals, including the production of insect suppressive agents. The use of transgenic crops in pest management has raised several sociological, economical and ethical issues. Nevertheless, transgenic crops have gone a long way to contain pest populations and reduce the pesticide load in the environment.

Integrated pest management. Integrated pest management (IPM) is a pest population management system that utilizes all suitable techniques either to reduce pest populations and maintain them at levels below those causing economic injury, or to so manipulate the populations that they are prevented from causing such injury. There are three phases in the development of an IPM strategy, viz. problem definition, research and implementation, of which the first is the most important. To be most effective, IPM requires the input of as much information as possible, not only about the agroecosystem, but also about the socioeconomic framework of the farming system in which the pest problem occurs.

Integrated crop management. The aim of further developments in crop protection is integrated crop management, which may be defined as the economical production of high quality crop, giving priority to ecologically safe methods of crop cultivation, minimizing the undesirable side effects and use of crop protection products. In fact, integrated pest management acts as a springboard to integrated crop management. Integrated crop management is the basis for sustainable agriculture, a production system which may be used continuously for many years, is soundly based on the potential and within the limitations of a particular region, does not unduly deplete its resources or degrade its environment, makes best use of energy and materials, ensures good and reliable yields, and benefits to local population at competitive costs.

CONCLUSIONS

Insects are the most dominant group of organisms on Earth and excel all other animals in both diversity and magnitude. They have attained this status by virtue of certain attributes acquired by them over a period of time. In the course of their evolution, many species of insects have adapted themselves to feed on agricultural crops, livestock and stored products. The losses caused by insect pests have increased tremendously during the Green Revolution era. A number of techniques have been devised and refined from time to time to contain the pest populations. However, the greatest challenge facing mankind is to reduce the losses due to pests so as to maintain food and environmental security on sustainable basis.

PART–II

PEST MANAGEMENT TACTICS

- Physical, Mechanical and Legal Control
- Cultural Control
- Biological Control : Predators and Parasitoids
- Biological Control : Microbial Pathogens
- Botanical Pest Control
- Chemical Control : Pesticides and their Application
- Chemical Control : Pesticide use and Management
- Insect Growth Regulators and other Biorational Insecticides
- Behaviour Modifying Chemicals : Semiochemicals and Insecticides
- Host Plant Resistance
- Genetic Control
- Biotechnological Approaches
- Integrated Pest Management : Concetps and Principles

INTRODUCTION

Physical and mechanical control were one of the first methods to be used for reducing the incidence of insect pests. Drying of grains before storage, handpicking of lice and collection and destruction of pest-infested plant parts were the routine methods that were employed since long. Similarly, some legal measures were also adopted to overcome certain pests which were otherwise difficult to contain. For example, as early as 1911, removal of cotton sticks by 1st August every year was made compulsory by law to minimise the incidence of pink bollworm on cotton in the erstwhile Madras state. All these methods were improved and refined to enhance their efficacy against various insect pests.

PHYSICAL CONTROL

These methods aim to reduce pest populations by using devices which affect them physically or alter their physical environment.

Hot or Cold Treatment

Application of dry heat including exposure to sun rays during hot summer months of April-June helps in killing a number of pests in seeds and stored commodities. Stored grain pests can be killed by exposing them to 55°C for three hours. Exposure of cotton seeds to sun heat in thin layers for 2-3 days during April helps in killing diapausing larvae of pink bollworm. Treatment of sugarcane setts with heat therapy units either as hot water or hot air treatment kills the scale insects carried over through the setts. Hot water treatment of plant storage organs like roots, corns, bulbs, etc. helps to kill concealed pests such as bulb flies and eelworms. Steam sterilization of soil is done to kill soil insects and nematodes. The use of flame throwers is useful for destroying locust hoppers and adults. Low temperature (below 4°C) makes the insects inactive and is thus, helpful in preventing the damage. Cold storage of fresh and dry fruits and vegetables is often resorted to for escaping fruit fly, potato tuber moth and pathogen damage. A temperature of 10°C for several days kills fruitfly maggots.

Moisture

Insects are highly sensitive to reduction in air moisture content but manipulation of humidity is generally not feasible under field conditions. The method is, however, useful in case of stored grain pests and under greenhouse conditions. Well-dried grains (moisture content < 8–10%) stored in a cool dry place escape insect damage. The increase in the loss of moisture from the body of insects can be manipulated for their control. Kaolinic clay offers successive activation with acid and heat can be mixed with grains. The clay minerals absorb the lipid layer over the insect cuticle, and the insects lose their body moisture and die of desiccation. A material called 'Drie-Die', marketed in USA, consisted of a highly porous, finely divided slica gel and caused abrasion of the insect cuticle, thus encouraging the loss of moisture from its body, resulting in ultimate death of the insect. It was mainly used against stored product pests.

Radiant Energies

Radiant (solar) energies which have been tried in the control of insect pests are: (*i*) radio-frequencies, (*ii*) infrared light, (*iii*) ultraviolet and visible light, (*iv*) x-rays and (*v*) γ-ray (Fig. 2.1). Energies of the longer wavelengths (*i* – *iii*) produce heating effect, while those of the shorter wavelengths (*iv* and *v*) produce chemical effects including ionisation of atoms of the absorbing media. These radiations can be used mostly for pests of stored grain and their products. Barring visible light, most of above energies have not been commercially feasible on account of their high costs. Nevertheless, the manner in which the energies affect the pests, will be of some interest to know.

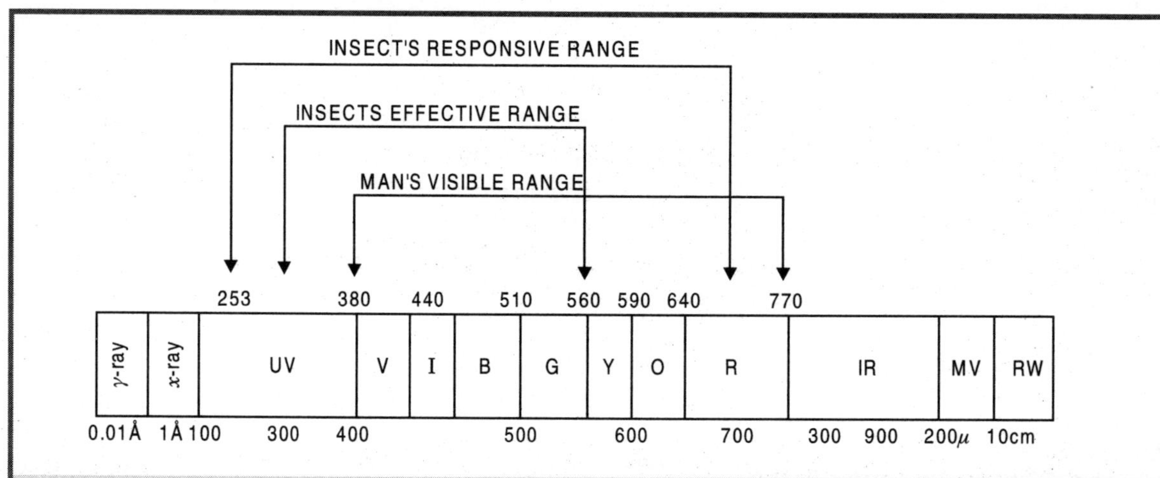

Fig. 2.1 Visible ranges of insects and man in the solar spectrum. Wave lengths are in nanometer (nm) except where mentioned (1 μm = 1/1000 mm, 1 nm = 1/1000 μm, 1Å = 1/10,000 nm)

(*i*) Radio-frequencies (RF). The RF (presently, employed in radio communication, radar navigation, diathermy, etc.) produce differential heating in the hosts (grains) and the infesting pests. This is due to the difference in the moisture content or humidity and dielectric properties of the two. The heating, therefore, kills the pests (possibly by synaptic blocking, vacuolisation, coagulation of nervous system or change in amino acid content) without much damage to the seeds. High frequency radio waves generate temperature of about 80°C in grains to kill granary weevils and confused flour beetles in 15-20 seconds. Some of the pests against which this method has been found encouraging are wood-infesting beetles like *Lyctus* and store grain insects like *Tribolium, Trogoderma* and *Sitophilus*.

***(ii)* Infrared (IR).** The IR radiation is intermediate between RF and a visible part of the electromagnetic spectrum (wavelength 10,000Å or 1μ). It is produced from hot bodies (like IR lamps) and has two uses : for killing by heating and for attracting the insects. Insects like moths and mosquitoes possess IR sensors in their antennae and can be drawn to an IR source and then killed by conventional means. It may be mentioned in the passing that in case of the moth *Hyalophora*, the thermocouple tied under the thorax of the female records an increase in body temperature by atleast 6°C above the ambient temperature. This increase is detected by the male at a considerable distance.

***(iii)* Visible light and ultraviolet (UV).** While man is able to see the colours violet to red (380-770 nm wavelengths) of the solar spectrum, the insect's responsive range lies between below UV to red (253-700 nm). In general, the UV to blue-green (300-560 nm) region of the spectrum is the most effective in attracting insects while red, orange and yellow are not attractive. For this reason, yellow colour in particular is used to repel insects and the UV lamp is used to attract nocturnal iinsects. Visible light can be used in three ways to control pests: (*a*) by producing phototaxis—positive (to attract) or negative (to repel), (*b*) by inducing diapause by altering the photo period, and (*c*) by modiying behaviour—ovipositional in particular. The most practical application of light is that of attracting (positive phototaxis) certain economic species to be killed by conventional methods. For this purpose, various types of light-traps have been devised. A light-trap basically consists of a source of light mounted above a funnel and an insecticide containing collection-can below. In the USA, field trials with many borers (corn borer, tobacco borer and tomato horn borer) with light traps, have met with some success. Theoretically speaking, the fields can be floodlit to extend the day length and to prevent the onset of diapause in insects. The insects which would otherwise, have survived by diapausing would fail to do so and perish in adverse weather. In California (USA), exposure of apple plants to artificial light interfered with the egg-laying of the codling moth and thus considerably reducing the damage to apples.

***(iv)* Ionising radiations.** The x-rays and γ-rays are ionising radiations which provide prospects of controlling stored-grain pests. This, they can do two ways, viz. by killing them outright or by sterilising them, so that their populations go down. Of the two radiations, γ-rays produced by isotopes like 60CO, are more penetrating and, therefore, more promising in the control of stored grain pests. The gamma radiation from 60CO source were used to sterilise the pupae of screw worm, *Cochliomyia hominivorax* in cattle in Curacao island of USA. The sterile males obtained were released at 400 males per square mile (2.59 square km) for 7 weeks to get 100 per cent sterile egg masses, meaning a total eradication of the pest. However, the cost of producing these radiations is prohibitive enough to render them commercially unprofitable.

MECHANICAL CONTROL

The reduction or suppression of insect populations by means of manual devices is referred to as mechanical control.

Collection and Destruction

Hand-picking and destruction of large sized, conspicuous, immature or mature stages of insects is the most ancient method which can prove fairly effective under certain conditions. The egg masses of rice stem borer and groundnut red hairy caterpillar can be picked up and destroyed. Collection and destruction of egg masses of top borer in first and second brood during March and May in ratoon and autumn planted sugarcane crops, if done over compact block, reduces top borer damage in endemic pockets. Destruction of infested cane stocks harbouring larvae of Gurdaspur and plassey borers in gregarious phase over an area wide basis is useful for reducing the incidence of these borers.

Handpicking is also generally useful for the management of hairy caterpillers, leaf rollers, tobacco caterpillar, cabbage butterfly, mustard sawfly, *Epilachna* beetle, white grubs, cockchafer beetles, etc. Collection and destruction of fallen infested fruits is effective against fruitflies and fruit borers. Manual removal of pink bollworm-attacked rosetted flowers, withered and drooped terminals infested by spotted bollworms, flared up squares, stressed and shed floral bodies attacked by bollworms, leaves with egg masses or younger instars of tobacco caterpillars can reduce the incidence of these pests in cotton crop. Pruning and destruction of infested shoots and floral parts is effective in checking the multiplication of scales, mealy bugs and gall midges attacking fruit trees like grapes, citrus, *ber*, fig, custard apple, etc. The clipping of infested rice seedlings helps to reduce the incidence of rice hispa. The insects like leafhoppers, earhead bugs and grasshoppers can be netted and killed. Adults of rhinoceros beetle are hooked out from the coconut crowns by means of iron hook. Passing a rope across a rice crop is sometimes done so as to dislodge the caseworms over the standing water which is then drained out to collect the pest at the mouth of the field.

Preventive Barriers

Digging of 30 to 60 cm wide and 60 cm deep trenches or erecting 30 cm high tin-sheet barriers around field is useful for protecting them from moving bands of locusts, hairy caterpillars and armyworms. Fruits wrapped in paper bags or cloth or straw remain protected to the extent of nearly 95 per cent against fruitflies. Paper and tin collars are placed around small plants like potato and tobacco to protect them from cutworms. Tin bands are fixed over coconut palms to prevent damage by rats. Pomegranate fruits are protected from fruit borer attack by covering them with paper or polythene bags. Putting fences around crop fields in the normal way or charged with low voltage electricity will keep away animal pests like rats and jackals. Stems and fruits could be surrounded by wiregauge screens to prevent attack by insects, particularly the borers. Screens and other barriers like mosquito nets and fly-proof cages are used to prevent flies, mosquitoes and other insects.

Stem-banding devices could be employed to prevent insect pests from climbing to the tree tops, so as to destroy inflorescence or to descend back to the soil to lay eggs (mango mealy bug). For instance, a band of some sticky material could be painted directly on the stem or on a waxed paper strip wound round the stem (Fig. 2.2A). Even two metallic cones with their mouths in opposite directions and insides painted with a sticky substance could be fitted around the stem to check both ascending and descending insects (Fig. 2.2B).

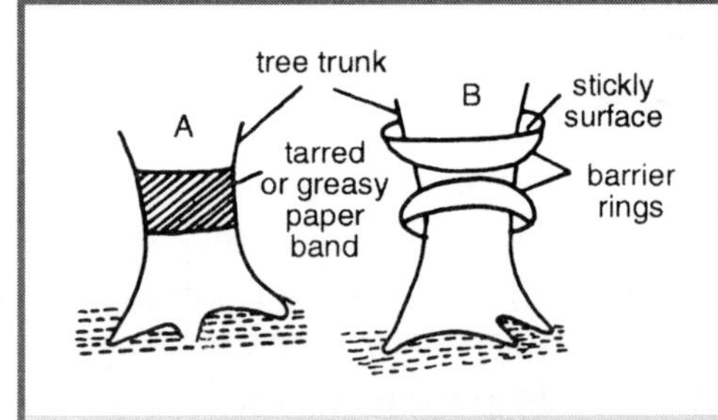

Fig. 2.2 Mechanical barriers to prevent movement of insects. A. Sticky band B. Sticky cones

Trapping

Any number of traps can be devised to exploit a dominating or fixed instinct of an insect: (*i*) *light traps* are used to attract night (nocturnal) insects which are strongly phototoxic, (*ii*) *food preferences* are exploited for baiting, (*iii*) *sticky traps* could be made by painting surfaces with some substances sticky enough to hold the insects striking it, (*iv*) *window-pane traps* consisting of a vertical glass-pane with an insecticide trough below, are specially suitable for coleopterans which react by falling into the trough after hitting the pane, (*v*) *vacuum trapping* or *suction devices* are used to suck the pest in; a portable motor, run on petrol, propels a blower which creates a sucking force, (*vi*) *pheromone traps* are used to attract the males, and (*vii*) *sound trapping* devices are used to scare the insects away; for example, the cotton bollworms have a natural enemy in bats which feed on them. These insects can perceive ultraosnic waves produced by the bats. Therefore, the ultrasonic waves are recorded and played in the fields to scare the insects away–a sort of a sound "scarecrow".

LEGAL CONTROL

Legal control involves the enactment of laws to regulate the entry, establishment and spread of pests. In early days, there were no restrictions on the transport of plants and animals from one country to another, because the danger involved in it, was either not realised or appreciated. This resulted in introduction of certain pests from countries of their origin to other countries, where the pests were not known to occur earlier. In many countries, quite a number of dangerous pests have been found to be the foreign pests and they inflict much severe damage than the indigenous ones. Cottony cushion scale, woolly aphid, San Jose scale, golden cyst nematode of potatoes and the giant African snail are some of the exotic pests that have been into India. The important foreign pests of which our country is free are the Mediterranean fruit fly, the grapevine phylloxera and the Mexican cotton boll weevil. The codling moth is restricted to Ladakh region of Jammu and Kashmir.

The importance of imposing restrictions on the movement of pest-infested plants or plant material from one country to another was realized when the grape phylloxera got introduced into France from USA by about 1860, and the San Jose scale spread into the USA in the later part of the 19th century and caused severe damage. This necessitated passing legislation and the first quarantine act in the USA came into operation in 1905. The first Act in India was passed in 1906 under the Sea Customs Act of 1878 to stop the entry of Mexican cotton boll weevil. This was followed by the "Destructive Insects and Pests Act of 1914", to prevent the introduction into our country of any insect, fungus or other pest destructive to crops.

The legislative measures in force in different countries can be grouped into five classes :

- Legislation to prevent the introduction of new insect pests, diseases and weeds from foreign countries.
- Legislation to prevent the spread of already established insect pests, diseases and weeds from one part of the country to another.
- Legislation to enforce upon the farmers, the application of effective control measures to prevent damage by the already established insect pests, diseases or weeds.
- Legislation to prevent the adulteration and misbranding of insecticides and to determine their permissible residue tolerances in food stuffs.
- Legislation to regulate the activities of men, engaged in pest control operations and the application of hazardous insecticides.

Historical Acts

The history of pest-control legislation in India is very interesting and various acts have been enacted from time to time.

1. The first Act in this country was passed in 1906 under the Sea Customs Act of 1878 to stop the entry of the Mexican cotton boll weevil. It was followed by the present Destructive Insects and Pests Act No.II passed on 3rd February 1914 at the instigation of Bombay Chamber of Commerce. Thus, provisions were made for preventing the entry of foreign insect pests, like the American cotton boll weevil, *Anthonomus grandis* and others that might be harboured in agricultural products. The entry of such plant material as sugarcane and unginned cotton was banned totally. Plants and seeds, in general, could be imported under certificates of health through notified ports where they could be inspected by qualified staff, fumigated properly and kept in quarantine before being released. There, they could be examined for the presence of eggs of pests or for the presence of bacteria, fungi and other pathogens, which are normally not killed by fumigation. The import of useful insects such as parasites was permitted only to scientific institutions.
2. According to various amendments of the Government of India Act, 1914, provisions were made for adopting control measures against local and exotic pests in centrally administered territories and states after first obtaining sanction from the President of India or from the Governor. Before control measures could be adopted by the state, it was considered necessary to (*i*) declare the organism to be injurious, (*ii*) place the infested area under quarantine, and (*iii*) ensure that preventive and remedial measures were prescribed. In this Act, provisions were also made for the state governments to pass their own legislation for adopting remedial measures. Accordingly, the then Madras Government enacted the Madras Agricultural Pests and Diseases Act in 1919, which was perhaps the first Act passed by any state in the country. This Act was brought into force from time to time to prevent the spread of five pests, viz. cottony cushion, scale, *Icerya purchasi*; black-headed caterpillar, *Opisina arenosella*; coffee berry borer, *Hypothenemus hampei*; sugarcane top borer, *Scirpophaga excerptalis*, and the cattle fly, *Stomoxys calcitrans*. The East Punjab Agricultural Pests, Diseases and Noxious Weeds Act was passed in 1949. Other states have passed similar legislation.
3. According to notification No. 1581, dated 1st October, 1931, under the Destructive Insects and Pests Act, 1914, provisions were made to restrict the imports of cotton from America and the West Indies, and to bring air freight within the scope of the Act. The import of cotton was allowed, provided it was fumigated and disinfected at the port of entry. The import of plant material by air was prohibited except under strict quarantine for scientific purposes, with prior permission of the Government of India. Similarly, fruits and vegetables from Afghanistan were allowed to be imported, provided they were accompanied with certificates of health issued by a competent authority. The import of seeds by air was exempted, but the entry of some of the seeds, namely cotton, Egyptian clover, flax, rubber, coffee and sunflower was banned. The import of potato seed from areas infested with golden nematode and wart disease was prohibited.

   Under this Act, notifications were also issued from time to time for the inspection, disinfection or destruction of plant material to be transported by road or by rail within the country. This checked the further spread of pests and diseases that might be present in certain plant parts. A number of such plants and plant material harbouring various pests were listed and the station masters of railway stations and other inspection authorities were given legal powers. The owners causing hindrance to the inspection of material at the destination were liable to be prosecuted and punished with fine up to Rs 1000. These provisions were made to restrict the spread of San Jose scale, *Quadraspidiotusperniciosus*; cottony-cushion scale, *Icerya purchasi*, the potato-wart disease, water hyacinth, lantana, spike disease of the sandal tree and the bunchy-top disease of banana.

4. According to the provision of the East Punjab Agricultural Pests, Diseases and Noxious Weeds Act 1949 (and other similar state acts), the state government could enforce, when necessary, control measures for the eradication of pests, diseases or weeds, such as locusts and grasshoppers, hairy caterpillars, rats, pyrilla and the Gurdaspur borer of sugarcane, *Bissetia steniella*, ergot of pearl-millet, *pohli (Carthamus oxycantha*), water hyacinth (*Eichhornia crassipes*) and other weeds.

The government would issue a notification, declaring the pest or weed to be noxious, specifying the area and the period for which it would remain in force, giving proper directions for carrying out control measures, and for adopting other practices against the introduction, reappearance or spread of the pest, disease or the weed concerned. The sowing of a particular crop for a given period could also be prohibited. The farmers of the notified area would be bound to carry out the preventive or remedial measures. If, on inspection, it was found that a given farmer did not carry out these instructions and the pest was still present, the inspector would issue a notice that the operations must be carried out within a specified period, failing which the inspector with his staff would perform this job at the expense of the farmer. The amount involved would be recoverable as arrears of land revenue. It would appear that the procedures laid down were lengthy and it would be rarely possible to enforce, in case of default, the measures recommended during a crop season. For that resaon, the implementation of the Act has not been very effective and *pohli*, for example, remained in the fields after the harvest of wheat fields throughout north India. It was only because of double-cropping and intensive agriculture since 1965 that this weed gradually disappeared in Punjab and other states.

In other cases where free pesticides were supplied for the control of pests, the success was greater. Anti-rat campaigns have been carried out by the Department of Agriculture and the Community Development Organization, and the cutting of sugarcane tops for the control of the Gurdaspur borer has been adopted in the factory zones

(10 km of sugar factory) of the Punjab and Haryana with considerable success.

The Prevention of Food Adulteration (PFA) Act, 1954 was enacted on September 1954, for prevention of adulteration of food. In view of the fast-expanding pesticide industry and the widespread use of these highly poisonous chemicals, more specific provisions were needed to safeguard public interests and even human life. Consequently, a special legislation to regulate the manufacture, transport, handling, sale and use of pesticides was envisaged and a new Bill, namely the Insecticide Bill was passed by the Indian Parliament in September 1968. Under this Act, provisions have been made for the compulsory registration of pesticides and for the establishment of pesticide laboratories to carry out various functions under the legislation. Recently, Pesticides Management Bill, 2008, has been introduced in the Rajya Sabha, and it will replace the Insecticides Act, 1968.

Prevention of Food Adulteration Act, 1954

The Prevention of Food Adulteration (PFA) Act was enacted on September 29, 1954 for prevention of adulteration of food. Rule 65 under Part XIV 'Insecticides and Pesticides' of Prevention of Food Adulteration Rules, 1955, specifies restrictions on the use of insecticides. It also specifies tolerance limits of pesticides on different raw agricultural products which move in commerce. The Central Committee for Food Standards (CCFS) under the Ministry of Health and Family Welfare renders advice to central and state governments on (*i*) formulation of rules, regulations and standards of food articles, and (*ii*) ensuring uniform administration of the Act throughout the country. The CCFS recommends the quality of food commodities under the PFA Act. Among its various sub-committees, Pesticide Residue Sub-committee advises CCFS on (*i*) tolerance limits for pesticides in different articles of food based on use pattern, dietary habits and nutritional status of our population, and (*ii*) restriction on sale of insecticides by the persons manufacturing, storing or selling food.

The Plant Protection Adviser to the Government of India, is the chairman of this sub-committee. Before tolerance limits for any pesticide are considered, the same needs to be approved and registered by the Registration Committee, constituted under the Insecticides Act, 1968. Based on the recommendations of Pesticide Residue Sub-Committee and after the approval of the CCFS, the Ministry of Health and Family Welfare has so far notified tolerance limits for 71 pesticides under Rule 65(2) of PFA Rules 1955.

Insecticides Act, 1968

The Insecticides Act was passed by Parliament on September 2, 1968 to regulate the import, manufacture, sale, transport, distribution and use of insecticides with a view to prevent risks to human beings or animals, and for matters connected therewith. The Act was enforced throughout the country with effect from August 1, 1971 and the rules were framed and brought into force on October 30, 1971 for effective implementation of the Act. The Act was amended in 1972 and 1977 to overcome teething problems in its implementation. During the administration and implementation of the Insecticides Act, 1968 during the last three decades, several practical difficulties were experienced for administration and enforcement of the Act. Consequently, a bill was introduced in the Parliament and amendments to the Insecticides Act were notified in the Gazatte of India on August 7, 2000.

The term 'insecticide' has been defined under the Act to include any substance in the Schedule or such other substances or preparations intended for the purposes of preventing, destroying, repelling or mitigating any insects, rodents, fungi, weeds and other forms of plant and animal life not useful to human beings. The central government on the recommendation and approval of the Central Insecticides Board can include substances in the Schedule from time to time. Applications for the registration of insecticides can be made for those chemicals, which are included in the Insecticides Schedule.

The Insecticides Act has been enforced in the country to achieve some of the under mentioned objectives :

- To register only safe and efficacious pesticides.
- To ensure that the farmers/users get quality product for controlling the pests.
- To prescribe usages of pesticides both from ground and air, and also important precautions for their handling and use.

- To minimise health hazards from the pesticide residues through contaminated food, water and air.
- To ensure that the pesticide industry manufacture, transport, distribute, store and sell the pesticides as per the prescribed regulations, failing which legal action is taken.
- To ensure that the pesticides are properly packed and labelled to avoid any leakage of the hazardous pesticides in transit and to provide enough instructions for their safe handling and use.

In order to achieve these objectives, the Government of India and state governments have created suitable machinery both at the centre and the state-level for implementing this Act. Under this Act, both the central and the state governments have powers to make rules in consultation with the Central Insecticides Board in the manner prescribed. Some of the most important functionaries prescribed and the regulatory procedures laid down under this Act are as follows :

A. Central Bodies and Laboratories

(i) Central Insecticides Board. This Board advises the central and state governments in all technical matters such as manufacture, formulation, storage, transport, distribution, sale, and safe use of insecticides. The Board also fixes tolerance limits for insecticide residues, safety period and shelf life, based on the data provided by the manufacturers and also based on research findings of the scientists in the country. The Board has 29 members representing various Ministries and Departments of the Government of India, and some specialists. The Director General of Health Services is the Chairman of the Board.

(ii) Registration Committee. This Committee consists of a Chairman, and not more than five persons from amongst the members of the Central Insecticides Board, including the Drugs Controller and the Plant Protection Advisor. The person appointed as Secretary by the central government functions as secretary of the Board and of this Committee. The secretary is assisted by seven technical officers namely, an Entomologist, a Plant Pathologist, an Agronomist, a Medical Toxicologist, a Senior Chemist, a Packaging Engineer, and a Law Officer and other ministerial staff.

Before these can be sold in India, all insecticides have to be approved and registered by this Committee. Registration is done after scrutinizing and verifying the formulae and their efficacy, and safety to human beings and animals. In addition, the Committee may also specify the precautions to be taken against poisoning by the use and handling of the particular insecticide.

(iii) Other Committees. The Board has constituted the following Committees and Expert Panels: (*a*) Pesticides Environmental Pollution Advisory Committee, to advise the Board on all hazards emanating from the use of pesticides for agriculture, public health, grain storage or for any other purpose. The Committee has 20 members including the Chairman. (*b*) Six different Expert Panels have been constituted to finalise the approved usages of insecticides (organophosphates, carbamates and organochlorinated hydrocarbons), fungicides, herbicides and fumigants, and rodenticides. The manufacturers of pesticides are obliged to give these usages and bio-effective qualities on leaflets.

B. Registration of Insecticides

A prospective manufacturer or an importer of a given insecticide, first applies to the Secretary, Registration Committee and Central Insecticides Board for consideration and acceptance of the product by the Registration Committee. The Committee, after making enquiries on the claims of the manufacturer or the importer as to the effectiveness and safety of the insecticide to human beings and animals, registers the insecticide on payment of prescribed fee and allots its registration number and issues a Certificate of Registration. This certificate is given within a period of 12 months from the date of receipt of the complete application. This period can be further extended to a maximum of six months when it is to be decided to register or reject application.

The general policy of the Government of India is that the insecticides approved should, as far as possible, be manufactured in the country. The new insecticides which are introduced in the country for the first time are generally registered provisionally for import and formulations for a period of 2 years. This period can be further extended in exceptional cases. During this time, the complete data are required for regular registration of the insecticide. Simultaneously, the laboratory and the field tests are also made in the Central Insecticides Laboratory or the Regional Laboratories and other scientific institutions. After an insecticide has been tried and found to be effective and safe, a regular registration is granted for its import or indigenous manufacture.

C. Licences for Manufacture and Sale

Any person desiring to manufacture or to sell, stock or exhibit for sale or distribute any insecticide or to undertake commercial pest control with the use of any insecticide, must first get a licence from the Licensing Officer of the state government. Such a licence can be granted for a specific period on receipt of an application on prescribed forms and on the payment of prescribed fee. The licence can be renewed from time to time, and may even be cancelled if it is found that there was some misrepresentation made as to some essential facts or in the event of failure to comply with the conditions on which the licence was granted.

D. Central Insecticides Laboratory

Under the provision of the Act, the Government of India has set up a Central Insecticides Laboratory under the control of a Director. The Director of this Laboratory is responsible for the following duties and functions :

- To analyse the samples of insecticides sent by any officer or authority of the central or state government.
- To analyse samples of materals for insecticide residues.
- To carry out such investigations as may be necessary for ensuring the conditions of the registration of insecticides.
- To determine the efficacy and toxicity of insecticides.
- To carry out such other functions as may be entrusted to him by the central government or by state governments with the permission of the Insecticides Board.

E. State Insecticides Testing Laboratory

Every state and union territory of India is required to establish one or more insecticides testing laboratories to test the quality of pesticide samples sent by Insecticide Inspectors. There is a network of 45 State Insecticide Testing Laboratories in 18 states and union territories with an annual analysis capacity of about 56,000 samples. The required staff and suitable laboratory equipment to carry out the analysis of the pesticide samples have been provided for each such laboratory. The Insecticide Analyst acts as the Incharge of the Laboratory and is required to deliver a test or analysis report, in duplicate, duly signed within a period of 30 days, for insecticide samples submitted to him by the Insecticide Inspector.

Pesticides Management Bill, 2008

A Bill seeking to encourage production of good quality and safe pesticides at affordable rates while curbing sale of spurious products was introduced in the Rajya Sabha on 20th October, 2008. The new Bill, which would replace the Insecticides Act, 1968, was needed to provide for better management of pesticides to respond to the need for faster agricultural growth. The proposed law aims to regulate the import, manufacture, export, sale, transport, distribution, quality and use of pesticides in the country. The new law is being enacted with a view to minimize the contamination of agricultural commodities by pesticide residues. The government will allow the use of a pesticide only after assessing its efficacy and safety. The Bill enables the government to constitute the Central Pesticides Board to advise on scientific and technical matters arising out of the administration of the proposed law.

For the first time, the government has defined household pesticides to enable delicensing of their retail sales for easy availability to the consumers. The Bill will also prohibit field application of household pesticides. Under the Bill, there is provision to accredit private laboratories to carry out all functions of the Central Pesticides Laboratory. It has also provided an elaborate procedure for drawing pesticide samples and their inspection. Under the proposed law, the government has made punishment more stringent to check production and sale of mis-branded, sub-standard and spurious pesticides.

The salient features of the proposed bill are as follows :

- To improve the quality of pesticides available to the Indian farmers and introduce new, safe and efficacious pesticides.
- More effective regulation of import, manufacture, export, sale, transport, distribution and use of pesticides, to prevent risk to human beings, animals and the environment.
- Detailed categorization of offences and punishment for greater deterrence to violators.
- De-licensing of retail sale of household pesticides.
- Timely disposal of time-barred pesticides in an environmentally safe manner.

CONCLUSIONS

A number of physical and mechanical control measures are in use ever since the evolution of agriculture. Some of these methods were modified and refined over time to increase their efficacy. In general, these measures are cost effective, easy to adopt and compatible with other pest management tactics. Moreover, these measures do not cause any adverse effect on the environment. Nevertheless, some of the physical control measures are costly and are beyond the reach of individual farmers. Some of the methods like handpicking of egg masses, cutting and removal of affected plant parts, and trapping of insects are recommended, but their scope is limited only to small cropping area and hence are not becoming popular among the farmers. Research efforts are needed to substantiate the usefulnes of these methods as an economical way of controlling pests at different stages of crop growth. There is a need to identify and apply these measures in specific situations, where other measures like the application of pesticides is not possible or uneconomical. Some of the legislative measures have played a pivotal role in preventing the introduction of exotic pests or spread of the indigenous pests to new areas. There is a need to apply these laws more stringently to avoid potential pest problems. The problem of sale of spurious pesticides is quite serious in India, where farmers had to suffer heavy losses. It is hoped that with the enactment and implementation of the proposed Pesticides Management Bill, 2008, good quality and safe pesticides would be available at affordable rates, to prevent risk to human beings, other non-target organisms and the environment.

☆☆☆☆☆

CULTURAL CONTROL

INTRODUCTION

Cultural practices include all the crop production and management techniques which are utilized by the farmers to maximize their crop productivity and/or farm income. It includes decisions on crops/varieties to be grown, time and manner of planting, tillage, field and crop sanitation, application of fertilizers and irrigation, harvesting times and procedures, and even off-season operations in fallow/cropped fields. Historically, cultural practices were the farmers' most important method of preventing crop losses. Prior to the emergence of crop protection sciences and even before the broad outlines of the biology of pests were understood, the farmers evolved many cultural practices largely through trial and error experiences to minimise the damage caused by insect pests. The prophylactic practices included field and plant sanitation, good seeds, proper cultivation, manuring, water management, etc. The curative methods consisted of deep ploughing, flooding, weeding, trap crops, etc. On the other hand, cultural practices like closer plant spacings, sowing times, rotations, harvesting procedures, etc. developed as part of the modern agricultural technology for exploiting the full genetic yield potential of high yielding varieties, have simultaneously proved favourable to most of the insect pests. To overcome these problems, some of the traditional practices have again been modified and modern cultural methods developed to strengthen pest management and enhance crop productivity.

The manipulation of farming practices for reducing or avoiding pest damage to crops is known as cultural control. Since cultural control manipulations are based on habitat management and require a thorough understanding of different components of the agroecosystem in which the pests thrive, this approach has also been called as ***ecological managementor environmental control***. The purpose of cultural control practices is to make the environment less favourable for the pest and and/or more favourable for its natural enemies.

The following are the main characteristics of cultural practices which should be viewed in the context of IPM.

- Cultural practices are simple modifications or adaptations of regular farm operations. The extra cost of their incorporation into pest management system is minimal in most cases. These are often the only control options economically feasible for low-value crops.
- Cultural practices generally produce no or negligible undesirable ecological consequences.
- Cultural control is primarily aimed at prevention and reduction of pest outbreaks.
- The results of cultural practices are often difficult to quantify primarily because ecological relationships within crop systems are poorly understood.
- Cultural control tactics are an effective means of pest control. These do not result in total elimination of the pest thus allowing for conservation of beneficial insects.
- Most cultural practices indirectly affect the pests and these are relatively slow acting and thus cannot resolve a pest outbreak. These are, however, important in minimizing pest damage by preventing pest build-up, rather than relieving an already existing pest problem.
- Cultural practices make cropping systems less friendly to the establishment and proliferation of pest populations.
- Cultural practices are designed to have positive effects on farm ecology and pest management, however, negative impacts may also result due to variations in weather, changes in crop management or perturbations in agroecosystems.
- Timing is critical to the success of most cultural practices, accordingly, the implementation of cultural control tactics requires thorough knowledge of pest ecology and its interaction with the cropping system.
- An area-wide deployment of cultural practices is essential for the effectiveness of the practice in IPM.
- Cultural practices are often pest-, crop and region-specific. Care should be exercised in transferring tactics to a region with markedly different agroecological conditions.

PLANTING TIME

The manipulation of planting time helps to minimise pest damage by producing asynchrony between host plant and the pest or synchronizing insect pests with their natural enemies or crop production with available alternate host plants of the pest or by production followed by destruction of crop residues before the insects can enter diapause. The classical example is that of Hessian fly, *Mayetiola destructor* control in USA by establishment of planting dates during 1930s. Hessian fly eggs are laid on the upper surface of young winter wheat leaves. By delayed planting, suitable hosts were not available until most of the overwintering adult flies emerged and died.

Similarly, the development of agronomically acceptable early-maturing varieties has received considerable emphasis in cotton-breeding programmes. The short-season, rapidly-fruiting cotton variety matures about 2-3 weeks earlier than the long-season cotton. The United States cotton industry survived the boll weevil plague of the early 1900s by using early-maturing varieties. When an early harvest was coupled with area wide stalk destruction before mid-September, the over-wintering populations of diapausing insects were drastically reduced by as much as 90 per cent.

In north India, the optimum sowing period of cotton is from mid April to mid May but more than 30 per cent sowing is delayed due to non-availability of canal irrigation. The sowing usually continues for 2-3 months that prolong the growing period and pests get continuous food for longer period. Due to staggered sowing, pests are able to compete 1-2 additional generations in the season. It is estimated that in case of pink bollworm the population increases by 20-fold from generation to generation and this indicates heavy build up of population during last 4-5 generations that could be avoided by timely sowing of cotton. Similarly, *Helicoverpa armigera* and *Bemisia tabaci* are late season pests and by sowing till mid-May, crop can escape damage from these pests.

In India, early planting has been found to reduce gall midge and leaf folder damage in rice; shootfly and headbug damage in sorghum and millets; whitegrub damage in groundnut and mustard aphid damage in *Brassica* crops. Timely and synchronous planting has been found to reduce bollworm damage in cotton and stem borer damage in sugarcane. The early and late sown cotton crop suffered higher damage due to pink and spotted bollworms. Early sowing can be used to minimize pod borer, *H. armigera* damage to chickpea in north India. Two peaks of *H. armigera* occur during December and March in the *rabi* season. During the second peak, the pest inflicts severe damage to chickpea crop. Early (October) sown crop escapes with least damage. Late-sowing (December and January) matures during late-March to April and suffers heavy damage. November-sown crop also suffers moderate damage.

SEED RATE

Adoption of appropriate seed rate ensures proper stand, spacing and crop canopy that helps in adoption of proper spray technology and checks the unwanted growth of crop. Use of high seed rate is recommended in those crops where removal of infested plants is helpful in minimising the incidence of insect pests, viz. maize borer in maize and sorghum shootfly in sorghum and other crops. The farmers in north India use 25-50 per cent less seed rate in cotton to avoid thinning. Low seed rate along with untimely rain and high temperature during sowing, drought conditions, termite attack and incidence of root rot, further reduce the plant stand. The plant stand estimated at the time of harvest is 12-30 per cent less than the recommended plant population. The use of appropriate seed rate in cotton leaf curl virus affected areas helps to maintain proper crop stand even after roguing of the diseased plants at an early stage. Besides this, too low or high seed rate adversely affects spraying operation.

PLANT SPACING

The major objective in spacing crop plants is to obtain maximum high quality yield per unit area per unit time. But spacing may also influence the population and damage of many insect pests by modifying the micro-environment of the crop or affecting health, vigour and strength of the crop plants or pattern and duration of crop growth and development. Closer spacing has been reported to increase the incidence of planthoppers, viz. brown planthopper and whitebacked planthopper, gall midge and leaf folder in rice crop. The percentage of plants showing hopper burn symptoms ranged from 100 in closer spacing (10 × 10 cm) to 7-67 in wider spacing (23 × 10 cm). Detailed multilocation trials have shown that stem borer and gall midge were more in closer spacings (10 × 10 cm and 10 × 15 cm) than in wider spacings (20 × 15 cm, 20 × 20 cm and 30 × 30 cm). On the other hand, closer spacing resulted in lower incidence of green leafhopper, rice hispa and whorl maggot.

The closer spacing in cotton results in bushy growth of the crop that affects penetration of light, results in vertical growth of the plant, hinders spraying operation and also results in higher relative humidity that favours higher incidence of sucking pests and bollworms. In closer plant spacing (45 × 30 cm), jassid population has been observed to be high as compared to wider spacing (60 × 45 cm). Incidence of bollworms is also higher in closer plant spacing (15 cm) in *hirsutum* cotton varieties LH 886 and F 505 than in wider plant spacing (30 cm).

Closer spacing in groundnut lowered the incidence of thrips, jassids and leafminer, and also increased parasitism in the latter. On the other hand, in cotton it increased the damage by jassid, whitefly and bollworms. In *hirsutum* cotton, the incidence of pink bollworm was 5.2 and 17.1 per cent at 75 × 20 cm and 50 × 20 cm, respectively. Larval population of podborer, *H. armigera* on chickpea was 4 times as large at closest (33 plants/m2) as at widest (3 plants/m2) spacing. There was little advantage of more than 8 plants/m2 in chemically protected crop. In soybean, damage by a number of insect pests including *Spilosoma obliqua, Melanagromyza sojae* and *Bemisia tabaci* was greater in closely planted crop. In sugarcane, closer spacing resulted in higher incidence of shoot, internode and stalk borers. In contrast to all these studies, population of *Aphis craccivora* on chickpea was more in widely spaced crop (60 × 20 cm) than in closer spacing (30 × 10 cm).

TILLAGE

The type and timing of tillage can markedly influence the soil environment and affect the survival of insect pests or their natural enemies. Fall ploughing is often helpful in reducing the overwintering population of *Helicoverpa* spp. and several species of cutworms that undergo diapause in the soil during winter. Deep ploughing immediately after harvest of wheat crop in April-May is helpful in exposing the resting grubs of rice root weevil to their natural enemies like birds and to the action of sun and wind. Deep ploughing is also helpful in minimising the infestation of armyworm in cereal crops, white grubs attacking groundnut and chillies, pupae of hairy caterpillars attacking groundnut, green gram, etc. Raking up and hoeing of the soil around melon plants, mango and other fruit trees serve to destroy pupae of fruit flies. A disc plough treatment caused upto 73 per cent mortality of overwintering larvae of *Dectes texanus,* a pest of sunflower compared to 40 per cent mortality recorded using a sweep plough. Light earthing at the early stage of sugarcane crop during May-June is helpful in checking the shoot borer.

PLANT DIVERSITY

Deterrence of colonisation is probably one of the most promising means of controlling insect pests through intra-field diversity, because only a little additional diversity in the crop field may have a profound effect on colonization by insects. The diversity of a crop system can be increased by intercropping, trap cropping, presence of weeds or by crops grown in the adjacent fields. When interplanted crops or weeds in the crop are also suitable host plants for a particular pest, they may reduce feeding damage to the main crop by diverting the pest. On the other hand, these may also serve as an essential source of food or shelter at some point in the life cycle or during some part of the season, enabling the pest to maintain or build up its numbers in the field and so attack the main crop more severely.

Intercropping

Some of the examples of intercropping systems that help in preventing pest outbreaks are listed in Table 3.1.

Table 3.1 Selected Examples of intercropping systems that effectively prevent insect pest outbreaks

Intercroping system	Pest(s) regulated	Factor(s) involved
Beans grown in relay intercropping with winter wheat	*Empoasca fabae* and *Aphis fabae*	Impairment of visual searching behaviour of dispersing aphids
Brassica crops and beans	*Brevicoryne brassicae* and *Delia brassicae*	Higher predation and disruption of oviposition behaviour
Brussels sprouts intercropped with fava beans and/or mustard	Flea beetle, *Phyllotreta crucifecae* and cabbage aphid, *Brevicoryne brassicae*	Reduced plant apparency trap cropping, enhanced biological control
Cabbage intercroped with white and red clover	*Erioischia brassicae*, cabbage aphids, and imported cabbage butterfly (*Pieris rapae*)	Interference with colonization and increase of ground beetles
Intercropping of *Cajanus cajan* with red, black and green gram	Pod borers, jassids, and membracids	Delayed colonization of herbivores
Cassava intercropped with cowpeas	Whiteflies, *Aleurotrachelus socialis* and *Trialeurodes variabilis*	Changes in plant vigour and increased abundance of natural enemies
Cauliflower strip cropped with rape and/or marigold	Blossom beetle, *Meligethes aeneus*	Trap cropping
Corn intercropped with beans	Leafhoppers (*Empoasca kraemeri*), leaf beetle (*Diabrotica balteata*) and fall armyworm (*Spodoptera frugiperda*)	Increase in beneficial insects and interference with colonization
Corn intercropped with fava beans and squash	Aphids, *Tetranychus urticae* and *Macrodactylus* sp.	Enhanced abundance of predators
Corn intercropped with clover	*Ostrinia nubilalis*	Unknown
Corn intercropped with soybean	European corn borer, *nubilalis*	Differences in corn varietal resistance
Corn intercropped with sweet potatoes	Leaf beetles (*Diabrotica* spp.) and leafhoppers (*Agallia lingula*)	Increase in parasitic wasps
Intercropping corn and beans	*Dalbulus maidis*	Interference with leafhopper movement
Cotton intercropped with forage cowpea	Boll weevil (*Anthonomus grandis*)	Population increase of parasitic wasps (*Eurytoma* sp.)
Intercropping cotton with sorghum or maize	Corn earworm (*Helicoverpa zea*)	Increased abundance of predators
Cotton intercropped with okra	*Podagrica* sp.	Trap cropping
Strip cropping of cotton and alfalfa	Plant bugs (*Lygus hesperus* and *L. elisus*)	Prevention of emigration and sychrony in the relationship between pests and natural enemies
Strip cropping of cotton and alfalfa on one side and maize and soybean on the other	Corn earworm (*H. zea*) and cabbage looper (*Trichoplusia ni*)	Increased abundance of predators
Intercropping cowpea and sorghum	Leaf beetle (*Oetheca benningseni*)	Interference of air currents

Cucumbers intercropped with maize and broccoli	*Acalymma vittata*	Interference with movement and tenure time on host plants
Groundnuts intercropped with field beans	*Aphis craccivora*	Aphids trapped on epidermal hair of beans
Maize intercropped with canavlia	*Prorachia daria* and fall armyworm (*Spodoptera frugiperda*)	Not reported
Maize-bean intercropping	*Spodoptera frugiperda* and *Diatraea lineolata*	Lower oviposition rates, trap cropping
Strip cropping of muskmelons with wheat	*Myzus persicae*	Interference with aphid dispersal
Oats intercropped with field beans	*Rhopalosiphum* sp.	Interference with aphid dispersal
Peaches intercropped with strawberries	Strawberry leafroller (*Ancylis comptana*) Oriented fruit moth (*Grapholita molesta*)	Population increase of parasites (*Macrocentrus ancyclivorus, Microbracon gelechise*, and *Lixophaga variabilis*)
Peanut intercropped with maize	Corn borer (*Ostrinia furnacalis*)	Abundance of spiders (*Lycosa* sp.)
Sesame intercropped with corn or sorghum	Webworms (*Antigostra* sp.)	Shading by the taller companion crop
Sesame intercropped with cotton	*Heliothis* spp.	Increase of beneficial insects and trap cropping
Soybean strip cropped with snap beans	*Epilachna varivestis*	Trap cropping
Squash intercropped with maize	*Acalymma thiemei, Diabrotica balteata*	Increased dispersion due to avoidance of host plants shaded by maize and interference with flight movements by maize stalks
Tomato and tobacco intercropped with cabbage	Flea beetles (*Phyllotreta cruciferae*)	Feeding inhibition by odours from non host plants
Tomato intercropped with cabbage	Diamondback moth (*Plutella xylostella*)	Chemical repellency or masking

Source : Altieri and Nicholls (2004)

In central and southern India, intercropping of cotton with black gram, green gram, onion, cowpeas, etc. is reported to divert the population of sucking pests and American bollworm from cotton. Monoculture of cotton was also found to harbour more insect pests than cotton intercropped with groundnut, cowpea and soybean. The intercrop of cowpea in cotton helped in the colonization of coccinellids and also enhanced the parasitism of spotted bollworm. On the other hand, okra, *mung* and pigeonpea as intercrops with cotton increased the population build up of jassid, whitefly, spotted bollworms and American bollworm.

Intercropping of groundnut with pearlmillet reduced the incidence of thrips, jassid and leaf miner whereas the same with sunflower and castor increased the incidence of thrips and jassid, respectively. When pearlmillet was grown as an intercrop in groundnut, the parasitic activity of *Goniozus* sp. was considerably enhanced. The pollen grains of the millet were preferably used as food by the adult parasitoids.

Tomato intercropped with cabbage has been reported to inhibit or reduce egg laying by diamondback moth. A planting pattern of one row of cabbage and one row of tomato (cabbage planted 30 days later than tomato), afforded maximum reduction of diamondback moth and leafwebber larvae on cabbage. Reduction in insect incidence was attributed to possible release of volatile substances from late crop growth stages of tomato which inhibited oviposition by incoming moths. Even the female moths which entered the mixed crop laid fewer eggs probably because of tomato foliage spread over every row of cabbage.

Intercropping of *taramira* in *raya* reduced the incidence of mustard aphid in the latter crop due to the allelopathic influence of the former. Similarly, trials conducted under the All India Coordinated Pulses Improvement Project at several locations demonstrated that the sole crop of chickpea attracted more *Helicoverpa* compared to intercrops with wheat, barley, linseed, mustard and safflower. On the other hand, lentil and field peas as inter-crops enhanced infestation in chickpea. Crop mixtures were more effective than row plantings.

In Kenya, intercropping maize with the non-host molasses grass, *Melinus minutiflora* decreased levels of infestation by stem borers, *Chilo partellus* and *Busseola fusca* and also increased larval parasitization of stem borers by *Apanteles sesamiae.* In field trials, *M. minutiflora* planted in alternate rows with maize significantly reduced stem borer infestation of the main crop (damaged maize plants : single crop 39.2%, intercropped with *M. minutiflora* 4.6%). There was also a significant increase in parasitization by the larval parasitoid, *A. sesamiae* (parasitized larvae in maize : single crop 5.4%, maize with *M. minutiflora* intercrop 20.7%). Volatile agents produced by *M. minutiflora* repelled female stem borers and attracted foraging female *A. sesamiae.*

Intercroping system

Beans grown in relay inter-cropping with winter wheatBrassica crops and beans Brussels sprouts intercropped with fava beans and/or mustardCabbage intercropped with white and red cloverIntercropping of *Cajanus cajan* with red, black and green gramCassava intercropped with cowpeasCauliflower strip cropped with rape and/or marigoldCorn intercropped with beansCorn intercropped with fava beans and squashCorn intercropped with cloverCorn intercropped with soybeanCorn intercropped with sweet potatoesIntercropping corn and beansCotton intercropped with forage cowpeaIntercropping cotton with sorghum or maizeCotton intercropped with okraStrip cropping of cotton and alfalfaStrip cropping of cotton and alfalfa on one side and maize and soybean on the otherIntercropping cowpea and sorghumCucumbers intercropped with maize and broccoliGroundnuts intercropped with field beansMaize intercropped with canavliaMaize-bean intercroppingStrip cropping of muskmelons with wheatOats intercropped with field beansPeaches intercropped with strawberriesPeanut intercropped with maizeSesame intercropped with corn or sorghumSesame intercropped with cottonSoybean strip cropped with snap beansSquash intercropped with maizeTomato and tobacco intercropped with cabbageTomato intercropped with cabbage

Pest(s) regulated

Empoasca fabae and *Aphis fabaeBrevicoryne brassicae* and *Delia brassicae*Flea beetle, *Phyllotreta crucifecae* and cabbage aphid, *B. brassicaeErioischia brassicae*, cabbage aphids, and imported cabbage butterfly (*Pieris rapae*)Pod borers, jassids, and membracidsWhiteflies, *Aleurotrachelus socialis* and *Trialeurodes variabilis*Blossom beetle, *Meligethes aeneus*Leafhoppers (*Empoasca kraemeri*), leaf beetle (*Diabrotica balteata*) and fall armyworm (*Spodoptera frugiperda*)Aphids, *Tetranychus urticae* and *Macrodactylus* sp.*Ostrinia nubilalis*European corn borer, *O.nubilalis*Leaf beetles (*Diabrotica* spp.) and leafhoppers (*Agallia lingula*)*Dalbulus maidis*Boll weevil (*Anthonomus grandis*)Corn earworm

(*Helicoverpa zea*)*Podagrica* sp.Plant bugs (*Lygus hesperus* and *L. elisus*)Corn earworm (*H. zea*) and cabbage looper (*Trichoplusia ni*)Leaf beetle (*Oetheca benningseni*)*Acalymma vittataAphis craccivoraProrachia daria* and fall armyworm (*S. frugiperda*) *S. frugiperda* and *Diatraea lineolataMyzus persicaeRhopalosiphum* sp.Strawberry leafroller (*Ancylis comptana*), Oriental fruit moth (*Grapholita molesta*)Corn borer (*Ostrinia furnacalis*)Webworms (*Antigostra* sp.)*Heliothis* spp.*Epilachna varivestisAcalymma thie mei, Diabrotica bal-teata*Flea beetles (*Phyllotreta cruciferae*)Diamondback moth (*Plutella xylostella*)

Factor(s) involved

Impairment of visual searching behaviour of dispersing aphidsHigher predation and disruption of oviposition behaviourReduced plant apparency, trap cropping, enhanced biological controlInterference with colonization and increase of ground beetlesDelayed colonization of herbivoresChanges in plant vigour and increased abundance of natural enemiesTrap croppingIncrease in beneficial insects and interference with colonizationEnhanced abundance of predatorsUnknownDifferences in corn varietal resistanceIncrease in parasitic waspsInterference with leafhopper movementPopulation increase of parasitic wasps (*Eurytoma* sp.)Increased abundance of predatorsTrap croppingPrevention of emigration and sychrony in the relationship between pests and natural enemiesIncreased abundance of predatorsInterference of air currentsInterference with movement and tenure time on host plantsAphids trapped on epidermal hair of beansNot reportedLower oviposition rates, trap croppingInterference with aphid dispersalInterference with aphid dispersalPopulation increase of parasites (*Macrocentrus ancyclivorus, Microbracon gelechiae,* and *Lixophaga variabilis*)Abundance of spiders (*Lycosa* sp.)Shading by the taller companion cropIncrease of beneficial insects and trap croppingTrap croppingIncreased dispersion due to avoidance of host plants shaded by maize and interference with flight movements by maize stalksFeeding inhibition by odours from non-host plantsChemical repellency or masking

Trap Cropping

Trap cropping is the planting of a crop to protect the main cash crop from a certain pest or several pests. The trap crop can be from the same or different family group, than that of the main crop, as long as it is more attractive to the pest. There are two types of the trap crops; perimeter trap cropping and row intercropping. Perimeter trap cropping (border trap cropping) is the planting of trap crop completely surrounding the main cash crop. It prevents a pest attack that comes from all sides of the field. It works best on pests that are found near the borderline to the farm. Row intercropping is the planting of the trap crop in alternating rows within the main crop.Even early or late plantings of the same crop in the main crop may also serve as traps. Thus trap crops are plant stands that are grown to attract insects or other organisms so that the target crop escapes pest attack. Protection is achieved either by preventing the pests from reaching the crop or by concentrating them in certain part of the field where they can easily be destroyed. The attractiveness of trap crops may be enhanced by use of insect pheromones, plant kairomones or insect food supplements. Depending on the seasonal cycle, insects may be left to develop in the trap or killed with an insecticide.

The major benefit of trap cropping is that insecticides are seldom required to be used on the main crop and this enhances the natural control of pests. Moreover, trap crops may also attract natural enemies thus enhancing natural control. The overall use of pesticides is clearly less than in conventional farming, making the strategy environmentally attractive. However, it needs to be emphasized here that the trap crop may also serve as a pest nursery for the target pest or some other pest(s). Some highly mobile natural enemies may be attracted to and aggregate on the trap crop just as on their host or prey. They are likely to be destroyed by insecticide sprays. A thorough understanding of the agroecocystem is, therefore, essential for recommending trap cropping as a means for minimising pest damage.

Globally, trap cropping has proved successful in experimental studies in a number of crops and has been recommended for large scale utilization (Table 3.2). Trap cropping has been successfully employed on a large scale in four crop ecosystems, viz. cotton and soybean in USA, potatoes in CIS (erstwhile USSR) and Bulgaria, and cauliflower in Finland. In cotton/ sesame intercrop trials in USA, row strips of sesame, constituting 5 per cent of the total acreage, were used as a trap crop to attract *Heliothis* spp. from the main crop of cotton. Sesame, which is highly attractive to *Heliothis* species from the seedling stage to senescence, attracted large numbers of insects away from the cotton. It also attracted the parasitoid, *Campoletis sonorensis* which ultimately parasitized large numbers of *Heliothis* insects. In rice, trap cropping of rice for green leafhopper control resulted in 12 per cent higher economic return than chemical control and 29 per cent higher than the untreated control.

Table 3.2. Examples of trap cropping practices applied in agroecosystems

Trap crop	Main crop	Method of planting	Pest(s) controlled
Alfalfa	Cotton	Strip intercrop	Lygus bug
Basil and marigold	Garlic	Border crops	Thrips
Castor plant	Cotton	Border crop	*Heliothis/Helicoverpa* sp.
Chervil	Vegetables, ornamentals	Among plants	Slugs
Chinese cabbage, mustard, and radish	Cabbage	Planted in every 15 rows of cabbage	Cabbage webworm, flea hopper, mustard aphid
Beans and other legumes	Corn	Row intercrop	Leafhopper, leaf beetles, stalk borer, fall armyworm
Chickpea	Cotton	Block trap crop at 20 plants/ m2	*Heliothis/ Helicoverpa* sp.
Collards	Cabbage	Border crop	Diamondback moth
Corn	Cotton	Row intercrop, planted in every 20 rows of cotton or every10-15m	*Heliothis/Helicoverpa* sp.
Cowpea	Cotton	Row intercrop in every 5 rows of cotton	*Heliothis/Helicoverpa* sp. Stemborer
Desmodium	Corn, cowpea, millet, sorghum	Row intercrop	Striga
Dill and lovage	Tomato	Row intercrop	Tomato hornworm
Green beans	Soybean	Row intercrop	Mexican bean beetle
Horse radish	Potato	Intercrop	Colorado potato beetle
Hot cherry pepper	Bell pepper	Border crop	Pepper maggot
Indian mustard	Cabbage	Strip intercrop in between cabbage plots	Cabbage head caterpillar
Marigold (French and African marigold)	Solanaceous, crucifers, legumes, cucurbits	Row/strip intercrop	Nematodes

Medic, *Medicago litoralis*	Carrot	Strip intercop in between carrot plots	Carrot root fly
Napier grass	Corn	Intercrop, border crop	Stem borer
Nasturtium	Cabbage	Row intercrop	Aphids, flea bettle, cucumber beetle, squash vine borer
Okra	Cotton	Border crop	Flower cotton weevil
Onion and garlic	Carrot	Border crops or barrier crops in between plots	Carrot root fly, thrips
Radish	Cabbage family	Row intercrop	Flea beetle, root maggot
Rye	Soybean	Row intercrop	Corn seedling maggot
Sesbania	Soybean	Row intercrop at a distance of 15 m apart	Stink bug
Sickle pod	Soybean	Strip intercrop	Velvet bean caterpillar, green stink bug
Soybean	Corn	Row intercrop	*Heliothis/Helicoverpa* sp.
Sudan grass	Corn	Intercrop, border crop	Stem borer
Sunflower	Cotton	Row intercrop in every 5 rows of cotton	*Heliothis/Helicoverpa* sp.
Tansy	Potato	Intercrop	Colorado potato beetle
Tobacco	Cotton	Row intercrop, planted in every 20 rows of cotton or every10-15m	*Heliothis/Helicoverpa* sp.
Cowpea	Cotton	Row intercrop in every 5 rows of cotton	*Heliothis/Helicoverpa* sp. Stemborer
Desmodium	Corn, cowpea, millet, sorghum	Row intercrop	Striga
Dill and lovage	Tomato	Row intercrop	Tomato hornworm
Green beans	Soybean	Row intercrop	Mexican bean beetle
Horse radish	Potato	Intercrop	Colorado potato beetle
Hot cherry pepper	Bell pepper	Border crop	Pepper maggot
Indian mustard	Cabbage	Strip intercrop in between cabbage plots	Cabbage head caterpillar
Marigold (French and African marigold)	Solanaceous, crucifers, legumes, cucurbits	Row/strip intercrop	Nematodes
Medic, *Medicago litoralis*	Carrot	Strip intercop in between carrot plots	Carrot root fly
Napier grass	Corn	Intercrop, border crop	Stem borer
Nasturtium	Cabbage	Row intercrop	Aphids, flea bettle, cucumber beetle, squash vine borer
Okra	Cotton	Border crop	Flower cotton weevil
Onion and garlic	Carrot	Border crops or barrier crops in between plots	Carrot root fly, thrips
Radish	Cabbage family	Row intercrop	Flea beetle, root maggot
Rye	Soybean	Row intercrop	Corn seedling maggot
Sesbania	Soybean	Row intercrop at a distance of 15 m apart	Stink bug
Sickle pod	Soybean	Strip intercrop	Velvet bean caterpillar, green stink bug

Soybean	Corn	Row intercrop	*Heliothis/Helicoverpa* sp.
Sudan grass	Corn	Intercrop, border crop	Stem borer
Sunflower	Cotton	Row intercrop in every 5 rows of cotton	*Heliothis/Helicoverpa* sp.
Tansy	Potato	Intercrop	Colorado potato beetle
Tobacco	Cotton	Row intercrop, planted in every 20 rows of cotton	*Heliothis/Helicoverpa* sp.
Tomato	Cabbage	Intercrop (tomato is planted 2 weeks ahead at the plots' borders)	Diamondback moth
Vertiver grass	Corn	Perimeter crop	Corn stalk borer

Source: www.oisat.org/control_methods/cultural_pract/trap_cropping.html

Planting Sudan grass (a commercial fodder grass), *Sorghum vulgare sudanense* around maize fields reduced infestation on maize by *Chilo partellus* and *Busseola fusca* in Keyna, as considerable number of stem borers were trapped on Sudan grass. There was increase in maize yield (4.45 t/ha) due to reduction in stem borer damage as compared to control (3.44 t/ha). Planting grass around maize fields also increased parasitization of borers by *Apanteles flavipes* and *A. sesamiae.* As compared to maize mono field where only 4.8 per cent *C. partellus* and 0.5 per cent *B. fusca* larvae were parasitized, 18.9 per cent *C. partellus* and 6.17 per cent *B. fusca* larvae were parasitized in maize surrounded by grass.

Okra can be used as a trap crop around cotton for cotton jassid, American bollworm and spotted bollworms. The infested fruits that have large population of bollworms should be removed periodically and destroyed, and jassid can be easily controlled by spraying with any systemic insecticide. Marigold and *Nicotiana rustica* grown as trap crops are also preferred hosts of *H. armigera.* Planting of castor as trap crop diverts the population of *Spodoptera litura* from cotton.

Crop Location

Another way in which crop diversity can be affected is by varying the type of crops growing in adjacent fields. Many insects can move quickly from one field to the next and between botanically related crops to obtain their requisites. Location of botanically dissimilar crops adjacent to one another will moderate pest movement as insect species would not find requisites in both. Large scale monoculturing of cotton, paddy, sugarcane and vegetable crops in India has resulted in a rapid increase in number and intensity of insect pests. Monoculturing of cotton continuously over large areas was an important factor contributing to *H. armigera* and whitefly outbreaks in South India during late 1980s.

Presence of Weeds

The presence of diverse vegetation within or near the field may add essential resources for predators or parasites and so enable them to find all their requirements near the pest population. Such resources include food, cover or alternate prey. Conversely, weeds may also adversely affect the orientation of predators and parasites to their prey. The weeds may even directly contribute to pest multiplication by providing preferred surface for oviposition. *Vicia sativa* is a common weed associated with chickpea in northern India. Removal of the weed at a time when maximum eggs are laid substantially reduces the incidence of pod borer, *H. armigera.* Weeds may also aid in chemical repellence, interference in movement of insects or provide alternate host for natural enemies (Table 3.3).

Table 3.3 Examples of crop pest population management through weed-crop diversity

Agroecosystem	Pest(s)	Factor(s) (suggested or proved)
1. Cotton and cowpea strip planted with weeds	Boll weevil, *Anthonomus grandis*	Greater parasitic wasp, *Eurytoma* sp. population
2. Vegetables grown among wild carrot (*D. carota*)	Japanese beetle, *Popillia japonica*	Greater activity of the parasitic wasp, *Tiphia popilliavora*
3. Peach and ragweed (*Ambrosia* sp.), smart weed (*Polygonum* sp.) and lambs quarter (*Chenopodium album*), golden rod (*Solidago* sp.)	Oriental fruit moth, *Grapho-litha molesta*	Alternate hosts for the parasite, *Macrocentrus ancylivorus*
4. Sugarcane with *Borreria verticillata* and *Hyptis atrorubens*	Cricket, *Scapteriscus vicinus*	Nectar source for the parasite, *Larra americana*
5. Apple trees grown with *Phacelia* sp. and *Bryngium* sp.	San Jose scale, *Quadraspi-diotus perniciosus* and various species of aphids	Greater abundance and activity of the parasites, *Aphytis proclia*
6. Collards, *Brassica oleracea* and other brassicas grown among weeds	*Pyllotreta striolata, Myzus persicae, Brevicoryne brassicae, Pieris rapae*	Camouflage
7. Cotton grown with ragweed (*Ambrosia* sp.)	Bollworm, *A. grandis*	Alternate hosts for the parasite, *Eurytoma tylodermis*
8. Alfalfa with natural bloom-ing weed complex	Alfalfa caterpillar, *Colias eurytheme*	Increased activity of *Apanteles medicaginis*
9. Apple plants with weeds	Tent caterpillar, *Malacosoma americanum* and *Carpocapsa pomonella*	Increased activity and abundance of parasitic wasps
10. Strip cropping cotton and alfalfa	Plant bugs, *Lygus hesperus* and *L. elisus*	Rentention of natural enemy and synchronizing intense natural enemy activity with pest population
11. Grape wines with weeds	Pacific mite, *Eotetranychus williamettei*	—
12. Brussels sprouts with weeds (hoed or cut back to 15 cm)	*M. persicae, B. brassicae, Aleyrodes brassicae, P. rapae*	Camouflage
13. Cruciferous crops with quick flowering mustards	Cabbage worm, *Pieris* sp.	Increased activity of the parasite, *Apanteles glomeratus*
14. Beans with goose grass, *Eleusine indica* and red spra-gletop, *Leptochola filiformis*	Leafhopper, *Empoasca kraemeri*	Chemical repellency or masking
15. Collards and ragweed, *Ambrosia artemislifolia*	Flea beetle, *Phyllotreta cruciferae*	Chemical repellency and masking
16. Cotton and ragweed plus *Rumex crispus*	*Heliothis* sp.	Greater predator population
17. Vineyards with wild blackberry, *Rubus* sp.	Grape leafhopper, *Erythroneura elegantula*	More alternate hosts for *Anagrus epos*
18. Collards in "diverse" row in an old field	*P. cruciferae, M. persiscae, B. brassicae, P. rapae*	Resource concentration

19. Cabbage with white and red clover	*Erioischia brassicae, B. brassicae, P. rapae*	Less colonisation and greater predator population of *Harpalus rufipes, Phalangium* sp.
20. 1, 10, 100 plant monocultures, 10 plant plots in old mowed field	*P. cruciferae, P. striolata,* aphids and *P. rapae*	Camouflage
21. White clover undersown in brussels sprouts	*E. brassicae, B. brassicae, P. rapae*	Camouflage and greater predation
22. Mungbeans grown among weeds	Bean fly, *Ophiomyia phaseoli*	Camouflage
23. Corn grown with giant ragweed	European corn borer, *Ostrinia nubilalis*	Alternate hosts for *Lydella grisesens*
24. Sugarcane with *Euphorbia* sp.	Sugarcane weevil, *Rhabdo-scelus obscurus*	Nectar and pollen sources for *Lixophaga sphenophori*
25. Brussels sprouts grown among natural weeds complex	*P. rapae, B. brassicae*	Camouflage and more predation
26. Mungbean grown among natural weed complex	Bean fly, *O. phaseoli*	Less colonisation
27. Beans growing among weeds or surrounded by weedy borders	*E. kraemeri, Diabrotica balteata*	—
28. Brussels sprouts grown with *Spergula arvensis* weeds	*M. brassicae, Evergestis forficalis, B. brassicae*	Lower colonization and greater predator population
29. Collards grown among weeds, mainly *Amaranthus retro-flexus, Chenopodium album, Xanthium stramonium*	Green peach aphid, *M. persicae*	Greater abundance of predators, *Chrysoperla carnea*
30. Soybean grown with *Cassia obtusifolia*	The green stink bug, *Nezara viridula,* and velvet bean caterpillar, *Anticarsia gemma-talis*	Greater abundance of predators

Source **:** Altieri and Nichollos (2004)

CROP ROTATION

The use of crop rotation involving cereals and pulses to minimise the damage caused by insect pests has been advocated since a century back. Generally, crop rotation is most effective against pests that have a narrow host range and dispersal capacity. The introduction of paddy crop in northern India has resulted in the practice of paddy-wheat rotation. In Punjab and Haryana alone, this rotation is followed on 2.4 million ha, besides 4 million ha in other parts of the country. The wheat crop serves a host for the survival of a number of insect pests including stem borer, pink borer and shootfly during winter months. This has resulted in increasing attacks of these pests on both the crops. In Tamil Nadu and other parts of South India, cotton is grown in 2-3 seasons throughout the year, thus, providing a continuous supply of food for the development and multiplication of pests. Cotton should be rotated with non-preferred hosts like *ragi,* maize, rice, groundnut, cowpeas or soybean to minimise the incidence of insect pests. Similarly, rotation of groundnut with non-leguminous crops is recommended as a method for minimising the damage by leafminer.

NUTRIENT MANAGEMENT

Irrigation, mulching, manuring and fertilization are practices that, in general, promote rapid growth and shorten the time the susceptible stage is available for attack, providing the crop with greater tolerance and opportunity to compensate for insect damage. However, such practices may also change the physiology of host plants, making them lush and succulent, and thus enhancing pest survival and multiplication.

Excessive use of inorganic nitrogenous fertilizers generally creates congenial conditions for many insect pests. High levels of nitrogen fertilizers significantly increase the incidence of most of the insect pests including yellow stem boer, leaf folder, gall midge, green leafhopper, brown planthopper, whitebacked planthopper, earhead bug, rice hispa, whorl maggot, etc. on the rice crop. In cotton also it results in greater attack of leaf folder, whitefly and bollworms. In sugarcane, this practice builds up internode and stalk borer, and *Pyrilla* populations. On the other hand, application of potash and sometimes phosphorus also, either singly or in combination with nitrogen results in lower incidence of many insect pests.

Growing of radish under controlled conditions in a nutrient medium revealed that the fecundity of mustard aphid increased with increase in nitrogen concentration from 6 to 18 m Eq l–1 and phosphorus from 1 to 13 m Eq l–1 while increasing potash from 3 to 15 m Eq l–1 resulted in reduction in fecundity. It has been found that potash application enhanced protein synthesis resulting in reduced amino acid content of the plant sap thus making the plant less suitable for development and multiplication of sap sucking insects. Field level studies have also revealed that increasing dosage of nitrogen (0 to 80 kg N/ha) increased the build up of mustard aphid, while increasing phosphorus (0 to 30 kg P2O5/ha) resulted in a decrease in its population on Indian mustard and *sarson*.

Similarly, a reduction in the incidence of a number of insect pests including *Empoasca kerri, Autographa nigrisigna* and *Spodoptera litura* on cowpea; green leafhopper, brown planthopper and whitebacked planthopper on rice ; aphid and thrips on chillies, and *Empoasca* sp., *Therioaphis trifolii* f. *maculata* and *Aphis craccivora* on lucerne following increasing application of K either singly or in combination with P has been reported.

In contrast to inorganic fertilizers, organic manures release nitrogen in small quantities over a longer period and hence their application does not generally lead to pest outbreaks. Special efforts are needed to produce large quantities of organic manures. Green manures and biofertilizers based on *Rhizobium, Azolla, Azospirillium,Azobacter* and VAM can serve as important components of organic manuring. Another alternative involves the use of slow-release nitrogenous fertilizers like neem-cake coated urea and coal tar coated urea. Integrated nutrient management (INM) must, therefore, form an integral part of IPM programmes.

WATER MANAGEMENT

The amount of moisture in the soil has a profound effect on the survival of many insect pests. The quality and quantity of nutrients available in the host plants are also greatly affected due to changes in the soil moisture level.

Flooding of fields has been recommended for reducing the attack of cutworms, armyworms, termites, whitegrubs, etc. On the other hand, draining the rice fields for 3-4 days during infestation controls the whorl maggot and brown planthopper populations. Alternate drying and wetting at 10-day intervals starting from 35 days after transplanting drastically reduced brown planthopper and whitebacked planthopper incidence in contrast to continuous standing water (5 cm). However, the incidence of gall midge was less in continuous flooding.

Early termination (by end of September) of irrigation to *hirsutum* cotton crop in Punjab helps in reducing the diapausing larval population of pink bollworm while late irrigation keeps the crop green and more conducive to late season buildup of whitefly and American bollworm, besides delaying the maturity of the crop. Late irrigation to *arboreum* variety LD 230 also resulted in higher incidence of bollworms.

Sap sucking insects like aphids, jassids and whitefly are especially sensitive to changing water levels in their host plants. Maximum fecundity of mustard aphid reared on *sarson* (*Brassica campestris* cv. yellow *sarson*) and *raya* (*B. juncea*) host plants was recorded when the water level was maintained continuously above the field capacity. The concentration of acidic amino acids and amides increased significantly under lower soil water regimes. Nutritional imbalance created by this higher concentration coupled with increasing burden on the excretory mechanisms of the aphid were mainly responsible for reduction in the fecundity of the aphid under such conditions. Due to this reason, economic threshold of the pest in the field was reached only at the highest soil water regime.

Indian mustard irrigated once harboured significantly higher aphid population than the unirrigated one. However, increase in number of irrigations from one to two did not result in a further increase in aphid incidence. In case of *B. campestris* cv. Chinese cabbage, the incidence of mustard aphid increased considerably with the increase in number of irrigations from 3 to 6. The build up of aphid in relation to irrigation levels may, thus, vary in different *Brassica* spp. Waterlogging enhances the multiplication of a number of borers including stalk borer, internode borer, plassey borer and the whitefly on sugarcane crop. Increase in soil moisture level due to frequent irrigation also helped in buildup of *Pyrilla* population on this crop, while blackbug damage is maximum in unirrigated fields.

SANITATION

Clean cultivation as a method for minimising the incidence of insect pests was advocated more than a century ago. Destroying or removing crop residues from fields is one of the basic ways to eliminate pest overwintering sites and reduce the spread of infestation. This may be achieved by ploughing directly or shredding and chopping, burning residues or raking and scooping them into piles for burning. Removal of cotton sticks by 1st August every year was enforced under the Cotton Pests Act, 1911 which helped in reducing the incidence of pink bollworm in erstwhile Madras state. The incidence of boll weevil, *Anthonomus grandis* on cotton ; European corn borer, *Ostrinia nubilalis* and South-western corn borer, *Diatraea grandiosella* in corn and Hessian fly, *Mayetiola destructor* in wheat in USA was reduced by sanitation measures.

In India, sanitation measures have helped to reduce the incidence of planthoppers, leafhoppers, leaf folder, rice hispa, gall midge and stem borer on rice crop. Removal and destruction of rice stubbles has been found highly effective in minimising overwintering populations of many species of stem borers. It has been estimated that stubbles left in a field on one hectare with 6.8 per cent population of immature stages is a potential source of emergence of 1,20,000 moths. Burning of rice stubbles has been reported to reduce the stem borer infestation on the subsequent crop by 67 per cent. Removal of damaged plant parts and uprooting of infested plants including those showing deadhearts at thinning time have been recommended to lower maize borer, shootfly, armyworm, pyrilla, aphids, cutworms and termite incidence in maize crop.

In sorghum, destruction of alternate host plants helps to reduce incidence of shootfly, stem borers and head bugs. Similarly, removal of alternate host plants of spotted bollworms (*Abutilon indicum* L., *Malvastrum tricuspidatum* L., *Sida* sp.), white fly (*Abutilon* sp., *Sida* sp., *Datura* sp., *Achyranthus aspera* L., *Acalypha indica* L.) and American bollworm (*Datura metal* L., *Cynandropsis gynandra* L., *Acanthospermum hispidium* DC, *Chenopodium album* L.), etc. in and around cotton fields has been reported to reduce the incidence of these pests on cotton crop.

Detrashing of dry leaves from August onwards reduces the attack of pyrilla and scale insect on sugarcane crop. Detrashing at fifth, seventh and ninth months checks internode borer damage and detrashing in October and November results in the reduction of stalk borer damage. Destruction of water shoots protects the crop from the ravages of stalk borer and internode borer. Burning of trash after harvest of the crop up to specific period before the pest migrates to nearby crop kills the carryover population of pyrilla, black bug and scale insect to some extent.

Avoiding ratooning of pigeonpea during off-season helps in reducing the carryover of pod fly and eriophyiid mite, *Aceria cajani,* an important vector of pigeonpea sterility mosaic virus. Selective pruning of pigeonpea can be useful in reducing the incidence of leaf folder and spotted caterpillar. Cotton sticks followed by cotton seeds are the major sources for the carryover of pink bollworm in the Punjab. Following measures have been recommended to reduce the carryover population of pest :

- After the last picking, sheep and goats should be allowed to graze on unopened leftover green bolls and shed material in the field.
- The leftover bolls, wherever feasible, should be removed manually before cutting the sticks. These bolls may be kept on roofs of houses, in thin layer for opening to extract good quality seed cotton and the remaining unopened and small bolls should be burnt.
- During summer months, on an average, 50.7 per cent (31.6–71.4%) of the larvae in cotton sticks died due to high atmospheric temperature which may go as high as 49°C in some years. The mortality of larvae in cotton stacks put in the open was higher (53.5%) than those kept under tree shade (32%). Similarly, mortality of larvae in stacks stored in bundles in upright position was higher (53.6%) than in sticks stored untied horizontally (37.7%). The cotton sticks with leftover bolls should be stacked in the open away from tree shade in the villages, preferably after tying them in bundles and storing in upright position.
- The ginning of seed cotton and extraction of oil from cotton seeds should be accomplished by end of April and May, respectively, so that diapausing larvae in the seed cotton and cotton seeds are killed during these processes well before the onset of fruiting bodies in the ensueing cotton crop.

HARVESTING PRACTICES

Harvesting practices involving crop maturity, time of harvest or cutting practices, selective harvesting and strip harvesting can be of considerable assistance in suppressing a variety of insect pests and/or conserving their natural enemies.

The harvesting time of cotton is very important in case of pink bollworm which diapauses during winter in the last larval instar mainly in the seeds of bolls that remain in the field after harvest. The onset of diapause is controlled by photoperiod and begins in September-October. The place and time of diapause in pink bollworm can be used to suppress the overwintering population by modification of cultural practices. In USA, the crop termination is achieved by use of defoliants and desiccants so that bolls open at nearly the same time and are promptly harvested. Soon after harvest the plants are shredded mechanically and ploughed deeply in the soil. In India, application of defoliant, folex (tributyl phosphorotrithioate) at 3 l/ha at 60 per cent boll bursting, has been found to increase boll opening by 16.8 per cent and accelerate maturity of crop by 12–15 days without affecting cotton productivity. Application of chloroflurenol eliminates the population of pink bollworm by suppressing the formation of new reproductives without affecting cotton productivity.

In erstwhile Madras state (India), removal of cotton stalks by 1st August every year was enforced under the Cotton Pests Act, 1911 and it helped in reducing the incidence of pink bollworm. Now-a-days also in south India, defoliants are recommended to hasten crop maturity. In Punjab and other northern States, early termination of the crop followed by other cultural practices are recommended to reduce the carryover of pink bollworm to the next year. Sheep, goats and other farm animals should be allowed to feed on unopened bolls and plant debris. Deep harvesting of cane fields which are to be ratooned provides protection to the crop from root borer and scale insect damage. Damage of pod borer, *Helicoverpa armigera* in chickpea and pigeonpea can be significantly reduced by growing early maturing varieties (first week of March) instead of traditional late maturing types.

Another modification of harvesting practices which has been used for lowering pest damage is the practice of strip harvesting. Movement of *Lygus* bug from alfalfa to cotton in California (USA) is heavy after alfalfa crop is harvested. To reduce this movement, alfalfa can be harvested in alternate strips. When a strip is cut, strips on either side of it are half grown and serve as trap for the bugs. Since natural enemies of *Lygus* also move from strip to strip, there is no increase in bug population in alfalfa. This procedure also favours natural enemies of other pests, *e.g.* more effective natural control of pea aphid, *Acyrthosiphon pisum* is achieved due to greater population of its parasitoid, *Aphidius smithi.*

INTEGRATION WITH OTHER TACTICS

Cultural practices are generally compatible with other pest management tactics. In fact, cultural control is a cornerstone for most biointensive IPM programmes, where each component complements and often augments the effects of others (ecological synergism). One of the greatest successes achieved in recent times in the development of IPM has been the integrated use of trap cropping and botanical pesticides for the control of diamondback moth (DBM) and other pests of cabbage. Growing of Indian mustard in paird rows at the beginning and after every 25 rows attracted more than 80 per cent of DBM infestation besides almost entire population of leaf webber, stem borer, bugs and aphids. To control the remaining attack of DBM, a 4 per cent neem seed kernel extract (NSKE) is applied at primordial or head initiation stage of the crop. Two or three post heading sprays (NSKE) may also be applied at 10-15 days intervals depending on population pressure. Spraying of NSKE is also safe to *Apanteles plutellae* which is the dominant natural enemy found in the cabbage ecosystem.

The entomologists at the Indian Institute of Horticultural Research (IIHR), Bangalore have also been successful in developing an IPM system for the control of tomato fruitborer, *Helicoverpa armigera.* Trap cropping of marigold after every 8 rows of tomato attracts most of the ovipositing moths to the former crop. The use of conventional insecticides on the trap crop reduces their attractiveness to the pest. Therefore, the pest on the trap crop has to be removed mechanically. The residual pest population on both the crops is controlled by sprays of *H. armigera* nuclear polyhedrosis virus (HaNPV) at 500 larval equivalents (LE) ha–1.

Trap crops like cowpeas, okra, corn, marigold and castor can be used to increase the efficiency of natural enemies in cotton ecyosystem. Planting Sudan grass around maize fields increased parasitization of *C. partellus* by *A. flavipes* and *A. sesamiae* from 4.8 per cent (maize only) to 18.9 per cent (maize surrounded by grass). Similarly, intercropping maize with molasses grass increased parasitization of stem borers from 5.4 per cent (mono maize) to 20.7 per cent (maize intercropped with grass).

High plant nitrogen levels are generally favourable to pest insect populations due to greater survival, increased feeding rate and increased fecundity resulting in faster population growth. A study on the effect of nitrogen fertilizer on the development of brown planthopper on rice indicated that nitrogen favoured population growth, regardless of the level of resistance in the host plant ; but the increase was limited at the higher levels of resistance as indicated by the highly resistant variety IR60. This indicates the need for planting resistant cultivars when high nitrogen levels are needed to maximize production.

The efficacy of insecticides against insect pests can be increased by manipulation of cultural practices. The mustard aphids, *Lipaphis erysimi*, feeding on potted *Brassica* plants grown at lower soil-water regimes were found to be more susceptible to insecticides than those from higher soil-water regimes. In field studies, lower dosages (250 and 500 ml/ha) of oxydemeton methyl were at par with higher ones (750 ml and 1 l/ha) after 2 and 15 days of spraying, in case of Indian mustard crop growing under water stress conditions. There was no difference in yield of crop under water stress and non-stress conditions. In another study, normal sown crop of *B. juncea* (RLM 619) and *B. campestris* (BSH 1) required one spray for the control of mustard aphid under no water stress conditions. But under moderate and high water stress conditions, no spray was required for aphid control on these crops.

Similarly, application of potash has also been reported to increase the efficacy of insecticides against mustard aphid. In case of potted *B. campestris* and *B. juncea* plants, the relative susceptibility of mustard aphid to dimethoate, endosulfan, carbaryl and fenvalerate increased with increase in rate of application from 50 to 100 and 200 ppm. Application of 200 ppm potash increased the susceptibility of the aphid to dimethoate by 2.83 to 3.27 times on *B. campestris* and *B. juncea* host plants, respectively.

CONCLUSIONS

In developing countries like India with surplus labour and abundant sunshine, the cultural methods appear to be very useful and economical components for use in IPM. Cultural control practices are generally prophylactic in nature and are frequently the first line of defence against crop pests. The major advantages of the use of these practices are as below :

- Most cultural practices result in little or no added production cost, because they are merely variations in the timing or manner of performing operations that are normally necessary to the production of the crop. Some of the techniques are, however, labour intensive, and, therefore, become highly expensive if the labour is costly.
- These tactics are environmentally safe as they do not have significant distruptive effects on the non-target organisms and environmental quality.
- These are usually compatible with other components of IPM like resistant varieties, bicontrol agents and even insecticides.
- Usually, the chances of development of resistance to a cultural practice are considered remote. But there has been atleast one recent example from USA where insects have

developed resistance to a cultural control practice. Monocropping of corn promoted the spread of rootworms, *Diabrotica virgifera* and *D. barberi*. A two year rotation cycle of corn and soybean was used to effectively eliminate the problem but the insects have responded by developing strains which remain dormant in the egg stage for two years and, thus, the two year rotation cycle has become ineffective. Rotation with longer cycles and involving more crops may now be required to manage these new rootworm strains. This example shows that the insects have the ability to defeat almost any tactic adopted by humans to defeat them.

In spite of these advantages, cultural practices are not widely used in modern agriculture due to a number of limitations.

- A thorough knowledge of the ecology of the host plant, insect pest, natural enemies and their interactions is required for developing suitable cultural control practices. The generation of this information requires long term exhaustive studies.
- The measures have to be taken long in advance of the pest attack and in many cases even before sowing the crop.
- In most cases, cultural practices alone are not sufficient to bring insect pest populations below economic injury level and hence these have to be supplemented by other methods.
- These practices have to be developed locally as their effect on the pest may vary with various climatic and biotic factors.
- Many of the practices are obstacles to farmers' aspirations to intensify and mechanise their holdings.
- A cultural control practice directed against one pest may well increase the chances of survival and multiplication of another pest. This is akin to secondary pest outbreaks in case of pesticide application.
- Many of the cultural practices are effective only when undertaken on an area- wide basis. Ideally, all farmers may adopt a useful cultural practice voluntarily but unfortunately some farmers generally hold out. Such farmers called 'spoiler holdouts' may impair the success of a programme by failing to adopt a necessary practice. This can only be corrected by enacting and enforcing suitable legislative measures. This is often difficult in a democratic set up.

Many of the traditional cultural practices may not be useful under modern, intensive agriculture. Sustained research is needed to develop improved cultural control measures which have great potential for use in sustainable agroecosystems. Suitable combinations of different cultural control practices can help to lower the general equilibrium position of many insect pests. If properly managed, some of these practices may obviate the need for insecticidal applications.

☆☆☆☆☆

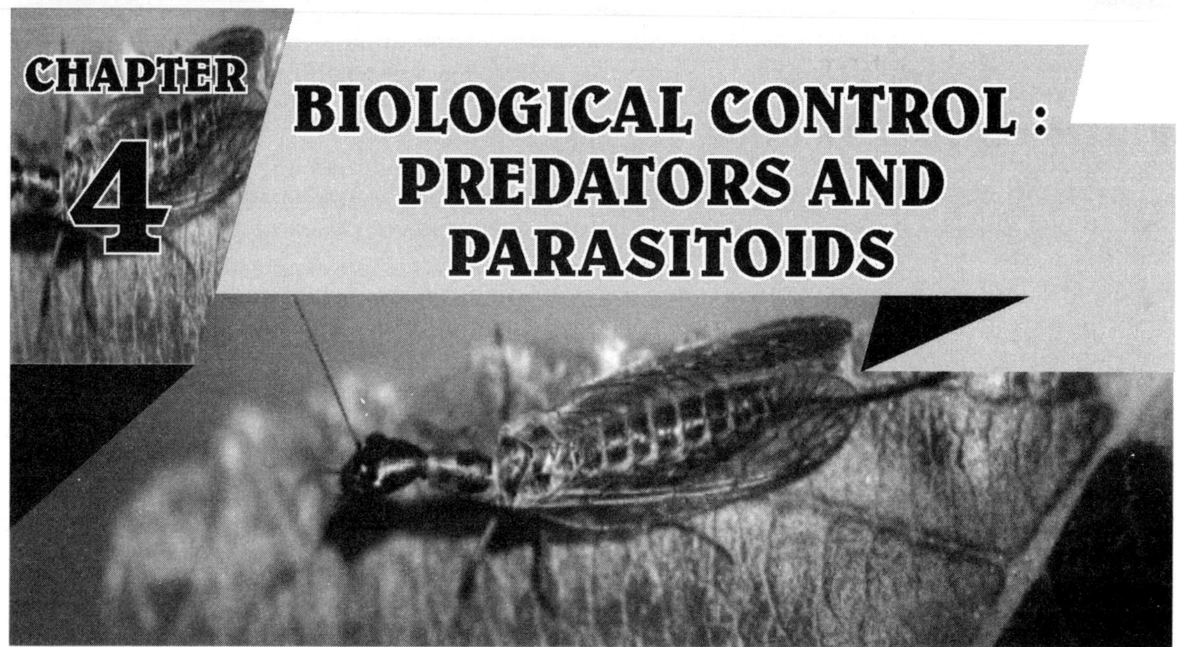

CHAPTER 4 BIOLOGICAL CONTROL : PREDATORS AND PARASITOIDS

INTRODUCTION

The predators and parasitoids are the natural enemies that attack various life stages of insects, resulting in the regulation of herbivore numbers in a particular ecosystem. This regulation has been termed 'biological control', and is defined as the action of parasitoids, predators, or pathogens in maintaining another organism's population density at a lower average than would occur in their absence. In the applied sense, it may be defined as the utilization of natural enemies to reduce the damage caused by noxious organisms to tolerable levels.

Some estimates have suggested that natural enemies control about 99 per cent of all potential pests. It has been generally realized that the green revolution technology has led to the destruction of the relationship between naturally occurring bioagents and pests that is often responsible for pest outbreaks. The aim of using biocontrol agents is to restore and/or enhance this relationship. Within the context of biological control, it is important to recognize that the term 'control' does not mean eradication, but it reflects population suppression to a level where the pest is no longer economically damaging. For stable plantation agroecosystems, it is likely that long-term control (more than one season) would be desirable. However, for temporary or unstable annual crops, it may be enough that the control lasts until harvest. Biocontrol is most suited to pest species with a relatively high economic injury level because a minimum prey density is usually required to support a permanent natural enemy population. Even where a permanent association is not the aim, it will still be necessary to have a relatively higher economic injury level since natural enemies are rarely able to exploit the prey to the point of extinction.

Success in biological control is measured as complete, substantial, or partial according to the extent of population regulation achieved. Complete success is achieved when the populations of the target pest are maintained below economical levels in an extensive area so that pesticide treatments become rare, if ever, necessary. Substantial success is achieved if only occasional pesticide treatments are required to maintain the pest population below economically damaging levels. Partial success refers to cases in which pesticide application remains necessary but less frequent or where complete success is achieved in only a major portion of the pest-infested area.

HISTORICAL PERSPECTIVE

The use of natural enemies for combating phytophagous insects has a long historical background (Table 4.1) The first account of natural enemies being used as insect management tool dates back as early as 900 A.D., when the Chinese citrus growers placed ants, *Oecophylla smaragdina,* on trees to protect them from foliage feeding caterpillars. The Chinese also placed bamboo rods as runways or bridges between trees to aid inter-tree movement of the ants. The ants built large paper nests in the trees and were apparently quite effective in suppressing various lepidopteran pests of citrus. These ants were also reportedly available for purchase till 1970s. Although the predatory behaviour of some insects was recognized long ago, there are conflicting reports about the first documented case of parasitism. Currently, the credit for the earliest reported correct interpretation of parasitism goes to Martin Lister who in 1685 realized that the adult ichneumon wasps emerging from caterpillars came from the eggs laid in the caterpillars by adult female wasps.

The first successful introduction of a natural enemy from one country to another is the import of mynah bird, *Gracula religiosa,* from India to control red locust, *Nomadacris septemfasciata,* in Mauritius in 1762. The first deliberate movement of parasitoids from one location to another was conducted by C.V. Riley, who distributed the parasitoids of the weevil, *Conotrachelus nenuphar* around the state of Missouri in 1870. The first predatory arthropod to be transported from one continent to another was the mite, *Tyroglyphus phylloxerae,* which was shipped from USA and established in France in 1873 to control grape pylloxera, *Viteus vitifoliae.* However, it failed to suppress the populations of the target pest. The first parasitoid to be successfully moved and established

from one continent to another (England to USA) was *Apanteles glomeratus* for suppression of *Pieris rapae* by the U.S. Department of Agriculture in 1883. Two other international movements of natural enemies included shipment of several aphidophagous natural enemies to New Zealand, including *Coccinella undecimpunctata* and importation of *Trichogramma* spp. from USA to Canada for control of the gooseberry saw fly, *Nematus ribesii.*

The first scientifically well-planned and successful biological control attempt involves the control of cottony cushion scale, *Icerya purchasi,* in California during the late 1800s. *I.purchasi* was introduced into California in 1869 and threatened to destroy the entire southern California citrus industry by 1886. No chemical treatments known at that time could control the scale. Efforts were made to look for the natural enemies of the scale during 1887 and 1888, in Australia, native home of the pest. Two insects, the Vedalia beetle, *Rodolia cardinalis* and a parasitic fly, *Cryptochetum iceryae,* were imported to California for field release in 1888. From initial releases of about 500 beetles, the scale insect rapidly declined in importance. It is not known precisely how many flies were released, but these were also helpful in controlling the pest in some areas. The initial releases took place in 1888 and by the summer of 1889, control of the pest was just complete. The total cost of the programme was about US $ 5000. Complete control of the pest was achieved within 18 months. The beetle and the fly still keep this scale under check, even over 100 years after the initiation of the project. The beetle is the dominant biocontrol agent in the interior and the fly is dominant in the coastal regions. Following the success of this programme, the beetle has been imported to control this scale insect in over 50 other countries.

Table 4.1 A chronology of salient events in biological control

Time	Event
Pre-scientific era (pre-1880)	
'Ancient' China	Releases of ants for control of citrus pests.
'Medieval' Arabia	Transportation of ant colonies from mountains to date groves.
1762	*Mynah* (a bird) from India imported for the control of locusts in Mauritius.
1855	A. Fitch reported the role of ladybird beetles, green lacewings and other predaceous insects in the control of insect pests of crops.
Classical era (1880-1939)	
1888	First major classical biological control success, importation of Vedalia beetle to California from Australia for the control of cottony cushion scale
1919	The term 'biological control' coined by H.S. Smith.
1920s	Commercial production of *Encarsia* for greenhouse control of whitefly.
1932	Prickly pear brought under control in Australia.
1939	*Bacillus thuringiensis* Berliner first used as a microbial insecticide.
Pre-green revolution era (1940s-mid 1960s)	
1940s	Commercial production of *Encarsia* for greenhouse control of whitefly ceases as a result of pesticide availability.
1940s	Decline in number of classical biological control introductions.
1950s	Extensive commercial production of Bt products.
1959	Concept of integrated control involving integration of chemical and biological control introduced.
Green revolution era (mid 1960s-late 1980s)	
1964	Publication of the book *Biological Control of Insect Pests and Weeds* by Paul DeBach, which established biological control as a separate discipline in Entomology.
1967	FAO formalises the concept of integrated control of pests.
1970s	Commercial production of *Encarsia* for greenhouse control of whitefly reintroduced and begins period of rapid growth in popularity.
1971	First deliberate introduction of a pathogen for weed control.
1975	Elcar (*Helicoverpa* NPV) registered for the control of bollworm and tobacco budworm on cotton.
1980s	Devine and Collego mycoherbicide products marketed.
Late 1980s	Worldwide sales of Bt estimated to exceed US$ 50 million.
Post-green revolution era (1990-till date)	
1992	BIOCAT database includes 4,769 introductions of insect natural enemies with 421 pest species controlled.
1995	Dr H.R. Herren awarded the World Food Prize for developing and implementing the world's largest biological control project for the control of cassava mealy bug in Africa.
1996	Publication of *Code of Conduct of Importation and Release of Exotic Biological Control Agents* (FAO).
1996	Cumulative total of 1,150 deliberate releases of 365 invertebrate and fungal species onto 133 weed species in 75 countries.
2004	BIOCAT database includes 5634 introductions of entomophagous arthropods to control 597 pest species.

Source : Dhaliwal and Koul (2010)

Although the primary focus of early efforts in biological control was importation of natural enemies, other methods of manipulating parasitoids and predators were also considered. The first practical attempt toward augmentation of natural enemies in Western Europe was probably made in 1899, when F. Decaux made use of release of field collected ichneumonid wasps in apple orchards. Mass rearing and periodic release of natural enemies in North America began in 1916, when mealy bugs and black scale were reared successfully on potato sprouts. Another early augmentation effort involved *Cryptolaemus montrouzieri*, which was mass-reared in insectary and distributed to citrus grooves for control of mealy bugs. A number of workers throughout the history of biological control considered conservation and enhancement of natural enemy population. However, concerted effects towards augmentation and conservation of natural enemies did not begin in earnest till the mid-20th century.

In India, the earliest attempt at introduction of a natural enemy was made in 1898 when a coccinellid, *C. montrouzieri*, from Australia was released against coffee green scale, *Coccus viridis*. It established but failed to control the scale. It is now a common mealy bug predator in South India. However, concerted efforts at setting an insect to kill an insect began in 1920s and soon many successes were obtained in India and other Asian countries (Tables 4.2, 4.3, 4.4). The establishment of Regional Station of Commonwealth Institute of Biological Control at Bangalore in 1957 gave a fillip to bicontrol work in India. Field surveys were initiated to identify important natural enemies of major crop pests. The beneficial role of parasitic and predacious organisms in regulating pest populations and practical methods of using them in the field were investigated. This work got a further boost with the establishment of All India Coordinated Research Project on Biological Control of Crop Pests and Weeds (AICRPBC) in 1977. The AICRPBC was upgraded to the level of Project Directorate of Biological Control (PDBC) in 1993. Recently, PDBC has been further upgraded and named as National Bureau of Agriculturally Important Insects (NBAII).

Table 4.2 Important examples of successful biological control of insect pests by use of introduced natural enemies

Year	Region or country	Crop	Insect pest	Natural enemy	Country from where imported
1925-26	Kgushu Island (Japan)	Citrus	Spiny black fly, *Aleurocanthus spiniferus*	*Encarsia smithi*	Japan Mainland
1925-29	Fiji	Coconut	Coconut moth, *Levuana iridiscens*	*Bessa remota*	Malaysia
1928-29	Fiji	Coconut	Coconut scale, *Aspidiotus destructor*	*Cryptognatha nodiceps**	Trinidad
1920s	Assam (India)	Apple	Woolly apple aphid, *Eriosoma lanigerum*	*Aphelinus mali*	England
1929-31	India	Wattle of commerce, *Acacia decurrens*	Cottony cushion scale, *Icerya purchasi*	*Rodolia cardinalis**	USA
1930s	Cheju Island (Korea)	Citrus	Cottony cushion scale, *I. purchasi*	*R. cardinalis**	Australia
1933-34	Fiji	Coconut	Coconut leaf-mining beetle, *Promecotheca coeruleipennis*	*Pediobius parvulus*	Java

1934-35	Korea	Apple	Woolly apple aphid, *E. lanigerum*	*A. mali*	Japan
1940s	Various islands in Japan	Citrus	Redwax scale, *Ceroplastes rubens*	*Anicetus beneficus*	Uncertain, observed in Japan
1958-60	India	Apple	San Jose scale, *Quadraspidiotus perniciosus*	*Prospaltella perniciosi*	China
1960	India	Apple	*Q. perniciosus*	*Aphytis diaspidis*	USA
1964	India	Castor	*Achaea janata*	*Telenomus* spp.	New Guinea
1965	India	Coconut	*Oryctes rhinoceros*	*Platymeris laevicollis**	Zanzibar
1975	Korea	Citrus	Wax scale, *C. rubens*	*Anicetus beneficus*	Japan
1980-86	Japan	Citrus	Arrowhead scale, *Cinaspis vanonesis*	*Physcus fulvus* *Aphytis yanonensis*	Taiwan Taiwan
1981-95	Africa (30 countries)	Cassava	Cassava mealy bug, *Phenacoccus manihoti*	*Epidinocarsis lopezi*	Paraguay
1989-97	Africa (30 countries)	Cassava	Cassava green mite, *Mononychellus tanajoa*	*Neoseiulus idaeus** *Typhlodromalus manihoti** and *T. aripo**	South America

Natural enemies with asterisk (*) are predators, others are parasitoids
Source :Dhaliwal and Koul (2010)

Table 4.3 Natural enemies introduced against different pests into India (1898-1992)

Pest 1	Nos. 2	Year(s) 3	Remarks 4
Scale insects			
Sugarcane scale, *Melanaspis glomerata madagassa*	25	1972-83	None established or recovered but for *Sticholotis*
San Jose scale, *Quadraspidiotus perniciosus*	6	1959-66	Substantial control through *Encarsia perniciosi*, especially Russian & Chinese strains.
Cottony cushion scale, *Icerya purchasi*	2	1926-48	Good control achieved with *Rodolia cardinalis*
Green scale, *Coccusviridis*	1	1898	Not established
Mealy bugs			
Sugarcane mealy bug, *Saccharicoccus sacchari.*	1	1970	Not established
Mealy bugs, *Planococcus citri*, *P. lilacinus* *Ferrisia virgata*, *Maconellicoccus hirsutus*	3	1898 1980	*Cryptolaemus montrouzieri* and *Leptomastix dactylopii* well established
Aphids			
Woolly apple aphid, *Eriosoma lanigerum*	1	1930-37	*Aphelinus mali* - substantial control
Cowpea aphid, *Aphis craccivora*	1	1966	Not established
Psyllids			
Subabul psyllid, *Heteropsyllacubana*	1	1988	*Curinus coeruleus* – substantial control
Lepidopteran tissue borers			
Sugarcane bores	43	1959-92	Most not established or recovered except *Trichogramma*

Maize stem borer, *Chilo partellus*, pink bollworm, *Pectinophora gossypiella*	3	1969-80	*Bracon kirkpatricki* , *Chelonus blackburni* & *Trichogramma brasiliensis* established
Codling moth, *Cydia pomonella*	3	1978-88	*Trichogramma* spp. recovered
Potato tuber moth, *Phthorimaea operculella*	15	1944-80	At least 10 recovered. Some like *Copidosoma* spp. & *C. blackburni* doing very well.
Castor semilopper, *Achaea janata*	3	1963-64	*Telenomus remus* recovered
Teak skeletoniser, *Eutectona machaeralis*	5	1937-38	Results not clear
Coconut caterpillar, *Opisina arenosella*	2	1960-81	*Spoggosia bezziana* recovered
Diamondback moth, *Plutella xylostella*	2	1969-92	Results not clear
American bollworm, *Helicoverpa armigera*	13	1968-85	*Eucelatoria bryani* established
Tobacco caterpillar, *Spodoptera litura*	5	1963-83	*Cotesia marginiventris* recovered, *T. remus* doing well, *Steinernema carpocapsae* established
Rhinoceros beetle, Giant African snail & mites			
Rhinoceros beetle, *Oryctes rhinoceros*	2	1965-79	*Platymeris laevicollis* recovered.
Giant African snail, *Achatina fulica*	2	1962-73	None established
Spider mite	2	1965-84	*Phytoseiulus persimilis* recovered
Tea mite	2	1961	None established
Weeds			
Prickly pear, *Opuntia* spp.	3	1926-75	Good control by *Dactylopius* spp.
Crofton weed, *Ageratina odenophora*	1	1963	Partial control
Lantana camara	10	1919-71	Several established but poor control
Broomrape, *Orobanche* sp.	1	1982	None recovered
Siam weed, *Chromolaena odorata*	1	1984	No definite impact
Carrot weed, *Parthenium hysterophorus*	1	1983	Well established, exerting fair control
Water hyacinth, *Eichhornia crassipes* established in other	3	1982	Spectacular results in Bangalore, states also
Water fern, *Salvinia molesta*	2	1982	Good control in Kerala

Source : Ramani *et al.* (2004)

Table 4.4 List of natural enemies introduced into India after 1992

Host insect/weed	Natural enemy	Year of origin	Country/ Place	Remarks
Hypothenemus hampei	*Cephalonomia stephanoderis*	1995	Mexico	Established
	Prorops nasuta	1995	Mexico	Not established
	Phymastichus coffea	2001	Colombia	Under field test
Liriomyza trifolii	*Diglyphus begini*	1997	California	Not established
Aleurodicus dispersus	*Encarsia guadeloupae*	1999	Lakshadweep Islands	Good control
Chromolaena odorata	*Cecidochares connexa*	2002	Indonesia	Under quarantine tests
Mikania macrantha	*Puccinia spegazzinii*	2003	U.K. (ex. Trinidad)	Under quarantine tests
Helicoverpa armigera and others	*Trichogramma mwanzai*	2004	Kenya	Under quarantine tests

Source : Ramani *et al.* (2004)

BIOLOGICAL CONTROL AGENTS

The insects that subsist on animals can be divided into two broad categories, *i.e.* true parasites and entomophages. The true parasites feed on animals other than their own kind and the entomophages feed on insects. It has been estimated that only 15 per cent of all entomophages have so far been identified. This is because of the fact that most research on entomphages is directed to a small proportion of insects that are of economic importance. The entomophages that are of interest to biocontrol can be grouped into two categories, viz. predators and parasitoids (to distinguish them from true parasites) (Table 4.5). A predator is a free-living organism throughout its life, it kills its prey and consumes it rapidly (seconds to minutes) and requires more than one prey to complete its development. A parasitoid (means 'parasite-like') may be external or internal feeder, which kills its host and consumes it more slowly (hours to days). Most parasitoids complete their juvenile development within a host (which is killed) but are free-living as adults. Most parasites, however, do not kill their hosts, at least in the short term, but may irritate, weaken or otherwise debilitate the host, and occasionally cause its death.

Table 4.5 Properties of insect categories subsisting on animals

Property	True parasites	Parasitoids	Predators
Size	Smaller than host	Same size as that of host	Larger than host
Feeders on host	Both larvae and adults	Only larvae, adults free living and vegetarian	Both larvae and adults
No. of hosts needed for maturity	One	One	More than one
Injury to host	Feed without killing	Paralyse to oviposit	Kill to devour
Activity	Function at low host density, so efficient	Function at low host density, so efficient	Function at higher host density, so not as efficient
Time of activity	Diurnal or nocturnal	Diurnal	Crepuscular
Host-specificity	Great	Great	Not so great
Suitability for biological control	Not suited	Best suited	Suited
Examples	Mosquitoes, lice, bed bugs	Parasitic wasps, tachinid flies	Mantids, ladybird beetles

India is very rich in biodiversity of biocontrol agents. A total of 120 natural enemies have been recorded on *Helicoverpa armigera,* followed by *Scirpophaga incertulas* (72), *S. excerptalis* (61), *Chilo infuscatellus* (50), *Oryctes rhinoceros* (45), *Spodoptera litura* (42), and *Opisina arenosella* (41). In addition, the spiders have been recorded from different crop ecosystems; maximum number of spiders were recorded from rice ecosystem (191), followed by cotton (106), sugarcane (58), maize (39), coconut (26), tobacco (23), legumes (19), wheat (14) and mango (11). Of the 218 species of predatory mites recorded in India, 150 species are from the family Phytoseiidae. More than 450 species of coccinellids, 60 species of chrysopids and 26 species each of trichogrammatids and anthocorid bugs have been described from India.

Predators

The insects that prey on other insects and mites occur in many insect orders, the most prominent being Coleoptera, Neuroptera, Hymenoptera, Diptera, Hemiptera, and Odonata (Table 4.6). In addition, there are several species of mites and spiders feeding on a wide range of insects and mites. Some predators use biting or chewing mouth parts to devour their prey (e.g. praying mantids, dragonflies, beetles), whereas others use piercing and sucking mouth parts to feed upon the body fluids of their prey (e.g. assassin bugs, lacewing larvae, and hover fly larvae). The sucking type of feeders often inject a powerful toxin that quickly immobilizes their prey.

Table 4.6 List of some common predators found in agroecosystems

Order	Family	Predator	Prey
Dictyoptera	Mantidae	Praying mantids	Large and small insects
Dermaptera	Labiduridae	Earwigs	Caterpillars, many others
Thysanoptera	Aleolothripidae	Predaceous thrips	Spider mite eggs
Hemiptera	Anthocoridae	Minute pirate bugs	Insect eggs, soft-bodied insects, small insects
	Lygaeidae	Big-eyed bugs	Insect eggs, soft-bodied insects, small insects
	Miridae	Plant bugs	Insect eggs, soft-bodied insects, small insects
	Nabidae	Damsel bugs	Insect eggs, small insects
	Reduviidae	Assassin bugs	Small insects, caterpillars
	Pentatomidae	Predaceous stink bugs	Small caterpillars
	Miridae	*Cyrtorhinus lividipennis*	Rice hoppers
	Veliidae	*Microvilea atrolineata*	Rice hoppers
Neuroptera	Chrysopidae	Lacewings	Aphids, soft-bodied insects
Coleoptera	Coccinellidae	Ladybird beetles	Aphids, soft-bodied insects, insect eggs
	Carabidae	Ground beetles	Insect eggs, soft-bodied insects, cater-pillars
	Staphylinidae	Rove beetles	Small insects
	Melyridae	Soft-winged flower beetles	Insect eggs, soft-bodied insects, small caterpillars
	Cicindelidae	Tiger beetles	Various insects on the ground surface
Diptera	Cecidomyiidae	Predaceous midges	Aphids
	Asilidae	Robber fly larvae	Soil insects
	Syrphidae	Hover flies	Aphids
Hymenoptera	Formicidae	Ants	Insect eggs, soft-bodied insects, small insects
	Vespidae	Hornets, yellow jackets	Caterpillars, small insects
Odonata	Many	Dragonflies, damselflies	Mosquitoes
Acari	Phytoseiidae	Predatory mites	Phytophagous mites and thrips
Araneae	Many	Spiders	Polyphagous
Vertebrates	Many	Birds more effective	Polyphagous

Source :Modified from Dhaliwal and Koul (2010)

Predatory insects feed on all host stages, i.e. egg, larval (or nymphal), pupal, and adult stages. Many species are predaceous in both larval and adult stages, although not necessarily on the same kinds of prey. Others are predaceous only as larvae, whereas the adults may feed on nectar, honeydew, etc. Often the non-predaceous adult female seeks the prey for her larvae by depositing eggs among the prey. This is because their larvae are sometimes incapable of finding the prey on their own. Many predators are agile, ferocious hunters, actively seeking their prey on the ground or on vegetation, as do beetles, lacewing larvae, and mites, or catching it in flight, as do dragonflies or robber flies. Certain hunters have specially adapted seizing organs, such as the barbed forelegs of mantids or the labial mask of aquatic dragonfly nymphs. Other predators may use various traps to catch their prey, of which the webs of spiders and sand pitfalls of ant lions are perhaps the best known.

The searching behaviour of predators is important in understanding predator-prey interactions in biological control. Adult predators may be monophagous (feeding on one prey species), oligophagous (feeding on several species), or polyphagous (feeding on many species). Polyphagous predators may shift to the most abundant prey species, which can stabilize prey populations in a community. If highly mobile, polyphagous predators may be effective in providing control of pests in disturbed systems; monophagous or oligophagous predators tend to be associated with prey in more stable systems. While many predators are carnivorous both as immatures and adults, some feed on nectar, honeydew, or plant food as well. Eggs of predators are often deposited by females in close proximity to their prey. Predators often use visual and chemical cues to locate plants with prey, and may also use prey pheromones as cues. Predators often concentrate on the more abundant prey species, which may make them less effective in controlling a pest at low densities but could make them particularly effective in suppressing pest outbreaks.

Parasitoids

The majority of the parasitoids utilized in biological control of insect pests belong to two orders, namely, Hymenoptera (especially wasps of the superfamilies Chalcidoidea, Ichneumonoidea and Proctotrupoidea), and Diptera (flies, particularly of the family Tachinidae) (Table 4.7). About 66 per cent of all successful biocontrol programmes have involved parasitoids that belong to the insect order Hymenoptera. One of the reasons for the success of these species is their having a modified ovipositor that can be used to lay eggs, to secrete venom to paralyse prey, to secrete feeding tubes and to locate prey via sensitive neural receptors. In general, the dipteran parasitoids in the family Tachinidae appear to be less host-specific. For example, some species of tachinid fly have been found to attack more than 100 different host insects. However, tachinids have not been used extensively in biological control programmes as yet.

Parasitoids may be classified depending upon whether they are external feeders (ectoparasites) or internal feeders (endoparasites). Ectoparasitic species are generally found in situations where the host is protected, i.e. leafminers or scale insects. In these circumstances, the adult parasitoid may simply deposit an egg inside a feeding tunnel (e.g. leafmine) or near the host without making a direct contact with the host. Endoparasitism is much more common with hosts that are not protected, such as aphids or caterpillars. In these situations, the adult parasitoids directly deposit the eggs inside the host with their ovipositors. Most insects parasitic upon other insects are protelean parasites, that is, they are parasitic only in their immature (larval) stages and lead free lives as adults. They usually consume all or most of the host's

Table 4.7 List of common parasitoids found in agroecosystems

Order	Family	Host	Internal/External
Diptera	Tachinidae	Beetles, butterflies and moths	Internal
	Nemestrinidae	Locusts, beetles	Internal
	Phoridae	Ants, caterpillars, termites, flies, others	Internal
	Cryptochaetidae	Scale insects	Internal
Hymenoptera	Chalcididae	Flies and butterflies (larvae and pupae)	Internal or external
	Encyrtidae	Various insect eggs, larvae or pupae	Internal
	Eulophidae	Various insect eggs, larvae or pupae	Internal or external
	Aphelinidae	Whiteflies, scales, mealy bugs, aphids	Internal or external
	Trichogrammatidae	Moth eggs	Internal
	Mymaridae	True bugs, flies, beetles, leafhopper eggs	Internal
	Scelionidae	Insect eggs of true bugs and moths	Internal
	Ichneumonidae	Larvae or pupae of beetles, caterpillars and wasps	Internal or external
	Braconidae	Larvae of beetles, caterpillars, flies and sawflies	Internal (mostly)
	Pteromalidae	Larvae and pupae of Lepidoptera and Coleoptera	Internal

Source : Modified from Hagler (2000)

body and then pupate, either within or external to the host. The adult parasite emerges from the pupa and starts the next generation afresh by actively searching for hosts in which to oviposit. Most adult parasitoids require food such as honeydew, nectar, or pollen and many feed on their hosts' body fluids, whereas others require free water as adults.

Parasitoids may have only one generation (univoltine) to one generation of the host or two or more generations (multivoltine) to one of the host. Life cycles are generally short, ranging from 10 days to 4 weeks or so in summer but correspondingly longer in cold weather. However, some require a year or more, if they have hosts with a single generation per year. In general, they all have great potential rates of increase. The parasitoids may be either solitary (when only one larva develops per individual host) or gregarious when more than one larva normally develops upon a single host). However, this is not always clear-cut, as many species may develop facultatively as solitaries upon a small host and gregariously upon a larger one. Adult parasitoids seek out their hosts in the environment using a variety of cues from the target host and its habitat. Visual, olfactory, and tactile cues are used by parasitoids to find their hosts. When a host is found, the female lays an egg in, on, or near the host. Parasitoid larvae feed on host tissues but may not kill their host until the host has fed and developed to adult stage. Parasitoids pupate in or near the host, and emerging adults mate and disperse to search for hosts or other food sources.

Some species of parasitoids are polyembryonic, in which a single egg gives rise to many embryos. Other parasitoids display ***superparasitism***, in which more than one adult of the same species attack the host, and ***multiparasitism*** where more than one species attack the same host. Both super- and multiparasitism are generally regarded as undesirable situations, since much reproductive capacity is wasted. When a parasitoid is attacked by another parasitoid, the phenomenon is called ***hyperparasitism***. They are called secondary if they attack primary parasitoids and tertiary if they attack secondary parasitoids. Secondary parasitism is usually harmful as it reduces the efficacy of primary parasitoids. Tertiary parasitism is not quite common and is usually not of much consequence, though theoretically it may prove useful, if we are so unfortunate as to need control of secondary parasitoids.

The structure of hyperparasitoid communities has been studied for a spectrum of phytophagous insects. There are two multitrophic systems with a well-studied hyperparasitoid ecology, i.e. (*i*) the heteronomous hyperparasitoids of the genus *Encarsia* attacking scale insects and whiteflies, and (*ii*) the aphid-parasitoid-hyperparasitoids community. In heteronomous hyperparasitoids or adelphoparasitoids, only males develop as hyperparasitoids, attacking females of their own or another parasitoid species. Aphid hyperparasitoids generally develop as obligate hyperparasitoids. It is of utmost importance to develop a conservation policy in biological control programme in order to exclude exotic facultative hyperparasitoids, so that they do not interfere drastically with biological control by exotic primary parasitoids.

BIOLOGICAL CONTROL APPROACHES

There are three basic tactics used in biological control, viz. (*i*) classical biological control, (*ii*) augmentation, and (*iii*) conservation. ***Classical biological control***consists of the foreign exploration for exotic natural enemies, their importation, and release to control a pest that has been accidentally or erroneously introduced. ***Augmentation***is defined as the effort to increase populations of natural enemies either by propagation and release or by environmental manipulation. The tactics of biological control by augmentation have two approaches, viz. inoculative and inundative releases. These approaches have different applications depending on the adaptability of the natural enemy and the environment in which it must operate. (*a*) *Inoculative releases.* These include the intentional release of a living organism as a biological control agent with the expection that it will multiply and control the pest for an extended period but not permanently. In this cases the control is expected to result from the progeny of the released natural enemies. (*b*) *Inundative releases.* In this case, the control is expected to be achieved exclusively through the direct activities of the natural enemies released. ***Conservation***is defined as actions to preserve and increase natural enemies by environmental manipulation. To be effective, conservation tactic requires the presence of appropriate natural enemies within the agroecosystem. In cases where this condition is not met, natural enemies must first be introduced.

A. Classical Biological Control

The intentional introduction of an exotic, usually co-evolved, biological control agent for permanent establishment and long-term pest control is referred to as classical biological control. The basic approach in this technique is to identify natural enemies that control a pest in its home location and introduce these enemies in the pest's new location. It is usually used to control species that have attained pest status following invasion of a new geographical location. Importation of biological control agents has been widely practiced since the initial spectacular success of the Vedalia beetle in 1889-90. The approach has yielded some of the best-known examples of biological control.

Procedures in Classical Biocontrol Programme

Procedures followed in natural enemy introduction programmes are fairly standard and generally include exploration for agents in areas of pest origin, pre-introduction studies (such as species identification, biological and ecological characterization, and rearing procedures), quarantine of agents for introduction, release and evaluation (Fig. 4.1). The salient features of the processes involved in establishing such programmes are enumerated below :

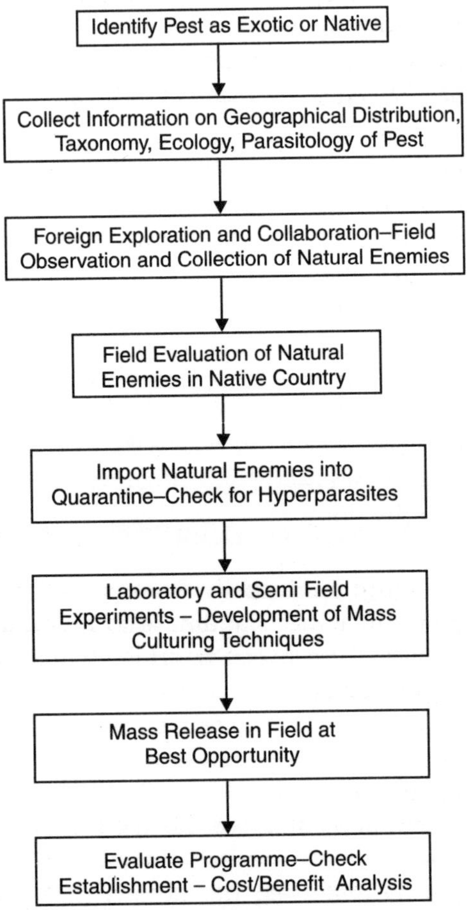

(*i*) Identification of pest. The first stage in the procedure is to establish the taxonomic identity of the pest and to determine whether the pest species concerned is of native or foreign origin. This will require information about pest's history, geographical distribution, ecology, taxonomy and if possible, parasitology. Improper identification of the pest can seriously hamper exploration efforts and delay the success of the programme. Moreover, it is important to assess the published information on natural enemies of the pest in order to determine whether biocontrol agents are available and if no, whether these might be acquired.

Identify Pest as Exotic or Native
↓
Collect Information on Geographical Distribution, Taxonomy, Ecology, Parasitology of Pest
↓
Foreign Exploration and Collaboration–Field Observation and Collection of Natural Enemies
↓
Field Evaluation of Natural Enemies in Native Country
↓
Import Natural Enemies into Quarantine–Check for Hyperparasites
↓
Laboratory and Semi Field Experiments – Development of Mass Culturing Techniques
↓
Mass Release in Field at Best Opportunity
↓
Evaluate Programme–Check Establishment – Cost/Benefit Analysis

Fig. 4.1 Stepwise procedure for establishing a classical biological control programme (After Thacker, 2002)

(*ii*) Foreign exploration. If the pest is exotic, the next stage is to collect information on the pest's status in its home location and its natural enemies. Exploration may involve transport of scientists to the country in question or collaborative work with scientists working in the country to be explored. The assistance of international agencies such as the International Organization for Biological Control (IOBC), Commonwealth Institute of Biological Control (CIBC) or the European Biological Control Laboratory (EBCL) may also be sought. During field collection, it is essential to collect species with as much genetic diversity as possible. This can usually be achieved by making collections over a number of sites in the geographical area, rather than collecting a number of individuals from a single site. Following collection, natural enemies are first tested in experiments in their native countries before importation.

(*iii*) Importation. After appropriate candidate organisms have been found, it is necessary that these may be properly exported and subsequently imported in the targeted country in preparation for release. This requires shipment of natural enemies in appropriate life stages and under proper environmental conditions to permit survival until these arrive at their destination. Imported organisms are held in quarantine facilities subsequent to their arrival in the country of intended release.

***(iv)* Quarantine.** Imported organisms are held in quarantine, typically for one or several generations, for the removal of unwanted pathogens and to permit evaluation of the vulnerability of non-target organisms to attack by the imported organisms. Quarantine facilities are carefully designed to permit efficient propagation of natural enemies while precluding their escape. The quarantine period also provides an opportunity to assess life-history attribute of natural enemies prior to release.

***(v)* Testing.** Following release from quarantine, further trials in the laboratory and semi-field (i.e using glasshouses, field cages, etc.) conditions are then undertaken while methods for mass rearing are developed. Mass rearing may not always be straight forward, which may involve growing of plants to support pest populations that then support natural enemy populations. Moreover, it is also important to acclimatize natural enemies prior to their release.

***(vi)* Mass release.** Once the numbers of the imported natural enemy are increased considerably through rearing programmes, it can then be mass-released. Efforts are made to release the natural enemies into a variety of regions and habitats to increase the opportunities for establishment. During this process care should be taken to ensure that for the natural enemies to develop upon, the pest population exists. If the natural enemies, particularly adults, require alternative food sources such as nectar, these should be made available. The number of individuals released should also be considered as there is an association between the percentage of successful introductions and the number of individuals released.

***(vii)* Evaluation.** This is the final stage in the process which comprises the post-release phase in which the aim is to monitor and determine whether the releases have been effective or not. Evaluation of released natural enemies could be of great value for assessing what factors determine success or failure to establish and suppress the target pest. Unfortunately, such studies are rare because of the limited resources provided for such work. Where post-release studies have been undertaken the data collected have proven invaluable. Evaluation of the effectiveness of the natural enemy is done by (*i*) comparing the host population of the pest before and after the release; (*ii*) correlating population changes of the natural enemy and the host, (*iii*) comparing the population on plots with and without the natural enemy, and (*iv*) by analysing the life and mortality data of the natural enemy.

Retrospective studies of biological control programmes have sought to determine factors affecting establishment of released natural enemies. These include (a) number of natural enemies released and frequency of releases, (b) biogeographical influences such as the ready accommodation of islands for new species as opposed to resistance exhibited by continents, (c) geographical origin of the agent and climatic suitability of the new range, (d) taxonomic order of the agent and its propensity to establish and proliferate, (e) environmental climatic events and catastrophes (e.g. storms and volcanoes), (f) biotypes and genetic constitution of founding populations, and (g) impact of resident organisms on population growth of exotics through either direct attack or competitive exclusion. Therefore, some evaluation should accompany each biocontrol project, and a few selected ones should be studied intensively.

Successes in Classical Biological Control

From 1890 through 1960, about 2300 species of predators and parasitoids were introduced in about 600 different situations worldwide for suppression of arthropod pests. The overall level of establishment of these natural enemies was calculated to be 34 per cent, with complete suppression of target pests occurring in 16 per cent of situations and some level of pest suppression achieved in an additional 42 per cent of situations. These rates have apparently not increased over the last 100 years, although the percentage of complete successful projects has reportedly risen since the 1930s. A computerized record of natural enemies imports maintained by the International Organisation of Biological Control (IOBC) has revealed that till the end of 1988, 4221 importations were done, of which 1251 natural enemies were established, 2038 failed and fate of another 932 was still not known. Thus, 38 per cent of the attempts with known outcome have been successful in establishing the natural enemies in exotic environments.

The BIOCAT database contains records of the introductions of entomophagous insects for the control of insect pests worldwide since 1880. A review of the database up to March 2004 reveals that there have been 5634 recorded releases of 2119 species of entomophagous arthropods to control 597 pest species. However, 'complete' (no other control measures needed; n=212) or 'substantial' (other control measures rarely required; n = 419) control was recorded in only 631 out of 5634 cases (11.2%). The primary target pests in classical biological control programmes have belonged to Homoptera (n=2420 releases) followed by Lepidoptera (1772), Coleoptera (596), Diptera (533), Hymenoptera (137) and Heteroptera (96); the Homoptera have been the most successful group controlled (429 releases or 17.7% were successful). The primary agents in classical biological control programmes have belonged to Coleoptera (n=1168), Diptera (457) and Hymenoptera (3887); the success rates recorded were 9.2, 8.1 and 12.3 per cent for these groups, respectively. In India, 163 exotic bioagents have been studied for utilization against crop pests and weeds. Of these, 69 species were recovered after releases, 4 provided partial control, 4 substantial and 6 recurring benefits worth millions of rupees. Among insect pests, maximum degree of success has been achieved with homopterans pests (46.7 %) (Dhaliwal and Koul, 2010).

A variety of reasons have been mentioned for the failures in classical biological control programmes, which include inadequate procedures, climate, predation or parasitism by natural fauna, lack of alternate hosts or food, feeding niche of target pest, inadequate knowledge of taxonomy of natural enemy and target pest, and insufficient amount of time or effort devoted to these projects. A systematic analysis of case histories of failures of introduced natural enemies revealed that in 23.5 per cent cases, the cause was climate related, viz. summer too hot, winter too cold, heavy rainfall, etc. In another 20 per cent of cases, existing native parasitoids attacked the released predator (parasitism) or parasitoid (hyperparasitism) rendering them ineffective. Lack of alternate hosts when pest numbers were low contributed to 17 per cent failures while non-acceptability of the particular pest strain by the introduced strain of the natural enemies was responsible for 11 per cent failures. The physical inacceptability of host (prey) from natural enemies resulted in 9 per cent failures. The minor causes like lack of adult food (nectar, etc.), low reproductive rate of the released natural enemy, emigration from release sites, etc. prevented establishment in 7 per cent of the cases.

Most successes in classical biocontrol have been in agroecosystems that permit species to form stable predator-prey relationships and where the pest species is exotic. One of the reasons for failure of classical biocontrol with native pests is that the introduced natural enemies have to compete with pre-existing natural enemy complexes. As a general rule, the best natural enemies are those that have evolved with the pest to be controlled. However, in some cases it has been possible to control field-based native pests of annual crops using classical approaches. These cases, although exception rather than the rule, do demonstrate the wide applicability of the classical biological approach to pest control.

Economics of Successful Programmes

Ultimately, the success or failure of a programme would be determined by its economic success. Economic assessments of classical biological control programmes are multidimensional, with a range of economic effects and, therefore, can be a complex undertaking. The components which should be considered for economic assessments include the type and degree of damage by the pest, efficiency of biological control agent, market price for the crop, cost savings for producers, profit increases, cost of programme, value of land, lowered cost of product and risk aversion of producers. The most common method of determining the economic benefits of biological control programmes is through cost-benefit analyses. Economic assessments of the use of introduced natural enemies have been made for several arthropod pests (Table 4.8).

Undoubtedly, classical biological control programmes have produced some of the highest benefit-to-cost ratios of any pest management approach, exceeding billions of dollars in terms of total savings. For example, a recent introduction programme initiated against the ash whitefly, *Siphoninus phillyreae*, in California resulted in benefit : cost ratio ranging between US$ 270:1 and 344:1. The cost and benefit of the release programme against cassava mealy bug, *Phenacoccus manihoti* in Africa, accumulated over 40 years (1974-2013), was estimated to be US$ 49 million and 9.4 billion, respectively, with a cost: benefit ratio range of 1:170 to 1:431, depending on the scenario. There was an average cost: benefit ratio of 1:9.4 (for the period 1960-2000) for three importation biological control programmes conducted against insect pests in Australia, as compared to 1:2.5 cost:benefit ratio for non-biological projects conducted during the same period. The economic benefits of classical biological control are enhanced by the fact that the programmes are self-sustaining and permanent, so that benefits continue to accrue annually without any additional cost.

Table 4.8 Economics of successful classical biological control programmes

Pest	Country	Cost	Benefit/Saving
Rufous scale	Peru	$1789	$226916 p.a. in 1977 on chemical control
Sugarcane scale	Tanzania	$11976	$67832 p.a. in 1974 in increased yields
Coconut leafminer	Sri Lanka	$35783	$12.4 million p.a. in 1977 in yield increases
Potato tuber moth	Zambia	$35732	$547560 p.a. in 1974 in yield increases
Mango mealy bug	Tago	$175000	$3.9 million p.a. in 1994
Cassava mealy bug	Africa	$49 million	$9.4 billion (1974-2013)

Soruce : Dhaliwal and Koul (2007)

Obstacles to Classical Biological Control

A number of impediments limit the application of classical biological control, some of which are discussed below :

Lack of prediction. It is difficult to predict whether an introduced natural enemy would establish and suppress the target population. A number of factors may prevent or enhance the establishment of an imported natural enemy: its adaptability to the climate in the release area, synchrony of the natural enemy's phenology with that of the target pest, availability of alternate hosts or food compatibility of the habitat (e.g. overwintering sites) with the introduced natural enemy, competitive ability of the natural enemy, complex of indigenous natural enemies attacking the imported one, and the genetic structure of the imported population. The compatibility of the imported natural enemy with the environment can be improved by considering the following points : (*a*) Efforts should be made to match the climate of the collection area and the released areas. (*b*) It is advisable to collect natural enemy species from a wide range of habitats to increase the chances of obtaining a genotype suited to the area of release. (*c*) Host-specific organisms are more effective natural enemies (particularly at low host/ prey densities) than are more polyphagous species. (*d*) The most dominant natural enemy in the targeted pest's native habitat would likely to be more effective in the release area.

Environmental impact. Importation of natural enemies has come under increasing scrutiny, as the environmentalists have shown high sensitivity to the conservation of natural species. Various scientists have expressed concerns about the potential effects of natural enemies on non-target organisms. The potential risks of classical biological control include predation or parasitism of non-target species, competition with native species community and ecosystem effects, and unexpected effects such as loss of species dependent on the target species of biological control efforts. Post collection studies of candidates for introduction should be conducted rigorously during quarantine to determine the safety of the proposed agent to the environment into which it would be released. The relative safety of a natural enemy is generally assessed by evaluating its host range to determine its potential impact on target and non-target populations in regions proposed for release. The more polyphagous the natural enemy, the greater is the probable risk to non-target species. It is believed that the few documented cases of non-target impacts, compared with the number of natural enemy introductions, may be more the result of a lack of monitoring and documentation than a lack of actual impacts. Hence, the current regulations and protocols seem to be inadequate and should do more to assess potential effects on non-economic species and ecosystems, as well as compare the effects of target pests with the potential non-target impacts of natural enemies prior to release.

Several avenues are currently being pursued to enhance the potential success of biological control projects, which can be measured in terms of pest suppression and lack of non-target impacts. These include (*a*) improved regulatory oversight to enhance project safety and efficacy, (*b*) developing reliable testing methods to predict natural enemy safety and efficacy, (*c*) employing risk management techniques to better effect, (*d*) improving monitoring of past projects to determine project efficacy, (*e*) genetic manipulation of natural enemies, and (*f*) extending biological control to non-agroecosystems to encompass 'non-traditional' targets.

Examples of Classical Biological Control

Some of the examples of classical biological control are described below.

Cassava mealy bug. Cassava is an exotic crop that was introduced to Africa over 500 years ago. It is native to tropical Central and South America. It is now the staple food of over 200 million people in an area known as the cassava belt, which extends from 150 N to 25°S. Cassava had remained relatively pest free until the 1970s. In the early 1970s, however, the cassava mealy bug, *Phenacoccus manihoti,* was accidentally introduced from South America to Africa. It has been estimated that since its first detection in Zaire (DPR of Congo) in the early 1970s, it spread at a rate of about 300 km per year. By 1986, it had reached 27 countries (70% of the cassava belt) in Western and Central Africa.

The cassava mealy bug spread throughout Africa and became a serious pest of cassava, causing tuber yield losses up to 84 per cent and nearly 100 per cent loss of foliage. In the mid-1970s, scientists began exploring South America for natural enemies of the cassava mealy bug. Initial searches for natural enemies were seriously handicapped by misidentification of the mealy bug-the parasitoids were collected from the wrong host species and the natural enemies were unable to reproduce on the cassava mealy bug. Finally, in 1981, specimens of cassava mealy bug were located in Paraguay and their natural enemies were collected; among the parasitoids was the encyrtid wasp, *Epidinocarsis lopezi,* which was selected for use in a biological release programme for cassava mealy bug control. With funding from the International Fund for Agriculture Development, the Africa-wide Biological Control Project (ABCP) was initiated at the International Institute of Tropical Agriculture (IITA) in Nigeria, headed by Dr Hans Rudolf Heren.

E. lopezi was first released in Nigeria in 1981 and in less than 1.5 years spread to areas as far away as 170 km from the original sites. By the end of 1984, *E.lopezi* was found in almost 70 per cent of cassava fields spread over an area of more than 2,00,000 km2 in southwestern Nigeria. Subsequently, the wasp was sent to several other countries and by the end of 1985, over 50 releases had been made in 12 African countries. It was established over a total area of more than 7,50,000 km2 in 16 African countries by 1986. By 1990, *A. lopezi* was established in 24 countries covering an area of more than 12.7 million km2. Currently, cassava mealy bug has been virtually eliminated in 30 African countries and no longer poses a serious threat to most cassava growing regions.

The cost and benefit of the biocontrol programme in Africa, over the 40 years period (1974-2013), has been estimated to be US$ 49 million and 9.4 billion respectively, with a cost:benefit ratio ranging between 1:170 to 1:431, depending upon the scenario. Even the most conservative estimates indicate that the project yielded a cost:benefit ratio of 1:149. The release programme, under the direction of Hans R. Herren, not only saved one of Africa's major staple crops and farmers billions of dollars, but also demonstrated the potential of classical biocontrol approach to control serious insect pests in agriculture. In view of the outstanding success of the programme, Hans R. Herren was awarded the World Food Prize in 1995.

Cassava green mite. The notable success of encyrtid parasitoid to control the cassava mealy bug has probably overshadowed the role of predatory mites in controlling the cassava green mite, *Mononychellus tanajoa* in several African countries. In the early 1970s, this mite was discovered attacking cassava in East Africa. This exotic mite quickly spread throughout the cassava belt causing up to 80 per cent reduction in yield. Since the mite is of South American origin, search was made by various research agencies for predators that could be used as biocontrol agents. Between 1984 and 2001, more than 11.6 million predatory phytoseiid mites of several species of Brazilian origin were released at 847 sites in 16 countries (Table 4.9). Three of these species, viz. *Neoseiulus idaeus, Typhlodromalus manihoti* and *T. aripo* are now established in Africa. *N. idaeus* became established in Benin and Kenya, *T. manihoti* became established in Benin, Burundi, Ghana and Nigeria, and *T. aripo* became established in 20 countries spanning the cassava belt of Africa. *T. aripo,* a predator confined to be growing tip of cassava plants, has been the big surprise. This predator has spread beyond most of the original release sites and *M. tanajoa* populations have been reduced by more than 50 per cent and yields increased by more than 35 per cent where *T. aripo* is present.

Ash whitefly. The ash whitefly, *Symphoninus phillyreae,* appeared in southern California in 1988 and spread rapidly throughout California and adjacent states. Because of its broad host range, the pest caused severe damage to many economically important trees and shrubs. The source of the whitefly was found to be the palearctic region and an intensive search was initiated for its natural enemies. Two species of natural enemies, viz. the aphelinid parasitoid, *Encarsia inaron* and the coccinellid beetle, *Clitosthetus arcuatus,* were imported and released. The females of *E. inaron* seem to be highly efficient in locating incipient populations of the whitefly.

Table 4.9 Phytoseiid species imported from South America and released and recovered in Africa from 1984 to 2001

Phytoseiid species	No. of countries	No. shipped	No. of release sites	Rate of recovery
Amblyseius aerialis	7	142,066	27	0.00
Euseius concordis	8	170,262	44	0.00
Galendromus annectens	10	516,728	41	0.13
Neoseiulus anonymus	10	2,029,983	71	0.30
N. californicus	8	443,512	30	0.28
N. idaeus	12	5,556,846	241	0.45
Phytoseiulus mexicanus	1	726	1	0.00
Typhlodromalus aripo	16	400,587	220	0.90
T. limonicus	3	144,000	20	0.00
T. manihoti	9	2,130,519	159	0.54
T. tenuiscutus	1	33,452	4	0.00

Source **:** Vincent *et al.* (2007)

Moreover, the parasitoid appears to be capable of over-wintering in deciduous habitats, whereas the whitefly must seek the foliage of alternate, evergreen hosts during the writer. Thus, when the whitefly returns to its preferred deciduous hosts in the spring, the parasitoid is already present there and ready to initiate reproduction simultaneously with that of the whitefly.

B. Augmentation

Augmentative biocontrol is focused on enhancing the numbers and/or activity of natural enemies in agroecosystems. This strategy involves mass multiplication and periodic release of natural enemies so that they may multiply during the growing season. The processes of augmentation or inoculation with natural enemies occur where natural enemies are absent or where they exist at levels that are ineffective for pest control. The aim is to establish a natural enemy population that is able to suppress pest numbers below economically damaging levels until harvest. The rationale for this approach to biological control is that many effective natural enemies cannot survive on a year-round basis on a crop. However, they are able to survive and effect control at certain times of the year, hence the need for annual releases. The critical difference between this approach and that of classical biological control is, therefore, that it is not long term. Ecologically, the general equilibrium of the pest population is not altered as in case of classical biological control. The releases have to be repeated periodically and only temporary suppression of the pest is achieved.

Several issues must be considered before releasing natural enemies for augmentation programmes.

- The cost and the anticipated benefits of using biocontrol relative to alternative tactics (e.g. pesticides), must be weighed carefully.
- The overall crop production system should be considered; releases may not be of any use if crop production practices are inimical to the use of natural enemies.
- The information on the most appropriate species or strain, most effective means of application (e.g. method of release, number of releases per unit area or per pest, evaluation of efficacy, etc) must be available.

More than 125 species of natural enemies are commercially available at global level for augmentative biological control. This form of control is applied in the open field in crops that are attacked by only a few pest species, and it is particularly popular in greenhouse crops, where the whole spectrum of pests can be managed by a suite of natural enemies. When compared with chemical control, augmentative control does not cause any phytotoxic effects on young plants, premature abortion of flowers and fruits does not occur, release of natural enemies takes less time, several key pests can be controlled only by natural enemies, and there is no safety or re-entry period after release of natural enemies, this allows continuous harvesting without danger to the health of greenhouse personnel.

The tactics of biocontrol by augmentation have two approaches, viz. inoculative or inundative releases. These approaches have different applications depending on the adaptability of the natural enemy and the environment in which it must operate. Inoculative releases are used in cases in which control is expected from the progeny and subsequent generations and not from the release itself. The natural enemies are released in relatively low numbers to establish or bolster local populations of resident natural enemies for either short-or long-term suppression of a target pest or pest complex. These may be made as infrequently as once a year to re-establish a species of natural enemy which is periodically killed out in an area by unfavourable conditions during part of the year, but operates very effectively the rest of the year. Inundative releases involve mass culture and release of natural enemies to suppress the pest population directly as in the case of conventional insecticides. In this case, large numbers of natural enemies are released to obtain rapid pest suppression. These are most economical against pests that have only one or at the most a few discrete generations every year. These two approaches impose different demands on production and release technologies. From an economic point of view, inoculative releases are generally cheaper because natural enemies will reproduce once released. By contrast, inundative releases require culturing or rearing of natural enemies, which adds to the cost of the control method.

As the aim of augmentative biocontrol is not usually long term, using natural enemies as a temporary measure is often expensive, particularly in comparison to the costs involved in conventional pesticide application. The expenses are incurred in rearing, distributing and applying the natural enemies. Hence, the use of natural enemies for augmentation has largely been restricted to situations where released natural enemies could be confined. Such situations often come across with high-value crops grown in greenhouses. The use of biocontrol agents in field situations where the natural enemies can easily disperse is generally limited, although some successes have been achieved with *Trichogramma* spp., that parasitizes the eggs of many lepidopteran pests. The use of *Encarsia formosa* Gahan against the greenhouse whitefly, *Trialeurodes vaporariorum* (Westwood), in greenhouses and the predatory mite, *Phytoseilus persimilis* Athias-Henriot against the two-spotted spider mite, *Tetranychusurticae* Koch, in both greenhouses and in some orchard crops is very well established throughout Europe.

In 2010, about 230 species of invertebrate natural enemies from ten taxonomic groups—were used in pest management worldwide. The majority of these species belonged to the Arthropoda (219 out of 230 species = 95.2%). An overview of the most important applications of augmentative biological control at global level is given in Table 4.10. In Europe, about 40,000-60,000 ha of orchard, vineyard and vegetable crops are treated with natural enemies annually. Greenhouse pests are presently managed through augmentative biological control on about 14,000 ha of about 300,000 ha of protected cultivation worldwide. Over 80 per cent of biological control in greenhouses is applied on cucumber, tomato and sweet pepper, and all vegetables together account for 90 per cent of the natural enemy market. Other greenhouse crops in which natural enemies are used are strawberries, eggplant, melon, watermelon, and beans. Since the 1990s, use of augmentative biocontrol has been growing steadily in cut flowers (gerberas, orchids, roses and chrysanthemum) and pot plants (e.g. poinsettia). In gerberas, the developments have been particularly fast and natural enemies were used on 78 per cent of the Dutch gerbera area in 1998. Augmentative biocontrol was applied on more than 10 per cent (600 ha) of the total Dutch greenhouse area planted with flowers and ornamentals in 1998. In USA, augmentative releases of natural enemies take place on about 10 per cent of greenhouses, 8 per cent of nurseries, 19 per cent of cultivated fruit and nut acreage and 3 per cent of the vegetable acreage. On one high-value crop, strawberries, beneficial mites are used for spider mite suppression on about 50-70 per cent of acreage in California alone.

Table 4.10 Worldwide use of augmentative biological control

Natural enemy/ enemies	Pest(s) and crop(s)	Area of use (million ha) & location(s)
Trichogramma spp.	Lepidopteranpests in field vegetables, cereals, cotton	10.0, former USSR
Trichogramma spp.	Lepidopteran pests in field crops, forests	2.0, China
Trichogramma spp.	Lepidopteran pests in corn, cotton, sugarcane, tobacco	2.0, Mexico
Trichogramma spp.	Lepidopteran pests in cereals	0.3, SE Asia
Trichogramma spp.	Lepidopteran pests in cereals, cotton, sugarcane	0.7, S. America
Cotesia spp.	Sugarcane borers	0.2, China, S. America
Trichogramma spp.	Lepidopteran pests in cotton, sugarcane and forests	0.1, N America
Trichogramma spp.	European corn borer in corn	0.05, Europe
Trichogramma spp.	Spider mites, other mites in vineyards	0.04, Europe
Suite of 5 spp.	Lepidoptera, Homoptera, spider mites in orchards	0.03, Europe
Aphytis spp.	Scales in citrus	0.02, USA
Phytoseiulus persimilis	Spider mites in open-field strawberries.	<0.02, USA, W. Europe
Encarsia formosa	Whiteflies in greenhouses	0.006, worldwide
P. persimilis	Spider mites in greenhouses	0.006, worldwide
Suite of 10 spp.	Aphids, leafminers, etc. in greenhouses.	0.003, worldwide
Suite of >10 spp.	Various pests in greenhouses.	0.003, worldwide
Suite of > 20 spp.	Interior plantscapes, botanical gardens	No data, W. Europe, N. America
Spalangia and others	Flies in cattle farms, poultry housing	No data, USA, W. Europe

Source : van Lenteren (2000)

Requirements for Augmentation

Although the practice of augmenting parasitoids and predators for pest management has been modest but notable throughout the world, impediments to increased implementation remain. As this technique involves the collection, rearing and release of natural enemies, this means that procedures need to be developed to produce, store, distribute and apply these agents while ensuring that they remain viable. Rearing is often expensive because tritrophic culturing systems are required in which plants are grown to support pest populations that can then support natural enemy populations. It is also important that species mass-reared or released should not suffer any loss of fitness as a result of laboratory culturing. Storage is also usually expensive because it is much difficult to keep a living organism alive than to keep a pesticide viable for a shelf-life of about two years. Some of the requirements for promoting the cause of augmentation are outlined below.

(*i*) Selection of natural enemy. The first requirement for a release programme is to select an appropriate natural enemy species or strain for the pest target. The natural enemy must be amenable to mass rearing and storage, and it must be matched to conditions under which it would be used.

(*ii*) Mass rearing. The development of cost-effective and efficient mass- rearing methodology is essential for the success of an augmentative biocontrol programme. The availability of large numbers of natural enemies is necessary and they must be produced economically. Some of the impediments to these systems include a lack of artificial rearing media and systems for efficient delivery of artificial media, limited automation, as well as the need for properly designed facilities, effective quality controls and improved management systems. There are numerous efficacious species for which no artificial rearing media or procedure for storage are available. A total of 19 species of egg parasitoids, about 15 species of larval parasitoids and fewer than 10 species of predators have been reared on artificial media.

(*iii*) Quality. Poor quality of the released natural enemies or incorrect release rates can lead to unsatisfactory pest suppression and contribute to unpredictability of the release programme. Natural enemies must perform consistently at a high level, commensurate with their cost and with the relative costs of alternative control strategies (e.g. insecticides). There are three components of insect mass production quality controls, viz.(a) production control, monitoring general procedures of rearing processes (e.g. equipment maintenance and environmental conditions); (b) process control, monitoring quality of the unfinished product (e.g. proportion of hatch, larval, and pupal weights, proportion of pupation); and (c) monitoring quality of the final product (e.g. quantity, size, sex ratio, fecundity, and other biological and behavioural characteristics.

Examples of Augmentative Releases

Massive releases have been attempted in several programmes involving natural enemies like the parasitoids, *Trichogramma* spp. and *Encarsia* spp., and the predators, *Chrysoperla carnea* and lady beetles, *Hippodamia convergens* and the predatory phytoseid mite, *Phytoseiulus persimilis*. The most important natural enemies used in greenhouses include *Encarsia formosa* (accounting for 25% of the total natural enemy market), followed by *P. persimilis* (12%) and *Amblyseius cucumeris* (12%).

Trichogramma. The release of mass-produced egg parasitoids of *Trichogramma* to control lepidopteran pests has gained increased attention worldwide in the last few years. These parasitoids have several advantages, including relative ease of rearing and causing death of their host in the egg stage before it causes feeding injury. However, there are certain significant shortcomings associated with the use of *Trichogramma* spp. Accurate species determination is difficult with this genus because of highly conserved morphological characters and the prevalence of biotypes. This characteristic poses a threat to non-target species. Secondly, the most frequently used species, e.g. *T. minutum* and *T. pretiosum* are polyphagous and widely distributed. This feature complicates evaluations, i.e. whether the outcome was due to released or naturally occurring parasitoids. Thirdly, timing of releases is often critical because of the rapid embryonic development in many insect pests and the resulting changes in suitability for parasitism as the host eggs age.

More than 100 species of *Trichogramma* occur in agroecosystems throughout the world. Globally, approximately 20 species of *Trichogramma* are regularly used in augmentative biocontrol programmes to control pests on at least 22 crops and trees on an estimated 32 million ha in 30 countries. Most of these species are released in large numbers, i.e. inundative releases in order to rapidly suppress the target pests. *Trichogramma* spp. have been extensively used in inundative releases in Europe, South America and Asia. Most *Trichogramma* used in western Europe are for suppression of the European corn borer, *Ostrinia nubilalis*. Currently, about 58,000 ha of corn are treated annually with *T. brassicae*, 84 per cent of which is supplied by BIOTOP in Valbonne, France. In 1998, between 400,000 and 500,000 ha of corn in France were treated with some type of pesticide for *O. nubilalis* suppression, about 10 per cent (45,000 ha) of which was *T. brassicae*. Sales of *T. brassicae* by BIOTOP have consistently increased each year from 1988, when *T. brassicae* first appeared on the market as a crop protection agent.

The former USSR ranked first in application of *Trichogramma* (27.6 million ha), followed by China (2.1 million ha) and Mexico (2.0 million ha). In contrast to the western European situation, an estimated 140,000 to 350,000 of various crops were treated with *Trichogramma* annually in the USA. Large scale trials with *T. pretiosum* to manage populations of the cotton bollworms, *Helicoverpa zea* and *Heliothis virescens*, have provided variable results, with some suggesting good pest suppression and others indicating poor suppression. In addition to the numbers released, effectiveness of *Trichogramma* may be influenced by the population density or dynamics of the pest species or strain of *Trichogramma* released, vigor of the parasitoid released, method of distribution, crop phenology, number of other bioagents present and proximity to crops receiving insecticide and drift of insecticides into *Trichogramma* release areas. *Trichogramma* spp. were released annually in over 2 million ha of crop and forest systems in China. Similarly, over 8 million ha of crops received *Trichogramma* spp. annually in the erstwhile USSR. Estimations of applications with *Trichogramma* in all other countries except former USSR, China and Mexico, are in the order of 300,000-400,000 ha. Inundative releases for the control of lepidopteran pests are being studied in more than 50 countries.

All *Trichoglamma* programmes must address the following four aspects for success: (*i*) Selection of the appropriate parasitoid population should be based on inter-and intra-specific variation as well as parasitoid quality. (*ii*) Mass rearing should be optimised taking into account both host and parasitoid components. (*iii*) Strategies for use in the field should vary according to the approach desired (classical or augmentative control), timing, frequency and rate of release, and multiple factors that affect release such as weather, crop, host, predation, dispersal and pesticides. (*iv*) Effective implementation of *Trichogramma* in the field requires the support of extension and advanced technology.

Green lacewing. The green lacewing, *C. carnea* has been utilized worldwide to suppress various pests including aphids, lepidopteran eggs and larvae, and other soft-bodied insects. Several biological features of green lacewings make them excellent agents for release programmes: (*i*) they are generalists capable of developing and reproducing on a wide variety of prey, (*ii*) they tend to be more tolerant of insecticides than many other entomophagous arthropods, and (*iii*) they can be mass reared and stored. Lacewings are typically released as eggs or pre-fed neonate larvae and have demonstrated high efficacy in some production systems when released in high numbers.

Augmentative Biocontrol in India

Some of the successful examples of augmentative biocontrol in India have been listed in Table 4.11. The status of augmentative biocontrol in selected crops is briefly presented herein.

Rice. Releases of mirid bug @ 100 bugs or 50-75 eggs/m2 at 10-day intervals have been found effective for the control of brown planthopper. Inundative releases of exotic *Trichogramma japonicum* at 50,000 ha-1 during egg laying period of rice stem borer reduced borer damage and increased crop yield. It has been found that 7-9 releases of *T. chilonis* and *T. japonicum* @ 1,00,000/ha, starting at 30 days after transplanting proved as effective as the standard insecticide treatment for the control of stem borer and leaf folder. A total of 11 releases of *T. japonicum* and *T. chilonis* @ 50,000 per ha per week on a long duration variety of rice (Swarna) reduced the tiller damage caused by yellow stem borer and folded leaves by rice leaf folder, to the tune of 50.1-61.3 and 63.8-75.5 per cent, respectively. Similarly reduction in tiller damage and folded leaves varied from 78.1 to 81.6 and 72.6 to 81.8 per cent, respectively, when the egg parasitoids were released @ 1,00,000 per ha per week during the season.

Sugarcane. The relatively stable sugarcane agroecosystem provides ideal conditions for the colonization of natural enemies. During recent years, releases of *T. chilonis* have been found effective for the management of various shoot and stalk borers in different parts of the country. The parasitoid releases @ 1,25,000 ha-1 are recommended against shoot borer in Andhra Pradesh. Weekly releases at 1,25,00 parasitic wasps per ha from 4th to 11th week stage of the crop provided effective control of internode borer, *Chilo sacchariphagus indicus* in Tamil Nadu. The release of 12 ml of parasitoid adults (3,00,000) per ha in six split doses effectively checked internode borer infestation in an area of about 500 ha. In Punjab, the sequential releases of *T. chilonis* (12 releases @ 50,000/ha at 10-day intervals) and *Cotesia flavipes* (6 releases @ 10,000/ha at 10-day intervals) during July to October proved very effective for the control of stalk borer. For the control of shoot borer, *Chilo infuscatellus*, 6-9 releases of *T. chilonis* during April to June at 10-day intervals @ 50,000/ha proved effective. Similarly, stalk borer and Gurdaspur borer have been controlled in parts of sub-tropical India by large-scale releases of *T. chilonis.*

In addition to egg parasitoids, field releases of the larval parasitoid, *Isotima javensis* exercised effective control of top borer in Tamil Nadu and Karnataka. Releases of *Sturmiopsis inferens* at 312 gravid females per ha provided effective control of

C. infuscatellus in coastal areas of Tamil Nadu. Sugarcane pyrilla has been effectively controlled by redistribution and periodic release of 8000-10,000 cocoons or 8,00,000-10,00,000 eggs per ha of parasitoid *E. melanolenca.* In 1999 there was an outbreak of pyrilla in 6 lakh ha in north India, perhaps due to indiscriminate burning of trash. However, the parasitoid overpowered the pest within 20 days and the spraying cost of about Rs 480 million crores was saved.

Cotton. A number of promising natural enemies have been found attacking cotton pests in the country. However, large-scale use of insecticides has reduced the population of most of these natural enemies to insignificant levels. In the fields where biocontrol was practiced, 25 natural enemies were recorded as compared to only 2 in the fields sprayed with insecticides. Releases of *Trichogramma* spp. at 1,50,000 parasitized eggs ha-1 at weekly intervals have proved

Table 4.11 Examples of successful augmentative biological control systems in India

Crop/Pest	Biotic agent(s)	Dosage per ha	Frequency of application	Application method	Remarks
1	2	3	4	5	6
Sugarcane					
Chilo spp.	*Trichogramma chilonis* Ishii (Bio SC_1)	50,000	Every 10 days, 8-10 times starting on 30-day old crop for shoot borer and 60 days for other borers or during egg laying period	Stapling parasitized egg card bits on lower surface of the leaf	If pheromone traps are available, initiate the first release on trapping the first moth in the pheromone traps
Melanaspis glomerata	*Pharoscymnus horni* (Weise), *Chilocorus nigrita* (Fabricius), *Sticholotis madagassa*	1,500 adult beetles or grubs	The first release is made on noticing the infestation, subsequent releases are made based on the population levels	The adult beetles are spread or released on infested canes through-out the fields.	The release of eggs about to hatch or grubs will be more effective because the grubs will feed and develop in the sugarcane ecosystem
Pyrilla perpusilla	*Epiricania melanoleuca*	2-3 egg masses or 5-7 cocoons in 40 selected spots/ha	The releases are initiated before the onset of rainy season	The egg masses or cocoons are uniformly spread in 40 selected spots/ha. In endemic areas the dosage is increased by 10 times	Drought conditions are not conducive for the development of parasi-toid. Hence the release should be made during the humid periods.
Rice					
Scirpophaga incertulas	*Trichogramma japonicum*, *T.chilonis*	100,000	30,37 and 44 days after transplanting (DAT)	Releasing adults or stapling parasitized egg card bits	Distributing the adults, parasitized egg card bits uniformly and spraying monocroptophos @ 1000 ml/ha on 58,65 and 72 DAT give better results.
Nilaparvata lugens	*Cyrtorhinus lividipennis*	100 adults or 50-75 nymphs/m^2	The predator is released on noticing the incid-ence of leaf-plant- hopper	The adults or nymphs are released on leaf or plant- hopper infested spots in the field	If the predator-host ratio reaches 1:4, no action is required
Maize					
Chilo paitellus (Swinhoe)	*T. chilonis*	100,000	Release parasitoid on 10-15 days old crop	Stapling parasitised egg and bits on underside of the central whock leaves in evening hours	Use only selective pesticidbles as part of biointensive IPM

Crop/Pest	Biotic agent(s)	Dosage per ha	Frequency of application	Application method	Remarks
1	2	3	4	5	6
Cotton					
Helicoverpa armi-gera, Earias spp., *Pecti-nophora gossy-piella*	*T. chilonis* (Bio C_1 or Bio C_3)	1,50,000	Weekly 6 times starting from 40th day after planting or during the egg laying period	Stapling parasitised egg card bits on lower sur-face of the leaf	Use only selective pest-icides as part of bio-intensive IPM
Tobacco					
Spodoptera litura	*Telenomus remus*	1,20,000	Five times at weekly interval	Releasing adults	Distribution of the para-sitoids uniformly throug-hout the nursery by tapping the tube conta-ining adult parasitoids while walking briskly along nursery beds gives the best results.
	Chrysoperla or *Apertochrysa*	60,000	Starting from 4th week at weekly interval	Releasing 2nd instar larvae	More useful in case sucking pests also create problems.
Myzus persicae, M. nicotianae	*Chrysoperla* or *Apertochrysa*	6/plant	November	Releasing six 2nd instar larvae per plant in the field crop	
Coconut					
Opisina arenosella	*Goniozus nephantidis*	3,000 adults	Need based or for each generation	Releasing adults	In case *G. nephantidis, Elasmus nephantidis* and *Brachymeria nosatoi* put together are present in the parasitoid-host ratio of 2:5 or one *G.nephantidis* is present for every five *O. arenosella,* no action is required; otherwise the same ratio has to be created
Arecanut					
Ischnaspis longirostris	*Chilocorus nigrita*	20 or 50 adults/ plant	Release as soon as infestation is noticed	Releasing adults	Identify the endemic areas, mark the infested trees and release

Crop/Pest	Biotic agent(s)	Dosage per ha	Frequency of application	Application method	Remarks
1	2	3	4	5	6
Coffee					
Mealy bugs (*Planococcus* spp. & *Pseudococcus* spp.)	*Cryptolaemus montrouzieri*	2-10 beetles / infested plant	After the blossom	Releasing adult beetles	Ant suppression operations should be adopted
Apple					
Eriosoma lanigerum	*Aphelinus mali*	1000 adults or mummies/infested tree	Once, as soon as infestation is noticed	Releasing adults or placing mummies	The parasitoid is effective against aerial population of woolly aphid, it is more effective in valleys than on slopes.
Quadraspidiotus perniciosus	*Encarsia perniciosi*	2000 adults/ infested tree	Once, in spring	Releasing adults on infested plants	In endemic areas, repeat release if necessary
	Chilocorus infernalis	20 adults or 50 grubs per tree	Once in April-May	Releasing adults on grubs	In endemic areas, repeat release if necessary
Cydia pomonella	*Trichogramma embryophagum*	2000 adults / tree	Releasing at weekly interval	Releasing adults	First release should be initiated once the first moth is caught in pheromone traps or eggs noticed.
Citrus					
Icerya purchasi	*Rodolia cardinalis*	10 beetles/infested plant	Once on noticing adults or infestation	Releasing adults	Ant suppression operations should be adopted in the orchard
Planococcus citri	*Cryptolaemus montrouzieri*	10 beetles/infested plant	After the blossom	Releasing adults	Ant suppression opera-tions should be adopted in the orchard; ringing the trunk with diazinon granules one foot away is essential for getting best results.
	Leptomastix dactylopii Howard	3000 adults	Need based; under expert supervision	Releasing adults	Ant suppression operations should be adopted in the orchards; ringing the trunk with diazinon granules one foot away is essential for getting best results.

Crop/Pest	Biotic agent(s)	Dosage per ha	Frequency of application	Application method	Remarks
1	2	3	4	5	6
Grapes					
Maconellicoccus hirsutus	*C. montrouzieri*	2500-3000 beetles/ha or 10 beetles/infested vine	Once, as soon as the infestation is noticed	Releasing adults	Adopt ant suppression measures in vineyards, repeat release in case necessary.
Guava					
Chloropulvinaria psidii	*C. montrouzieri*	10-20 beetles/ infested plant	Once, as soon as infestation is noticed	Releasing adults	Adopt ant suppression measures in the orchard. One release is enough because the beetle prefers guava ecosystem.
Beans					
Tetranychus spp.	*Phytoseiulus persimilis* Athias-	10 adults/ plant or 1-6 leaves containing predatory mites are released	Once, 30 days after germination	Releasing adults	Release 30 days after germination or as and when infestation is noticed. This predator is also effective against tetranychid mites on brinjal and strawberries.
Tomato					
H. armigera	*Trichogramma brasiliensis* Ashmead, *T. pretiosum* Riley / *T. chilonis* $BioH_1$	50,000	Weekly interval/6 times from 25th day after transplanting or during egg laying period.	Releasing adults or stapling parasitized egg cards	
Weeds					
Eichhornia crassipes	*Neochetina eichhorniae* Warn., *N. bruchi*	1000-5000 adults/ water body	Release weevils in ponds/lakes/canals, once at the onset of monsoon	Releasing adults or infested weed mats	Take up area wide operations to achieve best result.
	Orthogalumna terebrantis	10,000-50,000 mites/water body	Release mites in ponds/lakes/canals, once at the onset of monsoon	Scattering mite infested leaves on weed mats	Take up area wide operations to achieve best results.
Salvinia molesta	*Cyrtobagous salviniae*	1000-5000 adults/ water body	Pond/lake/canal to be infested with weevils once at the onset of monsoon	Releasing adults or infested weed mats	Take up area wide operations to achieve best results.
Subabul					
Heteropsylla cubana	*Curinus coeruleus*	20-25 adults/tree	Twice during July and October	Releasing adults	Inoculate as many places as possible.

Source **:** Modified from Singh et al., (2001)

promising for bollworm control. The green lacewing, *C. carnea,* can be released @ 2 larvae per plant during the peak egg hatching of cotton bollworms. Sucking pests may be checked by releasing chrysopids at 1 lakh per ha at fortnightly intervals. Recently, a new parasitoid, *Aenasius bambawalei,* has been reported to cause 50-80 per cent parasitization of the nymphs of mealy bug, *Phenacoccus solenopsis*. The parasitoid could kill the mealy bugs within a week, which turned into reddish dark brown mummies. The parasitoid population could be augmented in cotton through collection of mealy bug mummies from various host plants and releasing them onto the cotton plants.

Horticultural crops. Augmentative and inoculative release of two exotic parasitoids, *Encarsia perniciosi* and *Aphytis* spp. *proclia* group @ 2000 per infested tree have given promising results for the suppression of San Jose scale on apples. The Russian strain of *E. perniciosi* proved effective in Himachal Pradesh while Chinese and American strains proved better in Uttar Pradesh. *Aphelinus mali* was found effective against woolly apple aphid in Kullu Valley but subsequent releases in Shimla Hills, Chaubattia, Conoor and Shillong were not successful. Similarly, releases of exotic parasitoid, *Leptomastix dactylopii* have proved effective for the control of citrus mealy bug, *Planococcus citri* in Karnataka. Mass rearing and release of the Australian coccinellid predator, *Cryptolaemus montrouzieri* have been found effective against citrus mealy bug, grape mealy bug, guava scale and other scales in a number of plantations.

In case of vegetable pests, inundative releases of egg parasitoid, *Trichogramma brasiliensis* @ 4000 adults ha-1 for six weeks suppressed the attack of fruit borer on tomato. Phytophagous mites on okra and brinjal can be effectively checked by augmentative releases of phytoseiid mites, *Phytoseiulus persimilis* and *Amblyseius tetranychivorus* @ 10 adults plant-1.

Plantation crops. Inundative release of native parasitoids, *Goniozus nephantidis* and *Bracon brevicornis* at 3000 and 4500 per ha, respectively, has given encouraging results for the management of *Opisina arenosella* on coconut. The inoculative release of coccinellid, *Curinus coerulens,* against subabul psyllid, *Heteropsylla cubana* has proved very effective in the management of this pest.

C. Conservation

Conservation of biological control agents refers to modification of the environment or existing practices to protect and enhance specific enemies or other organisms to reduce the effects of pests. In contrast to classical biological control and augmentative releases, conservation does not involve collection and rearing of natural enemies for release. Rather, this approach involves creating conditions under which natural enemies are able to enhance their efficacy as biocontrol agents. Conservation is often the least emphasized of the three major approaches to biological control. However, it can constitute the most important approach because of two reasons; (*i*) The practices conducive to natural enemy conservation influence the success of native, imported and periodically released natural enemies. (*ii*) Conservation of natural enemies enables farmers to utilize beneficial species that exist in the agroecosystem. Thus, it serves to strengthen farmers' appreciation of biological control and their understanding of the natural enemies' ecology in relation to the crop production systems.

Agroecosystems are characterized by many agricultural practices and designs that have the potential to enhance the functional biodiversity of natural enemies and many others that negatively affect it. In general, there seem to be reluctance on the part of farmers to modify their production practices to accommodate or promote natural enemies. This may be because many a time, such practices conflict with conventional crop production or protection methods.

The farmers are also not fully convinced about the potential of natural enemies for pest suppression. Most importantly, there is often very little knowledge about the environmental factors that limit or encourage the effectiveness of natural enemies. Conservation requires detailed knowledge of the natural enemy's phenology and resource requirements. Moreover, knowledge of interactions of various management practices, both agronomic as well as pest management techniques, with natural enemy populations is essential. At present, such information is available only for a few species and systems. The most important strategies to conserve natural enemies within an agroecosystem are cultural control by habitat manipulation and rational use of pesticides.

Habitat Management

Modern crop systems are often inhospitable for proliferation of natural enemies. Habitat manipulation can enhance natural enemy survival by providing alternative hosts or prey, food in the form of pollen/or nectar for parasitoids, refugia from winter or higher-order predators, and a continuous source of primary host or prey. Special efforts in cultural practices and habitat manipulation, particularly in monoculture annual crops, may be required to achieve establishment of natural enemies. It is imperative to have detailed knowledge of the natural enemy's phenology and resource requirements to make advantageous modifications of their environment. In addition, the complexity of agroecosystems demands the understanding of the interactions of various management practices with natural enemy populations, to select the most appropriate manipulation strategies. The following environmental modifications can be incorporated into agricultural or silvicultural practices for protecting or enhancing natural enemies.

Plant biodiversity. Increasing diversity in time and/or space within the agroecosystem by multiple cropping, intercropping, trap cropping, strip harvesting, selective retention of weeds or conservation of wild plants at field margins helps the conservation of natural enemies by satisfying their biological requirements. It is not the crop diversification *per se,* but rather the interaction of crops, predator dietary preferences, and specific plant resource and alternative prey densities and dispersions that determine the outcome. Wild *Brassica vulgaris* and *B. kaber* in the vicinity of cabbage fields may enhance the survival of the ichneumonid, *Diadegma insularis,* a parasitoid of the diamondback moth, *Plutella xylostella,* by providing floral nectar reserves. Parasitization of the European corn borer, *Ostrinia nubilalis,* by the ichneumonid wasp, *Ereborus terebrans* and other larval parasitoids was significantly greater near woodlands than in fields next to open spaces or in field interiors. The adult food, alternate host species or favourable microclimates associated with wooded borders might have encouraged the effectiveness of the natural enemies. The presence of prune trees within vineyards significantly increased densities of *Anagrus epos,* a mymarid egg parasitoid of the western grape leafhopper, *Erythroneura elegantula* in California. Prune trees provided overwintering sites for *A. epos* and friendlier environment for the parasitoids by their wind-breaking effect.

In Kenya, intercropping maize with non-host molasses grass, *Melinus minutiflora,* increased larval parasitization of stem bores, *Chilo partellus* and *Busseola fusca,* by *Apanteles sesamiae,* from 5.4 (sole maize) to 20.7 per cent (intercropped maize). The volatiles produced by *M. minutiflora* repelled female stem bores and attracted foraging female. Beetle banks were developed in the UK in the 1990s as artificial hedgerows that were established within fields with plants known to be favoured by overwintering carabid beetles. The beetle banks also provide overwintering cover for insectivorous birds and habitats for spiders and flowers, which act as nectar sources for natural enemies.

Conservation tillage. Conservation tillage practices appear to increase the diversity and abundance of natural enemy populations by providing food, reducing mechanical injury, eliminating dust or other deleterious effects. The soil-inhabiting predators, including spiders and ground beetles, had a substantially greater impact on black cutworms in reduced and no-tillage corn than in conventionally tilled corn. The presence of flowering weeds in minimum-till corn increased the longevity, reproduction and parasitization rates for the cutworm parasitoid, *Meteorus rubens*. The effectiveness of the parasitoid, *Catolaccus grandis* against the boll weevil, *Anthonomus grandis*, in cotton is greatly reduced by mechanical cultivation, which buries fallen infested cotton buds and protects the immature weevils from parasitism. Southern corn rootworm immatures suffered heavier depradations from acarid mites, centipedes, carabid and staphylinid larvae, and ants in no-till compared with conventionally tilled corn.

Artificial structures. Pieces of gunny bags tied around citrus trees help in trapping and protecting coccinellid predator, *Cryptolaemus montrouzieri* of mealy bugs. Similarly, nesting boxes for predatory birds and wasps, placed at suitable sites, encourage the build up of population of these predators. Eggs of paddy, sugarcane, corn and sorghum tissue borers as well as of several other lepidopterans which lay their eggs in clusters, are placed in wire mesh cages, which permit the egg parasitoids to emerge and escape, but not the host larvae. Similarly, overwintering eggs of *Pyrilla perpusilla* in sugarcane trash, hibernating larvae of *Chilo partellus* in stubble of corn and sorghum, hibernating *Eriosoma lanigerum* and *Quadraspidiotus perniciosus* infested twigs on apple are collected and kept in specially designed cages covered with meshes of different size. During spring, these cages are placed in the field, the parasitoids emerge to parasitize the respective pests early in the season and the hosts emerge and die in the cage itself. In sugarcane, rice, cotton, groundnut and sunflower ecosystems, conservation of spider predators by placing bundles of dried grass on the bunds has been found to increase their efficiency.

Cover crops. The ground cover crops can provide a continuous source of prey and perhaps, a more favourable microclimate for generalist and specialist predators that attack spider mites, aphids and lepidopteran pests on orchard crops. Some cover crops can provide an early-season habitat from which beneficial organisms may subsequently move into the crop. This approach seeks to provide alternative hosts, prey nutrition, and/or favourable habitats for the entomophagous species within or adjacent to the crop system. Straw mulch uniformly spread on the soil surface may dramatically increase predator numbers, with concomitant reductions in herbivore numbers and increased crop yields. The use of straw-mulch in potato fields significantly increased the densities of soil-inhabiting predators and reduced defoliation damage by Colorado potato beetles. The mulch initially induced an increase in carabid predators early in the season, but by June and July, *Coleomegilla maculata, Hippodamia convergens, Chrysoperla carnea* and *Perillus bioculatus*, comprised 75 per cent of the predators found in foliage and accounted for 86 per cent of the observed predation. In a tropical rice system, weed residue led to increase in population of spiders, coccinellids and chrysopids.

Crop varieties. The use of resistant plant varieties tends to increase the effectiveness of parasitoids against phytophagous insects by increasing their development time and thereby increasing vulnerability to larval parasitoids. The parasitism of fall armyworm, *Spodoptera frugiperda*, was significantly higher on resistant than on susceptible varieties of corn. The use of nectariless cotton varieties is known to cause a significant reduction in natural enemy densities. The fecundity, survival and parasitism rate of *Campoletis sonorensis* were lower in nectariless cotton varieties than in nectaried varieties owing to the lack of extra floral nectarines that provide needed carbohydrates.

Pesticide Management

The most common human influence that negatively impacts natural enemies in agroecosystems is pesticide application. As a result, modification of pesticide use practices is the most commonly implemented form of conservation biological control. Pesticide use can be modified to favour natural enemies in a variety of ways, including treating only when economic thresholds dictate, use of active ingredients and formulations that are selectively less toxic to natural enemies, use of lowest effective rates of pesticides, proper timing of pesticide application, and temporal and spatial separation of natural enemies and pesticides. The role of some of these modifications in conservation of natural enemies is discussed below :

Selective pesticides. The use of selective pesticides is perhaps the most powerful tool by which pesticide use decisions can be modified to favour natural enemies. Selectivity of pesticides can be classified as physiological or ecological. Physiological selectivity is defined as differential toxicity between animal taxa due to organism's biochemical processes. Ecological selectivity is the judicious use of pesticides, based on critical selection, timing, dosage, placement, and formulation of pesticides with the goal of maximizing beneficial arthropod mortality. The differential toxicity is usually common in pesticides that require ingestion by the target pest. The pesticide abamectin, a natural product derived from the actinomycete, *Streptomyces avermitilis,* was found to be selective against the greenhouse whitefly, *Trialeurodes vaporariorum,* causing minimal mortality to its parasitoid, *Encarsia formosa. T. vaporariorum* susceptibility is due to its feeding on treated plants and parasitoid survival on whitefly pupae is explained by the lack of plant feeding during this development stage. In the Cauca Valley, Colombia, 22-28 insecticide treatments were carried out in cotton, in 1977, most of them to combat *Heliothis virescens*. However, combining early season releases of parasitoids with more selective pyrethroid insecticides since 1977, has reduced insecticide use in the country overall by nearly 70 per cent and steadily increased yields of cotton.

Timing of applications. Timing of pesticide applications is often the most effective and economical method to reduce the disruption of natural enemies. This requires the proper understanding of the phenology and colonization potential of important natural enemies. In cotton fields of southeastern United States, widely separated applications of pyrethroids during the middle and later periods of the growing season are less disruptive than early-season treatments. During the later part of the season, when pest pressure is most severe, large populations of beneficial species from the surrounding diverse habitats rapidly recolonize the cotton fields. The detrimental effect of insecticides on the parasitism of *Ceutorhynchus assimilis* on winter oilseed rape, by the parasitoid, *Trichomalus perfectus,* could be minimized by timing the applications before parasitoid migration to the fields, which occurs 3-4 weeks after *C. assimilis* migration.

Method of application. The method of pesticide application is an important factor in natural enemy conservation. Aerial application often delivers only a fraction of the pesticide to the target pest, but spreads pesticides kilometers away by wind-induced spray drifts. Ground sprayers provide better accuracy and control of delivery of pesticides, allowing their strategic placement within the field. Restricting the pesticide to a specific field location (spot treatment) or to a specific plant part minimizes the impact on natural enemies.

Non-intervention decision. One of the important tools of conservation concerning selective use of pesticides is the non-intervention decision tactic. This tactic consists of monitoring natural enemy densities and understanding their impact on pest populations to make decisions about the use of pesticides. The use of simulation models to assess the impact of key mortality factors operating in the field can aid in the decision-making processes. The mortality factors affecting boll weevil populations in Texas have been studied in detail. It has been established that density of 0.4 red imported fire ants, *Solenopsis invicta,* per plant provides boll weevil control about 90 per cent of the time. Eliminating the use of pesticides helps to conserve the populations of natural enemies that maintain control of secondary pests 95 per cent of the time in Texas and California.

Examples of Conservation Biological Control

Cotton aphid. Cotton aphid, *Aphis gossypii,* was considered a minor pest of cotton in USA, until insecticide applications for boll weevil control in 1930s caused population outbreaks, as a result of elimination of natural enemies. The development and use of organophosphates decreased the frequency of outbreaks. However, cotton aphid has reemerged as one of the most serious pests of cotton in USA during 1999s, primarily due to the development of insecticide-resistant populations and elimination of natural enemies with broad-spectrum insecticides targeted against other pests. During 1995-97, about 89 million pounds of cotton were lost to aphids nationwide, with about 29 per cent of U.S. cotton treated for aphids.

As against the national average, generally less than 1 per cent of cotton acreage in North Carolina has been treated annually for aphid control since detection of insecticide resistance in 1992. There are three factors which have predominantly contributed to this situation. Firstly, majority of aphid populations in North Carolina are resistant to insecticides, except imidacloprid. Secondly, the aphid is attacked by a variety of natural enemies, the most important of which appear to be the parasitoid wasp, *Lysiphlebus testaceipes* and the entomopathogenic fungus, *Neozygites fresenii.* This natural enemy complex is very effective in keeping aphid populations below economic thresholds and pesticide applications are recommended only at very high aphid populations in the absence of either of the natural enemy.

Thirdly, there are very few early to mid-season pest populations in cotton that require insecticide treatment in North Carolina. With elimination of boll weevil as an economic pest, over 90 per cent of cotton average is treated with a systemic insecticide at planting and mid season populations are too low to need any application. This allows natural enemy populations to increase and maintain aphid populations below economic thresholds. Foliar insecticides are applied for heliothin control towards mid to late July and by this time, *N. fresenii* is present in most fields, producing epizootics and suppressing late season aphid populations. The conservation of cotton aphid natural enemies saves growers about $ 5,000,000 annually on about 2,68,000 ha of cotton grown in North Carolina.

Apple mites. Biological control of phytophagous mites in Ouebec (Canada) orchards may be placed in two time periods. The first phase was from 1979 to 1990 and was based on the rearing and inundative releases of *Neoseilus fallacis* (Phytoseiidae). The second phase was from 1990 to date, and it was the development of a more robust and grower-friendly programme.

The first phase of the project was executed in four studies (*i*) The first study involved screening for naturally selected organophosphate (OP) resistance, mass rearing, maintenance of OP resistance and effects of other pesticides used in orchards on the selected strain of predators. (*ii*) The second study established the most appropriate time for release and the number of predators to be released. The most practical release threshold was established at 100 *N. fallacis* per tree at 2.2 European red mite (ERM), *Panonychus ulmi* (Tetranychidae), per leaf. (*iii*) The third study was the integration of the techniques and know-how gained in the previous studies in an experimental block in an orchard. This study mastered the mass rearing of OP-resistant *N. fallacis*, eliminated acaricide treatments completely or had them applied at very low rates, estimated release numbers of predators per tree, reduced the rate of insecticide treatments to manage other arthropods, and reduced the cost of protection by 34 per cent. (*iv*) The fourth study was to scale-up the rearing of predators and to evaluate the programme in a commercial context.

The emphasis in strategy during the second phase was changed from inoculation to conservation and augmentation. The main strategy was to create entire orchards that were friendly for the natural recolonisation and propagation of predacious mites from the perimeters of commercial orchards. Orchards where biological control of mites was well established were used as natural nurseries. Winter and summer-pruned wood from an orchard where biological control has been established was used to accelerate the recolonisation of orchards where biological control was in the process of being established. After the release of beneficial mites in an orchard, growers were advised to use pesticides that have minimal effects on predatory mites. As the conservation and augmentation technique is based on a complex of predators, viz. *N. fallacis*, *Typhlodromus caudiglans*, *Agistmus fleschneri*, *Balaustium* sp., *Anystis baccarum* and *Hyaliodes vitripennis*, it is far more stable than the approach used in early 1980s. This approach was initiated on less than 10 ha in 1991 and by 2006, most apple orchards in Quebec had not been treated for mites for atleast 5-10 years.

ATTRIBUTES OF EFFECTIVE NATURAL ENEMIES

Natural enemies that are considered effective usually possess one or more traits that play a vital role in pest suppression. These may include good searching ability (particularly at low pest population density), high population growth, and ability to perform over a broad range of climatic conditions. It is noteworthy that no one species or strain will possess all the ideal attributes. The intended use of a natural enemy is the key determinant of which biological characteristics are most important. For example, amenability to mass rearing is generally required of a natural enemy that is intended to be used in an augmentation programme. However, a natural enemy that has been imported for establishment against an exotic pest may be successful without a large scale rearing effort, although the release of a large number of genetically diverse natural enemies may increase the chances of colonization and establishment. Similarly, the ability to kill pests quickly is desirable in most augmentation programmes, whereas qualities that ensure persistence of the natural enemy and sustainable suppression of the pest population are more important in classical biological control programme.

Natural enemy attributes should be compatible with phenology of the pest, and biological and physical structure of the agroecosystem. A natural enemy that is a good searcher and has a high capacity for population growth would take care of a pest that occurs sporadically, but with a tendency to undergo explosive population growth. These characteristics may not be important against a pest that begins its season at low densities, exists in the same area from year to year, and has only moderate population growth. In areas where natural enemies of the proposed biological control agent exist, defense mechanisms, a capability for offsetting population losses (e.g. through reproduction) or caging during establishment, may be necessary. If natural enemies of the pest occur, choosing species with high competitive abilities may also be necessary. In general, greater the physical extremes (e.g. temperature, moisture, etc.), the more important it is to choose natural enemies that possess adaptations to survive and function under rigorous climatic conditions.

GENETIC IMPROVEMENT OF NATURAL ENEMIES

Genetic improvement involves directed purposeful genetic alterations to enhance the efficacy of the natural enemies for biological control. Genetic improvement may be achieved by artificial selection, hybridization to achieve heterosis effects or the use of recombinant DNA techniques. Entomophagous insects may be improved for climatic tolerance, sex ratio, host finding ability, host preference, increased host range, increased pesticide resistance, etc. *Aphytis lingnanensis* is the most important natural enemy of California red scale, *Aonidiella aurantii*, damaging citrus. A strain of the parasitoid possessing enhanced temperature tolerance was developed through artificial selection for over 100 generations. Phytoseiid mite, *Metaseiulus occidentalis* is the most important natural enemy of spider mites in deciduous orchards in USA. A pesticide resistant strain called COS strain (carbaryl-OP-sulphur-OP resistant strain) of the phytoseiid mite was selected, commercially mass reared and released in California almond orchards. It has been estimated that this strain has resulted in an annual saving of about $ 21, 256,000 to the almond growers alone. Subsequently, the strain was also used on other orchard crops. Other strains of phytoseiid species are also being selected and tested in field trials.

National Bureau of Agriculturally Important Insects (NBAII) (formerly Project Directorate of Biological Control), Bangalore has developed superior strains of *T. chilonis* such as Bio Sc1 for graminaceous tissue borers, Bio H3 for *H. armigera* and Bio C1 for cotton bollworms. Some of these strains are 60-100 per cent more fecund than the strains hitherto used. An endosulfan resistant strain of *T. chilonis* termed 'endogram' has been developed through artificial selection. This strain is tolerant to 2.5 ml/1 of endosulfan. The 'endogram' technology is registering a gradual spread and by now 20,000 ha of cotton and vegetables have been treated in six states. This strain has been further developed for the multiple resistance to monocrotophos and fenvalerate. A monocrotophos tolerant strain of *C. carnea* has also been developed. These pesticide tolerant strains will be very useful in cotton and other crop ecosystems.

Recently, a low temperature adapted strain of *T. chilonis* has been developed after rearing for 30 generations under laboratory conditions at 18-24°C, which has shown better host searching and can be successfully utilized under a low temperature regime. Similarly, a high temperature tolerant strain of *T. chilonis* has been developed, which gives high parasitism and increased longevity at 36°C and 60 per cent relative humidity. High temperature tolerant strain can be utilized when temperatures are more than 35°C. It is useful against the sugarcane shoot borer and top borer, and also other pests on cotton and vegetable crops during hot months. This strain has proved effective against sugarcane stalk-borer, *Chilo auricillius* and early shoot-borer, *Chilo infuscatellus* even at a lower dose (40,000 parasitoids/ha) as compared to the local strain (50,000 parasitoids/ha) under Punjab conditions.

It has been reported that populations of *Cotesia plutellae* from high pesticide use areas in Malaysia possessed 10-12 fold tolerance to dimethoate. It will be desirable to select pesticide resistant strains of the natural enemies to overcome the problems caused by the use of pesticides. The examples outlined above indicate that ecologically skilled deployment of genetically improved parasitoids and predators of phytophagous insects can play an important role in furthering biological control.

COMMERCIALIZATION

Commercial biological control laboratories can play an important role in meeting the ever-increasing demand for predators and parasitoids. These are essentially biofactories where the natural enemies are mass produced with professional expertise and made available at reasonable prices with necessary handling instructions. Efforts are on for *in vitro* rearing to reduce costs and make rearing possible under optimum nutritional conditions on a large scale. *In vitro* production of *Trichogramma* spp., coccinellids, chrysopids, geocorids, tachninids, etc. has been attempted with varying degree of success in different countries. Internationally, more than 125 species of entomophagous arthropods are commercially available for augmentative biological control programmes, including 37 commonly used species, such as the spider mite predator, *Phytoseiulus persimilis*; the whitefly parasitoid, *Encarsia formosa* and the moth egg parasitoid, *Trichogramma* spp. Based on sale figures of the natural enemies used, the main pest species targeted for augmentative biological control in glasshouse crops are whiteflies (33%), thrips (22%), spider mites (16%), aphids (13%) and others (16%).

There are many commercial insectaries operating in USA, Canada, and the erstwhile USSR, which, in turn, are supported by several smaller production units. Similar insectaries also exist in the Netherlands, Germany and other countries. In the People's Republic of China, mass production centers are located in the communes of several provinces. These produce millions of predators and parasitoids of a variety of pests and supply them to the needy farmers. The industry providing natural enemies has grown tremendously over the last 30 years in the USA. There are more than 142 commercial suppliers over 130 different species of beneficial organisms, of which 53 are arthropod predators and 46 are parasitoids. The categories of organisms included 17 predatory mites, 4 stored product pest parasitoids and predators, 17 aphid parasitoids and predators, 9 whitefly parasitoids and predators, 23 greenhouse pest parasitoids and predators, 7 scale and mealy bug parasitoids and predators, 12 insect egg parasitoids, 6 moth and butterfly larvae parasitoids, 8 filth fly parasitoids, 4 other insect parasitoids and 21 general predators. Annual sales of natural enemies in the USA amount to about $ 9-10 million and about 60 million globally.

In Europe, major use of parasitoids and predators has been for the control of insect pests in greenhouses. As early as 1968, *P. persimilis* was commercially produced and released for the control of two-spotted spider mite, *Tetranychus urticae* in glasshouse cucumber. Presently, more than 20 species of biological control agents are sold commercially for use in cucumber, tomato, sweet pepper, eggplant, bean, melon, strawberry and ornamentals. Europe has 15 natural enemy producers including the world's three largest, whereas there are about 50 commercial producers worldwide. The three largest companies serve more than 75 per cent of the greenhouse biological control market. Of the about 125 biological control agents that are marketed internationally, about thirty make up 90 per cent of the total sales. The total market for greenhouse natural enemies at end-user level was estimated to be more than US $ 30 million in 1997. The most important markets are The Netherlands, UK and France, followed by North America. Together these countries account for about two thirds of the total market. The largest commercial producer of biological control agents (Koppert Biological Systems, The Netherlands) rears about 15 billion arthropod natural enemies annually, with production of about 600 million individuals during a peak week and about 300 million individuals in more quiet weeks. Production of 15 billion natural enemies demands the rearing of 60 billion host insects. Based on these data, it has been estimated that the world wide commercial production of arthopod natural enemies concerns about 30-40 billion organisms per year.

In India, the first state run biofactory was established in 1930 to produce trichogrammatids. The first private insectary Biocontrol Research Laboratory was established at Bangalore in 1981. Since then, numerous companies have come up countrywide, producing predators (mainly coccinellids and chrysopids) and a variety of parasitoids (notably *Trichogramma* spp. and its various strains). There are 26 Central Integrated Pest Management Centres (CIPMC) in different states to produce bioagents for augmentation. The National Bureau of Agriculturally Important Insects (NBAII) has compiled an infobase on both private and government run bioagent producers in India. According to this, there are 128 organisations producing bioagents, of which 80 are private companies, 26 pest management centers, 10 agricultural universities, 8 ICAR institutes, and 4 breeding laboratories. A maximum of 34 units are involved in the production of various species of *Trichogramma,* mainly *T. chilonis*. There are 11 predators, mainly *Cryptolaemus montrouzieri* and *Chrysoperla carnea,* which are produced by different firms.

CONCLUSIONS

The potential of biological control has largely remained untapped because it has been under-used, under-exploited, under-estimated and often untried and, therefore, unproven. In fact, the use of parasitoids and predators should be a primary consideration in any pest management programme. It is generally said that if it works, biological control is the best method of control based on ecological and environmental considerations. For example, a new species of parasitoid, *Aenasius bambawalei,* is known to parasitise 50-80 per cent of the cotton mealy bug, *Phenacoccus solenopsis,* under natural conditions. This parasitoid has the potential of keeping the mealy bug under check, which is emerging as a major pest of cotton in India and Pakistan.

Biological control is highly economical. It rarely costs more than a few lakh rupees as against billions of rupees required to develop an insecticide. Moreover, once the method is developed, it is usually free of charge for the farmer as biocontrol agents are self sustaining. However, as in case of pesticides, indirect costs of biological control should be considered in any economic analysis. These include pre-release studies, post-release monitoring for efficacy and impacts on non-target organisms, and the delay in achieving control after release. The biological control method is usually selective with no side effects. There, however, have been a few instances of secondary problems due to biological control attempts. On one occasion, a serious disease of sugarcane was introduced into Trinidad on the ovipositor of a parasitoid being imported for biological control purposes and in at least two other cases, after controlling the intended prey, biological control agents have switched over to other related herbivores, which were important in controlling weeds. Biological control is self-propagating and self-perpetuating. Pest resistance to natural enemies is virtually unknown. There are no harmful effects on humans, livestock and other organisms. Biological control is virtually permanent. The successes achieved more than half a century ago continue to work to this day. Biological control agents possess the ability to search for their prey (pest). The use of parasitoids and predators is usually compatible with most other tactics of pest management except the use of broad-spectrum synthetic organic insecticides.

Although biological control has been successful in a number of cases, these still represent a small proportion of all pest control situations. It has been estimated that only about 4 per cent of insect pests worldwide have been controlled by biological methods. The reasons for the relatively low level of success with biocontrol agents are numerous as this method suffers from several drawbacks. Usually, the natural enemies do not control the pest completely and a low population of the pest continues to exist. The residual pest population is determined by the characteristics of the pest, its natural enemies and the environment. When this level is not acceptable economically, it has to be lowered by alternative means. Biocontrol is a specific form of control and attracts little interest from companies that want to market products that can be used to control a wide range of pest species. The success of biological control limits the subsequent use of pesticides for the same or other pests in the agroecosystem. Biocontrol agents take time to work and they do not have the immediate and dramatic effects that many pesticides do. However, the period of development of a pesticide from preliminary screening to commercial production is generally much greater than that required for a biological control project. Biological control attempts may require more labour and more specialized knowledge than is required with chemical pesticide applications.

Biological control can be elegant, sustainable, non-polluting and inexpensive, but the success rate has not been particularly high, especially for biological control of arthropods. A lot of work needs to be done to optimise the utilisation of predators and parasitoids in IPM. Better understanding of the ecological aspects of natural enemies is vital for improving the performance of predators and parasitoids, especially in tropical regions. Little is known regarding the biodiversity, ecology, community structure and host relationships in most tropical ecosystems and assessment of the impact of biocontrol agents is difficult under these conditions. Heat and cold tolerant strains have to be developed in case of a number of biocontrol agents. Environmental implications of the release of these organisms must be studied, especially in case of introductions and genetically engineered organisms. There is an urgent need to establish a network of large scale multiplication units, so that the natural enemies ae made available to the farmers at reasonable cost. With increasing concerns about the impact of conventional insecticides, predators and parasitoids are likely to play a prominent role in future IPM progammes.

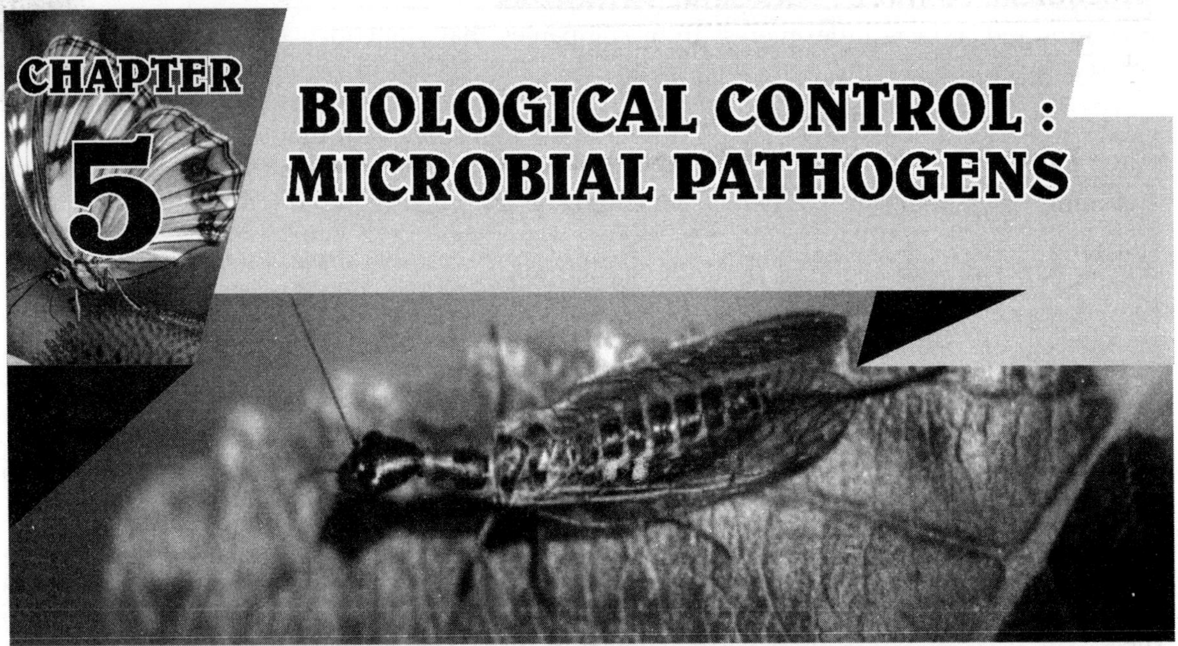

CHAPTER 5 BIOLOGICAL CONTROL : MICROBIAL PATHOGENS

INTRODUCTION

Microbial pathogens consist of disease causing microorganisms, which are disseminated in the pest populations in large quantities in a manner similar to application of chemical pesticides. The exploitation of disease causing organisms to reduce the population of insect pests below the damaging levels is referred to as microbial control. Insects, like other organisms, are susceptible to a variety of diseases caused by different groups of microorganisms including viruses, bacteria, fungi, protozoa, and nematodes (Table 5.1). Although not strictly microbes, nematodes have been included with entomopathogens, particularly since some of these are associated with insect-pathogenic bacteria. The following qualities go to make a microorganism suitable for the control of insect pests.

- **Strain.** Even within the same species one strain of microorganism may be more effective as a control agent than the other. It is fortunate for us that microorganisms occur in many strains so as to allow a suitable selection. Strains are more common in bacteria and fungi than in viruses and protozoa.
- **Virulence.** Virulence is the power of the pathogens to invade and produce disease in their hosts. The faster it can spread, the more virulent it will be. Virulence can be artificially enhanced by (*i*) passing the pathogens successively through susceptible hosts, (*ii*) introducing chemicals that may aid in increasing the invading power of the pathogens, (*iii*) associating it with other microorganisms that may render it more capable of invading tissues, and (*iv*) changing nutritional factors and culturing conditions.
- **Toxins.** Toxin producing pathogens are effective in two ways : by their own virulence and by the poisonous nature of the toxins they produce. Toxins could themselves be utilised as insecticide and, therefore, toxin-producing pathogens which are largely bacteria and fungi, are attracting the attention of the scientists to a greater extent. Toxins are extracted, purified, analysed and then synthesised for field operations.

- **Persistence.** Persistence is the quality which enables a microorganism to retain its viability and virulence on storage. The spores of bacteria, fungi, protozoa and polyhedral inclusions of viruses are known to possess a long shelf-life.

Table 5.1 Main groups of insect pathogens, their hosts and symptoms

Group	Example	Host and symptoms
Bacteria	*Bacillus popilliae* (milky disease of Japanese beetle)	Larvae develop milky white appearance, become sluggish and eventually die, but action is alow; attack coleopterans of the family Scarabaeidae
	B. thuringiensis	Attack lepidopterans larvae; larvae stop feeding, regurgitate, suffer from diarrhoea, and paralysis
Viruses	Nuclear polyhedrosis virus	Primarily a lepidopteran disease but can occur also in Diptera and Hymenoptera; symptoms appear only when the larvae are near their death; they stop feeding, become sluggish, pale, flaccid and fragile; tend to take higher position on the plant before death.
	Granulosis virus	Lepidoteran larvae; larvae become water-soaked, blackened; body disintegrates after death releasing fluid loaded with virus particles.
Protozoa	*Nosema bombycis*	Causes pebrine disease in mulberry silkworm eggs and larvae which develop black spots, get retarded, and wrinkled
	Nosema apis	Causes dysentery in honey bees during winter, body becomes dull grey-white instead of brownish red or yellowish
Nematodes	*Neoaplectana carpocapsae*	Affects wide range of phytophagous insects, develops inside by eating away the body tissues
Fungi	*Entomophthora* spp.	Affect caterpillars, bees, aphids, flies mosquitoes, grasshoppers; fungal hyphae and conidiophores can be seen projecting out from the body wall, small insects like aphids get stuck to leaf surface.

HISTORICAL PERSPECTIVE

Diseases of honey bees and silkworm have been known in China and India since ancient times. The observations of diseased silkworms were recorded in China as far back as 2700 B.C. The first documentation of insect diseases is usually attributed to the descriptions of honey bee maladies recorded by Aristotle somewhere between 330 and 323 B.C. Most of the earlier work on insect pathology is devoted to these two domesticated insects, viz. the silkworm, *Bombyx mori* and the honey bee, *Apis mellifera*. In 1835, Agostino Maria Bassi published his great work on white muscardine disease of the silkworm. In his treatise, Bassi demonstrated that the disease was communicated by food, contact and even by contaminated air. The disease could be transmitted to caterpillars of another species in similar manner. When it was transferred back to silkworm, it always produced identical symptoms, which gave an idea that man could communicate agents of disease to susceptible insect pests at will. Agostino Bassi is called the 'Father of Insect Pathology' for this monumental work. The fungus responsible for this disease was later on named as *Beauveria bassiana*.

The early descriptions of insect pathology were the fungi since the fruiting bodies were easily visible to naked eye. The first published record of a diseased insect appears to be that of the 'Chinese plant worm', described and illustrated by Rene-Antoine Ferchault de Reaumur in 1726. He understood the 'stem like vegetable growth', emerging from a noctuid larva to be the root of a plant. In 1749, Franciscan friar in Cuba described dead wasps with little trees growing out of their bellies. This was a fungus now known as a member of the genus *Cordyceps*.

Lie Conte in 1873, advocated for the first time the use of diseases as a means of insect control. Taking up this idea, a Russian entomologist, Metschnikoff, conducted the first systematic experiments on the control of injurious insects with microorganisms by infecting grubs of the grain beetle, *Anisoplia austriaca,* with the green muscardine fungus, *Metarhiziumanisopliae,* in 1879. Krassilstschik in 1888 mass produced spores of the fungus and applied them in the field. The fungus was found to be even more effective against the sugarbeet curculio, *Cleonus punctiventris* but the real breakthrough in the development of microbial control came with the discovery and practical application of the milky disease bacteria, *Bacillus popilliae,* for the control of the Japanese beetle, *Popillia japonica* on turfs in USA during 1940s. The term microbial control was coined by E.A. Steinhaus in 1949.

Upto the early twentieth century, only a few attempts were made to utilise microbial pathogens. However, many species of bacteria, viruses and nematodes were evaluated between 1920 and 1960. So far over 3000 microorganisms have been reported to cause diseases in insects. But scientists familiar with specific pathogen groups agree that a very large number of insect pathogens remain undiscovered or unidentified. It is very likely that insect pathogens outnumber the species of insects. The research and development in microbial pathogens got a boost in 1990s. In 1998, there were 59 species of microbial pathogens registered as pesticides worldwide. Thirty six species were registered to control animal pests (i.e. insects, mites, slugs and nematodes), 6 fungi and 1 microsporidia. Twenty species were registered to control plant diseases, 15 fungi and 5 bacteria. Three fungal species were registered as mycoherbicides. In India, about 110 entomopathogenic bacteria, 22 viruses, 92 fungi and 60 isolates of nematodes have been recorded. To-day, the world biopesticide market is claimed to be around US$ 350 million, representing little more than 1 per cent of the total world pesticide market. During the last decade, the world biopesticide scenario has undergone a drastic change. The growth in microbial pest control is now running at around 10 per cent per annum as against 1-2 per cent for chemical insecticides. Some estimates have even projected growth for microbial pesticides to be as high as 25 per cent per annum.

BACTERIAL PATHOGENS

Bacteria are prokaryotic, unicellular organisms varying from less than 1 μm to several μm in length. Those with rigid cell walls may be spherical (cocci), rod-shaped (bacilli) or spiral (spirilla, spirochaetes), whereas those without cell walls (mollicutes) are pleomorphic. More than 100 bacteria have been identified as arthropod pathogens. Most of the insect pathogenic bacteria occur in the families Bacillaceae, Pseudomonadaceae, Enterobacteriacae, Streptococcaceae, and Micrococcaceae; in the order Rickettsiales and class Mollicutes. Members of Bacillacae, particularly *Bacillus* spp., have received maximum attention as microbial control agents.

A. *Bacillus thuringiensis*

Bacillus thuringiensis (*Bt*) is a gram-positive, rod shaped aerobic, endospore forming, ubiquitous soil bacterium and produces a proteinaceous parasporal crystal in the sporangium at the time of sporulation. *B. thuringiensis* was first isolated in 1902 from diseased larvae of the silkworm, *Bombyx mori* in Japan by Ishiwata. However, Berliner who reisolated it from the Mediterranean flour moth, *Ephestia kuehniella* in Thuringia, Germany, first gave the name *B. thuringiensis* in 1915. The parasporal inclusions in sporulating cultures of *B. thuringiensis* were first described by Honnay in 1953 who later demonstrated that these inclusions were proteinaeous and might have insecticidal activity. *B. thuringiensis* is widely distributed in nature, and is being discovered repeatedly from different geographical areas and habitats frequented by varied complex of class Insecta. Dead insects, litters of sericultural farms, soils, waters, dusts, etc., form the so-called resource materials for the worldwide isolation of this bacterium. There are only a few reported cases of natural eipzootics of *B. thuringiensis* in lepidopetran forest/crop pests. Nevertheless, it is the most widely exploited microbial control agent.

It was not until mid 1920s that Btwas field-tested for efficacy against lepidopteran pests. The first trials were conducted against the European corn borer, *Ostrinia nubilalis*. In 1942, three years before the introduction of DDT, Steinhaus attracted the attention of applied entomologists worldwide by demonstrating the potential of this bacterium in pest suppression. Since then, there have been over 30 subspecies of *B. thuringiensis* classified, containing over 140 described crystalline toxins. These toxins have not only shown activity against Lepidoptera, Diptera and Coleoptera, but recent isolates have exhibited activity against nematodes, mites, lice, aphids and ants.

Bt Toxins

Bt produces a parasporal body within its cells during sporulation. This parasporal body contains one or more proteins, typically in a crystalline form. These proteins possess insecticidal properties and are called Bt toxins, δ-endotoxins or insecticidal crystal proteins (ICPs). It is not a single toxin but a class of toxic proteins produced from protoxins (crystal proteins) that are degraded by proteolytic enzymes to form smaller toxic peptides.Insecticidal crystal proteins kill insects by binding to and disnipting their midgut epithelium membranes, yet do little or no harm to most other organisms, including humans, wildlife and other insects. These insecticidal crystal proteins are classified into five classes, viz.,(*i*) CryI (Lepidoptera specific), (*ii*) CryII (Lepidoptera and Diptera specific), (*iii*) CryIII (Coleoptera specific), (*iv*) Cry IV (Diptera specific), and (*v*) CryV (Coleoptera and Lepidoptera specific).

Besides the δ-endotoxin, *B. thuringiensis* also produces a number of exotoxins. The α-exotoxin is a proteinaceous, thermolabile exotoxin which is highly toxic to some insects by oral and intrahemocyclic inoculations. It is also toxic to mice and other vertebrates. β-extoxin or thuringiensin is a thermostable toxin that kills insects by *per os* and parenteral inoculations. It is formed during vegetative phase of the bacteria and is secreted into the medium. Thuringiensin affects a broad spectrum of insects in the orders Diptera, Lepidoptera, Hymenoptera, Coleoptera, Isoptera, Orthoptera, Hemiptera and Neuroptera. The δ-endotoxin is the most widely studied of all entomocidal toxins.

Mode of Action

When the Bttoxins are ingested by insects, the crystalline inclusions initially dissolve in the midgut, releasing proteins (27-140 kDa) called delta endotoxins. These toxins have active and structural fragments. The toxins with these two components are termed as protoxins. Protoxins are cleaved by midgut proteases into toxic polypeptide which is usually of 65-68 kDa, and is the toxic protein. The toxic protein fragment can be divided into three domains, first is involved in spore formation, the second determines the receptor binding and third is involved in protection to the toxin from proteases. The toxin protein binds to specific receptors present in the midgut epithelial membranes. Upon receptor binding, the domain one inserts itself into the membrane leading to the pore formation. The disturbances in osmotic equilibrium and cell lysis lead to insect paralysis and death.

On the basis of sensitivity to Bt toxins, insects have been divided into three types. In type I insects, the first sign of poisoning following the ingestion of crystalline endotoxin is the paralysis of gut and mouth parts, leading to cessation of feeding, regurgitation and diarrhoea followed by general body paralysis. The death of insects occurs in 1-7 h. The symptoms of poisoning appear within minutes before activation of protoxins. In type II insects, death occurs within 2-7 days which is proceeded by gut paralysis. In type III insects, on ingestion endospore germinates in the host midgut at pH below 9, producing bacterial cells which migrate into haemocoel. In haemocoel, they multiply, invade and destroy certain tissues. The death occurs as a result of septicemia.

Host Range and Field Efficacy

The known range of Bt is restricted mainly to insect pest species amenable to laboratory bioassay and for which Bt or its products have potential as microbial pesticides. Most families of Lepidoptera include species susceptible to Cry I and Cry II crystal proteins produced in particular by subspecies *kurstaki* and *aizawai*. In general, species of the Sphingidae and Pieridae are highly susceptible, whereas those of the Tortricidae and Nocuidae are less susceptible. Since the discovery of the dipteran-specific subspecies *israelensis*, the recorded host range of Bt has expanded considerably with the addition of more than 100 susceptible species of mosquitoes and black flies. The more recently discovered subspecies *tenebrionis* and *sandiego* produce δ-endotoxins specific in their activity against coleopterans. Bt toxins other than δ-endotoxins are generally less host specific. The most notable of these toxins, thuringiensis, is highly toxic to dipteran insects. Bt is also reported to produce nematocidal toxins active against various stage of free-living plant and animal parasitic nematodes.

Bt has been recommended for the suppression of *Plutella xylostella* and *Pieris brassicae* on cabbage; *Crocidolomia binotalis* on cauliflower; *Helicoverpa armigera* on tomato, tobacco, sunflower and pulses; *Spodoptera litura* on tobacco, cabbage and beetroot; *Athalia lugens* on radish; *Papilio demoleus* on citrus; *Achaea janata* on castor; and *Amsacta moorei* and *A. albistriga* on pulses and oilseeds. *B. thuringiensis* has been widely applied for the control of diamondback moth, *P. xylostella*. In large-scale field trials, the pest was effectively controlled by two applications of Dipel 8L/Biolep/Biobit, all at 0.75 litres or kg/ha to cauliflower crop in Punjab, India. In Bt treatments, larval mortality five days after the second spray, was more than 80 per cent as compared to 59 per cent in endosulfan and fenvalerate (standards).

Bt based biopesticides were also moderately effective against other lepidopteran pests including head borer, *Hellula undalis*; tobacco caterpiller, *Spodoptera litura* and

H.armigera attacking cabbage and cauliflower crops. Control of H. *zea* in sweet corn has been reported with heavy doses of Bt. An encapsulated formulation and clay granular and emulsifiable formulation of Bt were effective against the European corn borer. The tobacco hornworms and budworms were successfully controlled. Moderate to high level of control was also achieved in case of a number of other pests including cotton bollworms, rice stem borer, brinjal fruit and shoot borer and cabbage semilooper. Some of the states such as Karnataka, West Bengal and Assam are hesitant to use *B. thuringiensis* on a large scale because of well-developed sericulture industry in these states.

Resistance to Bt Toxins

Microbial insecticides have not escaped the imbroglio of insecticide resistance that many hoped would be limited to conventional chemicals. Within the last few years, at least 16 insect species have been selected for resistance to Bt *delta*-endotoxins. These include *Aedes aegypti, Cadra cautella, Choristoneura fumiferana, Chrysomela scripta, Culex quinquefasciatus, Ephestia cautella, Ephestia kuehniella, Heliothis virescens, Homoeosoma electellum, Leptinotarsa decemlineata, Ostrinia nubilalis, Pectinophora gossypiella, Plodia interpunctella, Plutella xylostella, Spodoptera exigua, Spodoptera littoralis* and *Trichoplusia ni*. Among these reported cases of resistance only three involve resistance among wild populations. The Indian meal moth, *P. interpunctella,* evolved low levels of resistance in grain bins because of treating the grain with Bt. The diamondback moth, *P. xylostella* is possibly the most notable because it evolved high levels of resistance in the field as a result of repeated use of Bt in intense control programmes. Recently, the cabbage looper, *T. ni* has been reported to develop resistance to Bt in vegetable greenhouses in British Columbia, Canada.

The reports of development of resistance in the field populations of *P. xylostella* are essentially from the countries where *B. thuringiensis* is extensively used, viz. China 1000 tons, Philippines 300 tons, Malaysia 250 tons, and North America about 1000 tons per annum. In Japan also, high level of resistance to *B. thuringienis* was observed in *P. xylostella* collected from watercress plant. This occurred because watercress was grown throughout the year with a frequent use of *B. thuringiensis* formulations (15-20 times a year). In India, the populations collected from Tamil Nadu showed significantly high resistance to *B. thuringiensis,* whereas populations obtained from Delhi, Uttar Pradesh, Punjab and Maharashtra showed a high level of susceptibility despite their high level of resistance to many synthetic insecticides. Increased susceptibility to *B. thuringiensis* has been reported to be associated with synthetic insecticide resistance possibly involving monooxygenases in increasing susceptibility of resistant insects to *B. thuringiensis.*

The first report of development of field resistance to Bt in *T. ni* populations came from the commercial vegetable greenhouses in British Colombia, Canada. In a 3-year survey initiated in 2000, several greenhouse populations were surveyed multiple times within a growing season to monitor the rate at which resistance developed within a year in response to the grower Bt sprays. Bt resistance levels were directly correlated to the amount of Bt applied, and Bt resistance was observed to evolve repeatedly within one year as a consequence of grower spray programmes. The application of high doses of Bt greatly intensified the rates of resistance evolution. It is likely that the greenhouse environment plays a significant role in contributing to the development of resistance to Bt. The favourable environmental conditions and longer growing season in greenhouses increase the exposure period of *T. ni* to Bt, thus increasing the selection intensity for Bt resistance. Greenhouses probably also enhance Bt persistence by protecting Bt from sunlight degradation and rain. Furthermore, once resistance is present, the problem may be exacerbated by the application of high doeses.

Resistance management strategies have been proposed as a means to decrease the rate at which resistance evolves and hence, to keep the frequency of resistance genes sufficiently low for insect control.

- An effective monitoring programme to detect, as early as possible, shifts in pest susceptibility that could be abated in the initial stages.
- Use of mixtures of toxins with different mechanisms.
- Use of synergists to increase toxicity.

- Mosaic application to resort to time alterations rather than space alterations.
- Rotation of toxins to reduce the frequency of resistant individuals.
- Ultra-high doses of toxins that kill resistant heterozygotes and homozygotes.
- Refuges to facilitate survival of susceptible individuals.
- Generally, resistance to Bt is the consequence of a mutation(s) that alters an insect midgut receptor protein (s), so that it no longer binds to the cry protein. However, if a toxin gene was engineered, so that toxin is bound to other midgut cell surface proteins, then resistance might be less likely to arise.

B. *Bacillus sphaericus*

Bacillus sphaericus Neideis an aerobic, rodshaped, gram-variable bacterium that was first described by Neide in 1904 and produces terminally or subterminally swollen spherical spores. This bacterium is ubiquitous and cosmopolitan in soil and soil-aquatic systems. It has attracted particular attention due to its longer environmental persistence and excellent control over *Culex, Psorophora* and *Mansonia* mosquito larvae.

B. sphaericus toxicity has been found to be correlated with the sporulation process. The absence of toxicity in asporogenous mutants was correlated to the absence of crystal formation in the exosporium when the cells were induced to attempt sporulation. These crystals were produced during sporulation in the wild type cells and found to be proteinaceous in nature. This material accumulated as polyhedral body within the exosporium adjacent to the spore. The crystal proteins are known to be activated by proteolytic enzymes. After ingestion of a high concentration of *B. sphaericus* cells or spores, midgut cells swelled to lie against the body wall, throwing the peritrophic membrane with its food contents into zigzag folds. Intoxicated cells rounded up, became swollen and phase-dark, and then detached from support.

B. sphaericus has a relatively narrow active spectrum, having toxicity only to mosquitoes, not to black flies or any other insects. Its activities to about 40 mosquito species belonging to 7 genera (*Culex, Anopheles, Aedes, Mansonia, Psorophora, Toxorhychitis, Armigeres* and *Uranotaenia*) have been evaluated in laboratory and field conditions. It was indicated that the high toxic strains exhibit high activity to *Culex, Psorophora* and *Mansonia* spp; medium activity to *Anopheles* spp. and poor or no activity to *Aedes* spp. *B. sphaericus* is considered as a promising agent for mosquito control, especially for *Culex* control in urban regions in developing countries. In some tropical countries like Cameroon, Brazil, Cote d'Ivoir, India, Sri Lanka, Thailand and Tanzania, *B. sphaericus* has been used for filariasis vector, *Culex quinquefasciatus* control for many years. In China, about 150 tons of the formulation based on *B. sphaericus* has been used as larvicidal agent each year in the last two decades. Approximately 8,000 ha of different mosquito producing habitats have been treated with *B. sphaericus* each year.

C. *Bacillus popilliae*

A number of bacilli multiply and sporulate in the haemolymph of scarabaeid larvae. The haemolymph becomes turbid and the posterior portion of the larval body turns opaque and milky white; thus the name, milky disease. The syndrome was first described in grubs of the Japanese beetle, *Popillia japonica* in 1933. The bacteria causing type A and type B milky disease were identified as *Bacillus popilliae* and *B. lentimorbus*, respectively. *B.popilliae* is the most important of the various bacilli causing milky disease. Its host range within the scarabaeids is broad infecting about 70 insect species. Unlike other *Bacillus* species, the milky disease organisms are obligate pathogens.

The ingested spores germinate in the larval digestive tract and the rods penetrate into midgut cells. The bacteria multiply and invade into the haemocoel where multiplication continues. In the laboratory, milky disease undergoes four developmental stages. In phase 1, all bacterial cells are in the vegetative phase, while in phase 4, 95 per cent of the cells contain spores. The insect turns milky while in phase 4, and more than 70 per cent of the infected grubs die before reaching this phase. Following death, the host distintegrates and spores are released into the soil. Larvae with obvious symptoms of milky disease are common in the field after peak feeding of third instar. Symptoms develop in 3 to 4 weeks but underfed larvae succumb to the disease without exhibiting external symptoms. Milky disease develops best at 20-25°C and is inhibited at less than 15°C and more than 30°C. The cause of death is unknown and is considered to be caused by depletion of essential nutrients and the presence of heat-labile toxins or by a disturbance of oxidative enzymes.

Presently, 10 biovars of *B. popilliae* are known throughout the world including USA, New Zealand, Australia, India and Europe. These biovars differ in the morphology of sporangia, spores and parasporal bodies. All are, however, fastidious in their cultural requirements and only limited production is possible *in vitro*. The spores are mass-produced by injection of spores into the hemocoel of grubs. The *in vivo* production technique makes the product very expensive. Unlike the type A disease, when the grubs are infected by *B. lentimorbus,* they continue to grow and moult. Type B syndrome resembles type A except for the overwintering grubs that turn milky-brown and remain active for sometime before dying. *B. popilliae* is known to occur naturally on whitegrubs in India. It has been found effective under field conditions against *Holotrichia consanguinea, H. serrata* and *Leucopholis lepidophora.* The treatment is more effective in areas where winter temperatures do not fall below 15°C.

VIRAL PATHOGENS

A virus is a set of one or more nucleic acid template molecules, normally encased in a protective coat or coats of protein or lipoprotein that is able to organize its own replication only within suitable host cells. Viruses have been isolated from more than 1000 species of insects from at least 13 different insect orders. Entomogenous viruses fall into two categories, viz. inclusion viruses (IV) producing inclusion bodies in the host cell and non-inclusion viruses (NIV) which do not do so. The IV are further subdivided into polyhedroviruses (PV) or polyhedroses, which produce polyhedral (*i.e.* many-sided) bodies and granulosis viruses (GV) which produce granular bodies. Polyhedroses could inhabit the nucleus and are called nuclear polyhedrosis viruses (NPV) or the cytoplasm which are called cytoplasmic polyhedrosis viruses (CPV).

Viral diseases are one of the most widely investigated infections in insects. According to the International Commission on Nomenclature of Viruses, those pathogenic to insects belong to at least eleven families. However, viruses in the family Baculoviridae, a diverse family of more than 600 viruses, are the best known of all the insect viruses. This is because they are very common in some of our most important insect pests, disease symptoms are easily recognized and they have the most potential for development as microbial insecticides. The major reason for interest in baculoviruses is their environmental safety. They are often genus or species specific. Consequently, they are safe to all non-target organisms including humans, animals, plants and even beneficial insects.

Baculoviruses are infectious *per os* (by mouth) and exhibit efficient horizontal transmission. They replicate rapidly and cause extensive cell and tissue destruction in the host cell and thus are virulent mortality agents. They are capable of causing natural epizootics and infecting a large proportion of insects in a population. Baculoviruses encase their virions in large proteinaceous crystals, known as occlusion bodies (OBs). The OBs are consumed by the insect and the proteinaceous capsule is hydrolysed in the alkaline gut, releasing the virions. The virions enter the midgut cell nucleus, at which point they replicate and destroy the cell or else the virions pass through the cell into the haemocoel and infect cell nuclei of other tissues, replicate, encapsulate and rupture the cell. The OBs show great persistence in water and other carriers, as well as in soil. This enables formulation and application of virus-based pesticides just like chemical pesticides. On the other hand, the cost of development and registration is low as compared to chemical pesticides. Baculoviruses can be mass-produced by simple cottage industries in contrast to chemical pesticides, which require sophisticated industrial plants for manufacturing and formulation.

Classification of Baculoviruses

Baculoviruses (Family Baculoviridae) have only been isolated from invertebrates. Most examples have been found in insect species but there are some reports of baculoviruses that are pathogenic for Crustacea. Baculovirus infections have been described in over 700 species of invertebrates including Lepidoptera (455), Hymenoptera (31), Diptera (27), Coleoptera (5), Neuoptera (2), Trichoptera (1), Thysanura (1), Siphonaptera (1), besides Crustacea. So far, 19 relatively well characterized baculoviruses have received species status including AcMNPV, SeMNPV, LdMNPV, HzSNPV and

T. ni GV. Until 1995, family Baculoviridae was subdivided into two subfamilies: Eubaculovirinae, which included the occluded nuclear polyhedrosis virus (NPV) and granulosis virus (GV); and Nudibaculovirinae, encompassing the non-occluded baculoviruses. Currently, Baculoviridae is divided into two genera: *Nucleopolyhedrovirus* and *Granulovirus*.

NPV contains many virions occluded within occlusion body called polyhedra, while GV contains only one or rarely two or more virions in occlusion body called granules. Nucleocapsid envelopment of occluded virion occurs either within the nucleus (NPV) or in the nuclear–cytoplasmic milieu after rupture of the nuclear membrane (GV). Among NPVs, the viruses are further designated as SNPV or MNPV depending on the single (S) or multiple (M) packaging of the nucleocapsids in the virion. The phylogenetic analysis based on several viral genes indicated that the NPV could be divided into two groups. Group I contains the relatively well characterized baculoviruses, like *Autographa californica* (AcMNPV), *Orgyia pseudotsugata* (OpMNPV) and *Bombyx mori* (BmNPV), while *Lymantria dispar* (LdMNPV), *Spodopteraexigua* (SeMNPV), *Helicoverpa zea* (HzSNPV) and *H. armigera* (HaSNPV or Hear NPV), are included in group II. NPVs have limited host ranges, usually being restricted to one host species or genus, with the exception of the NPVs of *Autographa californica, Anagrapha falcifera* and *Mamestra brassicae*. GVs are more specific than NPVs as they have been reported only from Lepidopera.

Structure of Baculoviruses

The nucleopolyhedroviruses consist of packaged nucleocapsids, either as one (SPNN) or many (MNPV), within a single viral envelope (virions). These are randomly distributed within the electron dense occlusion body (OB). OBs may vary in size from 0.15 to 15 μm. The type species of the genus is multinucleocapsid nucleopolyhedrovirus of *Autographa california* (AcMNPV). There are 15 recognized species and 482 tentative species. The granuloviruses are, on average, smaller than the NPVs and consist of a single nucleocapsid within a virion each individually occluded. They range in size from 0.13 to 0.5 μm and contain a single molecule of dsDNA. The type species is *Plodia interpunctella* (PiGV). There are 4 recognized species and 131 tentative species.

Baculoviruses have a large, double-stranded, covalently closed, circular DNA genome of between 88 and 200 kbp. This is associated with a highly basic (arginine-rich) protein of 6.5 KDa. The DNA-protein complex is contained by a rod-shaped nucleocapsid comprising a 39 KDa capsid protein and an 87 KDa capsid protein. The nucleocapsids may be occluded within a crystalline matrix, referred to as a polyhedron or granule. Polyhedra consist largely of a single protein (polyhedrin) of about 30 KDa which are formed in the nucleus of infected cells. Virions that have been released from polyhedra are called polyhedra derived (PDV) in the mid-gut tissues of susceptible insect, whereas virions that are released from cells without occlusion are called extracellur virus (ECV) or budded virus (Fig. 5.1) Granulin, the major granule protein in GVs is similar to polyhedrin in function.

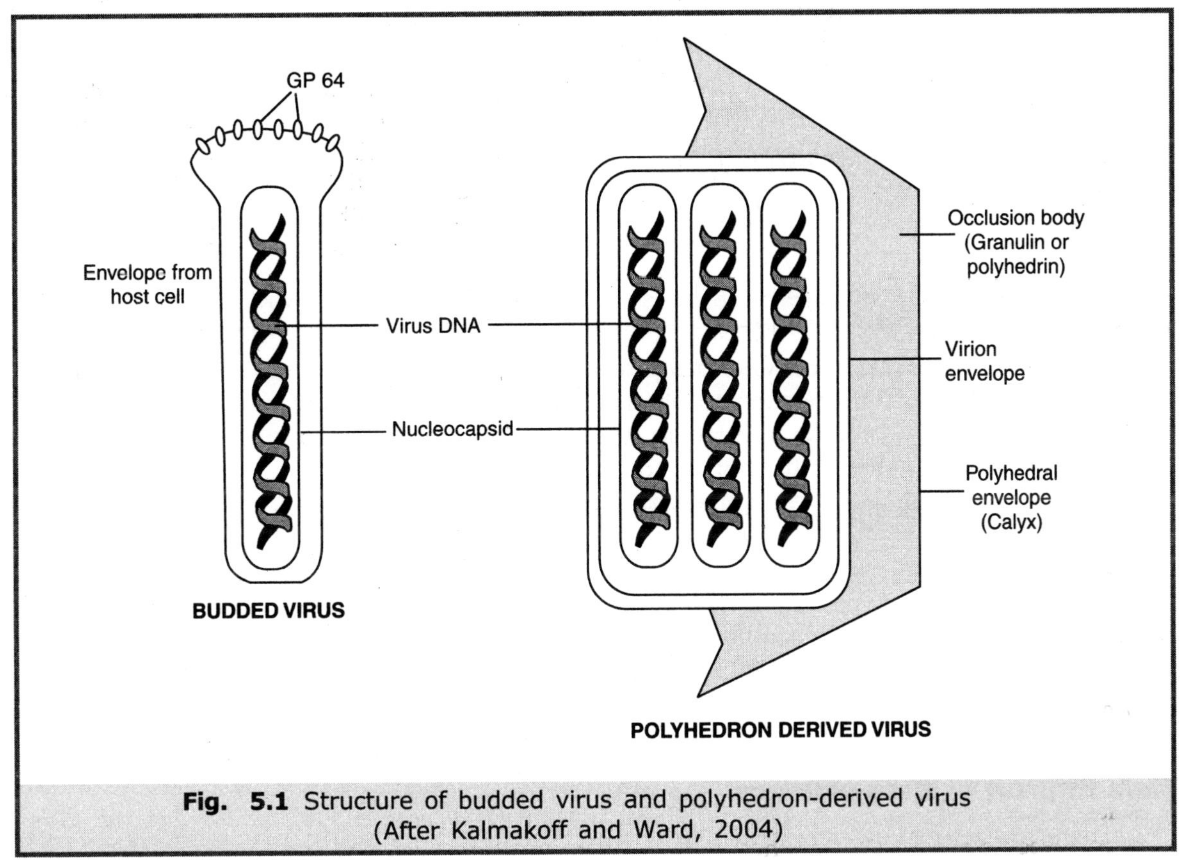

Fig. 5.1 Structure of budded virus and polyhedron-derived virus (After Kalmakoff and Ward, 2004)

Mode of Action

Most baculoviruses infect only the larval stages of susceptible insects, exceptions are NPVs that infect Hymenoptera and the non-occluded virus of *Oryctes*. These viruses infect the adult as well as the larval stage. Baculoviruses must be ingested to infect the larvae, so they are used mainly to control open-feeding species. The occlusion bodies dissolve in the highly alkaline host mid-gut and the virus infects the host epithelial cells. The basic virus infection process is shown in Fig. 5.2. The virus replicates within the nuclei of susceptible tissue cells. Tissue susceptibility varies greatly between viruses with some NPVs being capable of infecting

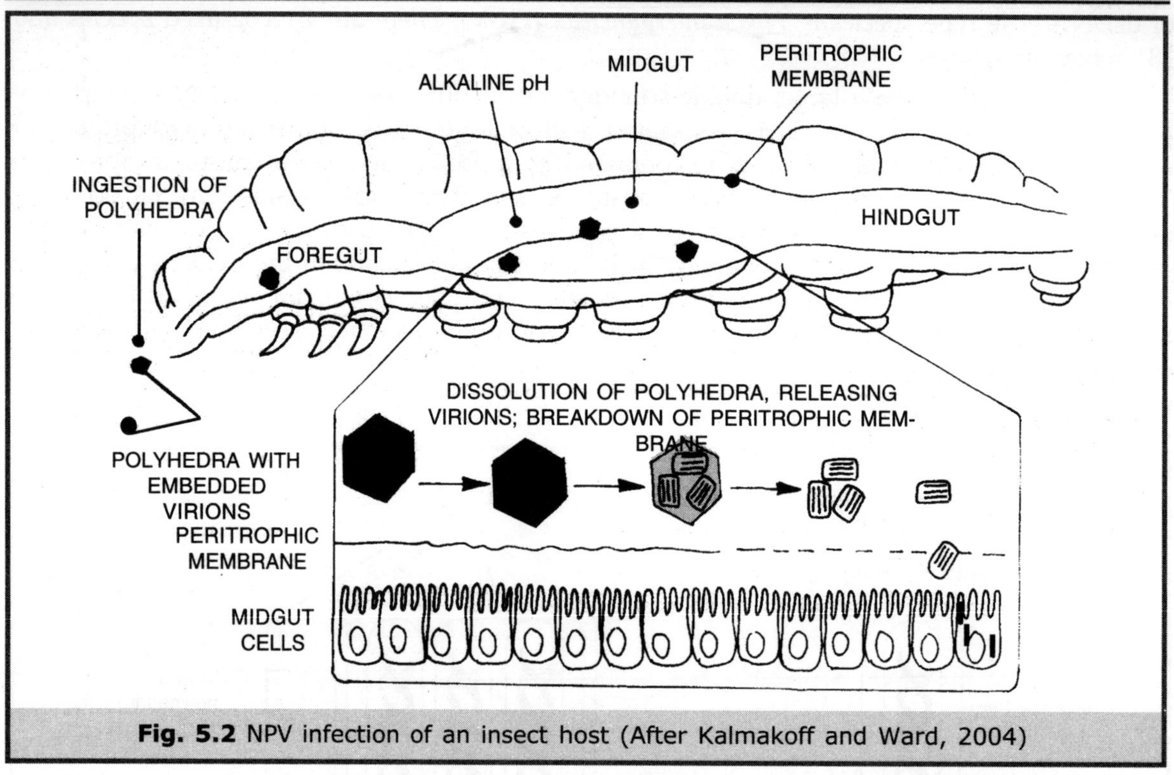

Fig. 5.2 NPV infection of an insect host (After Kalmakoff and Ward, 2004)

almost all tissue types and most GVs being tissue-specific replications (e.g. fat body cell only). The budded virus initiates infection to other tissues in the hemolymph, i.e. fat bodies, nerve cells, haemocytes, etc. The cells infected in the second round of virus replication in the insect larva also produce budded virus, but in addition occlude virus particles within polyhedra in the nucleus. The accumulation of polyhedra within the insect proceeds until the host consists almost entirely of a bag of virus. In the terminal stages of infection, the insect liquefies and thus releases polyhedra, which can infect other insects upon ingestion. A single caterpillar at its death may contain over 109 occlusion bodies from an initial dose of 1000. The infected larvae exhibit negative geotropism before succumbing to the virus infection, thereby facilitating widespread dissemination (Fig. 5.3). The speed with which death occurs is determined in part by the environmental conditions. Under optimal conditions, target pests may be killed in 3-7 days, but death may be caused in 3-4 weeks, when conditions are not ideal .

Field Efficacy of Baculoviruses

There are four strategies, which have been employed for using baculoviruses for pest supression. (*i*) The virus spreads from limited applications and permanently regulates the insect population through a classical biological control. (*ii*) An epizootic is established through vertical and horizontal transmission, but reapplication may be necessary because control is not permanent. (*iii*) A vertical inoculum in the environment is conserved and reactivated through environmental manipulation. (*iv*) Repeated applications are used to control an insect population because there is no horizontal transmission of the virus.

Bculoviruses, particularly NPV, are known to occur extensively in different groups of insects though predominantly among the lepidopterans. World over about 525 insect species in 52 families and eight orders are known to be infected by NPV and of this large number of

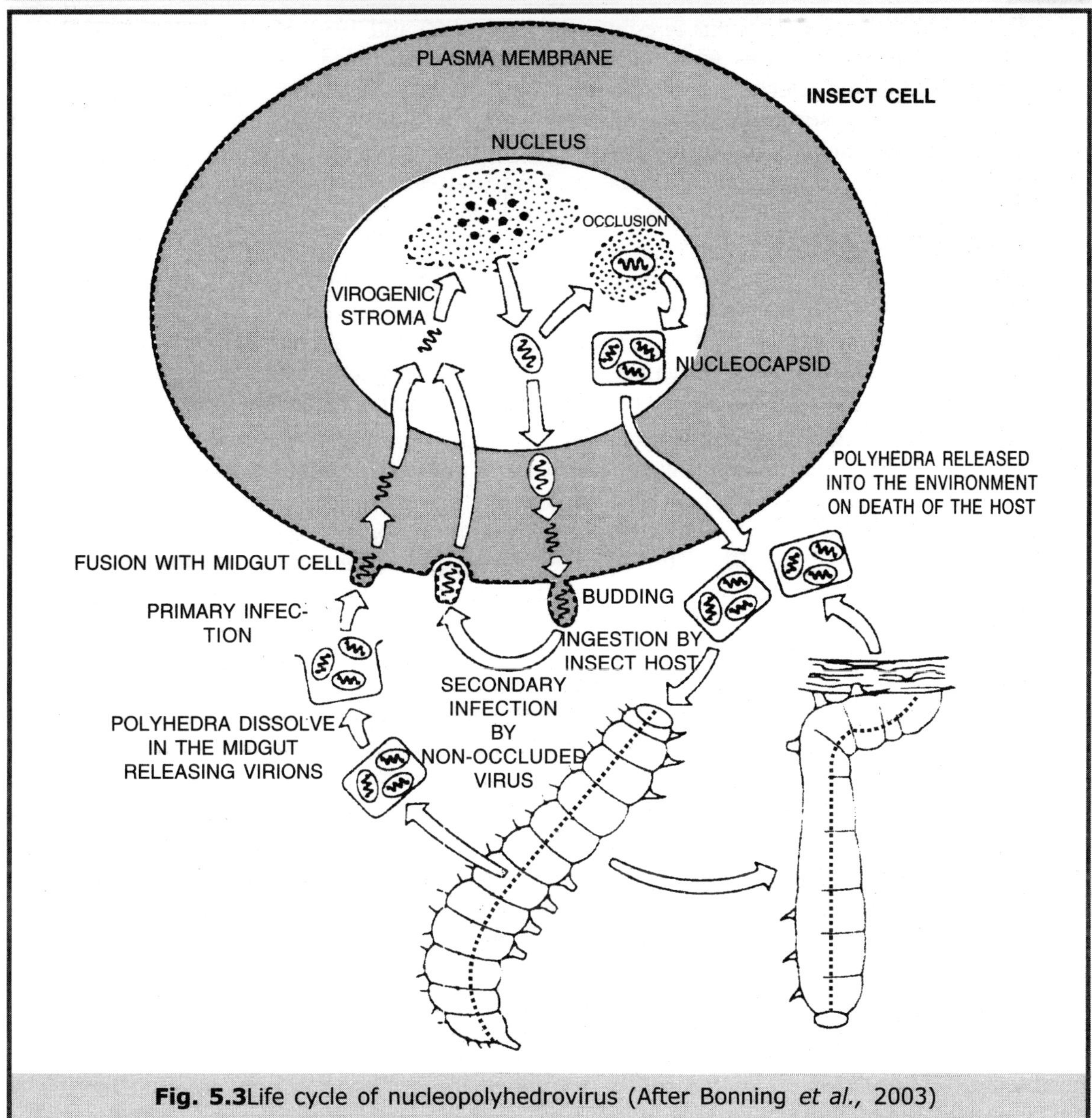

Fig. 5.3 Life cycle of nucleopolyhedrovirus (After Bonning *et al.*, 2003)

species, 455 belong to Lepidoptera. Among the lepidopterans, noctuids comprise the largest family with 107 species. In India, NPV has been recovered from several insects, many of them of economic importance and a majority of them under noctuidae. A rich genetic diversity also exists within each of these viruses as documented in the case of *Helicoverpa armigera* NPV (HaNPV), *Amsacta albistriga* NPV (AaNPV), *Chilo infuscatellus* granulosis virus (CiGV) and *S. litura* NPV (SlNPV). The widespread occurrence of baculoviruses and their diveristy make them attractive candidates as microbial insecticides.

Some of the examples of baculoviruses that have been extensively studied or reached the point of field testing are given herein.

***Helicoverpa/Heliothis* complex.** The genera *Helicoverpa* and *Heliothis* contain some of the most destructive pests of agricultural crops including *Helicoverpa armigera,*

H. assulta, H. zea and *Heliothis virescens*. Between 1960 and 1980, about 200 field tests were conducted in various countries with NPV, for the control of these pests on different crops. It was evident that crop selection was important and success on cotton was less evident than on maize, control on sorghum was frequently better and control on soybean and chickpea was the best of all. In case of sorghum, a single application of the virus at 11.6 × 1010 OBs per 0.4 ha showed excellent control of the pest. Virus treatment significantly increased cotton yields over untreated checks and it was at least as good as the insecticides in a majority of cases. Four sprays of HzNPV at

100-250 LE/ha (one LE or larval equivalent corresponded to 6 × 109 POBs/ml) provided effective control (90-96%) on soybean in USA. In China, 100, 000 ha of cotton and hot pepper are treated annually with HaNPV from *H. armigera*. In India, a large number of field trials have been conducted with NPV for the management of *H. armigera* on tomato, chickpea, sunflower, cotton, groundnut and several other crops providing partial to effective control of the pest.

Soybean caterpiller. The soybean caterpiller, *Anticarsia gemmatalis* is a major pest of soybean in Brazil. The AgNPV occurs naturally in Brazil in *A. gemmatalis* population with pathogenesis similar to otherNPVs. Its development and implementation as a microbial insecticide was carried out by EMBRAPA (Brazilian Agricultural Research Corporation). In pilot scale field trials with AgNPV at 50 LE/ha (1.5 × 1011 OBs/ha), reductions of over 80 cent of *A. gemmatalis* larval populations were obtained and yields were on a par with insecticide-treated plots. Approximately, 2000 ha were treated in 1982-83 season, which increased to 500,000 ha in 1986-87, and to 1 million ha 1989-90. With the commercialization of the AgMNPV by private companies, use of the biological insecticide increased to approximately 1.5 million ha in 1995, with most of the production being produced in the field during each soybean season. The virus is presently used on 2.0 million ha of soybean in Brazil, representing the largest programme worldwide for the use of an entomopathogen to control a pest on a single crop.

The use of AgMNPV in Brazil has generated substantial economic, ecological and social benefits. The current annual savings at the soybean grower level are over US $14 million. Since implementation of the programme in 1982-83 up to 2004-05, it is estimated that cumulative use of AgMNPV reached approximately 23,000,000 ha, which represents savings to growers of about US$161 million. Most importantly, since the beginning of the programme, more than 23 million litres of chemical insecticides were not sprayed in the environment, resulting in considerable ecological benefits to society. Also, the hand-picking of the virus-killed larvae during the soybean seaon has provided an additional source of income to poor families, which has contributed to their socio-economic improvement. With recent achievements in commercial production of AgMNPV under controlled laboratory conditions, it is expected that the use of the biological insecticide may reach 4.0 million ha per year within 5 years.

***Spodoptera* complex.**Several species in the genus *Spodoptera*, including *S.litura, S.frugiperda, S. littoralis, S. sunia* and *S.exigua,* are important pests on many crops. In Brazil, an indigenous isolate of SfNPV at 2.5 × 1011 OBS/ha provides effective control of early larval instars of *S. frugiperda* on maize. The virus is applied in approximately 2000 ha annually. In USA, Crop Genetics International (CGI) commercially produces SPOD-X (SeNPV) for control of *S.exigua* on cotton and vegetable crops. NPVs have also been developed and used against *S.litura* (China, India, Taiwan), *S.littoralis* (Egypt), *S.exigua* (USA, Guatemala, Thailand) and *S. sunia* (Guatemala). Three weekly sprays of SlNPV at 375 LE/ha caused more than 95 per cent mortality of *S. litura* larvae on cauliflower crop in large scale field trials in India. This treatment also conserved the braconid and ichneumonid parasitoids which were killed in the insecticide-treated plots.

Pests of plantation crops. A non-occluded virus (OrV) of the rhinoceros beetle, *Oryctes rhinoceros*, a major pest of coconut palms, has been successfully used in pest control in South-East Asia and the Pacific. The virus known as *Rhabdinovirus oryctes* is used as an inoculative agent by pre-infecting adults with the virus. Adults from the field or reared in the laboratory are infected by immersing them in a viral suspension and then allowed to crawl through saw dust mixed with the virus. The infected adults do not feed but are attracted to breeding and feeding sites. The infected adult midgut cells produce large numbers of viral particles that are disseminated with the faeces. When an infected adult beetle visits the breeding site for oviposition, it defecates and the larvae already present in the breeding site become infected upon ingestion of the contaminated faecal matter.The virus was first used in Malayasia in 1967 and since then has been used in over 40 other countries worldwide. In India, the virus has effectively controlled the beetle in the Andaman Islands, causing 80-90 per cent reduction in beetle damage. More recently, the virus has been successfully used in the Middle East country of Oman to control rhinoceros beetle on datepalm. In all of the above cases, the beetle population has been reduced to a point where it no longer represents an economic threat to farmers. Once introduced, the virus seems to maintain itself adequately without additional intervention.

Field Stability and Persistence

Entomopathogens are highly susceptible to damage by desiccation, and by exposure to sunlight, or to ultraviolet (UV) radiations. Various additives/adjuvants (like charcoal, India ink, egg-albumin, mollases, optical brightener, etc.) have been suggested to be used along with formulations of various entomopathogens including baculoviruses. *Heliothis* NPV-bait formulations when used on cotton remained active for at least 6 days during hot, dry and sunny weather. The addition of crude sugar (15%) to the HaNPV spray fluid increased the persistence of the virus both under natural sunlight and shade.

Under north Indian conditions, an NPV of *Spilarctia obliqua*, lost a total of 33.3 to 50 per cent of its original activity on the sunflower foliage in comparatively shorter exposure periods ranging between 4 and 12 h. Beyond this, up to a period of 72 h exposure to sunlight, the virus could still persist with 25 per cent activity. The loss of activity was about 75 per cent at the maximum exposure period (4 days). The SlNPV persisted on the sunflower foliage for a period of 6 days with 6.6 per cent of its original activity kept intact. An evening spraying of NPV helped significantly to minimize the photoinactivation of this virus on cotton foliage besides allowing its greater ingestion by *S. litura* larvae.

Certain substrates such as boric acid, chitinase, extracts of neem tree and optical brighteners of the stilbene group have enhanced baculovirus activity. Mixtures of baculoviruses with optical brighteners of the stillbene group seem to have excellent potential for use in formulated products because they can enhance viral activity at concentrations as low as 0.01 per cent, reduce time to kill the host, and provide protection against UV solar radiation. These substances have enhanced the activity of NPVs of *Autographa californica, Anagrapha falcifera, Anticarsiagemmatalis, Heliothis virescens, Helicoverpa zea, Lymantria dispar, Spodoptera exigua* and *Trichoplusia ni*. Among 8 optical brighteners (Blankophor HRS, P167, BBH, RKH, BSU, DML, LPG and Tinopal LPW) of the stilbene group, five compounds acted as enhancers and the most active brighteners (BBH, RKH and LPW) reduced LC50 of gypsy moth, *L. dispar* NPV by 800 to 1300-fold. The most effective compounds were those exhibiting the greatest fluorescence. The brightener acts on the insect midgut and has no effect on the virus *per se*. The virus and the optical brightener must be ingested. Within 48h the insects stop feeding, midgets are clear and the gut pH is greatly reduced. The brightener allows the virus to replicate in a nonpermissive tissue (columnar cells of the midgut). More importantly, the host spectrum of the baculovirus can be expanded by the use of these compounds.

FUNGAL PATHOGENS

The fungi include a large group of organisms and the extent of biodiversity within fungi is often underestimated. There are over 72,000 described species and the total number of species in the world may be as high as 1.5 million. The first pathogens found to cause diseases in insects were fungi because of their conspicuous macroscopic growth on the surfaces of their hosts. Towards the end of nineteenth century, Agostino Bassi demonstrated that the fungus *Beauveria bassiana* was the causal agent of the white muscardine disease of the silkworm, *Bombyx mori*. Since then, over 800 species of entomopathogenic fungi have been identified. These fungi are specific to insects, often to a particular species, and do not infect animals or plants. While bacteria and viruses must be ingested to cause disease, fungi can cause infection by penetrating the outer structure of insects. Fungi provide the only satisfactory microbial means of biocontrol of plant-sucking insects such as aphids and whiteflies which are not susceptible to bacteria and viruses.

Mode of Infection

The most common portal entry of fungi is through the integument though invasion via the respiratory or alimentary tract is also reported. The infective unit in most fungi is a spore, usually a conidium. In favourable conditions, the conidium, germinates into a short germ tube which gives out small swellings called *appressoria* (Fig. 5.4) The appressorium attaches itself to the cuticle and sends out an infection peg which provides a firm attachment that the fungus needs to physically force its way into the host. The hyphae then penetrate the layers of the integument by enzymatic dissolution of chitin and protein, ramify first in the cuticle and then reach the haemocoel and internal organs. The invasion by the fungal mycelium continues until the insect is virtually filled with the fungus and becomes quite firm to touch. Conidiophores are then produced which erupt through the cuticle

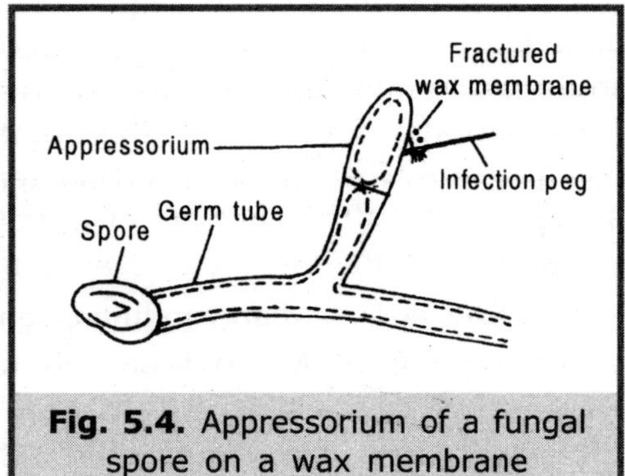

Fig. 5.4. Appressorium of a fungal spore on a wax membrane

(Fig. 5.5) and produce spores on the outside of the insect, infecting nearby healthy insects also. Death of the host is by obliteration (choking) of the tissues and also by the toxins produced by the fungus.

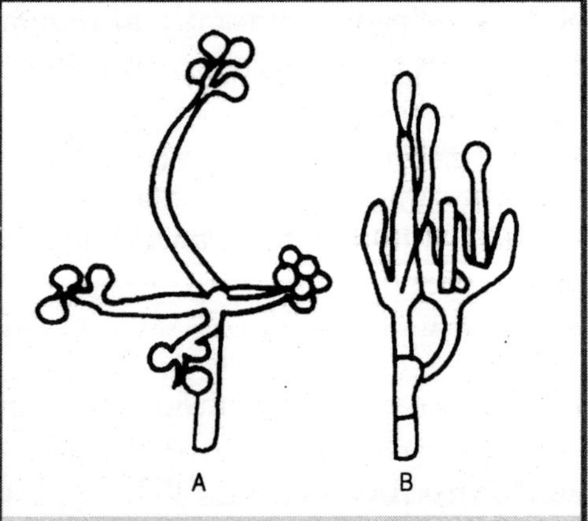

Fig. 5.5. Some important entomogenous fungi; A, *Beauveria bassiana*; B, *Metarhizium anisopliae*

Entomogenous fungi belong to four main classes of fungi, viz. Phycomycetes, Ascomycetes, Basidiomycetes and Deuteromycetes or Fungi imperfecti. The more potent fungi that can be used for insect control belong to the class, Fungi imperfecti (examples : *Beauveria bassiana, Metarhizium anisopliae*). These cause *muscardine disease* in insects (forming a fungal mat on the outer surface of the body), exist in many strains, are internal parasites of insects and reproduce by conidia. Different tissues and organs are not attacked simultaneously, some of them are spared until death. While some fungi confine themselves to blood, others can penetrate tissues like muscles, tracheae, gut fat body, etc.

Loss of appetite and an attempt to climb higher, are the early symptoms of the fungal disease. They are followed by decreased irritability, general or partial paralysis, discoloured patches on integument and increased acidity in the blood. The body hardens and the insect is upright on its legs at the time of death. Death occurs within a week or even within 24 hours. Death may result due to hyphae forcing apart muscles, blood cells stopping circulation due to increased hyphae, blockage of the gut and the toxins produced by the fungus.

Host Range

The fungi infect individuals in most of the orders of insects like Hemiptera, Diptera, Coleoptera, Lepidoptera, Orthoptera and Hymenoptera. The immature stages are more commonly infected than the adults and in some cases the reverse is true. The pupae are infrequently attacked and the eggs rarely succumb to fungal infection.

Beauveria bassiana. The white muscardine fungus, *Beauveria bassiana* (Balsamo) Vuillemin occurs throughout the world and it has the largest host range among the fungi imperfecti. It has been detected from over 700 insect species and also occurs in the soil as a ubiquitous saprophyte. *B. bassiana* mainly infects insects belonging to Lepidoptera, Coleoptera and Hemiptera. It also occurs in Diptera and Hymenoptera. A related species *B. brongniartii* is the most abundant white grub pathogen and exhibits a much wider host range among whitegrub species.

B. bassiana and *B. brongniartii* produce toxins, some of which might become as novel insecticidal compounds. The toxins indentified include beauvericin, bassianolide, beauverolides, isarolides, pigments like tenellin and bassianin, and oxalic acid. The toxins produced by *B. bassiana* cause swelling and stiffening in insect larvae. Some toxins, which are high molecular proteases, either directly damage the principal functions of the haemolymph or cause damage indirectly by producing a toxic byproduct in the insect. Beauvericin causes alternation in the nuclei and affects cell migration in the cell lines. Bassianolide, the cyclodepsipeptide, is toxic when inoculated into the haemocoel or when fed to the larvae. The secondary metabolites, which are anibiotics, may prevent bacterial putrefaction and thus, permit fungal mummification of the insect.

B. bassiana has been extensively evaluated against different pest species both in the laboratory and field conditions in various parts of the world. It has been found effective against the Colorado potato beetle, *Leptinotarsa decemlineata*; European corn borer, *Ostrinia nubilalis*; codling moth, *Cydia pomonella*; Japanese beetle, *Popillia japonica*; pod borer, *Helicoverpa armigera*; mango mealy bug, *Drosicha mangiferae*; boll weevil; *Anthonomus grandis;* cotton leahopper, *Psallus seriatus*; cotton whitefly, *Bemisia tabaci*; chinch bug, *Blissus leucopterus*; cabbage caterpillar, *Pieris bassicae;* tarnished plant bug, *Lygus lineolaris;* aphids, *Aphis gossypii* and *A. craccivora;* brown planthopper, *Nilaparvata lugens;* rice leaf-folder, *Cnaphalocrocis medinalis;* and yellow stem borer, *Scirpophaga incertulas*.

Metarhizium anisopliae. The green muscardine fungus, *Metarhizium anisopliae* (Metschnikoff) Sorokin is a common and widely distributed fungus with a wide host range. It was isolated in 1879 by Metschnikoff from the beetle, *Anisoplia austriaca*. It has been detected from at least

300 species of insects belonging to different orders. It is especially active against chrysomelid, curculionid and scarabaeid beetles (Table 5.2). A related species *M. flavoviridae* has been found promising for the control of locusts and grasshoppers.

Table 5.2 Major target pests of *Metarhizium anisopliae*

Insect order	Insect species	Country
Coleoptera	Chrysomelids	Taiwan
	Brontispa longissima	
	Curculionids	Europe
	Otiorhynchus sulcatus	
	Scarabaeids	Australia
	Adoryphorus couloni	
	Antitrogus couloni	
	Antitrogus parvulus	
	Aphodius tasmaniae	
	Oryctes rhinoceros	South Pacific, Philippines
Homoptera	Spittlebugs	Philippines
	Aeneolamia spp.	Brazil
	Nilaparvata lugens	
	Mahanarva posticata	
	Zilia spp.	
Isoptera	Termites	Australia
Orthoptera	Locusts, grasshoppers	Europe/Africa
	Locusta migratoria migratorioides	
	Schistocerca gregaria	
	Cockroaches	USA
	Periplaneta americana	

Source : Zimmermann (1993)

M. anisopliae has been found to be effective against the sugarcane spittle bug, *Mahanarva posticata*; brown planthopper, *Nilaparvata lugens*; Japanese beetle, *Popillia japonica*; rhinoceros beetle, *Oryctes rhinoceros*;sugarcane pyrilla, *Pyrilla perpusilla* and diamondback moth, *Plutella xylostella*. The fungus has been extensively used in Brazil since 1972 for the control of *M. posticata*. In India, the overwintering population of *P. perpusilla* was found to be readily infected by the fungus application and the infected individuals were capable of spreading the infection and inducing an epizootic. The fungus was found to be safe to the principal parasite of *Pyrilla*, viz. *Epiricania melanoleuca*. *M. anisopliae* has also been found effective against *Plutellaloylostella*, *Spodoptera litura* and *Spilarctia obliqua*.

Verticillium lecanii. *Verticillium lecanii* is a common pathogen of scale insects in tropical and subtropical environment. It also infects aphids, thrips, whiteflies, mites and nematodes. *V. lecanii* has been found to be effective against greenhouse whitefly, *Trialeurodes vaporariorum*; guava scale, *Chloropulvinaria psidii*; thrips and red spider mite, *Tetranychus urticae*. Studies conducted in India showed that *V. lecanii* @ 6×106 spores per ml caused high mortality of *C. viridis*. With two fortnightly applications, maximum mortality of 73 per cent was noticed at two weeks after application. The fungus was comparatively less effective during the drought period and addition of humectant, glycerol 0.1 per cent, increased the mortality of *C. viridis*.

Nomuraea rileyi. *Nomuraea rileyi* (Farlow) Samsonis pathogenic to a majority of the noctuids, especially the larvae. It has the ability to cause spectacular epizootics under favourable environmental conditions. Farmers in Brazil refrain from spraying insecticides when they observe natural incidence of *N. rileyi* on velevetbean caterpillar, *Anticarsia gemmatalis*, in soybeans. They generally resort to late plantings of soybeans for the management of *A. gemmatalis* as *N. rileyi* has been reported to cause late season epizootics. These epizootics generally result in a relatively heavy load of soil-borne conidia that act as natural reservoir for the seasonal initiation of *N. rileyi* epizootics in soybean caterpillars.

In India, epizootics have been observed on *Spodoptera exigua, Helicoverpa armigera* and *Junonia orthiya.* Epizootics of *N. rileyi* were facilitated by favourable environmental conditions of temperature (21-28°C) and humidity (68-93% RH). *N. rileyi* is a key mortality factor in the population of *S. litura* in coastal Andhra Pradesh. In field trials, *N. rileyi* was found effective against *S. litura* as foliar spray as well as soil application Persistence of *N. rileyi* is reported to increase with the addition of sunflower, saffflower and groundnut oils. Early instar larvae of *S. litura* and *H. armigera* were more susceptible (80-95% mortality in Ist and 2nd instars) to *N. rileyi* infection.

Neozygites fresenii. *Neozygites fresenii* is an efficient natural pathogen of cotton aphid, *Aphis gossypii.* It was observed in 1990 that the aphid populations were being decimated by *N. fresenii* (an obligate pathogen of aphids) and it led to years of basic research on the epizootology of this pathogen. Billions of aphids across vast cotton fields, counties and states in USA were being killed by the pathogen. The epizootics were very widespread in the mid-southern states of Arkansas, Lousiana, Misissippi and Tennessee, and the south-eastern states of Albama, Florida, Georgia, North Carolina and South Carolina. The epizootics occurred regularly each year within a 5-week period, during June and July, and once epizootics began, aphid populations declined to economically unimportant levels within about a week. Several biological aspects of *N. fresenii,* viz. rapid life cycle, one spore sufficient to infect a host, large numbers of spores produced per host, spores discharged from the host on to other hosts and into air, combine to result in epizootics. The Cotton Aphid Fungus Sampling Service was started in 1993, for diagnosis of aphid samples from fields, providing information on fungus prevalence level and advising farmers to delay pesticide applications for aphid control if the fungus level in the field was 15 per cent or higher. Thousands of farmers have taken advantage of this service till 2006 and in many years, the fungus has saved growers in the mid-south and south-east millions of dollars in input costs.

NEMATODE PATHOGENS

The entomopathogenic nematodes have received increased attention as biological control agents in recent years. Beneficial nematodes are microscopic (0.6 mm) roundworms found associated with most of the insect orders. The two major groups of entomopathogenic nematodes that attack insects are *Steinernema* and *Heterorhabditis.* The primary nematode species are about 55 of *Steinernema* the world over and a dozen of them occur in India. Among *Heterorhabditis,* about 12 species are on record and the most common in India is *H. indica.* The nematode-bacterium complex has attained the status of a potential biopesticide because of their impressive attributes. They are unique due to their symbiotic relationship with bacteria in the genera *Xenorhabdus* or *Photorhabdus.* All species of *Steinernema* are associated with bacteria of the genus *Xenorhabdus* and all *Heterorhabditis* with *Photorhabdus* species.

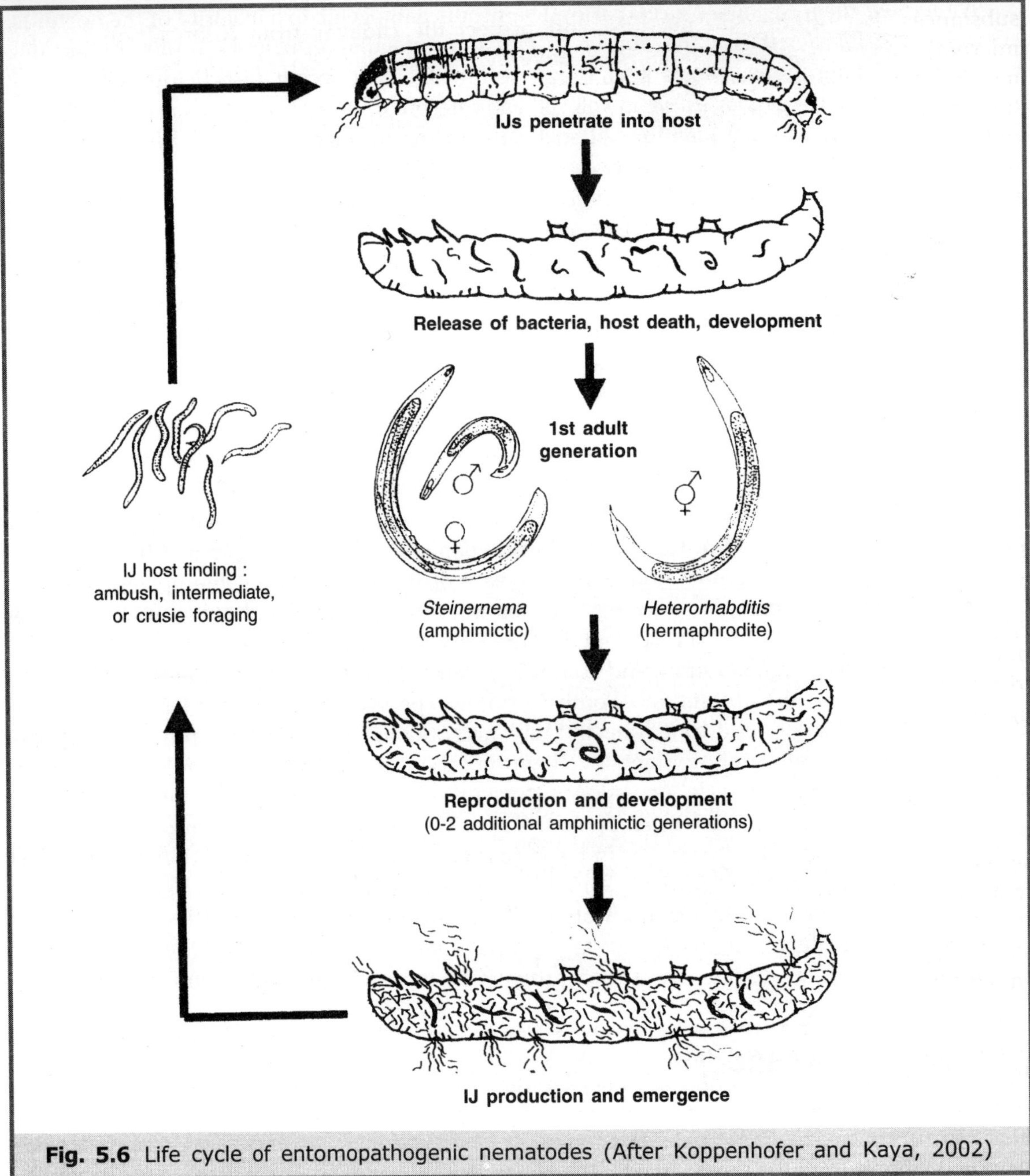

Fig. 5.6 Life cycle of entomopathogenic nematodes (After Koppenhofer and Kaya, 2002)

Steinernema and Heterorhabditis are obligate pathogens in nature. The only stage that survives outside of host is the non-feeding third stage infective juvenile (IJ) or dauer juvenile. The IJs carry cells of their bacterial symbiont in their intestinal tract. After locating a suitable host, the IJs invade it through natural openings (mouth, spiracles, anus) or thin areas of the host cuticle (common only in *Heterorhabditis*) and penetrate into the host hemocoel. The IJs recover from their developmental arrestment, release the symbionts, and bacteria and nematodes cooperate to overcome the host's immune response. The bacteria propagate and produce substances that rapidly kill the host and protect the cadavar from colonization by other microorganisms. The nematodes start developing, feed on the bacteria and host tissues metabolized by the bacteria, and go through 1-3 generations. Depleting food resources in the host cadavar leads to the development of a new generation of IJs that emerges from the cadavar in search of a new host. The major difference between *Steinernema* and *Heterorhabditis* is that *Heterorhabditis* adults are hermophrodites in the first generation but amphimictic in the following generations, whereas *Steinernema* adults are always amphimictic (Fig. 5.6).

Each nematode species is specifically associated with one symbiont species, although a symbiont species may be associated with more than one nematode species. This specificity has been demonstrated to operate at two levels. (*i*) Although the nematode can develop on other bacteria, but reproduction occurs on their natural symbiont.

(*ii*) Natural symbiont cells are retained better than cells of other bacteria. In this association, the nematode is dependant upon the bacterium for (*a*) quickly killing its insect host, (*b*) creating a suitable environment for its development by producing antibiotics that suppress competing secondary microorganisms, and (*c*) transforming the host tissues into a food source. The bacterium requires the nematode for (*a*) protection from the external environment, (*b*) penetration into the host's hemocoel, and (*c*) inhibition of the host's antibacterial proteins.

Efficacy Against Target Pests

Entomopathogenic nematodes have been tested against a large number of insect pest species with results varying from no effect to excellent control. Nematodes have been applied most successfully in habitats that provide protection from environmental extremes, especially in soil, their natural habitat, and in cryptic habitats. Excellent control has been accomplished against insects that bore into plants; apparently their cryptic habitats contain less limiting factors (natural enemies of nematodes) than soil and can more easily be manipulated to the nematodes' advantage. Low or highly variable efficacy has been achieved in manure contents like ammonia on IJs. Control attempts in aquatic habitats have not been successful because the nematodes are not adapted to directed motility in this environment. Lastly, on foliage and similar habitats, the IJs are exposed to detrimental conditions that can be only marginally remedied by adjuvants. Nematodes have been evaluated for the control of a number of coleopteran (flea beetles, root weevils, root worms), dipteran (leaf miners, sciarid flies) and lepidopteran (cutworms, armyworms, peach borer, crown borers, stem borers) pests on a variety of crops. A few examples are discussed below:

Cryptic habitats. Cryptic habitats are considered as most favourable for entomoparasitic nematodes as these enhance infectivity, survival and persistence of nematodes by minimizing their death from desiccation and ultraviolet radiation. One of the most successful examples is from Tasmania where thousands of hectares of pine trees were infested by the wood wasp, *Sirex noctilio,* which implants to the trees the fungus, *Amylosereum aerolatum.* The fungus killed many susceptible trees. A specific tylenchid nematode, *Deladenus siridicicola,* was mass-reared and introduced into the trunks with wood wasp larvae. Usually over 70 per cent of the emerging wood wasps were parasitized by nematodes, which were established in most of the treated areas and spread up to 19 km in a single year and reduced damage of pine forests significantly in the following years.

Application of entomogenous nematode, *Steinernema feltiae,* in July caused 32 per cent mortality of overwintering larvae of codling moth, *Cydia pomonella,* settled in corrugated paper bands around tree trunks. However, October and Feburary applications increased mortality to 80 and 95 per cent, respectively. This high efficacy may be attributed to rainfall during the autumn and winter period, and the water retention properties of the paper bands. The cryptic habitats can be considered as moisture-retaining stations that often contain food attractants. Under such conditions, *S. carpocapsae* survived for weeks and significantly reduced the numbers of the German cockroach, *Blatella germanica*.

Soil ecosystems. In recent studies, *S. feltiae* @ 2.5-5.0 billion/ha was effective in reducing *Delia radicum* larvae on cabbage and increasing the yield of cauliflower 2.3–fold. *S. riobrave* has been found very effective for controlling the prepupae and pupae of the corn earworm, *Helicoverpa zea*. *S. carpocapsae* has provided 9 per cent mortality of larvae of codling moth, *Cydia pomonella*, whereas mortality by *S. riobrave* and *H. bacteriophora* was 80 and 83 per cent, respectively. *S. riobrave* also provided better control of larvae of pink bollworm, *Pectinophora gossypiella*, than did *S. carpocapsae*. Similarly, *S. riobrave* has been considered as a better control agent of the citrus root weevil, *Diaprepes abbreviatus*, than *S. carpocapsae*. The control potential of *D. abbreviatus* with *S. ribobrave* was higher than 90 per cent under greenhouse conditions and 50-75 per cent mortality in field caged *D. abbreviatus* larvae beneath mature citrus trees.

Foliar habitats. Field applications of entomoparasitic nematodes against foliage-feeding insects have resulted in varying degrees of efficacy. Nematodes require high relative humidity, water drops on leaves and avoidance of direct sunshine. Tropical conditions and rainy periods enhance nematode survival on the foliage, but in temperate and dry areas, nematode application has limited success. The emergence of the spruce bud moth, *Zeiraphera canadensis* was reduced upto 82 per cent with water spray containing IJs of *S. carpocapsae*. Foliar application of *S .feltiae* under glasshouse conditions, when relative humidity was >90 per cent, suppressed the outbreak of *Liriomyza huidobrensis*. Similar mortality level of 75 per cent for *L. trifolii* was obtained with *S. feltiae* on chrysanthemum. Similar levels of controls of *L. trifolii* were obtained under greenhouse and foghouse tests, with up to 69 per cent mortality by *S. feltiae* and >65 per cent by *S. carpocapsae* AII strain. The control of leafminers can be successful if the nematodes enter leaf mines before desiccation. In India, *S. carpocapsae* has proved effective against *Amsacta albistriga* on groundnut and *Leucinodes orbonalis* on brinjal in field trials.

Aquatic habitats. Mermithid nematodes are regarded as potential candidates for control of water inhabiting stages of mosquitoes, black flies and midges. There have been several field releases of *Romanomermis culicivorax*, which had successfully reduced mosquito populations in rice fields and in small ponds in Louisiana. *R. culicivorax* were also released into mosquito-breeding ponds in Maryland. The mermithid nematodes, originating from the warmer areas of Louisiana, probably established and overwintered in the region where the temperatures go down to -190C in January. It was able to self-reproduce and caused mortality of mosquitoes to a level of 50-100 per cent. There have been several studies utilizing steinernermatid and heterorhabitid nematodes against aquatic insects. However, these nematodes are not adapted to swim and their host-finding ability in water is limited.

PROTOZOAN PATHOGENS

More than 1000 species of protozoa pathogenic to insects have been described and many more remain to be discovered. The entomogenous protozoa are commonly found in the digestive tracts of insects as commensals or they are in a mutualistic association with insects. The infected insect is usually lethargic, small in size, has reduced feeding and morphological deformities, and fails to moult or pupate. Of the numerous protozoans associated with insects, pathogenic species are found in all the major groups of protozoa, viz. Sarcomastigophora,

Apicomplexa, Microspora and Ciliohora. However, majority of the emtomophilic protozoa described are from the phyla Apicomplexa and Microspora. The efficiency and control potential of these protozoans is considered to be limited because of the chronic nature of infection produced in their host. Since relatively few of the entomophilic protozoa are highly virulent or fast acting, they have been considered to offer little potential to short term, quick action microbial insecticides and to be more appropriate as agents for long term control programmes with high economic injury level. However, in recent years, there has been a renewed interest in search of entomophilic protozoans for the control of insect pests.

In recent times, most studies on protozoa have been focussed on *Nosema* spp., due to the successful commercial production and use of *N. locustae* against grasshoppers. Another protozoan, *Vairimorpha necatrix*, which infects a number of important noctuid pests, appears quite promising for development as a biopesticide.

***Nosema* spp.** *Nosema* is one of the major genera of sporozoa exploited for biological control of insect pests. Three species of *Nosema*, viz. *N. locustae, N. acridophagus* and *N. cuneatum* have been known to parasitize acridids. Being intracellular, the organism redirects the metabolism of host cells to form more of *Nosema*, similar to the effect of viruses on host cells. *N. locustae* normally invades the fat body as well as the pericardium of grasshoppers, thereby disrupting the host's intermediary metabolism and competing with the insect for energy resources. Pathogenicity is normally expressed in many ways, among which increased mortality rates, reduced fecundity, delayed development, decreased activity and reduced food consumption are regarded as indicative parameters for successful control of the pests. Infected insects often show various cytopathological effects such as nuclear and cellular hypertrophy, formation of neoplastic-like xenomas, and extensive alteration of cytoplamsic organelles such as chromosomes, endoplasmic reticulum, mitochondria, ribosome bodies, protein granules and vacuoles.

Nosema probably spreads by transovum or transovarial transmission or by cannibalism of diseased individuals. *N. locustae* has been applied at concentrations ranging from 1 × 108 to 5 × 109 spores/ha and this application is known to reduce the population by 50-60 per cent with 35-50 per cent infection among survivors. Although the effect of *N. locustae* infection is debilitating rather than rapid mortality, the infection reduces the fertility of the sperm in males and fecundity in females. 'Noloc' is the formulation bsed on *N. locustae* produced by M/s Sandoz Inc. for use against grasshoppers. Other examples of *Nosema* considered for biological control of harmful insects are *N. acridophagus,N.cuneatum, N. heliothidis,N. disstriae, N. fumiferanae* and *N. furnaclis. N. fumiferanae* is being exploited for the management of the spruce budworm, *Choristoneura fumiferana*. One of its major attributes is that, once applied it would perpetuate itself in the pest populations. Similarly, *N. heliothidids,* within a few days of larval infection, becomes a continuous source of infection since fresh spores are excreted in the faeces for the continuation of the infection. Thus, infected adults and larvae can serve as a bioresource and disseminators of spores until death.

Vairimorpha necatrix. *V. necatrix* is a highly virulent species, infecting 36 lepidopteran pests among which 20 are noctuids. It primarily infects the fat body of the lepidopteran larvae such as *Pseudaletia unipuncta, Helicoverpa zea, Spodoptera exigua* and *Trichoplusia ni*. It causes two different types of diseases resulting in mortality in its hosts, viz. (*i*) mortality due to damage of the gut, followed by bacterial septicemia, and (*ii*) mortality due to microsporidiosis after ingestion of even a low spore dose. A low dosage results in a chronic infection of mainly the fat bodies and some muscular tissues, whereas high doses produce an acute infection of mainly mid gut tissues. In the advanced stage of infection, the abnormally large, white fat body is usually conspicuous, and a dorsal swelling may appear on the last two or three abdominal segments. Both ID50 and LD50 for *V. necatrix* are very low, i.e. less than 100 spores per larva, for most host species. It can be mass produced at reasonable cost and stored for short periods. When formulated with sunlight protectant, spores survive sufficiently in the field. However, application time as well as the cost of *in vivo* production are the major bottlenecks in the commercial production of this pathogen.

GENETIC IMPROVEMENT

The basic objective of genetic improvement of microbial pathogens is to alter their genetic make-up to improve their effectiveness as biocontrol agents without producing a hazard to non-target organisms. In general, pathogens can be made more effective by increasing rate of reproduction, speed of transmission and infective ability, or increasing the quantity of toxins produced.

Bacillus thuringiensis

It has now been nearly three decades since Bt *delta*-endotoxin gene was first cloned and expressed in *Escherichia coli* demonstrating for the first time the potential of genetic engineering technology for microbial control. Since that time, Bt toxin genes have been cloned and expressed in a wide variety of microorganisms (baculoviruses to cyanobacteria) as well as in plants in attempts to improve their delivery and efficacy against insect pests. Progress has been rapid, and in 1991, the United States Environmental Protection Agency (USEPA)'s registration of two genetically engineered products (MVP and M-Trak), based on Bt *delta*-endotoxin expressing *Pseudomonas fluorescens*, in which the cells are killed before use, was an important step in the process of commercializing recombinant or transgenic microbial pesticides. Thus, the microencapsulation of Btcrystal, i.e. 'biopacking' by *P. fluorescens* (Pf) cell wall, the process called 'cell up' will protect the endotoxin from the environmental factors. In the process of biopacking (*i*) the gene coding for δ-endotoxin protein is removed from the Bt cell, (*ii*) the gene is incorporated into a plasmid that contains genetic information to allow for expression of the protein, and (*iii*) the plasmid is inserted into a Pf cell. The process results in an active, stable, biotoxin encapsulated within a non-viable cell. These products are environmentally benign because the microorganism cannot spread from the site of application or transfer its genetic information.

Improvement in host range. Nearly 525 insect species belonging to 13 orders were reportedly found to be infected by Bt around the world in mid eighties. Since then the host range is constantly expanding with increasing commercial interest and the extensive screening programmes in progress. Recent efforts to improve insecticidal activity have been based on transfer of Bt genes into non-homologous isolates of Bt as a means of combining *delta*-endotoxins to produce either additive or synergistic effects and thus expand the host range. Thecloned Btgenes were introduced into native isolates of Btthus increasing their host spectrum, using electroporation and the resulting organism demonstrated activity towards mosquitoes and beetles as expected, but also showed unexpected activity against *Pieris brassicae*, a lepidopteran pest. It has shown through their novel approach the expansion of insecticidal host range in Bt via *in vitro* genetic recombination. This has been achieved by inserting the sequence IS232 to deliver *cry3A* gene into an isolate producing CryIA toxin resulting in a strain, which displayed insecticidal activity against both Lepidoptera and Coleoptera. The transconjugant "Foil", a bioinsecticide product marketed by Ecogen Inc. for application on potatoes and egg plants possessed both coleoteran and lepidopteran activity and it was considered by regulatory agencies to be genetically manipulated rather than genetically engineered and hence it was approved for use by USEPA in 1990.

Improvement in foliar activity and delivery. To improve delivery and residual activity, the researchers have expressed Bt toxins in plants and in plant-colonizing organisms. Crop Genetics International product, known as "Incide", involved endophytic *Clavibacter xyli* var. *cynodontis* as toxin delivery system for Bt toxin genes. It has been field-tested and no adverse environmental effects have been reported. In another approach, the 'cellcap' system was also used to increase the residual activity of Bt *delta*-endotoxins. The final step in 'cellcap' encapsulation process is a fixation step, which kills the transgenic *P. fluorescens* cells while they are still in the fermenter, and in this way the regulatory restrictions on the release of otherwise living recombinants are removed, and the products can be effectively used. Recently, the scientists from Madurai Kamraj University, Tamil Nadu, have isolated an organism-strain RSI-identified as *Bacillus* sp., which is capable of colonizing in cotton leaves and found to be an excellent colonizer of cotton phyllosphere. By conjugal transfer, *cryIAa* gene of Bt has been introduced into it. It has been shown that transconfugation colonizes cotton plants for a prolonged period and it protects the plant from the attack of *Helicoverpa armigera* for more than 30 days.

Improvement in soil activity and delivery. Microbes, which normally occur in close association with the roots of crop plants, can be used for engineering these bacteria to produce the appropriate Bt toxin(s). A cloned Bt endotoxin gene has been introduced into the corn root colonizing bacterium, *Pseudomonas fluorescens*. This, in principle is to deliver the lepidopteran active (CryIAb) toxin crystals beneath the surface of the soil in areas where root feeding insects do the most damage. In an innovative approach towards improving delivery to soil insects, the symbiotic relationship between pigeonpea, *Cajanus indica*, a legume crop, and the nitrogen-fixing bacterium, *Bradyrhizobium* was exploited. It was possible to reduce the *Rivellia angulata* infestation on pigeonpea through the development of transgenic *Bradyrhizobium* cells that expressed the dipteran active CryIVD gene.

Baculoviruses

The ability to transform or genetically engineer baculoviruses may provide a means of correcting the perceived defects in the efficiency and marketability of virus pesticides although some of these defects could also be alleviated with a more sophisticated IPM strategy including early sensing of population dynamics. It should be possible to optimize their genetics so that the transformed or modified baculoviruses may perform specific pesticide functions in a predictable manner. Different strategies have been tried to improve the baculovirus properties, focused on increasing the speed of action, enhanced virulence and extended host range. These approaches include expressing physiological effectors (hormones, enzymes or antisense), interrupting the normal metabolism of the insect, expressing insect specific toxins such as neurotoxin and Bt or deleting baculoviral genes that may ineract with the reaction of the viruses to the insect.

Improvement in host range. Although baculoviruses infect over 600 insect species, individual isolates normally show a limited host range and infect only closely related species. Thus, baculoviruses, in general, have narrow host specificity. This property makes baculoviruses, potentially very useful biocontrol agents. To increase their usefulness as effective biological insecticides, it is desirable to alter these viruses genetically to be more virulent and infect a broader host range.

The recombinant DNA technology has its current applications in inserting foreign genes into insect baculoviruses and achieving their rapid and efficient expression in the recipient host systems. The most common approach for the construction of recombinant baculoviruses involves the cotransfecion of an insect cell line that supports viral replication with naked viral genomic DNA and a plasmid transfer vector. The transfer vector consists of a viral genomic restriction fragment containing the desired alteration. The effective host range of a baculovirus might be expanded by inserting an insect-specific neurotoxin and/or behaviour-modifying gene into the baculovirus genome so that the gene is under the control of a promoter that is expressed early on virus entry into cells. This would not actually alter the host range for virus replication but could alter the ability of the virus to influence host behaviour and thereby increase the "effective" host range of virus as a pesticide. The necessity for application of a variety of viruses to protect those crops affected by a multitude of pests could be avoided by specifically broadening the host range of one virus. It is envisaged that this may be achieved by engineering specific genes from one NPV into the genome of another. A future approach would be to synthesize biologically active and authenticated insect pheromones and other behaviour-modifying proteins that are used in IPM, by way of expressing the genes responsible for pheromones in insect cells through baculovirus vector instead of depending on *in vitro* production technique, which is cost-prohibitive and time consuming. Engineering viruses to insecticidal proteins in many cases should also result in expanded host range.

Improvement in speed of kill. A virulent NPV sprayed at an appropriate rate will kill the first and second and in some cases the third instar larvae within 2-4 days. But the advanced instars may live for a week or more, causing further damage to the crop. Current approaches improving the efficacy of viral insecticides, therefore, are aimed at developing broad-spectrum viruses that will cause cessation of feeding within 24-48 h of infection. Candidate genes for hyperexpression in the baculovirus insecticide system include those encoding insect-specific hormones, toxins, or enzymes as well as antipeptides. Recombinant baculoviruses expressing such genes have been constructed and their insecticidal activity assessed *in vivo*. However, the first genes that were inserted into baculoviruses that successfully altered their biology were insect-selective toxin genes derived from other arthropods, namely the North African scorpion, *Androctonus australis*, and the predatory mite, *Pyemotes tritici*. *Helicoverpa zea* NPV has been improved by way of inserting mite toxin gene and expressed the toxin during infection resulting in 50 per cent mortality within 40 hours after virus treatment. This is said to be the fastest acting recombinant baculovirus reported to-date.

The deletion of *egt* gene from viral genome results in a faster acting viral pesticide exhibiting decreased crop damage following application. Deletion of *egt* gene of AcNPV reduces the LT50 approximately by 20 per cent. The percentage of reduction in larval feeding for *egt*-deleted versus wild-type AcNPV is approximately 40 per cent or roughly twice that of the observed percentage of reduction in LT50. An AcNPV derivative lacking *egt* was the first genetically improved recombinant baculovirus to be approved by the USEPA for field-testing in the USA and was first field tested by American Cyanamid in 1993. In contrast to *egt* deletion variant of AcMNDV, AaIT insertion recombinants have notably increased field efficacy and resulted in considerably reduced crop damage. Thus, the recombinant baculoviruses hold possible commercial potential

Improvement in photostability. One of the major obstacles to expansion of the use of commercial baculovirus preparations for control of crop pests is their sensitivity to photodegradation. Insect viruses have been selected for resistance to UV irradiation and for an increased rate of vertical transmission. One such strain of GV of codling moth(CpGV) was quite resistant to the effect of UV irradiation both under natural sunlight and in laboratory conditions. The modified strain was 5.6 times as resistant toUV light as the original isolate and remained infective for twice as long in the field. A UV-resistant strain of an NPV of *Lymantria dispar* has also been obtained. The genes that might be responsible for the effective DNA repair system, if isolated, inserted, and expressed into the genomes of baculoviruses, can produce UV-resistant baculoviruses. Considering the available biodiversity in the tropics, such investigations in tropical agroecosystems will bring fruitful dividends.

The laboratory bioassays have shown that the AcMNPV recombinant expressing AaIT reduces time to death by approximately 25 per cent. The field trials with AcMNPV against cabbage looper, *Trichoplusia ni* revealed that the recombinant virus acted more quickly and significantly reduced the crop damage compared with an unmodified virus.

Nematodes

Entomopathognic nematodes are promising biological control agents, but limitations like susceptibility to environment extremes and diverse host-finding behaviour hamper their optimum utilization. One solution to this problem is to develop genetically improved strains with enhanced traits for biological control. Strategies for genetic manipulation include artificial selection, hybridization, mutagenesis and recombinant DNA technology.

Selection. Selection is employed to find genetically superior nematode species. A heat tolerant strain of *H. bacteriophora* designated as IS5 was discovered in Negev desert, Israel in 1996 and was found superior to HP88, a commercially available strain of *H.bacteriohora*. Artificial selection has also been successful in selecting entomopathogenic nematodes for increased infectivity at low temperature and increased nematicide resistance. Genetic selection of *H. bacteriophora* strain HP88 resulted in an 8-9 fold increase in resistance to phenamiphos and avermectin, and 70 fold increase in resistance to oxamyl. The enhanced resistance was stable and continued even after the selection was relaxed. The challenges to selective breeding are (*i*) the selected strain may become laboratory adapted, (*ii*) relaxed selection may lead to loss of a field-adapted trait, and (*iii*) an overall fitness cost to the animal.

Hybridization. The transfer of beneficial genes by hybridization can provide a powerful approach for genetic improvement of entomopathogenic nematodes. Once beneficial traits are found in a natural population, and shown to be heritable, those traits can be combined through hybridization to produce superior strains. A trait for heat tolerance was transferred from *H. bacteriophora* strain designed IS5 discovered in the Negev Desert in Israel to the wild-type *H. bacteriophora* HP88 strain. The hybrid progeny were confirmed by use of a marker mutant isolate and by backcrossing. More importantly, there was no loss of fitness in the hybrid progeny relative to the parental strain.

Mutagenesis. The isolation of mutant nematodes with distinct morphological characteristics can serve as genetic markers for the analysis of mutants displaying desired traits or for the mapping of beneficial genes. *H. bacteriophora* is particularly suited for mutagenesis because it has a short generation time and is self-reproducing hermaphrodite. Homozygous development from a single parent allows pure lines to be obtained and maintained easily, and the appreciable male production of subsequent generations provides the vehicle for the exchange of genetic material between individuals. The *C. elegans* mutagenesis protocol, using ethyl methanesulfonate (EMS) has been routinely used in the development of entomopathogenic mutants. It has been demonstrated that in situations where a suitable and non-labour intensive screening method can be devised, chemical mutagenesis can provide an accessible, robust and inexpensive means of entomopathogenic nematode strain improvement. Mutagenesis aimed at induction of beneficial mutations is also a viable approach for genetic improvement as a desiccation tolerant mutant of *H. megidis* has been evolved. Overall, the use of mutagenesis has been under-exploited for improvement of entomopathogenic nematodes. However, the enormous amount of information available on mutations and genes in *C. elegans* should be invaluable for studying corresponding mutations and genes in entomopathogenic nematodes.

Genetic transformation. Genetic engineering of entomopathogenic nematodes offers a significant advantage over selective breeding and mutagenesis, making it possible to produce small defined beneficial changes in the genotype. A heat-inducible *Caenorhabiditis elegans* heat-shock gene, *hsp* 70A, has been transferred into *H. bacteriophora* HP88. The 70-kDa heat shock protein encoded by the gene enables cells to eliminate or renature proteins damaged by high temperatures. Overexpression of the gene results in an enhanced thermotolerance in transgenic nematodes. The transgenic nematodes were 18 times more tolerant of heat shock than wild type nemaodes. The genetically engineered *H. bacteriophora* had improved heat tolerant character without affecting other important characteristics like infectivity, reproductive capacity, etc. and the transgenic nematode was safe to mice when injected intraperitoneally. Although the transgene was inherited extrachromosomally, the transformation was stable for 15 generations. Desiccation and osmotic tolerance was enhanced in adult *S. feltiae* nematodes transformed using a heat-inducible promoter derived from *C. elegans* and the *tsp-1* gene. Beside using the nematode directly, another approach has been to use the 'toxin A' isolated from *Photorhabdus luminescens. Arabidopsis thaliana* was recently transformed to express the 'toxin A' gene at extremely high levels, and transformed plants had good insecticidal activity against at least one lepidopteran pest and moderate activity against a coleopteran pest.

Fungi

Genetic improvement in fungi can be used to enhance the pathogenicity and effectiveness in biological control. Various techniques such as mutagenesis, transformation using plasmid vectors and protoplast fusion are used for this purpose. This helps in combining the complimentary characteristics to enhance biological control. Protoplast fusion technique has been used to derive *Beauveria* strains, which were effective at lower temperature and humidity. Benomyl or carbendazim resistant isolates have been obtained by treating susceptible strains with ultraviolet light and mutagenic agents. A hybrid of *B. bassiana* was formed through protoplast fusion which could grow on benomyl and several antibiotics while parent material was susceptible to this fungicide and most of the antibiotics. Some hybrids proved more efficient in producing enzymes required to attack the insect cuticle. Similarly, hybrids were produced through protoplast fusion of diauxotrophic mutants of *B. bassiana* (entomopathogenic strain) and *B. sulfurescens* (toxicogenic strain), which were significantly different from parents in pathogenicity and some of the hybrids were hyper virulent and killed the insects more quickly.

The DNA mediated transformation of *M. anisopliae* to benomyl resistance using cosmid p50 which harbours *betatubulin* gene from *Neurospora crassai* and *ben A3* gene from *Aspergillus nidulans,* respectively, has also been obtained. The transformants were mitotically stable when subcultured on non-selective agar and retained the ability to infect and kill the larvae of *Manduca sexta* which will pave the way for concurrent use of this fungus with fungicide on the crop when needed.

M. anisopliae normally takes 5-10 days to kill a host insect. In order to enhance insecticidal efficacy, additional copies of the *PrI* gene, which encodes a subtilisin-like protease involved in host cuticle penetration were engineered into the genome of *M. anisopliae.* A constitutive promoter, *gpd* from *A. nidulans* was used to drive expression. Infection with the recombinant strains resulted in partial hydrolysis of hemolymph proteins and extensive melanization of the larvae. *PrI* was found to activate trypsins, which in turn activated the phenoloxidase system involved in initiation of the melanization process and tyrosine metalbolism in general. The larvae infected with the recombinant strains died from these effects 25 per cent sooner than the larvae infected with wild type *M. anisopliae* and feeding damage was reduced by 40 per cent. Although it would be possible to incorporate other insecticidal genes into *M. anisopliae,* use of homologous gene such as *PrI* may be more acceptable from a regulatory viewpoint.

COMMERCIALIZATION

The organisms that comprise the microbial pest control market are bacteria, viruses, fungi, nematodes and protozoa. The annual market for microbial pesticides has been steady at around £ 20-25 million. However, the scenario has changed during the last decade. While the current growth in the chemical insecticide market is around 1-2 per cent per annum, the growth in the microbial pest control market is now running at around 10 per cent per year. Some estimates have even projected growth for microbial pesticides to be as high as 25 per cent per annum.

Bacteria

Although more than 100 bacteria have been identified as arthropod pathogens, only *Bacillus thuringiensis* has achieved commercial success for pest suppression. This bacterium has been registered for use on a diversity of pests in over 100 different formulations throughout North America and Europe. Two other bacilli, *B. popilliae* and *B. sphaericus* have been used in more specialised niches, and are likely to undergo further commercial development in the future. The only nonbacillus microbial insecticide to have been registered for use on an insect pest comprises the application of *Serratia entomophila* to control the pastureland grub, *Costelytra zealandica,* in New Zealand. To date, bacterial pesticides have been used to control an enormous diversity of lepidopteran, dipteran and coleopteran pests in agriculture, forestry and public health.

Registration of Bts has been comparatively easier because they are naturally occurring insect pathogens with relatively less effects on non-target organisms. They have been registered for use on a wide variety of crops, including many niche markets not available to synthetic insecticides. The Bts are currently registered in USA on over 50 vegetable crops, 10 small fruits and berries, 20 nuts, citrus, pome and stone fruits, 9 legumes, 30 field crops, 15 herbs and spices, bedding plants, flowers, ornamentals, turf, forestry, landscape trees and shrubs, and various tropical crops. Most of the current products registered for the control of lepidopteran pests are based on Btk strain HD-1 (Table 5.3).

In India, the credit for production of an indigenous Bt product on a pilot scale in 1968 goes to Prof. S.K. Majumdar and his team of research workers at the Central Food Technological. Research Institute (CFTRI), Mysore and it was named as Lepidopterocide. Subsequently, indigenously isolated Bt strains were obtained from various crop pests at many places but no serious efforts were made to exploit these bacteria anywhere in India. Recently, the interest in production and utilization of these eco-safe locally available Bt isolates has again picked up. Several Bt-based products are being marketed in India by various agrochemical industries,

Table 5.3 Commercially available bacterial pesticides

Commercial name 1	Bacteria species 2	Producer 3
Lepidoptera		
Bactospeine	*B.t.kurstaki/* HD-1	Abbott
Biobit	*B.t.kurstaki/* HD-1	Abbott
Dipel	*B.t.kurstaki/* HD-1	Abbott
Florbac	*B.taizawai*	Abbott
Foray	*B.t. kurstaki/* HD-1	Abbott
XenTari	*B.t.aizawai*	Abbott
Cordalene	*B.t. kurstaki/* HD-1	Agrichem
BMP 123	*B.t. kurstaki/* HD 263	Becker
Biobest-Bt	*B.t. kurstaki/* HD-1	Biobest
Bacticide	*B.t. kurstaki/* HD-1	Cequisa
Worm Wipper	*B.t. kurstaki/* HD-1	Cape Fear Chemicals
Collapse	*B.t. kurstaki/* HD-1	Calliope
Baturad	*B.t. kurstaki/* HD-1	Cequisa
Condor	*B.t. kurstaki/* EG2348	Ecogen
Crymax	*B.t. kurstaki/* EG7841	Ecogen
Cutlass	*B.t. kurstaki/* EG2371	Ecogen
Lepinox	*B.t. kurstaki/* EG7826	Ecogen
Raven	*B.t. kurstaki/* EG2424	Ecogen
Ecotech Bio	*B.t. kurstaki/* EG2371	Ecogen/AgrEvo
Ecotech Pro	*B.t. kurstaki/* EG2348	Ecogen/AgrEvo
Jackpot	*B.t. kurstaki/* EG2424	Ecogen/Intrachem
Rapax	*B.t. kurstaki/* EG2348	Ecogen/Intrachem
Forwarbit	*B.t. kurstaki/* HD-1	Forward International
Bio-Worm Killer	*B.t. kurstaki/* HD-1	Green Light Co.
Bactospeine Koppert	*B.t. kurstaki/* HD-1	Koppert
Guardjet	*B.t. kurstaki/* Cry1Ac	Mycogen/Kubota
Maatch	*B.t. kurstaki/* Cry1Ac & *B.t. aizawai*/Cry1C	Mycogen
M/C	*B.t. aizawai*/Cry1C	Mycogen
M-Peril	*B.t. kurstaki/* Cry1Ac	Mycogen
MVP	*B.t. kurstaki/* Cry1Ac	Mycogen
MYPII	*B.t. kurstaki/* Cry1C	Mycogen
Bactec BT 16	*B.t. kurstaki/* EG 2348	Plato Industries
Bactec BT 32	*B.t. kurstaki/* HD-1	Plato Industries
Insectobiol	*B.t. kurstaki/* HD-1	Samabiol
Bactosid K	*B.t. kurstaki/* HD-1	Sanex
Soilserv BT	*B.t. kurstaki/* HD-1	Sil Serv Inc.
Agrobac	*B.t. kurstaki/* HD-1	Tecomag

Able	*B.t. kurstaki/* M-200	Thermo Trilogy
Agree	*B.t. aizawai/* GC-91	Thermo Trilogy
Costar	*B.t. kurstaki/* SA-12	Thermo Trilogy
Delfin	*B.t. kurstaki/* SA-11	Thermo Trilogy
Design	*B.t. aizawai/* GC-91	Thermo Trilogy
Javelin	*B.t. kurstaki/* SA-11	Thermo Trilogy
Thuricide	*B.t. kurstaki/* HD-1	Thermo Trilogy
Turex	*B.t. aizawai/* GC-91	Thermo Trilogy
Vault	*B.t. kurstaki/* SA-11	Thermo Trilogy
Larvo-Bt	*B.t. kurstaki/* HD-1	Troy Biosciences
Troy-Bt	*B.t. kurstaki/* HD-1	Troy Biosciences
Ringer BT	*B.t. kurstaki/* HD-1	Verdant Inc.
Safer BT	*B.t. kurstaki/* HD-1	Verdant Inc.
BT 320	*B.t. kurstaki/* HD-1	Wilbur Ellis Inc.
Diptera		
Bactimos	*B.t. israelensis*	Abbott
Gnatrol	*B.t. israelensis*	Abbott
Skeletal	*B.t. israelensis*	Abbott
VectoBac	*B.t. israelensis*	Abbott
VectoLex GC	*B. sphaericus*	Abbott
Acrobe	*B.t. israelensis*	American Cyanamid
Aquabac	*B.t. israelensis*	Becker Microbial
BMP	*B.t. israelensis*	Becker Microbial
Bactis	*B.t. israelensis*	Caffaro
BTI Granules	*B.t. israelensis*	Clarke Mos. Cont.
Prehatch SG	*B.t. israelensis*	Meridian
Vectocide	*B.t. israelensis*	Sanex
Summit Bactimos	*B.t. israelensis*	Summit Chemicals
Summit Mosquito Bits	*B.t. israelensis*	Summit Chemicals
Teknar	*B.t. israelensis*	Thermo Trilogy
Doom	*B. popilliae*	Fairfax
Coleoptera		
Ditera	*B.t. tenebrionis*	Abbott
Novodor	*B.t. tenebrionis*	Abbott
Raven	*B.t. kurstaki* (EG2424)	Ecogen
Invade	*Serratia entomophila*	Industrial Research Ltd.
M-Trak	*B.t. tenebrionis*/Cry3A	Mycogen
M-One	*B.t. sandiego*	Mycogen
Trident	*B.t. tenebrionis*	Thermo Trilogy

Source : Flexner and Belnavis (2000), Lewis (2007)

which are mainly effective against lepidopteran pests (Table 5.4). Pilot-scale production of *B.t. israelensis* has been successfully accomplished in 100 litre fermentation chambers in South India. Local strains of Bt are being investigated for development of bacterial insecticides in many agricultural universities/research institutes in India.

Table 5.4. *Bacillus thuringiensis* (Bt) products available in India

Bt variety	Trade name	Target pest(s)	Crop(s)
Bt var. *kurstaki*	Halt	Diamondback moth, lepidopteran caterpillars	Cabbage
	Biolep	Cotton bollworms	Cotton
	Bioasap	Cotton bollworms	Cotton
	Delfin	Cotton bollworms	Cotton
		Tobacco caterpillar	Castor
	Dipel	Cotton bollworms	Cotton
		Fruit borers	Tomato, brinjal, okra
	Biobit	Lepidopteran caterpillars	Several
Bt var. *galleriae*	Spicturin	American bollworm,	Cotton
		Tobacco caterpillar	Chillies
		Diamondback moth	Cabbage, cauliflower,
		Leaf folder	Rice
Bt var. *aizawai*	Xentari	Lepidopteran caterpillars	Vegetables
Bt var. *morrisoni*	Foil	Coleopteran beetles	Vegetables
	Novodor	Coleopteran beetles	Vegetables
	Trident	Coleopteran beetles	Vegetables
Bt var. *israelensis*	Vectobac	Mosquitoes	Breeding water
	Taknar	Black flies	Breeding water

Viruses

A number of viral pesticides have been registered for commercial use for control of lepidopteran pests of agricultural and horticultural crops (Table 5.5). However, the most successful use of viruses to date has been against the temperate forest pests where high damage thresholds and limited pest complexes exist. For example, both the pine sawfly, *Neodiprion sertifer* and Douglas fir tussock moth, *Orgyia pseudotsugata,* are successfully controlled by baculovirus pesticides. It is because these products are usually registered for use by government departments and they are not available to the general public. To date, no virus-based pesticides have been developed for the control of mosquitoes, flies or other dipteran pests.

The first viral insecticide to be developed for commercial use was the single-nucleocapsid nucleopolyhedrovirus of *Helicoverpa zea* (HzSNPV) registered in 1971. It was commercialized by International Minerals and Chemical Corporation (Virion-H®), who sold it to Sandoz (Elcar®) in the mid-1970s. Elcar was infective against all the major *Helicoverpa/Heliothis* species and provided efficient control of soybean, sorghum, maize, tomato, chickpea and navybeans. The advent of synthetic pyrethroids in late 1970s resulted in reduced interest in Elcar and production was stopped in 1982. However, during the last two decades several viral insecticides have been registered in different countries for use in pest control. HzSNPV is currently produced and marketed as Gemstar® by Thermo Trilogy. By far the most successful viral insecticide used to-

Table 5.5 Commercially available viruses for lepidopteran control

Commercial name	Viral species	Target pest(s)	Producer
Granupom	*Cydia pomonella* GV	Codling moth	AgroEvo
Carposin	*Cydia pomonella* GV	Codling moth	Agrichem
VPN-80	*Autographa californica* MNPV	Lepidopteran larvae	Agricola Ei Sol
Gusano	*Autographa californica* MNPV	Alfalfa looper	Thermo Trilogy
Polygen	*Anticarsia gemmatalis* MNPV	Velvet bean caterpillar, sugarcane borer	Agroggen
Capex 2	Andermatt Biocontrol	*Adoxophyes orana* GV	Summer fruit tortrix
Madex 3	*Cydia pomonella* GV	Codling moth	Andermatt Biochemical
Ness-A	*Spodoptera exigua* MNPV	Beet armyworm	Applied Chemical
Ness-E	*Spodoptera exigua* MNPV	Beet armyworm	Applied Chemical
Leconteivirus	*Neodiprion sertifer/ N. lecontei* MNPV	Sawfly larvae	Canadian Forestry Service
Multigen	*Anticarsia gemmatalis* MNPV	Velvetbean caterpillar, sugarcane borer	EMBRAPA
Monisarmio-virus	*Neodiprion sertifer/ N. lecontei* MNPV	Sawfly larvae	Kemira
Virin-EKS	*Mamestra brassicae* MNPV	Lepidopteran larvae	NPO Vector
Virin-GYAP	*Cydia pomonella* GV	Codling moth	NPO Vector
Carpovirusine	*Cydia pomonella* GV	Codling moth	NPP/Calliope
Mamestrin	*Mamestra brassicae* MNPV	Lepidopteran larvae	NPP/Calliope
Virox	*Neodiprion sertifer/ N. lecontei* MNPV	Sawfly larvae	Oxford Virology
Elcar	*Helicoverpa zea* SNPV	Heliothines	Novartis
Cyd-x	*Cydia pomonella* GV	Codling moth	Thermo Trilogy
Gemstar	*Helicoverpa zea* SNPV	Heliothines	Thermo Trilogy
Biotrol	*Helicoverpa zea* NPV	Heliothines	Thermo Trilogy
Not determined	*Anagrapha falcifera* MNPV	Lepidopteran larvae	Thermo Trilogy
Spod-X	*Spodoptera exigua* MNPV	Beet armyworm	Thermo Trilogy
Otienem-S	*Spodoptera exigua* NPV	Beet armyworm	Thermo Trilogy
Gypcheck	*Lymantria dispar* MNPV	Gypsy moth	U.S. Forest Service
TM Biocontrol-1	*Orygia pseudotsugata* MNPV	Douglas-fir tussock moth	U.S. Forest Service

Source :Flexner and Belnavis (2000), Lewis (2007)

date is the multi-nucleocapsid nucleopolyhedrovirus of *Anticarsia gemmatalis* (AgMNPV), applied to over 2 million ha annually for the control of velvet bean caterpillar, *Anticarsia gemmatalis,* in Brazil. In India, commercial formulations of NPVs of pests such as *Helicoverpa armigera* and *Spodoptera litura,* and GV of *Chilo influscatellus,* are widely available and used by the farmers.

Fungi

Of over 800 species of fungi known to be pathogenic to insects, only seven have been commercialized (Table 5.6). The first mycoinsecticide to be registered was *Hirsutella thompsonii* produced by Abbott Labs under the trade name of Mycar®. It received full registration in USA in 1981, which was cancelled in 1988. Subsequently, a British firm registered two strains of *Verticillium lecanii;* Vertalec® was effective against aphids and Mycotal® was targeted for the control of greenhouse whitefly. Currently, the most widely used fungal insecticide is *Beauveria bassiana.* There are at least three major strains of *B. bassiana* being marketed in USA, Europe and South America. *B. bassiana* strain Bb-147 is registered on maize (Ostrinil®) in Europe for the control of the European corn borer, *Ostrinia nubilalis* and the Asiatic corn borer, *Ostrinia furnacalis*. *B. bassiana* strain GHA is registered in USA for control of aphids, whitefly, thrips and mealy bugs (Mycotrol® and Botanigard®). *B. bassiana* strain ATCC 74040 is registered against many soft-bodied insects in the orders Homoptera and Coleoptera (Naturalis®).

There are currently two registered fungal insecticides in the genus *Metarhizium. M. anisopliae* is registered in USA for use in roach traps (Biopath®) and for control of termites (Bioblast®). *M. flavoviride* has been registered by the International Institute of Biological Control for the control of grasshoppers and locusts in Africa and the tropics. *Paecilomyces fumosoroseus* has recently been registered in USA for the control of whitefly, thrips, aphids and mites. Three species of fungi, viz. *B. bassiana, M. anisopliae* and *Paecilomyces* sp. are currently commercially available in India.

Nematodes

More than 300 nematode-insect relationships have been described to-date. However, mainly two families of the nematodes, Heterorhabditidae and Steinernematidae, have been extensively used to develop commercial formulations. The first commercially available formulation was *Romanomermis culicivorax,* which was registered against mosquitoes in USA in 1976. The registration was subsequently cancelled due to the success of alternative products. Currently, there are eight species of nematodes (7 for insect pests and 1 for slugs) that are available for pest control (Table 5.7). These are from three genera and are being sold/and or manufactured

Table 5.6 Commercially available fungi for insect control

Commercial name	Viral species	Target pest(s)	Producer
Ago Bio. Bassiana	*Beauveria bassiana*	Soft-bodied insects	Ago Biocontrol
Ago Bio. Metarhizium 50	*Metarhizium anisopliae*	Coleoptera & Lepidoptera	Ago Biocontrol
Ago Bio. Verticillium 50	*Verticillium lecanii*	Greenhouse pests	Ago Biocontrol
Laginex AS	*Lagenidium giganteum*	Mosquitoes	Agraquest Inc.
Engerlingspilz	*Beauveria brongniartii*	*Hoplochelis marginalis* & *Melolontha melolontha*	Andermatt
Lagenidium giganteum	*Lagenidium giganteum*	Mosquitoes	CA Dept. of Health
Bay Bio 1020	*Metarhizium anisopliae*	Soil inhabiting beetles and termites	EcoScience
BioBlast	*Metarhizium anisopliae/* ESF 1	Termites	EcoScience

BiPath	*Metarhizium anisopliae/* ESF 1	Cockroaches	EcoScience/ Terminex
Green Muscle	*Metarhizium flavoviride*	Grasshoppers & locusts	Int. Inst. Biol. Cont.
Mycotal	*Verticillium lecanii/* whitefly strain	Whitefly	Koppert
Vertalec	*Verticillium lecanii/* aphid strain	Aphids	Koppert
Botanigard	*Beauveria bassiana*/GHA	Whitefly, thrips, aphids, & mealy bugs	Mycotech
Mycotrol	*Beauveria bassiana*/GHA	Whitefly, thrips, aphids, & mealy bugs	Mycotech
Betel	*Beauveria brongniartii*	*H. marginalis* & *M. melolontha*	NPP/Calliope
Ostrinil	*Beauveria bassiana/* Bb-147	*Ostrinia nubilalis* & *O. furnacalis*	NPP/Calliope
PFR-97	*Paecilomyces fumoso-roseus/* Apopka 97	Whitefly, thrips, aphids & spider mites	Thermo Trilogy
Naturalis	*Beauveria bassiana/* ATCC 74040	Homoptera, Coleoptera, & Heteroptera	Troy Bioscience
Naturalis-L	*Beauveria bassiana*	Homoptera, Coleoptera & Heteroptera	Mycotech
Naturalis-O (ornamentals)	*Beauveria bassiana*	Homoptera, Coleoptera & Heteroptera	Mycotech
Naturalis-T (turf)	*Beauveria bassiana*	Homoptera, Coleoptera & Heteroptera	Mycotech

by over a dozen companies offering 36 different products. The attributes of these nematode based formulations that make them amenable to production and use are ease of mass production, efficacy comparable to synthetic pesticides and safety to non-target organisms.

Table 5.7 Commercially available nematodes for insect control

Commercial name	Nematode	Target pest(s)	Producer
1	2	3	4
Dickmaulrussler-nematoden	*Heterorhabditis megidis*	Soil insects primarily *Otiorhynchus sulcatus*	Andermatt
Traunem	*Steinernema feltiae*	Sciarid flies, and other soil insects	Andermatt
EcoMask	*S. carpocapsae*	Root weevils, cutworms, fleas, borers, fungus gnats	BioLogic
Heteromask	*H. bacteriophora*	*Popillia japonica* larvae and other insects	BioLogic
Hortscan	*S. carpocapsae*	Root weevils, cutworms, fleas, borers, fungus gnats	BioLogic
Termask	*S. carpocapsae*	Termites	Biologic
Scanmask	*S. feltiae*	Sciarid flies, and other soil insects	Biologic/IPM Laboratories
Nema-BIT	*H. bacteriophora*	*P. japonica* larvae and other insects	BIT

Cruiser	*H. bacteriophora*	*P. japonica* larvae and other insects	Ecogen
Otinem S	*S. scapterisci*	Mole crickets	Ecogen
Nema-top	*H. bacteriophora*	*P. japonica* larvae and other insects	e-nema
Nema-green	*H. bacteriophora*	*P. japonica* larvae and other insects	e-nema
Nema-plus	*S. feltiae*	Sciarid flies, and other soil insects	e-nema
Steinernema glaseri	*S. glaseri*	White grubs	Greenfire
Guardian	*S. carpocapsae*	Root weevils, cutworms, fleas, borers, fungus gnats	Hydro-Gardens
Lawn Patrol	*H. bacteriophora*	*P. japonica* larvae and other insects	Hydro-Gardens
Steinernema glaseri	*S. glaseri*	White grubs	Integrated Pest Management
Larvanem	*H. megidis*	Soil insects primarily *O. sulcatus*	Koppert
Entonem	*S. feltiae*	Sciarid flies, and other soil insects	Koppert
Sciarid	*S. feltiae*	Sciarid flies, and other soil insects	Koppert
Nemasys	*S. feltiae*	Sciarid flies, and other soil insects	MicroBio/Biobest
Nemasys-H	*H. megidis*	Soil insects primarily *O. sulcatus*	MicroBio/Biobest
Nemasys-M	*S. feltiae*	Sciarid flies, and other soil insects	MicroBio/Biobest
Nemaslug	*Phasmarhabditis hermaphrodita*	Slugs	MicroBio
Heterorhabditis megidis	*H. megidis*	Soil insects primarily *O. sulcatus*	Neudorff
Steinernema carpocapsae	*S. carpocapsae*	Root weevils, cutworms, fleas, borers, fungus gnats	Neudorff
Steinernema feltiae	*S. feltiae*	Sciarid flies, and other soil insects	Neudorff
Exhibit SC-WDG	*S. carpocapsae*	Root weevils, cutworms, fleas, borers, fungus gnats	Novartis BCM
Exhibit SF-WDG	*S. feltiae*	Sciarid flies, and other soil insects	Novartis BCM
Steinernema glaseri	*S. glaseri*	White grubs	Praxis
Bio Safe WG	*S. glaseri*	Root weevils, cutworms, fleas, borers, fungus gnats	Thermo Trilogy
Millennium	*S. carpocapsae*	Root weevils, cutworms, fleas, borers, fungus gnats	Thermo Trilogy
Savior WG	*S. carpocapsae*	Root weevils, cutworms, fleas, borers, fungus gnats	Thermo Trilogy

Magnet	*S. feltiae*	Sciarid flies, and other soil insects	Thermo Trilogy
X-Gnat	*S. feltiae*	Sciarid flies, and other soil insects	Thermo Trilogy
Bio Vector 355	*S. riobrave*	Root weevils, mole crickets, and plant nematodes	Thermo Trilogy
Devour	*S. riobrave*	Root weevils, mole crickets, and plant nematodes	Thermo Trilogy

Source : Flexner and Belnavis (2000)

In general, steinernematids and heterorhabditids have shown excellent results in habitats where high humidity could be maintained, e.g. soil inhabiting insects and borers. *Steinernema glaseri* is still marketed in USA for grub control by Praxis.

S. ribobrave has recently been registered by Thermo Trilogy for the control of mole crickets, *Scapteriscus* spp.; sugarcane rootstalk borer, *Diaprepes abbreviatus* ; citrus root weevil, *Pachnaeus litus*, and the blue-green weevil, *P. opalus*. *S. scapterisci*, which was isolated from mole cricket in South America, was originally produced by BioSys (now Thermo Trilogy), who licensed it to Ecogen. There are two species of heterorhabditids that are currently commercially available. *Heterorhabditis megidis* is sold mostly in Europe for weevil and soil insect control. *H. bacteriophora* is effective against a wide range of soil insects but is sold primarily for the control of Japanese beetle.

In India, both steinenematidis and heterorhabditids are marketed by Bio-Sense Crop Protection (Eco-Max Agrosystems Ltd.), Mumbai. *Steinernema* sp. is commercially available for the control of Amercian bollworm, pink bollworm, tobacco caterpillar, white grub, shoot borer, stem borer, tuber moth, spotted bollworm and leaf eating caterpillar on crops like cotton, groundnut, sugarcane, rice, potato, tomato, chilies, okra, sunflower and legumes. *Heterorhabditis* sp. is available for the control of white grub, flea beetle, grey weevil, and red palm weevil on groundnuts and coconut.

Protozoa

At present, there is only one registered protozoan insecticide targeted against grasshoppers and the Mormon cricket. The microsporidian *Nosema locustae* is known to infect at least 60 species of grasshoppers and crickets. It is sold in the western USA as Nolo Bait® by M & R Durango and Grasshopper Control Semaspore Bait® by Beneficial Insectary. Both the products are formulated on bean that is consumed by the grasshoppers. However, the utility of *N. locustae* as a grasshopper control agent remains questionable and after more than a decade of use, its field effectiveness in USA, Canada and Africa is known to vary. Moreover, protozoan formulations are very expensive to manufacture and tend to cause chronic rather than acute infections.

STRATEGIES FOR UTILIZATION OF MICROBIALS

There are four basic strategies for using microbial pathogens in insect pest management.

Introduction and Establishment

The introduction and establishment of microbials in an environment is intended to result in permanent suppression of the target pest. Most of the successes of viruses in insect control have been by this method. There have been at least 16 successful introductions of viruses, 5 in row crops and 11 in more stable ecosystems primarily forests. In the 1930s, an NPV of the European spruce sawfly, *Gilpinia hercyniae* was introduced accidentally into Canada alongwith parasitoids, which were imported from Scandinavia and released for control of the pest. Later this NPV was also multiplied and applied in selected locations. The NPV was remarkably successful and no control measures have been required against the pest in Canada for the last 50 years. Its success was attributed to the relative stability of the forest ecosystem and host populations as well as to efficient horizontal and vertical transmission of the virus. Later, the European pine sawfly, *Neodiprion sertifer* and the red-headed pine sawfly, *N. lecontei* were also successfully controlled with one or two introductions of respectiveNPVs into field populations. AnNPV of *Chrysodeixix includens* is possibly the best example of a baculovirus implemented as a classical biological control agent in a crop. ThisNPV was released on 200-250 ha of soybean in USA and provided control 12-15 years later.

Milky disease bacterium, *Bacillus popilliae,* has been successful microbial control agent against the Japanese beetle, *P. japonica* on turfs and pastures. The bacterial spores once established in the soil either through natural dispersal or application persist in the soil through recycling for many years. *Steinernema scapterisci* from South America was successfully introduced into Florida for the control of mole cricket pests in large scale field trials.

Seasonal Colonization

It is a modification of the introduction and establishment approach. It involves the incoculative release of microbial pathogens to control insect pests for more than one generation, although subsequent releases are required when the pathogen populations decline. It requires efficient replication and transmission of the pathogen in host populations. Most important example is the control of velvet bean caterpillar, *Anticarsia gemmatalis* on soybean by application of AgNPV. The virus is applied on 2 million ha annually in Brazil. TheAgNPV occurs naturally in Brazil in *A. gemmatalis* populations with pathogenesis similar to other NPVs. Currently, it is produced directly on the farmers' fields. It involves virus application on soybean infested with *A. gemmatalis* larvae, collection of the dead larvae, and storage in large rooms at –4 to –8°C until processed as a formulation. Cost of the formulated product is US$ 0.7 per ha and it reaches the farmer at a mean cost of US$ 1.2–1.5 per ha, which is lower than the cost of chemical insecticides. Considering that the cost of AgMNPV is about 20-30 per cent lower than the average cost of chemical insecticides and that the virus usually provides control during the season with only one application, compared with an average of two applications for chemical insecticides, the economic returns from the use of virus may reach approximately US$ 7.0 per ha per season.

Another notable success is the use of non-occluded virus of the rhinoceros beetle, *Oryctes rhinoceros* on coconut palms in the Pacific Islands. The virus is spread by releasing infected adults of the beetle in the field. The infected adults do not feed but are attracted to breeding and feeding sites. The virus is also transmitted during mating when the uninfected adult ingests virus-laden faecal material from its sexual partner. The GV of *Plodia interpunctella,* a pest of stored grain and grain products, has potential for long-term control in storage bins. The GV is protected from environmental extremes and persists in the stored grains.

Environmental Manipulation

It involves changing the host habitat to favour conservation or augmentation of pathogens in a system where they either occur naturally or have been introduced. Modified cultural practices enhance prevalence of pathogens in insect populations by aiding in persistence or assisting their transport from the soil to the insects' feeding substrate. These practices include changes in cultivation, grazing, sowing and chemical use to increase natural control of *Wilseana* sp. by NPV in New Zealand pastures. Movement of cattle similarly enhanced NPV transport and natural control of *Spodoptera frugiperda* in Louisiana pastures. Environmental manipulation has also been found useful for enhancing the efficacy of non-occluded virus in case of rhinoceros beetle on coconut palms. Viral spread and control of the beetle populations are enhanced if some of the dead palms are left standing and others are piled and overgrown with crops rather than left lying around the plantation. Sites having a relatively high air humidity have more fungal epizootics of insects than neighbouring dry sites and are predisposed to the use of fungi. Shade trees in coffee plantations facilitated fungal epizootics of *Coccus viridis* and *Saissetia coffeae* by *Cephalosporium* species.

Microbial Pesticides

Most microbial pathogens are suitable for use as microbial pesticides. The industry also has maximum interest in this approach, because the multiple applications create the best opportunity for product sales. *B. thuringiensis* is a classical example of a microbial pesticide. It is being produced by a number of commercial companies for use against pests of agricultural crops, stored products, forestry as well as against pests of medical and veterinary importance. The NPVs and GVs of lepidopteran caterpillars as well asNPVs of several species of saw flies provide short-term control comparable to that obtained with conventional insccticides. Some of the species of fungi, protozoa and nematodes are also being utilized as microbial insecticides on a variety of crops. The estimated market for bioinsecticides in 1995 was US$ 380 million including $ 3-4 million for viruses. By 2000, the market for bioinsecticides was predicted to have increased by $116-141 million, with viruses making up $ 5-6 million of the total. Presently, the microbial biopesticides account for 2–5 per cent of the world pesticide market. The market is dominated by products based on *B. thuringiensis* and nematodes, which occupy about 90 per cent of the total share of microbial pesticides.

CONCLUSIONS

Current problems with the use of chemical insecticides and emphasis on low-input sustainable agriculture, have pushed the microbial agents to the fore-front for use in IPM systems. The microorganisms provide certain distinct advantages over many other control agents or methods. The major advantage of exploiting microorganisms for pest control is their environmental safety primarily due to the host specificity of these pathogens. Microorganisms have natural capability of causing disease at epizootic levels due to their persistence in soil and efficient transmission. Many insect pathogens are compatible with other control methods including the chemical insecticides and parasitoids. The cost of development and registration of microbial insecticides is much less than that of chemical insecticides. There is minimum effect on non-target organisms. There is a long-term regulation of a pest population in most of the cases whereas in others fairly a good check of pest population has been established. Their large-scale culture and application is relatively easy and inexpensive in most cases. Generally, resistance in insects to pathogens is not developed, however, it may develop slowly as compared to insecticides.

Many problems arise in the use of microorganisms for pest control. The relatively slow speed with which microorganisms kill their hosts has hampered their effectiveness as well as acceptance by potential users. This time period may be 7 days or more in case of viruses. A wide range of environmental factors affects the efficacy of microbial insecticides. Development of resistance to viruses and *B.thuringiensis* is a matter of serious concern although resistance seems to be less stable than most cases of chemical-insecticide resistance. However, the use of both naturally occurring and genetically engineered microorganisms may increase their effectiveness against the less susceptible species. It is necessary to correctly time the applications as most pathogens cause disease after a definite incubation period, which varies in different stages of insects. In view of the marked specificity of certain insect pathogens, spectrum of effectiveness is narrowed down. While this may be desirable from the point of view of their use in IPM, this is also the major reason for their being not economically competitive with chemical insecticides. It is necessary to maintain the virulence and viability of the pathogens till use. Some pathogens like protozoa and viruses are difficult to mass-produce. Until *in vitro* techniques are developed for mass production of viruses, the production process will remain laborious and costly.

Recent accelerated growth of microbial pesticides emanates from their relatively improved performance and cost competitiveness in the face of ever-increasing arthropod resistance to chemical insecticides, environmental hazards and lack of synthesis of new pesticidal chemical molecules. More recently, major agrochemical companies have taken a greater interest in biopesticides, particularly microbial pesticides. However, detailed studies are required to understand the basic host-pathogen relationships for effective use of entomopathogens in IPM. A better understanding of the mechanisms of microbial control activity is necessary if rational strain improvement is to become a reality in case of all entomopathogens. There is a need to understand the ecology of indigenous pathogens and exploit their attributes to manage a pest insect.

The main areas for improvement of microbial pathogens comprise production and environmental stability. In order to increase the utility of microbial pathogens in IPM programmes, systematic surveys should be undertaken in different agro-ecological zones to identify naturally occurring pathogens. Detailed studies are necessary on the properties, mode of action and pathogenecity of insect pathogens. Ecological studies on the dynamics of diseases in insect populations are necessary because the environmental factors play a significant role in development of diseases and ultimate control of insect pests. Efforts should be made to minimize the loss in infectivity of certain pathogens due to photo-inactivation. Studies on safety of insect pathogens to higher animals, beneficial insects and plants should be undertaken. Finally, interaction of insect pathogens with other methods of pest control should be thoroughly studied to develop better IPM strategies. The self-perpetuating nature of most of the pathogens in both space and time would certainly prove to be an asset in sustainable agriculture.

☆☆☆☆☆

BOTANICAL PEST CONTROL

INTRODUCTION

Insects and plants originated almost simultaneously about 500 million years ago, and ever since both these groups of organisms have been fighting for their survival. This fight is still on between the attacker (insect) and the attacked (plant). During this long evolutionary history of attacker and attacked, plants have developed ways and means to combat attacker. Plants cannot run away nor can they fight physically, hence nature during this evolutionary period provided plants with highly sophisticated in-built defense mechanisms to resist/desist attack by insects and other pests. The greatest testimony that they are not helpless is that even the plant species considered most susceptible survive well in the nature. Of the various defense mechanisms developed, chemicals elaborated by the plants are the most important for defense. Plants are nature's 'chemical factories', providing the nature's richest source of chemicals on earth.

The chemicals that plants produce to protect themselves against insect attack belong to a group that includes compounds known as secondary plant substances. These chemicals are a subset of what are known as phytochemicals (plant-based chemicals). Within the context of pest control, they are referred to as botanical pesticides. Secondary plant substances are produced as byproducts of major biochemical pathways and chemically, they include alkaloids, terpenoids and phenolics as well as a number of other compounds. These chemicals repel approaching insects, deter feeding and oviposition on the plants, disrupt behaviour and physiology of insects in various ways and even prove toxic to different developmental stages of many insects.

Botanical pesticides are either naturally occurring plant materials or products derived rather simply from such plant materials. In their simplest form, botanical pesticides may be crude preparations of plant parts ground to produce a dust or powder that may be used full-strength or diluted in carrier such as clay, talc or diatomaceous earth. Only slightly more sophisticated are water extracts or organic solvent extracts of insecticidal components of plants. These extracts or resins are then prepared as liquid concentrates or applied to talc or clay to use as insecticidal dusts. The most processed forms of botanical pesticides are purified insecticidal compounds that are isolated from plant materials by a series of extractions and distillations.

HISTORICAL PERSPECTIVE

The use of plants as pesticides has been practiced since times immemorial. For thousands of years, people in India placed neem leaves in their beds, books, grain bins, cupboards and closets. The Hindu book, the *Rig Veda,* written in India in 2000 BC, makes a mention of the use of poisonous plants for pest control. It is quite probable that the exploitation of the toxicological properties of plants has an even older history. Prior to the onset of agriculture, local peoples had already deified trees and many plant-based extracts were believed to possess special powers, particularly for healing. With the development of agriculture, links would have rapidly been made between food production and pest control. These links might have provided an opportunity for this specialised knowledge to be used directly for protection of crops against pests.

Crude botanical pesticides have been used for several centuries and were known in tribal or traditional cultures around the world before being introduced to Europe. Those with long histories of traditional use include neem in India, rotenone in East Asia and South America, pyrethum in Persia (Iran), and sabadilla in Central and South America (Table 6.1). The explorations of the New World and the opening of trade routes with Asia led to the exploitation of pesticidal plants. For example, the first explorers of the Americas observed that native Indians in Venezuela were using the powdered seeds of lily, *Sobadilla officinarum,* to protect crops against insect attack. This led to the export of this crop to Europe and to the use of the extract for pest control up to the middle of the twentieth century. Similar events happened with the discovery that nicotine was widely used in North America for pest control, that quassia (from *Quassia amara*) was widely used in Central America and the sweet flag (*Acorus calamus*) was widely used in China and India.

Table 6.1 Botanical pesticides traditionally used for pest control in agricultural crops in different countries

Pesticide	Main source	Country/Region
Neem	*Azadirachta indica* A.Juss.	India
Dharek	*Melia azedarach* L.	China, India
Pyrethrum	*Tanacetum cinerariaefolium* (Treviranus)	Middle and near East; later introduced into Europe
Rotenone	*Derris elliptica* (Roxb.) Benth. *Lonchocarpus nicou* (Aubl.) DC *Tephrosia vogelli* Hook f. *Amorpha fruticosa*	East Africa, China South America Eastern and Southern Africa, China China
Nicotine	*Nicotiana tabacum* Linnaeus *N. rustica* Linnaeus *N. glauca*	Europe Europe Argentina, Uruguay
Ryanodine	*Ryania speciosa* Vahl.	South America
Pellitorine	*Anacyclus pyrethrum* DC	Algeria
Quassin	*Quassia amara* L.	Central America, Brazil
Sabadilla	*Sabadilla officinarum* Brant, *Veratrum sabadilla* Retz.	Venezeula, Central and South America, Mexico

The earliest documented examples of plants being used as pesticides occur in China, Egypt, Asia and Europe. None of these uses involved large-scale commercial production of botanical pesticides till the sixteenth century when European explorers began to discover the plants that the native cultures were using for pest suppression. Widespread commercial use of botanical pesticides in Western Europe and North America continued from the sixteenth century till the Second World War. From the late 1800s to the 1940s, botanical pesticides were used extensively on several high value fruit and vegetable crops in USA. Nicotine-based insecticides were prominent before 1900, whereas pyrethrum, rotenone, sabadilla, and ryania became more popular in the 1930s and 1940s. Beginning in the 1940s and 1950s, the discovery and increasing development of synthetic insecticides led to virtual abandonment of botanical pesticides in commercial agriculture in most of the developed countries. Some large scale plant screening programmes did take place throughout the 1940s, 1950s and 1960s, particularly in the USA and China. Although many of these programmes identified a number of potentially useful extracts, most lacked sufficient funding to be sustained. However, in the 1980s and 1990s, there was a renewed interest in the use of botanical pesticides, primarily because of the environmental problems created by the widespread use of synthetic pesticides.

PROMISING PLANT SPECIES

Plants are biochemists *par excellence.* During their long evolution plants have synthesized a diverse array of chemicals to prevent their colonization by insects and other herbivores. It is estimated that there are about 2,50,000 to 5,00,000 different plant species in the world today. Only 10 per cent of these have been examined chemically indicating that there is enormous scope for further work. Over the years, more than 6000 species of plants have been screened and more than 2500 plant species belonging to 235 families were found to possess biological activity against various categories of pests (Table 6.2). The highest number of pesticidal plants belong to Meliaceae (>500), followed by Myrtaceae (72), Asteraceae (70), Euphorbiaceae (63), Leguminosae (60), Fabaceae (57), Ranunculaceae (55), Apocyanaceae and Rutaceae (39 each), and Rosaceae (27). This number seems to be far less than the actual number of naturally occurring pesticidal plants as this is just 0.77 per cent of the total 3,08,000 species of plants or 0.87 per cent of 2,75,000 species of flowering plants. It is thus likely that novel and potent

Table 6.2 Type of pest control activity reported in various plant species

S.No.	Pest control activity	No. of species of plants	S.No.	Pest control activity	No. of species of plants
1.	Insecticidal	1053	9	Fungicidal	100
2.	Antifeedant	230	10	Bactericidal	4
3.	Repellent	225	11	Molluscicidal	6
4.	Growth inhibitor	32	12	Herbicidal	14
5.	Attractant	27	13	Antiseptic	35
6.	Rodenticidal	29	14	Fish poison	147
7.	Acaricidal	2	15	Arrow poison	90
8.	Nematicidal	58	16	Poisonous	69

Source : Grainge and Ahmed (1988)

molecules that can be used for pest suppression remain to be discovered from many plant species.

Plants are known to produce a diverse range of secondary metabolites such as terpenoids, alkaloids, polyacetylenes, flavonoids, unusual amino acids, sugars, etc. The structures of more than 600 alkaloids, 3000 terpenoids, several thousands of phenylpropanoids, 1000 flavonoids, 500 quinones, 650 polyacetylenes, and 4000 amino acids have already been elucidated. Many of these chemicals protect the plants from pests and pathogens. But in addition to high insecticidal activity, plant species must possess some other characteristics for development into an ideal botanical insecticide, viz. safety to plant and animal life, biodegradability with sufficient residual action, ready availability of the plant or capability for cultivation with a reasonably short gestation period, economical isolation procedures for the active component(s) or capacity for formulation of crude extracts obtained from plant parts, and yield products of consistent quality.

Some of the insecticidally promising plants alongwith their bioactive components and the types of effects produced in target pests are listed in Table 6.3. The most promising ones suitable for development as botanical pesticides are discussed here.

Neem

Neem, *Azadirachta indica* A. Juss. (Fam. Meliaceae) is indigenous to India from where it has spread to many Asian and African countries. For centuries, the tree has been held in esteem by Indian folk because of medicinal and insecticidal value. A breakthrough in the insecticidal application of neem was made by Pradhan *et al.* (1962) who successfully protected the standing crops at Indian Agricultural Research Institute, New Delhi, by spraying them with 0.001 per cent neem seed kernel suspension during a locust invasion. Due to its legendry insect-repellent and medicinal properties, it has been identified as the most promising of all plants by the National Research Council, Washington, USA. Neem has assumed the status of an international tree which is evident from the fact that it has been a subject of discussion at nine global conferences, viz. Rottach-Egern, Germany (1980), Rauischolzhausen, Germany (1983), Nairobi, Kenya (1986), Bangalore, India (1993), Queensland, Australia (1996), Vancouver, Canada (1999), Mumbai, India 2002), Kunming, China (2006) and Coimbatore, India (2007).

All parts of the neem tree possess insecticidal activity but seed kernel is the most active. Neem bark, leaf, fruit and oil as well as extracts with various solvents especially ethanol have been found to exhibit activity against insect pests. Neem products exhibit almost every conceivable type of activity against insects (Fig. 6.1). Till today, 450 to 500 species of insects have been tested with neem products at global basis and 413 of these are reportedly susceptible at different concentrations (Table 6.4). The repellent and antifeedant effects of neem have been reported against a wide range of insect pests including desert locust, *Schistocerca gregaria* ; migratory locust, *Locusta migratoria*; rice planthoppers, *Nilaparvata lugens* and *Sogatella furcifera*; rice leaf folder, *Cnaphalocrocis medinalis*; ear cutting caterpillar, *Mythimna separata*, etc. It has been found that even starved *N. lugens* avoided feeding on plants sprayed with neem oil and spent most of their time searching for suitable sites. Concentrations ranging from 0.001 to 0.4 per cent of various neem seed kernel (NSK) extracts have generally been found to deter feeding of most of the insects evaluated so far.

The growth inhibitory effects of neem derivatives result in various developmental defects and even mortality. The larvae of various lepidopteran and coleopteran pests like *Plutella*

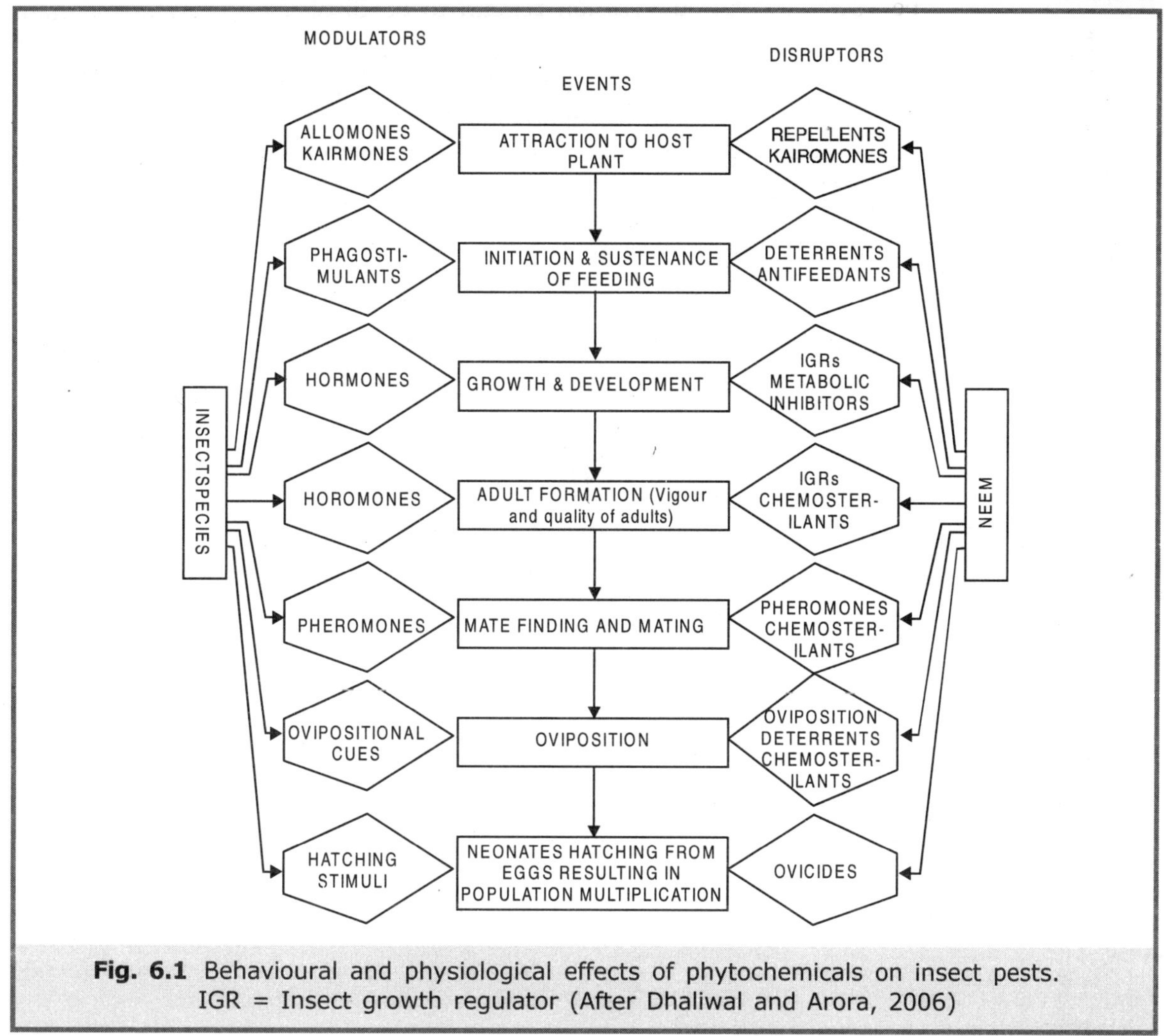

Fig. 6.1 Behavioural and physiological effects of phytochemicals on insect pests. IGR = Insect growth regulator (After Dhaliwal and Arora, 2006)

xylostella, Spodoptera frugiperda, Helicoverpa zea, Pectinophora gossypiella, Epilachna varivestis and *Ephestia kuehniella* show impaired development on neem treated diet. The developmental abnormalities could be attributed to reduced feeding and/or disturbances in the neuro-endocrine system of insects caused by azadirachtin.

Neem products also affect insect vigour, longevity and fecundity. Females of *E. varivestis* and *Leptinotarsa decemlineata* were sterilized by neem compounds, while reproductive maturation was inhibited in *N. lugens* males. At higher concentrations, most females did not emit normal male eliciting signals. During the last decade, neem products have been found to act as ovipositional deterrents for *Bactrocera cucurbitae, H. armigera, Spodoptera litura, Callosobruchus* spp., etc. Ovicidal activity of neem products has been reported in *Corcyra cephalonica, Earias vittella* and *S. litura*. Strong contact effects of neem oil leading to transformation of gregarious nymphs to intermediate and solitary forms have been recorded in locusts. Direct contact toxicity of neem products has been demonstrated against termites, *Macrotermes* sp. and aphids, *Lipaphis erysimi* and *Rhopalosiphum nymphae*, etc.

Table 6.3. Selected list of promising plant species with pesticidal properties

S.No.	Plant	Family	Biologically active Component (s)	Insect pest (s)	Type of activity
1	2	3	4	5	6
1.	*Acarus calamus*	Araceae	*Trans*-asarone, *cis*-asarone, isoasorone	*Athalia proxima*, *Tineola bisselliella*	Antifeedant, repellant, toxicant
2.	*Aglaia elaeagnoidea*, *A. Odorata*	Meliaceae	Rocaglamide, aglaroxin A	*Spodoptera litura*, *Helicoverpa armigera*	Toxicant
3.	*Allium sativum*	Amaryllidaceae	Diallyl sulfide, diallyl trisulfide	*Culex pipiens*, *Epilachna varivestis*, *Plutella Xylostella*, *S. litura*	Antifeedant, repellent, toxicant
4.	*Annona squamosa*	Annonaceae	Annonacin, annonin, annonelliptine, annonidines, asimicin	*Attagenus megatoma*, *Aphis fabae*, *Dicladispa armigera*	Feeding deterrent moderately toxic
5.	*Azadirachta indica*. *A. indica siamensis*, *A. excelsa*	Meliaceae	Limonoids, azadirachtins, salanin, nimbin	*Schistocerca gregaria*, *H. armigera*, P. *Xylostella*	Antifeedant, oviposition deterrent, behaviour and physiological disturbances, toxicant
6.	*Citrus limon*	Rutaceae	Limonin, nomilin, obacunone	*Helicoverpa zea*, *Leptinotarsa decemlineata*, *P. Xylostella*	Antifeedant, toxicant
7.	*Curcuma longa*	Zingiberaceae	Termerone, dehydrotermerone, a-phellandrene	*Spilarctia obliqua*, *P. Xylostella*, *Tribolium castaneum*	Growth inhibitor, oviposition deterrent, toxicant
8.	*Melia azedarach*, *M. toosendan*, *M. Volkensii*	Meliaceae	Tetranor triterpenoids, tossendanin, meliandiol, melianone, meliantriol, nimbolidin A, volkensin	*S. litura*, *P. Xylostella*, *Bemisia tabaci*, *H. armigera*	Antifeedant, oviposition deterrent, antifertility, toxicant
9.	*Mentha spicata*	Labiatae	Carone, pulegone, menthol	*Earias insulana*, *Microcerotermes* crassus	Antifeedant, toxicant
10.	*Nerium oleander*	Apocynaceae	Cardiotonic, oleandrin, neridin	*S. gregaria*, *Lymantria dispar*	Antifeedant, toxicant
11.	*Nicotiana tabacum*	Solanaceae	Nicotine, nornicotine, analbasine	Soft bodied insects like aphids, thrips, whiteflies, leafhoppers, mites, etc.	Contact toxicant, fumigant

12.	*Parthenium hysterophorus*	Astoceae	Parthenin	*Dysdercus ungulaturs*, *S. litura*, Callosobruchus Chinensis	Feeding deterrent, growth inhibitor
13.	*Piper nigrum*	Piperaceae	Piperine, pipericide, guinesseine, retrofractamide, dehydropipericide, pellitorine, piperlonguminine	H. zea, *Anthonomus grandis*	Toxicant, oviposition deterrent
14.	*Pongamia pinnata*	Fabaceae	Karanfin	*S. litura, Papilio demoleus, Nilaparvata lugens, Rhyzopertha dominica*	Antifeedant, juvenile hormone agonist, toxicant repellent
15.	*Quassia amara*	Simaroubaceae	Quassin	*Heliothis virescens, E. varivestis*	Antifeedant, toxicant
16.	*Ryania speciosa*	Flacourtiaceae	Ryanodine, dehydroryanodine	*Cydia pomondla, Ostrinia nubilalis S. Liture*	Feeding deterrent, repellent toxicant
17.	*Schoenocaulon officinale*	Literature	Cevadine, veratridine	Vegetable and fruit pests, particularly squash bug and citrus thrips	Toxicant
18.	*Tanacetum cinerariaefolium*	Asteraceae	Pyrethrins, cinerins, jasmolins	House flies, mosquitoes, fleas, lice, etc.	Quick knock
19.	*Tephrosia vogelii*	Fabaceae	Rotenone, tephrorin, 5-methoxy isolon chocarpin	*Chilo partellus, spodoptera littoralis, Eldana saccharina*, household pests	Feeding deterrent
20.	*Zingiber officinale*	Zingiberaceae	Gingerdione, paradole, gingerol, shogaol	*S. obliqua*	Antifeedant, growth inhibitor

Source. Dhaliwal and Koul (2007)

Table 6.4 Number of neem sensitive insects in different orders

India		World	
Order	**Number**	**Order**	**Number**
Coleoptera	28	Blattodea	6
Dictyoptera	1	Caelifera	21
Diptera	9	Coleoptera	79
Hemiptera	23	Dermaptera	1
Hymenoptera	1	Diptera	49
Isoptera	1	Ensifera	3
Lepidoptera	32	Heteroptera	32
Orthoptera	5	Homoptera	50
Siphonaptera	1	Hymenoptera	8
Thysanoptera	2	Isoptera	6
		Lepidoptera	136
		Phasmida	1
		Phthiraptera	4
		Siphonaptera	4
		Thysanoptera	13
Total	**103**		**413**

Source : Singh (2000)

Nearly 100 protolimonoids, limonoids or tetranor-triterpenoids, pentanortri- terpenoids, hexanortriterpenoids and some non-terpenoids have been isolated from various parts of the neem tree and still more are being isolated. Azadirachtin

(Fig. 6.2), the most important biologically active component of neem shows phagorepellent and toxic effects at 0.1 to 1000 ppm when incorporated into diets of different insect species. Azadirachtin was synthesised in the laboratory by scientists of the University of Cambridge (UK) in 2007, after 22 years of research when structure of azadriachtin was determined in 1985.

Inspite of these impressive strides, large scale practical utilization of neem in pest management still faces several hurdles. There is an urgent need to characterize best ecotypes of neem tree for different environmental conditions. Intensive breeding and selection work needs to be undertaken for economic production of various high quality raw materials required for insecticide production. The development of new techniques for harvesting, depulping, drying and storage of neem seeds is a necessary pre-requisite for large scale production of neem-based pesticides.

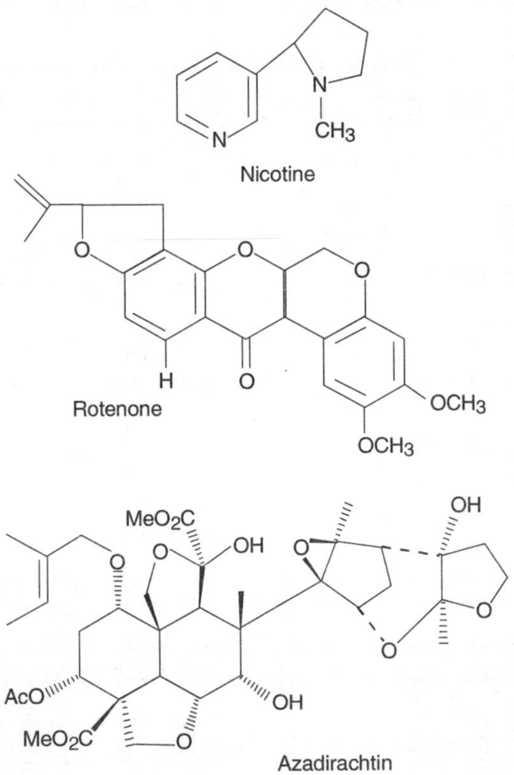

Fig. 6.2. Structures of nicotine, rotenone and azadirachtin.

Ironically, the neem tree itself is attacked by 60 species of insects besides mites, nematodes, mammals and 16 phytopathogens. Some of these like *Pulvinaria maximaAonidiella orientalis, Helopeltis antonii* and *Rhizoctonia solani* are already causing serious damage in some areas. As commercially high quality genotypes are introduced on a large scale, the pest and pathogen problems may be aggravated. It is, therefore, imperative that the neem ecosystem is thoroughly studied to manipulate various biological components and cultural practices to keep the damaging organisms in check. Another problem facing the utilization of neem is the phytotoxic effects recorded in several crops, viz. cabbage, onion, muskmelon, potato, tobacco, tomato, etc. Dose-response relationships need to be worked out for all the crops where neem products appear to be useful for use in IPM.

Commercialization of neem-based pesticides is expanding at a rapid rate. Nearly one hundred products are either being marketed or are awaiting commercialization in India (Table 6.5). However, lack of standardized and reliable formulations is an important constraint in increased use of neem products for pest control. To overcome these difficulties, the Central Insecticides Board in 1991 approved the guidelines and data requirements for registration of neem based pesticides. Formulated neem products are required to contain at least 1500 ppm of a.i. azadirachtin in kernel based formulations and 300 ppm in neem oil based ones. Recently, neem formulations with 10,000 and 50,000 ppm of azadirachtin have been introduced. Surveys conducted in India have shown that farmers usually buy commercial products, which are also difficult to obtain in the local market. Improved local production units, which incorporate inexpensive equipment and chemicals would probably make neem pest control attractive to many more farmers.

Table 6.5 Commercially produced neem-based pesticides in India

Trade name	Formulation(s)	Manufacturer
1	2	3
Achook	0.5% aza, nimbicinol, epinimbocinol	Godrej Agrovet Ltd., Mumbai
Aphidin	Soapy humus extract	Eco-Max Agroecosystems Ltd., Mumbai
Aza	0.15% aza	SOM-IPM Systems (India) Ltd., Hyderabad, A.P.
Azadit	0.3% aza	Pesticides (India) Ltd., Udaipur, Rajasthan.
Bioneem	0.03% aza	Ajay Biotech Laboratories Pvt. Ltd., Pune, Maharashtra
Bionema	—	Bioved Research & Communication Centre, Allahabad, U.P.
Biopest	0.15% aza	Bioved Research Society, Allahabad, U.P.
Biosol	Oil	A.V. Thomas Pvt. Ltd., Chennai, Tamil Nadu
Econeem, Econeem Karnataka	0.3% aza, 1.0% aza,	Margo Biocontrol Pvt. Ltd., Bangalore,
Plus, Ecotin, Tricure	5.0% aza, 0.03% aza	
Field Marshal	0.3% aza	Khetiwadi Corner, Shiyabave, Vadodra, Gujarat
Fortuna Aza	0.15% aza	Fortune Biotech Ltd., Hyderabad, A.P
Jai Neem	0.03% aza	Jai Chemicals, Faridabad, Haryana
Jawan	0.03% aza	Mc DA Agro. Pvt. Ltd., Mumbai
Jeevan Crop Protector	0.05% aza	Mc DA Agro. Pvt. Ltd., Mumbai

Juerken	0.03% aza	Madurai Chemicals and Agro Industries Ltd., Madurai, Tamil Nadu
Limonool Bangalore,	75EC (0.03% aza)	Bio-Multi Tech Pvt. Ltd., Ganganagar, Karnataka
Margocide-CK	20 EC (0.15% aza)	Monofix Agro Products Ltd., Hubli, Karnataka
Margocide-O	80 EC (0.03% aza)	Monofix Agro Products Ltd., Hubli, Karnataka.
Neem Gold Ltd.,	0.15% aza	Southern Petrochemical Industries Corporation Chennai, Tamil Nadu
Neem Hit	0.15% aza	Sky Lark Agro Chemicals, Thane, Maharashtra
Neem Oil	0.03% aza	Six Agro Research Laboratories, Mumbai
Neem Oil	2% aza	National Organic Chemical Industries Ltd., Mumbai.
Neem Plus	0.15% aza	B.D. Keathen & Co., Mumbai
Neem Top	0.03% aza	Sri Krishna Co., Coimbatore, Tamil Nadu
Neemactine	0.15% aza	Wockhardt Ltd., Mumbai
Neemarin 1.0% aza	0.03%, 0.15%, 0.5%,	Biotech International Ltd., New Delhi
Neemark	0.03% aza	West Coast Herbochem Pvt. Ltd., Bangalore, Karnataka
Neemax	Seed powder (300 ppm aza)	Eco-Max Agrosystems Ltd., Mumbai
NeemAzal-F	5% aza	E.I.D. Parry (India) Ltd., Chennai, Tamil Nadu
Neemgaurd	0.03% aza	Garda Chemicals Pvt. Ltd., Mumbai
Neemicide	300 ppm aza	Sanvardhini Agro Pvt. Ltd., Satara, Maharashtra
Neemocide	0.03% aza	Vinayak Fats & Proteins (P) Ltd., Kolkatta
Neemol	0.03% aza	Ramson Laboratories, Vijayawada, A.P.
Neemolin	0.15% aza	Khatau Agro. Tech., Mumbai
Neemosan	0.03% aza	Agronule Industries, Trichy, Tamil Nadu
Neemox	80% EC aza	Parkash Farm Chemicals, Mumbai
Neempourn	0.15% aza	Prabhakar Oil Mills, Trichy, Tamil Nadu
Neemrich	0.03% aza	National Chemical Laboratory, Pune, Maharashtra
Neemta	0.15% aza	A.J. Chemicals, Kisan Brothers Pvt. Ltd., Ahmedabad, Gujarat.
Neethrin	0.03% aza	Amitul Agro Chem. Pvt. Ltd., Gorakhpur, U.P.
Nim-76	0.05% aza	Defence Institute of Physiology & Applied Sciences, New Delhi.
Nimbasal	0.15% aza	Nimba Foods & Agro Chemicals Division, New Delhi.
Nimbasal	0.03% aza	Pesto-Chem India Ltd., New Delhi
Nimbecidine	0.03% aza	T. Stanes & Co., Coimbatore, Tamil Nadu
Nimbitor (ZA-199)	0.03% aza	Zandu Pharmaceutical Works Ltd., Mumbai
Nimbo Bas Pennadam	0.03% aza, 0.15% aza	Basarass Biocontrol Research, Eraiyur R.S., Cuddalore Distt., Tamil Nadu

Nimbosol	0.15% aza	Victoria Laboratories, Salem, Tamil Nadu
Nimlin	0.03% aza	Sunline Agro Chemicals Pvt. Ltd., Dhulia, Maharashtra
Ozoneem	300, 1500, 3000, 10,000, 50,000 ppm aza	Ozobiotech Pvt. Ltd., Faridabad, Haryana
Phytowin	0.03% aza	Phyto Products Ltd., Thiruthparipoondi, S.A. District, Tamil Nadu
Rakshak	0.15% aza	Murkumbi Bio Agro Pvt. Ltd., Belgaum, Karnataka
RD-9 Repelin	100 EC aza, *Pongamia, Annona*	I.T.C. Limited, Hyderabad, Andhra Pradesh
Replin 555	93 EC aza	Micro Chemicals Ltd., Madurai, Tamil Nadu
Shaktiman	0.03% aza, nimbin	Gujarat Krishna Bio-Tech. Pvt. Ltd., Rajkot, Gujarat
Shaktiman	0.05% aza	Osho Worship Centre, Rajkot, Gujarat
Sukrina	0.03% aza, meliantriol	Conster Chemicals Ltd., Adayar, Tamil Nadu
Suneem	0.03% aza	Sunida Exports Ltd., Mumbai
Swaticure	0.03% aza	Swathi Industries Ltd., Mumbai
Tric	0.03% aza	Amitul Agro Chem. Pvt. Ltd., Gorakhpur, U.P.
Vapacide	0.03% aza	Indian Institute of Chemical Technology, Hyderabad, A.P.
Wellgro	0.03% aza	I.T.C. Limited, Rajahmundry, A.P.

Many times neem products have shown inconsistent results in the field. The products available in the market and/or prepared locally vary widely in quality and quantity of different active components. A survey of neem oil samples in Canada revealed that 2 samples completely lacked detectable amounts of azadirachtin while remaining samples contained 200 to 4000 ppm (0.02-0.4%) azadirachtin. In another study, one sample containing 6800 ppm was also detected. There is an urgent need to monitor market samples of neem products so that farmers are able to get consistent and reliable results while using neem based pesticides.

Chinaberry

Melia azedarach L., commonly known as *Dharek*, Chinaberry tree, China tree, Persian lilac or 'Pride of India' is a close relative of neem tree. Very strong antifeedant effects of the tree against locusts (*S. gregaria*) were discovered during the locust invasion of Palestine in 1915. It was observed by an adolescent, Rachel Shpan-Gabrielith, that while all other vegetation was nearly completely devoured, the Persian lilac, was almost undamaged. Subsequently, laboratory studies by her established that the foliage remained untouched by locusts even after one week of starvation. The hot water extracts of the plant applied to wheat bran also prevented feeding by the locusts. She subsequently successfully used this technique to save several crops during later invasions (1945, 1951) by locusts.

The work on active principles established that several tetranortriterpenoids (limonoids) related to azadirachtin were present in *M. azedarach*. The compounds isolated included melianone, melianol, meliantriol, tossendanin, meliacarpinin, etc. A wide range of behavioural, physiological and toxic effects were observed against several insect species including *Epilachna varivestis,Nilaparvata lugens,Mythimna separata, Plutella xylostella*, etc. Extracts in different solvents as well as pure compounds were found to exhibit phagodeterrent, oviposition deterrent, fecundity and longevity reducing, development disrupting and toxic effects. Limited work on natural enemies also revealed that Chinaberry products are comparatively safe to coccinellids and predatory mites, *Amblyseius sewsami*.

Chrysanthemum

Pyrethrum, derived from the dried flowers of *Tanacetum* (*Chrysanthemum*) *cinerariaefolium* (Fam. Asteraceae), has been used as an insecticide since ancient times. The original home of the plant is Middle and Near East. Its commercial use originated in Persia from where it was introduced to Europe, America and Japan in the nineteenth century. After the first world war, its cultivation was taken up in Africa and presently Kenya followed by Tanzania, Rwanda and Zaire are the major producers of pyrethrum. A related plant, Persian insect flower, *T. roseum*, is the basis of the pyrethrum industry in Papua New Guinea. Worldwide annual production of pyrethrum now averages 30,000 tonnes.

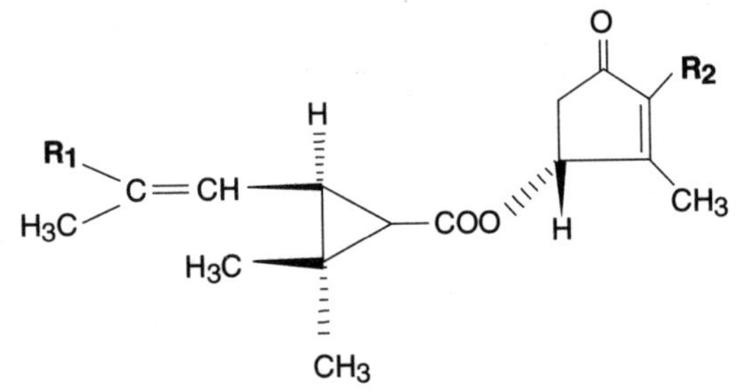

	R_1	R_2
Pyrethrin I	$CHCH_3$	$CH_2CH{=}CHCH{=}CH_2$
Pyrethrin II	$COOCH_3$	$CH_2CH{=}CHCH{=}CH_2$
Jasmolin I	CH_3	$CH_2CH{=}CH_2CH_3$
Jasmolin II	$COOCH_3$	$CH_2CH{=}CHCH_2CH_3$
Cinerin I	CH_3	$CH_2CH{=}CHCH_3$
Cinerin II	$COOCH_3$	$CH_2CH{=}CHCH_3$

Fig. 6.3. Structures of major insecticidal constituents of pyrethrum

Pyrethrum is a highly effective insecticide against common household insects. It is safe to mammals and is easily broken down to non-toxic metabolites. The insecticidal principals in pyrethrum comprise pyrethrins I and II, cinerins I and II, and jasmolins I and II (Fig. 6.3). Pyrethrin I is the most effective. Pyrethrins act quickly on the insect central nervous system, causing a knockdown effect. Addition of sesame oil or synergists like piperonyl butoxide enhances the insecticidal activity of pyrethrins. The use of pyrethrum in agriculture is mainly restricted to some vegetable and fruit crops due to its high cost and photo-instability. Efforts were, therefore, made from 1940s onwards to develop photostable analogues resulting in the development of synthetic pyrethroids.

Tobacco

Tobacco, *Nicotiana tabacum*, has been cultivated by the American Indians for at least 1000 years and it remained a part of their religious ceremonies. Long before people knew of nicotine alkaloid (Fig. 6.2) in tobacco, the latter was being used as a dust or water extract to control phytophagous insects, some three hundred years ago. Nicotine has by now been isolated from at least 18 species of plants. *Nicotiana rustica* containing 18 per cent nicotine is a better source than the more familiar *N. tabacum* containing 6 per cent nicotine. Many of these plants also contain the related alkaloids, nornicotine and anabasine. *N. glauca* grown in Argentina and Uruguay contains a higher amount of anabasine. Systematic use of nicotine sulphate started with the introduction of a standardized pesticide formulation containing 40 per cent actual nicotine around 1910. Before the second world war, nicotine sulphate was a very popular insecticide around the globe. With the advent of synthetic insecticides, it lost its ground due to less persistence and high cost. Now that interest in botanicals is being revived, nicotine sulphate has also resurged as a preferred pesticide.

On a world-wide basis, about 600,000 kg of nicotine sulphate and 75,000 kg of pure nicotine were being produced annually till recently, mostly in UK, India, Germany and the Netherlands. India manufactures around 800 tonnes of nicotine sulphate annually and exports the entire quantity to Japan and Europe. The cost may be a prohibitive factor in its use in India. But the pesticide could be obtained from 35-40 million kg of tobacco waste produced in the country annually. Recently, cost effective methods have been developed for extraction of nicotine sulphate from tobacco waste.

Nicotine sulphate is effective against a wide range of pests. Its efficacy against soft bodied insects like aphids is well known, but it has also been found effective against whitefly, thrips and bollworms in cotton; brown planthopper and green leafhopper in rice; grubs in brinjal, potato and cauliflower. Recently, nicotine sulphate (0.2 and 0.4 % a.i.) has been found highly toxic to eggs and neonate larvae of *Helicoverpa armigera* and *Spodoptera litura*. It was also found highly effective against *Bemisia tabaci* under field conditions.

Nicotine sulphate is safe to coccinellids but toxic to chrysopids. It does not leave any residue on the crop. However, its low persistence necessitates a repeated number of sprays for effective control of insects. It may prove very useful for use on fruit, vegetable and edible oilseed crops, where residues of pesticides are not acceptable.

Pongram

Pongamia pinnata (Syn. *P. glabra*), variously known as *karanja*, puna oil tree, Indian beech or Pongram is also indigenous to India. The active component in pongram has been identified as karanjin, a furaflavone. Karanja oil applied as a surface protectant effectively checked the infestation of pulse beetles, *Callosobruchus maculatus* and

C. chinensis and other storage pests like *Rhyzopertha dominica* and *Sitotroga cerealella*. A concentration of 1 per cent afforded complete protection even after 150 days and did not alter taste and smell of the grains. Pongamia cake was found effective in controlling the attack of ground beetles on tobacco. It also did not leave any of harmful residues in the soil. Pongamia cake water extract was found effective for protecting tobacco seedlings from *S. litura* damage.

The oil of karanja repelled brown planthopper in rice and significantly reduced its ingestion and assimilation of food. Both brown planthopper and whitebacked planthopper suffered heavy mortality but green leafhopper was less susceptible. Other pests which have been reported susceptible to powders or extracts of Pongamia are *Epilacha vigintioctopunctata, Amsacta moorei, Chilo partellus, Papilio demoleus, Leucopholis lepidophora,* etc. Various types of bioactivity observed were antifeedant, fecundity curtailing and toxicity.

Custard Apple

Annona squamosa and other related plants contain a number of mono- or sesquiterpenes like α-pinene, β-pinene, germacrene-D, etc. Powdered seeds applied to wheat and rice grains act as a protectant against *Sitophilus oryzae* and *C. chinensis*. The plant extracts act as a feeding deterrent against *A. moorei, Oncopeltus fasciatus, N. lugens, Dicladispa armigera, Nephotettix virescens, S. litura* and *E. vigintioctopunctata*. As with other botanical insecticides, disruption of growth, reduced oviposition, reduced adult emergence and moderate toxicity has also been observed in different species. Annonine, an alkaloid found in the stems and leaves of custard apple, has been found effective in checking the infestation by termites, root grubs, etc. Other compounds isolated recently which may prove to be biologically active are annonacin and annonidines.

Rotenone Containing Plants

Rotenone (Fig. 6.2) and related alkaloids occur in the roots of *Derris* and *Lonchocarpus* plants and in leaves and seeds of *Tephrosia* plants, all belonging to family Fabaceae. *Derris* is native to East Asia, *Lonchocarpus* to American tropics and *Tephrosia* to Eastern and Southern Africa. Traditionally, all these plants were used as fish poisons by the people for centuries. The commercially important species *Derris elliptica.* contains

4-5 per cent rotenone while *Lonchocarpus nicou* contains 8-10 per cent rotenone in dried roots. The vogel tephrosia, *Tephrosia vogelii* is regarded as a more promising source of rotenone than *Derris* and *Lonchocarpus*.

In addition to rotenone, these plants contain a number of other flavonoids like deguelin, tephrosin, elliptone, sumatrol, toxicarol, malaccol, etc., which show toxic as well as various behavioural and physiological effects on the insects. Low in mammalian toxicity, rotenone is mainly active as a contact poison with some action as a stomach poison. It mainly acts as a site I respiratory inhibitor. Its rapid degradation in sunlight has limited its utility in crop protection. Synthetic rotenoids have so far proved very costly because of the complex chemical structure.

EFFECTS ON NON-TARGET ORGANISMS

Natural Enemies

Work on the effect of botanical pesticides on non-target organisms has picked up only in recent years. The biological activity of neem products against natural enemies has been summarised in Table 6.6. The application of NSKE for the control of *S. litura* did not affect the emergence of the egg parasitoid, *Telenomus remus*, and predator, *Brinckochrysa scelestes*. However, longevity of the parasitoid was reduced in case of oviposition on pretreated egg masses. Topical application of seed oil of neem, Chinaberry and custard apple showed no adverse effect on predatory spider, *Lycosa pseudoannulata* and was only slightly toxic to the mirid bug predator, *Cyrtorhinus lividipennis* at and above 10 μg/female.

An active neem seed kernel fraction evaluated against sorghum pests was found to be safe to midge (*Contarinia sorghicola)* parasitoid, *Tetrastichus* sp. and predator, *Orius* sp. It was, however, toxic to *Apanteles ruficrus*, a larval parasitoid of *M. separata*. Field trials with neem oil for the control of sorghum aphid, *Melanaphis sacchari* did not show any adverse effect on syrphids and coccinellids.

Neem formulations, Repelin and Neemguard, were relatively safe at lower concentrations to the egg, larval and pupal parasitoids, viz. *Trichogramma australicum*, *Bracon hebetor* and *Tetrastichus israeli* of *Opisinia arenosella*. Repelin, Neemark and nicotine sulphate were safe to the predatory coccinellid, *Menochilus sexmaculatus* but highly toxic to its hyperparasitoid, *Tetrastichus coccinellae*. Neemark and Repelin worked as good acaricides against *Tetranychus macfarlanei* on okra, but were safer to predatory mites.

In laboratory trials with NSKE on bean leaf discs, predatory phytoseiid mite, *Phytoseiulus persimilis* was less affected than the casmine spider mite, *Tetranychus cinnabarinus*. In the same trials, predatory clubionid spider, *Chiracanthium mildei* was unaffected. Neem formulations, viz. Neemark, Repelin, Wellgro, neem seed kernel suspension (NSKS) and Neemrich did not show

Table 6.6 Effect of neem on parasitoids and predators

	Parasitoids			Parasitoids	
Species	**Neem concentration**	**Effect**	**Species**	**Neem concentration**	**Effect**
Telenomus remus	Aqueous NSKE (2%)	+	*Cyrtorhinus lividipennis*	Neem oil (3%), aqueous NSKE (5%)	+
Trichogramma pretiosum	NSKE (2.5% and 3%)	–	*Orius majusculus*	NeemAzal-T/S 1: 200, 1: 100, 1:50)	+
Trichogramma chilonis	Aqueous, ethanolic and hexane extracts NSK @ 0.3 to 5.0%	+ & -	*Coccinella septem-punctata*	NeemAzal and Rakshak Gold (0.5, 1.0 & 2.0 l/ha)	+
T. pretiosum	NSK based extract NIM-20	+	*Coccinella undecimpunctata*	Neem oil (1%)	+
T. chilonis	NeemAzal-F 5% (1 ml/lit), NeemAzal-T/S, NSKE (5%) (50 g/lit)	+	*Cryptolaemus montrouzieri*	NSKE (5%)	+
Diaeretiella rapae *Aphidius cerasieola*	NSKE (5%)	+	*Menochilus sexmaculatus*	Neem oil (20-200 ppm)	+
			M. sexmaculatus	NeemAzal and Rakshak Gold (0.5, 1.0 & 2.0 l/ha.	+
Bracon hebetor	Neem oil (5%)	+	*Brinkochrysa scelestes*	NSKE (2%)	+
B. hebetor	Repelin and Neemguard	+	*Chrysoperla carnea*	AZT-VR-K (1000 ppm) with mixture of neem oil (250-30,000 ppm)	+
B. hebetor	Aqueous, ethanolic and hexane extracts of NSK @0.3, 0.6, 1.2, 2.5 & 5.0%	+ & -	*C. carnea*	NeemAzal and Rakshak Gold (0.5, 1.0 & 2.0 l/ha	-
Diadegma semiclausum	NSKE (0.1-5%)	+			
Apanteles glomeratus	Higher concentration (40 ppm) of azadirachtin and of azadirachtin free fraction, and 50 and 100 ppm of enriched product	–	*Typhlodromus athiasae, Amblyseius barkeri A. zakuri*	Margosan-O, Azatin, Repelin	+
Tetrastichus israeli	Neem seed kernel suspension (5%) and neem oil 50 EC (3%)	+	*Lycosa pseudoannulata*	NSKE (5%), neem oil (3%) or aqueous extract of neem cake (10%)	+

- = Adverse effect, + = Beneficial or no effect

Source : Dhaliwal and Koul (2007)

toxic and ovicidal effects against the green lacewing, *B. scelestes* but acted as oviposition repellents against the females. On the other hand, nicotine sulphate was toxic to adults and showed ovicidal activity against the eggs of the lacewing. Parasitization of whitefly, *Bemisia tabaci* nymphs by *Eretmocerus* spp. was not affected by application of botanical insecticides, viz. mineral oil, neem oil, nicotine sulphate, saradine oil, etc.

The plant extracts of some rice varieties were found to be highly toxic to important rice pests including *Chilo suppressalis, Nilaparvata lugens* and *Sogatella furcifera* but were safe to predators of hopper complex, viz. *L. pseudoannulata* and *C. lividipennis*. In the rice field trials, application of neem seed bitters as ULV sprays had no detrimental effect on a number of natural enemies including the black cricket predator, *Mettioche vittaticollis*; ground beetle predator,

Ophionea nigrofasciata and lady beetle predator, *Conocephalus longipennis*. Predation of leaf folder, *Marasmia patnalis* eggs by *M. vittaticollis* was unaffected in treated fields. The parasitization of *Cnaphalocrocis medinalis* larvae was relatively unaffected in rice fields sprayed with 50 per cent neem oil (ULV application) than in control fields.

Normal male and female *Macrocentrus philippinensis* emerged from parasitized leaf folder, *C. medinalis* larvae which had been confined to rice leaf cuts treated with partially purified neem fractions. Similarly, emergence of braconid predator, *Lysiphlebus testaceipes* from parasitized aphids, *Aphis gossypii* was unaffected by application of Margosan-0 to *Hibiscus* leaf discs in laboratory studies. Neem oil 50 per cent sprayed at rates up to 20 ml of spray fluid (recommended rate 3 ml/l) had no adverse effect on *Chrysoperla carnea* and *Tetrastichus howardi*.

There have been reports indicating moderate to high adverse effects of neem products on natural enemies. Coccinellid predator, *Delphastus pusillus* preferred untreated eggs of *B. tabaci*. The emergence of aphelinid parasitoid, *Eretmocerus californicus* from treated *B. tabaci* was reduced by more than 50 per cent. Untreated whiteflies were attacked at a rate three times more than that for treated ones. Emergence of eulophid parasitoid, *Tetrastichus howardi* from pupae of *M. patanalis* treated with 1000 ppm neem seed bitters decreased. A dose of 50 μg/female of neem seed bitters proved lethal to the parasitoid, *Goniozus triangulifer*. The emergence of parasitoids from treated leaf folder, *M. patanalis* hosts as well as the fecundity of such parasitoids were reduced. Treatment of cocoons at 2.5 per cent or higher concentrations of neem oil reduced emergence of braconid parasitoid, *Apanteles plutellae* in the laboratory.

The population of sword-tail cricket predator, *Anaxiphla longicornis* was significantly reduced following application of neem oil in rice fields. Neem oil 50 per cent was found to be more toxic (LC50=2.88%) to the predatory black mirid, *Tytthus parviceps* than malathion. It also reduced the emergence and longevity of the scelionid parasitoid, *Telenomus rowani*. NSKE (5%) altered the sex ratio of *Telenomus howardi* adults that emerged from treated pupae of the striped stem borer, *Chilo suppressalis*.

Other Organisms

Recent studies have shown that neem leaf extract completely stopped aflatoxin production by *Aspergillus flavus* and *A. parasiticus*. These fungi which grow widely on various foods are one of the most deadly organisms on earth and the aflatoxins produced by them are highly carcinogenic. The use of neem for inhibiting aflatoxin production may open the door to a simple, inexpensive method for protecting stored foods using locally produced materials, even in the remotest villages.

Ground neem leaves and kernel incorporated in the potted soil showed positive effect on weight and survival of earthworms, *Eisenia foetida* but exerted a short-term repellency effect in slowing their entry into the soil. Both the neem products in the soil caused no negative side effects on nematodes. Applications of neem extracts alongwith urea resulted in a decline in the population of nitrifying bacteria.

Neem oil extracts at 0.005 per cent used as a mosquito larvicide were non-toxic to insectivorous fish, *Gambusia* sp. Concentrations upto 0.01 per cent were essentially non-toxic to the fish. However, at 0.04 per cent concentration, 80 per cent tadpole mortality was obtained within 24 h and 100 per cent in 48 h. The LC50 values of Margosan-0 to rainbow trout, *Salmo gairdneri* and blue sunfish, *Lepomis macrochirus*, 96 h after treatment were 8.8 and 37 mg/l of water, respectively. The 96 h no effect concentrations for the two species were 5 and 20 mg/l, respectively. Young guppies, *Lebistes reticulatus* tolerated 100 ppm AZI-VR-K/l of water. It has been reported that toxicity of Margosan-0 to fish and other aquatic organisms is caused by its petroleum oil content (15%) or probably another compound used for its formulatiom.

Margosan-0 is also toxic to the water flea, *Daphnia magna* and other invertebrates that inhabit stagnant water.

An IRRI-ADB project measured the effects of neem on several common aquatic species inhabiting tropical rice fields. Studies in the Philippines showed that the recommended dose (5%) of NSKE was toxic to Nile tilapia, *Oreochromis niloticus* but neem oil 50 per cent (3 ml/l) did not appear to harm the fish. In laboratory assays, the LC50 of neem oil for carp, *Cyprinus carpio* was 302.7 ppm 24 h after treatment. Studies in India found that NSKE or neem oil 50 per cent were non-toxic to Java tilapia, *Oreochromis mossambicus* when applied upto 0.01 per cent and *Bufo* sp. up to 0.1 per cent.

The feeding of water extract of neem berries to poultry birds resulted in toxicity symptoms like sluggish movement, dropping head, etc., and in many cases even death. The liver underwent degenerative changes with focal congestions, retention of bile in gall bladder and congestion of kidney with localized haemorrhages. The hepato- and nephro-toxic effects may prove lethal. Trial feeding of neem seed to starter chicken caused severe heptatitis with necrotic patches, mild to severe nephritis with congestion and slight inflammation in intestine. However, compared to synthetic insecticides, the toxic effects were produced at higher dosages. The acute LD50 of Margosan-0 to mallard duck, *Anas platyrhynchos* is 16.0 mg/kg. Acute oral LC50 of this compound to bobwhite quail, *Colinus virginianus* and mallard duck is in excess of 7000 ppm in a 5-day test period.

Traditionally, neem-based preparations have been used for the treatment of a wide range of disorders in domestic animals and livestock. Neem leaves contain appreciable amounts of protein, minerals and carotene, and adequate amounts of trace minerals except zinc. Incorporation of 20 per cent neem cake in sheep diet increased the growth rate. But neem leaves have also been reported to cause toxic effects on sheep, goats and guinea pigs. The acute oral LC50 of Margosan-0 against rat, *Rattus* sp. is 5.0 ml kg–1 and acute inhalation LC50< 43.9 mgl/h. *Lantana camara* is toxic to sheep when given orally at 60 mg/kg body weight. Affected animals show depression and anorexia, a few days after ingesting. Death occurs a few weeks later and may be due to renal failure.

Horses, cattle and sheep die after eating the leaves of *Nerium oleander* in quantities as little as 0.005 to 0.015 per cent of their body weight. Pyrethrum which was widely used before the advent of synthetic insecticides was safe to higher animals and there was never any casuality of a pet or a farm animal due to pyrethrum toxicity.

Man

Neem preparations have been used since ancient times in unani medicine for the treatment of a wide range of human ailments due to their anti-inflammatory, concoctive, blood purifying, anti-leprosy, anti-arthritic, anti-pyretic, anti-microbial and antihelminthic actions. Injections of sodium nimbidinate at 1 g and its oral administration up to 7 g to human beings did not produce any harmful effects. Cases of neem seed oil intoxication have, however, been reported. The intake of oil resulted in vomitting, drowsiness, metabolic acidosis, etc. It has been reported that the oil uncouples mitochondrial oxidative phosphorylation, thus inhibiting respiratory chain. Normal human cells in culture were not affected by neem extracts at 5 mg/ml while tumor-originated cells degenerated.

In USA, Margosan-0 underwent comprehensive toxicological tests prior to registration by US Environmental Protection Agency (EPA). Tests for skin irritation, inhalation, mutagenicity, and immune response were low enough to allow EPA registration. There have been a number of reports of death of children and adult human beings after consuming neem oil in South India. These poisonings apparently resulted because the neem seeds from which the oil was extracted had been contaminated with aflatoxin producing fungus, *Aspergillus flavus*. When extracted from clean and fungal-free seed kernels, neem oil did not cause any oral toxicity in laboratory rats at 500 mg/kg body weight.

Neem preparations have been found to have no teratogenic and carcinogenic effects. In the standard Ames mutagenicity test, azadirachtin showed no mutagenic activity on strains of *Salmonella thyphimurium* castellanichalmers. There are extensive records on human exposure and response to pyrethrum used as an insecticide and these establish the negligible hazards to the users of pyrethrum products. On the other hand, several other plants are known to be highly toxic to humans and other mammals. A single leaf of yellow oleander, *Nerium oleander,* is potentially lethal to humans. Affected persons become dizzy and drowsy, heart beat becomes progressively weaker and irregular leading to dyspnoea and coma.

ENVIRONMENTAL IMPACT

The use of botanical pesticides for plant protection has assumed greater importance in recent years all over the world due to environmental deterioration and health hazards associated with the use of synthetic pesticides. It is hoped that extensive use of plant-based pesticides in integrated pest management will help in conserving environmental quality.

The neem tree has answers to several environmental problems such as the rehabilitation of degraded ecosystem and wastelands, reduction in the use of agro-chemicals such as fertilizers and synthetic pesticides, and generation of income for all small farmers with limited resources. The neem-based pesticides are relatively safe and do not leave any residues on agricultural produce. As the pesticidal preparations using neem seeds, leaves or cake are very simple, farmers may make direct use of these products locally. The use of neem products for plant protection will help in minimizing atmospheric pollution and prevent food poisoning. It will also reduce the demand for costly chemical pesticides.

Neem oil has found a wide range of industrial applications in India. Due to its antiseptic properties, it has been a major ingredient in soaps for atleast 50 years. In addition, pharmaceutical preparations like emulsions, ointments, poultices and liniments as well as cosmetics such as creams, lotions, shampoos, hair tonics and gargles have been prepared. Neem toothpaste and neem sticks are also widely used for cleaning of teeth and as a mouth freshner. Neem oil is non-drying and is, therefore, used to grease cast wheels.

Neem is a valuable forestry species in India. Being a hardy species, it is ideal for reforestation programmes and for rehabilitating degraded, semiarid and arid lands and coastal areas. During a severe drought in Tamil Nadu during June-July, 1987, it was witnessed that neem trees remained luxuriant while all other vegetation dried up. Neem is useful as windbreaks and in areas of low rainfall and high windspeed, it can protect crops from desiccation. Neem is also a preferred tree along avenues, in markets and near homelands because of the shade it provides. It can grow in and even neutralize acid soils that plague much of the tropics. It may also act as an important source of fuel. Neem oil is burned in lamps. The wood has long been used in firewood. The husk from seeds produced as a waste during pesticide manufacture can also be used as fuel. The neem timber is durable and resistant to attack of termites and other pests. It can be used for making fence posts and poles for house constructions.

It is, thus, clear that all parts/products of the neem tree find a variety of uses in agriculture, and as raw materials for the manufacture of household articles, pharmaceutical preparations and other products. Even the industrial by-products have found application in agriculture and as fuel. Due to its successful cultivation even under adverse environmental conditions and utilization of all its products so that no waste material is left, neem growing can be an important component in environmental protection programmes.

PEST RESISTANCE TO PHYTOCHEMICALS

The naturally occurring phytochemicals exert a wide range of behavioral and physiological effects on insects and there is, thus less likelihood of development of resistance to these pesticides. Ironically, the neem tree itself is attacked by 60 species of insects besides mites, nematodes and 16 phytopathogens. Some of these like *Pulvinaria maxima, Aonidiella orientalis, Helopeltis antonii* and *Rhizoctonia solani* are already causing serious damage in some areas. This indicates that some insects might adopt to limonoids in the future but in laboratory tests two genetically different strains of the diamondback moth, *Plutella xylostella,* treated with neem seed extract showed no signs of resistance in feeding and fecundity tests up to 35 generations. In contrast, deltamethrin-treated lines developed resistance factors of 20 in one line and 35 in the other. There was no cross resistance between deltatamethrin and neem seed extract in the deltamethrin resistant lines. However, two lines of *Myzus persicae* of the same origin, when treated with pure azadirachtin, developed a 9-fold resistance to azadirachtin compared to non-selected control line after 40 generations.

Some resistance to pyrethrins has been reported among a few agricultural pests, particularly those with resistance to organochlorines, organophosphates and carbamates District. However, the diversity of neem compounds and their copmbined effects on insects seem to confer a built-in resistance prevention or delay mechanism in neem. Even then, the farmers should refrain from exclusive and extended application of single bioactive materials such as azadirachtin. Also, for durability sake, even novel neem-rich insecticides should be applied within the framework of integrated pest management programmes.

INTEGRATION WITH OTHER TACTICS

The use of pesticides of plant origin for the control of agricultural pests has a long history but has assumed greater importance in recent years due to environmental deterioration and health hazards associated with the use of synthetic pesticides. Botanical pesticides exert a range of behavioural and physiological effects on the colonization, development, growth, survival and multiplication of insects. In view of their environmental safety, these pesticides offer an attractive alternative to synthetic pesticides for use in IPM. Botanical pesticides can be integrated with the use of parasitoids and predators, microbial pesticides and even synthetic chemical pesticides to achieve greater efficiency in pest control.

The application of neem seed kernel extract (NSKE) for the control of *S. litura* did not affect the emergence of the egg parasitoid, *Telenomus remus*, and predator, *Brinckochrysa scelestes*. Topical application of seed oil of neem, Chinaberry and custard apple showed no adverse effect on predatory spider, *Lycosa pseudoannulata* and was only slightly toxic to the mirid bug predator, *Cyrtorhinus lividipennis* at and above 10 μg/female in rice crop. An active neem seed kernel fraction evaluated against sorghum pests was found to be safe to midge, *Contarinia sorghicola* parasitoid, *Tetrasictus* sp. and predator, *Orius* sp. It was, however, toxic to *Apanteles ruficrus*, a larval parasite of *M.separata*. Field trials with neem oil for the control of sorghum aphid, *Melanaphis sacchari* did not show any adverse effect on syrphids and coccinellids.

The plant extracts of some rice varieties were found to be highly toxic to important rice pests including *Chilo suppressalis*, *Nilaparvata lugens* and *Sogatella furcifera* but were safe to predators of hopper complex, viz., *Lycosa pseudoannulata* and *Cyrtorhinus lividipennis*. In the rice field trials, application of need seed bitters as ULV sprays has no detrimental affect on a number of natural enemies including the black cricket predator, *Mettioche vittaticollis*; ground beetle predator, *Ophionea nigrofasciata* and lady beetle predator, *Conocephalus longipennis*. Predation of leaf folder, *Marasmia patnalis* eggs by *M. vittaticollis* was unaffected in treated fields. The parasitization of *Cnaphalocrocis medinalis* larvae was relatively unaffected in rice fields sprayed with 50 per cent neem oil (ULV application) than in control fields.

Normal male and female *Macrocentrus philippinensis* emerged from parasitized leaf folder, *C. medinalis* larvae which had been confined to rice leaf cuts treated with partially purified neem fractions. Similarly, emergence of braconid predator, *Lysiphlebus testaceipes* from parasitized aphids, *Aphis gossypii* was unaffected by application of Margosan-0 to *Hibiscus* leaf discs in laboratory studies. Neem oil 50 per cent sprayed at rates up to 20 ml of spray fluid (recommended rate 3 ml/l) has no adverse effect on *Chrysoperla carnea* and *Tetrastichus howardi*.

Botanical pesticides have been found to be compatible with synthetic chemical insecticides. The use of neem formulations in combination with conventional insecticides resulted in better control of pink bollworm and spotted bollworm on cotton. The use of neem pesticides and alphamethrin on cotton proved as good as the sprays of alphamethrin alone in cheking the menace of bollworms and increasing the seed cotton yield. Similarly, alternate application of high potency neem-based insecticides and synthetic insecticides led to the effective management of cotton whitefly. Neem and other plant products have also been found to increase the efficacy of microbial control agents like baculoviruses, *B. thuringiensis* and fungi.

CONCLUSIONS

At present, many plant species are used for the production of pest control formulations. Some estimates put the number of plant species in use as source of botanical pesticides at over 2500. Despite this, it has been argued that resource poor farmers in many developing countries could make far more use of these free, naturally occurring products. The use of botanical pesticides offers several advantages over the synthetic pesticides.

As plants have developed these chemicals in response to the combined selection pressure of phytopathogens, insects and other herbivores, many of these pesticides are effective against diseases, nematodes and other organisms in addition to phytophagous insects. The naturally occurring phytochemicals exert a wide range of behavioural and physiological effects on the insects, and, therefore, it is difficult for insects to develop resistance to these pesticides. The limited number of studies conducted so far indicate that neem and other botanical pesticides are comparatively safe to natural enemies and higher organisms. The available evidence indicates that botanical pesticides are biodegradable in contrast to persistent synthetic insecticides. Many botanical pesticides can be developed from indigenous plants, and, therefore, it will save valuable foreign exchange. Moreover, village cooperatives can take up the formulation of locally available plants and, thus, farmers will be saved from spending large sums of money for the purchase of costly synthetic agrochemicals. There is great demand in international market for residue-free cotton garments, fruits, vegetables and beverages. The large scale utilization of botanical pesticides will certainly help us in meeting international standards of quality and safety in these products.

However, the large scale utilization of botanical pesticides in IPM is limited by several factors. Numerous species show some antifeedant/repellent activity. The identification of promising plant species suitable for utilization as botanical pesticides is, therefore, a difficult task. Standardized bioassay procedures need to be developed for efficient screening of plants for different types of toxic, morphogenetic, behavioural and physiological effects. The results obtained with botanical pesticides are usually inconsistent. In many cases this problem is due to a lack of quality control and could be overcome by developing suitable guidelines for registration of botanical pesticides. The mortality obtained is usually moderate and the required degree of control is not achieved in many cases. The trees like neem and *dharek* have to be planted many years in advance. There is a long gestation period and only after that can these trees be used for obtaining pesticidal products.

A lot of work needs to be done before large scale utilization of botanical pesticides in IPM becomes a reality. The programmes are needed to familiarise the farmers with the pesticidal properties of naturally occurring plants. Plants should be identified that can be used as source of botanical pesticides and their positive qualities should then be emphasised. For example, plants that can be used for pest suppression and also have additional complementary uses, should be preferred, which are often critical for convincing the farmers to grow such species. After identification of potentially useful species, intensive breeding and selection work will have to be undertaken for economic production of various high quality raw materials required for insecticide production. Simple formulation technology will have to be developed so that ready-to-use pesticides can be produced at the local level. Quality control in botanical pesticides is a major problem. There is wide variation in the quality and quantity of extractives obtained from a plant due to variation in ecotypes, environmental factors, etc. Such variations affect the performance and shelf life of formulated products. There is an urgent need to develop and prescribe suitable standards for registration of these products.

Phytotoxic effects of neem have been reported in a number of crops including cabbage, onion, mustard, muskmelon, potato, tobacco, and tomato. Dosage-response relationships need to be worked out carefully so that the farmers do not suffer any losses. The safety and selectivity of other botanical pesticides also should not be taken for granted. The new pharmacological and biochemical tools developed for evaluating the hazards of synthetic pesticides must be utilized for testing the promising botanical pesticides. These efforts will certainly enable us to identify selective, diverse, renewable, cheap and environmentally acceptable plant products from the repository of 'mother nature' for use in IPM programmes.

☆☆☆☆☆

CHAPTER 7 CHEMICAL CONTROL : PESTICIDES AND THEIR APPLICATION

INTRODUCTION

The cultural and other agro-technical practices are quite often not sufficient to keep the pests at such a level that economic losses are avoided. Therefore, chemical agents are resorted to both as preventive and curative measures to minimise the pest incidence and damage. The chemicals to combat different kinds of pests are called pesticides. Based on the target organisms, these pesticides are grouped into various categories, viz. insecticides (insects), herbicides (weeds), fungicides (fungi), nematicides (nematodes), rodenticides (rodents), etc. A good pesticide should be cheap to produce and potent against pests. It should not endanger the health of man and domestic animals, and should ultimately break down into harmless compounds, so that it does not persist in the environment. Prior to the World War II, mostly botanical and inorganic pesticides were used to fight the menace of pests. Subsequently, many of the potent synthetic organic pesticides were developed which revolutionised pest control in agriculture and public health.

HISTORICAL ASPECTS

The use of chemicals to control pests can be traced back to atleast 4000 years. For example, the *Rig Veda,* a Hindu book written in India in 2000BC, mentions the use of poisonous plants for pest control. For thousands of years, people in India placed neem leaves in their beds, books, grain bins, coupboards and closets to keep away the troublesome insects. The plants are known to be used as sources of insecticidal compounds by the Egyptians during the time of the Pharaohs. Ancient Romans are credited with having used false or white hellebore as a rodenticide. Homer, in 1000BC, makes a reference to the use of arsenic, soda or olive oil. The Arab scholar Abu Mansur in 970 AD, described over 450 plant products with toxicological and/or pharmacological properties.

In addition to the plant-based products, some inorganic compounds began to become more widely available and hence, more widely used. For example, arsenic mixed with honey was used as bait for the ants from the mid-1600s onwards. Copper arsenite, lead arsenate and calcium arsenate became widely available from the end of the nineteenth century onwards. In 1867, Paris green, a crystal compound of acetate and arsenate of copper, was successfully used for the control of Colordo potato beetle in USA. Another arsenic compound, lead arsenate, was first used against gypsy moth in USA in 1892. A number of other inorganic compounds containing sodium, mercury, copper and tin were also used as stomach poisons during this period. In the early 1900s, sodium fluoride and cryolite replaced some arsenicals because of lower phytotoxicity. Many of these inorganic chemicals had high mammalian toxicities and they acted as stomach poisons. Both these characteristics led to a decline in their use and they were eventually replaced by more selective and effective synthetic organic compounds.

The first synthetic organic insecticide to be developed and marketed was the dinitrophenol compound, potassium dinitro-o-cresylate. The insecticide was marketed in Germany in 1892, as a moth-proofing agent by Fredrich Bayer and Co. Further refinement of the molecule subsequently led to the synthesis of dinitro-orthocresol (DNOC), an insecticide that is still in use today. This is a non-systemic insecticide and acaricide that is toxic to moths, scale insects and spider mites.The second group of synthetic organic insecticides to be developed, comprises the alkyl thiocyanates, which were developed in 1930s. Some of these compounds are still in use today, although they have been replaced by safer compounds in many parts of the world. It is believed that these chemicals were never fully exploited as insecticides because of the dramatic success achieved by the compounds that superseded them (Table 7.1).

Table 7.1 Salient historical events in evolution of chemical control of pests

Year	Event(s)
Pre-scientific era	
1000 BC	Homer referred to sulphur, used in fumigation and other forms of pest control.
100 BC	The Romans applied hellebore for the control of rats, mice and insects.
900 AD	Chinese used arsenic to control garden insects.
1649	Rotenone used to paralyse fish in South America.
1690	Tobacco extracts used as contact insecticide.
1773	Nicotine fumigation by beating tobacco and blowing smoke on infested plants.
1787	• Soap mentioned as insecticide. • Turpentine emulsion recommended to repel and kill insects.
1800	• Persian louse powder (pyrethrum) known to the Caucasus. • Sprays of lime and sulphur recommended for insect control. • Whale oil prescribed as scalecide.
1820	Fish oil advocated as insecticide.
1822	Mixture of mercuric chloride and alcohol reommended for bed-bug control.
1825	Quassia used as insecticide in fly baits.
1848	Derris (rotenone) reported being used in insect control in Asia.
1854	Carbon disulphide tested experimentally as grain fumigant.
1867	Paris green used as an insecticide.
1868	Kerosene emulsions employed as dormant sprays for deciduous fruit trees.
1877	Hydrogen cyanide (HCN) first used as fumigant in museum cases.
1880	Lime sulphur used against San Jose scale in California.

1882	Naphthalene cakes used to protect insect collections.
1892	• Lead arsenate first prepared and used to control gypsy moth in Massachusetts, USA. • First use of a dinitrophenol compound, the potassium salt of 4-6-dinitro-o-cresol, as insecticide.
1897	Oil of citronella used as a mosquito repellent.
Pre-green revolution era	
1902	The value of lime sulphur for apple scab control discovered in New York, USA.
1907	Calcium arsenate in experimental use as an insecticide.
1909	First tests with 40% nicotine sulphate made in Colorado, USA.
1912	Zinc arsenite first recommended as an insecticide.
1922	Calcium cyanide begins commercial use.
1931	Thiram, first organic sulphur fungicide, discovered.
1932	Methyl bromide first used as a fumigant in France.
1936	Pentachlorophenol introduced as wood preservative against fungi and termites.
1938	TEPP, first organophosphate insecticide, discovered by Gerhardt Schrader.
1939	DDT discovered as an insecticide by Paul Muller in Switzerland.
1941	Hexachlorocyclohexane (HCH) (benzene hexachloride, BHC) discovered to be insecticidal in France.
1942	Introduction of 2, 4-D, the first of the hormone (or phenoxy) herbicides.
1943	First dithiocarbamate fungicide, zineb, introduced commercially.
1944	Introduction of 2, 4, 5-T for brush and tree control and warfarin for rodent control.
1945	Chlordane, the first of the persistent, chlorinated cyclodiene insecticides, introduced.
1946	First resistance in house flies to DDT observed in Sweden.
1947	• Toxaphene insecticide introduced, to become the most heavily used insecticide in U.S. agricultural history. • Passage of Federal Insecticide, Fungicide and Rodenticide Act (FIFRA).
1948	Aldrin and dieldin, first produced; the best of the persistent soil insecticides.
1949	• Captan, first of the dicarboximide fungicides, appears. • Synthesis of first synthetic pyrethroid, allethrin.
1950	• Malathion introduced, probably the safest organophosphate insecticide. • Maneb fungicide introduced.
1951	First carbamate insecticides, viz. isolan, dimetan, pyramat and pyrolan, introduced.
1952	Fungicidal properties of captan first described.
1953	Insecticidal properties of diazinon described in Germany.
1956	Introduction of carbaryl, the first successful carbamate insecticide.
1958	Atrazine, first of the triazine herbicides, and paraquat, first of the bipyridylium herbicides, introduced.
1961	Introduction of chlorophacinone rodenticide and mancozeb fungicide.
1962	Publication of *Silent Spring* by Dr Rachel Carson.
1964	Fungicidal properties of thiabendazole described.
1965	Development of Temikâ, first soil-applied insecticide-nematicide.

Green Revolution Era	
1966	• Carboxin, the first systemic fungicide, developed. • Methomyl insecticide and chlordimeform acaricide-ovicide introduced.
1967	Introduction of second group of systemic fungicides with benomyl.
1968	Discovery of tetramethrin, resmethrin and bioresmethrin, synthetic pyrethroids with greater activity than natural pyrethroids.
1969	Arizona (USA) places a moratorium on the use of DDT in agriculture.
1971	Glyphosphate herbicide first introduced.
1973	• Development of first photo-stable synthetic pyrethroid, permethrin. • Cancellation of virtually all uses of DDT by the EPA. • Registration of first JHA (Juvenile hormone analogue), Altosid for commercial use in USA
1975	Cancellation of all uses of aldrin and dieldrin, except as termiticides.
1983	EPA cancels most uses of ethylene dibromide.
1984	• EPA cancels most registrations for endrin. • Discovery of first neonicotinoid, imidacloprid.
1985	First registration of azadirachtin as an insecticide for non-food use.
Post-green revolution era	
1986	EPA cancels all agricultural uses of toxaphene.
1988	Chlordane and heptachlor use as termiticides cancelled.
1990	Azadirachtin uses expanded.
1991	• EPA cancels most uses for ethyl parathion due to human hazard. • The first neonicotinoid, imidacloprid, marketed for the first time.
1992	California creates state Environmental Protection Agency (CalEPA) in USA.
1993	Neemix® granted EPA exemption on food.
1994	California initiates 100% use reporting for all commercial pesticide applications.
1996	• US Federal Food Quality and Protection Act (FQPA) enacted. • The neonicotinoid, acetamiprid, commercially developed.
2001	The neonicotinoid, thiamethoxam, commercially developed.
2005	Flonicamid, a novel insecticide with a rapid inhibitory effect on aphid feeding was launched in the world market
2007	Azadirachtin synthesised in the laboratory by Dr Steven V. Ley and colleagues, University of Cambridge (UK).
2012	Sudan adopts cultivation of Bt cotton
2014	Commercial cultivation of Bt binjal (egg plant) allowed in Bangladesh, the first developing country in the world to grow a genetically engineered food crop.

Source: Modified from Dhaliwal and Koul (2010).

CLASSIFICATION OF PESTICIDES

Insecticides can be grouped in various ways, viz. according to the mode of their entry (stomach poisons, contact poisons and fumigants), their mode of action (physiological poisons, protoplasmic poisons, respiratory poisons and nerve poisons) or according to their chemical composition. As an insecticide may enter and act in an insect body in more than one way, it may be desirable to group them according to their chemical nature.

Chemically, the types of insecticides are : (*i*) elements, such as sulphur, phosphorus, thallium, mercury, etc.; (*ii*) inorganic compounds such as lead arsenate, sodium fluosilicate, zinc phosphide, Paris green, etc.; (*iii*) organic compounds; (*a*) compounds of plant origin such as pyrethrum, nicotine, rotenone, etc.; (*b*) animal and mineral oils such as fish oil, diesel oil, etc., (*c*) synthetic organic compounds such as DDT, malathion, carbaryl, etc.; (*iv*) poisonous gases such as hydrogen cyanide, ethylene dichloride, carbon tetrachloride, methyl bromide, phosphine, etc., used as fumigants.

For those interested in insect control, however, it is more meaningful to enlist these compound according to their mode of entry in the insect body and lethal action on the pests. The above mentioned compounds could, therefore, be rearranged under the following categories:

Stomach Poisons

Stomach poisons are generally used against insects with chewing type of mouthparts and under certain conditions against those with sponging, siphoning, lapping or sucking mouthparts. Some of these poisons are also mixed with food for killing higher animal pests, such as rodents, jackals and birds.

The stomach poisons are applied in many ways. The foliage or other natural food is thoroughly covered with poison or the poison is mixed with food along with an attractant, which makes the mixture very acceptable. Sometimes, these poisons are sprinkled in the runways of insects. As the insects move about, they pick up the poison on their feet or antennae and while cleaning these parts with mouth, they ingest the poison. Certain organophosphates act as systemic insecticides, which are taken up by the plant or animal system, and are translocated into tissues. When insect pests feed on these tissues, they die because of the poisoned cell sap.

For the stomach poisons to be acceptable in common use, they should have certain pre-requisites :

- ❐ The concentration which is applied to the plant for insect control should not be injurious to the foliage.
- ❐ The non-systemic compound should generally be insoluble in water, otherwise it might be absorbed through leaves and roots and, thus, poison the plants.
- ❐ It should be potent so as to kill the pest quickly and, thus, save the crop.
- ❐ It should be inexpensive and be easily available in large quantities.
- ❐ The compound should not be distasteful to the insects, so that they may not be repelled.
- ❐ Chemically, the compound should be stable, so that it does not lose its toxicity while in shipment, in storage or after it has been applied to the plants.
- ❐ It should also not break down too easily when mixed with other chemicals.
- ❐ The insecticide should have the physical properties of adhering to the plant surface on application and yet, after a certain period, it should disintegrate or be washed away by rain, etc., so that it does not persist on the plants for long periods and, thus, endanger the health of farm animals or of human beings.

The stomach poisons are applied as aprays, dusts, dips or baits. These poisons include inorganic and organic compounds. Among the inorganic compounds are the lead arsenate, calcium cyanide, Paris green (copper acetoarsenite), sodium flouride, sodium fluosilicates and sodium aluminofluoride (cryolite) and borax.

Systemic Poisons

Systemic insecticides are toxicants which can penetrate plant tissues and migrate from the point of application to other parts of the plants in quantities that will continue to remain toxic to insect pests for a long time after use. While most modern insecticides have the property of penetrating plant tissues by combining with a lipoid cuticle, it is only the systemic insecticides that can migrate (translocated) long distances, making the whole plant insecticidal. An insect with piercing mouthparts sucks cell-sap through its proboscis which it embeds into the plant or animal tissue. The only way a poison can reach its stomach is through the plant or animal system. It is only in recent years that some highly effective systemic insecticides have been discovered. A systemic insecticide when applied to seeds, roots, stems or leaves of plants, is absorbed and translocated to various parts of the plant in amounts lethal to insects, which feed on them. Some of them are quite specific to certain groups of insects. The systemic insecticides have a great value in an integrated approach to pest control, because through their application, the parasitoids, predators and other natural enemies of the pests escape damage. Most of these insecticides act primarily as stomach poisons, and they include oxydemeton methyl, dimethoate, phosphamidon, aldicarb, phorate, carbofuran and others.

According to the decomposition of insecticides inside the plant, systemic insecticides may be classified into three types :

(*a*) **Stable systemic.** Systemic insecticides which do not decompose or change inside the plant tissue are stable systemics *e.g.*, selanium.

(*b*) **Endolytic systemic.** Systemic insecticides which go unchanged from the plant into the insect body and change into a toxicant inside the latter are endolytic systemics *e.g.*, schradan, dimefox.

(*c*) **Endometatoxic systemic.** Systemic insecticides which are partly or wholly metabolised into other toxicants inside the plants themselves are endometatoxic systemics *e.g.*, demeton. The process is accelerated at a higher temperature because the latter increases the physiological activity of the plant.

An ideal systemic insecticide should have the following qualities : (*i*) it should be liposoluble to allow easy penetration into the plant tissues; (*ii*) it should also be adequately water soluble to allow translocation (migration) inside the plant tissues; (*iii*) it should be stable inside the plant tissue in order to be able to act for a longer time, and (*iv*) it should easily decompose into non-toxic substances.

The efficiency of a systemic insecticide depends upon the active participation of the plants in the following three ways : absorption, translocation and detoxification.

Absorption. The insecticides are absorbed by all the parts of a plant—through seeds, roots, stem and leaves, of which the roots and leaves are the more important absorbing organs. Seeds are either coated or soaked in the toxicant, the latter being more effective. Large seeds will obviously absorb more of the toxicant and, therefore, the length of protection varies with the weight of the seed. The toxicant is first absorbed by the seed coat and then stored in the cotyledons whence it reaches the seedling and protects it.

The absorption of the insecticide by the roots takes place best in a solution, less in sand and the least in soil. This may be due to : (*a*) the difference in contact between the roots and the insecticide in these different media; (*b*) the greater affinity of the insecticide for the molecules of the media, or (*c*) the selective absorption by the roots—materials with a lower lipoid solubility, for instance, are more readily accepted by the roots. An increase in the temperature and thus, in the physiological activity of the plant enhances absorption by roots.

Leaves absorb systemic insecticides either through the leaf surface (cuticular penetration) or through stomata, the former being more important for highly liposoluble material. It should be noted that young leaves and undersurfaces are more absorptive than older leaves and upper surfaces. The amount of material absorbed by the leaves is regulated by the weather (temperature and light), leaf age, leaf surface, leaf type, and light and heat reflecting properties of the leaf surface. These factors not only affect the amount of insecticide retained per unit area of the leaf surface but also cell permeability. In case of the woody plants, bark absorption of the insecticides has been found to be more effective than root absorption possibly because the material can enter the cambium more easily in case of bark.

Translocation. Transport of the insecticides through the conducting tissues (phloem and xylem) of the plant is called translocation. The force that draws it upwards is transpiration through the leaf-surface, which is, therefore, dependent on temperature and humidity. Greater temperature and lower atmospheric humidity will mean greater transpiration and, therefore, faster translocation of the systemic insecticides. The rate of transpiration also depends upon the nature of the chemical itself, some chemicals travelling faster and longer than others. Dimefox, for instance, travels through the roots of the willow, *Vicia falsa*, at the rate of only 11 cm/h while demeton travels at the rate of 3.2 m/h.

Detoxification. Decomposition of the systemic insecticides into different compounds inside the plant body is referred to as detoxification. This is done by the plant's enzymes. The compounds could be detoxified into metabolites that are entirely non-toxic to insects or those that are more toxic to insects than the parent material. A compound that combines the latter trait with a low mammalian toxicity is favoured. Transpiration, evaporation or diffusion through the plant surface also make the insecticides more potent by enhancing their concentration in the plant tissues.

Inert Dusts

Fine dusts of various compounds have been used for a long time to control insect pests of crops and stored grains. These dusts are mixed with the grain or dusted on a surface from where the insects pick up the fine particles which cause irritation and abrasions in the cuticle, particularly at the body articulations. It results in excessive loss of moisture from the body of an insect, which ultimately dies of desiccation. These dusts are based on fine sand, powdered cowdung ash (which also acts as a hygroscopic compound), calcium carbonate, silica, aerogel, etc.

Contact Poisons

The other most effective and most prevalent method of insect control lies in Ine use of contact poisons, a large number of which are now available. The contact poisons are applied as sprays or dusts, either directly onto the body of insects or to the places frequented by them. These poisons kill the insects either by clogging spiracles and respiratory system or by entering through the cuticle into the blood and acting as nerve or general tissue poisons. It has been shown that the insect cuticle possesses very high absorptive properties, so that the lethal dose applied externally is almost the same as the quantity required to kill by injecting it into the body. The contact insecticides, even though applied in the form of emulsions, suspensions or dusts, are highly lipophilic and are readily absorbed by the lipids present in the epicuticle of insect exoskeleton. The residual film of a contact insecticide may kill an insect by its action on the sensory organs present in the tarsi of its legs.

Like the stomach poisons, the contact poisons also must have certain qualities before they can be accepted for use. Some of them are also phytotoxic. Others, like mineral oils, are so lethal to the foliage, that they can only be applied in winter as dormant sprays when there are no leaves on the plants. Even among the milder insecticides which are used as summer sprays or dusts, some have phytotoxic effect. For instance, high doses of DDT and HCH are known to cause phytotoxicity in plants. Most of the insecticides damage citrus inflorescence and, therefore, they cannot be applied when plants are in blossom. Some of these compounds are also toxic to mammals and are readily absorbed through the skin, for instance, parathion and endrin, when sprayed on crops in the field during the monsoon, can easily cause death of the operators, if due precautions are not taken. Insecticides like DDT and HCH, which do not act as acute poisons, may cause very serious chronic ailments among mammals. Because of their slow breakdown over time, they are preferably deposited in the adipose tissue and are secreted through milk. Thus, the babies are exposed to the risk through contaminated food.

There is a wide range of contact poisons available in the market today. Among the inorganic compounds, sulphur, sodium fluoride and arsenicals may be mentioned, but these are very limited in use. The mineral oils, including diesel oil, kerosene oil, crude oil and animal fats, including fish oil or the soaps prepared from them, are also used as winter and summer sprays. A number of complex organic compounds which are extracted from various plants, have the remarkable property of being very safe for man and domestic animals. These compounds include nicotine in sulphate form, anabasine, rotenone, pyrethrum, neem extract, *dharek* extract, etc. A wide spectrum of new synthetic organic compounds have revolutionised the modern practices of pest control. The major groups include chlorinated hydrocarbons (DDT, HCH, aldrin, etc.), carbamates (carbaryl, aldicarb, carbofuran, etc.), and the organophosphates (malathion, oxydemeton-methyl, monocrotophos, etc.).

Fumigants

Poisonous gases, derived from either solids or liquids, are used as fumigants to kill insect pests of stored grains and other products in warehouses, museums, godowns, etc. They are also used to kill insect pests found in animal sheds or human dwellings; soil-infesting grubs and nematodes, the scales infesting nursery stock, the borers found in trees or wooden structures; to control all kinds of greenhouse pests and even worms found inside the intestines of animals. Since practically all the fumigants are deadly poisonous, great care is needed in their use. Some of the common fumigants, both old and new, include nicotine, hydrogen cyanide, carbon bisulphide, sulphur dioxide, paradichlorobenzene, naphthalene, ethylene dichloride and carbon tetrachloride mixture, methyl bromide, phosphine, DBCP, D-D (dichloropropane-dichloropropene) mixture, etc.

The kill obtained is determined to a great extent by the temperature and atmospheric pressure at which the fumigation is done. In a partial vacuum, the penetration is very much enhanced and at lower temperatures, a longer exposure is required to kill the pests than at room temperature (21-37°C). The duration of effective exposure depends upon the gas used. This is determined by its toxicity, dose, rate of penetration, its absorption by the food stuffs, tainting or discolouration of products, chemical composition and moisture content of the materials to be fumigated.

Miscellaneous Chemicals

Under this group are a number of chemicals, both new and old, which cause changes in the physiology and behaviour of insects and are, thus, used either to repel them or to kill them. Chemosterilants such as apholate, tepa and metapa are fed to the insects along with food and through their physiological action, they cause sterility and ultimately the pest population declines. Antifeedants, such as neem seed extract or 4'-(dimethyl triazene acetanilide), when sprayed on plants or mixed with food, make them distasteful to the insects who stop eating and ultimately die of starvation.

Repellents are another group of chemicals which are only mildly poisonous, but prevent damage by making the food unattractive or offensive. These substances generally have a specific effect and are effective against certain groups of insects only. Trichlorobenzene is effective against crawling insects such as termites and ants, and is applied in the basement, to provide protection to buildings. Adhesive tapes, carrying bichloride of mercury, when fixed around the legs of a table, also provide protection against ants. Heavy oils applied at the base of poultry roosters act as barriers against poultry lice and mites. Bordeaux mixture and lime-sulphur wash, repel leafhoppers and certain chewing insects. Oil citronella or dimethyl phthalate (Odomos) when applied as liquid or mixed with a vanishing cream, keeps mosquitoes away from human beings. Smoke keeps biting flies away from cattle. Oil of cedar, naphthalene or dry leaves of neem (*Azadirachta indica* A. Juss.) protect warm clothes and carpets against the attack of moths and beetles. There are still other chemicals which repel insects from sitting on wounds and laying eggs there. For example, pine-tar oil and diphenylamine, when applied to the skin near the wounds of animals, keep the screwworm flies away, so that they do not oviposit. The wheat crop can be protected against damage by birds like sparrows, by spraying it with Thiuram (tetramethyl thiuram disulphide).

When insects are to be poisoned through baits, it is advantageous to mix an attractant with the food, which gives olfactory stimulation. Many such attractants occur naturally either in the food, or as pheromones, which are secretions released by other members of the same species that promote aggregation, mating and other types of behaviour. Apart from these natural attractants, a number of other chemicals are also known to be effective. In United States, a mixture of 9 parts of geraniol and

1 part of eugenol serves as a food lure for the Japanese beetle, *Popillia japonica*. Fermented sugar or syrups act as attractants for moths and butterflies. Sometimes, the addition of a chemical makes this food even more attractive. For example, the essential oil anethol is particularly luring to the codling moth, *Cydiapomonella* and isoamyl salicylate to the tomato and tobacco hornworm moths, *Protoparce* spp. Ammonia strongly attracts many insects and its slow liberation from a mixture of glycine and sodium hydroxide has been used in United States for luring the walnut husk fly, *Rhagoletus completa*. Sometimes, closely related species of insects exhibit a marked preference for one chemical over the other. The Oriental fruit fly, *Bactrocera dorsalis*, is attracted to methyl eugenol, whereas the melon fruit fly, *Bactrocera cucurbitae*, is attracted to anisyl acetone. Metaldehyde which is lethal by itself also acts as an attractant in poison baits for snails and slugs.

There is still another group of chemicals which, when fed to rodents and other mammals, produces physiological changes in the blood and inhibits coagulation. When chemicals, like warfarin, fumarin, coumafuryl (Rodafarin) are fed to rats, they die of internal haemorrhage.

FACTORS INFLUENCING EFFECTIVENESS OF PESTICIDES

Pesticides are applied in various forms, depending upon the type of pest, the situation under which they are to be applied and the hazards involved. Apart from the physical properties of these formulations, a number of factors, both inherent in the pest and those of the environment, also influence the effectiveness of chemicals.

Formulations

Pesticides are available as dusts, wettable powders, emufsifiable concentrates, water soluble concentrates, granules, solutions, soluble powders, low volume concentrates (LVC), aerosols, mists, fumigants, etc. For common use, the pesticides are rarely, if ever, marketed in pure form. They are always marketed in a reduced concentration which can be further diluted at the time of application.

Dusts. Dusts are fine powders, mixed with various types of carriers, *i.e.* walnut-shell flour or pulverised minerals such as talc, pyrophyllite, bentonite, diatomite, etc. The finished product is generally available in the concentration varying from 0.1 to 25 per cent of the active material. In general, the toxicity of insecticides increases as the particle size decreases.

When used as dusts, a number of properties affect the efficiency of the insecticides. In the powdered insecticides, the particle shape varies. It may be spherical, polyhedral, tubular, irregular, and if ground further, the shape changes and becomes more spherical and, therefore, desirable because when various shapes of particles are present in a particular preparation, they may segregate during application and act in different ways.

Particle size is also important in stomach poisons. It is believed that 10 micro-metre (μm) is the right size, as it gives a sufficiently large surface area and provides good adherence to the foliage or other parts dusted. If the particle size is too small, the dust settles down very slowly and has a tendency to drift at the time of application. The particle density determines the carrying power, segregation of the dust components and settling of the suspension of particles. If the particles are too dense, they do not spread easily.

The particle size, shape, density and chemical composition of the mixture determine the flowability of the dust. A good dust should have a higher feed-rate through the dusting equipment. Dusts with fibrous or needle-shaped particles have a slow feed-rate, whereas those with spherical particles, have a faster rate. These properties also determine the sticking quality of the dust, even though dusting is done when the plants are wet with dew. If the particles have a high sorptive capacity, they might have a tendency to form aggregations, which will not be desirable. If the particle size is too small, again there will be a tendency for the dust to granulate.

When a dust is applied with a machine, an electrical charge is produced by friction among the particles, and between the particles and the dusting equipment. A high charge will make the dust to stick to the machine and not have a good flow. The magnitude of the charge depends chiefly upon the composition of the dust, material of which the equipment is made, amount of agitation of the particles, temperature and humidity at the time of application.

Sprays. Spray fluids are prepared by dissolving insecticides in water or oil or by the dilution of wettable powders (WP), emulsifiable concentrates (EC) and water soluble concentrates (WSC) in water. In wettable powders, it is not desirable that the solid particles should settle down too rapidly. Therefore, some dispersing agent or deflocculator is added to the powder to keep its particles in suspension. The common materials used are gelatin, glue, gum, etc. Insecticides are also available in the form of wettable powders which have to be mixed with water at the time of application and diluted to the desired concentration. The particle size in such cases, must be less than 10 μm. in diameter and in some preparations, a particle size up to 1 μm is also available.

Emulsions are made by the dispersion of oil droplets in water, there being a protective film of emulsifier around the oil droplets. The size of droplet is important in many ways and it is governed by the kind and amount of the emulsifier used. If the size is large, the emulsion is unstable and the oil tends to rise and float on the surface, when allowed to stand for sometime. If the droplet size is very small, the emulsion becomes very stable and the oil does not rise even on standing for hours. However, in insecticides it is desirable to have an emulsion that is sufficiently stable in the spray tank but on leaving the nozzle or upon contact with the surface being treated, the film of the emulsifier should break and the oil droplet should stick to the surface or to the insect pests. In case the film does not break, the oil droplet drains off. The effectiveness of a spray is influenced by a number of other factors as well like the leaf surface, prevailing temperature, insect species involved, rate of break down of the chemical, etc.

On spraying, a surface becomes wet when the liquid comes into direct and persistent contact with the surface of a solid, there being no layer of air in between. Immediately after wetting, the liquid forms a persistent liquid-solid intersurface, solely by surface tension and, thus, the spread of the liquid is obtained. The surface of the foliage, in some cases, is wetted more readily than in others, depending upon the waxy layer on the cuticle. A high-quality spreader is used in the preparation of an insecticide when maximum coverage is desired in the field. Where it is desirable to have the residual effect, the spreader is replaced by an adhesive such as protein or a similar colloid, which is absorbed on the particle of the insecticide and provides adhesion to a solid surface. Other adhesives used are hydrophilic inorganic compounds, molasses, dextrin, sugar, starch, wheat flour, gum, linseed oil, fish oil, etc.

Where solid particles are suspended in a spray, the size of the particle determines the efficieny of an insecticide. The principle involved is the same as discussed under dusts. When the fluid is actually sprayed, the droplet size varies according to the fineness of the spray. It is 400 μm or above in a coarse spray, 100-400 μm in a fine spray and 50-100 μm. in a mist spray. An emulsifiable concentrate of an insecticide available in the market has to be diluted to the desired concentration by adding water. The percentage of active material is written on the packing and the dilution is done as follows:

The concentration of the active material in the product used is divided by the concentration required in the spray fluid. The figure obtained indicates how many parts of water are to be added to one part of the product, either by weight or by volume. Malathion which is available as 50 per cent emulsifiable concentrate is generally applied to a crop at the concentration of 0.05 per cent, i.e. one part of the insecticide is added to 1000 parts of water.

Depending upon the type of vegetation, kind of pest to be controlled, nature of the terrain where the control is to be exercised, type of pesticide formulation, and availability of water, the following volumes of spray liquid per hectare of land are normally used :

Low-volume spray. Refers to 5-400 litres/ha of the spray liquid used. Normal aerial dose is 15-75 litres/ha and ground dose, 100-200 litres/ha.

High-volume spray. Refers to more than 400 litres/ha of the spray liquid used.

Ultra-low volume (ULV) or low-volume concentration (LVC) spray. Refers to the use of less than 5 litres/ha of the spray liquid. Here, the technical grade insecticide is dissolved in a non-volatile organic solvent having a high viscosity and a high specific weight. The formulation thus prepared is not diluted with water, but applied as such in a highly concentrated form and so the name ULV or LVC. To compensate for the (small) volume, the concentrate is broken down into extremely fine particles by special equipment. They are sprayed by aircrafts from a high altitude. Thus, a fall from a greater height, the fineness of the particles and their being heavier in weight and abundant in number enable a greater coverage with smaller amounts of the insecticide. The technique was first conceived soon after the World War II, during locust control in East Africa. Its efficacy on crops was demonstrated by the USDA (United State Department of Agriculture) in 1963 and since then the technique has spread throughout the world including India where it was first tried out in 1965.

Unfortunately, however, not many insecticides can be employed as ULV sprays, the best known insecticide which offers itself to ULV being the malathion concentrate (with a 95 per cent active ingredient). Due to lack of proper equipment, ULV spray has so far been used only in aerial spraying (both by fixed-wing aircrafts and helicopters) though, recently, attempts have been made to develop ULV ground-spraying equipments (like Aspee's modified mist-blower and knapsack). The ULV technique offers many advantages : (i) uniform coverage with a particle size that is more toxic to pests, (ii) economy in pesticide (only a few grams needed per ha) and in labour, (iii) more area can be covered per day, and (iv) minimisation of hazards to pilots and ground workers due to the need for higher flight altitude than the conventional (aerial) techniques (Table 7.2).

Table 7.2 Comparison of parameters of ultra-low volume (ULV) with those of conventional techniques

S.No.	Parameter	ULV	Conventional techniques
1.	Application rate (litres/ha)	0.5	28
2.	Swath width, i.e. width of area sprayed at any moment (m)	328	10.5
3.	Flight altitude (m)	5-8	1.0
4.	Load carried per trip (litres)	250	500
5.	Number of trips made	1	28
6.	Hectares treated per trip	500	18
7.	Total volume applied (litres)	250	14,000
8.	Total time taken	2 h 46 min	11 h 6 min

Granules. The granular formulations are discrete aggregates of dust particles which disperse gradually and, thus, last longer and are very effective when placed at strategic sites, i.e. in the soil near the root-zone or in the whorl of leaves in maize or sorghum plants. The granule size is expressed as 30/60 or similar figures for other sizes. This figure indicates that all the granules pass through a 30-mesh sieve (30 meshes per linear inch or 2.5 cm) and only a negligible number of particles will pass through a 60-mesh sieve.

Aerosols. The aerosol 'bombs' (non-explosive) are produced for use in houses or stores for killing flying insects. An aerosol consists of minute particles of insecticides suspended in the air as smoke, fog or mist. The particle size varies from 0.1 to 50 μm. The dispersion of the insecticide is achieved by burning a dry insecticide material or an insecticide in a volatile oil-base, by atomising mechanically, a liquid insecticide, or by pushing with force an insecticide through an orifice 0.03-0.06 cm in diameter, with the help of a liquid convertible into gas. In the latter case, the liquid evaporates and the insecticide particles are dispersed in the airas a fine mist. These 'bombs' are very useful in the kitchen, pantry, living-rooms, bedrooms, cellars, etc., and before use the doors and windows are closed. If an aerosol is opened for

6 seconds in a room of 30 m^3, mosquitoes, house flies, sand flies, moths, etc. are killed and, if released for 15 seconds, fleas, wasps, hornets, etc. are also killed. The particle size is important for obtaining the maximum effectiveness. If it is too small, the particles are deflected from the flying insects, and if too large their dispersion is poor and they settle down too rapidly. A particle size of 10-15 μm is the optimum.

Pesticide Additives

Pesticides are seldom used in pure and technical forms, firstly, because only small amounts of them per unit area are needed to kill the pests, secondly, because they need to be evenly spread on the treated surface for a better contact with the insect body and thirdly, because they are costly. They are, therefore, mixed with inert materials or additives. The mixture thus formed, is called a formulation and the additives vary accordingly, as the formulation is a solid (dust), liquid (spray) or gas (fumigant). The nature and function of the commonly used additives are being given below :

Dust additives. Dusts are prepared by mixing insecticides with carriers (also called extenders, diluents, or vehicles). Sometimes, a distinction is made in the type of the carriers. When an insecticide is adsorbed on the particle surface of the diluent, the latter is called a carrier, otherwise a filler. The effectiveness of a dust formulation depends upon the evenness of the application which, in turn, depends upon the particle size of the carrier—smaller the particles, more potent the toxicant. However, particle size is not always kept the smallest. For different purposes, different particle sizes are needed and the size of the particle largely determines the choice of the carrier. Dust carriers which are normally employed, fall into two categories: (*i*) organic compounds such as flours of walnut, shell, soybean, woodbark, and (*ii*) inorganic minerals such as sulphur, calcium oxide (lime), calcium sulphate (gypsum), silicon oxide (diatomite), silicates (like talcum - H_2O 3MgO $4SiO_2$, pyrophyllite— H_2O Al_2O_2 $4SiO_2$), clays [like bentonites—$(OH)_4Al_4Si_8O_{20}$, kaolins—$(OH)_8Al_4Si_4O_{10}$, attapulgites—$(OH)_4OH_2Mg_5Si_8O_{20}4H_2O$)] and volcanic ash. Some alkaline carriers inactivate certain insecticides and are, therefore, incompatible.

Spray additives. Organic insecticides are mostly insoluble in water and, therefore, to prepare a spray out of them, the following additives need to be added :

(i) Solvents. Organic insecticides are fully or partially dissolved in various solvents. The more commonly used solvents are kerosene oil (crude, refined or deodorised), diesel oil, petroleum, xylene, cyclohexanone, carbon tetrachloride, chlorobenzene, pine oil, ethyl and amyl acetates and ethylene dichloride. Some of the solvents themselves have an insecticidal property, some are toxic to plants, some inflammable and some incompatible with certain insecticides. These facts need to be kept in view while choosing a solvent. A good solvent : (*a*) should have a high solubility factor, (*b*) should not be inflammable, (*c*) should not be phytotoxic, (*d*) should be compatible with the insecticide to be dissolved in it, and (*e*) should be odourless and cheap.

(ii) Wetting agents. Agricultural insecticides are normally used as aqueous sprays (are not dissolved in organic solvents). Since most of the organic insecticides are insoluble in water, it is necessary to add to them a dust carrier which itself is soluble or partly soluble in water (*i.e.* is wettable). The carrier is called a wettable agent and the formulation prepared after adding to it, a water dispersible powder (WDP) or simply wettable powder (WP) which may contain up to 75 per cent or more of the toxicant. Thus, the purpose of adding a wettable agent to an insecticide is to convert a water-insoluble toxicant into a soluble or partly soluble one.

(iii) Emulsifiers. Most of the organic insecticides are water insoluble, and, therefore, are first dissolved in a solvent (generally, a mineral oil) and then mixed with water for making a final spray. But in doing so, there is the possibility of the insecticide settling down in water (being insoluble in it). This is avoided by adding an emulsifer, which keeps the insecticide emulsified (suspended) as small particles (oil-in-water-type suspension) in water, making it possible to formulate an aqueous spray out of an insoluble insecticide. Thus, the emulsifiers are substances that prevent a solvent—dissolved insecticide from precipitating out. The common emulsifying agents are : soap such as sodium oleate, amines such as triethanolamine (superior to soap), sulphates of long chain alcohols such as sodium lauryl sulphate, sulphonated aliphatic esters and natural agents such as proteins, gums, lipids, saponins, blood albumin, casein, etc.

Commercially, many insecticides are sold as an emulsifiable concentrate (EC = mixture of insecticide + solvent + emulsifer) to which the recommended amount of water (mentioned on the container) is added at the time of use. The emulsion tends to separate or "break" into its component parts on storage and this could be regulated by agitating the liquid or by using a proper amount and type of the emulsifer. For crop-spraying, a fairly quick-breaking emulsion is useful, since it limits the run-off of the insecticide from the surface of the foliage. The advantages of adding an emulsifier are: (*a*) it makes an insoluble insecticide partly soluble in water, and (*b*) it reduces surface tension at the insect body and spray interface, enabling the spray to spread and make intimate contact with the insect body. If an emulsifier is not added, the aqueous spray tends to form discrete droplets on the surface of the waxy (hydrophobic) cuticle of the insect and foliage and thus, lose efficacy.

(iv) Spreaders* or *deflocculators. Because of the waxy smooth or oily nature of the foliage surface, it may not be easily wetted. This problem is overcome by adding spreaders such as calcium caseinate, soybean flour, sulphated alcohols or sulphonated compounds that improve wetting as a result of their spreading property achieved by reducing surface-tension at the spray-foliage-interface.

(v) Stickers. Compounds that ensure spreading or wetting may also accelerate the washing-off of insecticide coating by rain or dew. Therefore, to make the spray containing a spreader stay longer on the treated surface and to ensure that it does not get washed off, adhesives or stickers like gelatin, resin, glue, sugar, starch, soybean flour, casein, blood albumin, mineral, fish or vegetable oil, fine clay, etc., are added to the formulation.

(vi) Stabilisers. These are substances that retard rapid decomposition of those organic insecticides which are unstable. Some of the stabilisers are isopropyl cresols, hexamethylene tetramine and epichlorohydrin. These prevent decomposition of pyrethrins, endrin and aldrin, respectively.

(vii) Softeners. These are substances that reduce phytotoxicity of insecticides. Examples are sulphur, zinc sulphate, lime, casein, etc.,

(viii) Maskers* or *deodorants. These are used to suppress (mask) the unpleasant odours of certain insecticides (like pyrethrins, thiocyanates) when used for household purposes. Examples are cedar oil, pine oil, etc.

Synergists

The term 'synergist' is derived from the Greek word '*synergos*' meaning together. Synergists are chemicals which have little or no insecticidal property of their own, but when added to an insecticide, enhance its toxicity manifold. The enhanced toxicity is greater than the sum of the toxicities of the two components reckoned separately to more than the additive (total) toxicity of the two taken together. This phenomenon, first discovered in 1938, is known as "synergism" and the substance producing it, a synergist. A substance, that has the opposite effect, i.e. that which reduces the toxicity of an insecticide, is called an "antagonist".

Synergists are known for only some insecticides like pyrethrins, rotenoids and certain organophosphates. The best and the first known synergists are those relating to pyrethrins and, therefore, only these will be mentioned here. Pyrethroid synergists fall into three classes of chemicals : (*i*) Methylene dioxyphenyl compounds such as sesamine derived from the oil of *Sesame indicum*, pipeline obtained from black pepper, piperonyl cyclonene or cyclohexonone (good for field crop insecticides), piperonyl butoxide (good for livestock insecticides), piperonyl amides, propyl isome, and fagaramide, (*ii*) N-substituted amides like N-isobutylundecylenamide or IN 930, and (*iii*) terpene derivatives like thanite, terpene diacetate and pine oil. Some of these synergists are also the synergists for organophosphates. For example, piperonyl cyclonene, sulphoxide, piperonyl butoxide, piperonyl isome are good synergists for coumaphos, and piperonyl butoxide and sulphoxide for diazinon.

Certain substances increase the efficiency (not the toxicity) of pyrethrins by stabilising the droplet size of their sprays and thus, ensuring better and persistent contact with the insect body achieving a better rate of killing. They are referred to as pesudosynergists. Examples are oleic acid, lubricating oils and the oil part of the sesame and pine oils from which the actual synergist has been removed.

The mode of action of synergists has not been clearly understood. Three possible mechanisms are suggested : (*i*) Synergists may produce two types of effects; i.e. inductive and non-inductive effects. Through the inductive effect, they activate their enzyme system which then enhances the toxicity of the insecticide. This is a slow process taking a long time to operate and, therefore, not useful for synergism. Non-inductive effects are those in which synergists inhibit the enzymes that detoxify the insecticide and thus, enhance the killing power of the latter. (*ii*) Synergists may improve penetration of the insecticides through the insect cuticle and the nervous system. This is indicated by the fact that synergism occurs only when application of the synergist precedes that of the insecticide. If the synergist is applied later than the insecticide, no synergism is seen. (*iii*) Synergists may be protecting the insecticide from weathering effects, thereby increasing the residual action and thus, the amount of kill.

Penetration of Insecticide

Apart from its entry through spiracles and the alimentary canal, the insecticide is also absorbed directly through the cuticle. The penetration and effectiveness of an insecticide depend upon the quality of the cuticle and chemical composition of the insecticide. This is so, because most of the insecticides are lipophilic and are absorbed by wax in the epicuticle. However, some lipid-insoluble materials, such as arsenicals and flourides may also find their way through the cuticle. If the thin waxy layer of the epicuticle is dissolved in some organic solvent like ether, chloroform, xylene, etc., penetration becomes even faster. The most vulnerable regions for action of contact insecticides are the head, neck, thorax or other intersegmental parts where the cuticle is thin and there are vital nerve centres. Other such parts are antennae, bases of wings, trochanters, tarsi and intersegmental membranes. The body characters that provide protection against contact insecticides are the hard elytra of beetles, hair-coating of hairy caterpillars, thick waxy secretions of mealy bugs, some aphids and coccids. All these mechanisms are normally meant to keep water away.

After penetrating the cuticle, a contact insecticide like pyrethrum, may directly affect the hypodermal cells, reach the haemolymph and destroy haemocytes. It may be deposited in various tissues as in the case of DDT or may be transported along the lipid sheaths of the nerves, starting from the nerve endings, as in pyrethrum.

Whether the insecticide is lipophilic or not, the undissociated molecule has a much faster penetration than the dissociated ionic component. The type of carrier used also determines to a great extent the rate of penetration. An oil solution or an oil-in-water emulsion has better penetration than an aqueous suspension. Water, because of its high surface tension, is unable to enter the tracheae, whereas mineral oils or aqueous solutions of the wetting agent having reduced surface tension, can enter the breathing tubes.

Susceptibility of Insects

Different species of insects have a wide range of susceptibility to insecticides. An insecticide can act only, if it hits the vital part of an insect. Lepidopteran tissue-borers or weevils that feed while hiding inside plant tissues, naturally escape the topical application. The habitat and the behaviour of the species play an important role. A very mobile insect like the cockroach or another having a strong sense of smell will stay away from a treated area.

Different developmental stages of a pest species are also affected differently by an insecticide. In the pupal stage, an insect neither respires very much nor feeds and is often protected by a cocoon or by an earthen cell and hence, it escapes being hit directly. In contrast, a larva, which feeds exposed, is very highly vulnerable to stomach as well as to contact insecticides.

Weather Conditions

The various components of weather influence the effectiveness of insecticides. If the wind is blowing at a speed of 8-10 km per hour, it will interfere with spraying. Dusting from an aircraft is best done early in the morning or in the evening, when there is only a slight wind. On the other hand, when the sun is up, the rising currents tend to carry the dust away from the crop. If aerosols are to be applied, wind velocity of 1.5-6.0 km per hour is useful and again cooler temperatures near the ground in the morning or after sunset are suitable. A few metres higher up, the atmosphere is warm and the aerosol cloud has a tendency to rise and drift. In general, extremes of temperature are not favourable. Certain chemicals, when applied in hot weather, may injure the plants. The rate of metabolism is fast at high temperatures, so the insects have an inherent capacity to resist the poison. If the weather is too cold, the oil sprays may cause injury to foliage.

If insecticides do not contain a good adhesive and the spray does not stick to the plants effectively, it may be washed off by rain. Dusts are more easily washed-off than sprays but if dusting is done when there is dew on the plants, the insecticide sticks quite well.

Field Conditions

The condition of the plant, location of the pest, time of application and amount of insecticide applied, all determine the effectiveness of an operation. Some plants grow faster than others, still others grow faster in one season than in another, and the fruits grow much faster in the early stages than in the later stages. In these cases, if the entire surface is to be kept covered with an insecticide, naturally the frequency of application has to be changed accordingly. Even where it is not necessary to maintain a deposit, it is desirable to time the application properly. Spraying or dusting is to be done when the pest is in a vulnerable stage;

if done too early, the maximum kill may not be obtained; if too late, much damage to the crop may have already been caused. In general, crops should not be sprayed while in blossom, because the flowers in which seed is to set may be damaged or the bees and other insects, so important for the pollination of crops, may be killed, thus causing reduction in yield instead of an expected increase. The structure of the leaf is also important; hairy leaves are more easily covered while those having smooth and waxy surface, have to be sprayed with more sticky insecticides.

Since the pest is to be directly hit, the method or site of application of the poison would depend on its location. Insects feeding on the lower surface of the leaves, have to be reached by the spray, those feeding on the roots, have to be killed by mixing insecticides with the soil, and those rising up the trunks of the trees have to be intercepted with sticky or poison bands.

Various insecticides are effective for different durations. As a rule of thumb, the duration of effectiveness of dusts is for about one week and that of the sprays for about two weeks. The excessive use of insecticides is expensive and wasteful, and can be injurious to plants or non-target animals in the soil. Even pond life can be affected by the run-off from treated fields. The selection of an insecticide and the frequency of its application should be such that the near maximum kill is obtained with the least quantity, so that the natural enemies of the pests can be spared as far as possible.

Compatibility

Since the farmer is interested in protecting the crop both from pests and diseases, the insecticides and fungicides or even some weedicides might have to be mixed together before spraying. Some chemicals are compatible, whereas others are not; the latter should not be mixed because they might become ineffective or damage the foliage. The mixing should be done with the full knowledge of their compatibility or in consultation with an expert. Based on the compatibility of various compounds, a miscibility chart should always be consulted at the time of mixing the chemicals.

Pesticide Application

Apart from precautions for spraying and dusting, there are many other points that should be considered for obtaining the best results. A given preparation of insecticide has instructions printed on the packing and these should be followed strictly. For example, an oil-base insecticide meant for use on walls, furniture, wooden structures and floors should not be sprayed on plants and again the one meant for use on dormant trees cannot be used on those having foliage. Arsenicals (and chlorinated hydrocarbons) persist in the soil for many years and may accumulate in quantities sufficient to injure the plants under temperate conditions. The organophosphates are generally very toxic to man and domestic animals, but they have the advantage that they do not persist for long and are detoxified in the soil after 2 or 3 months. They are also generally destroyed when the food is cooked.

The old saying that "If little is good, more is better" does not apply in the case of insecticides. The right dose (quantity per hectare) or the right potency (concentration of an insecticide) should be applied at right intervals. To get the best results a preparation has to be applied in optimum quantity. This is possible if the machine is correctly calibrated. It is particularly important with the power-operated sprayers and dusters. With the manually operated high-volume sprayers, generally 600-1000 litres of the fluid is required per hectare, whereas with the low-volume sprayers (carried on the back or on a trolley) only 125-200 litres is sufficient, hence the concentration is increased. Since the rate of flow is important in power sprayers and power dusters, it should be measured by noticing the amount of the insecticide used on a known crop area. The rate of flow can then be increased or decreased by making adjustments in the apertures.

MAJOR GROUPS OF PESTICIDES

Based on the their chemical structure, pesticides may be classified into two broad categories, viz. inorganic and organic pesticides. Organic pesticides may further be divided into five major groups, viz. organochlorines, organophosphates, carbamates, synthetic pyrethroids and neonicotinoids. Besides, there are several fumigants, acaricides, nematicides and nematicides, which are used for the control of various groups of animal pests.

A. INORGANIC PESTICIDES

Arsenic Compounds

Arsenites derived from arsenious acid [$As(OH)_3$] and arsenates derived from arsenic acid [$O = As(OH)_3$] are both toxic to insects, the former more so than the latter. It is believed that the actual toxicants are the arsenite ions and, therefore, arsenates must be reduced to arsenites in order to be effective. Some workers, on the other hand, also believe that both chemicals are interconvertible in the living system and are equally effective. However, since arsenates are less phytotoxic, they are preferred as insecticides. The following are examples of arsenates that are commonly used as insecticides :

Lead arsenates. Lead arsenates were discovered in 1892 in the USA. They exist in acidic and basic forms. Acid lead arsenate (PbHAsO4) or white arsenic burns the tender parts of the plants and is, therefore, used where plants are not a consideration such as in orchards, forests, shade trees, shrubs, etc., for the control of chewing insects. Basic lead arsenate [$Pb_2(PbOH)$ (AsO_4)] is sold as a mixture of arsenic compounds. It is more stable and less toxic to insects, but it needs to be used in greater amounts and takes a longer time compared to the acidic compound.

Calcium arsenate. Discovered in 1920, calcium arsenate is a white fluffy powder. It also exists in acid calcium arsenate ($CaHAsO_4$) and basic tricalcium arsenate [$Ca_3(AsO_4)_2$] forms. The plus points of these compounds are that they are cheaper, they possess a high arsenical content, are fine, affording a better spread and are more toxic to insects as compared to lead arsenates. But their negative point is that they are more phytotoxic. Other arsenates are sodium, copper, magnesium, zinc, manganese arsenates, arsenic trioxide (AS_2O_3) and arsenous oxide (AS_2O_2). The latter is cheaper, but phytotoxic and, therefore, has a limited use as a poison bait for grasshoppers, ants, armyworms and cockroaches.

Paris green. This is copper acetoarsenate [$Cu(C_2H_3O_2)3Cu(AsO_2)_2$] used first in the USA in 1865 as a stomach poison for the Colorado potato beetle. It is expensive, burns foliage and, therefore, has limited use as mosquito larvicide. It also forms one of the constituents of the Bordeaux mixture.

Fluorides

Fluorides were developed as substitutes for arsenates. They are highly active and do not leave highly poisonous residues on food crops as the arsenates do.

Sodium fluoride (NaF). This was discovered in 1915. The pure mineral is a white powder, but its insecticidal product is always coloured green to remove confusion with flour. It is used particularly against ectoparasites like chewing lice on animals and poultry, and in baits for cockroaches and ants. It is, however, toxic to warm-blooded animals and irritating to the skin and the respiratory passage.

Sodium fluosilicate (Na_2SiF_6). This is a white, odourless and granular powder. It has been widely used as poison bait for grasshoppers, crickets, cutworms, and weevils. A saturated water solution of this compound is used in moth-proofing for woollens. However, it is not as effective as NaF and is phytotoxic.

Cryolite or sodium fluoaluminate (Na_2AlF_6). This is a white crystal discovered as an insecticide in 1929. It is found naturally as a mineral in Greenland and is manufactured synthetically. It is effective against chewing lice, codling moths of apples, pumpkin beetles, blister beetles, etc.

Sulphur

Elemental sulphur (S). Sulphur is the only element used as an insecticide. It has been widely applied as dust for the control of mites, thrips and some fungi, and also as a carrier for other insecticides. By adding wetting agents, sulphur can also be formulated as a spray.

Lime-sulphur wash or liquid lime sulphur. This is prepared by boiling two parts of sulphur and one part of freshly slaked (hydrated) lime to give a paste. The paste is then diluted and used as a spray. The active ingredients seem to be calcium (tetra and penta) sulphides (CaS_4 and CaS_5).The wash is used as fungicide against scale insects, aphids and mites. It may be mixed with a stabiliser and evaporated to dryness to form dry lime sulphur which is easier to handle but less effective than its liquid form.

Miscellaneous Compounds

Bordeaux mixture or Bordeaux. Pronounced as "bordo", this was discovered in 1882 and is a mixture of copper sulphate, lime, and water in the ratios of 6, 10 and 100, respectively. This is primarily used as a fungicide, but is also recommended as a repellent for the cucumber beetles and leafhoppers.

Sodium selenate (Na_2SeO_4). This is applied in the soil and acts as a systemic poison. It controls aphids and mites.

Mercury compounds. Both mercurous (Hg_2Cl_2 or calomel) and mercuric ($HgCl_2$ or corrosive sublimate) chlorides are used to control roost-infesting insects (lice) and cabbage and onion maggots. Mercuric chloride is also used in book-binding and coated on tapes to repel ants, cockroaches and termites. Both compounds are, however, dangerous for mammals.

Phosphorus (P). Phosphorus, yellow or white, mixed with a sweet syrup, forms a good poison bait for cockroaches, rats and mice. However, phosphorus is highly toxic and easily ignites and, therefore, should be handled with great care.

Thallium sulphate (TI_2SO_4). This is mixed with a sweet substance and used as a poison bait for ants.

Borax or sodium tetraborate ($Na_2B_4O_7$). This is used to kill maggots of house flies in manure. It prevents breeding of mosquitoes in water which is not to be drunk. Boric acid (H_3BO_3) has been used in cockroach baits.

Formaldehyde. An aqueous solution of 40 per cent formaldehyde is a good poison bait for houseflies.

B. Organic pesticides

The organic pesticides are classified into natural and synthetic compounds.

I. Natural Compounds

The natural compounds are further divided into petroleum oils and botanicals.

Petroleum Oils

Petroleum or mineral oils comprise kerosene, petrol, lubricating oils, asphalt, tar, etc. They are derived from sedimentary rocks and are important in insect control. Petroleum oils are composed of saturated and unsaturated hydrocarbons. The unsaturated hydrocarbons are volatile and readily react to form compounds with plants. Therefore, lesser the content of unsaturated hydrocarbons, safer is that oil for the plants.Sulphonationis the process to determine the amount of unsaturated hydrocarbons. This is brought about by boiling the oil with concentrated sulphuric acid. The unsaturated hydrocarbons react and sink to the bottom and the unsulphonated or unreacted residue (UR) is measured in percentage. Oils with a UR value of 50-90 per cent are called dormant oils and being less purified are phytotoxic, while those with a UR value of 90-96 per cent called summer oils, are highly purified and, therefore, safer.

There are three oil formulations in general use : (*i*) Oil emulsions are mixtures of oil, a small quantity of water and an emulsifier (soap, blood albumin, etc.) to make oil somewhat miscible with water. This makes a stock spray (commercially emulsifiable oils) to which a recommended amount of water is added at the time of use as a spray. (*ii*) Emulsive oils contain only oil and an emulsifier but no water. They are emulsified by agitation in spray tanks. (*iii*) Tank-mix oils wherein the emulsifier and water are added separately only at the time of use and, by a violent agitation, an emulsion is prepared to be diluted with water and sprayed.

Oils are used in two ways : as an insecticide carrier (*e.g.* for DDT) and as insecticides themselves. The advantages of oils are as follows : (*i*) they are relatively cheaper than other insecticides; (*ii*) they possess good spreading quality; (*iii*) they are easy to mix and to handle; and (*iv*) they are safe for animals. The disadvantages are as follows : (1) they possess low insect toxicity; (2) they are unstable on storage; (3) they are phytotoxic and, therefore, largely used as solvents for domestic insecticides; and (4) they damage insecticide equipment — rubber hoses and other parts of sprayers.

Botanical Pesticides

The botanicals are plant products that have been used as insect repellents in our country from ancient times. Dried end powdered leaves of neem are used against wool moths, *Calotropis* against white ants and turmeric against rodents and mosquitoes. Sandal dhoop, likewise, a plant product, is often used as a fumigant in Indian houses though in a religious garb. Many tribal people still use plant toxins to poison their arrows. Plants yield the following products that are used in insect control; (*i*) toxi-cants or insecticides, (*ii*) attractants (geraniol, eugenol), (*iii*) repellents (oils of citronella and cedar), (*iv*) solvents for insecticides (cotton seed oil), and (*v*) dust carriers (soybean and walnut shell flours). Botanical pesticides have been discussed in detail in Chapter 6

II. Synthetic Organic Pesticides

The development of synthetic organic pesticides during and following the World War II revolutionised the control of pests. Chemists had been looking for chemicals with persistence in sunlight and low toxicity to man, which would kill pests quickly. As a result, several groups of pesticides were developed, which played a pivotal role in ushering in the green revolution.

Chlorinated Hydrocarbons

The chlorinated hydrocarbons were the first widely used group of synthetic organic pesticides. Compared with the inorganics and the botanicals, these chemicals were more efficacious against a broader spectrum of arthropod pests, provided longer residual control due to environmental persistence, and were more economical.

1. DDT. DDT (dichlorodiphenyl trichloroethane) was the first organochlorine pesticide developed and is probably the best-known insecticide in the world. DDT was first prepared as a chemical in 1874 by a German graduate student, Othmar Zeidler. The insecticidal properties of this chemical were discovered in 1939 by Paul Muller, a Swiss chemist working for the Geigy Chemical Co. Paul Muller was awarded the Nobel Prize for Medicine in 1948 in recognition of his life-saving discovery of the toxic properties of DDT.

The first use of this compound was made in Switzerland in 1941 on the Colorado potato beetle and then in Naples (Italy) in 1944 on the body louse, *Pediculus humanus*, spreading typhus fever amongst the civilians living in crowded conditions due to war bombings and killing by the thousands. In both cases, DDT proved an instant success and became famous as an insecticide overnight and hailed by no less a personality than Sir Winson Churhill as "that miraculous DDT powder". It may be mentioned that before the advent of DDT, typhus had been a scourge of war. In the World War I, 25 per cent of the Serbian soldiers and several millions of Russians died of this disease.

DDT was used during the war to protect troops from diseases such as yellow fever, typhus, elephantasis and malaria. The success of the pesticide proved far better than expected and after the war, it was widely used to combat these diseases in the civilian population. For example, in India alone cases of malaria declined from 75 million to less than 5 million per annum in a decade. After the war, DDT was also widely used in agriculture to protect crops from pests.

Crude DDT is a mixture of about 14 isomers, of which para-para or p, p'-DDT are the main ones. Technically, DDT contains 65-80 per cent of the active p, p'-DDT and 15-21 per cent of the nearly inactive o, p'-DDT. Therefore, what we call DDT is in fact the p, p'-DDT, which is a cream to white coloured amorphous powder. It is highly stable, resistant to destruction by light and oxidation. Its residues, when applied indoors, may remain effective for as long as one year. Outdoor application on plants, however, is less durable, lasting from a month to a growing season due to weathering and slow decomposition by light and traces of metals. The unusual stability offers an advantage of a long residual action as well as a disadvantage of killing beneficial (non-target) insects, contaminating edibles (fruits, vegetables, crop products), and polluting the environment. DDT has great affinity for lipids (oils) and, therefore, is easily absorbed by skin in an oil solution-a cause for taking precautions while handling oil solutions of this insecticide. It is safe for most plants but toxic to cucurbits, tomatoes, and some others. Mode of action of DDT is complex, but it destroys the delicate balance of sodium and potassium within the neuron, thereby preventing it from conducting impulses normally.

The impact of DDT on pest control is unmatched by any other synthetic pesticide and nearly 1.5 billion kg of DDT was used during the three decades following its introduction in agriculture during 1940s. By 1961, there were over 1200 brands of DDT registered for use on 334 agricultural commodities against 240 species of insect pests in USA. Peak production of DDT occurred in 1963 with 81, 646, 200 kg of the material being formulated DDT became popular because it is relatively cheap to produce, has a broad spectrum of activity and is selective in its toxicity. However, it has now been banned in many countries due to its persistent nature, but continues to be used for vector control in many developing countries.

2. DDT analogues. These are compounds closely related to DDT and were developed in the search for a less toxic insecticide to vertebrates than DDT. Some of the more important analogues are the following :

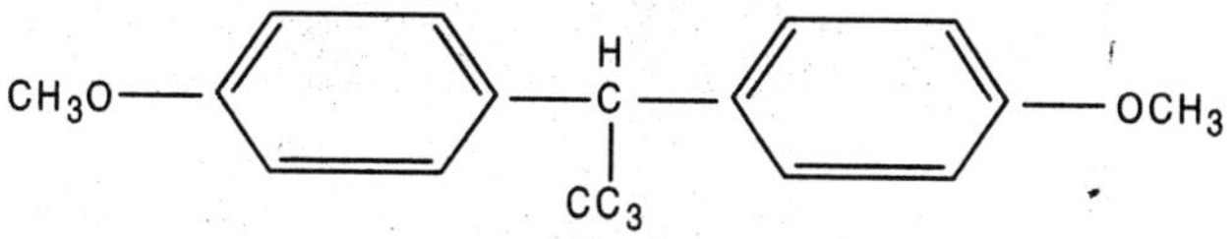

CH_3O H C OCH_3 CC_3

Methoxychlor

Methoxychlor ($C_6H_{15}Cl_3O$). This, again a Geigy product, is a white powder, producing a more rapid knock-down in insects than DDT, but is less toxic. Its oral LD50 for the rat is 7000 mg/kg compared to 250 mg/kg of DDT. It does not accumulate in fat and is favoured for this property. It is good for vegetable crops and livestock pests.

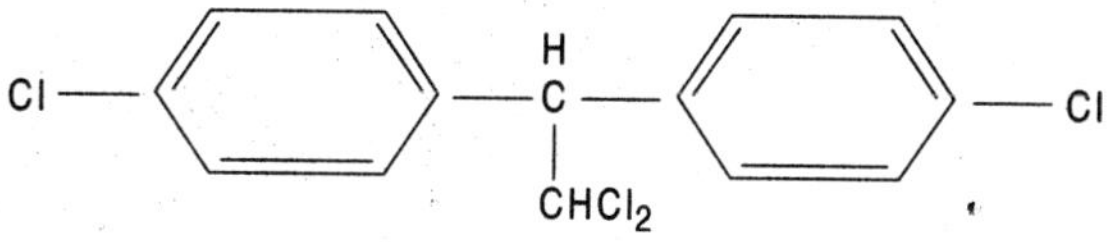

Cl H C Cl $CHCl_2$

DDD (or TDE)

DDD or TDE. Dichlorodiphenyl dichloroethane (DDD), also called tetrachlorodiphenyl ethane (TDE), is one of the impurities of technical DDT. It is less toxic to vertebrates than DDT, but has a damaging effect on the adrenal cortex of some mammals (dog) though not on that of others (*e.g.* rat). Its oral LD50 for rat is 3400 mg/kg.

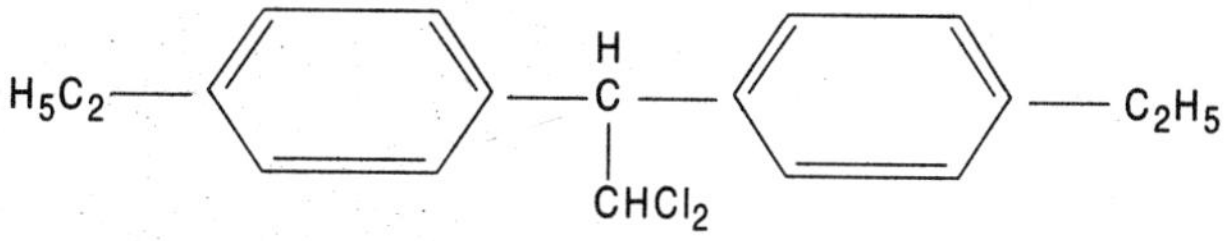

H_5C_2 H C C_2H_5 $CHCl_2$

Perthane

Perthane. This is very closely related to DDT and was developed for application where a very low, acute and chronic toxicity was required. Its oral LD50 for rat is 8170-9340 mg/kg.

Nitroparaffin analogues. Prolan and Bulan are nitrogen-containing compounds found to be better than DDT against some insects. These are, again, less toxic to vertebrates than DDT, their oral LD50 for rat being 4000 and 330 mg/kg, respectively. A mixture of these two compounds is commercially sold as "Dilan".

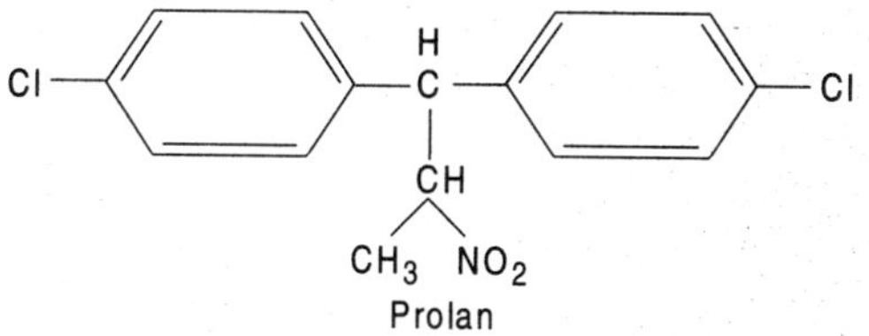

Cl H C Cl CH CH_3 NO_2

Prolan

Cl H C Cl CH C_2H_5 NO_2

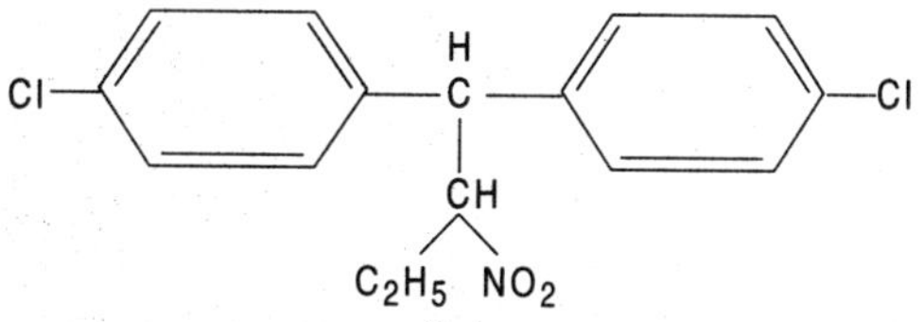

Bulan

Dicofol ($C_{14}H_9Cl_5O$), chlorobenzilate ($C_{16}H_{14}C_{12}O_2$) and dichlorodiphenylethanol ($C_{14}H_{12}C_{12}O$) are some of the DDT analogues which act as acaricides.

3. HCH. The discovery of the toxic properties of DDT spawned research into the toxic properties of related organic molecules. Hexachlorocyclohexane (HCH), which was earlier erroneously called benzene hexachloride (BHC) made a land mark in agricultural pest control. BHC was first synthesized by Michael Faraday in 1825 but its insecticidal properties were discovered by the British and French scientists in 1942. BHC is a mixture of 6 isomers, viz. alpha (α, 55-70%), beta (β, 5-14%), gamma (γ, 10-18%), delta (δ, 6-8%), eta and epsilon (η and ε, 3-4%). Of these, the beta and epsilon isomers are inactive; alpha, beta

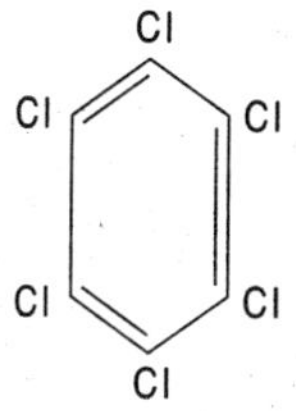

Cl Cl Cl Cl Cl Cl

BHC (HCH)

and eta isomers, slightly to moderately active, and the gamma isomer is the most active. The toxicity to arthropod pests is due to the gamma isomer or lindane, derived from the name of Van der Linden, who first, isolated the pure compound in 1912. Mode of action of HCH is similar to that of DDT. Ulike DDT, lindane is still widely used as an insecticide in agriculture and in the control of both public health pests and animal ectoparasites, particularly in many developing countries.

4. Chlorinated terpenes. These are derived by chlorinating naturally occurring terpenes.

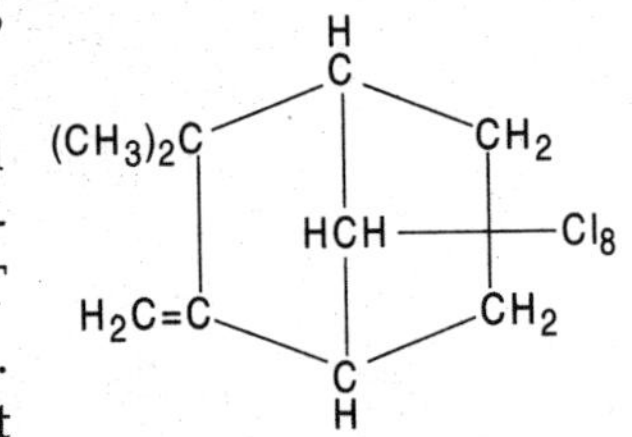

Toxaphene ($C_{10}H_{10}C_{18}$). It was discovered in 1948 by Parker and Beacher, is produced by chlorinating camphene (so mildly camphor-like in smell), is an amber coloured, waxy solid, less active than DDT and HCH, but four times more toxic to mammals than the former. Though it is a broad spectrum insecticide like DDT, it does not accumulate in the animal fat. Unlike DDT, it is specially effective for grasshoppers (and other orthopterans), cutworms, cotton insects, etc. It is compatible with a mixture of methyl parathion and DDT or with DDT alone.

Toxaphene

Strobane ($C_{10}H_{11}C_{17}$). This is a product of similar composition prepared by chlorinating a mixture of camphene and pinene to contain 66 per cent chlorine and is a straw-coloured liquid.

5. Cyclodienes. The insecticidal properties of cyclodienes were discovered in 1945 and this group includes aldrin, dieldrin, endrin, chlordane, endosulfan, etc. These are relatively persistent pesticides that have been widely used to control soil pests and termites. Like DDT, most of these insecticides are not in use now. This is because of their high mammalian toxicity, persistence (and hence residue problems in food), and development of resistance in pest species. The Environmental Protection Agency (EPA) in the USA had cancelled the registration of cyclodienes for agricultural use between 1975 and 1980. However, endosulfan is still being used for the control of crop and pubic health pests, particularly in many developing countries. In general, cyclodiens act upon central nervous system. Insects treated with these insecticides react violently followed by trembling, convulsions, and paralysis finally leading to death. The cyclodienes probably release excessive acetylcholine which is responsible for loss of nerve coordination.

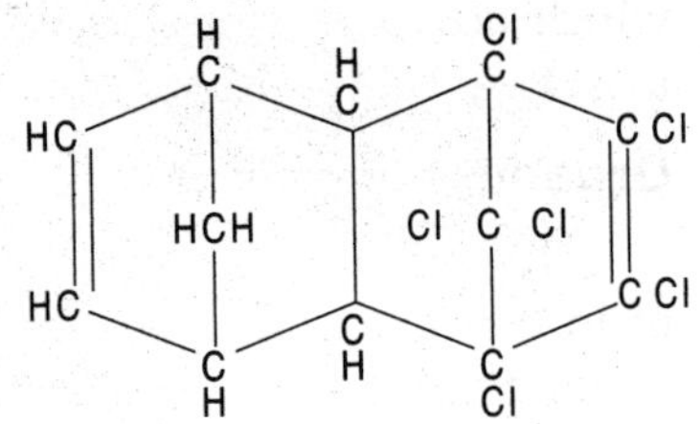

Aldrin ($C_{12}H_8C_{16}$). Aldrin (also called octalene) is named after Kurt Alder whose work with Otto Diels made the synthesis of cyclodienes possible. They received the Nobel Prize in 1950. Technical material is a white crystalline compound. An acid inhibitor, epichlorohydrin is added to prevent its impurities from changing into HCl on storage. Like other organochlorines, it is insoluble in water and variously soluble in organic solvents (benzene, CCl_4, kerosene, xylene, acetone, etc.). Formulated as 5 per cent dust, 25-50 per cent EC and 25 per cent WDP, it is effective against grasshoppers and soil insects.

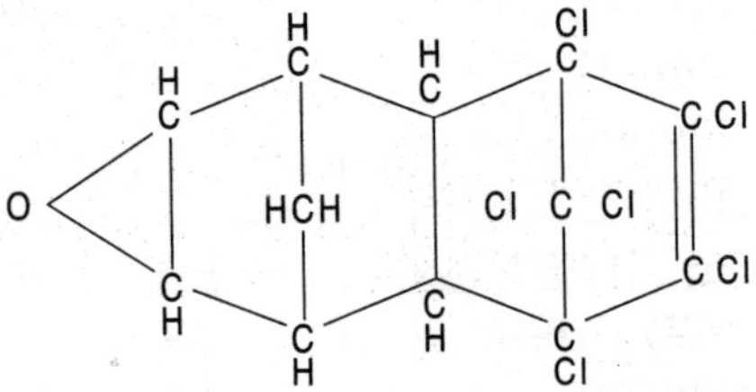

Aldrin

Dieldrin ($C_{12}H_8C_{16}O$). This is named after the German chemist, Otto Diels. It is buff to light brown coloured powder, very stable even in alkalis and has a long residual action. Formulated as 2 per cent dust, 50 per cent WDP

Aldrin

and 99 per cent EC, it is effective against household pests (flies, mosquitoes, bedbugs), crop pests (cotton, fruit, vegetable), soil insects, especially termites, and is also used for moth-proofing).

Endrin ($C_6H_8C_{16}O$). This is an endo-endo isomer of dieldrin, but less stable than the latter. Formulations are, therefore, stabilised by the addition of small amounts of hexamethylene tetramine. Formulated as 2-5 per cent dust, 25 per cent WDP and 10 per cent ED, it is, especially effective against aphids and caterpillers. But, being the most toxic chlorinated hydrocarbon (oral rat LD50, only 10 mg/kg), it was not applied on edible portions of crops.

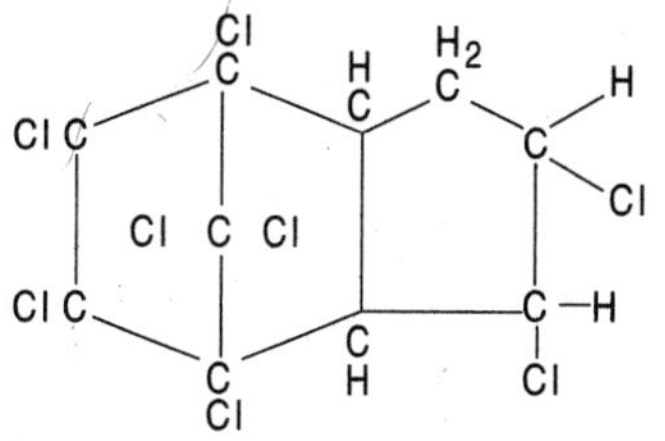

Chlordane ($C_{10}H_6C_{18}$). Chlordane was discovered in 1945 and is a brown viscous liquid smelling like cedar but unstable in alkalis. Formulated as 2-5 per cent dust, 40-50 per cent WDP by adsorption on clays and 20 per cent EC, it is effective against ectoparasites (lice, fleas, ticks), household pests (flies, carpet beetles, clothes, moths, ants, cockroaches, silverfish) and crop pests (cotton pests, grasshoppers, leaf miners, soil insects, termites).

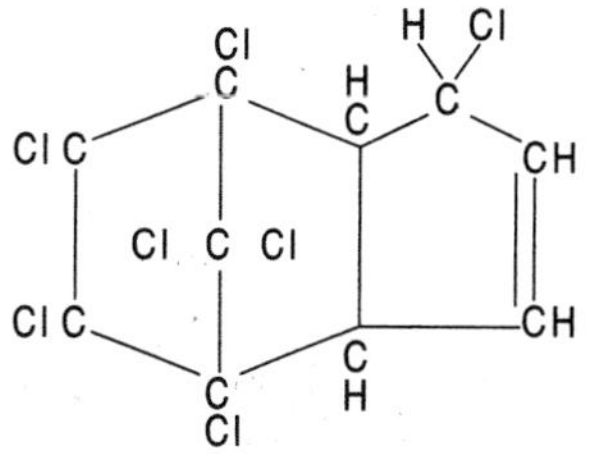

Heptachlor

Heptachlor ($C_{10}H_5C_{17}$). This is a soft waxy solid, very stable even in alkalis. Formulated as 1-2 per cent dust, 25 per cent WDP and 25 per cent EC, it is highly toxic to insects as also to man. It was recommended for grasshoppers, soil insects, termites and was mixed with fertilisers.

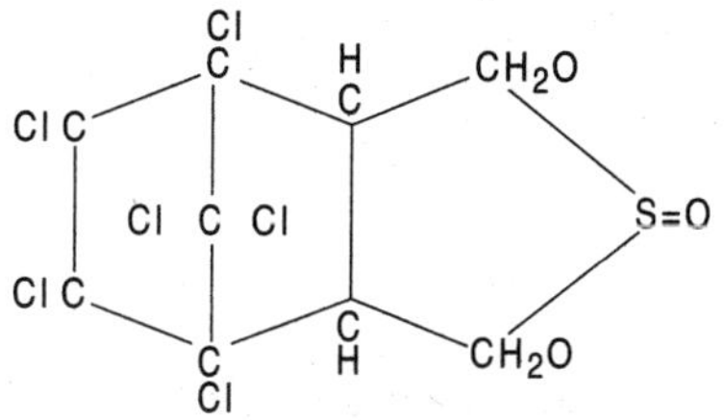

Endosulfan

6. Miscellaneous compounds. Endosulfan (Thiodon), chlordecone (Kepone), and Mirex are some of the other organochlorines which have heterogeneous chemical structures. Endosulfan ($C_9H_6C_{16}O_2S$) is a brown crystalline solid and is both, a chlorinated hydrocarbon and an organic sulphite. Formulated as 3 percent dust, 6 per cent WDP and 35 per cent EC. It is effective against tissue bores, bark-eating caterpillars, semiloopers, armyworms, cutworms, leaf-rollers, hairy caterpillars, plant bugs, pyrilla, aphids, thrips, whiteflies, leafhoppers and gall midges. It is highly toxic to fish, but is comparatively safer to bees and wildlife. Chlordecone is a white to brown solid which acts as a stomach poison against ants, grasshoppers and houseflies. Mirex kills similar insects as the earlier two but has a lower toxicity to animals than the other two.

Organophosphates

It was almost at the same time when organochlorines were developed that the discovery of insecticidal properties of organophosphates was made. A German chemist G. Schrader was looking for a replacement for nicotine, that was in short supply. He finally synthesised the first organophosphorus compound, schradan in 1941 and parathion in 1944. These compounds opened the door for the development of a group of insecticides numbering more than 100 active ingredients in over 10,000 different formulations. These include malathion, phorate, dimethoate, trichlorfon, naled, diazinon, chlorpyriphos, ethion, disulfoton, demeton, monocrotophos, dichlorvos, dicrotophos, acephate, methyl parathion and more recently profenofos and sulprofos.

Organophosphates is the most successful group of insecticides ever to be developed. They vary widely in their structure, chemical and biological properties. Many are fast-acting and quickly degradable, others are stable enough for use as systemic toxicants in plants and animals. Unlike organochlorines, organophosphates are much less environmentally persistent, more biodegradable, less subject to biomagnification and usually unstable in the presence of sunlight. Organophosphates have played a pivotal role in the green revolution and have been widely used in agriculture for the control of all types of insect pests including sap suckers, foliage feeders, tissue borers and soil insects. Many of these pesticides are still in extensive use today all over the world.

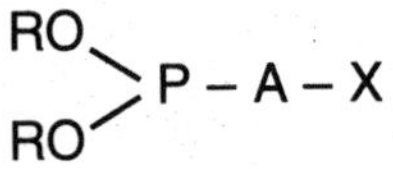

$$\begin{matrix} RO \\ RO \end{matrix} > P - A - X$$

Most organophosphates are esters of alcohols with phosphoric acid or anyhydrides of phosphoric acid with some other acids (Table 7.3). The general formula for an organophosphate is represented by, where R represents a methyl or ethyl group, A represents S (sulphur) or O (oxygen) and X represents a greatly diversified group. Compounds with P = O bond are more active than those with P = S bond because of their being more electrophilic. The generic name of on organophosphate is employed for all compounds containing phosphorus (P), but in cases where side chains attached to P are very complex, the naming of the side chain gets priority. Organophosphorus compounds have higher anticholinesterase activity, as they are structurally similar to acetylcholine. The function of cholinesterases is to hydrolyse acetylcholine. The insecticidal activity of the organophosphates is attributed to their capacity to inhibit cholinesterase in insect nervous tissue. The inhibition is irreversible, which results in accumulation of acetyl choline and disruption of the normal functioning of the nervous system and finally leading to death.

Table 7.3 Classification of organophosphates according to their chemical structure

S.No.	Group	Structure	Example(s)
1.	Phosphate	$\begin{matrix} O \\ O \end{matrix} > \overset{O}{\overset{\|}{P}} - O$	TEPP, dichlorvos, naled, mevinphos, monocrotophos, phosphamidon
2.	Phosphonate	$\begin{matrix} C \\ O \end{matrix} > \overset{O}{\overset{\|}{P}} - O$	Trichlorphon
3.	Phosphorothionate	$\begin{matrix} O \\ O \end{matrix} > \overset{S}{\overset{\|}{P}} - O$	Parathion, methyl parathion, diazinon, demeton, fenitrothion
4.	Phosphorothiolate	$\begin{matrix} O \\ O \end{matrix} > \overset{O}{\overset{\|}{P}} - S$	Oxydemeton methyl, fenthion, quinalphos, chlorpyriphos, triazophos
5.	Phosphorodithiolate	$\begin{matrix} O \\ O \end{matrix} > \overset{S}{\overset{\|}{P}} - S$	Phorate, dimethoate, malathion, phosmet
6.	Phosphoramidate	$\begin{matrix} O \\ O \end{matrix} > \overset{O}{\overset{\|}{P}} - N$	Schradan, crufomate
7.	Miscellaneous		EPN, dimefox, methamidophos

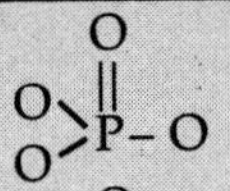

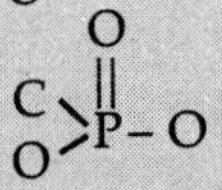

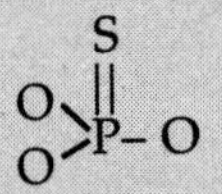

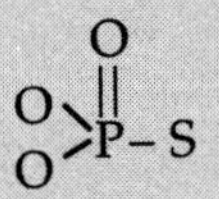

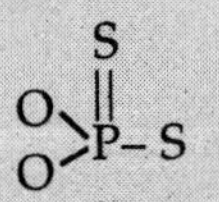

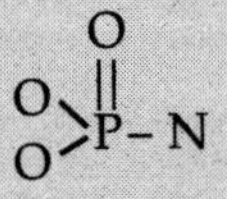

1. Phosphates

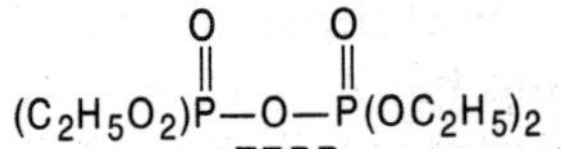

TEPP ($C_8H_{20}O_7O_2$). TEPP (tetraethyl pyrophosphate) was first synthesised by Clermont in 1854, but its insecticidal property was discovered in 1939 by the German chemist Gerhard Schrader. TEPP is

$$(C_2H_5O_2)\overset{O}{\overset{\|}{P}}-O-\overset{O}{\overset{\|}{P}}(OC_2H_5)_2$$

TEPP

a colourless, odourless, hygroscopic liquid, miscible with water and soluble in most organic solvents. It is rapidly hydrolysed into non-toxic compounds which are highly acidic and corrosive to equipments. Therefore, the insecticide should be prevented from exposure to moisture to preserve its insecticidal property and after formulation, should be used as soon as possible. It has a short residual action and hence leaves no harmful residues on plants. However, it is the most toxic of all other insecticides to mammals (oral rat LD50 is only 0.85 mg/kg) and, therefore, should be handled with care and if contacted, should be washed immediately. It is a contact action insecticide effective against aphids and plant mites.

Dichlorvos or DDVP ($C_4H_7O_4C_{12}P$). This is a pleasant smelling liquid, soluble in water and organic solvents, rapidly hydrolysed in an alkaline medium and slowly in neutral and acidic media. It has a contact, stomach and slow fumigant action. It also has a quick knock-down, is broad spectrum insecticide effective against public health insects (flies, mosquitoes), crop pests (locusts, caterpillars, miners, sucking insects) and is also used against dairy, bakery, and stored grain pests, but is highly toxic to bees.

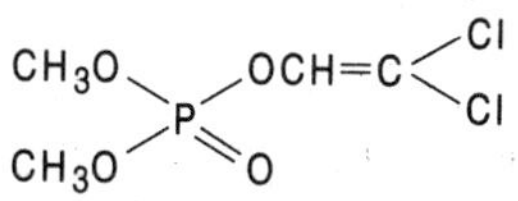

Dichlorovos

Naled ($C_4H_7Br_2Cl_{22}P$). In the technical form, this material is a straw-coloured liquid but in the pure form, it is a white solid, slightly pungent in smell, poorly soluble in water and aliphatic solvents and is unstable in alkalis. Approved for ULV formulation, it is effective against vegetable pests and not recommended for certain fruit crops like apple, grape, cherry, etc.

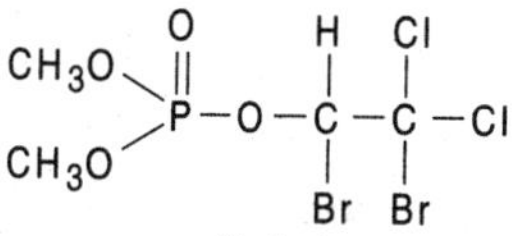

Naled

Mevinphos ($C_7H_{13}O_6P$). This is a colourless liquid, miscible with water and solvents, has powerful contact and fumigant action, is rapdily hydrolysed inside plants and so, is of short residual action and not harmful; it is broad spectrum in the range of killing.

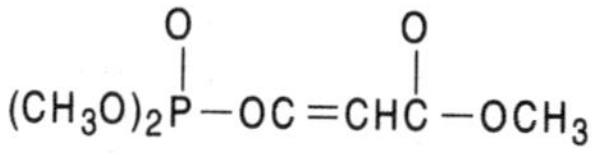

Mevinphos

Monocroptophos ($C_7H_{14}O_5NP$). This is a colourless, crystalline solid with a mild odour, miscible with water, less soluble in xylene and the least in kerosene, is rapidly hydrolysed by alkalis, systemic in action, corrosive to metals, suitable for ULV application and effective against thrips, aphids, crop mites, etc.

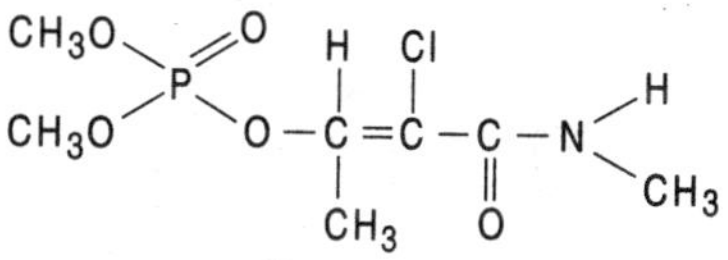

Monocroptophos

Phosphamidon ($C_{10}H_{19}O_5NCIP$). Technical material is brown and commercial material a violet liquid due to the addition of a dye. It is faint, but pleasant smelling, miscible with water and most organic solvents, systemic in action, toxic to bees and effective against rice stem borers and sucking insects.

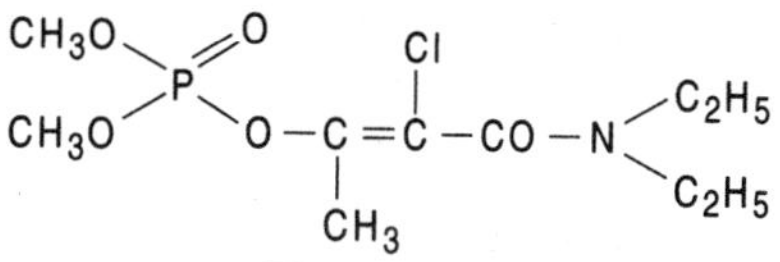

Phosphamidon

2. Phosphonates

Trichlorphon ($C_4H_8C_{13}O_4P$). This is a white crystalline solid, soluble in water, alcohol, aromatic hydrocarbons and insoluble in CCl_4, petroleum and ether. It is unstable, readily converts into dichlorvos, contact and mild fumigant in action, quick-acting, effective against dipterans (flies), hemipterans (bugs), lepidopterans (caterpillars) and has a low bee toxicity. Its granular formulation is effective against borers on maize and sugarcane.

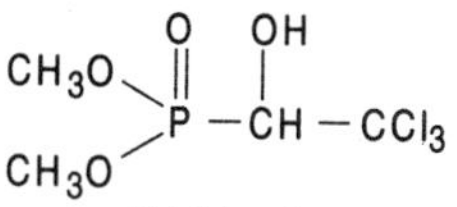

Trichlorphon

3. Phosphorothionates

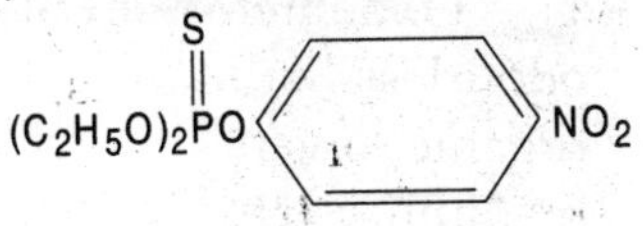

Parathion ($C_{10}H_{14}NO_5PS$). This insecticide was also discovered by Schrader. It is a dark brown to pale yellow liquid with a strong garlic smell, slightly soluble in water, insoluble in kerosene, soluble in xylene, unstable in an alkaline medium, contact and slow fumigant in action, has a broad spectrum and a short residual action and so, is safe for edible parts of plants. It is highly toxic to mammals (oral rat LD50, 3-6 kg/kg) except ruminants, whose rumen enzymes hydrolyse it; if contacted, skin should be washed at once. Formulated as 0.25-2 per cent dust, 25 per cent WDP, and 50 per cent EC, it is effective against a wide range of insects, especially cotton bollworms. While handling this insecticide, rubber gloves, goggles and a respirator should be used.

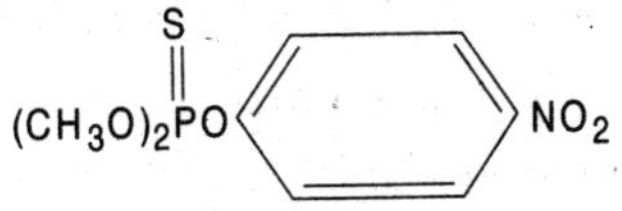

Parathion

Methyl parathion ($C_8H_{10}NO_5PS$). This was developed as a less toxic substitute of parathion. It is a white solid, less stable than parathion, but with a similar broad spectrum action, more toxic to insects and less to mammals. Methyl parathion forms a compatible mixture with DDT (the mixture sold as dust and EC) and toxaphene, which was particularly recommended for the cotton bollworms.

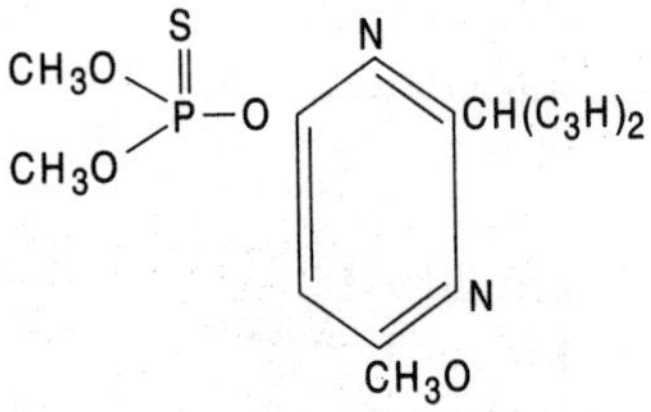

Methyl parathion

Diazinon ($C_{12}H_{21}N_2O_3PS$). This is a colourless liquid with a slight odour, very slightly soluble in water, soluble in ether, alcohol, deodorised kerosene, petroleum ether, unstable in acidic and alkaline media, contact in action and a broad spectrum general purpose insecticide with a long residual action. Formulated as 25 per cent WDP and 25 per cent EC, it is effective against borers, resistant flies, field circkets, onion maggots and excellent for the livestock ectoparasites.

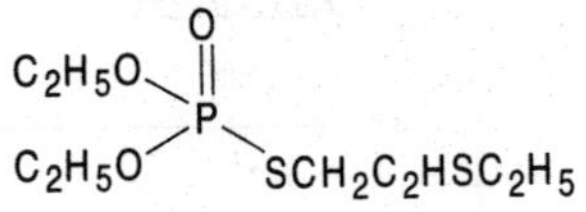

Demeton ($C_8H_{19}O_3PS_2$). This is a colourless to yellowish viscid liquid with slight odour, slightly soluble in water, soluble in organic solvents, unstable in an alkaline medium, contact and systemic in action, being used as seed systemic also, and is as highly toxic to mammals as parathion. Disytoxis a derivative of systox and is a better seed systemic.

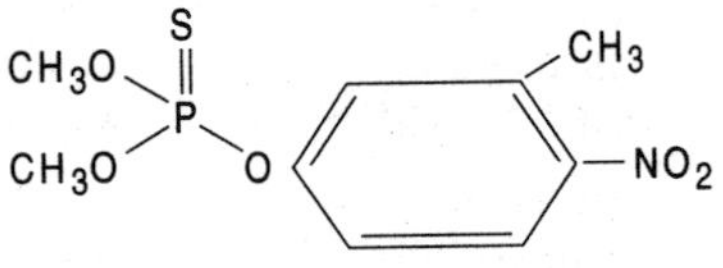

Demeton

Fenitrothion ($C_9H_{12}O_5NPS$). This is a yellow-brownish liquid developed in Japan. It is insoluble in water, soluble in alcohol, unstable in alkaline medium and contact and stomach poison being suitable for ULV application, good for rice pests, mosquito larvae, bed bugs, poultry lice, fleas, ticks and ectoparasites of livestock but toxic to bees.

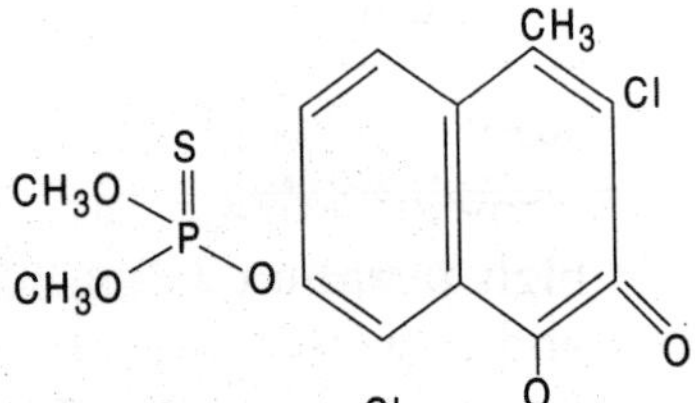

Fenitrothion

Coumaphos. This is a tan crystalline solid, which is insoluble in water, soluble in organic solvents and systemic in action being also used as an animal systemic (as 0.25-0.5 per cent spray).

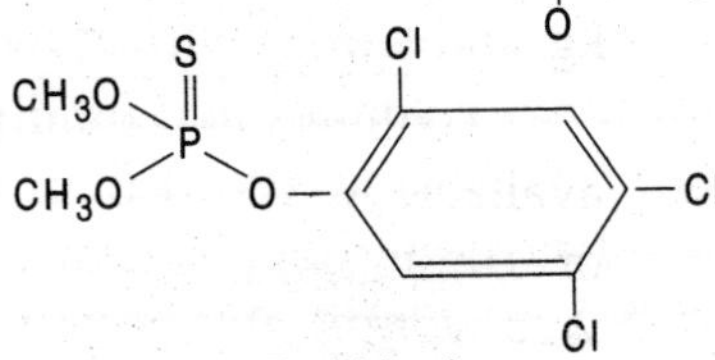

Fenchlorphos ($C_8H_8Cl_3O_3PS$). This is insoluble in water, soluble in organic solvents and is a general purpose insecticide, being also used as an animal systemic (dose 100 mg/kg of animal weight) to kill both ectoparasites and endoparasites of livestocks.

Fenchlorphos

4. Phosphorothiolates

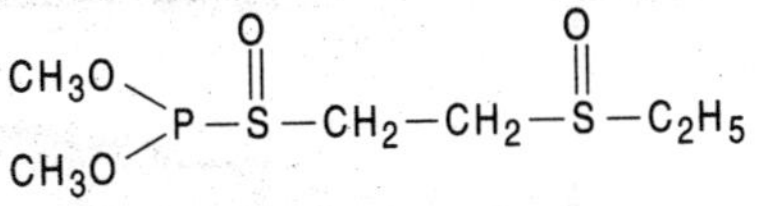

Oxdemeton-methyl ($C_6H_{15}O_4PS_2$). This is a yellowish odourless liquid which is miscible with water, soluble in most organic solvents except petroleum ether, unstable in an alkaline medium, systemic in action, effective against sucking insects and harmful to bees.

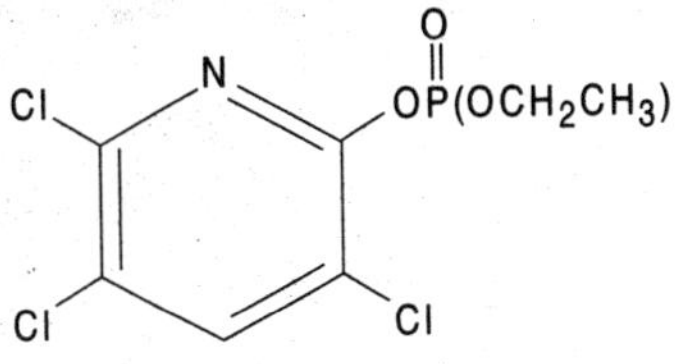

Oxydemeton-methyl

Chlorpyriphos ($C_9H_{11}Cl_3NO_3PS$). It was introduced in 1965 by the Dow Chemical Co. under the code number Dowco 179. It is a contact insecticide and acaricide especially for the control of soil pests. It persists in soil for 2-4 months. The acute oral LD50 for male rats is 155 mg/kg and the acute dermal LD50 for rabbits is about 2100 mg/kg. It is rapidly detoxified in the animal body.

Chlorpyriphos

Chlorpyriphos is sold under the trade name of Dursban and is available in the form of EC and granules. It is applied at the rate of 200-250 g a.i. per ha. As a spray, it is used in the concentration of 0.06 per cent on field crops. As a soil insecticide, it is used in higher doses against termites and white grubs. It is effective against black bug, tobacco caterpillar, termites, white grubs and ground weevils.

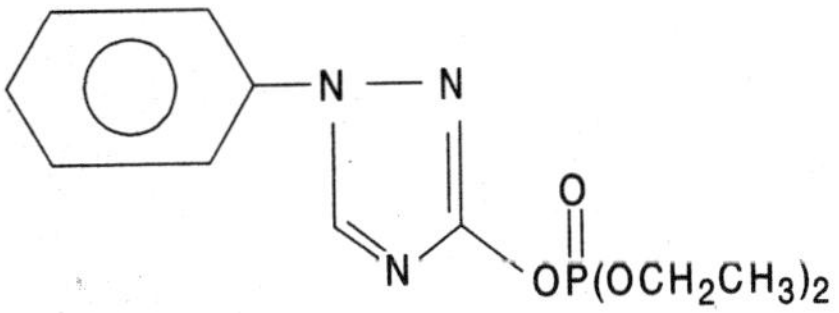

Triazophos ($C_{12}H_{16}N_3O_3P5$). It is a broad spectrum insecticide/acaricide with contact and stomach action. It is effective against aphids, thrips, lepidopteran larvae, etc., on crops like cotton, vegetables, etc. The registered formulations are 20% EC and 40% EC. The acute oral and dermal LD50 for rat is 57-68 and 2000 mg per kg, respectively. It is toxic to honey bees.

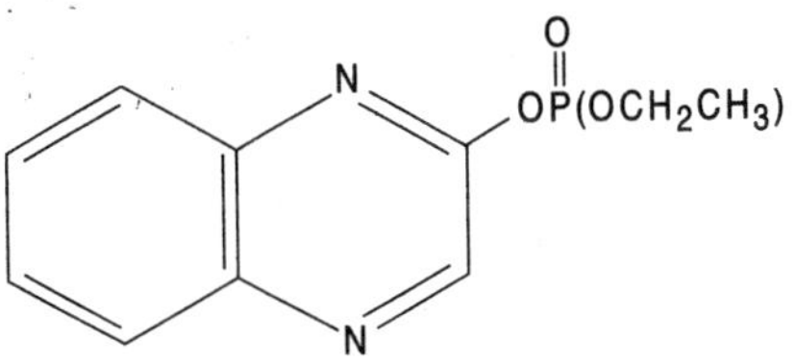

Triazophos

Quinalphos ($C_{12}H_{15}O_3H_2PS$). It is a contact and stomach insecticide and acaricide. It was introduced by Bayer in 1969 under the code No. Bayer 77049. Its acute oral LD50 and acute dermal LD50 for rats is 62-137 and 1250-1400 mg/kg, respectively.

Quinalphos

Quinalphos is sold under the trade name of Ekalux and is available in various formulations including EC, granules and dust. It is applied at the rate of 125-500 g a.i. per ha in concentrations varying from 0.025 to 0.2 per cent on a large number of crops. It is effective against the bollworm complex, armyworms, diamondback moth, hairy caterpillars, tissue borers, thrips, leaf miners, web-worms, mealy bugs, *hadda* beetles, etc.

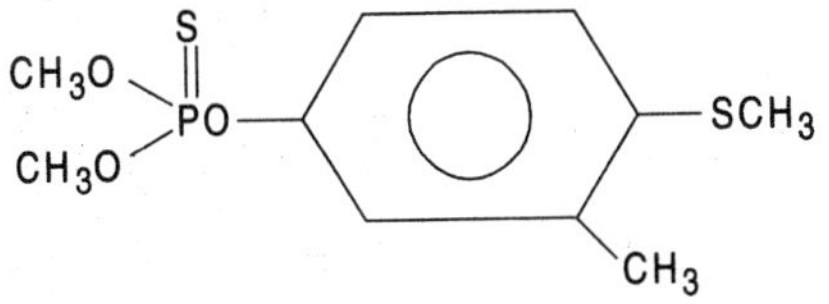

Fenthion ($C_{10}H_{15}O_3PS$). It was introduced in 1957, by Farbenfabriken Bayer A.G. under the code numbers Bayer 29493 and 51752. It is a systemic and contact insecticide. By virtue of its low volatility and stability to hydrolysis, it has high persistence. It may be phytotoxic on sensitive cotton, and apple varieties such as 'golden' or 'delicious'. The acute oral LD50 for male rats is 215 mg/kg and the acute dermal LD50 per male rats is 350 mg/kg.

Fenthion is sold under the trade names of Lebaycid, Baytex, Entex and Tiguvon, and is available in the form of EC. It is applied at the rate of 625-1250 g a.i. per ha in concentrations of 0.05 to 0.1 per cent on many field crops. It is effective against the tingid bug, leaf-folders, web-worms, thrips and leafhoppers.

5. Phosphorodithiolates

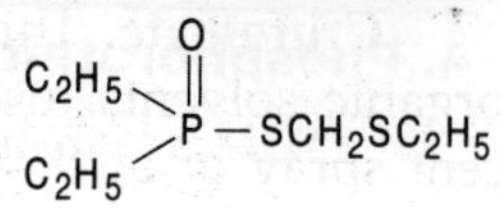

Phorate ($C_7H_{17}O_2PS_3$). This is a colourless liquid, which is less soluble in water, miscible with many organic solvents (xylene, alcohols, CCl_4, etc.), unstable in alkaline and humid conditions, and contact, systemic and slow fumigant in action. It changes into toxic compounds (sulphoxides and sulphones) inside the plants and is compatible with HCH (the mixture sold as Peddigard and used against paddy pests). Besides insects, it is also effective against nematodes and mites.

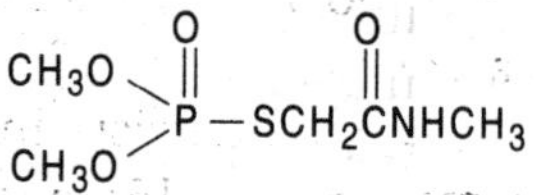

Phorate

Dimethoate ($C_5H_{12}O_3PS_2N$). This is a white crystalline solid with slight odour which is less soluble in water, soluble in some organic solvents (chloroform, acetone, benzene, alcohol, etc.), unstable in an alkaline medium, contact and systemic in action, suitable for ULV application and phytotoxic to some plants (figs, begonia, chrysanthemum).

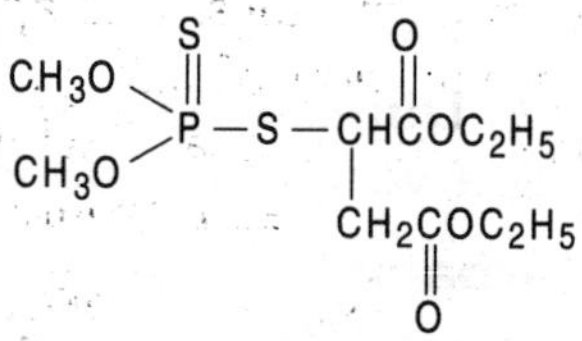

Dimethoate

Malathion ($C_{10}H_{19}O_6PS_2$). This is a light yellow to dark-brown liquid with a strong offensive odour which is slightly soluble in water and mineral oil, soluble in most organic solvents, unstable in an alkaline medium and is a contact and stomach poison. It has a low phytotoxicity and the lowest to mammals as compared to all other organophosphates. It is suitable for ULV application. Formulated as 5 per cent dust, 25 per cent WDP, 50 per cent EC and aerosol, it is effective against crop pests (aphids, psyllids, plant bugs, caterpillars, household pests (flies, mosquitoes, bedbugs) and livestock pests (lice, fleas, ticks).

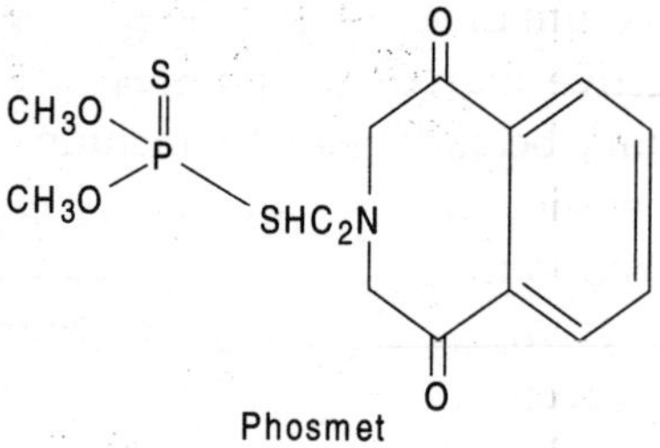

Malathion

Phosmet ($C_{11}H_{12}O_4NPS_2$). This is a white crystalline solid, acting both as an insecticide (for weevils, beetles, leafminers) and an acaricide (for mites and ticks).

Azinphosphomethyl. This is a white solid, soluble in organic solvents, is persistent with a long residual action and is a general purpose insecticide.

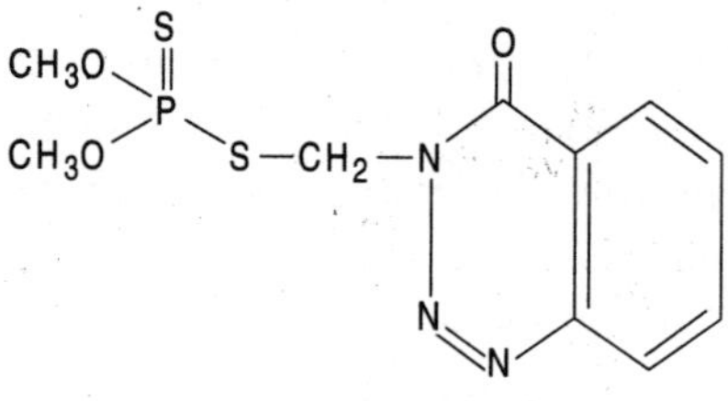

Phosmet

Azinphosphomethyl

6. Phosphoramidates

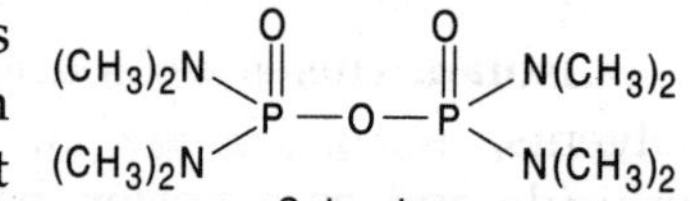

Schradan ($C_8H_{24}N_4P_2O_3$). Named after Schrader, this insecticide is a brown liquid, miscible with water and soluble in most organic solvents, quite stable in an alkaline medium, but unstable in an acidic medium, weakly contact but good systemic in action, provides protection to plants for several months and effective against hemipterans and mites.

Schradan

Crufomate. This is insoluble in water, but soluble in organic solvents, used as an animal systemic as 0.75 per cent spray or at the rate of 20-25 mg/kg of animal weight.

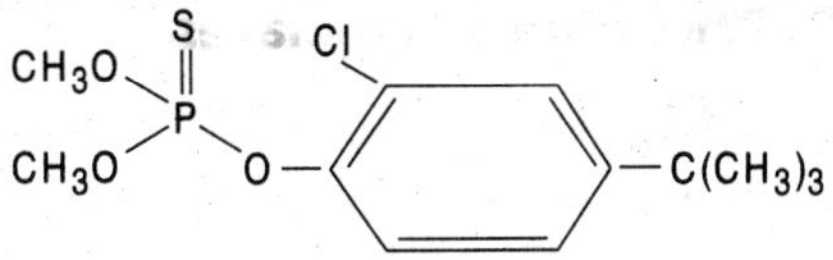

Crufomate

7. Miscellaneous compounds

EPN. EPN (ethyl 4-nitrophenyl phenyl-phosphnothionate) is a yellowish crystalline solid when pure, and a brown liquid, when it is of a technical grade. It is insoluble in water but soluble in organic solvents. Formulated as 25 per cent WDP, it is a general purpose insecticide.

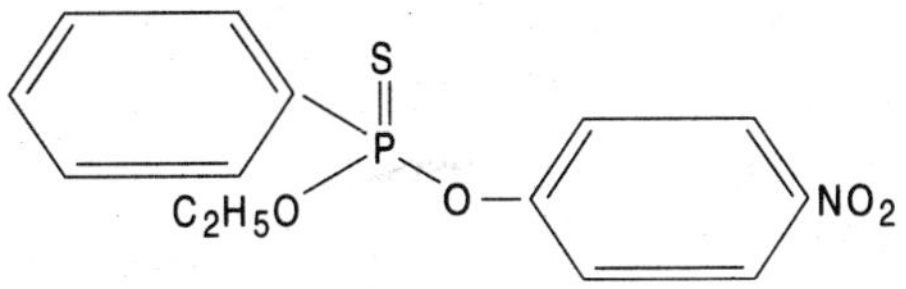

EPN

Methamidophos ($C_2H_8NO_2PS$). This is a yellowish crystalline substance readily soluble in water, alcohols, aliphatic chlorinated hydrocarbons, insoluble in petroleum, has good contact, stomach and systemic action and is effective against aphids, whiteflies and lepidopteran larvae.

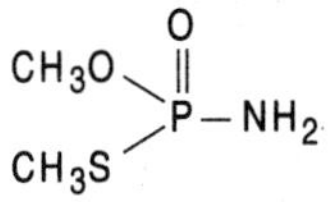

Dimefox. This is a colourles liquid, which is water soluble, volatile and so has a very short residual action and is not suited for foliage application.

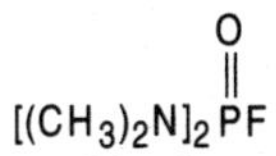

$[(CH_3)_2N]_2P(=O)F$

Dimefox

Carbamates

The carbamate insecticides were originally developed by the Geigy Corporation in 1951, but it was not until 1956 that the first commercial product, carbaryl was marketed by the Union Carbide. Carbaryl became one of the most widely adopted insecticides owing to its low mammalian toxicity and broad spectrum activity against insects. Overall, about 30 different active ingredients have been developed since 1956. Some of the most important carbamates to have been developed, include carbaryl, carbofuran, methiocarb, pirimicarb, propoxur, thiodicarb, bendiocarb and aldicarb. The carbamate insecticides, which include a number of systemic compounds, have been used to control a wide variety of pests of agricultural, medical and veterinary significance. Many of these pesticides are relatively nonpersistent, do not bioaccumulate and tend to have lower mammalian toxicity. The carbamates inhibit the enzyme acetylcholinesterase. Blockage of this enzyme results in failure of the nervous system due to accumulation of acetylcholine in the nerve synapse. The inhibition of cholinesterase is reversible as against irreversible inhibition in case of organophosphates.

Carbamate insecticides are derived from carbamic acid containing —OCONOCON group and represented by the general formula , where R represents an alkyl group and X, a diversified group. In their properties and mode of action, they are similar to organophosphates.

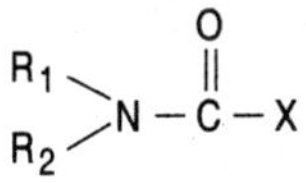

$R_1R_2N-C(=O)-X$

Carbamates are classified as heterocyclic carbamates, phenyl carbamates and oxime carbamates.

1. Heterocyclic carbamates

Isolan. This is a colourless liquid which is soluble in water and organic solvents, is volatile and so has a short residual action. It is used as an aphicide and as a poison bait for flies.

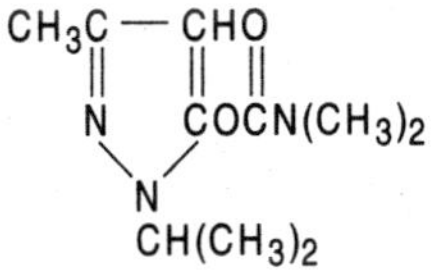

Other examples of this group are pyrolan, dimetilan, pirimicarb and dimetan.

Isolan

2. Phenyl carbamates

Carbaryl ($C_{12}H_{11}NO_2$). This is a white crystalline solid, which is almost insoluble in water and moderately soluble in some solvents (xylene, ketone, CCl_4, petroleum ether). It has contact and stomach, action, a broad spectrum, being effective against organochlorine resistant insects, cattle and poultry lice, ticks and mites of animals, crop pests (cotton, coconut, vegetables) and is also used in a mixture with HCH against paddy pests.

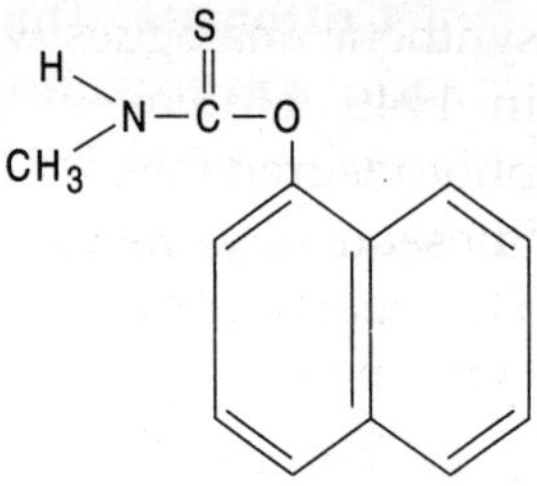

Carbaryl

Carbofuran ($C_{12}H_{15}NO_3$). This is a white crystalline solid with a phenolic smell, is unstable, has a poor solubility in water and a little better solubility in organic solvents, systemic and effective against sucking pests.

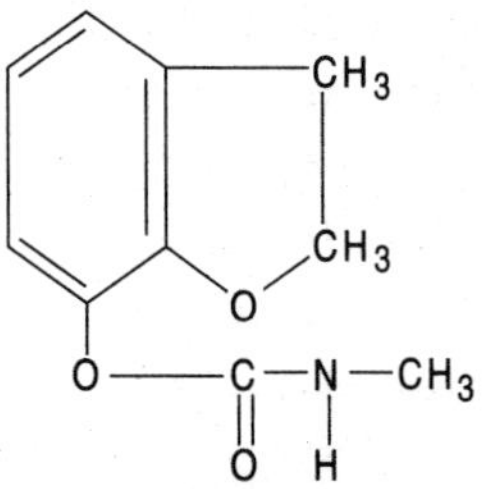

Carbofuran

Arprocarb ($C_{11}H_{15}O_3N$). This is a white to light yellow powder with a mild phenolic smell. It is readily soluble in organic solvents, very poorly in water, contact and stomach in action, causes a rapid knock-down, has a broad spectrum activity and is effective against household and public health pests. It can be used in hotels, bakeries, godowns, stables, military barracks, ships, aircraft, etc.

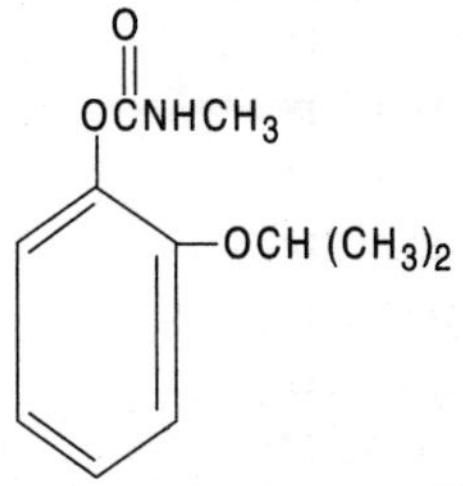

Arprocarb

Aminocarb ($C_{11}H_{16}O_2N_2$). This is a white crystalline solid which is odourless, slightly soluble in water, better in organic solvents, and effective against chewing insects, especially caterpillars.

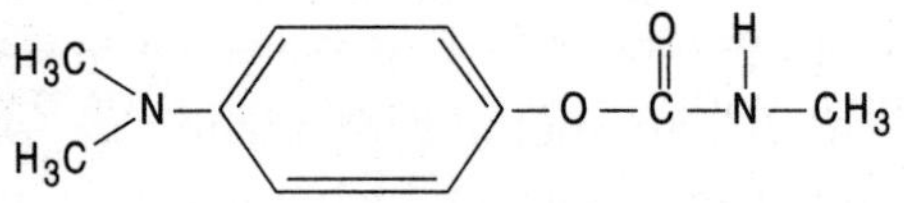

Aminocarb

Dioxacarb ($C_{11}H_{13}NO_4$). This is a white crystalline solid, which is odourless, persistent, has a stomach and contact action, is effective against cockroaches and other domestic pests, some beetles and aphids.

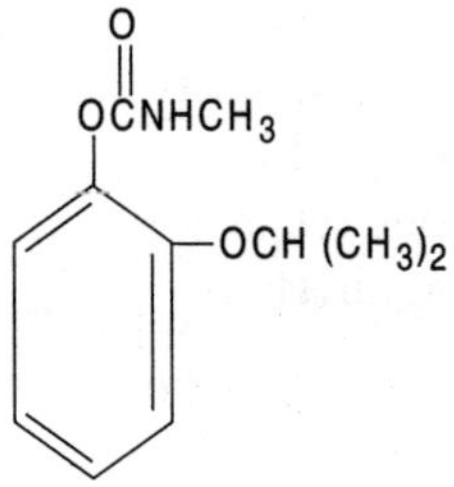

Dioxacarb

3. Oxime carbamates

Aldicarb ($C_7H_{14}N_2O_2S$). This is a crystalline white solid, with a slight sulphurous smell, which is slightly soluble in water, more in organic solvents, is systemic in action, has a wide spectrum activity and also acts as an acaricide and a nematicide. Inside the plants, it is first oxidised to its sulphoxide which is the actual toxicant and then to aldicarb sulphone, a less toxic substance.

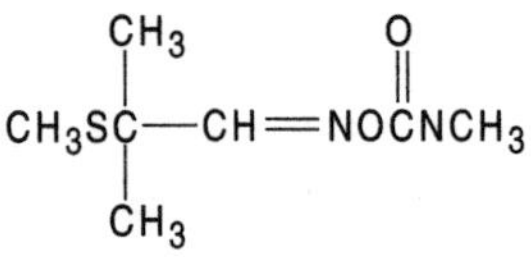

Aldicarb

Oxamyl. This is a solid substance with a sulphurous smell. It is systemic in action and effective against mites and root nematodes because of its ability to migrate to the roots when applied on the foliage.

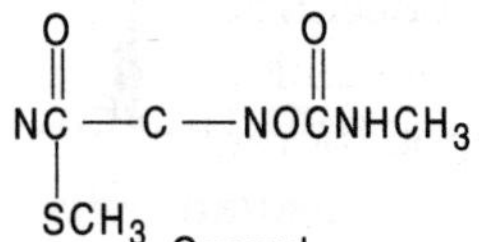

Oxamyl

Synthetic Pyrethroids

As the name indicates, synthetic pyrethroids are synthetic analogues of the naturally occurring botanical insecticide, pyrethrum. Pyrethrum is safe to mammals and possesses spectacular activity against insects. High photoinstability, however, prevented its widespread use in agriculture. Efforts were, therefore, made from 1940s onwards to develop synthetic analogues with photostability. The first synthetic pyrethroid, allethrin, was introduced in 1949. However, allethrin and the other early synthetic analogue tetramethrin were photodegradable. The first photostable analogue, permethrin, was developed only in 1972. Subsequently, more than 40 different active ingredients have been developed and marketed. The most important synthetic pyrethroids include resmethrin, phenothrin, cyfluthrin, cypermethrin, deltamethrin, fenvalerate, lambda-cyhalothrin, tralomethrin and tefluthrin.

The primary site of action by pyrethroids is the central nervous system symptomised by hyperactivity, lack of coordination, tremors and convulsions followed by paralysis and death. Control of Na+ ion permeability is through nerve membrane and is vital to nerve function. Pyrethroids act on a small fraction of the first voltage dependent Na+ ion channel in excitable nerve membranes on several parts of the insect nervous system. The major effect is to delay the closing of the Na+ ion channel agitation gate.

Synthetic pyrethroids offer a number of advantages over natural pyrethrins for pest control. Firstly, many synthetic pyrethroids are photostable, while the natural pyrethrins are not. Secondly, synthetic pyrethroids are comparatively cheaper, whereas the natural pyrethrins are relatively expensive. Thirdly, synthetic pyrethroids are more toxic to insects than natural pyrethrins and they can be applied at very low dosages. For example, the synthetic pyrethroid deltamethrin, can be applied at dose rates as low as 2.5 g per ha. A major limitation of synthetic pyrethroids is that these are generally not effective as soil insecticides. However, tefluthrin, a novel pyrethroid, is effective against a wide range of soil insects, but it does not persist in the soil. Synthetic pyrethroids have also been reported to cause resurgence in several groups of insect pests, especially whiteflies and aphids. Moreover, there has been a rapid development of resistance to synthetic pyrethroids in many important agricultural pests. Today, synthetic pyrethroids are the most widely used insecticides for pest control in many developed countries.

Cypermethrin. Cypermethrin is sold under the trade names of Ripcord, Cymbush, Cyperkill, etc., and is available as emulsifiable concentrate. It is applied at the rate of 50 g.a.i. per ha in low concentrations on cotton, arhar, sugarcane, gram, lentil, coffee, etc. It is effective against the bollworm complex of cotton, pod-borers of arhar, gram, lentil, etc.

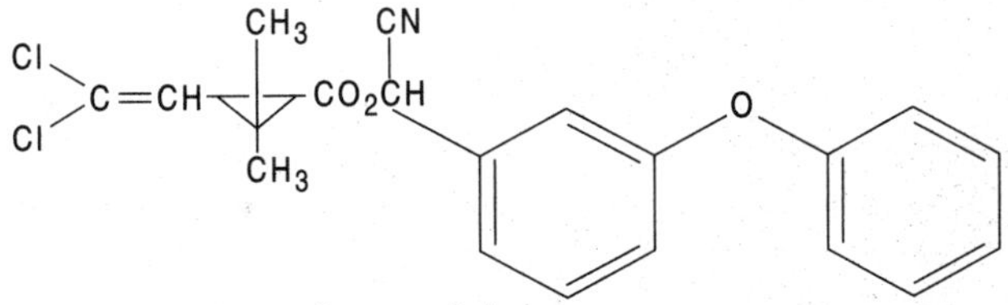

Sypermethrin

Permethrin. It is sold under the trade names of Permasect, Ambush, etc., as emulsifiable concentrate. It is applied at the rate of 50 g.a.i. per ha in low concentrations on cotton, arhar, vegetables and pulses. It is effective against the bollworm complex of cotton, tissue borers and pod borers.

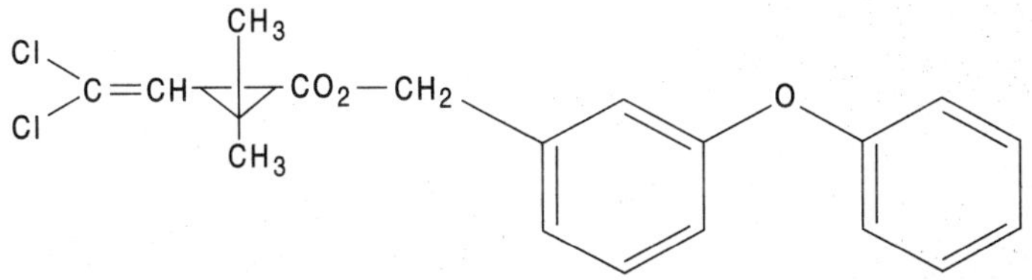

Permethrin

Deltamethrin. Deltamethrin is sold under the trade name of Decis, as an emulsifiable concentrate. It is applied at the rate of 10 g.a.i. per ha against the bollworm complex of cotton, pod borers and tissue borers of fruits, vegetables and pulses.

Fenvalerate. It is sold under the trade names of Sumicidin, Fenval, etc., as an emulsifiable concentrate. It is applied at the rate of 50 g.a.i. per ha in low concentrations against the bollworm complex of cotton, pod borers and tissue borers of fruits, vegetables and pulses.

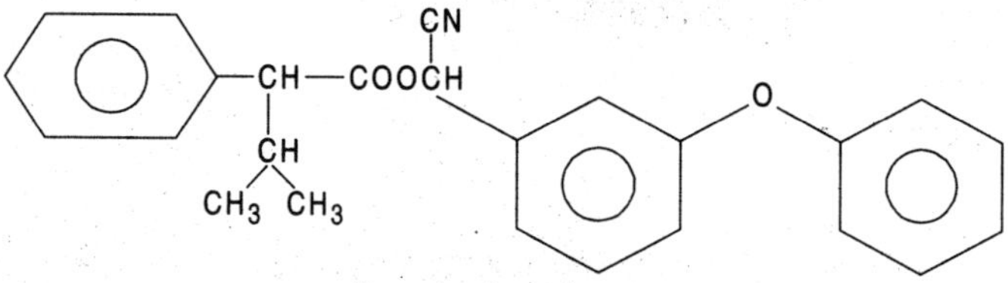

Fenvalerate

Neonicotinoids

Neonicotinoids represent the latest group of synthetic insecticides to be developed. They are so named because their development was based on the chemical structure of the alkaloid nicotine. Neonicotinoids represent a class of chemicals, nicotine mimics, in which the biochemical target is the nicotinic acetylcholine receptor of both the central and peripheral nervous systems. Like nicotine, these compounds bind to postsynaptic acetylcholine receptors resulting in hyperactivation, tremors, paralysis and death.

The first commercial neonicotinoid, imidacloprid, was discovered in 1984, and was commercially marketed for the first time in 1991, for the control of sucking pests. Since then, four more neonicotinoids—nitenpyram (1995), acetami-prid (1996), thiamethoxam (2001) and lately flonicamid (2005) have been commercially, developed.

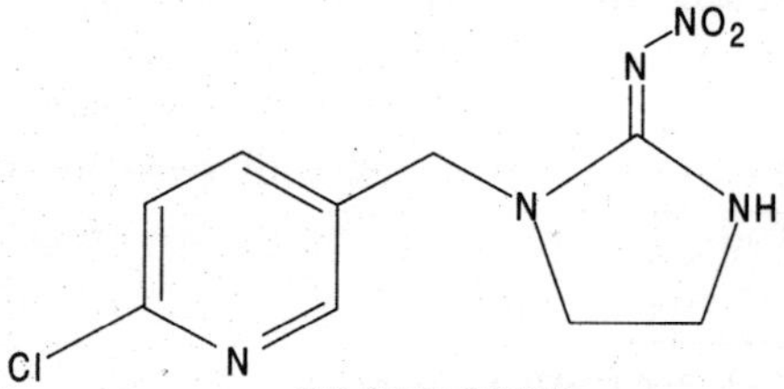

IMLDACLOPRID

Imidacloprid is a systemic and contact insecticide, exhibiting low mammalian toxicity. It has superior activity against sucking insects such as aphids, leafhoppers, planthoppers, thrips and whiteflies; it is also effective against some coleopteran, dipteran and lepidopteran pests. With excellent systemic and good residual characteristics, imidacloprid is especially appropriate for seed treatment and soil application. The other neonicotinoids are also effective against sucking pests, and a number of chewing and/or biting pests. The recently introduced novel insecticide, flonicamid, has selective activity against hemipteran pests such as aphids and whiteflies, and thysanopteran pests. This insecticide has antifeedant activity against aphids, regardless of differences in species, stages and morphs.

Miscellaneous Insecticides

Diflubenzuron. It is an 'insect growth regulator', more precisely a chitin synthesis inhibitor' that interferes with moulting process in the larvae leading to abnormal developments. It is effective against most leaf feeding larvae at 25-75 g a.i./ha and at 50-150 g a.i/ha against cotton bollworms. It is non-toxic to predators and honey bees. It is registered as 25% WP in India. Its oral LD50 for rat is 4640 mg/kg and dermal LD50 for rabbit 2000 mg/kg.

Pyriproxyfen. This is a 'juvenile hormone analogue' a sub-category of the 'insect growth regulators' that inhibits the process of metamorphosis in larvae and nymphs and its application leads to larval / nymphal adult intermediates or supernumerary larvae or nymphs. In the adult insects, application of pyriproxyfen affects the process of oogenesis resulting in gonadotropic effects. The analogue is registered in many countries including India and is commercially available for control of several insect pests such as whiteflies, beetles, midges, fruits, vegetables and cotton insect pests.

Cartap. It is commonly known as cartap hydrochloride (C7H16ClN3O3S2). Its insecticidal properties were reported in 1967. It is systemic insecticide with stomach and contact action. It acts on the central nervous system by ganglionic blocking action, resulting in paralysis, cessation of feeding and death due to starvation. It is effective against rice stem borer and leaf-folder, sugarcane shoot borer, diamondback moth, etc. It is registered in India as 50% SP and 4G. Its acute oral and dermal LD50 for rat is 325-345 and 1000 mg/kg, respectively.

Fipronil. Fipronil is a new phenylpyrazole insecticide that has excellent activity against many soil and foliar insect pests. Its insecticidal properties were discovered by Rhone-Poulene Ag. Co. in 1987. This broad spectrum insecticide is highly active via ingestion, contact and systemic routes. It has shown a great promise both as a soil and foliar insecticide against several important insect pests of cotton. Its unique action as a potent blocker of the GABA-gated chloride channel makes it effective against insects resistant to carbamate, organophosphate and pyrethroid insecticides. Acute oral LD50 for rats is 100 mg/kg and dermal LD50 is 72000 mg/kg.

Spinosad. It is a natural source insecticide containing a mixture of two components derived from fermentation technology produced by *Saccharopolyspora spinosa,* a species of actinomycete. It is formulated as 48SC and is active against *Helicoverpa armigera,* leafhopper, aphid and whitefly on cotton at 75-100 g a.i./ha.

Table 7.4 Number of chemicals screened, and cost involved to develop a new pesticide

Year	Number of chemicals screened	Approximate cost (million US$)
Pre-green revolution era		
1956	1,800	0.85
1964	3,600	2.55
Green revolution era		
1970	7,400	NA
1972	10,000	NA
1977	12,000	17.00
Post-green revolution era		
1987	16,000	17.00–25.50
1989	20,000	34.00
1996	30,000	51.00-76.50
1998	50,000	85.00-102.00

NA = Accurate data not available

Source : Thacker (2002)

Organochlorines, organophosphates and carbamates have played a major role in pest control during the green revolution, whereas the synthetic pyrethroids neonicotinoids, spinosad and some of the pesticides from organophosphate groups (*e.g.* monocrotophos, quinalphos, chlorpyriphos, triazophos, etc.), have been dominant during the post-green revolution period. The following three major changes can be characterised in terms of development of synthetic chemicals for pest control :

- There is a drastic decrease in the rate of application of pesticides. For example, in Europe, the rate of application of lead arsenate in the beginning of the twentieth century was 10 kg per ha, which has come down to 10 g per ha in case of alphacypermethrin at the end of the twentieth century.
- There has been considerable increase in the cost involved in research and development, associated with bringing a new active ingredient in the market (Table 7.3). The main reasons for this increase are the decline in the rate of discovery of novel molecules for pest control, and an increase in the number and complexity of tests required prior to product approval.
- There has been a decline in the number, but increase in size of the companies involved in pesticide research and development. For example, Hoechst and Rhone-Poulene merged to create Aventis towards the end of 1998. Zeneca and Novartis joined hands to create Syngenta.

C. Fumigants

Fumigants are insecticides in a gaseous form, that enter the body through the spiracles and spread all over via the tracheae and tracheoles. They kill insects in two ways : by clogging the tracheal system and cutting it off from the oxygen supply, and by their own toxic action interfering with the respiratory process. Fumigants, therefore, can kill all kinds of insects irrespective of their mouthparts or feeding habits.

A good fumigant should have the following qualities :

- It should be volatile with a deep penetrating power.
- It should not be corrosive to the equipment or household articles.
- It should not adversely affect the germinating quality of the seeds and should not harm man and plants.
- It should not be inflammable.
- It should be cheap.

Hydrogen cyanide (HCN). Hydrogen cyanide or hydrocyanic acid gas is a colourless gas with a bitter almond odour. It is lighter than air, not deeply penetrating and soluble in water. It tarnishes metals and is difficult to rid it off a treated surface, is highly inflammable, and non-toxic to plants at recommended doses, but is deadly to man and animals. It is prepared fresh at the time of use by heating concentrated H_2SO_4 with cyanides of Na, K or Ca by the followings methods :

Pot method. Carefully measured sulphuric acid is poured into water contained in a good quality glazed earthen vessel kept inside the tent or room to be fumigated. While the mixture is still hot due to its own reaction, a weighted amount of cyanide salt is dropped preferably by a remotely controlled device or else the operator must leave the room atonce after dropping the salt.

Machine method. Measured quantities of the constituents are introduced into a machine and the generated gas is led to the desired enclosure through pipes (hoses). This method has been found suitable for citrus plants covered with a portable tent.

Liquid method. In this method, liquid HCN is stored in a steel container and pumped into the desired enclosure to vaporise.

Dry method. Here, Ca $(CN)_2$ or liquid HCN is absorbed in dust (earth) or on paper discs which are then sealed in cans. When needed, the cans are opened and the contents scattered in the desired enclosure. Atmospheric moisture brings about the reaction and liberates the gas according to the reaction.

$$Ca(CN)_2 + 2H_2O \longrightarrow Ca(OH)_2 + 2HCN \uparrow$$

Commercially, HCN is available under the trade names Calcid (German product), in the form of bricks sealed in tins which contains 50 per cent HCN by weight, Cynogas (American product), in the form of a powder (Cynogas A) or granules (Cynogas G) in sealed tins, which contain 25 per cent HCN by weight and Cynag (British product) like Cynogas, in a form containing only 20 per cent HCN. The usual doses of HCN are low on account of its high toxicity and consquently, is less expensive. However, great care has to be taken in its application.

Carbon bisulphite or disulphite (CS_2). This is a colourless to yellowish liquid with an unpleasant odour. It is highly penetrating and, therefore, used for packed or heaped materials like bales, bins, stored grains and also for pests of fabrics, furniture, soil, borers and intestinal bots and worms. It is highly absorptive leaving a yellow stain on surfaces. Since it is highly inflammable, it is mixed with CCl_4.

Methyl bromide or bromomethane (CH_3Br). This is a colourless gas with a faintly sweetish smell. High penetrating power, great insect toxicity, non-inflammability and stability are the plus points which make it suitable for mills, warehouses, granaries, packed foodstuff and quarantine plants. However, it is toxic to mammals and being highly volatile, needs special equipments for its application.

Ethylene dichloride ($C_2H_4Cl_2$). This is a colourless sweet smelling liquid with a low mammalian toxicity, inflammable, and so, mixed with CCl_4. It has a moderate insect toxicity and is mainly used for stored grains.

Ethylene dichloride-Carbon tetrachloride mixture (EDCT). This can occur both in gaseous and liquid forms, can be safely stored and is free from hazards

Carbon tetrachloride (CCl_4). This is colourless liquid or gas with a chloroform-like small, has a low insect toxicity, and being non-inflammable and non-explosive, its chief use is as a fumigant additive to reduce inflammability.

Dichloropropene ($C_3H_4Cl_2$) and dichloropropane ($C_3H_5Cl_2$). Also called D-D mixture, it occurs in a liquid form and is commonly used as a soil fumigant for the control of plant nematodes and soil insects. It is, however, toxic to plants and gives an off-flavour to potatoes and, therefore, should be used much in advance of the harvest.

Paradichlorobenzene ($C_6H_4Cl_2$) and naphthalene ($C_{10}H_8$). Both these are white crystalline solids with a characteristic odour and a slow vaporising nature. They are popular as moth balls or flakes for moth control. Though mainly used to protect clothes, woollens carpets, museum specimens (of insects also), they can also be used as soil fumigants.

Hydrogen phosphide or phosphine. This is sold in the form of tablets, containing aluminium phosphide and ammonium carbamate, which on contact with the moisture in the air, gives out phosphine gas. It is widely used as a grain fumigant in bags or bins, but is highly toxic to mammals. A tablet or pellet of 3 g is enough for one ton of grain.

Chloropicrin (CCl_3NO_2). A colourless gas, it is also called tear-gas which is highly lachrymatory and poisonous to mammals. As an insecticide, it has limited use in flour mills, grain elevators, stored grain, against household pests and as a soil fumigant. It is extremely irritating to insects and drives them out of their hiding places.

Nicotine ($C_{10}H_{14}N_4$). This is commonly used as a greenhouse fumigant due to its being safe for both the plants and the operator. As a fumigant, only pure nicotine and not its sulphate is employed. It is heated in shallow pans or forced through heated pipes. Commercially, nicotine-impregnated material "Nicfume" is sold in containers in which holes are made and the material is ignited to smoulder into fumes.

Besides nicotine, other plants or their products like neem and *sandal dhoop* are also burnt to ward-off insects like mosquitoes. Smoke is a familiar fumigant used against the honey bees.

D. ACARICIDES

Chlorobenzilate. Ethyl 4, 4′-dichlorobenzilate ($C_{16}H_{14}C_3C_{12}$) was introduced as an acarcide by the Geigy Chemical Co. in 1952. It is a chlorinated hydrocarbon, closely related to DDT in structure. It is usually not phytotoxic, but sometimes it may cause injury to peach, plum, rose and prunus. Unlike DDT, it is not accumulated in body fat. The mammalian toxicity as LD50 is reported to be 1000 mg/kg.

It is also marketed under the trade names of Folbex, Akar and Acarben as 25 per cent wettable powder or emulsifiable concentrate. It is recommended for use on fruits, cotton, cucurbits, turfs and ornamental plants against all species of phytophagous mites. It is applied at the rate of 0.75-2.50 kg per ha. Being a selective acaricide, it is used against the tracheal mites, causing acarine disease in honey bees. The hives are fumigated by burning Folbex paper strips.

Dicofol. 1, 1-bis (p-chlorophenyl)-2, 2, 2-trichlorethanol ($C_{14}H_{13}OC_{15}$) was introduced as an acaricide in 1955 by Robin and Haas Chemical Co., under the trade name of Velthane. It is also related to DDT in structure. It differs from DDT only with respect to bridge 11, which is replaced by 'OH'. It is non-systemic with long residual activity. It is non-phytotoxic. The mammalian toxicity (LD50) is 684 mg/kg.

It is marketed as EC, WP and dust. It is applied at the rate of 1.0-2.5 kg per ha on all types of plants against mites. It gives good initial kill and long residual action. Its residue disappears in soil rapidly, but traces may persist for a year or more. It is compatible with most other pesticides.

A number of insecticides are equally effective against mites. These include thiometon, phorate, menazon, formothion, chlorpyriphos, etc.

E. NEMATICIDES

These chemicals are used for controlling plant parasitic nematodes. Some of the common nematicides are mentioned here.

Dibromochloropropane (DBCP). 1, 2-Dibromo-3-chloropropane ($C_3H_6Br_2Cl$) as soil fumigant was introduced in 1955, under the trade names of Nemagon and Fumazon by Shell Chemical Co. and Dow Chemical Co. It is also marketed as Memapaz and Namafume. As nematicide, it is particularly effective against root-knot nematodes when the soil temperature is 21-27°C. It is non-phytotoxic to most of the plants at normal concentrations. Some plants such as potato and tobacco are, however, sensitive to its action. It is irritating to eyes and its LD50 is reported to be 173 mg/kg.

It is available as EC and granules. The dose of its application varies from 12-30 litres per ha. It can be applied around the basin area of woody perennials. Also, it can be injected into soil or applied with irrigation water to the standing crops which are tolerant to its action.

This nematicide is very effective for the control of root-knot nematodes, cyst nematodes, stylet nematodes, root lesion nematodes and other ectoparasitic nematodes present in the rhizosphere of roots.

Dichloropropane-dichloropropene (D-D mixture). DD mixture is a by product of plastic manufacture which was first used as a soil fumigant in 1943 by Dow Chemical Co. and Shell Chemical Co. Since then, it has been in use as an effective nematicide in cooler climates (4-27°C). It is a mixture of 1, 3-dichloropropane and 1, 2-dichloropropene, and is phytotoxic. It is a dark liquid at ordinary room temperature. It does not accumulate in soil and is safe for the soil microorganisms. It has quite a high mammalian toxicity, LD_{50} being 140 mg/kg. Its contact with skin or inhaling of its fumes should be avoided. Its strong odour warns the operator and it should be stored away from food. Being inflammable, it should be used with great care.

The commercial names of this nematicide are DD, Vidden D and Telone. It is liquid fumigant and can be applied to the properly tilled soil by injecting it and later plugging the holes. A crop should be sown or transplanted after a period of three weeks so as to avoid phytotoxic effects. The dosage varies from 200 to 400 litres per ha. It is very effective for the control of cyst nematodes, *Heterodera* and *Globodera* spp.; the root-knot nematodes, *Meloidogyne* spp; the burrowing nematodes, *Rapopholus similis* and the root-lesion nematodes, *Pratylenchus* spp.

Ethylene dibromide. This chemical has been described in the section of 'Fumigants'. Its trade name is Dowfume W-85. This fumigant is in liquid form and should be applied by injection method upto a depth of 15 cm in rows 25-40 cm apart. The dose per hectare is 250 kg. After soil fumigation, a crop should not be sown or transplanted before a waiting period of 3 weeks in order to avoid phytotoxic effects. It can be employed for the control of the root-knot, root-lesion and cyst nematodes.

Ethoprop. It is marketed under the commercial name of Mocap by Mobile Chemical Co. and is available in granular or EC form. It is applied at the rate of 2.4 kg/ha.

Phenamiphos. It is commercially available under the name of Nemacur, and its formulations are both granular and EC. It is very effective for the control of root-knot and cyst nematodes. Being a systemic nematicide, it is capable of killing both ecto- and endo-parasitic nematodes. The application rate varies from 5 to 10 kg a.i.per ha and it can be applied before or at the time of sowing or transplanting a crop.

Metham sodium. Sodium N-methyl dithiocarbamate dihydrate ($C_2H_4NS_2Na_2H_2O$) was introduced in 1954 by Stauffer Chemical Company and E.I. Dupont de Nemours, under the trade name of Vapam. It is a soil fumigant for the control of fungi, bacteria, nematodes, weeds and soil insects. It is phytotoxic and in gaseous form, is irritating to eyes, skin and mucous membranes. The LD_{50} is reported to be 1260 mg/kg.

It is also sold under the trade names of Vitafume, Unifume, Sistan, Trimaton and Mapsol. It is available in water miscible form and the breakdown product is methyl isothiocyanate. The soil application is by injection method and it should be applied 2-3 weeks before transplanting the crop. The dose varies upto 1000 litres per ha. It controls the root-knot and lesion nematodes. It is not advisable to use this chemical in greenhouses. It is corrosive to brass and copper.

Methyl bromide (CH_3Br). Chemical and biological properties of this compound have been described under the section on 'Fumigants'. It is a gas fumigant and is available under the trade names of Embafume-C and Dowfume MC-2. Dowfume

MC-2 is a formulation of bromomethane and 2 per cent chloropicrin. It should be applied in the soil before transplanting or sowing of a crop at the rate of 100-400 kg per ha under a gas-tight cover. It is a broad spectrum nematicide and kills all types of plant parasitic nematodes.

Qamyl. The commercial name of the chemical is Vydate. It is available in the form of granules and as emulsifiable concentrate. The granules can be applied by broadcasting in the field before sowing or at the time of sowing. Emulsifiable concentrate can also be sprayed on plants for the control of stem and bulb nematodes, and also root-knot nematodes infesting vegetable crops.

Aldicarb. Aldicarb ($C_7H_{14}N_2O_2S$) was introduced as an insecticide-acaricide-nematicide in 1962 by the Union Carbide Corporation, USA. It is systemic in nature and at the recommended dose it does not damage seeds. It is highly toxic to mammals and the LD_{50} is only 0.93 mg/kg. It is marketed under the name Temik and is formulated as granules having 5 and 10 per cent active ingredient. It is very effective at the dose of 2-4 kg a.i. per ha and can be broadcast or drilled at the planting sites. The root-knot, cyst, root lesion and citrus nematodes can be controlled effectively. It has no phytotoxic effects and hence, can be applied on vegetable crops quite safely.

Carbofuran. Chemical and biological properties of carbofuran have been described under the section on Carbamates. It is available in granular and flowable formulations under the commercial name Furadan. The recommended dose is 2 to 4 kg a.i. per ha for the control of root-knot and lesion nematodes infesting vegetable crops. Flowable powder can be applied as seed treatment to provide protection to the newly emerging seedlings.

Dazomet. Dazomet ($C_5H_{10}N_2S_2$) was introduced by the Union Carbide Corporation, USA, in 1952, as a pre-plant soil fumigant under the trade name of Mylone. It is reported to be phytotoxic to growing plants. It is the breakdown product, methyl isothiocyanate, which is toxic to nematodes. Dazomet is irritating to skin and the mammalian toxicity as LD_{50} is reported to be 500 mg/kg.

It is also marketed under the trade names of Basamid, DMTT and Soil-Kare. It is available in the form of 50 and 85 per cent WP, 50 per cent granules, and 2 and 5 per cent dusts. It is recommended for use on tobacco and ornamental plants at the rates of 200-500 kg per ha. It controls all nematodes except the cyst forming nematodes. Since it is phytotoxic, it is applied 4 weeks before planting. It also kills some weeds.

12. Fensulfothion. Fensulfothion ($C_{11}H_{18}O_4PS_2$) was introduced as a soil insecticide and nematicide by Farbenfabriken Bayer, A.G. of Germany in 1964 under the trade name Dasanit. It is systemic and long-persistent. It is non-phytotoxic at the doses recommended for use. It is a highly toxic compound and the mammalian LD50 is reported to be 2.2 mg/kg.

It is available as emulsifiable concentrate and granules. It is recommended for use on cruciferous vegetables, tobacco, tomato, potato and ornamental plants. It is recommended for the control of root-knot and golden nematodes, when applied at the rate of 1-16 kg a.i. per ha. It protects the plants against soil insects and nematodes for 4 months. It should not be applied on the foliage or in the greenhouses. It is also toxic to fish in water.

13. Phorate. The chemical and the biological properties have been described under the section on Organophosphates. It is also a granular nematicide and is available as Thimet. For the control of root-knot and other ectoparasitic nematodes, it is recommended at the rate of 10 kg a.i. per ha. It is applied by broadcast method and then mixed into the soil.

F. RODENTICIDES

Strychnine. Strychnine ($C_{20}H_{20}N_2O$) was used as a rodenticide in Europe around 1930 Chemically, it was synthesised in 1954 in USA and was distributed by a number of companies. It is of botanical origin and was extracted from the seeds of *Strychnos* spp. It is a strong mammalian poison; the LD100 for rats is 1-30 mg/kg and for man is 30-60 mg/kg.

It is sold under the trade names of Sanaseed, Mousetox, Kwik-kill, Rodex, etc. It kills mice, squirrels, dogs, porcupines, rabbits, jackals, birds and other animals. It is marketed as a concentrated powder which is used for making baits. It is mixed with raw meat as a bait to kill jackals.. It can also be used by mixing it with grains, vegetables or fruits at the rate of 0.5 per cent by weight. Since it is a deadly poison, its handling needs utmost care by the users. One application is usually sufficient to kill the animals.

Zinc phosphide. Zinc phosphide (Zn_3P_2) was introduced by Hooker Chemical Co. in 1943. This rodenticide belongs to inorganic phosphide group and has long been in use. It is an acute poison for mammals and birds. It is stable when dry, but decomposes slowly to phosphine in moist air. It is a general poison and the mammalian toxicity at LD_{50} is reported to be 45.7 mg/kg. It is sold under the trade names of Rumetan, Mous-con and Kilrat as 80-95 per cent concentrated powder.

It is usually used in the concentration of 2.5 per cent as a bait for killing field rats, mice and other rodents. The bait is prepared by mixing one part of zinc phosphide with 40 parts of wheat-flour, adding sufficient water to make pellets. Alternatively, the poison can be coated on grains of wheat, maize, sorghum or *bajra* (the pearl millet, *Pennisetum typhoides*) after they are rinsed with a small quantity of some edible oil. It is an acute poison and only one dose is needed to kill the animal. The disadvantage of this compound is that rats come to know of its presence and they develop bait shyness.

Warfarin. Warfarin ($C_{19}H_{16}O_4$) is the first anti-coagulant coumarine derivative which was synthesized by Wisconsin Alumni Research Foundation in 1950. It was sold by S.B. Penick and Co. and Prentis Chemical Co. The mammalin toxicity as LD50 is reported to be 186 mg/kg as a single dose. On a multiple dose basis, the LD100 for rats is reported to be 0.2 mg/kg/day, for 5 days.

It is sold under the trade names of Rat-B-Gon, Warf, Warfarat, Dethmor and Duocide in numerous formulations such as concentrated powder, dust, bait, water miscible liquid, etc. It is used to kill rats and mice. The rats die of internal haemorrhage after eating it for about 5 days. It is applied in cereal baits at the rate of 0.025-0.05 per cent by weight. The 0.5 per cent powder is mixed with dry bait material at a 19:1 ratio to get the required concentration. It should be kept out of the reach of children, pets and other domestic animals. Vitamin K is an antidote. The other commonly used anticoagulant is Fumarin sold as Rodafarin and Ratafin.

G. MOLLUSCICIDES

Molluscicides may be classified into two broad categories, viz. aquatic and terrestrial. Aquatic molluscicides may be botanical, e.g. endod, or chemical, e.g. copper sulphate, niclosamide, sodium pentachlorophenate, trifenmorph, etc. Terrestrial molluscicides include carbamates, *i.e.* aminocarb, carbaryl, isolan, methiocarb, mercaptodimethur, mexacarbate, etc. and others, *i.e.* metaldehyde.

Metaldehyde (plymer aldehyde) is also known as metacetaldehyde and by the trade name Meta. The slug killing properties of metaldehyde were reported in 1936. Slugs are immobilised before they die. It is formulated as slug bait in a protein rich milling offall such as bran. Ordinary lime is also used as a molluscicide by sprinkling it on the ground, around the cropped area.

PESTICIDE APPLICATION EQUIPMENT

Pesticides are applied on crops to keep the pests under minimum biological activity. Insecticides are used against insect pests, fungicides are used against fungal crop diseases and herbicides are used against weeds in order to protect crops and avoid losses. It is necessary to select the most efficient equipment for securing a uniform deposit on the target in the least time with minimum labour and without appreciable wastage of material The concentration and quantity of the spray fluid or dust material to be applied will depend upon the type of machinery used The efficacy of a machine depends upon its ability to give the maximum pest control per unit area and time with the minimum dose of actual ingredient of the poison. The wastage and pollution of the environment should also be the minimum. Pesticides may be applied as dusts, sprays, mists, aerosols, smokes, etc. Various types of equipment used include dusters, sprayers, vapour and smoke generators, agricultural aircrafts, granule applicators, soil injectors, etc.

Pesticide appliances are essential for four reasons : (i) pesticides are costly and would be wasted if not applied by machines; (ii) pesticides need to be evenly spread on the target (foliage) surface which is possible only through appliances; (iii) appliances take less time and need less labour and, therefore, are economical; and (iv) pesticides can be aimed to impinge on the targets or reach tall trees only through appliances. It should be also remembered that appliances have played an important role in insect pest control and have undergone as much evolution in their variety and efficiency as the insecticides themselves.

Insecticide appliances can broadly be grouped as dusters (for applying solid formulations), sprayers (for applying liquid formulations), and miscellaneous appliances of which, the first two serve the main purpose. Dusters function by producing air blasts and sprayers by producing both air-blasts and hydraulic force. Though these two categories of appliances differ in their contraction, they are composed of five basic units : (i) a driving force which could be a blower (fan) in the duster and a pump and blower both in the sprayer; (ii) a container called 'hopper' in the duster and a tank in the sprayer to store formulations and normally provided with an agitator or a stirring device, to prevent caking in dust formulations or sedimentation in spray liquids; (iii) a delivery or discharge tube to guide the formulations out; (iv) a nozzle fixed at the end of the delivery tube to break (atomize) the formulations into proper-sized particles (or droplets) and also to provide proper shape to the outgoing formulation, and (v) miscellaneous accessories like the strainers to filter the spray liquids, valves to maintain the flow in one direction, pressure or air-chamber to allow a continuous flow, a spray lance to regulate discharge of the flow a continuous flow, a spray lance to regulate discharge of the flow through the nozzle and a boom to increase the number of nozzles. Both dusters and sprayers could be hand and power-operated.

I. Dusters

Hand-operated Dusters

(i) Plunger type duster. This is a simple pump to which a dust chamber is connected (Fig. 7.1). The pump generates an air-blast that is passed on to the dust chamber causing the dust to blow out through a delivery tube. It is suited for small-scale operations like kitchen gardens, poultry houses, cattle sheds, etc. The machine is also known as foot pump duster or cyanogas pump, since it can be employed in fumigating the rodent (rat) burrows with calcium cyanide (cyanogas) or sodium cyanide (cynamag).

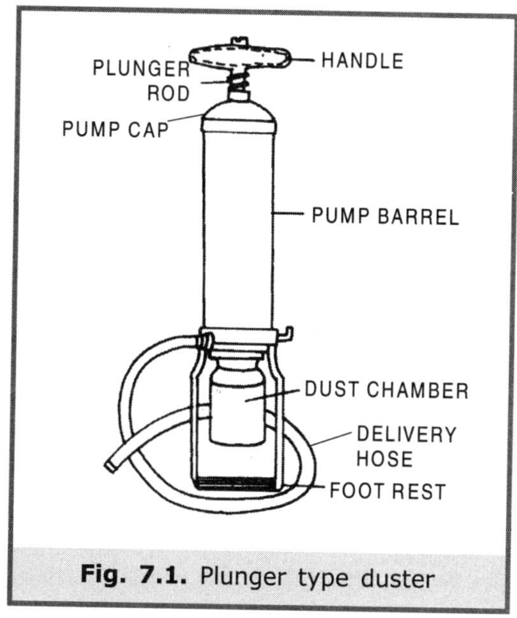

Fig. 7.1. Plunger type duster

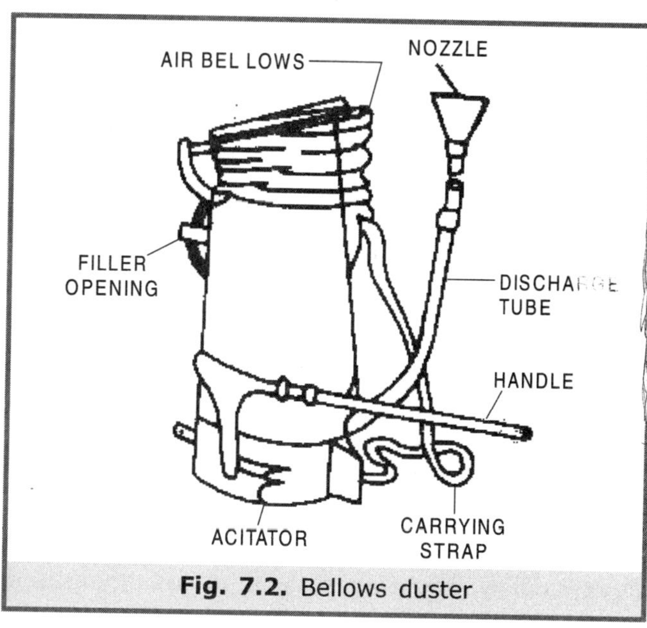

Fig. 7.2. Bellows duster

(ii) Bellows duster. This type of duster (Fig. 7.2) works on compressing bellows (which may be made of leather, rubber or plastic) to produce an air-blast for ejecting the dust out in small clouds. The machine comes in many shapes and models, and is suitable for domestic purposes or for kitchen gardens.

(iii) Rotary (crank) duster. In this machine, the air-blast is produced by employing a blower (fan) enclosed in a box. Through gears, the fan is connected to a handle (crank). The slow rotation of the crank is converted into fast rotation of the fan by the gears. The air-blast produced by the fan sucks the dust through a suction pipe, so as to pass it out through the discharge pipe. An agitator connected to the gears keeps the dust fluffy in the hopper to prevent blocking of the passage to the suction pipe. Two models of this duster are available: one, which rests on the belly of the operator and the other mounted on his shoulder. Rotary dusters are useful for treating small acreage and row crops like potatoes, tobacco, cotton, etc.

(iv) Traction dusters. For a large-scale dusting, the duster is mounted on wheels and the blower fan is connected to the wheel or wheels. Traction of the duster runs the fan which blows the dust out.

Power-operated Dusters

These dusters are provided with a petrol-driven motor which runs both the agitator inside the hopper and the blower (fan). The blower produces the air blast which, as usual, carries the dust particles to the delivery tube (hose) to be expelled out through the nozzles mounted on a boom. These appliances are used for much larger areas.

II. Sprayers

A sprayer is an appliance which atomises the spray fluid, which may be suspension, emulsion or solution. The sprayers function on three main principles : (i) by pressing the spray liquid directly through a plunger (piston) to force it out (hydraulic sprayers); (ii) by compressing a layer of air through a plunger which, in turn, presses the underlying spray liquid to force it out (compression or compressed, air or pneumatic sprayers, and (iii) by producing an air blast through a plunger or a blower (fan) which atomises the spray liquid and carries it along to the target (air-blast sprayers or spray blowers, when a blower is employed).

There are various types of nozzles to disperse the spray fluids. Nozzles are usually classified and named after the energy used to form droplets.

(i) Hydraulic nozzles. These nozzles are mostly used in sprayers in which large quantities of water are used in spray fluid. The liquid under pressure is fed through a nozzle. The pressure determines the rate of discharge, throw of the fluid and its atomisation. These nozzles usually produce coarse sprays and are of different types.

(a) *Impact or floodjet nozzles.* These operate at low pressures of 0.5-1 kg per cm^2 giving a coarse spray without any drift. These are used for spraying herbicides and liquid fertilizers.

(b) *Flat fan nozzles.* These are supplied with variable discharge rates varying from 500 to 3,000 ml per min at different angles (60-110°). Those most commonly used have a discharge of 1,500 ml per min at a pressure of 3 kg per cm^2 and an angle of 80°. These also give fine to coarse sprays without much drift and are most suitable for insecticidal and fungicidal spray for a good coverage.

(c) *Cone nozzles.* Generally, hollow cone nozzles rather than solid cone nozzles are used in agriculture. These are suitable for the application of insecticides and are most widely used because of their low price.

(ii) Gaseous/Pneumatic nozzles. These are usually used with mist blowers. The atomisation occurs by the impact of air-blast on the drop of pesticide falling with gravity. The ratio of fluid discharge to air is 1 to 1000 times for appropriate atomisation. These nozzles provide fine sprays suitable for low volume spraying.

(iii) Centrifugal nozzles. The spray fluid is fed to a rotating disc and the centrifugal force disintegrates it into droplets of very fine size. The nozzle is used in rotary disc ULV sprayers. The droplet size is inversely proportional to the speed and the size of the disc.

(iv) Thermal or hot tube nozzles. A fog composed of very fine droplets can be produced by condensing a pesticide which has been injected into a stream of hot gas to shear the liquid into droplets which are immediately vaporised. These vapours later on condense into very fine droplets which are suspended in the air for sometime, till they finally settle on a surface. This method is very suitable for controlling flying insects in enclosed spaces.

Like dusters, the sprayers are also hand and power-operated, the latter working on any one or combination of the above principles. Descriptions of the examples of these categories of sprayers are as follows:

Hand-operated Hydraulic Sprayers

(i) Syringes. These are the simplest hydraulic sprayers, consisting of a cylinder and a plunger. The liquid is drawn in by the upward (suction) stroke and passed out by the downward (compression) stroke of the plunger. These sprayers are tiring to use and are, therefore, suitable only for small areas like household flower beds and kitchen gardens.

(ii) Bucket (or stirrup) pump sprayers. These machines are composed of a plunger with a D or T-shaped handle, one or two barrels (cylinder), a stirrup and a footrest, In the single barrel pump, the spray is emitted only during the downward stroke, but in the double barrel pump, it is emitted in both downward and upward strokes because of the provision of a second (broader) barrel which acts as a pressure or air chamber, maintaining the spraying pressure even during the upward stroke. In the former, therefore, the spray is emitted intermittently and in the latter, continuously. There are two valves in the double barrel pump; a suction valve with a strainer at the bottom of the pump and a delivery valve at the bottom of the pressure chamber. These valves allow the flow in one direction only. The delivery tube is fitted on top of the pressure chamber extending inside it. The pump is dipped in a bucket, containing the spray liquid and retained in position by pressing the footrest. Two persons are needed to work this pump; one to operate the pump and the other to handle the delivery tube and the spray lance. The pump is suitable for spraying shrubs, low crops (vegetables) and nurseries.

(iii) Knapsack sprayers. This type of sprayer works on the same principle as the stirrup pump, but is provided with a tank that sits comfortably on the back of the operator. Accordingly, it is single or double-barralled and can be operated by a single person. It is suitable for hilly and muddy terrains, where the use of larger sprayers or power sprayers is not possible.

(iv) Foot (or pedal) pump sprayers. The piston of this type of sprayer is operated by foot and, therefore, the pump has been inverted to connect it to a pedal. Another change is that the pump itself has two sections ; the lower section containing the piston is the pump proper and the upper section functions as a pressure or air chamber. The liquid is sucked in by the pump through a strainer-fitted suction hose and passed on to the air chamber which, in turn, discharges it out through the delivery tube. The whole unit is fixed to an iron frame, provided with a hand grip to hold the pump, while the foot presses the pedal. The pump can develop pressure up to 900 g which can send the spray up to a height of 6 m. Therefore, this pump is suitable for spraying trees in the orchards, but can also be used for crops on medium-sized farms.

(v) Rocker sprayer. These sprayers function like foot sprayers, but here the piston is connected to a lever (instead of a pedal) which can be rocked to and fro to operate the piston. It has a larger and detachable air chamber.

(vi) Wheelbarrow-sprayers. A rocker or a pedal pump sprayer can be mounted on a trolley, provided with a tank to make a wheelbarrow sprayer. The advantage of this machine is that the operator is saved from carrying the weight of the machine and spray liquid and the disadvantage is that it is tiring to push the machine, particularly on uneven grounds.

Compression Sprayers

(i) Pneumatic hand sprayers. These sprayers employ air pressure to force the liquid out and, therefore, are kept partly empty to provide space for development of air pressure. They comprise a tank and an air pump to develop pressure and are provided with an air-check valve at one end and a delivery tube connected outside to a nozzle through a trigger-control valve (Fig. 7.3). The pressure developed by the pump forces the liquid to rise in the delivery tube and then go out through the nozzle, the flow being regulated by the trigger-control valve. The sprayer is suitable only for the household and for kitchen gardens. Its plus point is that due to the prior development of air pressure, pumping process during spraying is minimized and its negative point is that one has to bend over low plants which is tiring. These sprayers come in many shapes and models.

(ii) Pneumatic knapsac sprayers. These are composed of a strongly built brass or copper

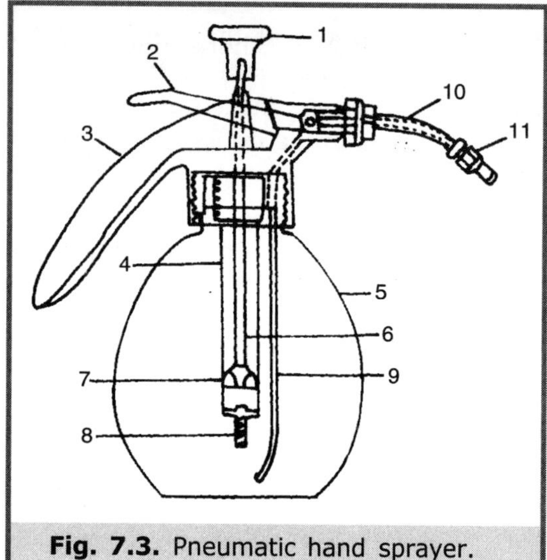

Fig. 7.3. Pneumatic hand sprayer. 1, knob; 2, cut-off valve; 3, handle; 4, pump; 5, tank; 6, plunger rod; 9, discharge tube 10, spray lance; 11, nozzle (courtesy Prof. O.S. Bindra and Harcharan Singh)

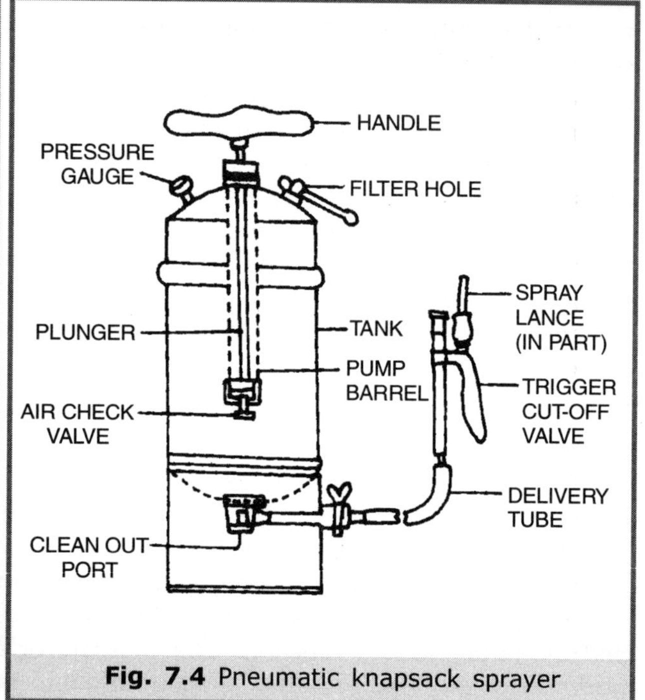

Fig. 7.4 Pneumatic knapsack sprayer

tank with a capacity of 7 to 22.5 litres, a vertical air pump passing through the top and tightly fixed to it, a pressure gauge to indicate pressure inside and a delivery tube with a spray lance (Fig. 7.4). The tank is filled only up to two-thirds to three-fourths, so as to leave an air space above spray liquid. The pump can produce a pressure of 55-60 psi (lb/sq in). The pump may then be loaded and strapped on the back and the trigger valve of the lance pressed to release the spray. It may be necessary to pump in air more than once to clear out all the liquid. The sprayer is good for large areas and is particulary useful in the control of public tiealth insects like mosquitoes, houseflies, etc.

Air Blast Sprayers

(*i*) Hand atomiser. This is the simplest air-blast sprayer which consists of a pump (with its usual barrel and plunger), bearing a minute hole called nozzle in the middle of its closed end, a small tank, a cap and a small delivery tube that rises above the cap up to lower-half of the nozzle hole and below it, upto the bottom of the tank. The barrel bears a small hole at its posterior end for the incoming and outgoing air. When the plunger is pushed forward (downstroke), the pump ejects a gust of air from its nozzle which in turn, drives the air above the delivery tube away, creating a momentary vacuum due to which, the spray liquid rises out of the tube. Now when the plunger is drawn backward (upstroke), fresh air enters the barrel through its nozzle only to be expelled out by the next downstroke. The outgoing (second) gust of air not only breaks (atomises) the oozed out spray liquid on top of the delivery tube into minute droplets, but also carries them along to the target. A succession of up and down strokes thus throws out intermittent jets of the spray liquid. Working the pump is a tiring process and, therefore, this appliance is suitable only for the household and kitchen gardens.

(ii) Spray blowers. (see below under Power-operated sprayers).

Power-operated Sprayers

(i) Hydraulic (power) sprayers. These machines are powered by 1-5 horse power petrol engines and are composed of a pump, a tank with an agitator, a pressure regulator valve, a pressure gauge, suction and delivery hoses (which may be 1-3 in number) haying a spray gun or lance with a nozzle or several nozzles mounted on a boom. According to their capacity to discharge liquids, they can be categorised as low-pressure, low-volume sprayers or high-pressure, high-volume sprayers. The low-volume sprayers produce a pressure of 15-125 psi and deliver 1-25 gpm (gallon/min; 1 gallon = 4½ litres) of the spray liquid. On the other hand, the high-volume sprayers produce a pressure of 400-1,000 psi and deliver 8-85 gpm of the spray liquid. High-volume spraying, (also called full coverage spraying) needs more water and obviously more labour, and is suitable for partially soluble or low dispersibility chemicals (like Bordeaux mixture) of highly soluble products (like nicotine sulphate).

Due to high degree of dilution, the danger of phytotoxicity is minimised and due to larger apertures of the nozzles, clogging is avoided. However, this is not suitable where there is water scarcity (arid areas) or difficulty in obtaining labour. In this type of spraying, one hectare of crop will need 500-1125 litres of spray liquid, which is quite a large amount. Low-volume spraying (also called concentrate spraying), on the other hand, needs 8-25 times lesser amount of water and chemicals, thus saving of labour and time, but still offering better coverage and efficacy of insecticide due to the smaller size of the droplets. A water-miscible liquid insecticide (like malathion) is more suitable for low-volume spraying since it can be atomised without the danger of sedimentation. In this type of spraying, one hectare will need only 12.5-125.0 litres of spray liquid. Semi-low-volume (or semi-concentrate) spraying needing 0.5-6.25 litres/ha is also carried out. But the recent trend is to use ULV (ultra-low-volume) spraying which requires less than 6.25 litres/ha of spray liquid. Sometimes, the insecticide is also used undiluted in this formulation. The decision to go in for the high-or low-volume spraying is taken on the basis of the type of crop, availability of water, labour cost, nature (solubility) of the chemical and the appliance available. To carry the power-operated sprayer on an uneven/muddy terrain, the appliance is mounted on a pair of handles and is then called stretcher or skid sprayer.

(ii) Spray blowers. The spray blowers combine a low-pressure low-volume hydraulic sprayer and an air blower. Atomisation of the spray liquid is first done by forcing the liquid to pass through a series of nozzles. The droplets thus atomised are further broken down into still smaller particles by an air-blast, produced by a blower, which also blows the particles to the target surface. A spray blower is rated in terms of the quantity of air, that it can blow out per minute at a certain speed of air. A low-volume spray blower delivers 7.5-900 cmm (cu metre/min) at an air velocity of 240km/h, and a high-volume one, 600-30,000 cmm at 60km/h. Since the spray is broken up into small (150-300 μ) droplets, the spray blowers are suited for concentrate spraying

III. Miscellaneous Appliances

(i) Mist blower. This appliance works on the same principle as the spray blowers—the spray liquid is atomised first by a hydraulic pump and then blown by an air-blast, produced by a blower. Here, the particle size is still smaller (50-150 μ) and dilution is reduced by 20-80 per cent. It is used for covering a larger area by employing smaller quantity of spray liquid and is suitable for spraying shade or orchard tress (with droplet size of 80-100 μ) or for area control as for mosquitoes (with droplet size of 50-70 μ). Majority of the mist blowers are motorised.

(ii) Fog generators. The droplet size in these machines is reduced to the minutest (1-50 μ) value which enables the droplets to remain floating in the air longer to kill the flying insects. These generators are generally used for treating very dense foliage or enclosed spaces to prevent drifting during the time that the fog takes to settle on the target surface. They are good for the control of mosquitoes, flies and other insects inside the buildings and for treating larger areas in shorter time with smaller quantities of the material.

(iii) Smoke generators. These are simple canisters in which some amount of insecticide is mixed with a slow burning material. About 60 per cent HCH mixed with about 40 per cent burning material (equal amounts of sucrose and potassium chlorate with a small amount of clay acting as retardant) are formulated as slow burning pellets. Smoke particles range from 0.001-0.1 μ which is smaller than most dust particles. These machines are employed mainly in confined areas like greenhouses and warehouses.

(iv) Liquefied gas aerosols (oraerosol bombs). Aerosol refers to a fine spray, ejected by pressurised can. The aerosol bombs are made of strong metal (tin) containers having a rapidly volatilizing and greatly compressed liquefied gas (such as dichlorodifluoromethane : Freon-12 or Genetron-12 or trichloromonofluoromethane : Freon-ll or Genetron-11 mixed with 10-20 per cent insecticide in a non-volatile oil and fitted with a delivery tube extending from the bottom. This ensures delivery of the insecticide solution which also lies at the bottom. The material is released through a capillary tube regulated by a triggering device. The vapour pressure of the liquefied gas provides the propelling force. As the gas volatilises, it leaves the oil solution of the insecticide in the form of an aerosol, having very fine droplets, which are expelled in great force by pressing the trigger. Aerosol bombs of synergised pyrethrum, methoxylchlor, lindane, dichlorovos, etc., have been developed. The bombs are useful in small enclosed spaces for killing flying insects like mosquitoes, flies, etc., particularly during outdoor camping (by soldiers, scouts, surveyors, etc.)

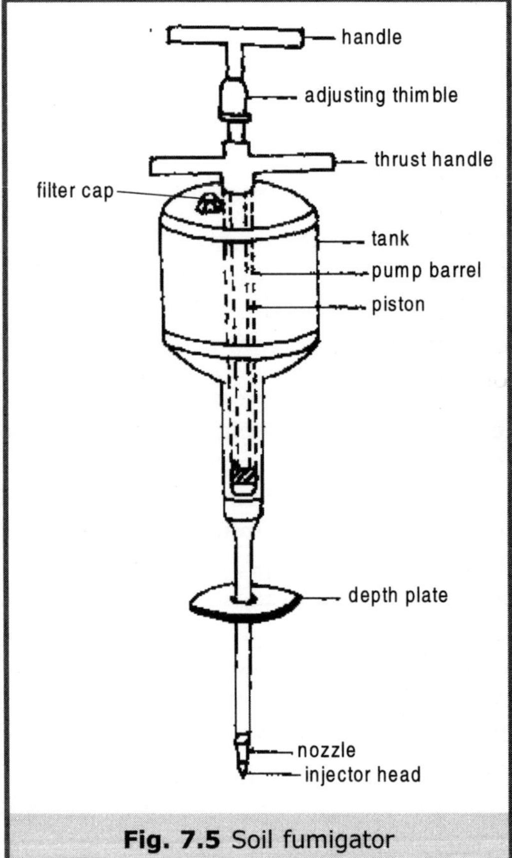

Fig. 7.5 Soil fumigator

(v) Soil injecting guns. Also called soil fumigators, these are simple pumps with their lancer modified to penetrate the soil (Fig. 7.5). Hand-operated injectors have a tank with a 2.25-3.5 litre capacity that can fumigate soil up to a depth of 15-20 cm. These are used for controlling soil insects and soil nematodes.

(vi) Dust applicator for burrows. The plunger type duster (Fig. 7.1) can also be used for driving dust into burrows. These are employed in rodent control.

Dusting and Spraying : Some Facts

Both dusting and spraying have their own advantages and disadvantages, the advantage of one turning out to be the disadvantage of the other. Dusting, for example, has the following advantages over the spraying : (*i*) the weight of the dust required per unit area is less than that of the spray, so that dusts are easy to carry on hilly and muddy terrains; (*ii*) dusting is more suitable in areas (*e.g.* arid), where there is scarcity of water and spray cannot be prepared (it may, however, be mentioned here that water requirement is greatly reduced in low-volume spraying and completely eliminated in ultra low-volume spraying); (*iii*) dusting requires fewer men, covers more acreage per day and so, saves on labour and time; (*iv*) dust residues get removed more easily from the surface of the edibles than spray ones; (*v*) dusting machines are generally lighter than the spraying ones and, therefore, are easy to transport; and (*vi*) dry dust is less corrosive to equipment than the wet sprays.

In spite of these advantages, dusts have the following disadvantages and the sprays score over them : (*i*) drifts (wind-carried dust particles) present health risks to people and animals which may assume greater significance in the case of very toxic products; (*ii*) unlike sprays, dusts cannot be aimed to impinge on the target—a sizeable portion of them may miss the target, resulting in a less effective deposit on its surface; (*iii*) being dry, the dusts do not stick to the target surface, a sizeable portion ot them may get knocked off the foliage as the plants rub against each other due to wind, particularly singificant in the case of dense crops such as sugarcane, maize, sorghum, etc. (to minimise this, dusting operations are recommended in the morning hours when the leaves are moist with dew and the atmosphere is calm); (*iv*) dusts need diluents which are costlier than water needed for sprays; (*v*) two or more spray formulations can be easily incorporated into a single formulation, which is not possible in the case of dusts for two reasons—great bulk of dusts preludes a uniform and thorough mixing and even if mixed, the carrier tends to separate out from the toxicant while in air; (*vi*) for the control of certain pests, dust formulations are simply not available; and (*vii*) dusts offer a greater hazard of inhalation by the operator than the sprays.

AERIAL APPLICATION OF PESTICIDES

Aerial application of pesticides has been in practice since the inception of aircraft itself in 1920. In India, an aircraft was first employed to control mosquitoes in Delhi in 1944-45 and to control desert locusts in 1951. Aircraft chosen for this purpose are small fixed-winged aeroplanes (single-winged monoplanes or double-winged biplanes, more commonly the latter) or helicopters. Helicopters are more advantageous, since they can fly slowly and at lower heights, possess greater manoeuvrability, can land on any piece of flat ground and do not need an airstrip. However, they are suited for spraying alone and have to be grounded for long periods to fix and test a spraying equipment. To overcome this difficulty, a detachable helicopter underslung spraying system (HUSS) has been developed that can be loaded, tested and quickly attached to the helicopter at the time of pesticide application. A simple plug-in electrical connection provides the controls to the pilot. However, helicopters are costlier to operate and maintain than the aeroplanes. Even by aeroplanes, the cost of pesticide application is very high, which cannot be afforded by the Indian farmers who have mostly small holdings. Neverthless, in India, there are about 28 agricultural aircraft of which 17 belong to the government and the rest, to private establishments treating an area of more than four lakh hectares.

Principle of Aerial Application

The spray droplets or dust particles dispersed from an aircraft largely follow the path of air flowing around the aircraft. This air flow is produced by the aircarft when it tries to rise off the ground. In order to go up or lift itself up, the wings of an aeroplane press the air downwards at a speed of about 180 m per min in the case of ordinary biplanes or 330 m per min in case of helicopters flying at 130-160 km per h. This force imports a downward motion to the air called downwash or downdraft. Due to downwash, the pressure below the wings becomes high and above them, low. These two antagonistic forces drive and wind sideways towards the wing-tips in a rotary fashion. This movement of the wind is called the wing-tip vortex. The downwash helps to carry the insecticide particles towards the ground (crop) while the wing-tip vortices tend to deflect them sideways producing the swath. The lower the plane flies, the greater the downwash and stronger the wing-tip vortices. Similar effects will also be produced if the plane's speed is reduced. However, the final course of movement of particles is governed by the factors described below.

Factors Affecting Aerial Distribution

(*i*) Particle size. Larger particles have a tendency to fall vertically downwards and the smaller ones, to deflect sideways; both sizes, however, suffering a greater deflection towards the wing-tips. Obviously, the dynamic catch (actual deposit of the insecticide) for larger particles will be more than that of the smaller ones. For instance, 85 μ particles (aerosols) may give a dynamic catch of 9 per cent, 200 μ spray droplets, 32 per cent, and 300 μ droplets, 50 per cent.

(*ii*) Wind velocity. The wind velocity is inversely proportional to the particle size in case of the dynamic catch. For instance, if a 50 per cent dynamic catch is obtained for the particles say, of 200 μ size at wind velocity of 8 kmh, then for the same recovery at a greater wind velocity, the particle size has to be reduced.

(*iii*) Aircraft height. The greater the height of an aircraft, the greater the lateral dispersion (swath width) of the insecticide. With conventional dusting planes, the swath width obtainable ranges from about 6.0 m across at 4.5 m height to 27.0 m at 15.0 m height. While it is possible to obtain swath widths up to 135 m by a large aircraft, the most practical swath width to control field and vegetable crop pests is about 12 m, beyond which, the insecticide deposit (dynamic catch) is not heavy and uniform enough to secure an adequate control. For small variations in height, the effect on the swath width is negligible.

(*iv*) Aircraft speed. A decrease in the aircraft speed increases the wing-tip vortex which, in turn, increases the swath width. But such an effect is more on smaller particles; for large particles the speed of the aircraft is not so important.

(*v*) Meteorological conditions. Meteorological conditions have a direct bearing on the wind, which has two components: longitudinal wind flowing parallel to the line of flight (*i.e.* to the aircraft) and vertical current (or turbulence) flowing at right angle to the line of flight. It is the latter, which is of greater consequence in the distribution of insecticide. Since it (turbulence) is the least in the early hours of the morning and an hour before the sunset (turbulence free or inversion condition), and more during the day (turbulent or lapse condition), the spraying or dusting operations should be carried out during the inversion condition.

Equipment for Aerial Application

(*i*) Aircraft. The aircraft most commonly used for commercial application of insecticides are the biplanes and less commonly, the monoplanes. However, helicopters score over these (fixed-winged) planes by offering certain advantages. The choice of aircraft, therefore, should be based on operational circumstances. In general, the following desirable traits should be incorporated into an applicator aircraft: (*a*) ability to carry a (formulation) load of atleast 35 to 40 per cent of its gross weight; (*b*) ability to take off and climb to 15 m within 0.4 km with full load; (*c*) safe operating speed of 96 to 160 kmh and minimum safe flying speed of 72 kmh; (*d*) emphasis on the aircraft's design for pilot's safety in a crash; his comfort to reduce fatigue; ventilation to avoid exposure to toxic pesticides; easy handling of controls with high manoeuvrability; excellent forward and lateral visibility, etc.; (*e*) facilities for quick and easy loading, and (*f*) simple rugged construction with simplicity in maintenance and repair.

(*ii*) Spraying equipment. The tank is made up of aluminium alloy, stainless steel or plastic impregnated with fibre glass for corrosion resistance with a capacity of about 180 litres in light aircraft and 900 litres in larger aircraft; the spray pump could be of centrifugal or gear type, corrosion resistant and with adequate seals. Wind-driven propeller (windmill) mounted in front of the aircraft and connected to the pump is the most widely used method to run the pump. The spray boom is of aluminium or steel tube best mounted about 30 cm below the lower wing. The nozzles numbering 20 to 30 are mounted progressively closer together towards the boom-tips. For a spray with a droplet size of 50-200 μ, hollow cone or flat fan spray nozzles are the most desirable.

(*iii*) Dusting equipment. The hopper is made-up of aluminium alloy, stainless steel or plastic coated with fibre glass for corrosion resistance with a capacity of 90-200 kg of dust, a sloping floor, an easily accessible loading door with tight sealing gasket, an air-vent and a small glass window to serve as a gauge for the pilot. The agitator in the hopper is powered by a wind-driven propellor (windmill) through a gear-box to reduce the speed and is regulated from the cockpit. An aluminium sliding gate at the bottom of the hopper and controlled from the cockpit regulates the rate of discharge of dust into box-shaped spreader or venturi. The venturi suspended underneath the aeroplane, is designed to concentrate the flow of air current through the delivery slots discharging the dust out in a wide swath. In order to obtain a more uniform distribution across the swath, dusting is ordinarily done at a somewhat greater height than spraying and also at rates greater than would be necessary with ground appliances to compensate for the drifts.

Formulations for Aerial Application

Dusts. Dusts with which the aerial rapplication of insecticides started, are less popular mainly because being composed of finer particles, they are at a greater mercy of the weather conditions and so can be applied only during a limited (inversion) part of the day. The easy drafts formed by them reduce the dynamic catch, making the operation costlier. Even though, these difficulties can be reduced to some extent by electrostatically charging the dust particles or wetting them as they are discharged, the use of dust is nowadays limited to dense vegetation (forests and orchards) and low crops like cotton where coverage of lower surface of the leaves, possible only by dusts, is required.

Sprays. The water dispersible powders are avoided in aerial spraying because they tend to block filters, spray lines, and nozzles. The emulsifiable concentrates overcome this difficulty and with water-in-oil type of emulsion (invert) where the viscosity is reduced, a smooth flow of the spray through the pump could be made possible. However, on storage or on addition of more water to make the spray cheaper and less phytotoxic, the viscosity rises making the passage through the pump impossible. Now a new technique called the 'bi-flon or bi-fluid' technique overcomes this problem. In this system, water-mixed insecticide is kept in one tank and the oil in another tank, and the liquids are mixed to form the emulsion only at the time of application. The ultra low-volume formulation, where very small amount or even no water is used, is the best suited for aerial application. But the limitation with this method is that not all insecticides can be converted into a ULV formulation.

Advantages and Disadvantages

Advantages. (*i*) Aerial application provides quick coverage of large areas,

200-800 ha or more per day; this assumes a greater significance in the case of greater infestations of pests and epidemics of plant diseases; (*ii*) no mechanical damage is caused to the crop unlike application from land; (*iii*) treatment is possible on hilly and muddy terrains or even after rains when the ground is soft and traction is not possible; (*iv*) aquatic insects like mosquito larvae, weeds like water hyacinth, and crops like paddy and jute on water-filled fields can be treated; (*v*) important plantations like tea and coffee grown on hills are more easily accessible; (*vi*) a dense crop like sugarcane through which insecticide appliances cannot move are better treated;

(*vii*) it is the only means to treat locusts in flight, tree tops and forests; (*viii*) a strong downwash created by a low and slow flying fully loaded aircraft, can disturb the leaves to enable treatment of their lower surfaces; (*ix*) there is minimum danger of exposure to toxic chemicals for the operator; and (*x*) the method saves on time and labour, making the treatment economical, particularly for large holdings.

Disadvantages. (*i*) Mechanical trouble developing at the nick of time can jeopardise aerial application of pesticides; (*ii*) unprofitable for small holdings which the Indian farmers have; (*iii*) problem of drift of toxic chemicals to distant places exists; (*iv*) a high degree of risk is involved both to the pilot and the men on ground due to low flying and possible crashes; (*v*) aerial application is dependent on optimum weather conditions since wind produces drift, high temperature produces a convention current, carrying the particles upwards and low humidity produces evaporation of water-based sprays; (*vi*) in certain areas and fields, aerial application may not be possible because of tall trees, electric and telephone poles etc.; and (*vii*) undersurfaces of the foliage are not as well covered as by spraying from the ground.

PESTICIDE APPLICATION : SOME NOVEL APPROACHES

Only a miniscule amount of the pesticide applied to the crop reaches the target pest. Various studies have demostrated that the insect pests may receive as low as

10–6 to 10–1 per cent of the pesticide applied. Over 99 per cent of the pesticide moves into the ecosystem to contaminate land, water and air. In view of these facts, the importance of application technology in pest management can hardly be overemphasised. Only some specialised application methods suitable for use in IPM are discussed here briefly.

Seed Treatment

Application of pesticides to seeds, before or at the time of planting, offers the most efficient and concentrated means of protecting the germinating seeds and seedlings. Such applications are minimal in dosage and, therefore, highly economical as well as least disturbing to the environment. Treatment of seeds of a wide variety of field and vegetable crops with lindane, chlorpyriphos or other insecticides is generally effective for the management of cutworms, shoot-fly, wireworms, white grubs, foliage feeding beetles, etc. Seed treatment with systemic insecticides like phorate and disulfoton protects the seedlings from the attack of aphids, thrips and leafhoppers for several weeks. Dipping of cane setts in 0.25 per cent lindane is effective for termite control, while dipping in 0.1 per cent malathion or dimethoate checks the infestation of scale insect.

Now-a-days, a number of seed treating machines are available for this purpose. An ideal machine should have accurate grain and liquid metering as well as an effective initial distribution. Equipments with the more vigorous re-mixing mechanisms are expected to produce a more uniform seed to seed distribution. A recent innovation is the technique of film coating; it involves the use of various natural or synthetic film-forming materials generally applied at a high volume. This method achieves a range of benefits not possible with traditional seed treatment methods. Better uniformity of distribution ensures that fewer seeds are either over- or under-dosed. As a result, all seeds are equally protected and likelihood of phytotoxicity is minimised. Since the products are bound onto the seeds in a film, retention of powders and flowable suspensions is dramtically improved.

Another recent development in the field is a slow release microcapsule suspension of tefluthrin for use as a seed treatment. Tefluthrin is a novel pyrethroid with physical and chemical properties which make it ideal for use as a soil insecticide. Application at a low rate of 20 g a.i./100 kg cereal seeds achieved a high level of control of wheat bulb fly, *Delia coarctata* with a wide range of drilling dates and soil types. Thus, new developments in formulations as well as application technology look set to provide a promising future to seed treatment techniques.

Seedling Dip Method

Whole seedling dip and seedling root dip methods have been found effective for the control of stem borer, gall midge and whorl maggot in rice crop. Seedling root dip treatment in 0.02 per cent chlorpyriphos for 12 h or in combination with urea 1 per cent for 3 h prior to planting, reduces the infestation of stem borer and whorl maggot up to 30 days after transplanting. The whole plant dipped for one minute in 0.05 per cent chlorpyriphos was even more effective than 12 h of root-dip method. Both the treatments are low cost techniques applicable in pest endemic areas and under late planting conditions, where insecticidal treatment is a must to prevent the early insect attack. The method is also selective and safe to the natural enemies.

Root-zone Placement

Root-zone placement also known as deep placement or band placement, was developed to reduce the quantity of insecticides applied to the rice crop in Asian countries. IRRI (International Rice Research Institute) entomologists found that systemic insecticides packaged in capsules and placed in the rice root zone, controlled common insect pests such as stem borers, leafhoppers, planthoppers and whorl maggots, cheaper and more effectively than when conventionally applied. The pesticide is absorbed more readily from the root zone and the covering layer of soil protects it from heat, sunshine, volatilisation, and damage with overflowing water. The insecticides could be applied to the root zone in the form of straw capsules, gelatin capsules, paper capsules, tablets and large granules. It was found that 2kg ha–1 of insecticide applied only once to the root zone, protected rice as much as 8 kg ha–1 broadcast in four dosages at 20-day intervals. Analysis of plant tissue, 10 days after treatment, showed that 10 times more insecticide was absorbed by plants, when applied to the root zone than when applied to the soil surface. Cabofuran, cartap and chlordimeform were most effective but similar results were obtained with a large number of other insecticides.

An additional advantage of the technique is that it is less hazardous to parasitoids and predators of rice pests, and to other non-targeted organisms in the rice agroecosystem than insecticides applied as foliar sprays or to the paddy water. The only limitation is that the method is highly labour intensive.

Whorl Application

Whorl application of insecticides has been found effective for a number of stem borers. Whorl application of lindane 10 G @ 1.2 kg a.i. ha–1 35 days after planting and chlorpyriphos 10G @ 1.0 kg a.i. ha–1 at 30 and 60 days is advocated for the management of shoot borer of sugarcane. Whorl application of granules has also been found effective for the control of maize borer on maize and sorghum, since early instar larvae feed in the whorls for 1-2 weeks before boring into the stem.

Electrostatic Spraying

The ULV spinning disc sprayer has been extensively used, but the need for reduced power consumption and greater control of droplet deposition led to the development of a hand-carried sprayer that used an electrostatic charge to produce spray droplets. The 'Electrodyn' sprayer was invented by Coffee in 1979. The commercially available Electrodyn sprayer uses pesticide prepackaged in a plastic container with the nozzle as an integral part of it to form a 'Bozzle'. This Bozzle' is screwed into the long tubular stick that contains four 1.5 VD size batteries and a high voltage generator. The formulation contains a vegetable or mineral oil/ solvent mixture to provide the appropriate resistivity, so that as it is fed by gravity through the annular slit nozzle, the liquid is charged at 24KV and forms series of ligaments as it emerges from the nozzle. The ligaments break up into droplets of remarkably uniform size. Under the influence of the charge on the nozzle, the subsequent space cloud effect and then the induced charge on plant surfaces, deposition of the spray on both upper and lower surfaces of leaves, stems and other parts of the crop canopy are good, provided there is an air space, into which, the charged droplets can move. The technique is, therefore, more suited to the treatment of small, well- spaced plants.

The 'wrap around' effect of a charged spray is particularly useful in controlling pests on the underside of leaves. Improved deposition has enabled effective use of dosages which are usually much less than those recommended for use in Knapsack sprayer. In many cases, very little spray is deposited on the soil surface under the canopy so survival of ground dwelling predators such as ants, spiders and carabids is better than in case of high volume sprays. The drift is also usually much less than with uncharged sprays. Trials using 'Electrodyn' sprayer on cotton have been reported in a number of countries including Brazil, China, Coted' Ivoire, India, Kenya, Malawi, Paraguay and Tanzania. In India, Electrodyn sprayer provided better deposition (15.2 ng cm–2) of the pesticide on the cotton crop as compared to Knapsack sprayer (1.64 ng cm–2). This resulted in better control of sucking pests as well as bollworms. The number of sprays is reduced to one-half, as compared to conventional hydraulic spraying. The only major limitation is that special 'ED' formulation is required which is presently available only for cypermethrin.

Chemigation

Chemigation is defined as the application of agrochemicals by injection into the water flowing through an irrigation system. Chemigation is possible with all types of irrigation (drip/trickle, flood, furrow, sprinkler) systems. Drip and subsurface irrigation systems may only be used for soil applications. On the other hand, sprinkler systems accommodate both soil and foliar application of agrochemicals. The minimum equipment required for chemigation is an irrigation system, a chemical injection pump and a chemical reservoir. In addition, safety devices are required to prevent potential contamination or backflow into chemical storage tank. The chemical injection pump is the heart of the chemigation system; it should be accurate, easily adjustable for different flow rates and constructed from non-corrosive materials.

In flood or furrow irrigation, a constant head siphon device can be used instead of an injection pump to meter a chemical into water. This siphon device consists of a valve or petcock and an appropriate metering orifice attached to a length of pipe and an air control valve that can be fitted into a chemical container, The changes in chemical flow rate are made by changing the meter orifice size, or altering the head pressure. This metering device requires no external power, but requires calibration for viscosity changes.

The major advantages of chemigation are (*i*) decreased application costs, (*ii*) improved pesticide coverage, (*iii*) decreased human contact with pesticides during application process, (*iv*) decreased energy consumption, and (*v*) more flexibility in time of day for application. The disadvantages are (*i*) lack of formulations approved for chemigation, (*ii*) need for flow valves and check systems to prevent contamination of water source, (*iii*) ineffectiveness of water soluble pesticides when applied via chemigaton, (*iv*) requirement of additional equipment and capital outlay, and (*v*) requirement for training of applicators for this purpose.

Infusion and Injection Methods

Infusion and injection are environmentally safe techniques for introducing pesticides into the xylem tisues of fruit and ornamental trees. In infusion method, the chemicals are introduced into the pre-drilled holes on the tree trunk and are fed into the holes with gravtiational force without applying any external pressure. Injection method employs mechanical force to introduce and distribute the chemical into the trees. This procedure helps in applying more quantity of liquid at faster rate. Application of dicrotophos, dimethoate, oxydemeton methyl, monocrotophos, fenitrothion, acephate and medicap by infusion and injection method has been found effective for the control of beetles, bugs, aphids, leaf miners, midges, hoppers, mealy bugs and mites attacking European elm, Douglas-fir, mango, *Ficus* and coconut trees.

Attract and Kill Devices

A promising approach for arthropod control is the development of attract and kill devices. For example, polyvinyl chloride (PVC) has been used to combine and slowly release a mixture of grandlure (sex and aggregating pheromone for the boll weevil) feeding stimulants, and a toxicant for boll weevil control. The PVC device is in the form of a cap that is placed on top of wooden stakes (commonly referred to as boll weevil bait sticks) that are placed in or around cotton fields. Field tests conducted during early season, indicated 15-67 per cent reduction in boll weevil trap captures in treated fields versus control fields.

CONCLUSIONS

There have been spectacular developments in the evolution of pesticides ever since the insecticide properties of DDT were discovered. These pesticides have played a prominent role to increase the world food supplies. Many of the pesticides were phased out in due course of time due to one reason or another. The new molecules with different mode of action and spectrum of activity took their place. While the rate of application has come down from 10 kg to 10 g per ha, the cost involved in research and development of a new molecule has increased from 0.5 to about 50 million pounds. There is a need to increase the availability of cheaper insecticides so that these become within the reach of resource poor farmers in developing countries. Further, it has been estimated that barely 1 per cent of the pesticide reaches the target pest and the rest of it contaminates different components of the environment. The observations of Ritter, made in 1955 that "crop protection chemicals are only as good as the techniques used to employ them" hold equally true even today as there have been few advances in the application technology during the last five decades. Therefore, there is a need to apply pesticides with precision not only to economise on the chemical, but also to safeguard the consumer and the environment. This will require a paradigm shift in the pesticide application technologies.

CHAPTER 8 CHEMICAL CONTROL : PESTICIDE USE AND MANAGEMENT

INTRODUCTION

Modern synthetic pesticides began to be used on a widespread basis in global crop protection following the end of the World War II. These chemicals gave mankind unprecedented manipulative power to suppress the pest populations. For the first time in the world history, a little more than 50 years ago, man had curative tools to fight agricultural pests and vectors of human diseases. Chemical weed control, provided an effective substitute for manual weed control, thus reducing dependence on human labour. In fact, green revolution was driven by a wide array of different chemical technologies including the synthetic organic pesticides. Availability of pesticides made cultivation of crops profitable in areas, where this was previously not possible because of pest problems. Increased agricultural productivity associated with high levels of pest control, improved crop and animal genetics, availability of fertilizers and mechanised production systems allowed food supplies to increase and standard of living to improve in many regions of the world.

PESTICIDE USE IN AGRICULTURE

The use of synthetic pesticidies in agriculture is the most widespread method of pest control. Farmers spend approximately $4.1 billion on pesticides annually on global basis. This high cost is justified by a direct return of $3-5 for every dollar spent on pesticides. Nearly two million tonnes of pesticides are used annually worlswide; while China is the major contributing country, followed by the USA and Argentina. It is estimated that by the year 2020, the global consumption of pesticides may increase up to 3.5 million tonnes. About 36 per cent of the total pesticide used are herbicides, 25 per cent insecticides, 10 per cent fungicides and 29 per cent other pesticide groups. About 34 per cent of the total pesticide is consumed in USA, 45 per cent in Europe and 20 per cent in developing countries. The Asia-Pacific region accounts for 16 per cent of the total pesticide consumption, out of which 75 per cent is used on rice, cotton and vegetable crops. About 85 per cent of all pesticide use in the world is for agriculture. However, the relative amount of each type of pesticide varies from country to country. For example, 75 per cent of the pesticides used in Malaysia are herbicides, and insecticides account for only 13 per cent. In the Philippines, insecticides account for 55 per cent of the total pesticide use, and fungicides account for 20 per cent. India with about 4 per cent of the world cropped area has a share of around 2 per cent of the global pesticide consumption. About 60 per cent of the pesticides used in India are insecticides. The cotton crop receives about 45 per cent of the total consumption of pesticides, followed by rice (20%), and vegetables and fruits (15%). The consumption of pesticides on many important crops like gram, jute, rapessed, mustard, soybean, sunflower and tobacco is less than 1 per cent.

India was one of the first countries in the third world to start large scale use of pesticides for the control of insect pests of public health as well as of agricultural importance. Initially, DDT and HCH were imported soon after independence. A moderate beginning in indigenous manufacture of pesticides was made with the setting up of a plant to produce HCH in 1952 at Rishra (West Bengal). This was followed by the indigenous production of DDT. At present, India is the largest producer of pesticides in South Asia with production of 82,000 metric tonnes in 2005-2006. It is the second largest manufacturer of basic pesticide chemicals in Asia next to China and at 12th place globally. The total installed capacity is about 124,000 metric tonnes for the manufacture of 62 technical grade pesticides which meet 95 per cent of the total need of the country. Uptil December 2006, 209 pesticides have been registered under Insecticide Act 1968 in India. Some of the most toxic and persistent pesticides have been banned or restricted for use (Table 8.3).

The consumption of pesticides for pest control in agriculture picked up after the introduction of high yielding varieties in 1966-67. The total amount of pesticides used in the country increased from 154 metric tonnes in 1953-54 to 61,357 metric tonnes in 1994-95. Earlier projections had put the pesticide demand at nearly 100,000 metric tonnes by the year 2000. But in view of the ban on DDT, HCH, aldrin, etc., high potency (and consequently lower required dosages) of new insecticides, especially synthetic pyrethroids and high priority being accorded to IPM, the pesticide consumption has shown a decreasing trend. during the last decade. Statewise consumption of pesticides in India is depicted in Table 8.1.

ENVIRONMENTAL IMPACT OF PESTICIDES

The synthetic organic insecticides widely used in agriculture are general biocides having innate ability to cause injury to all living organisms as well as to the quality of our environment. Although real full estimates of damage caused by pesticides are not available, it has been reported that every one dollar worth of pesticide used has caused an estimated 5-10 dollars worth of damage to environment and public health alone. The adverse effects of the pesticides on different components of the environment were first highlighted by Rachel Carson in 1962 in her famous book *Silent Spring*. The presence of residues of these pesticides in food commodities and other components of the environment has proved toxic to humans, domestic animals, birds, fishes and non-target fauna of agroecosystems. In addition to these side effects, the insect pest problems in many crops have aggravated following continuous application of pesticides. This, in turn, has further increased the consumption of pesticides resulting in the phenomenon of ***pesticide treadmill***.

Table 8.1. Consumption of chemical pesticides in various States/UTs during 2014-15 to 2018-19

As on 22.08.2019		Unit: Quantity in MT Tech. Grade				
S.No.	**States/UTs**	**2014-15**	**2015-16**	**2016-17**	**2017-18**	**2018-19 (Provisional)**
1	Andhra Pradesh	4050	2713	274	303	1359
2	Bihar	787	831	790	840	981
3	Chhattisgarh	1589	1625	1660	1685	1398
4	Goa	12	48	*NR*	24	25
5	Gujarat	1730	1980	1713	1692	1558
6	Haryana	4070	4100	4050	4025	4015
7	Himachal Pradesh	379	450	341	467	407
8	Jammu & Kashmir	1921	2251	2188	2430	2459
9	Jharkhand	650	493	541	619	650
10	Karnataka	1793	1434	1288	1502	1458
11	Kerala	910	1123	895	1067	1037
12	Madhya Pradesh	696	732	694	502	862
13	Maharashtra	8663	11665	13496	15568	11746
14	Orissa	1075	723	876	1318	1061
15	Punjab	5689	5743	5764	6362	5836
16	Rajasthan	2694	2475	2269	2307	1280
17	Tamil Nadu	2096	2096	2092	1929	462
18	Telangana	2862	2950	*NR*	4866	4777
19	Uttar Pradesh	9736	10457	10614	10824	11116
20	Uttarakhand	172	217	198	210	102
21	West Bengal	3060	3712	2624	2982	*NR*
	Sub Total	**54633**	**57819**	**52366**	**61522**	**52589**
North-Eastern						
22	Arunachal Pradesh	18	17	18	*NR*	14
23	Assam	190	*NR*	*NR*	241	385
24	Manipur	31	30	*NR*	27	*NR*
25	Meghalaya	28	*NR*	*NR*	*NR*	*NR*
26	Mizoram	805	*NR*	9	*NR*	74
27	Nagaland	20	20	20	20	*NR*
28	Sikkim	*NR*	*NR*	*NR*	*NR*	*NR*
29	Tripura	346	293	298	330	349
	Sub Total	**1437**	**359**	**345**	**617**	**822**
Union Territories						
30	Andaman & Nicobar	8	*NR*	*NR*	*NR*	*NR*
31	Chandigarh	*NR*	*NR*	*NR*	*NR*	*NR*
32	Dadra & Nagar Haveli	*NR*	*NR*	*NR*	*NR*	*NR*
33	Daman & Diu	*NR*	*NR*	*NR*	*NR*	*NR*
34	Delhi	*NR*	*NR*	*NR*	*NR*	*NR*
35	Lakshadweep	*NR*	*NR*	*NR*	*NR*	*NR*
36	Pondicherry	42	43	43	43	41
	Sub Total	**50**	**43**	**43**	**43**	**41**
	Grand Total	**56121**	**58221**	**52755**	**62183**	**53453**

Source: Statistical Database: Directorate of Plant Protection, Quarantine and Storage, India (ppqs.gov.in)

In view of the environmental concerns, restrictions have been imposed on the use of pesticides in both the industrialised and developing counteis (Table 8.2) including India (Table 8.3). The Stockholm Convention on Persistent Organic Pollutants (POPS), on May 31, 2001, adopted to reduce and eliminate the production, use and release of 12 chemicals, often called ***dirty dozen***. This list includes eight organochlorine pesticides, viz. aldrin, chlordane, DDT, dieldrin, endrin, heptachlor, mirex and toxaphene; two industrial chemicals, viz. hexachlorobenzene (HCB) and polychlorinated biphenyl (PCB) group; and two groups of industrial byproducts, viz. dioxins and furans. The Convention came into force on May 17, 2004 with ratification by an initial 128 parties and 151 signatories. Co-signatories agreed to outlaw nine of the 'dirty dozen' chemicals, limit the use of DDT to malaria control and curtail inadvertent production of dioxins and furans.

Plant protection chemicals currently cover about 30 per cent of the total cultivated area in India. The green revolution was possible in India due to the application of only a few

Table 8.2 Status of worlwide restrictions on selected pesticides

Pesticide	Restrictions
DDT	Banned or restricted in 56 countries. Illegal to import in 102 countries. Limited use, primarily for vector control, in Bhutan, India, Nepal, Philippines, Vietnam, Ethiopia, Guinea, Kenya, Madagascar, Mauritius, Sudan, Tanzania, Boliva, Brazil, Mexico and Venezuela. No reported legal use in Europe, the Middle East or North America.
2,4,5-T	Banned or restricted in 33 countries. Illegal to import in 69 countries. Limited use, primarily for road brush control in Tanzania, Japan European Union, Brazil and Suriname.
Paraquat	Banned or restricted in 10 countries. No import restrictions. Banned or restricted in Togo, Indonesia, Austria, Denmark, Finland, Germany, Hungary, Slovenia, Sweden and Kuwait. Registered uses in North America and Europe.
Methyl parathion	Banned or restricted in 10 countries. Illegal to import in 43 countries. Registered uses, usually for agricultural pests, in Algeria, Republic of Congo, Madagascar, South Africa, Sudan, Australia, China, India, New Zealand, Pakistan, Philippines, Thailand, Cyprus, European Union, Germany, Hungary, the Netherlands, Switzerland, Turkey, Brazil, Colombia, Costa Rica, Suriname and USA.
Ethylene dibromide	Banned or restricted in 36 countries. Illegal to import in 91 countries. Limited use acceptable in South Africa, Tanzania, Zimbabwe, Cook Islands, Fiji, India, Japan, New Zealand, Barbados and Brazil. No legal use in North America.
Dieldrin	Banned or restricted in 51 countries. Illegal to import in 99 countries. Limited use, primarily for termites or vector control, in Ethiopia, Libya, Sudan, Tanzania, Uganda, Zambia, Zimbabwe, India, Nepal, Sri Lanka, Brazil and Venezuela. No legal use in North America or Europe.
Carbaryl	Banned or restricted in four countries (Angola, Austria, Germany and Sweden). No import restrictions. Listed as registered in 12 countries (Madagascar, South Africa, Tanzania, Australia, New Zealand, India, Philippines, Hungary, Portugal, UK, Canada and USA).
Aldicarb	Banned or restricted in 13 countries. No import restrictions. Listed as registered for use in 11 countries (South Africa, Sudan, Australia, Germany, India, Hungary, the Netherlands, Portugal, UK, Argentina and USA).

Source **:** Luttrell (2007)

chemical pesticides and fertilizers, and this has led to serious soil-water problems. Today, there are more than 200 registered pesticides (majority of them are toxic insecticides and fungicides) available to the Indian farmers. Indian farmers apply more insecticides and fungicides as against developed countries which use more herbicides. On comparing toxicity levels (per unit basis) of various pesticide categories, insecticides and fungicides are several times more toxic than herbicides. Moreover, these toxic chemicals are used indiscriminately and, therefore, both environmental and health problems could be alarming in India.

Table 8.3. List of pesticides which are banned, refused registration and restricted in use in India: (as on 31.10.2019)

I. PESTICIDES / FORMULATIONS BANNED IN INDIA

A. Pesticides Banned for manufacture, import and use .

1. Aldicarb (vide S.O. 682 (E) dated 17th July 2001)
2. Aldrin
3. Benzene Hexachloride
4. Benomyl (vide S.O 3951(E) dated 8th August, 2018)
5. Calcium Cyanide
6. Carbaryl (vide S.O 3951(E) dated 8th August, 2018)
7. Chlorbenzilate (vide S.O. 682 (E) dated 17th July 2001)
8. Chlordane
9. Chlorofenvinphos
10. Copper Acetoarsenite
11. Diazinon (vide S.O 3951(E) dated 8th August, 2018)
12. Dibromochloropropane (DBCP) (vide S.O. 569 (E) dated 25th July 1989)
13. Dieldrin (vide S.O. 682 (E) dated 17th July 2001)
14. Endosulfron (vide ad-Interim order of the Supreme Court of India in the Writ Petition (Civil) No. 213 of 2011 dated 13th May, 2011 and finally disposed of dated 10th January, 2017)
15. Endrin
16. Ethyl Mercury Chloride
17. Ethyl Parathion
18. Ethylene Dibromide (EDB) (vide S.O. 682 (E) dated 17th July 2001)
19. Fenarimol (vide S.O 3951(E) dated 8th August, 2018)
20. Fenthion (vide S.O 3951(E) dated 8th August, 2018)
21. Heptachlor
22. Lindane (Gamma-HCH)
23. Linuron (vide S.O 3951(E) dated 8th August, 2018)
24. Maleic Hydrazide (vide S.O. 682 (E) dated 17th July 2001)
25. Menazon
26. Methoxy Ethyl Mercury Chloride (vide S.O 3951(E) dated 8th August, 2018)
27. Methyl Parathion (vide S.O 3951(E) dated 8th August, 2018)
28. Metoxuron
29. Nitrofen
30. Paraquat Dimethyl Sulphate
31. Pentachloro Nitrobenzene (PCNB) (vide S.O. 569 (E) dated 25th July 1989)
32. Pentachlorophenol
33. Phenyl Mercury Acetate

34. Sodium Cyanide (banned for Insecticidal purpose only vide S.O 3951(E) dated 8th August, 2018)*
35. Sodium Methane Arsonate
36. Tetradifon
37 Thiometon (vide S.O 3951(E) dated 8th August, 2018)
38. Toxaphene(Camphechlor) (vide S.O. 569 (E) dated 25th July 1989)
39. Tridemorph (vide S.O 3951(E) dated 8th August, 2018)
40. Trichloro acetic acid (TCA) (vide S.O. 682 (E) dated 17th July 2001)

B. Pesticide formulations banned for import, manufacture and use

1. Carbofuron 50% SP (vide S.O. 678 (E) dated 17th July 2001)
2. Methomyl 12.5% L
3. Methomyl 24% formulation
4. Phosphamidon 85% SL

C. Pesticide / Pesticide formulations banned for use but continued to manufacture for export

1. Captafol 80% Powder (vide S.O. 679 (E) dated 17th July 2001)
2. Nicotin Sulfate

D. Pesticides Withdrawn (Withdrawal may become inoperative as soon as required complete data as per the guidelines is generated and submitted by the Pesticides Industry to the Government and accepted by the Registration Committee. (S.O 915(E) dated 15th Jun,2006)

1. Dalapon
2. Ferbam
3. Formothion
4. Nickel Chloride
5. Paradichlorobenzene (PDCB)
6. Simazine
7. Sirmate (S.O. 2485 (E) dated 24th September 2014)
8. Warfarin (vide S.O. 915 (E) dated 15th June 2006)

II. PESTICIDES REFUSED REGISTRATION

S.No.	Name of Pesticides
1.	2,4, 5-T
2.	Ammonium Sulphamate
3.	Azinphos Ethyl
4.	Azinphos Methyl
5.	Binapacryl
6.	Calcium Arsenate
7.	Carbophenothion
8.	Chinomethionate (Morestan)
9.	Dicrotophos
10.	EPN
11.	Fentin Acetate
12.	Fentin Hydroxide
13.	Lead Arsenate
14.	Leptophos (Phosvel)
15.	Mephosfolan
16.	Mevinphos (Phosdrin)
17.	Thiodemeton / Disulfoton
18.	Vamidothion

III. PESTICIDES RESTRICTED FOR USE IN THE COUNTRY

S.No.	Name of Pesticides	Details of Restrictions
1.	Aluminium Phosphide	The Pest Control Operations with Aluminium Phosphide may be undertaken only by Govt./Govt. undertakings / Govt. Organizations / pest control operators under the strict supervision of Govt. Experts or experts whose expertise is approved by the Plant Protection Advisor to Govt. of India except 1Aluminium Phosphide 15 % 12 g tablet and 2Aluminum Phosphide 6 % tablet. [RC decision circular F No. 14-11(2)-CIR-II (Vol. II) dated 21-09-1984 and G.S.R. 371(E) dated 20th may 1999]. 1Decision of 282nd RC held on 02-11-2007 and, 2Decision of 326th RC held on 15-02-2012. The production, marketing and use of Aluminium Phosphide tube packs with a capacity of 10 and 20 tablets of 3 g each of Aluminium Phosphide are banned completely. (S.O.677 (E) dated 17thJuly, 2001)
2.	Captafol	The use of Captafol as foliar spray is banned. Captafol shall be used only as seed dresser. (S.O.569 (E) dated 25thJuly, 1989) The manufacture of Captafol 80 % powder for dry seed treatment (DS) is banned for use in the country except manufacture for export. (S.O.679 (E) dated 17thJuly, 2001)
3.	Cypermethrin	Cypermethrin 3 % Smoke Generator is to be used only through Pest Control Operators and not allowed to be used by the General Public. [Order of Hon,ble High Court of Delhi in WP(C) 10052 of 2009 dated 1407-2009 and LPA-429/2009 dated 08-09-2009]
4.	Dazomet	The use of Dazomet is not permitted on Tea. (S.O.3006 (E) dated 31st Dec, 2008)
5.	Dichloro Diphenyl Trichloroethane (DDT)	The use of DDT for the domestic Public Health Programme is restricted up to 10,000 Metric Tonnes per annum, except in case of any major outbreak of epidemic. M/s Hindustan Insecticides Ltd., the sole manufacturer of DDT in the country may manufacture IDDT for export to other countries for use in vector control for public health purpose. The export of DDT to Parties and State non-Parties shall be strictly in accordance with the paragraph 2(b) article 3 of the Stockholm Convention on Persistent Organic Pollutants (POPs). (S.O.295 (E) dated 8th March, 2006)

IV. PESTICIDES WHICH SHALL BE PHASED OUT VIDE GAZETTE NOTIFICATION NO. S.O. 3951 (E).

S.No.	Name of the pesticide	Insecticides to be phase out by 31st December, 2020
1.	**Alachlor**	(i) No new certificate of registration to manufacture shall be issued after publication of this Order. (ii) No person shall import, manufacture or formulate Alachlor with effect from the 1st January, 2019. (iii) The use of Alachlor shall be completely banned with effect from the 31st December, 2020. (iv) It is toxic to aquatic organism, hence a cautionary statement should be incorporatedon label and leaflets toxic to aquatic organism hence should not be used near water bodies, aquaculture or pisciculture area.
2.	**Dichlorovos**	(i) No new certificate of registration to manufacture shall be issued after publication of this Order. (ii) No person shall import, manufacture or formulate dichlorvos with effect from the January,

		2019. (iii) The use of dichlorvos shall be completely banned with effect from the 31st December, 2020. (iv) It is very toxic to aquatic organism, hence a cautionary statement should be incorporated on label and leaflets that it is toxic to aquatic organism, hence should not be used near water bodies, aquaculture or pisciculture area. (v) A warning may be incorporated in the label and leaflet stating that this product is toxic to honey bees so do not spray during active honey bees foraging period of the day.
3.	**Phorate**	(i) No new certificate of registration to manufacture shall be issued after publication of this Order. (ii) No person shall import, manufacture or formulate Phorate with effect from the 1st January, 2019. (iii) The use of Phorate shall be completely banned with effect from the 31st December, 2020. (iv) It is very toxic to aquatic organism, hence a cautionary statement should be incorporated on label and leaflets that it is toxic to aquatic organism, hence should not be used near water bodies, aquaculture or pisciculture area. (v) A warning may be incorporated in the label and leaflet stating that this product is toxic to honey bees so do not spray during active honey bees foraging period of the day. (vi) A cautionary statement should incorporate in label and leaflet that this product is toxic to birds.
4.	**Phosphamidon**	(i) No new certificate of registration to manufacture shall be issued after publication of this Order. (ii) No person shall import, manufacture or formulate Phosphamidon with effect from the 1st January, 2019. (iii) The use of Phosphamidon shall be completely banned with effect from the 31st December, 2020.
5.	**Triazophos**	(i) No new certificate of registration to manufacture shall be issued after publication of this Order. (ii) No person shall import, manufacture or formulate Triazophos with effect from the 1 st January, 2019. (iii) The use of Triazophos shall be completely banned with effect from the 31st December, 2020. (iv) It is very toxic to aquatic organism, hence a cautionary statement should be incorporated on label and leaflets that it is toxic to aquatic organism, hence should not be used near water bodies, aquaculture or pisciculture area. (v) A warning may be incorporated in the label and leaflet stating that this product is toxic to honey bees so do not spray during active honey bees foraging period of the day (vi) A cautionary statement should incorporate in label and leaflet that this product is toxic to birds
6.	**Trichlorfon**	(i) No new certificate of registration to manufacture shall be issued after publication of this Order. (ii) No person shall import, manufacture or formulate Trichlorfon with effect from the 1 st January, 2019. (iii) The use Trichlorfon shall be completely banned with effect from the 31st December, 2020. (iv) It is very toxic to aquatic organism, hence a cautionary statement should be incorporated on label and leaflets that it is toxic to aquatic organism, hence should not be used near water bodies, aquaculture or pisciculture area. (v) A cautionary statement should incorporate in label and leaflet that this product is toxic to birds.

Source: Statistical Database: Directorate of Plant Protection, Quarantine and Storage, India (ppqs.gov.in)

Human Toxicity and Health Effects

The toxicity of a pesticide is determined in terms of the median lethal dose (LD50), which refers to the minimum amount of insecticide required to kill 50 per cent of the population of the test animal. For animals (rats), it is expressed in mg/kg of the body weight and for insects, microgrammes per gramme of the insect's weight (μg/g). The oral LD50 of DDT for rats is 250 mg/kg which means that if this amount is fed to each rat of a large group, it should kill 50 per cent of its population. The higher the LD50 values, the lesser is the toxicity of the insecticide. The practical use of the LD50 values is the availability of comparative toxicities of various insecticides whose knowledge is helpful both in the formulation of insecticides and in taking precautions while handling them. Dermal LD50 values are higher than the oral ones and are more important to those who handle formulations or are likely to come in contact with insecticides. Likewise, median lethal concentration (LC50) values pertain to fluid medium and are expressed in mg/litre of air or water. The LD50 values (in mg/kg) for rats of some of the more important pesticides are given in Table 8.4, and symptoms of poisoning and their treatment are given in Table 8.5.

The most serious effects of pesticides are those on human life and health. It has been reported that 3 million acute poisoning cases caused by pesticides occur worldwide every year; 2 million of these are suicide attempts and the rest occupational or accidental poisoning cases. Despite the restrictions and regulations on pesticide use, India accounts for one-third of the total poisoning cases in the world. In the first major accident involving pesticides, 108 people died due to parathion poisoning in Kerala in 1953. The world's worst industrial disaster involving a chemical plant was the 'Bhopal Gas Tragedy' at the Union Carbide Plant in Bhopal (Madhya Pradesh) during 1984. Ironically, the plant manufactured carbaryl, which is considered to be one of the safest insecticides in use even now. Vapours of methyl isocyanate (MIC), an intermediate involved in the manufacture of carbaryl, leaked from the plant killing at least

5000 people, disabling and causing permanent damage to another 50,000 people. In all, about 2,00,000 people were affected. The long term teratogenic, mutagenic, carcinogenic and other effects involving vital body organs are even now being felt in the surviving population. Out of every 3 children born to women who were pregnant on the night of disaster, only one survived. Out of 1350 new born babies, 16 were physically deformed and 60 died prematurely.

In a landmark report, the Natural Resource Defense Council (NRDC) of USA reported that one out of every 3400 children between 1 and 5 years of age could one day get cancer because of the pesticides they ate as young children. If pesticides could cause so much damage to child health in the country which imposes the most stringent regulations on their use, the extent of damage in developing countries where the pesticide use is more or less unregulated, can be well imagined.

In fact, cases of blindness, cancer, diseases of liver and nervous system from pesticide poisoning have been identified in cotton growing areas of Maharashtra and Andhra Pradesh. A case study of occupational workers regularly involved in spraying of DDT and malathion revealed high incidence of psychological symptoms like anxiety, sleep disturbance, depression and severe headache. Some of the workers also suffered from impaired memory and retinal damage.

In case the poison is swallowed accidentally,the victim should be taken immediately to the nearest doctor or preferably to a hospital. It is most important that the insecticide container

Table 8.4. Acute oral and dermal LD_{50} values of different groups of pesticides

Name of pesticide	Oral LD_{50} (mg/kg)	Dermal LD_{50} (mg/kg)
Insecticides of plant origin		
Nicotine sulphate	84	285
Pyrethrum	470	1880
Rotenone	50-75	940
Chlorinated hydrocarbons		
Aldrin	39	98
BHC	1250	–
Chlordane	335	840
Chlorbenzilate	1220	5000
DDT	113	2510
D-D mixture	140	2100
Dicofol	1100	1230
Dieldrin	46	90
Endosulfan	43	130
Endrin	17.8	18
Ethylene dibromide	146	300
Ethylene dichloride	770	3890
Heptachlor	100	195
Isobenzan	5-10	–
Lindane	88	1000
Methoxychlor	5000	6000
Toxaphene	90	1075
Organophosphates		
Azinphos methyl	13	220
Bromophos	3750	2188
Carbophenothion	30	54
Chlorpyriphos	155	202
Demeton	6.2	14
Diazinon	108	900
Dichlorvos	80	107
Dimethoate	215	610
Disulfoton	6.8	15
Fenitrothion	250	1500
Fenthion	215	330
Formothion	300	1000
Leptophos	43	10,000
Malathion	1375	4444
Menazon	1200-1600	500
Mephosfolan	9	100
Methyl parathion	14	67
Mevinphos	6.1	14.7
Monocrotophos	21	112
Oxydemeton-methyl	65	100
Parathion	13	21
Phenthoate	200	700
Phorate	2.3	6.2
Phosalone	135	1390
Phosphamidon	23.5	143
Quinalphos	65	1250
Schradan	5	50-100
TEPP	1.05	2.4
Thiometon	100	200
Trichlorphon	630	2000
Carbamates		
Aldicarb	0.93	3
Carbaryl	850	4000
Carbofuran	8	1000
Synthetic pyrethroids		
Permethrin	>4000	>4000
Cypermethrin	247	>2000
Decamethrin	128	>2000
Fenvalerate	451	>5000
Herbicides		
DNOC (dinitrocresol)	40	600
MCPA	800	1000
PCP (pentachlorophenol)	280	150-350
2, 4, 5-T	300	–
2, 4-D	375	1000
Methabenzthiazuron	1000	–
Metoxuron	2000	–
Isoproturon	3600	–
Butachlor	3000	–
Thiobencarb	1903	2900
Nitrofen	2630	–
Fungicides		
Dithiocartamates-mamet, zineb, dithane	1000-8000	1000
Ethyl mercuric salt	30	200
Sulphur	Non-toxic	–
Thiram	700-1000	1000
Carbendazin	1500	–
Benomyl	9590	–
Carboxin	3200	8000
Oxycarboxin	2000	16000

from which the poison was swallowed should be shown to the doctor. The symptoms of poisioning and the medical treatment for each pesticide are given in Table 8.5.

Table 8.5 Symptoms and treatment of poisoning by pesticides

S.No. 1	Name of pesticide 2	Symptoms 3	Treatment 4
1.	DDT	Dizziness, paraesthesia of tongue, lip and face, benumbing of extremeties; incoordination and tremors. In severe poisoning, convulsion and partial paralysis of hands may develop. Pupils get dilated; the pulse becomes irregular and slow.	(*i*) Give universal antidote (activated charcoal 2 parts, magnesium oxide 1 part, tannic acid 1 part; 15 g of the mixture in half a glass of warm water) to absorb or neutralize poisons, to be followed by gastric lavage to evacuate stomach contents. If patient is vomiting, do not give an emetic, but give large amounts of warm water. If an emetic is needed, give 15 g sodium chloride in warm water and repeat until vomit fluid is clear. (*ii*) Give magnesium sulphate 30 g in water as a cathartic and force fluid. (*iii*) Give caffeine sodium benzoate 0.5 g subcutaneously or intravenously or give hot tea or coffee drink. (*iv*) Give calcium gluconate 10 ml of 10% solution intravenously for incoordination and tremors or pentobarbital sodium 0.1 g intravenously if necessary. (*v*) To prevent any liver damage, use diet having high carbohydrate and calcium.
2.	HCH	Headache, nausea, hyper-irritability,urticaria in some cases, cyanosis (blueness of skin), blood dyscrasias (disordered condition). In case of acute poisoning, leukocytosis and rise in blood pressure.	Same as for DDT.
3.	Aldrin, dieldrin, endrin, chlor-dane, endosulfan and other chlorinated hydro-carbon insecticides	Uneasiness, headache, nausea, vomiting, dizziness and tremors, convulsions, respiratory arrest, coma, leucocytosis and rise in blood pressure.	(*i*) If ingested, give universal antidote. (*ii*) Give a saline purgative, but not oil laxative. (*iii*) Give phenobarbital up to 0.7 g or pentobarbital 0.25-0.50 g per day to induce sedation and control convulsions. (*iv*) Give calcium gluconate 10% intravenously. (*v*) Oxygen therapy and artificial respiration may be needed during depression.
4.	Diazinon, dimethoate, form-othion, malathion, oxyde-meton me-thyl, methyl para-thion, parathion, phosph-amidon, thiometon, etc.	Headache, giddiness, vertigo (whirling), weakness, excessive mucous discharge from nose and sense of tightness are symptoms of inhaled exposures. Blurring of vision, fixed pin point pupils and ocular pain occurs when there is ocular exposure. Nausea	(*i*) Atropinize the patient immediately and repeat doses of 2-4 mg at 5-10 minutes intervals till the continuance of symptoms. As much as 50 mg of atropine may be given per day without any side effects. (*ii*) Administer 1g of 2-pyridine–2 aldoxine–N-methyliodide (2 P.A.M.) intravenously. This should

		followed by vomiting, abdominal contraction, diarrhoea and salivations are symptoms of ingestion. Loss of muscle coordination, speech defects, twitching of muscle, difficulty in breathing, hypertension, jerky movement, convulsions and coma indicate severeness of poisoning. Death may occur due to depression of respiratory centre.	be done very slowly in 5-10 minutes. (*iii*) Give gastric lavage with 5 per cent sodium bicarbonate. (*iv*) Wash contaminated skin and irrigate eyes with normal saline. (*v*) Maintain electrolyte balance but avoid large amounts of intravenous fluids. (*vi*) Apply artificial respiration if necessary to remove upper respiratory obstruction. (*vii*) Do not give morphine, theophyline or aminophyline.
5.	Zinc phosphide	Nausea, vomiting, diarrhoea, severe abdominal pain followed by symptom-free period of 8 hours or longer. On systemic toxic absorption, nausea, protracted vomiting and diarrhoea may occur which may be followed by haemorrhage in the skin, coma and delirium and damage to liver.	(*i*) Give gastric larvage with 1 : 5000 potassium permanganate solution. (*ii*) Give 0.02% cupric sulphate. This may act as an emetic and produce insoluble cupric phosphide which should be removed by lavage. (*iii*) Use morphine for sedation and salivation. (*iv*) Give large doses of vitamin K.
6.	Mercurial fungicides	Nervous symptoms like paracenesthesia of tongue, lips and toes. Fine tremors and incoordination, blisters on contacted skin.	(*i*) Give universal antidote as for DDT followed by gastric lavage. (*ii*) Give high colonic irrigation with sodium formaldehyde sulpho-xylate solution allowing small amounts to remain inside. (*iii*) Inject 100-200 ml of freshly prepared 5-10% sodium formaldehyde sulfoxylate solution intravenously. For later treatment, give sodium citrate 1-4 g every 4 hours by mouth. (*iv*) Give calcium gulconate 10 ml of 10% solution intramuscularly or intravenously for muscle spasm.
7.	Strychnine hydro-chloride	Stiffness of face and neck muscles, hyperactive reflexes, opisthotonous, repeated convulsions, respiratory arrest, leading to death.	(*i*) Give universal antidote followed by gastric lavage with 240 ml of potassium permanganate 1 : 1000 solution leaving one-fourth in the stomach. (*ii*) Give pentobarbital sodium 0.1 g intravenously. (*iii*) Do not use morphine or its derivatives.
8.	Metaldehyde	–	(*i*)Keep the patient lying and warm. (*ii*)Give sodium chloride 15 g in a glass of warm water, repeat until vomit fluid is clear and give 30 g of magnesium sulphate. (*iii*) Give strong tea or coffee or one tablespoonful of aromatic spirit of ammonia in water.
9.	Methyl bromide	The symptoms after inhalation of gas are dizziness and headache which are followed by loss of appetite, nausea, vomiting, abdominal pain, blurred speech, staggering gait,	(*i*) Correct the metabolic acidosia. (*ii*) Give artificial respiration and guard against respiratory infection. (*iii*) Inject caffeine sodium benzoate 0.5 g and if necessary epin-ephrine 0.5 ml 1 : 1000. (*iv*) Keep the mouth rinsed

		blurring of vision and even temporary blindness. Mental confusion, tremors and epileptiform convulsions may develop. The death may occur from respiratory complications.	with 10% solution of sodium thio-sulphate. (*v*) When revived, give hot tea or coffee.
10.	Aluminium phosphide	The symptoms of inhalation of gas are headache, giddiness, nausea, diarrhoea and mental confusion. If treatment is delayed, coma, loss of reflexes may develop and death may occur from respiratory or circulatory collapse.	(*i*) Take the patient immediately into air and let him lie down in a comfortable position. (*ii*) Apply artificial respiration, if necessary. (*iii*) Inject glucose solution.
11.	Ethylene dibromide	Inhalation of gas may cause pulmonary lesions, and pulmonary oedema. Respiratory and circulatory depressions occur. Damage to liver and kidney has been reported. Contact with liquid causes blisters on the skin if allowed to evaporate.	(*i*) Give oxygen therapy, respiratory stimulants such as nikethamide or caffeine. (*ii*) After acute nervous symptoms subside, give adrenergic blocking agents like bidenzyl betachloroethyl amine hydrochloride to prevent damage to liver and kidneys. (*iii*) If the poison has been swallowed, give gastric lavage and saline purgatives.

The following precautions should be followed to minimise the hazards by pesticides:

A. Precautions to Protect Man

(*i*) **Supervision.** Pesticides are highly toxic and should not be chosen unless absolutely necessary and, if chosen, should be applied under the supervision of trained personnel. If there is any doubt that the safety measures cannot be strictly enforced, methods other than pesticides should be adopted rather than risk the lives of the people.

(*ii*) **Evacuation.** During spraying or dusting—aerial in paticular—farmers, labourers, grazing animals, etc., should be evacuated from the vicinity.

(*iii*) **Personal apparel.** Face masks and respirators should be worn to avoid inhalation of poisons, and gloves and goggles should be used to avoid contact with poisons. Separate overalls (clothes meant only to be worn during pesticide application) should be worn to cover the body. The overalls should be changed and washed after application.

(*iv*) **Separate instruments.** Instruments (knives, scissors, etc.), used for opening tins and packages of pesticide should be kept separately and should not be used for any other purpose. Formulations should be mixed using long wooden handles and definitely not by hands. Parts of equipment (sprayers, dusters) should never be blown by the mouth.

(*v*) **Personal precautions.** Smoking and eating should not be carried out while applying pesticides. Also, spilling of pesticide and contact with it, should be avoided. One should wash atonce with plenty of clean water in case of spillage or contact and take a bath as soon as possible after application.

(*vi*) **Washing of equipment.** Pesticide equipment should never be washed near a source whose water is used for drinking (like wells, taps, tanks, pools, etc.).

(*vii*) **Disposal.** Empty tins or packages of pesticides should be disposed off, *i.e.* taken to safer places. It would be better to bury them.

(*viii*) **Safe storage.** Pesticide packets/tins should be clearly labelled with prominent danger marks and should be stored at places (preferably under lock and key) out of the reach of children, servants, and pets.

(*ix*) **Heed instructions.** All instructions on the label of the packings should be checked and heeded scrupulously.

(*x*) **Re-entry period.** Field workers should strictly observe the safe re-entry period after pesticide application.

(*xi*) **Antidote.** Antidotes are normally mentioned on the pesticide packings. They should be kept ready at hand and their proper use known beforehand in case they may be needed due to accidental poisoning.

(*xii*) **First-aid.** Field workers should be given first-aid training so that they can treat accidental poisoning. A doctor should be summoned as soon as possible in case of accident and the antidote should preferably be administered by a doctor if there is time. Field workers should be periodically checked by a doctor. To acquaint oneself with the safety measures, he should consult the guidelines of the Bureau of Indian Standards which deal with the first-aid to be given before the arrival of the physician, symptoms and diagnosis that help in identifying the exact pesticide that has affected and specific treatment to be given.

B. Precautions to Protect Environment

(*i*) **Minimum use.** The use of pesticides should be avoided wherever possible and attempts to do so should always be made.

(*ii*) **Rotation of pesticides.** The same pesticides should not be used for a long time; they should be kept substituted. This is likely to check/postpone the development of pesticide resistance.

(*iii*) **Consideration of economic levels.** The mere sight of pests does not call for a control measure. Control measures should be adopted only when the pest numbers are above economic levels.

(*iv*) **Excessive use unnecessary.** A 100 per cent control of pests is not necessary to protect crops, since the latter can tolerate some amount of pest attack. Therefore, an excessve use of pesticides with a view to eradicating a pest species is not only unnecessary but impossible to achieve.

(*v*) **Combination with other methods.** One way to minimise the use of pesticides is to use (integrate) other methods of control.

Pesticide Residues

Pesticides have become essential input in intensive agriculture. Some of the crops like grapes require as high as 20 sprays a year. Similarly, other crops such as small cardamom (12 insecticide and 6 fungicide sprays per year), irrigated chillies and cotton need 12 rounds of pesticide sprays per season. Pesticides account for a major share of the cost of cultivation of crops in India. According to a recent survey, they have a substantial share in cost of cultivation of cotton (36%), pomegranate (35%), vegetables (30%), cole crops (31%), paddy (26%), chickpea (25%), grapes (24%), mango (21%), wheat (14%), cardamom (8%) and apple (6%). Therefore, pesticides are being pumped into such agroecosystems in India. Only a small amount of the pesticide (< 1%) applied to a crop reaches the target pests and the remaining (> 99%) enters different components of the environment to contaminate soil, water, air, food, feed, forage and other commodities. The major source of human exposure to pesticides is food, but drinking water, inhaling air and dermal contact with pesticides may also leave residues in humans.

The following terms, which have relevance to pesticide residues, need to be defined:

Pesticide residue. The pesticide residue is a substance or a mixture of substances in food, feed, soil, water and air, originating from the use of pesticides, and includes the specified degradation and conversion products, metabolites, reaction products and impurities.

Deposit. The amount of pesticidal chemical, initially laid down on the surface, is called deposit (the amount of pesticide left over after a lapse of time is called residue).

Maximum residue limit. The maximum residue limit (MRL) or tolerance limit is the optimum safe concentration of the left over pesticide or its degradation products according to good agricultural practices.

Acceptable daily intake. The acceptable daily intake (ADI) is the daily exposure to a level of pesticide residue which does not manifest into an appreciable risk during the entire life time.

Waiting period. Waiting period is defined as the period required for the residue level of the pesticide to decline to the tolerance limit (MRL value).

Monitoring surveys in different parts of India have revealed the widespread contamination of all types of food products including cereals, pulses, vegetables, fruits, animal products, vegetable oils, milk and milk products, spices and honey with pesticide residues (Fig. 8.1). In many cases, the residues were above the legal maximum residue limits (MRLs). Twenty per

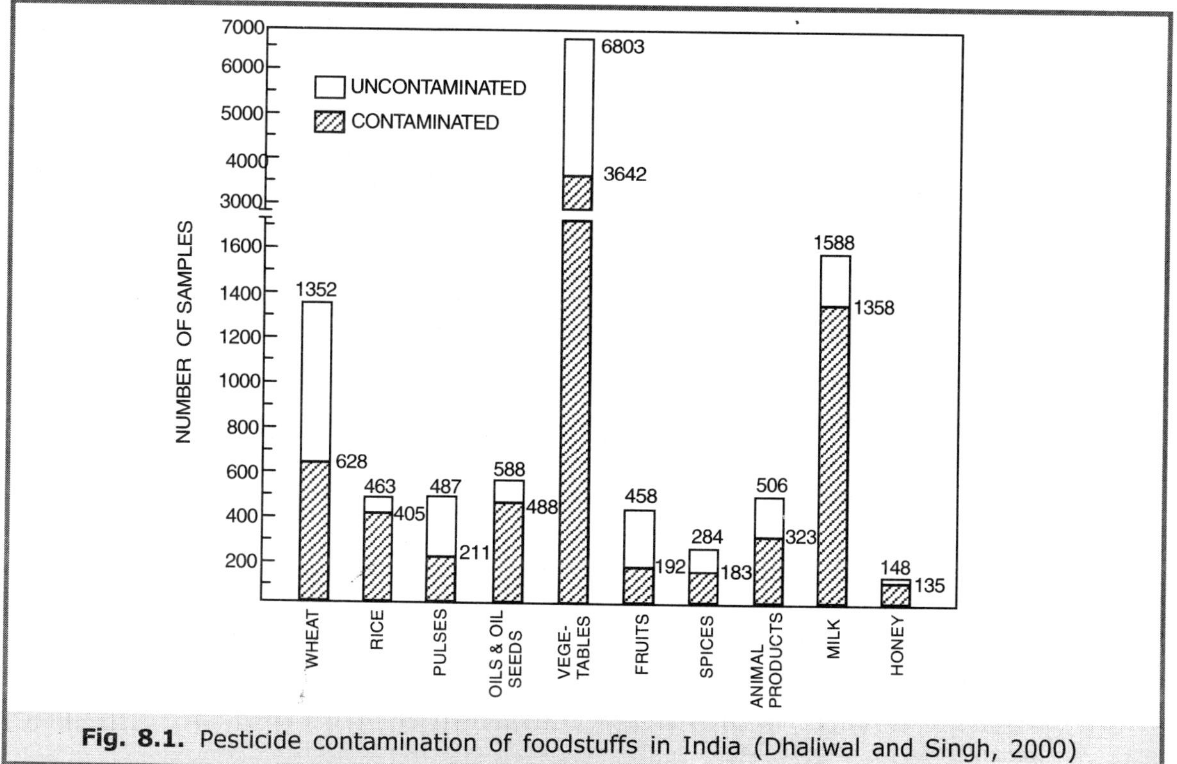

Fig. 8.1. Pesticide contamination of foodstuffs in India (Dhaliwal and Singh, 2000)

cent of the market samples of non-fatty food commodities were found to have residues above MRL. In case of milk, about 87 per cent samples were contaminated with DDT with 43 per cent above the MRL of 0.05 mg/kg. Similarly, 90 per cent of samples were cotainated with HCH, 78 per cent of which had total HCH above the legal limit of 0.01 mg per kg. In contrast to this, only 1-2 per cent of the samples of food commodities at the global level contained residues above the MRL. In California, the figure was found to be as low as 0.12 per cent and less than 18 per cent of the samples of 72 marketable commodities contained detectable residues. In India, even human breast milk samples were found to be contaminated with high levels of residues of DDT, HCH and aldrin.

Recent surveys conducted in Punjab reveal significant reduction in the residues of these insecticides in food commodities. However, lindane residues were found to be present in 53 per cent of milk above the legal limit. The presence of commonly used organophosphorus insecticides in 71 per cent samples of vegetables and 85 per cent of fruits is also a matter of concern.

The population of the developing countries is known to carry heavy burden of pesticides in their bodies. The principal source of these residues is believed to be the diet which contains significant quantities of persistent pesticides. Due to the ubiquitous presence of DDT and HCH residues in all food commodities, it has been estimated that the dietary intake of these pesticides exceeded the acceptable daily intake (ADI) in India. In addition to foodstuffs, soil and water samples from different parts of the country have been found to contain residues of both these pesticides. DDT has become so widespread in our environment that its residues have been detected even in antaractic snow.

Besides DDT and HCH, other organochlorine insecticides like aldrin, dieldrin, heptachlor and endosulfan have also been found in many of the samples of foodstuffs in India. After the ban on the use of DDT and HCH, the residues of these insecticides have started to show a declining trend. But lindane residues still exceeded the prescribed MRL of 0.01 mg kg–1 in 23 of the 24 milk samples examined during 1999-2000. In case of vegetables also a number of samples were found to contain residues of some commonly used organophosphorus insecticides like monocrotophos, quinalphos, trizophos, etc. above the prescribed MRLs. In addition, pesticide residues in agricultural commodities have a significant influence in the area of international trade. Commodities bearing pesticide residues above the legally permitted levels may be rejected by the importing country, thereby causing appreciable economic loss to the exporting country. Pesticides in tea, coffee and vanaspati have affected our export of these commodities. There is also a market for export of cotton fabrics and garments devoid of pesticide residues in Japan, Europe and America.

The levels of pesticide residues can be minimised if following precautions are followed :

- Pesticides should be used only when it is absolutely essential. The non-chemical methods of pest control should be encouraged.
- Only recommended pesticides should be applied at the right time and at the prescribed dosages.
- Preference should be given to the use of less persistent pesticides. Never use the banned or restricted pesticides.
- Ripe fruits and vegetables should be plucked before pesticide application. After pesticide use, the crop should be harvested only after the recommended waiting period.
- Pesticide residues on the produce can also be reduced by washing along with rubbing and peeling off vegetables.

Pesticide Resistance

Resistance is the development of an ability to tolerate a dose of a pesticide, which would prove lethal to the majority of the individuals in a normal population of the same species. This ability results due to genetic change in pest populations in response to toxicants that may impair their control in the field when applied at recommended rates. In sharp contrast to slow evolution of resistance to natural toxins, resistance to synthetic pesticides has developed rapidly, because pesticides have been used intensively in situations that otherwise favour rapid pest buildup.

The first documented case of resistance to insecticides appeared in 1914 when it was reported that San Jose scale became resistant to hydrogen cyanide. The introduction of each new class of synthetic organic insecticides, starting with DDT in 1940s, was followed by reports of insecticide resistance in some insects. In 1938, seven insect and mite species were known to be resistant to at least one pesticide; by 1950 this number had increased to 11. In 1969, 156 species were known to be resistant and by 1984 this number had increased to 447. By the end of 1990s, the number of resistant insects and mites had risen to about 600 species and by 2001, it had increased to over 700 species (Fig. 8.2). This trend is likely to continue in the twenty-first century. Many species have developed resistance to all the available groups of insecticides including DDT, cyclodienes, organophosphates, carbamates and pyrethroids. In diamondback moth which is notorious for its capability to develop resistance quickly, the resistance now extends to benzoyl phenyl ureas and *Bacillus thuringiensis*.

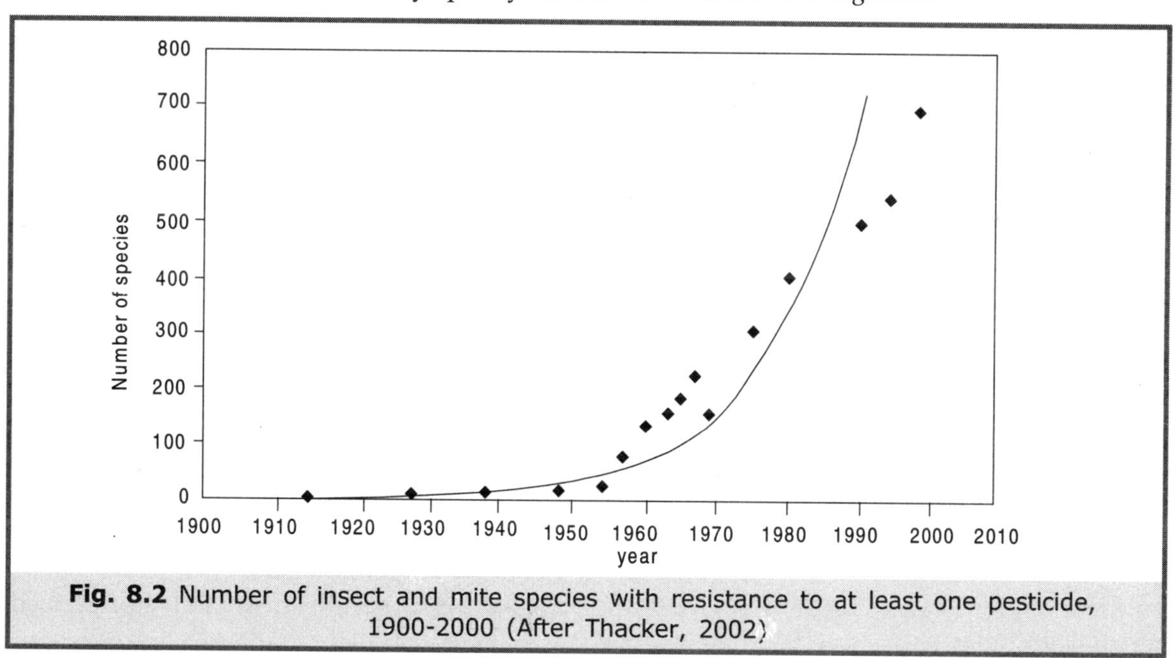

Fig. 8.2 Number of insect and mite species with resistance to at least one pesticide, 1900-2000 (After Thacker, 2002)

Resistance to organochlorine pesticides is most common and comprises approximately 66 per cent of the top 10 insecticides/acaricides or formulations that have a arthropod species resistant to them. Organophosphorous products make up an additional 29 per cent and the carbamates are 5 per cent of this total. The resistant species represent 15 different arthropod orders and among these, the top five orders (Diptera, Acari, Lepidoptera, Coleoptera and Homoptera) comprise approximately 90 per cent of the resistant species. Seven of the top 10 species to show resistance are agricultural pests, two are medically important and one is pest of farm animals (Table 8.6).

Table 8.6 Ten most resistant arthropod species to insecticides or acaricides

S. No.	Common name	Species	Host/economic impact	Number of pesticides	Number of cases
1.	Two-spotted spider mite	*Tetranychus urticae*	Cotton, fruits, ornamentals, walnuts	79	325
2.	Diamondback moth	*Plutellaxylostella*	Crucifers, nasturtium	76	278
3.	Peach-potato aphid	*Myzus persicae*	Crops, flowers, fruits, grains, trees, tobacco, vegetables	68	293
4.	Colorado potato beetle	*Leptinotarsa decemlineata*	Brinjal, pepper, potato, tomato	48	183
5.	House fly	*Musca domestica*	Urban	44	183
6.	Southern cattle tick	*Boophilus microplus*	Cattle	43	127
7.	German cockroach	*Blatella germanica*	Urban	42	213
8.	Cotton whitefly	*Bemisia tabaci*	Cotton and other crops	39	169
9.	Red spider mite	*Panonychus ulmi*	Fruits, trees	38	178
10.	Cotton aphid	*Aphis gossypii*	Cotton and other crops	37	103

Source **:** Onstad (2008)

A perusal of literature associated with arthropod resistance revealed that prior to 1980, there were 1613 reported cases of resistance (species × compound) to different pesticide classes. Prior to 1990, this had increased to 2325 reported cases, and prior to 2000 some 2585 cases of arthropod resistance to pesticides were recorded. About 49 per cent of the reported cases were species resistant to organophosphates. Resistance to organochlorines accounted for 33 per cent of the reported cases of resistance. Pyrethroids and carbamates accounted for 9 and 6 per cent of the arthropod resistance cases, respectively. Reports of resistance to a wide range of other pesticides, including the newer insect growth regulators and other chemicals, accounted for less than 1 per cent of the reported cases of arthropod resistance.

The impact of development of resistant pest species has varied world wide. Its impact has been greatest in tropical climates in developing countries where pest species reproduce rapidly and have numerous generations per year. Some of the best known examples of resistance development come from the cotton-growing regions of the world. For example, the development of resistance to insecticides in cotton pests led to near destruction of cotton growing in Russia, to make cotton growing completely uneconomical in the Yellow River valley in China, to a reduction in the cotton hectarage in Mexico in the 1960s from 2,80,000 ha to 400 ha, and to a decline in cotton yields in diverse countries such as Nicaragua, Peru, Egypt and India.

In Asian countries, the first report of development of pesticide resistance was reported from India where *Singhara* beetle, *Galerucella birmanica* was found resistant to DDT and HCH. Since then 14 other pests have been demostrated to become resistant to different insecticides in one or more countries (Table 8.7). Severe pyrethroid resistance in the cotton bollworm, *Helicoverpa armigera* was first recorded in eastern Andhra Pradesh in 1987-99 and in Punjab in 1990-91. Failure to control the pest with the existing conventional insecticides resulted in severe outbreaks on cotton and other crops in different areas of the country since then.

Extensive studies carried out on *H. armigera* collected between 1991-1995 from 51 locations from the Indian subcontinent including various locations in India, two locations in Nepal and

Table 8.7 Status of insecticide resistance in insect pests of crops in developing countries

Insect pest	Common name	Insecticide (s) to which resistant	Country
Aphis craccivora	Aphid	Carbamates, organophosphates	India
Bemisia tabaci	Whitefly	Cyfluthrin, cypermethrin, endosulfan, methamidophos, monocrotopos, quinalphos	India, Pakistan, Sudan
Empoasca kerri	Jassid	Carbamates, organophosphates	India
Galerucella birmanica	*Singhara* beetle	Aldrin, chlordane, DDT, dieldrin, HCH, malathion	India
Helicoverpa armigera	Gram pod borer	*Bacillus thuringiensis*, carbaryl, endosulfan, endrin, DDT + toxaphene, organophosphates, synthetic pyrethroids	Chad, China, India, Nepal, Indonesia, Pakistan, South Africa, Thailand, Vietnam, Zimbabwe
Laodelphax striatella	Leafhopper	Carbamates, cyclodienes, organophosphates	Korea
Lipaphis erysimi	Mustard aphid	Carbamates, cypermethrin, deltamethrin, dimethoate, endosulfan, fenvalerate, lindane, malathion, omethoate, parathion, phosphamidon	China, India
Myzus persicae	Peach aphid	Dimethoate, endosulfan, malathion	India
Nephotettix cincticeps	Green leafhopper	Organophosphates	China, Korea, Taiwan
Nephotettix virescens	Green leafhopper	Carbamates, DDT	Taiwan, Vietnam
Nilaparvata lugens	Brown planthopper	Carbamates, cyclodienes, DDT, organophosphates	Fiji, Malaysia, Philippines, SriLanka, Vietnam
Plutella xylostella	Diamondback moth	Abamectin, acephate, aminocarb, *Bt* subsp. *aizawi*, *Bt* subsp. *kurstaki*, carbaryl, carbosulfan, cartap hydrochloride, cyanofenphos, cypermethrin, DDT, diazinon, dichlorvos, ethyl parathion, fenitrothion, HCH, leptophos, malathion, methamidophos, methomyl, monocrotophos, parathion, permethrin, propoxur, prothiophos, quinalphos, trichlorfon	China, Malaysia, India
Recilia dorsalis	Zigzag leafhopper	Carbamates, DDT, organophosphates, synthetic pyrethroids	Taiwan
Sogatella furcifera	Whitebacked planthopper	Carbamates	Sri Lanka
Spodoptera litura	Tobacco catterpillar	DDT, endosulfan, fenitrothion, HCH, lindane, malathion, methyl parathion monocrotophos	India, Indonesia, Vietnam
S. exigua	Soybean caterpillar	Cypermethrin, deltamethrin, endosulfan, fenvalerate, methamidophos, monocrotophos, parathion methyl	Vietnam

Source : Mehrotra and Phokela (2000)

one in Pakistan, many locations being from Maharashtra and Andhra Pradesh, show that resistance to some pyrethroids is ubiquitous in this pest in the Indian subcontinent. The resistance levels to cypermethrin ranged from 5 to 6000-fold and to fenvalerate 16 to 3200-fold. Pyrethroid resistance levels were highest in central and southern India which are intense cotton and pulse growing areas where excessive application of insecticides is common. Resistance to organophosphates was low ranging from 2 to 59-fold to quinalphos and 0.4 to 3-fold to monocrotophos. Gene flow resulting from migration of moths from high input farming regions to other areas is most likely responsible for the apparent homogeneity of resistance to SPs and OPs over large areas of India. Widespread occurrence of resistance in this pest has also been reported from Indonesia and Thailand

Diamondback moth, *Plutella xylostella*, is another serious pest which has developed resistance to nearly all classes of insecticides used against it in south-east Asian countries. In India, as early as 1968, resistance to DDT and parathion was reported in *P. xylostella* damaging cauliflower crop around Ludhiana. By 1976, multiple resistance to a number of organochlorine and organophosphate insecticides was observed. In 1980s high levels of resistance to synthetic pyrethoids, cypermethrin (145-fold), fenvalerate (210-fold) and deltamethrin (194-fold) were reported from different parts of the country.

During 1990s, the levels of resistance have increased to 2880-fold in cypermethrin and 2700-fold in fenvalerate in Punjab. It now appears that *P. xylostella* has developed resistance to DDT, HCH, endrin, parathion, fenitrothion, malathion, quinalphos, endosulfan, cypermethrin, fenvalerate and deltamethrin. This suggests that the true multiple resistance has appeared in this pest in India. This multiple resistance calls for immediate attention with regard to evolving management strategies for this pest (Mehrotra and Phokela, 2000).

Similarly, another polyphagous pest, *Spodoptera litura,* damaging vegetables, oilseeds, cotton and tobacco crops, has been observed to be resistant to chlorinated hydrocarbons, organophosphates, carbamates and synthetic pyrethroids in India. In fact, the real development of pesticide resistance in this pest took place during 10-year period from 1971 to 1980. During 1980s, populations of *S. litura* collected from Guntur and Tenali districts of Andhra Pradesh showed low to moderate levels of resistance to DDT, HCH, lindane, endosulfan, malathion, methyl parathion and pyrethrum. A study on 22 strains of *S. litura* collected from groundnut crop of 8 locations in Andhra Pradesh between 1991 and 1996, reported resistance levels ranging from 0.2 to 197-fold to cypermethrin, 8 to 121-fold to fenvalerate, 1 to 13-fold to endosulfan, 1 to 29-fold to quinalphos, 2 to 362-fold to monocrotophos and 0.7 to 19-fold to methomyl.

There has been development of resistance in *S. litura* to the extent of 21-fold to pyrethrum, 15-fold to endosulfan and 23-fold to lindane between 1961 and 1995. Towards the organophosphates, development of resistance over the last quarter century between 1970 and 1995 was 2-fold to monocrotophos, 39-fold to fenitrothion, 9-fold to dimethoate, 4-fold to malathion, fenthion and methyl parathion. In case of synthetic pyrethroids, development of resistance was to the extent of 9 -, 1.45 - and 98-fold to cypermethrin, fenvalerate and deltamethrin, respectively, from 1987 to 1985 (Mehrotra and Phokela, 2000).

Brown planthopper of rice has been reported to have developed resistance to one or more pesticides in Fiji, Malaysia, Philippines, Sri Lanka and Vietnam. Moderate to high level of resistance to all the insecticides tested has been reported in *Bemisia tabaci* in Pakistan. Besides the individual OPs, SPs and endosulfan, resistance has extended to commercially available insecticide mixtures, Polytrin C (profenofos and cypermethrin) and Bathroid TM (methamidophos and cyfluthrin). Surprisingly, a strain of whitefly collected from brinjal crop was virtually immune to cyfluthrin and exhibited more than 300-fold resistance to cypermethrin. Even though pyrethroids are not specifically recommended against whitefly on cotton in Pakistan, heavy reliance on pyrethroid/OP mixtures for bollworm and other pests has resulted in extensive whitefly exposure to pyrethroids. In case of other pests, the problem is not yet widespread and can be tackled by undertaking timely remedial measures.

Evolution of resistance to insecticides is a threat to modern agriculture. An understanding of the dynamics of resistance is of utmost importance to tackle this problem. There is a general concurrence that the evolution of resistance is determined by a variety of genetic, biological and operational factors. The genetic and biological categories are inherent qualities of the population and, therefore, are beyond our control. Their assessment is, however, essential in determining the risk for resistance in a target population. The operational factors, on the other hand, are human-made and thus are within our control. They can be altered to any extent necessary and feasible, depending on the risk for resistance that is revealed by genetic and biological factors. The strategies used to delay the onset of resistance and to manage resistant populations are known as ***insecticide resistance management*** (IRM) and form an important component of IPM programmes. The three alternative strategies used for IRM are moderation, saturation and multiple attack.

(*i*) Moderation. Susceptible genes are a valuable and depletable resource that may be conserved by reduction of selection pressure. By applying a lower dose than that which kills all susceptible individuals, sufficient susceptible genes are preserved in the population. Incomplete coverage and leaving untreated areas also allows susceptible individuals to survive in untreated areas and helps in delaying the onset of resistance.

(*ii*) Saturation. It aims at rendering the R genes functionally recessive by applying dosages sufficiently high to be lethal to susceptible as well as heterozygous resistant genotypes. Use of synergists may help in suppression of detoxication in resistant individuals.

(*iii*) Management by multiple attack. Here control is achieved by action of several independently acting forces such that selection pressure by any one of them is below that leading to the development of resistance. This may be achieved by use of insecticide mixtures, insecticide rotations and optimal sequences of insecticides.

It needs to be emphasized here that IPM also contributes to a reduction of chemical selection pressure and, thus, helps in IRM. New chemicals provide us with diversification in available toxicants and enable us to avoid over-reliance on one specific compound or a group of compounds. However, these chemicals by themselves do not offer solution since none has been shown to be immune to the development of resistance. Breakthroughs in formulation and application technology may also help in reducing the selection pressure. A combination of these measures may help to increase the useful life span of pesticides as the rate of development of new pesticides is falling rapidly.

Pest Resurgence

Resurgence refers to an abnormal increase in pest population or damage following pesticide application often far exceeding the economic injury level. Pest resurgence may broadly be classified into two categories, *i.e.* primary pest resurgence and secondary pest resurgence (replacement).

Primary pest resurgence. Primary pest resurgence occurs when the target pest population responds to a pesticide treatment by increasing to a level atleast as high or higher than in an untreated control or higher than the population level observed before the treatment. The resurgence may occur after the first application or after several applications of the pesticide. Pest population outbreaks can be caused by many factors, but pest resurgence occurs after a treatment of the crop with a chemical, targeted at the pest population that is intended and expected to control the targeted pest.

Secondary pest resurgence. Secondary pest resurgence refers to the replacement of a primary pest with a secondary pest or a secondary pest outbreak occurs when a non-target, but injurious pest population increases in a crop, after it is treated with a pesticide to control a primary pest population. The increase is an unintended and unexpected consequence of the pesticide treatment. For example, pesticide sprays to control the codling moth, apple maggot and plum curculio on apple lead to resurgence of populations of white apple leafhopper, spotted tentiform leafminer, and European red mite. Season long sulphur sprays for control of powdery mildew on grapes often lead to resurgence of the red spider mite, *Tetranychus pacificus*.

Resurgence of insect pests following application of insecticides has been known for a long time. As early as 1956, more than 50 species of insect pests and mites whose populations showed resurgence after insecticidal treatments with diverse chemicals were known. Maximum cases of resurgence belong to Homoptera (44%) followed by Lepidoptera (24%) and phytophagous mites (26%). It is interesting to note that homopteran insects are protected from contact insecticides by a waxy covering and many of the Lepidoptera exhibiting resurgence are borers and leafminers which also escape direct contact with the insecticides. Interestingly, Homoptera (66%) and Lepidoptera (18%) head the list for classical biological control successes associated with each insect order. It thus appears that resurgence is associated with pests which have effective natural enemies and which are also less affected by contact pesticides than their natural enemies.

Maximum reports of resurgence pertain to planthoppers especially brown planthopper (BPH) of rice. BPH was a minor pest of rice crop during 1950s in India but extensive use of insecticides has elevated it to the status of a major pest not only in India but whole of Asia. Reports of insecticide-induced resurgence in BPH have been received from Bangladesh, India, Indonesia, and Solomon Islands. As many as 27 insecticides have been reported to cause resurgence in BPH (Table 8.8). The factors implicated in BPH resurgence include reduction in duration of nymphal stage, longer oviposition period, shortened life cycle, enhanced reproductive rate, higher feeding rate and destruction of natural enemies especially *Cyrtorhinus lividipennis*.

The use of synthetic pyrethroids on cotton during the last two decades has resulted in increasing incidence of serveral sucking pests including whitefly, aphid, red mite and mealy bugs. Over-reliance on SPs for the control of bollworms has been the major factor responsible for whitefly outbreaks in Andhra Pradesh, Gujarat, Tamil Nadu and other parts of the country.

SPs have also been reported to cause resurgence of mustard aphid infesting Indian mustard. It was found that the application of SPs to the host plants increased the concentration of glucose and some amino acids especially arginine, lysine, isoleucine, leucine and cystine. These changes might be responsible for stimulation of aphid reproduction and increased weight of such aphids. On the other hand, endosulfan did not affect the quality of leaf sap of the host plants but still caused enhanced reproduction in the aphid. It was found that endosulfan reduced the excretion of some amino acids in the honeydew of the aphid indicating that better utilization of these amino acids was responsible for the increased fecundity of such

Table 8.8 Pesticides causing resurgence of insect and mite pests of crops

Pest	Scientific name	Pesticide(s)	Mode of application
Cotton			
Cotton jassid	*Amrasca biguttula*	Chloropyriphos, quinalphos	Foliar
Cotton aphid	*Aphis gossypii*	Carbaryl	Dust
		DDT	Foliar
		Monocrotophos	Foliar
		Phorate, disulfoton, dimethoate	Soil
		Cypermethrin, deltamethrin, fenvalerate, flucythrinate, permethrin, S-524	Foliar
Whitefly	*Bemisia tabaci*	DDT, dimethoate	Foliar
		Monocrotophos	Foliar
		Cypermethrin, deltamethrin, fenvalerate	Foliar
		PP-321	Foliar
		Toxaphene	Foliar
Spider mite	*Tetranychus cinnabarinus*	DDT	Foliar
		Carbaryl	Foliar
		Cypermethrin, fenvalerate, fluvalinate	Foliar
Mealy bug	*Ferrisia virgata*	Deltamethrin, cypermethrin, fenvalerate, permethrin	Foliar
Rice			
Brown planthopper	*Nilaparvata lugens*	Diazinon, methyl parathion, miral, perthane, ethoprop, acephate, phorate, deltamethrin	Soil, water
		Vamidothion, phosphamidon, methomyl, azinophos methyl, triazophos, monocrotophos, fenthion, fenitrothion, phosalone	Foliar
		Chlorpyriphos	Foliar
		Carbaryl	Dust, foliar
		Carbofuran	Soil, water
		BPMC	Water
		Deltamethrin, permethrin, cypermethrin, fenvalerate, WL 8587, lambdacyhalthrin	Foliar
Green leafhopper	*Nephotettix virescens*	Phorate	Soil
		Deltamethrin	Foliar
Blue leafhopper	*Empoascanara maculifrons*	Acephate, dicrotophos, dimethoate, methyl demeton, monocrotophos, phosphamidon	Seed treatment, seedling root dip
Whitebacked planthopper	*Sogatella furcifera*	Deltamethrin, diazinon, methyl parathion	Foliar
		Cypermethrin, deltamethrin, fenvalerate	Foliar
Leaf folder	*Cnaphalocrocis medinalis*	Phorate, carbofuran	Soil
Striped stem borer	*Chilo suppressalis*	HCH, parathion	Dust, foliar

Vegetables and fruits			
Brinjal			
Aphid	*Myzus persicae*	Cypermethrin, deltamethrin	Foliar
Bitter gourd			
Aphid	*Aphis malvae*	Malathion, deltamethrin, permethrin	Foilar
Leafhopper	*Hishimonus phycitis*	Fenvalerate	Foliar
Muskmelon and watermelon			
Red spider mite	*T. cinnabarinus*	Fluvalinate	Foliar
Mustard aphid	*Lipaphis erysimi*	Phorate, disulfoton, dimethoate	Foliar
Potato			
Colorado potato beetle	*Leptinotarsa decemlineata*	DDT	Foliar
Grapevine			
Mealy bug	*Pseudococcus martimus*	DDT	Foliar
Okra			
Mite	*Tetranychus urticae*	Ethion	Foliar
Cabbage			
Diamondback moth	*Plutella xylostella*	Methomyl	Foliar
Chillies			
Yellow mite	*Polyphagotarso-nemus latus*	Monocrotophos, methyl demeton, thiometon, phosphamidon, formothion, neem cake extract	Foliar
		Acephate, cypermethrin, permethrin, fenvalerate, deltamethrin	Foliar
Mango			
Mite	*T. cinnabarinus*	Carbaryl	Foliar
Citrus			
False rust mite	*Phyllocoptruta oleivora*	Methidathion	Foliar
Strawberry			
Aphid	*Chaetosiphon fragaefolii*	Phorate, disulfoton	Soil
Miscellaneous pests			
Sugarcane scale	*Melanapis glomerata*	Endrin	Foliar
Western corn root worm	*Diabrotica virgifera*	Carbofuran, carbaryl	Foliar
Sorghum mite	*T. cinnabarinus*	Carbaryl	Foliar

Source : Dhawan *et al.* (2000)

aphids. It is, thus, clear that different insecticides may cause resurgence of the same insect by different mechanisms and even the same insecticides may produce variable effects at different sub-lethal concentrations.

The use of right type of insecticide, dosage, time and method of application can play a significant role in reducing the risk of insecticide resurgence. The agronomic practices like date of sowing, judicious use of fertilizer and irrigation water can help in reducing the insecticide-induced resurgence. The cultivation of healthy crop, conservation of natural enemies with the use of eco friendly insecticides, proper surveillance and making farmers IPM experts can help in avoiding insecticide-induced resurgence.

Toxicity to Non-target Organisms

Most of the popular pesticides used in agriculture are neurotoxicants which affect all living organisms in a similar manner. The whole range of living organisms including natural enemies, pollinators, domestic and wild animals, birds, fish and other aquatic organisms and even soil fauna are affected by the use of pesticides in agriculture.

Natural enemies. Parasitoids and predators are important components of agroecosystems and serve to regulate the populations of most insect pests. Unfortunately, many natural enemies are susceptible to a variety of pesticides used in crop protection. Such susceptibility often results in pest resurgences and outbreaks of secondary pests in the treated crops. Screening of commonly used pesticides for the control of major insect pests of agricultural crops has revealed that some of these are comparatively safe to the natural enemies (Table 8.9).

Table 8.9 Pesticides reported as comparatively safe to natural enemies

S.No.	Natural enemy	Insect pest	Safe pesticide(s) identified
1	2	3	4
	Egg parasitoids		
1.	*Telenomus remus*	Tabacco caterpillar	Monocrotophos, phosalone
2.	*Trichogramma achaeae*	Spotted bollworm	Deltamethrin, monocrotophos, permethrin, phosalone
3.	*Trichogramma brasiliense*	Gram pod borer	Cypermethrin, deltamethrin, endosulfan, fenpropathrin, fenvalerate, flucythrinate, monocrotophos, phosalone
4.	*Trichogramma chilonis*	Tissue borers of sugarcane, jowar and maize	DDT, deltamethrin, diazinon, diflubenzuron, endosulfan, fenvalerate, lindane, oxydemeton methyl, phosalone, phosphamidon
5.	*Trichogramma japonicum*	Top borer of sugarcane and yellow stem borer of rice	Endosulfan, lindane
6.	*Trichogramma perkinsi*	Tissue borers of sugarcane, jowar and maize	DDT, diazinon, endosulfan
7.	*Trichogrammatoidea armigera*	Gram pod borer	Phosalone
8.	*Trichogrammatoidea eldanae*	Tissue borers of sugarcane	Deltamethrin, oxydemeton methyl
	Egg-larval parasitoids		
9.	*Chelonus blackburni*	Cotton bollworms	Diflubenzuron, dimethoate, fenpropathrin, permethrin, phosalone
10.	*Tetrastichus pyrillae*	Sugarcane pyrilla	Endosulfan, quinalphos
	Larval parasitoids		
11.	*Allorhogas pyralophagus*	Tissue borers of sugarcane	Dicofol, mancozeb, phosalone, zineb
12.	*Apanteles angaleti*	Pink bollworm	Deltamethrin, fenvalerate, permethrin, phosalone, phosphamidon
13.	*Apanteles papilionis*	Lemon butterfly	Fenvalerate, permethrin, phosalone

14.	*Apanteles plutellae*	Diamondback moth	Cypermethrin, fenvalerate, monocrotophos, permethrin, phosalone
15.	*Bracon brevicornis*	Coconut black headed caterpillar	Endosulfan, phosalone
16.	*Bracon kirkpatricki*	Pink bollworm	Cypermethrin, deltamethrin, permethrin, phosalone
17.	*Eucelatoria bryani*	Gram pod borer	Cypermethrin, monocrotophos, phosalone
18.	*Parasierola naphantidis*	Coconut black headed caterpillar	Endosulfan, phosalone
19.	*Pediobius foveolatus*	Epilachna beetle	Extracts of *Acorus calamus* (rhizome), *Azadirachta indica* (seed oil), *Melia azedarach* (drupes)
20.	*Sturmiopsis inferens*	Tissue borers of sugarcane	Carbofuran, fenvalerate, lindane (whorl application of granules), chlorpyriphos (soil application)
	Parasitoids of sucking pests		
21.	*Adelencyrtus mayurai*	Sugarcane scale	Endosulfan, malathion
22.	*Aenasius advena*	Guava mealy bug	Diazinon
23.	*Allotropa japonica*	Grapevine mealy bug	Monocrotophos, phosalone
24.	*Anagyrus dactylopi*	Grapevine mealy bug	Cypermethrin, deltamethrin, fenvalerate
25.	*Aphelinus mali*	Woolly apple aphid	Endosulfan, phosalone
26.	*Aphytis proclia*	San Jose scale	Fenvalerate
27.	*Azotus* sp.	Sugarcane scale	Dimethoate
28.	*Coccidoxenoides peregrinus*	Citrus mealy bug	Deltamethrin
29.	*Epiricania melanoleuca*	Sugarcane pyrilla	Dimethoate, quinaphos
30.	*Leptomastix dactylopii*	Citrus mealy bug	Monocrotophos, phosalone
31.	*Platygaster* sp.	Gall midge	Phosalone
32.	*Tetracnemoidea indica*	Coffee mealy bug	Fenvalerate
	Predators		
33.	*Chrysoperla carnea*	Jassids, aphids	Endosulfan, fenvalerate, phosalone
34.	*Coccinella septempunctata*	Aphids	Alcoholic extract of *dharek* drupes and sweetflag rhizomes, methyl demeton
35.	*Cryptolaemus montrouzieri*	Mealy bugs	Alcoholic extract of *dharek* drupes and sweetflag rhizomes, endosulfan, endrin, methyl demeton
36.	*Cyrtorthinus lividipennis*	Brown planthopper	Phosalone, phosphamidon
37.	*Lycosa* spp.	Brown planthopper	Phosphamidon
38.	*Mallada boninensis*	Aphid,whitefly	Cypermethrin, dichlorvos, endosulfan, fenvalerate, fluvalinate, oxydemeton methyl
39.	*Menochilus sexmaculatus*	Aphid, whitefly	Endosulfan, Repelin

Source: Atwal and Dhaliwal (2009)

Bee toxicity. Besides yielding honey, honey bees and wild bees are vital to the pollination of deciduous fruits, vegetables, legumes, oilseeds, forage crops and natural plants. Indiscriminate use of insecticides on these crops has resulted in widespread mortality of honey bees. Laboratory studies with 50 insecticides revealed that 33 of these were highly toxic and 12 others moderately toxic to the honey bees. Only dialifos (0.3-0.6 kg/ha), bromophos ethyl (0.75 kg/ha), ethiofencarb (0.4-0.6 kg/ha), kolevan (0.18 kg/ha) and diflubenzuron (0.24 kg/ha) were safe to bees. Field studies in Punjab revealed that application of carbaryl, endosulfan, fluvalinate and monocrotophos for bollworm control caused 94, 74, 44 and 100 per cent mortality, respectively, of the bees present in the cotton fields. Residues of these insecticides also proved highly toxic to the bees but fluvalinate residues rapidly lost their toxicity. In *raya* crop, quinalphos, anthio and endosulfan caused 100, 98 and 25 per cent bee mortality, respectively, by direct spray method. Some of the commonly used pesticides have been categorized on the basis of their toxicity to honey bees (Table 8.10).

Table 8.10 Classification of pesticides on the basis of their toxicity to honey bees

Highly toxic (LD50 0.001 – 1.99 mg/bee)	
Carbaryl	Fenvalerate
Carbofuran	Monocrotophos
Carbophenothion	Oxydemeton-methyl
Chlorpyriphos	Parathion
Cypermethrin	Permethrin
Deltamethrin	Phorate
Dichlorvos	Phosphamidon
Dicrotophos	Quinalphos
Dimethoate	Thiometon
Moderately toxic (LD50 2.0 – 10.0 mg/bee	
Insecticides	
DDT	Hinosan
Diazinon	Lindane
Dieldrin	Malathion
Endrin	Metasystox
Ethyl parathion	Methyl demeton
Fenitrothion	Methyl parathion
Fenthion	Mevinphos
Formothion	Monocrotophos
HCH	Trichlorphon
Heptachlor	
Fungicides	
Bavistin	Difolitan
Carbendozin	Foltaf
Dithane	Hexcacap
Relatively non-toxic (LD50> 11.0 mg/bee)	
Insecticides	
Bacillus thuringiensis	Methoxychlor
Chlorobenzilate	Morestan
Dicofol	Nicotine

Dimite	Nuclear polyhedrosis virus
Endosulfan	Phosalone
Ethion	Pyrethrum
Menazon	Sabadilla
Fungicides	
Anilazine	Dinocap
Benomyl	Dodine
Bordeaux mixture	Folcid
Catafol	Polyram
Captan	Thiram
Cuprous oxide	Ziram
Herbicides, defoliants and desiccants	
Alachlor	Cynazine
Amitrole	Diuron
Ammate	Methazole
Atrazine	Nitrofen
Bromocil	Oil sprays

Source : Dhaliwal and Koul (2010)

In USA, it has been estimated that 5 per cent of the bee colonies are killed outright or die during winter as a result of pesticide damage, while another 15 per cent of the colonies suffer partial damage. Such data are not available regarding the extent of damage under the Indian conditions. However, as a result of heavy pesticide use on certain crops especially cotton, bee colonies are excluded from millions of hectares of good apiary locations.

Soil organisms. A number of microorganisms, insects, other arthropods, nematodes and annelids inhabit the soil. These small organisms are essential to the proper functioning of all ecosystems since they break down wastes permitting the vital elements to be recycled in the life system. Bacteria and blue algae make atmospheric nitrogen available to the plants. Earthworms and insects aid in turning over the soil. Only scanty information is available regarding the impact of pesticides on these soil organisms. Higher concentrations of DDT, HCH and carbaryl in the soil inhibit the nitrogen fixing activity of *Rhizobium* spp., *Azotobacter* and blue green algae.

Fish. Pesticides that run off treated cropland often drain into nearby aquatic ecosystems. Such pesticides are easily washed into streams and lakes. Pond, river and lake water at a number of locations in Delhi, Jammu & Kashmir, Karnataka, Madhya Pradesh, Punjab, Rajasthan and West Bengal have been found to be contaminated with DDT, HCH, aldrin, heptachlor and dimethoate. High concentrations of dimethoate (20-200 ppb) were recorded in Hoogly waters in West Bengal. Even low concentrations of pesticides in water may eliminate essential fish foods like insects and other invertebrates. Sublethal dosages of pesticides may also increase susceptibility of fish to disease, starvation and other environmental stresses. High concentrations may kill fish directly. Market samples of various fish species at Ludhiana (Punjab) were invariably contaminated with DDT and HCH residues. Fish samples at Bombay (Maharashtra) contained upto 34.1 ppm of DDT. Such residues are ultimately passed on to humans.

PESTICIDES AND HUMAN WELFARE : AN APPRAISAL

Pesticides have played a major role in raising world's food production. Availability of pesticides made cultivation of crops profitable in areas, where this was previously not possible because of pest problems, as for example with cotton in East Africa. Pesticide use almost universally brought about increased crop production by minimising pest damage and thereby, encouraging farmers to adopt better agronomic practices and obtain high yields. The development of high yielding varieties of crops which ushered in the green revolution was possible only under the protection provided by the pesticide umbrella.

In the green revolution era, pesticides were dominant component of pest management, mainly due to the constraints in adoption of cultural practices, non-availability of resistant cultivars and lack of efficient bioagents. Initially, persistent insecticides of organochlorinated group like endrin, aldrin, DDT, HCH and endosulfan dominated the pesticide market. Later on, organophosphates replaced the persistent insecticides, followed by the highly effective group of synthetic pyrethroids. The use of synthetic pyrethroids during 1980-95 increased the potential of existing cotton cultivars by 25-48 per cent due to effective management of pests. In addition, pesticide use increases farming efficiency and availability of fruits and vegetables, contributes to the supply of low-cost food and fibre for consumers, improves food quality and soil conservation, decreases losses in transport and storage, and ensures a stable and predictable food supply. It has been estimated that for every dollar invested in pest control, there is a return of four dollars.

In spite of their glorious past and great potential in future, pesticides face mounting public pressure due to increasing environmental problems caused by their use. The use of pesticides in early phase of the green revolution was based on fixed schedule, at one or two weeks interval. Subsequently, the economic threshold levels were fixed for differnt crops and these were by and large not adopted by the farmes, as these were not farmer friendly and they continued with indiscriminate use of insecticides. New problems, like insecticide resistance, resurgence of pests, loss of biodiversity and natural enemies, residues in food commodites, adverse effects on environment and human health highlighted the impact of indiscriminate use of insecticides.

Despite the various environmental problems caused by their use, pesticides continue to be the single most widely used method of insect pest control. Pesticides will continue to play an important part in most IPM programmes in the foreseeable future in view of a number of advantages over alternative means of pest control.

- Pesticides provide control of some pests where no other effective tactics were previously available.
- When an increasing insect population approaching ETL is observed in the field, insecticides are often the only means of preventing economic damage.
- Pesticides are easily available across the counter in convenient and ready to use packings.
- Pesticides often provide rapid remedial action against the targeted pest and allow rapid control of an existing pest problem.
- Depending upon the crop, insect-pest and nature of damage, a range of insecticides is available to choose from. Usually, there are several insecticides available and the grower can select one of these based on his requirements and investment capacity.

- Pesticides are easy to apply and large areas can be covered in a relatively short time.
- Even if there is a complex of several insect pests causing economic losses, a single insecticide or a combination of two insecticides in a single application may control the whole pest complex.
- When properly used under appropriate conditions, pesticides provide a relatively predictable level of control. There is often a greater level of uncertainty associated with the use of other tactics.
- Based on the cost of pesticides including application cost, usually the grower is able to get a high return on his investment in a short time. In USA, it has been estimated that cost:benefit ratio works out to 1:4. Now efforts are being made to assess the environmental, ecological and social costs of pesticide use and empirical estimates in USA have revealed that even after including these costs, the cost:benefit ratio may still be 1:3.
- Use of insecticides protects the crops from the ravages of insect pests and thus provides stability in yield as well as in farmers' income.
- Usage of pesticides can permit agricultural production in regions, where such production would not be feasible.
- The use of insecticides is compatible with other components of IPM under intensive agriculture and modern farming conditions.

Many problems arise with pesticide use and misue. The magnitude and importance of these problems vary considerably among pesticide categories. As with the advantages, some problems are real, but others are only perceived.

(*i*) The repeated usage of a single pesticide may lead to the selection of pests that are resistant to the pesticide. This is an enormous problem for use of all types of pesticides, but has been particularly important with insecticides, herbicides, fungicides, and bactericides (antibiotics).

(*ii*) When the pesticide (usually an insecticide) kills the targeted pest, but also kills beneficial insects, the pest population often will increase to a level, higher than the level preceding the application. The phenomenon is called pest resurgence. When the survivors of the targeted population begin to reproduce, their number grows exponentially because the beneficials that once limited population growth are no longer present.

(*iii*) When the pesticide kills the key pest, but not a minor (secondary) pest, the minor pest population may increase and become important. This is a problem for both insecticide and herbicide use.

(*iv*) Pesticides may have nontargeted effects, which occur at two levels :

- Pesticides may harm useful organisms, such as honey bees, or beneficial insects that are critical in the biologial control of pest populations. Some pesticides are toxic to wildlife.
- Pesticides may move from the place where they were applied, resulting in contamination of surface water or groundwater, and pesticide accumulation in the food-chain.

(*v*) Pesticide residues remain in the soil, and on or in harvested produce after the application of a pesticide. Residues may be of particular concern if pesticides are applied incorrectly. Drift occurs when pesticides are applied during unfavorable weather conditions. Wind may carry pesticides to areas, adjacent to the crop fields, resulting in damage to neighbouring plants and animals.

(*vi*) The possibility exists that pesticide residues in food lead to long-term, adverse health consequences for consumers. Residues are of particular concern on foods for infants, as tolerances may be quite different from those for adults.

(*vii*) Because pesticides are toxic chemicals, they have the potential to be toxic to humans, livestock and wildlife.

(*viii*) Due to their toxicity, pesticides have the potential to cause illness in farm workers, especially for those working in hand-harvested fresh market crops.

(*ix*) Although low cost may be a reason for the use of pesticides, in other situations pesticides are an expensive choice; this is especially true for management of certain insects where biological control is a feasible alternative. In many developing countries, the cost of pesticides is prohibitive. Often cheap laour offers alternatives to pesticides, as for example, in hand-weeding or in hand-picking worms on crop plants.

(*x*) Misuse of pesticides may lead to more frequent applications and require higher rates of the product needed to control the same pest. This phenomenon has been called the pesticide treadmill and it is the result of severe ecosystem disruption.

When several chemicals are available to ameliorate pest problems, selection of the actual chemical to be used, should be based on all the factors, affecting the benefit/risk equation. Although cost and efficacy tend to be the overriding factors, emphasis should also be placed on integrated pest management, insecticide resistance management, and environmental considerations, as these factors determine long-term efficacy and availability.

CONCLUSIONS

The development of modern synthetic pesticides has had an enormous impact on the lives of people all around the globe. Pesticides are likely to remain an integral and necessary component of pest management systems in the foreseeable future also, particularly in the annual cropping systems with multiple pests. Furthermore, the use of pesticides has made possible the profitable production of many commodities in the presence of potentially devastating pests. However, it is critical that the use of pesticides be viewed as a single component of an ecologically and biologically based system in order to conserve and prolong the utility of the declining pool of pesticides. New pesticides with more specific modes of action and reduced spectrum of activity may be more suited for large scale agricultural systems utilising a vast arsenal of chemical control options. The efficacy of existing pesticides can also be enhanced by developing more efficient formulations.

There is a need to regulate the use of pesticides in developing countries. A number of developing countries promote pesticide reduction through official policies or regulation. China introduced the Green Certificate programme and banned highly toxic pesticides from vegetable crops. Biological control is a national priority for Cuba; the new policy is intended to make integrated pest management (IPM) biointensive, with 80 per cent of pests managed through biological control. A National IPM Committee in Malaysia, is reducing pesticide use and increasing farmer knowledge of other pest management techniques. Iran constituted the High Council of Policy and Planning for Reduction of Agricultural Pesticides. India, Indonesia, Nepal, Philippines and Sri Lanka have adopted national IPM policies. The Food and Agriculture

Organization and the World Health Organization are collaborating with the international community and developing nations to develop pesticide policy, but many developing countries have only preliminary regulation of pesticide use.

Additional research efforts are required to obtain maximum benefits from the existing pesticides. Greater attention needs to be devoted to physiological effects of insecticides on the nutritional status of the host plants, and development and multiplication of surviving insects to overcome the problem of pest resurgence. Regular surveys need to be undertaken for early detection of insecticide resistance in major pests. Suitable insecticide resistance management (IRM) strategies should be developed as a component of the IPM, so that large scale epidemics are avoided by timely action and the useful life of the existing products is prolonged. Fundamental research on insect physiology and biochemistry needs to be strengthened to develop more selective pesticides for the future. With these efforts, pesticides will continue to play an important part as a component of sustainable IPM programmes.

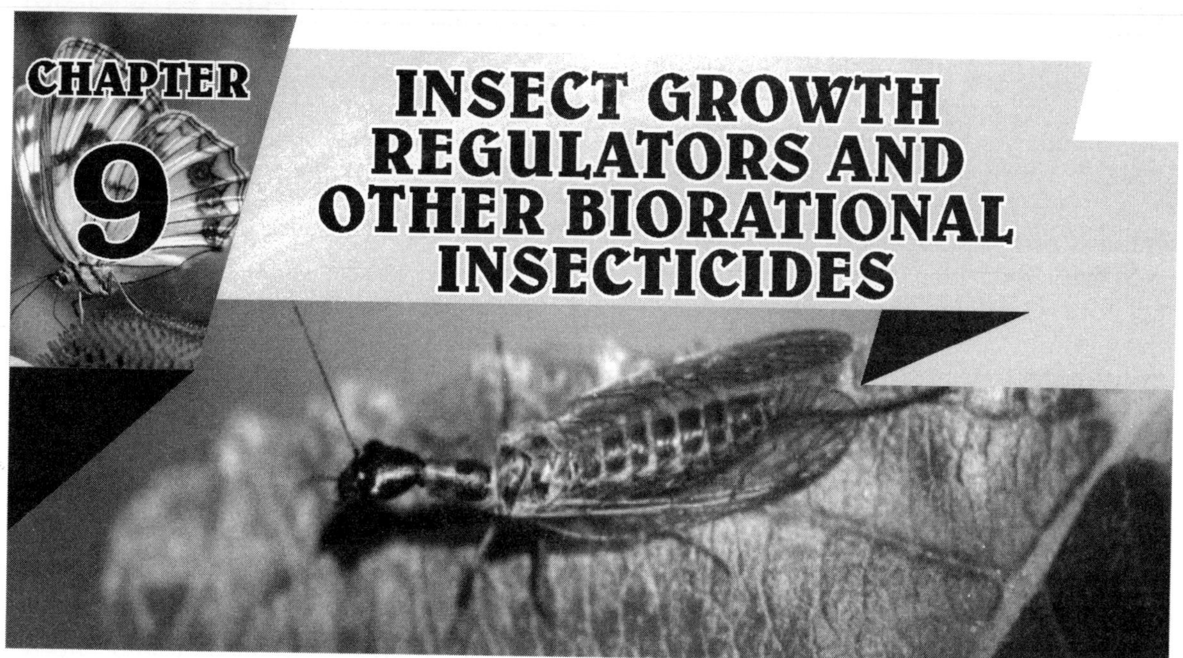

CHAPTER 9: INSECT GROWTH REGULATORS AND OTHER BIORATIONAL INSECTICIDES

INTRODUCTION

The threats arising due to indiscriminate use of conventional insecticides are really very challenging and demand serious attention of all concerned. Development of insecticide resistance and resurgence has made the management of insect pests extremely difficult apart from other environmental concerns such as residue in food and feed and influence on humans and other non-target organisms besides resulting in environmental pollution and contamination. Since decades, entomologists world over had been attempting to find eco-friendly and sustainable alternatives for management of insect pests with least disturbances to the environment. Out of various strategies tried, one is the application of Insect Growth Regulators (IGRs), which are known to be extremely safe due to their biodegradable nature, selective in action and have mode of action different from the conventional insecticides which make these compounds less prone to development of cross-resistance. IGRs comprises two sub-groups i.e. insect hormones and their analogues (neurohormones, juvenile hormone analogues, moulting hormone analogues etc.) and chitin synthesis inhibitors (CSIs).

Among all the insect hormones, the juvenile hormones and their analogues have proved to be the most successful in the management of insect pests with many commercial formulations of these available in the market. Though there are more than 50 neurosecretions (including the brain hormone or the prothoracicotropic hormone) that have been isolated from various insect species, but given to their proteinaceous nature and hence inability to penetrate through the insect cuticle, and its costly synthesis, future of the brain hormone for the control of insect pests does not look bright. The second category of insect hormones i.e. ecdysones or moulting hormones, are secreted by prothoracic glands of insects which sequester cholesterol from the circulating haemolymph and convert it into ecdysone; no moulting is possible without this hormone. Multiple number of commercial formulations of ecdysteroids are available in the market for use against several insect pests belonging to Lepidoptera, Coleoptera, Diptera and insects belonging to several other orders, but analogues of moulting hormones (MHAs) do not appear to have a bright scope in IPM programmes due to certain serious limitations. One of the very serious limitations is their steroidal nature which makes these compounds more hydrophilic than lipophilic, and hence restricts their penetration through the waxy layer of the insect cuticle making them ineffective when applied topically and must be fed orally to the target species. Moreover their complex steroidal structure also makes their synthesis costly and laborious. The amount required to affect precocious moulting is generally quite high which often deter feeding of insects on the treated material. More than all this, their regulatory role in the development of crustaceans and their close proximity to steroid hormones (found in man and other higher animals), is a matter of concern and hence we need to adopt a very cautious approach for their use in pest control programmes.

Juvenile hormones (JHs) secreted by the cells of corpora allata, and their analogues (JHAs) influence both the immature and mature insects, affecting morphogenesis in the former and gonads in the later, by playing a key role in the vitellogenin synthesis and its uptake by the growing oocytes. Any exogenous application of JHAs in the last instar larvae results in morphogenetic abnormalities by producing adultoids, larval-pupal intermediates or supernumerary instars, which rarely moult into proper adults. On the bases of such inferences, Williams, in 1967, raised the possibility of use of JHs as the 'Third Generation Pesticides' which led to the synthesis of a large number of JHAs. The natural JHs could not be of much use in IPM programmes due to their instability in UV light, rapid metabolism in insects apart from difficulties in their synthesis.. The JHAs are also compatible with the commercially available insecticides.

The second sub-category of IGRs i.e. chitin synthesis inhibitors (CSIs) are chemically benzoylphenylureas, which act by inhibiting the enzyme chitin synthetase required for polymerization of N-acetylglucosamine in the bio-synthesis of chitin during the process of moulting of insects. Scores of the CSIs are commercially available in the market and sveral of these have been registered in India for the control of various insect pests. On the whole, JHAs and CSIs have demonstrated their potential to become a viable component of IPM programmes.

Chitin Synthesis Inhibitors

Chitin synthesis inhibitors (CSIs) interfere with production of chitin, the structural polysaccharide found in insect cuticle, and thus affect the integrity of insect exoskeleton. Exposure causes improper attachment of the new cuticle during moulting and produces a cuticle that lacks some of the layers that normally occur. Most larvae die from ruptures of the new malformed cuticle, desiccation, starvation or predation. Scientists investigating the new derivatives of herbicide, diclobenil, discovered CSIs accidentally. It was found that 1-(2, 6-dichlorobenzoyl)-3-(3, 4-dichlorophenyl) urea (DU 19.111) possessed interesting insecticidal properties against several species of insects. Thereafter, a large number of structural analogues were prepared and screened against a variety of insect pests. Diflubenzuron [1-(4-chlorophenyl)-3-(2, 6-difluorobenzoyl) urea] (Fig. 9.1A) was the most successful analogue of the series and is effective against insect pests belonging to Coleoptera, Diptera and Lepidoptera. Subsequently, more potent BPUs have been developed and they are very effective in controlling insect pests of cotton, maize and vegetable crops such as *Spodoptera* and *Helicoverpa* spp. A new BPU insecticide, novaluron (Fig. 9.1D), has somewhat more contact and translaminar activity as compared with other BPUs, thereby affecting whiteflies and leafminers, in addition to lepidopteran and coleopteran larvae.

A. Diflubenzuron

B. Chlorfluazuron

C. Lufenuron

D. Novaluron

E. Buprofezin

Fig. 9.1 Structures of some important chitin synthesis inhibitors

The benzoyl phenyl urea (BPU) analogues are compounds with selective properties, affecting the larval stage. They mainly act as stomach toxicants and kill insects at the time of moulting. However, in some species they suppress fecundity and exihibit ovicidal and contact toxicity. The BPU analogues block the terminal polymerization step catalyzed by the enzyme chitin synthase during the process of biosynthesis of chitin (Fig. 9.2). However, the exact site of action is not yet clearly understood and a number of interesting hypotheses have been put forward to explain the effects produced by the application of BPU analogues. The most plausible explanation so far is that BPU analogues block the availability of substrates at the active sites of the membrane bound enzyme, chitin synthase, probably by altering membrane permeability. These compounds also inhibit a number of other enzymes and DNA biosynthesis in larval epidermal cells. BPUs generally affect the larval stages of insects, which synthesize chitin during their moulting processes. Hence, the adults of beneficial species,

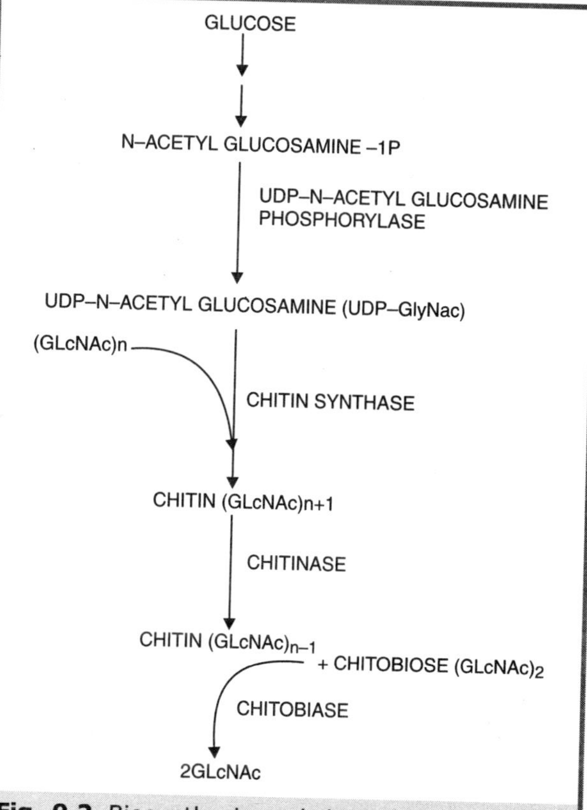

Fig. 9.2 Biosynthesis and degradation of chitin in insects (After Dhaliwal and Arora, 2006)

predators and parasitoids, are seldom affected. For this reason, BPUs are considered important components in IPM programmes.

Another compound, buprofezin, is a thiadizine like compound with long residual activity that also acts as chitin synthesis inhibitor. It has both contact and vapour activity, and acts on nymphal stages of sucking insects such as leafhoppers, planthoppers and whiteflies. Its mode of action resembles that of BPUs, although its structure is not analogous. The compound inhibits incorporation of 3H-glucose and N-acetyl-D-3H-glucosamone into chitin (Fig. 9.2). Because of chitin deficiency, the procuticle of the whitefly nymph loses its elasticity and the insect is unable to molt. As in case of BPUs, buprofezin is effective against immature stages and not adults. The compound has a mild effect on natural enemies and is an important component of IPM programmes for managing whiteflies in cotton, vegetables and ornamental plants.

In addition to BPU analogues, several other groups of compounds have also been reported to act as CSIs. Plumbagin is a naturally occurring CSI present in the roots of a tropical medicinal shrub, *Plumbago capensis* Thunb. It has been reported to possess novel mode of action like chitin and ecdysteriod inhibition thereby leading to growth inhibition in insects. Recent investigations have revealed that plumbagin possesses high ovicidal activity against eggs of *Dysdercus koenigii, Spodoptera litura, Corcyra cephalonica* and *Plutella xylostella*. Besides its activity as a CSI, plumbagin is toxic to *S. litura, P. xylostella* and *Helicoverpa armigera* larvae, and adults of *Myzus persicae*. Toxicity of plumbagin was at least 3-fold higher for winged than apterous adults in case of topical assays, and at least 1645-fold higher for pterous than that for apterous aphids in residual film assays.

Chitin Degradation Inhibitors

At each moult, chitin is degraded and new chitin is laid down. Two chitinolytic enzymes, viz. chitinase and chitobiase (Fig. 9.2) carry out degradation of chitin. The degradative process is necessary, first because the old cuticle must be weakened enough so that it can be ruptured along ecdysial lines and the insect can exit and, second, because many of the degradative products are recycled and utilized in the synthesis and deposition of the new cuticle.

Chitinases offer attractive opportunities for development of new biopesticides. Chitinases have been isolated from the tobacco horn worm, *Manduca sexta*, and several other insect species, and some of their physical, chemical and kinetic properties have been determined. A transformed entomopathogenic virus that produces the enzyme has been known to enhance insecticidal activity. Chitinase also potentiated the activity of Bt toxin against several insect pests, viz., spruce bud worm, *Choristoneura fumiferana* and gypsy moth, *Lymantria dispar*. Insect chitinase genes can be expressed in plants, thereby disrupting the feeding and growth of the insects feeding on the plant, or expressed in insect baculoviruses, enhancing the insecticidal activity and speed of kill of the viruses.

Sclerotization Inhibitors

Protein component of insect cuticle is extremely complex containing in excess of 20 proteins with different mobility on polyacrylamide gels. These proteins are stabilized by means of covalent bonds by a process called sclerotization. Sclerotization is the process of hardening the cuticle due to the tanning of proteins which follows eclosion (emergence of an immature stage from the egg) or ecdysis (shedding of the cuticle and subsequent expansion of an insect under hormonal control). The covalent linkage of adjacent polypeptide chains and the blocking of reactive groups by the tanning substances, phenols and quinones make the proteins hard, dark and insoluble. Such proteins are called the tanned proteins or sclerotins. Inhibitors of sclerotization may disrupt the metabolism and/or deposition of phenolic compounds, proteins or other components that participate in culticular stabilization mechanisms.

The only commercially available sclerotization inhibitor is MON0585 developed by Monsanto. It is a ditertiary butyl alcohol which is highly toxic to mosquitoes and other dipteran insects. It causes mortality at the time of pupation and dead pupae are white instead of tan colour because of failure of the organism to harden the pupal cuticle via arylation. Such failure to arylate is a result of loss of benzoid precursors to the rearing medium through faulty transport of precursors to the cuticle, and unavailability of receptor sites for arylating groups or side-chains destined for cross-linking. Another group of compounds with capacity to inhibit sclerotization are inhibitors of the enzyme 3, 4-dihydroxyphenyl alanine decarboxylase (DDC). DDC inhibitors like α-methyl DOPA cause mortality in dipteran larvae at the time of moulting. Accelerators of sclerotization process also exert a toxic effect on insects. Cryomazine, a substituted diaminotriazine produces necrotic lesions in the cuticle of blow fly and stiffens house fly larval cuticle by inserting an extra layer between the endo-and exocuticle, causing rod like puparia. The cuticle of *Manduca sexta* is unable to expand following treatment with cryomazine.

INSECT HORMONES AND THEIR ANALOGUES

Insect growth and development are regulated by a combination of hormones including the brain hormone (BH),juvenile hormone (JH), moulting hormone (MH), eclosion hormone (EH) and ecdysis triggering hormone (ETH). The brain hormone (secreted by neurosecretary cells in the brain of insects), moulting hormones (secreted by prothoracic glands) and juvenile hormones (secreted by corpora allata) form the endocrine axis in insects; any disruption in this axis results in physiological and morphological abnormalities in them. In fact, it is the brain hormone which induces secretion of mouting hormone by acting upon the prothoracic glands and hence also called prothoracicotropic hormone (PTTH). However, quality of the moult depends upon the quantum of secretion from the juvenile hormone from the corpora allata. Higher levels of junenile hormone helps the insect to retain juvenility i.e. larva moults in to larva; at lower levels of JH the larva would moult into pupa and adult moult will ensue in the absence of any JH (Fig. 9.3). Following the production of a new cuticle during moulting, eclosion hormone is released, followed by the release of ecdysis triggering hormone, and the

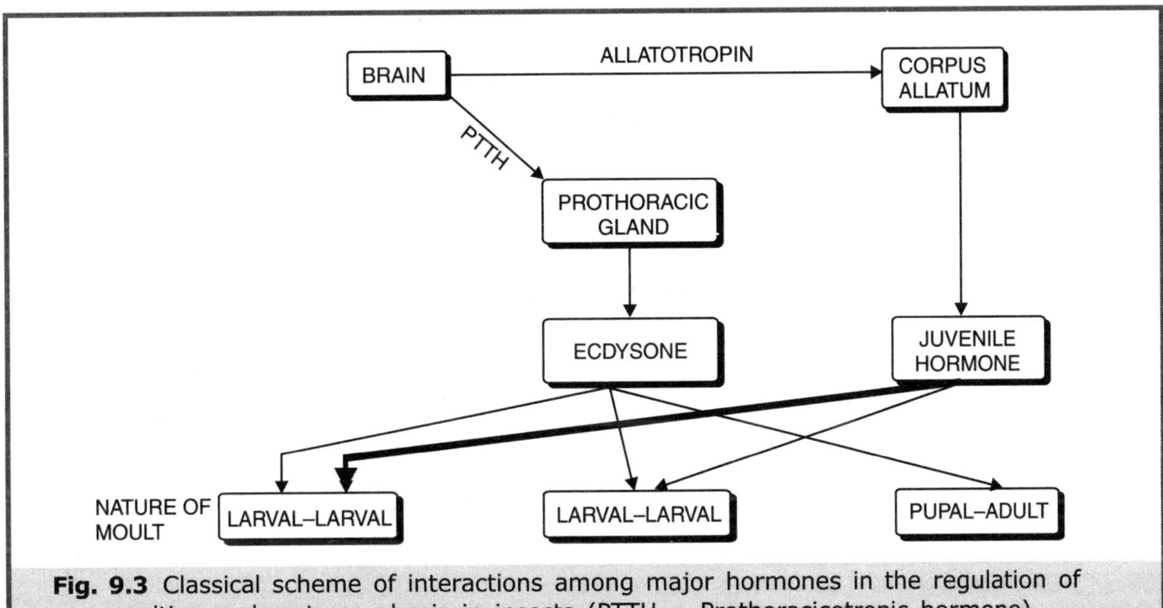

Fig. 9.3 Classical scheme of interactions among major hormones in the regulation of moulting and metamorphosis in insects (PTTH = Prothoracicotropic hormone)

insect sheds the old cuticle or exuvium. In Lepidoptera, the JH titer decreases to nondetectable levels in the last larval instar, providing a signal for release of a small prewandering MH peak and a switch from larval to pupal commitment. A larger prepupal peak of MH, which occurs in the presence of a low titer of JH, then stimulates synthesis of pupal cuticle and the insect makes transition to the pupal stage. Following pupation, MH is again produced to cause formulation of adult structure and the pupal cuticle is shed at adult eclosion. Due to the prominence of hormones in the insect life cycle, the administration of hormone agonists and antagonists provides exciting opportunities for disrupting the normal growth and development of insects.

Brain Hormones

Chemical messengers produced by the central nervous system to regulate various events in the body are known as brain hormones or neurohormones. The first insect neuropeptide proctolin was isolated from *Periplaneta americana* in 1975 and more than 50 such structures have been isolated from different insects during the three intervening decades. All the fully sequenced brain hormones happen to be oligopeptides or small protein molecules. The important brain hormones from practical point of view are diuretic and antidiuretic hormone, eclosion hormone, allatotropins and allatostatins, prothoracicotropic hormone and pheromone biosynthesis stimulating hormone. Since neuropeptides exert critical control over key developmental, reproductive, metabolic and behavioural functions, any disruption or removal of these neuropeptides can lead to mortality of the affected insects. The major problems in commercial exploitation of neuropeptides are their costly synthesis, inability to penetrate the insect cuticle and photoinstability. These problems may be overcome in a variety of ways to utilize these regulatory chemicals to the detriment of the insects:

- The synthesis of simpler peptide mimics which can penetrate the insect cuticle or gut and block or overstimulate the peptide-mediated responses in the target cells.
- Development of control agents that interfere with the secretion of neuropeptides.
- Incorporation of neuropeptide producing genes into microorganisms will make large scale production economical, and also help in overcoming stability and penetration problems.
- The neuropeptide producing genes could be directly inserted into the host plants of important insect pests.
- Development of insect neuropeptide receptor assays for rapid screening and identifying stable insecticidal compounds in culture broths or plant extracts.

Juvenile Hormones

The possibility of utilizing insect hormones as insect-specific environmentally benign pesticides was first suggested by C.M. Williams in 1967 who named these as 'third generation pesticides'. As of today, six closely related naturally occurring JHs have been isolated from insects. Of these, four (JH 0, I, II and 4-methyl JHI) appear to exist only in Lepidoptera. JH III seems to be present in all non-lepidopteran insects except higher Diptera where it is replaced by JH III-bisepoxide. Analogues of Juvenile hormones (JHAs) are sesquiterpenes and hence can easily penetrate the insect cuticle and hundreds of these compounds have been synthesised with many successful examples in insect control. Moreover, JHAs affect both mature and immature stages of the insect; while these affect morphogenesis and other physiological parameters in immature insects, embryogenesis is influenced in the mature insects

JH	R_1	R_2	R_3	R_4
JH 0	C_2H_5	C_2H_5	C_2H_5	H
JH I	C_2H_5	C_2H_5	CH_3	H
JH II	C_2H_5	CH_3	CH_3	H
JH III	CH_3	CH_3	CH_3	H
4-MeJHI	C_2H_5	C_2H_5	CH_3	CH_3
JH III bisepoxide	CH_3	CH_3	CH_3	H

(the epoxide group replaces the bond between C_6 and C_7)

Fig. 9.4 Structures of naturally occurring insect juvenile hormones

through the synthesis and intake of vitellogenin.Application of JHAs in the last instars produces adultoids, larval-pupal intermediates or supernumerary instars with varying degrees of morphogenetic abnormalities. In insects, JHs regulate a variety of functions including metamorphosis, vitellogenesis, diapause and polymorphism. The JHs are synthesized from acetyl COA via farnesyl pyrophosphate (FPP), an intermediate involved in the biosynthesis of sterols in higher animals and man (Fig. 9.5).

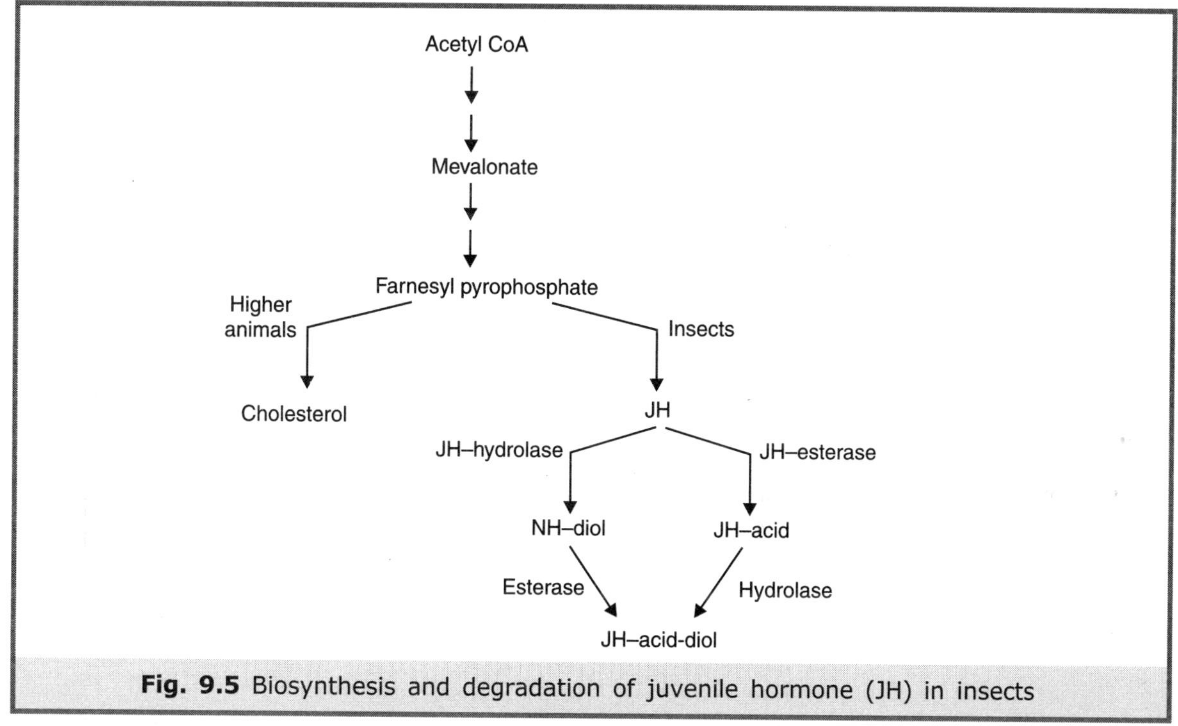

Fig. 9.5 Biosynthesis and degradation of juvenile hormone (JH) in insects

Interestingly, many plant products also exhibit JH activity. The search for JHAs among plants was stimulated by the accidental finding of a paper factor from American paper products having JH activity against *Pyrrhocoris apterus*. It was named as juvabione and was chemically identified as the methyl ester of todomatuic acid. Along with its analogue, dehydrojuvabione, it is found in the balsam fir tree, *Abies balsamea*. It was this research that led to the production of the first synthetic hormone, farnesol, for use in pest control. Despite the production of farnesol as a juvenile hormone mimic, its use in pest control has been limited. Unfortunately, farnesol does not penetrate insect cuticle well, it maintains insects in the juvenile (and possibly injurious) stage and it does not have a great deal of residual activity following application.

The natural JHs *per se* have limited scope in pest control because these are unstable in UV light and are rapidly metabolized by insects. Therefore, the juvenile hormone analogue (JHA) synthesis was directed towards the stabilization of the molecule by protection or substitution of the 2, 6 diene double bonds. Some of the earlier compounds showing promise as pest control agents were the substituted alkyl 2, 4-dienoates like methoprene (Fig. 9.6A), hydroprene (Fig. 9.6B) and kinoprene (Fig. 9.6C) which were commercialized. In newer compounds like fenoxycarb (Fig. 9.6D), pyriproxyfen (Fig. 9.6E) and diofenolan (Fig. 9.6F), linked phenoxy groups have substituted isoprene groups providing increased stability and substantially improved biological activity.

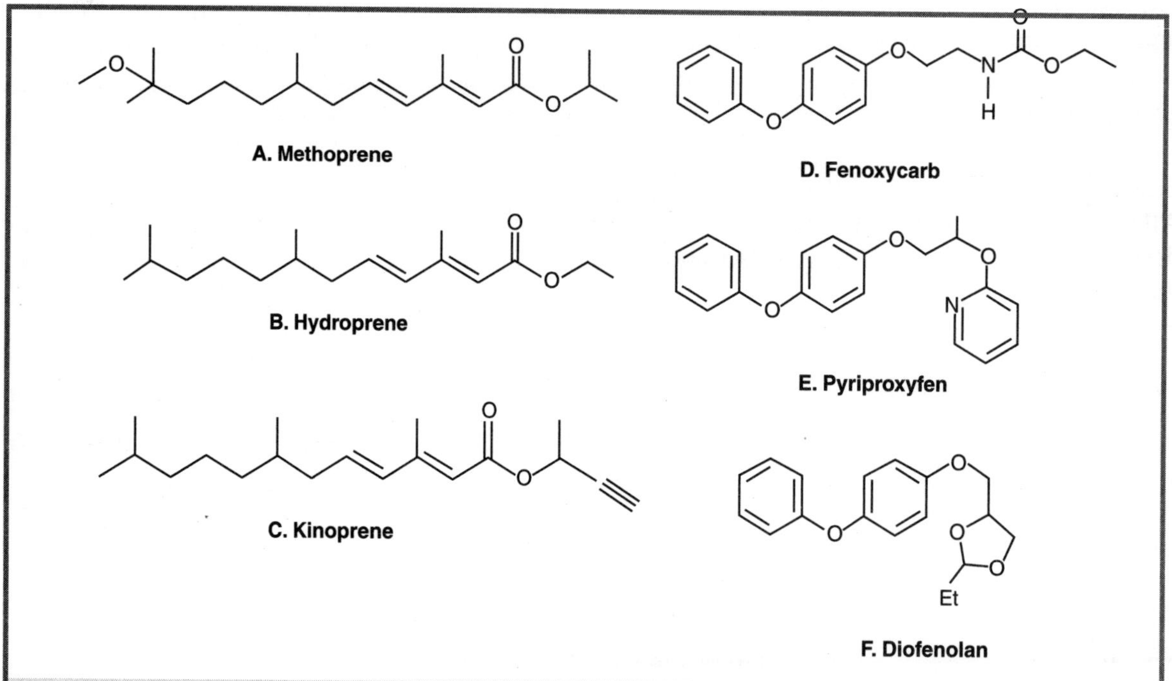

A. Methoprene

D. Fenoxycarb

B. Hydroprene

E. Pyriproxyfen

C. Kinoprene

F. Diofenolan

Fig. 9.6 Structures of some important juvenile hormone analogues

JHAs are highly effective insect growth regulators that cause a wide range of developmental derangements in susceptible species, affecting embryogenesis, larval development, metamorphosis and reproduction. The exogenous application of JH and its analogues to insects is known to result in their deranged development resulting in the formation of supernumerary nymphal/ larval instars, larval-pupal or pupal-adult intermediates and malformed adultoids. These abnormal forms are frequently unable to reproduce, feed or fly normally. In adult insects, the JH is again required for vitellogenesis in the ovaries and for the activation of accessory reproductive structures. Thus, application of JHAs to the adult females or eggs results in ovicidal and/or chemosterilizing effects. JHAs are far more potent than conventional insecticides in ovicidal activity. Hydroprene, for instance, has an LD50 of 0.0003 μg per egg in *Samia cynthia*, whereas no insecticide tested showed a value lower than 0.01 μg. Disruption of embryogenesis by application of JHAs has been reported in Lepidoptera, Orthoptera, Coleoptera and Hemiptera.

Methoprene disrupts embryogenesis and egg hatch as well as larval development in fleas and kills mosquitoes as larvae and as pupae prior to adult ecolsion. Methoprene acts to terminate adult reproductive diapause in house flies and induce reproductive development. It also acts on Lepidoptera to cause moulting to supernumerary instars and formation of intermediates. Fenoxycarb is a non-neurotoxic carbamate with a high level of JH-like activity in a wide range of insects, including Hemiptera, Lepidoptera, Hymenoptera, Coleoptera, Diptera, Dictyoptera and Isoptera. The administration of fenoxycarb has been reported to cause sterility, kill insect eggs, interfere with metamorphosis, induce permanent larvae, cause formation of nonviable intermediates and affect caste differentiation. Pyriproxyfen interferes with embryogenesis, disrupts metamorphic molt and causes morphological deformities in insects. The reproduction may be inhibited through oviposition inhibition as well as toxic effects on developing oocytes following treatment with pyriproxyfen. Recent studies have revealed that pyriproxyfen caused a significant inhibition of ecdysteroid amounts and of the thickness of the new cuticle formed in the mealworm, *Tenebrio molitor*.

The exogeneous application of JHAs is effective only when the endogenous JH titer in insects is low. This leaves the larval/nymphal stages of most insects unaffected. This limitation could be overcome by blocking the biosynthesis of natural JHs. The chemicals exhibiting this property are known as *antijuvenile hormone agents* (AJHAs) or *JH antagonists.* Interestingly, AJHAs were also initially isolated from a plant, *Ageratum houstonianum* Mill. These compounds designated as precocene I (Fig. 9.7A) and II (Fig. 9.7B) induced precocious metamorphosis in the milkweed bug, *Oncopeltus fasciatus*. Chemically, these were identified as chromene derivatives. Another related compound precocene III was isolated from *Ageratum conyzoides* L.

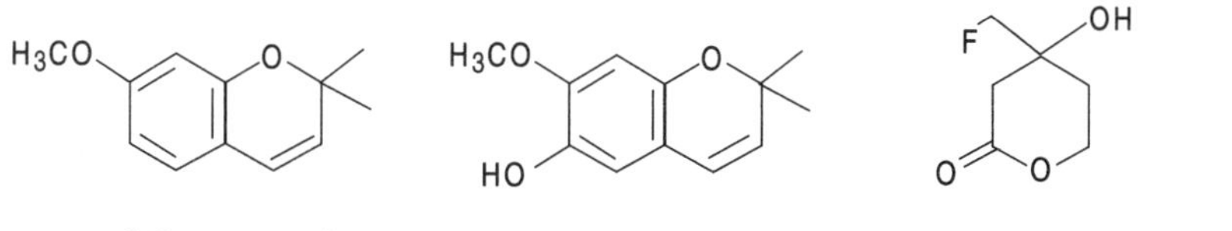

Fig. 9.7 Structures of some antijuvenile hormone agents

The precocenes are oxidized within the insect body into highly reactive metabolites which act as selective cytotoxins against corpus allatum, responsible for secretion of JH. This results in a variety of physiological and behavioural changes including precocious metamorphosis, sterilization of adult females, induction of diapause and inhibition of sex pheromone production. Precocenes represent just one of the ways in which AJHAs could be developed and their importance lies in the fact that they opened up another possible target in the insect body for attack. Vertebrate hypocholesterolemic agents like compaction and fluoromevalonate (Fig. 9.7C) also show AJH activity in insects. Additionally, a number of inhibitors of later steps in JH biosynthesis like piperonyl butoxide, imidazoles, acetylenic compounds and cyclopropyl amines also show AJH activity. Some other compounds like ethyl 4-[2-*tert*-butylcarboxyloxy) butoxy]-benzoate (ETB) and ethyl *E*-3-methyl-2-dodecanoate (EMD) act as JH-receptor antagonists.

More recently, many synthetic furanyl compounds were reported to possess AJH activity against *O. fasciatus.* These compounds appear to limit the development of corpora allata. The corpora allata of precocious adults are small and do not increase in size as occurs in normal adults. The exogenous application of AJHAs to insects not only shortens the life cycle of immature stages but also results in diminished feeding. Further, precocious males are unable to mate and inseminate normal females, while precocious females are sterile. AJHAs are thus effective against different developmental stages of insects which generally exist simultaneously in the field (Dhaliwal and Arora, 2006).

Moulting Hormones

Moulting hormones (MHs) represented by ecdysone, ecdysterone and other ecdysteriods (Fig. 9.8) are steroidal compounds secreted by prothoraic glands and are responsible for normal moulting, growth and maturation of insects. Depending upon the stage of insect, ecdysone acts as a hormone or as a precursor for the more active 20-hydroxy ecdysone, 20,26-dihydroxy ecdysone or 26-hydroxy ecdysone (Fig. 9.8). Makisterone A reported from Hemiptera, Hymenoptera and Diptera is unique among ecdysteroids in that it contains a methyl substituent at C-24 of the side chain and is not synthesized from either cholesterol or other ecdysteriods.

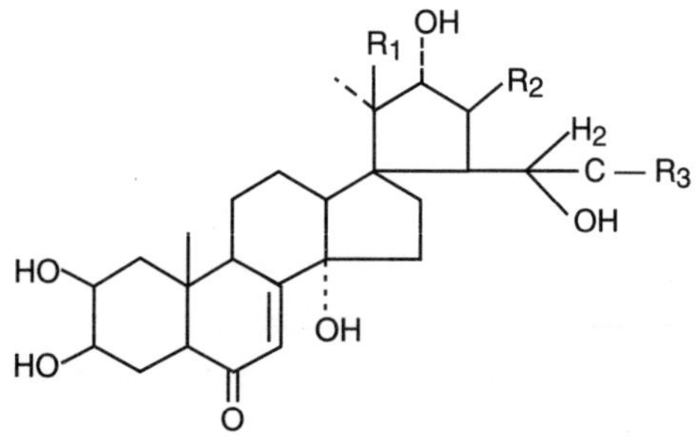

Ecdysteroid	R_1	R_2	R_3
Ecdysone	H	H	H
20-Hydroxyecdysone	OH	H	H
20, 26–Dihydroxyecdysone	OH	H	OH
Makisterone A	OH	CH_3	H
20-Deoxymakisterone A	H	CH_3	H

Fig. 9.8 Structures of insect ecdysteroids

The MHs are hydrophilic because of a number of hydroxy groups present on the molecule. So analogues of these hormones cannot penetrate the insect cuticle and hence cannot serve as effective pest control agents. However, blocking the biosynthesis of MHs can be used to disrupt the moulting process. In the insect body, moulting hormones are produced from cholesterol, which in turn is synthesized from a number of phytosterols via a common intermediate, desmosterol. Some compounds like triparanol and 22, 25-diazacholesterol block the conversion of demosterol to cholesterol by inhibiting the action of enzyme Δ24-sterol reductase. These inhibitors were found to disrupt growth and development of corn borer, *Diatraea grandiosella.* Subsequently, several azasterols were found to be potent inhibitors of sterol reductase system and inducers of abnormal growth and development in insects. Modified azasteroids, nitrogen-containing steroids and some non-steroidal secondary and tertiary amines also produce these effects. Interestingly, many of these amines and amides were also active as nematicides, miticides and antibiotics. However, none of these has got commercialized due to high cost of production, environmental instability and other problems. Nevertheless, several emerging compounds from this group hold promise of providing safe and selective pest control against a variety of organisms.

In recent years, Rohm and Haas have synthesized several nonsteroidal bisacylhydrazine ecdysone agonists (Fig. 9.9). The first ecdysteroid agonist (structure-A) was discovered in 1983 and subsequent chemical modification of this early lead produced a simple and slightly more potent analogue, RH-5849 (Fig. 9.9 B), followed by other more potent and cost-effective analogues like tebufenozide (Fig.9.9.C), halofenozide (Fig.9.9D) and methoxyfenozide (Fig.9.9E). These chemicals are much more potent than 20-hydroxyecdysone in inducing molting. They are also known to reduce feeding and weight gain. In lepidopteran insects, a lethal moult is induced following administration of the ecdysone agonist and the insect dies trapped within the exuvial cuticle. Feeding stops 4-6 hours after ingestion of toxic doses of the agonist, and molting is initiated in the absence of an ecdysteroid increase. Usually, the insect dies in the slipped head capsule stage following onset of apolysis. However, supernumerary larval molts may also occur, when the JH titer is high.

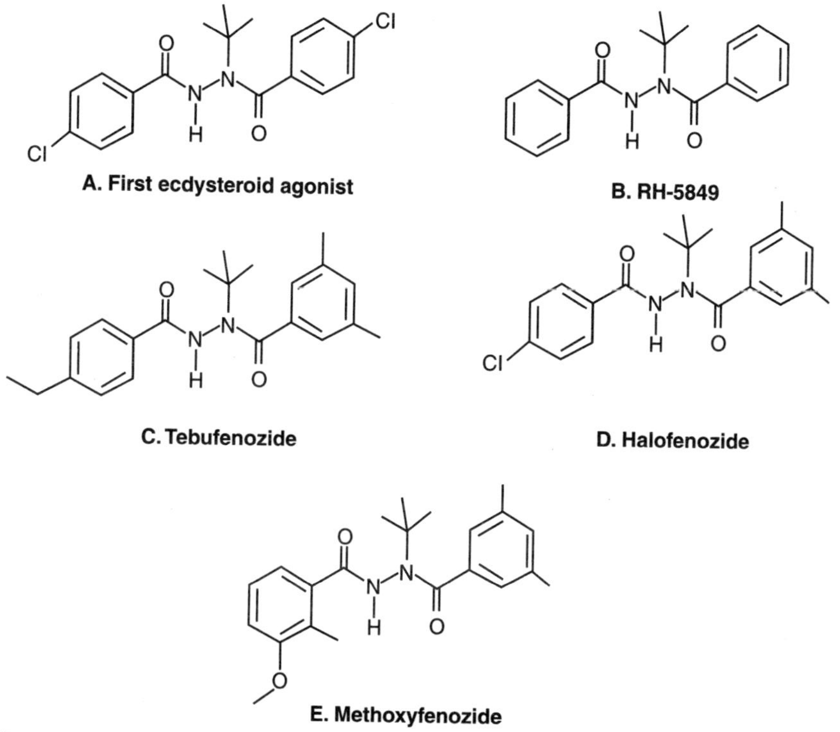

A. First ecdysteroid agonist

B. RH-5849

C. Tebufenozide

D. Halofenozide

E. Methoxyfenozide

Fig. 9.9 Structures of some bisacylhydrazine agonists

Ecysteroid agonists have been demonstrated to be active against many lepidopterans including *Manduca sexta, Pieris brassicae, Plodia interpunctella, Spodoptera exempta, S. littoralis* and *S. litura*. RH-5992 (tebufenozide) is more toxic to lepidopteran larvae than RH-5849. RH-0345 (halofenozide) has an overall insect control spectrum similar to that of RH-5849 but with accentuated soil systemic efficacy against scarabid beetle larvae, cutworms and webworms. RH-2485 (methoxyfenozide) is more potent than tebufenozide against lepidopteran pests of cotton, maize and other major agricultural crops.

Methoxyfenozide induces an immediate and fatal moult in *Spodoptera littoralis* when added to the diet of 2nd and 4th instar larvae at 1 ppm and to that of 6th instar larvae at 0.001 ppm concentration. Ten times lower doses fed to the larvae continuously allow an apparently normal larval development that is terminated by a supernumeracy larval moult. The other effects of methoxyfenozide include death during metamorphosis and impaired fertility of emerged adults. The number of progeny is reduced even with low doses, *e.g.* insects fed 0.0001 ppm since 2nd, 4th and 6th instars produce 72, 62, and 22 per cent, respectively, less progeny than the controls.

The ecdysone agonists have been tested in larvae and adults of more than 16 different insect orders, but these compounds have produced lethal effects mostly in lepidopteran, dipteran and coleopteran larvae. The high binding affinity of tebufenozide and methoxyfenozide to proteins in nuclear extracts of lepidopteran cells is correlated with their selective action on lepidopetran insects. By contrast, the ecdysteroid receptors of coleopteran insects bind tebufenozide with low affinity. This difference thereby explains the specificity of this compound for lepidopteran insects. Ecdysone agonists affect all larval stages but the effect induced depends on when the insect ingests or is treated with the compound during the time of application within a stadium. If treatment occurs early in an instar, an immediate lethal molt is induced, but if the insect is treated toward the end of an instar, first a normal moult will occur, which is then followed by the lethal moult. In adult stage insects, egg production and spermatogenesis may be adversely affected by exposure to the ecdysone agonists.

MICROORGANISM-DERIVED BIORATIONALS

Over the passt two decades, attempts have been made to produce biorational pesticides, derived from natural or biological sources. Several important classes of pesticides were produced, mostly from soil microorganisms by fermentation procedures. Among these classes are avermectins, spinosyns, polynactins and pyrrole insecticides.

Avermectins

Avermectins are a group of macrocylic lactones isolated from fermentation of the soil actinomycete microorganism, *Streptomyces avermitilis.* These compounds act as agonists for GABA-gate chloride channels. They bind with high affinity to sites in the neuronal membranes of various insect species. It was suggested that avermectins might bind to a common site in all gated chloride channels. Avermectins are among the most potent anthelmintic, insecticidal and acaricidal compounds known. These compounds exhibit a broad spectrum of activity against agricultural pests such as aphids, mites, caterpillars, and other pests that feed on crops and ornamental plants. They are also used in veterinary medicine for treatment of internal and external parasites, and mites of pests and livestock. Because of their low application dose, rapid degradation in the environment, strong binding and lack of bioccumulation in soil, the surface residues of avermectins are decomposed rapidly and thus do not pose environmental hazard to beneficial organisms.

Abamectin. Abamectin B1 (commercialized as abamectin) (Fig. 9.10A) is insecticidely most active among the eight analogues identified. It is a mixture of not less 80 per cent avermectin B1a and not more than 20 per cent avermectin B1b. It is a broad spectrum pesticide recommended for use on ornamentals, cotton, citrus, pome, nut crops, vegetables, potatoes and many other crops to control the motile stages of a wide range of arthropods, including spider mites, agromyzid leafminers, ants, cockroaches and selected lepidopteran species. It has contact and stomach action with only limited plant systemic activity, but some translaminar movement. Great differences in efficacy are reported for closely related insects. Although topical toxicity of abamectin to *Helicoverpa zea* and *Heliothis virescens* is similar, oral toxicity is 30-fold

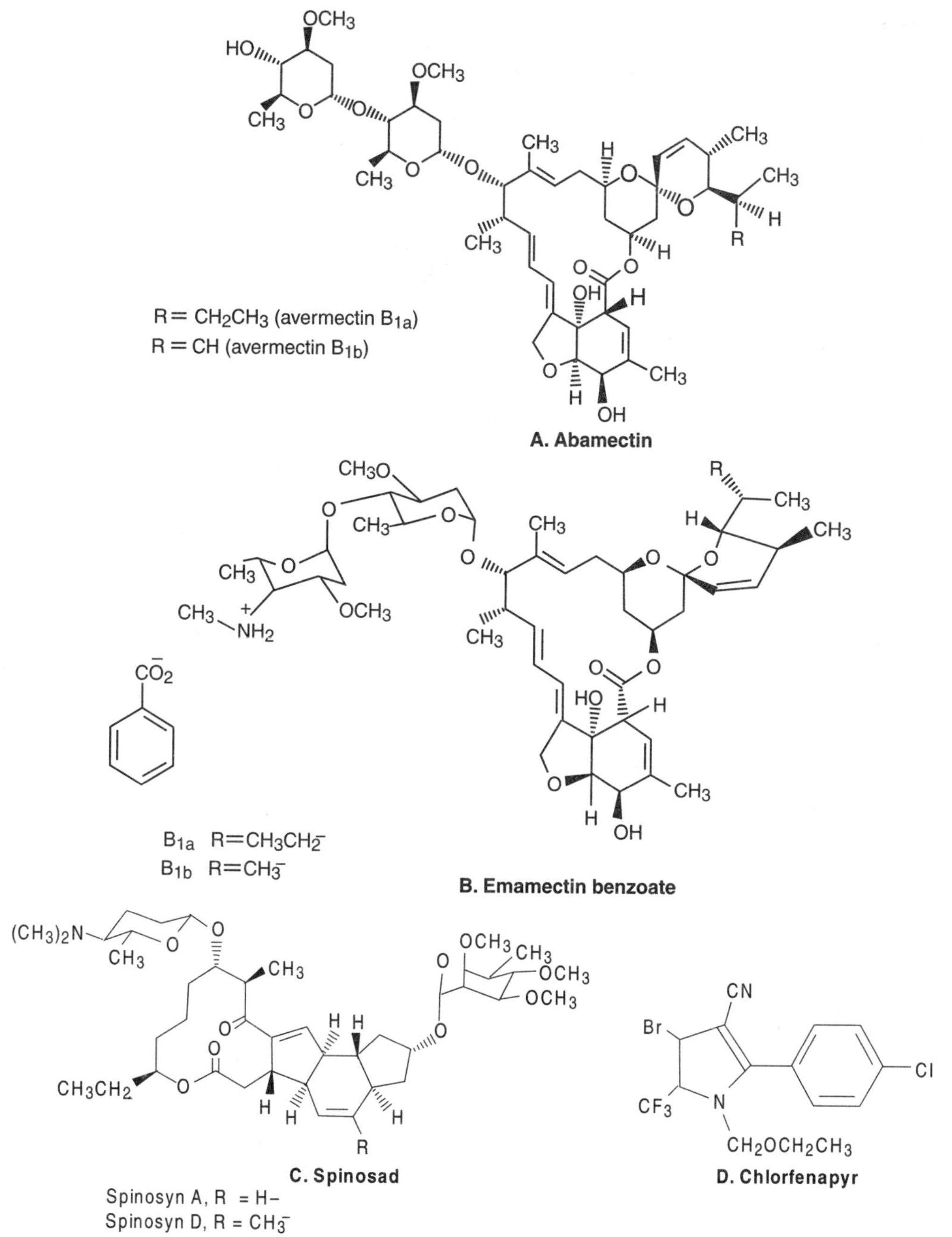

R = CH_2CH_3 (avermectin B_{1a})
R = CH (avermectin B_{1b})

A. Abamectin

B_{1a} R=CH_3CH_2–
B_{1b} R=CH_3–

B. Emamectin benzoate

C. Spinosad

Spinosyn A, R = H–
Spinosyn D, R = CH_3–

D. Chlorfenapyr

Fig. 9.10 Biorational pesticides derived from soil microorganisms

lower for *H. zea* compared to *H. virescens*. The differences in toxicity for the two species have been attributed to differences in GABA receptors, as other parameters such as penetration and metabolism are very similar. Abamectin shows some selectivity in practice because it is rapidly absorbed by plant tissue and does not persist as a contact poison. It has proved effective in controlling a leafminer, *Liriomyza trifolii* in celery without damaging the parasitoid complex which destroys up to 90 per cent of the leafminer larvae.

Abmectin is considered a selective pesticide with relatively low toxicity to many non-target arthropods. It is used at very low rates and degrades rapidly when exposed to light, especially when applied as a thin film on either insect surfaces or leaves. The half-life of a thin film of abamectin under laboratory light or sunlight is approximately 4-6 h regardless of type of surface or foliage. Despite its rapid photodecomposition following application, abamectin provides residual activity in the field due to its translaminar action; rapid penetration of abamectin into cotton leaves within a few hours after application has been observed. In addition, the use of mineral oil or surfactants in combination with abamectin, is known to extend its foliar residual toxicity, especially to phytophagous mites and whiteflies, both under greenhouse and field conditions (Horowitz and Ishaaya, 2004).

Althogh abamectin is relatively high in its mammalian toxicity, its high biological activity against insects and mites means that only very low rates are used, thereby retaining a wide margin of safety between targeted insects and non-targeted spcies and human beings.

Emamectin benzoate. Emamectin benzoate (Fig.9.10B) is a novel macrocyclic lactone insecticide derived from the avermectin family. Emamectin, obtained from abamectin via a five-step synthesis, was discovered after screening several hundred avermectin derivatives in an *in vitro* screening programme using *Heliothis virescens* and *Spodoptera eridania*. This compound was subsequently selected for further development in pest control. Later studies revealed that benzoate salt of emamectin had improved thermal stability and greater water solubility when compared with the original hydrochloride salt. As in case of abamectin, emamectin affects the nervous system of arthropods by increasing chloride ion flux at the neromuscular junction, resulting in cessation of feeding and irreversible paralysis.

Emamectin has exhibited broader spectrum of activity than abamectin. It is particularly effective against lepidopteran pests, with suppressive activity against mites, leafminers and thrips. It is recommended for use in vegetables, maize, tea, cotton, groundnut and soybean. It has been found to be effective against various lepidoptern pests such as *Plutella xylostella*, *Trichoplusia ni*, *Spodoptera exigua* and *H. virescens*. It has translaminar activity, providing a relatively prolonged residual activity. While abamectin acts specifically on mites, with low efficacy against lepidopterans, emamectin has shown considerable potency on diverse lepidopterans, controlling major pests on various crops at 8-16 g per ha. It is highly effective for controlling *Helicoverpa armigera*, *Spodoptera littoralis* and *Frankliniella occidentalis*. Recent studies conducted in India have revealed that emamectin benzoate @ 11 g per ha provided excellent control of tomato fruit borer, *Helicoverpa armigera* and increased the fruit yield. Emamectin benzoate reduced larval population by 89-92 per cent, reduced fruit damage by 89-91 per cent and increased fruit yield by 47-48 per cent. Emamectin has contact and stomach action with limited plant systemic activity, but exhibits translaminar movement. It has a lower mammalian toxicity than abamectin, but it is very active against beneficial insects such as honey bees and as such should not be sprayed during flowering.

Spinosyns

The spinosyns, a new class of insecticidal macrocyclic lactones, derived by fermentation of the soil actinomycetes, *Saccharopolyspora spinosa* are active against many pests of crops, ornamentals, forestry, greenhouse, garden and households. In addition, the spinosyns exhibit a favourable environmental and toxicological profile. Spinosyns initially cause spontaneous muscle contractions and tremors by exciting neurons in the central nervous system and they excite this system directly when applied to insect ganglia. These effects are consistent with the activation of both nicotinic acetylcholine receptors and GABA functions, which may increase their activity. However, the site of interaction on the acetylcholine receptors differs from that of neonicotinoids. The most effective insecticide of this group and the first entry into the market by DowElanco was spinosad (Fig. 9.10C). It is a mixture of spinosyn A and spinosyn D (85:15), and it has shown contact and stomach activity against Coleoptera, Diptera, Hymenoptera, Lepidoptera, Siphonaptera and Thysanoptera. It may be used on row crops (including cotton), vegetables, fruit trees, turf, vines and ornamentals.

Spinosad has translaminar activity, affecting hidden insect pests not targeted by the spray solution. It is very active against a wide range of agricultural insect pests, particularly lepidopterans such as the heliothine complex including *Heliothis virescens, Helicoverpa armigera* and *Helicoverpa zea*. It is one of the most powerful insecticides for controlling the western flower thrips, *F. occidentalis* and leafminers. Spinosad has been considered an effective and selective insect control agent for potential use in vegetables cultivated in greenhouses in Europe. This compound is also very effective for the control of lepidopteran pest complex of cabbage, viz. *Pieris rapae, P. xylostella* and *T. ni*.

The application of spinosad 2.5SC @ 25g a.i. per ha has proved very effective for the management of pod borer complex, viz. *H. armigera, Melanagromyza obtusa* and *Exelastis atomosa*, on pigeonpea. Seed treatment with spinosad @ 25 g a.i. per kg of seed provided excellent control of onion maggot, *Delia antiqua*, both during wet and dry seasons. Spinosad applied @ 0.5 or 1.0 mg per kg provided complete protection to wheat against *Rhyzopertha dominica*, during 9 months of storage, with 100 per cent adult mortality after 14 days of exposure. The contact toxicity of spinosad from 0.005 to 0.02 per cent concentrations caused 65.0 to 87.5 per cent mortality in 48h to third instar larvae of *H. armigera, Spodoptera litura* and *Earias vittella*. Field evaluation in three consecutive cotton trials revealed that spinosad @ 75, 100 and 125 g a.i per ha treated plots resulted in minimal incidence or damage by *H. armigera*. Spinosad @ 100 and 125 g a.i. per ha recorded higher *kapas* (cotton seed with lint) in comparison to treatments of chlorpyriphos, quinalphos, endosulfan and untreated check (Dhaliwal and Koul, 2007).

Unlike conventional biopesticides, spinosyns are relatively stable in water at pH-5-7 and when formulated have a shelf life of up to 3 years. Their low-to-moderate water solubility, low leaching potential and short persistence in the environment do not pose any threat to groundwater pollution. Their unique chemistry, favourable mammalian and environmental profile, insect selectivity, unique mode of action, lack of cross resistance, selectivity with respect to predaceous insects, short to moderate residual profile coupled with outstanding insect control properties against economically important pests and safety to mammals, fish, birds and beneficial insects, have made them increasingly sought after throughout the world.

Polynactins

Polynactins are secondary metabolities from the actinomycete *Streptomyces aureus* strain S-3466 and are a mixture of tetranactin, trinactin and dinactin. They are used to control spider mites, such as carmine spider mite, *Tetranychus cinnabarinus*; two-spotted mite, *T. urticae* and European red mite, *Panonychus ulmi* in orchard fruit trees. They are very effective in controlling spider mites under wet conditions. It is believed that the mode of action is through a leakage of basic cations (such as potassium ions) through the lipid layer of the mitochondrial membrane.

Water is considered essential to this toxic effect by either assisting penetration or accelerating ion leakage. The polynactins, are usually sold as combination products with other acaricides, in order to reduce the risk of development of resistance. Polyactins are not considered to be toxic to mammals and are relatively non-toxic to beneficial insects, although they do have a high toxicity to fish.

Pyrrole Insecticides

Pyrrole insecticides have been derived from a natural product, dioxapyrrolomycin, isolated from a strain of *Streptomyces.* Several pyrroles have been synthesized in Cyanamid's laboratory, using dioxapyrrolomycin as a template. However, chlorfenapyr (Fig. 9.10D) has been commercially developed because of its broad spectrum of activity against many species of Coleoptera, Lepidoptera, Thysanoptera and Acarina. Chlorfenapyr acts at the mitochondrial level by uncoupling oxidative phosphorylation. The activated compound disrupts the proton gradient across mitochondrial membranes and impairs the ability of the mitochondria to produce ATP, which leads to cell destruction and death of the affected pest arthropod. Chlorfenapyr is mainly a stomach toxicant, but has some contact activity. Field trials have demonstrated that foliar applications of chlorfenapyr were effective in controlling more than 70 insect pests and mites in cotton, cereals, vegetables, orchard trees and ornamental plants.

Milbemycin

Milbemycin (also known as milbemectin) is an insecticide and acaricide that is the fermentaion product from the soil-dwelling actinomycete, *Streptomyces hygroscopicus* subsp. *aureolacrimosus*. It is a mixture of milbemycin A3 and milbemycin A4 in the ratio of 3 : 7. It is used for the control of citrus red mite, *Panonychus citri*; pink citrus red mite, *Aculops pelekassi*; Kanzawa spider mite, *Tetranychus kanzawai* and other spider mites and also recommended for control of leafminers in citrus, tea and protected ornamentals. It has contact and stomach action with limited plant systemic activity, but it does exhibit translaminar movement. Milbemycin has a moderate oral mammalian toxicity, but is much less toxic via the dermal route. It does not persist in the environment and is considered to be relatively non-toxic to non-targeted organisms, although some beneficial insects are susceptible.

COMMERCIALIZATION

Among the insect growth regulators, juvenile hormone analogues (JHAs), and chitin synthesis inhibitors have been developed commercially. Methoprene (ALTOSID®) was the first commercially available JHA, marketed by Zoecon Corporation, California and approved by Environmental Protection Agency, USA for use against the California flood-water mosquito, *Aedes nigromaculus* (Linnaeus). It was made available in micro-encapsulated form and was effective at <1.0 ppb concentration in water, where the mosquitoes breed. Subsequently, under the trade name PHARORID®, it was also registered in UK in 1980 to control pharaoh's ants. Another formulation of methoprene (APEX®) has been used to protect mushroom cultures against sciarid flies. At present, scores of formulations of various JHAs are commercially available in the market for the management of a variety of insect pests; the important ones besides methoprene include hydroprene, kinoprene, fenoxycarb and pyriproxifen (Table 9.1). Pyriproxifen is also registered in India and is commercially available for the control of several insect pests. Hydroprene is marketed for the control of cockroaches and fire ants. Kinoprene is specific to Homoptera, but it does not compete economically with conventional insecticides and hence largely been withdrawn from use. Fenoxycarb is marketed for the control of a diversity of pest species while pyriproxyfen is marketed for the control of public health pests. Application of IGRs (JHAs and CSIs) result in various degrees of deformity in the target insects such as adultoids, larval/nymphal adult intermediaes and supernumerary instars (with additional moultings) apart from other secondary deformities in antennae, legs etc. (Fig. 9.11, 9.12)

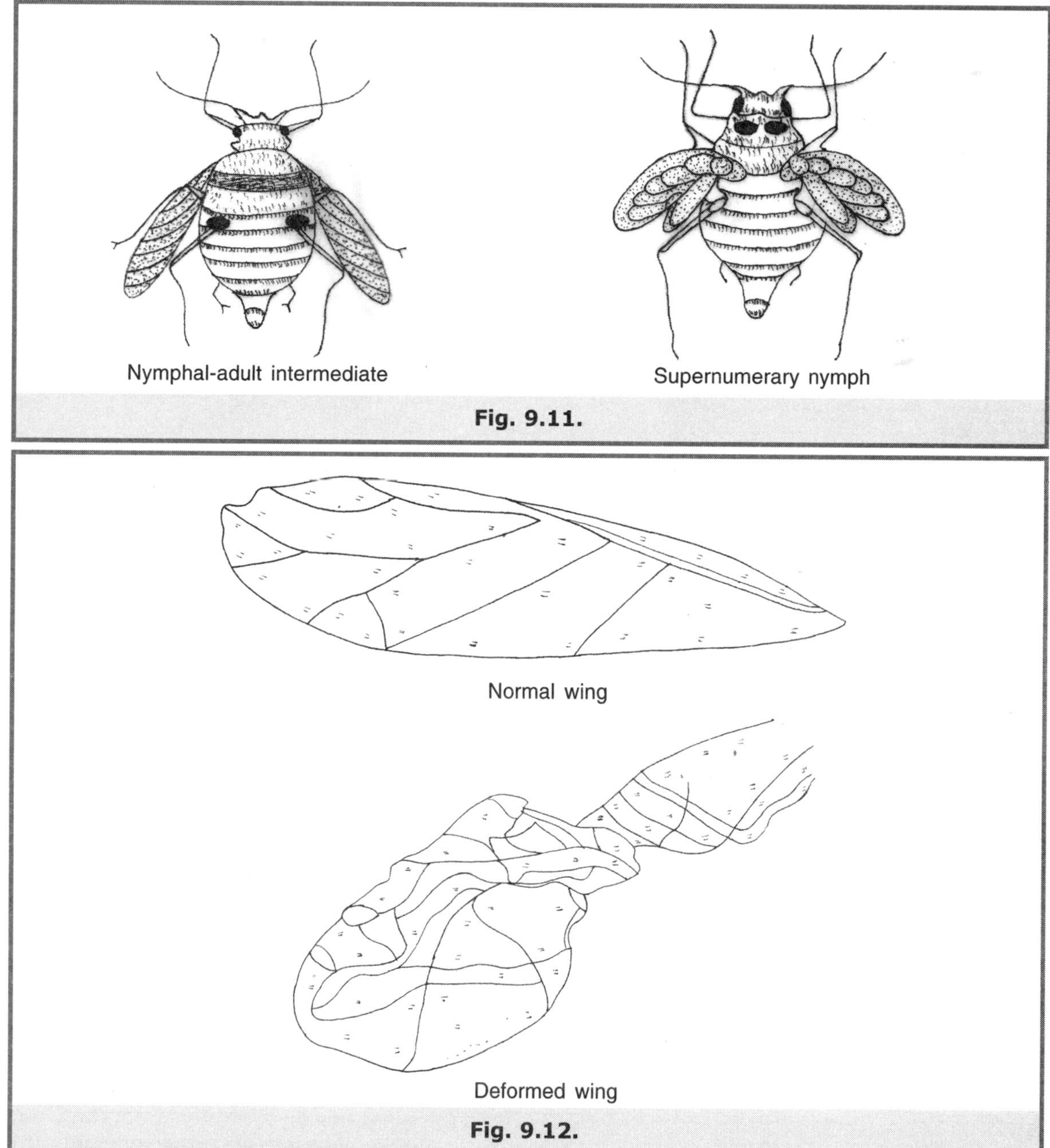

Fig. 9.11.

Fig. 9.12.

Among the chitin synthesis inhibitors, there are at least 10 different active ingredients (collectively referred to as benozphenylureas), that have been developed commercially (Table 9.1).

Table 9.1 Commercially available formulations of Insect Growth Regulators (IGRs)

Active ingredient	Trade name(s)	Target pests
Juvenile hormone analogues (JHAs)		
Methoprene	Altosid, Kabat, Apex, Pharoid, Precor, Minex, Dianex, Diacon, ZR 215, Inex, Extinguish	Mosquito larvae, horn flies, sciarid flies, pharaoh ants, flea larvae; vegetables, fruits and stored grain insect pests
Hydroprene	Gentrol, Gencor, Rockite, Mator	Cockroaches, *Tribolium* sp.
Kinoprene	Enstar II, Enstar 5E	Homopterous insect pests (aphids, whiteflies, mealy bugs)
Fenoxycarb	Insegar, Logic, Varikill, Torus, Pictyl, Precision	Mosquito larvae, fire ants, fleas, cockroaches, vine yards and orchards insect pests
Pyriproxyfen	Esteem, Admiral, Knack, Arc, Tiger, Distance, Nemesis, Lano	Mosquitoes, flies, beetles, midges, whiteflies; vegetables, fruits and cotton insect pests
Diafenolan	Aware, Context	Scale insects, vegetables, fruits and ornamental plants insect pests, eggs of Lepidoptera
Hydroprene + Permethrin	Gencor Plus	Cockroaches
Moulting hormone analogues (MHAs)		
Tebufenozide	RH 5992, Confirm, Mimic, Romdan	Rice leaf folder, codling moth, boll weevil, *Spodoptera* sp, *Helicoverpa sp.*
Halofenozide	RH 0345, Grub EX, Mach-2	White grubs, cutworms, armyworms
Methoxyfenozide	RH 2485, Runner, Interpid, Prodigy	Oriental fruit moth, codling moth, European corn borer, *Helicocerpa armigera*
Chromafenozide	Matric FL, Matric DL, Matricjoker	Larval Lepidopterans, Coleopterans and Dipterans
RH 5849	RH 5849	Larval Lepidopterans, Coleopterans and Dipterans
Chitin Synthesis inhibitors (CSIs)		
Diflubenzuron	Dimilin, Micro, Adept	Gypsy moth, boll weevil, citrus and vegetables insect pests, mosquitoes, midges
Chlorfluazuron	Atabron, Helix	Homoptera and Lepidoptera
Flufenozuron	Cascade	Phytophagous mites
Fluazuron	Acatak	Cattle ticks
Flucycloxuron	Andalin	Diptera and spider mites
Hexaflumuron	Consult,Recruit, Sentricon, Truneo	Termites, Coleoptera, Lepidoptera
Lufenuron	Match, Program	Vegetable and cotton insect pests, dog fleas
Teflubenzuron	Nomolt	Hemiptera and Lepidoptera
Triflumuron	Baycidal	Coleoptera and Dictyoptera
Novaluron	Rimon, Diamond,	Diptera and Lepidoptera
Buprofezin	Applaud, Accolade, Tribune, PI Bupro,	Cotton, vegetables and fruit insect pests, rice homopterans

ROLE IN PEST MANAGEMENT

The two main groups of insect growth regulators being used on a commercial scale are analogues of the insect hormones (juvenile hormone analogues, moulting hormone analoges) and chitin synthesis inhibitors.

Juvenile Hormone Analogues

The JHAs have been tested in large scale trials for the control of various pests of agriculture, forestry and public health importance. Five different formulations of methoprene are available commercially for the control of mosquitoes, manure breeding flies, cigarette beetle, pharaoh's ant, fungus gnat and flies. In house flies, adult emergence may be prevented by earlier treatment with methoprene. When administrated as a feed additive to cattle, methoprene controls horn flies and other veterinary pests that breed in dung. Other uses of methoprene include coleopteran and lepidopteran pests in stored tobacco, sciarid flies in mushrooms, flea larvae indoors, Homoptera on houseplants, pharaoh ants indoors and leaf-mining flies in vegetable and flower crops. Hydroprene is used indoors against cockroaches and in this case, exposure of nymphs to the material causes them to become sterile adults. Kinoprene is a strong highly selective JHA effective against aphids, whiteflies, scales and mealy bugs. In view of its environmental instability, it has been most successfully used on ornamental plants and vegetable seed crops in greenhouses and shade houses.

Different formulations of fenoxycarb have been developed for different groups of pests and used against number of coleopteran and lepidopteran pests of stored wheat and rice. It has also been found effective against several fruit pests such as grape moths, *Lobesia botrana* and *Eupoecilia ambiguella*; plum moth, *Cydia funebrana*; codling moth, *Cydia pomonella*; summerfruit tortix, *Adoxophyes orana*; pear sucker, *Cacopsylla pyricola*; fruit tree tortix, *Archips podanus*; tufted apple bud moth, *Platynota idaeusalis*; and a number of leaf rollers, pear psyllids and diaspidid scales. Foliar application of fenoxycarb on cotton provided satisfactory control of *Helicoverpa zea* and *Heliothis virescens*. It is also effective for the control of fire ants, fleas, cockroaches and mosquito larvae.

Pyriproxyfen (registered for commercial use in India) has proved effective against a number of sucking pests including whitefly, *Dialeurodes citri*; *Thrips palmi*; California red scale, *Aonidiella aurantii*; chaff scale, *Parlatoria oleae*; cottony-cushion scale, *Icerya purchasi*; sweet potato whitefly, *Bemisia tabaci*; greenhouse whitefly, *Trialeurodes vaporariorum*; green peach aphid, *Myzus persicae*; and pear psylla, *Cacopsylla pyricola*. It is also active against a number of mosquito species and as a feed-through compound in poultry, cattle and swine for the control of the house fly, *Musca domestica*; face fly, *M. autumnalis* and horn fly, *Haematobia irritans*. Pyriproxyfen also disrupts the development of horn fly following direct application to the fly.

A newer analogue, diofenolan is highly effective for the control of scale insects and lepidopteran pests attacking citrus, pome fruit, stone fruit, grape, mango, olive, nut, tea and ornamental plants. It shows excellent activity at 300 g a.i./ha against *A. aurantii, Quadraspidiotus perniciosus, Saissetia oleae, Planococcus citri, I. purchasi, Aulacapsis tubercularis, C. pomonella* and *C. molesta*. It is also effective against tea leaf roller, *Caloptilia theivora*. NC-196, a derivative of benzyl pyridazinone shows good systemic and contact activity against brown planthopper of rice. In Japan, application of NC-196 @ 300-600 g a.i./ha effectively suppressed brown planthopper populations for nearly one month.

Moulting Hormone Analogues

Both tebufenozide and methoxyfenozide are highly active in the field against a variety of vegetable, fruit and ornamental pests. Tebufenozide has been found to be highly effective against *Cydia pomonella* and miscellaneous leafrollers in apples, various leafrollers in treefruit,

Spodoptera exigua in cotton, *Choristoneura fumiferana* and *Lymantria dispar* in forestry, *Lobesia botrana* in grapes, *Cnaphalocrocis medinalis* and stem borers in rice, *Diatraea saccharalis* in sugarcane, *S. exigua, Helicoverpa* spp. and various other lepidopteran pests in vegetables and ornamentals. The use rates vary from 100 to 300 g a.i./ha, depending on the target pest and crop.

Halofenozide is highly effective against the soil-dwelling larval stages of scarabaeid beetles such as *Popillia japonica, Phyllophaga* spp., *Cyclocephala* spp. and *Hyperodes* spp. as well as various soil and sod-dwelling caterpillars such as cutworms and web worms. Halofenozide was effective against all stages of *P. japonica,* but its effects were stage dependent in case of European chafer, *Rhizotrogus majalis* and the Oriental beetle, *Anomala orientalis*. Generally, the effects were more pronounced when the applications were made in the egg or first larval stages. Methoxyfenozide has exhibited high field efficacy against lepidopteran pests of apple, cotton, grape, maize, rice, treefruit and vegetables.

Chitin Synthesis Inhibitors

Chitin synthesis inhibitors belonging to the acyl urea group are also being used commercially for the control of a number of foliage feeders and tissue borers. Satisfactory control of cabbage looper, *Trichoplusia ni*; cotton leaf perforator, *Bucculatrix thurbeviella* and Egyptian cotton leafworm, *Spodoptera littoralis* and boll weevil, *Anthonomus grandis* damaging cotton crop has been obtained with diflubenzuron. Foliar application of diflubenzuron has shown excellent residual activity against eggs of *H. armigera* and *S. litura.* In addition to its well known stomach toxicity, it has significant contact activity aginst some insect species including *H. armigera* and *S. littoralis.* Diflubenzuron is promising against a variety of other pests on several crops including soybean, citrus, vegetables and forests, and against nuisance and medical pests like flies, gnats, midges and mosquitoes.

Some new CSIs like XRD-473, IKI-7899 and IGR 1055 have shown excellent larvicidal activity against *H. armigera.* Teflubenzuron possesses high ovicidal action against the tortricid, *C. pomonella* on apple. Buprofezin has been found promising against homopteran pests of rice, cotton, citrus, potato and vegetables. Hexaflumuron is used primarily for termite control around houses and other buildings. Termites feed on hexaflumuron bait and die within 6-8 weeks during moulting. It is also effective against certain Lepidoptera, Coleptera, Homoptera and Diptera on cotton, potatoes and fruit trees. Lufenuron is prescribed by veterinarians for flea control on dogs. When a female flea bites a treated dog, lufenuron enters the flea's system, and prevents some eggs from hatching and prevents any enclosed larvae from becoming adults.

In India, several CSIs have been evaluated for their efficacy against *Helicoverpa armigera* infesting chickpea under field conditions. Lufenuron (0.006%) was found to be the most effective which recorded the least pod damage (11.9%) with highest efficacy (97.4%) and grain yield (2064.3 kg/ha). This was followed by flufenoxuron (0.008%), novaluron (0.01%), diflubenzuron (0.05%) and standard insectivide endosulfan (0.07%) with average efficiency of 94.8, 92,8, 89.9 and 65.9 per cent, respectively.

IMPACT ON NON-TARGET ORGANISMS

In general, insect growth regulators have no or very little adverse effect on non-target organisms. However, some of the compounds have exhibited little or moderate toxicity to certain natural enemies.

Among other mechanisms, selectivity of IGRs can result from penetration through the insect cuticle. This can explain the inhibition of egg hatch in the predator *Chrysoperla carnea,* after exposure to diflubenzuron and nontoxic effect observed in the ecdysone agonist, tebufenozide. In comparative assays, tebufenozide was harmless to *Orius insidious* and *Geocoris punctipes*, the predators of cotton pests, but it was found moderately toxic to predators of the diamondback moth, *Plutella xylostella*. In laboratory and field trials, tebufenozide was found nontoxic to the coccinellid predator, *Stethorus punctum*, but other IGRs, including fenoxycarb and teflubenzuron, were harmful to some stages of this predator. Fenoxycarb was also found to be toxic as an ovicide to the predator,

C. carnea. Tebufenozide and fenoxycarb are also safe for pollinators such as the honey bee, *Apis mellifera*. In greenhouse poinsettias, the use of IGRs (especially buprofezin) has reduced parasitoid release rates for controlling whiteflies. The introduction of two IGRs, pyriproxyfen and buprofezin, in Israel and Arizona (USA) has led to the replacement of broad spectrum insecticides, organophosphates and pyrethroids. This change had favourable impact on populations of natural enemies and allowed cotton growers to manage whiteflies with fewer disruptions to the environment and nontarget organisms.

Some other biorational compounds such as avermectins, spinosads and pyrrole insecticides have shown varying degrees of toxicity to natural enemies. Abamectin showed high mortality of various species of predators and parasitoids up to 6 days after application, thereafter the residual toxicity declined rapidly. In laboratory assays, spinosad was found toxic to two predators of spider mites; the thrips, *Scolothrips takahashii* and the lady beetle, *Stethorus japonicus*. In experiments conducted in Mexico, spinosad in a granular maize-flour formulation was toxic to the predaceous beetle, *Aleochara bilineata*, but larvae of *C. carnea* were not harmed.

In laboratory assays, spinosad did not harm two important predators of cotton pests, *O. insidiosus* and *G. puncticeps* and similar results were reported in cotton fields. In cotton field trials, spinosad exhibited marginal to good selectivity to various natural enemies, but was quite toxic to some parasitoids such as *Trichogramma* spp. and *Bracon* spp. Spinosad (0.005–0.02%) was safe to natural enemies, *T.chilonis, Cheilomenes sexmaculata, Chrysoperla carnea* and *Argiope catenulata*, under both contact and feeding toxicity tests.

Chlorfenapyr was found moderately toxic to predatory arthropods in cotton. The fresh residue of this compound caused very high mortality of *Diadegma semiclausum*, a parasitoid of *P. xylostella*, however, this toxicity did not persist long. Under laboratory conditions, chlorfenapyr was harmful to several beneficials, but the level of selectivity increased under semi-field conditions. However, under field conditions, chlorfenapyr was safe to most of the beneficials, such as bumble bees and various predatory mites.

RESISTANCE TO BIORATIONALS

Insects were believed to be less prone to the development of resistance to IGRs because of their novel mode of action and high level of safety to predators and parasitoids. However, several instances of resistance have been documented. Pyriproxyfen resistance has been generated in house flies selected for 17 generations for resistance. Resistance to pyriproxyfen has been observed in the whitefly, *Bemisia tabaci*, on cotton and rose.

A loss in efficacy of tebufenozide was observed in a laboratory strain of codling moth, *Cydia pomonella*, originally collected in southeast France and amplified for resistance to chitin synthesis inhibitor, difubenzuron. However, no such loss in tebufenozide susceptibility was observed in a different strain of the codling moth resistant to benzophenylurea. Similarly, no loss in tebufenozide susceptibility was observed in a pyrethroid resistant strain of cotton leafworm, *Spodoptera littoralis*, and organophosphate resistant strain of the tufted apple bud moth, *Platynota idaeusalis*.

There are also reports of development of resistance to spinosad. For example, studies with beet armyworm, *Spodoptera exigua*, populations have confirmed the vulnerability of spinosad to resistance. However, there was no reduction in the susceptibility of tobacco budworm, *Heliothis virescens* and bollworm, *Helicoverpa zea* to spinosad after 3 years of use in Mississippi, USA. Spinosad was incorporated in the Australian IPM-IRM strategy against *H. armigera* in the late 1990s, but resistance levels to this insecticide increased 30-fold after 5 years of use.

CONCLUSIONS

The use of insect growth regulators in place of broad spectrum conventional pesticides offers several advantages in IPM programmes. Most of these chemicals are more or less non-toxic to man and domestic animals. Methoprene, for example, has an acute oral LD_{50}(rat) of > 34600 mg/kg. These compounds do not persist or accumulate in the environment and are degraded to simple molecules that are unlikely to cause problems of environmental contamination. Many of these chemicals are species specific and have no adverse effect on parasitoids and predators. Among the IGRs, studies conducted so far indicate that these are also comparatively safe to natural enemies. Most of these compounds are active at very low concentrations and, therefore, prove economical in the long run. Since they affect more than one aspect of an insect's development and physiology, they could be effective against such insects, which are resistant to insecticides. These chemicals are most suitable for pest species with several successive short life cycles per season, for sedentary and non-migratory insects living in confined environments.

IGRs also suffer from several disadvantages, which limit their large scale utilization. Each of these compounds is effective against a single pest or a closely related group of pests. Therefore, the market potential of these chemicals is very limited. Development and registration of each new chemical requires huge investment in terms of resources and time. Therefore, investment in these chemicals is not profitable from a purely economic point of view. They have narrow physiological windows, *i.e.* they cannot be applied at all times, but need specific stages and periods. These chemicals disrupt the development of insects and do not provide immediate control of pests. The treated larvae/grubs continue to cause damage for a number of days. It is generally believed that prolongation of larval duration of lepidopteran insects increases crop damage. However, total amount of food consumed by the treated larvae is less than that of control larvae inspite of a prolongation of the larval duration in the former. Many of these compounds are photodegradable and, therefore, they rapidly loose their efficacy following their application to the crop. This problem has been solved in a number of cases by developing suitable protected, controlled release formulations which retain their effectiveness for a considerable length of time. As with other techniques, insects are capable of developing resistance to these chemicals. In many cases, insects already possess the ability to metabolize these compounds in the course of their normal development. Any selection pressure would, therefore, result in rapid development of resistance to such compounds.

At present IGRs play a limited role in overall pest management. However, it is highly likely that as our knowledge of insect growth and development expands, more opportunities for developing growth regulators for use in pest control will occur. On a long-term basis, the process of regulation of insect development needs to be understood in a sequential manner. There is a need for fundamental research on controlled release systems, which are cheap, non-toxic and biodegradable. Suitable application technology also needs to be developed for these formulations. Last decade has witnessed significant advances in most of these areas. On the whole, the IGRs are safe, selective, biodegradable and hence eco-fruendly pest control agents, but given to their limitations they can not completely replace the concentional inseticides. However, these compunds are very valuable tool in several IPM programmes where their judicious use along with the insecticides and other pest control techniques can help management of various noxious insect pests.

☆☆☆☆☆

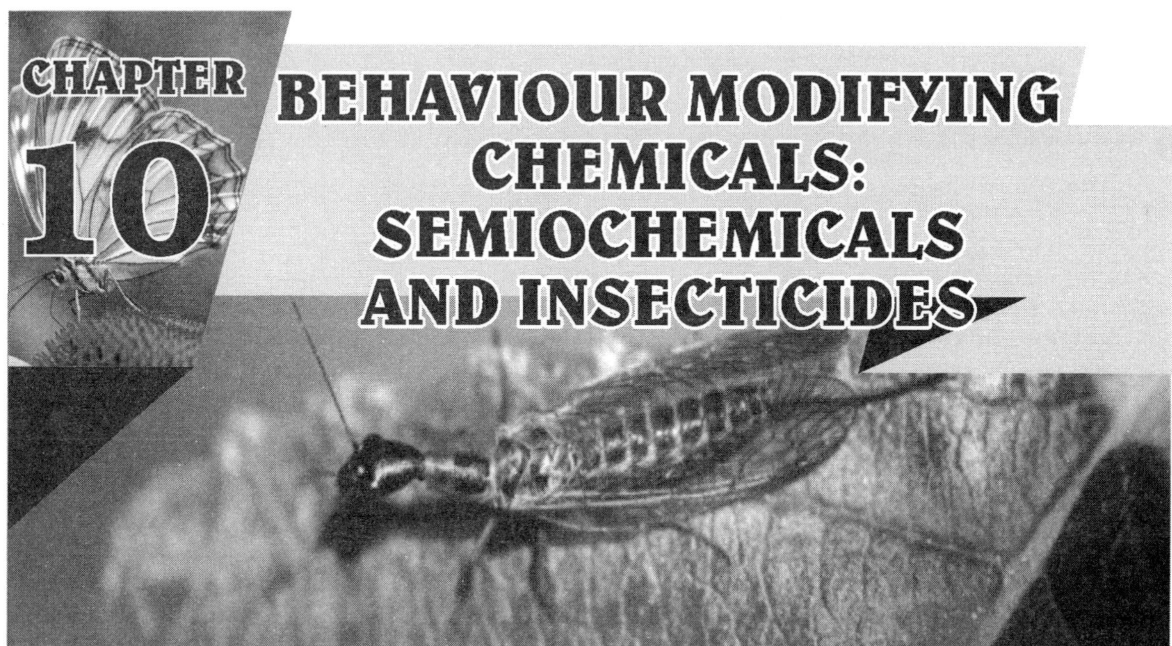

BEHAVIOUR MODIFYING CHEMICALS: SEMIOCHEMICALS AND INSECTICIDES

INTRODUCTION

Animal behaviour is elicited in response to visual, auditory, tactile, olfactory and gustatory-sensory information from the surrounding world. However, chemical communications appear to be the primary mode of information transfer in most groups of animals. A finely tuned olfactory system enables perception of even very weak signals from potential mates, and discrimination between acceptance and non-acceptance of host for feeding, mating and oviposition. Chemical messages that trigger various behavioral responses in the organisms are called semiochemicals. Semiochemicals can be used to mediate the behaviour of the target organism in a wide range of ways. Their potential for use in pest management was recognized quite early and several types of these chemicals and plant volatiles have been used for trapping insects for decades. Their successful use requires a good understanding of the behaviour of the target insect, including the underlying mechanisms that influence the behaviour. The increasing success rate of applications based on semiochemicals has occurred due to the development and application of new techniques of identification, chemical synthesis, new release techniques, and especially more detailed knowledge about the insect's behaviour and the parameters for their successful application.

Semiochemicals are divided into intraspecific and interspecific communication chemicals (Fig. 10.1, Table 10.1). The chemicals used for intraspecific communication are called pheromones. The term *pheromone* is derived from the Greek *pherein*, meaning to transfer and *hormone*, meaning to excite. Thus, a pheromone may be defined as a chemical or a mixture of chemicals that is released to the exterior by an organism and that causes one or more specific reactions in a receiving organism of the same species.

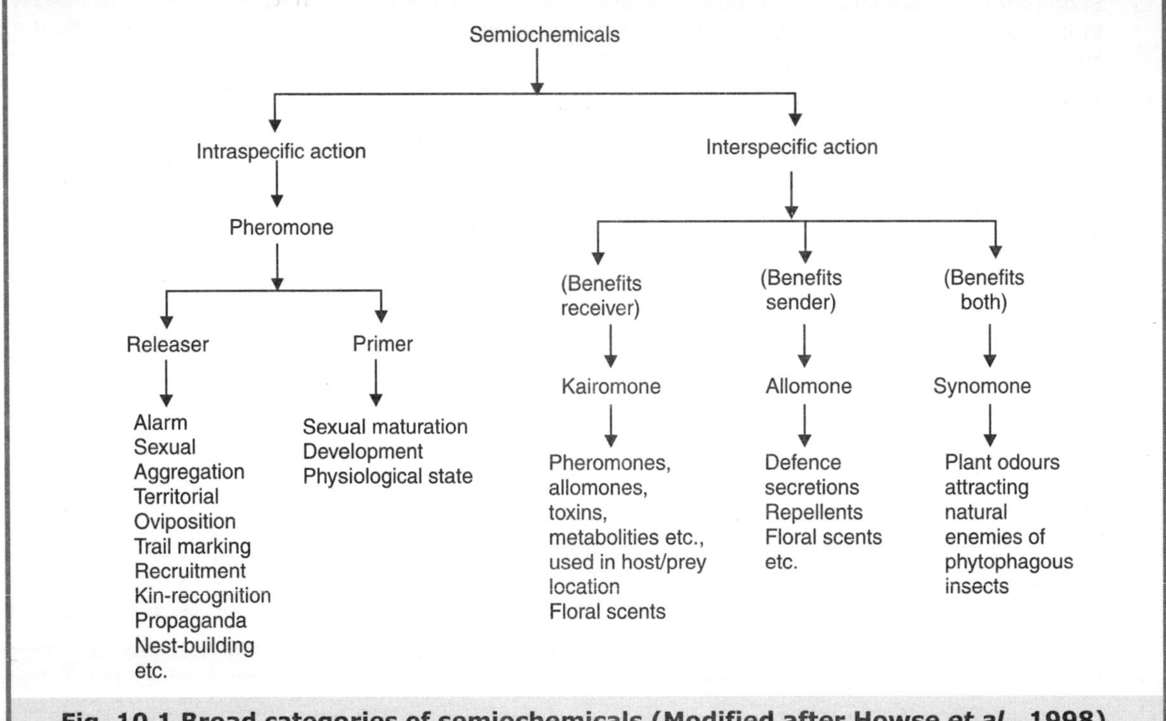

Fig. 10.1 Broad categories of semiochemicals (Modified after Howse *et al.,* 1998)

Table 10.1 Different types of semiochemicals involved in insect communication

Pheromone

A substance that is secreted by an organism to the outside and causes a specific reaction in a receiving organism of the same species.

- *Sex pheromone* - a substance generally produced by the female to attract males for the purpose of mating.
- *Aggregation pheromone* - a substance produced by one or both sexes, and bringing both sexes together for feeding and reproduction.
- *Alarm pheromone* - a substance produced by an insect to repel and disperse other insects in the area. It is usually released by an individual when it is attacked.
- *Parapheromone* - a substance of anthropogenic origin, not known to exist in nature but structurally related to some natural pheromone components that in some way affects the insect communication system.
- *Propheromone* - refers to photolabile adduct able to protect pheromone molecules under field conditions.

Allelochemical

A substance that is significant to organisms of a species different from its source, for reasons other than food.

- *Allomone* - a substance produced or acquired by an organism that, when it contacts an individual of another species, evokes in the receiver a behavioural or physiological reaction that is adaptively favourable to the emitter but not the receiver.
- *Kairomone* - a substance produced or acquired by an organism that, when it contacts an individual of another species, evokes in the receiver a behavioral or physiological reaction that is adaptively favourable to the receiver but not the emitter.

- *Synomone* - a substance produced or acquired by an organism that, when it contacts an individual of another species, evokes in the receiver a behavioural or physiological reaction that is adaptively favourable to both emitter and receiver.
- *Apneumone* - a substance emitted by a non-living material which evokes a behavioural or physiological reaction that is adaptively favourable to a receiving organism but detrimental to an organism of another species that may be found in or on the non-living material.

The possibility of disrupting the chemical communication of insect pests has initiated the development of new semiochemicals, *parapheromones,* which are compounds not found in insects, but structurally related to natural pheromone components and cause phenomone-like action. Such compounds have shown a large variety of effects, and accordingly have been called agonists, pheromone mimics, synergists and hyperagonists, or else pheromone antagonists, antipheromones and inhibitors. Thus parapheromones are the chemical compounds of anthropogenic origin, not known to exist in nature but structurally related to some natural pheromone components that in some way affect physiologically or behaviourally the insect pheromone communication system. A good example of parapheromone is the synthetic compound trimedlure, which is the best known attractant of the male Mediterranean fruit fly, *Ceratitis capitata.* This was found by routine screening of compounds and is a chlorine containing compound not known in nature. The other examples of parapheromones are methyl eugenol and cue-lure for *Bactrocera dorsalis* and *B. cucurbitae,* respectively (Fig. 10.2).

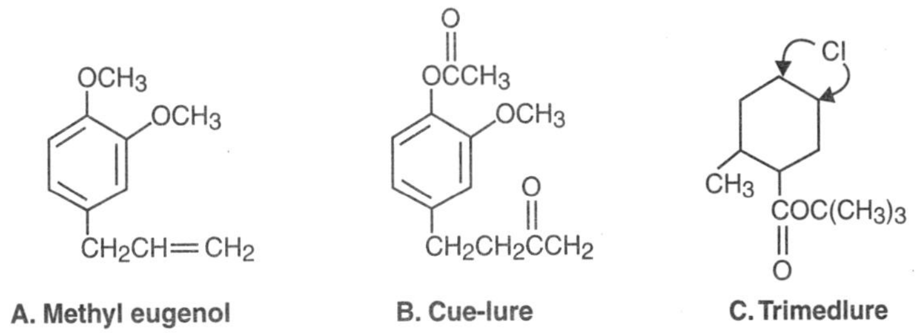

A. Methyl eugenol **B. Cue-lure** **C. Trimedlure**

Fig. 10.2 Parapheromones for tephritid fruit files

Chemicals involved in interspecific communication have been given the name of allelochemicals or allelochemics. Allelochemicals may be defined as non-nutrient substances originating from an organism (plant or animal) which affect the behaviour, physiological condition or ecological welfare of organisms of another species. Allelochemicals affect the survival, growth and development of herbivorous insects as well as their natural enemies. Based on the specific advantage they confer to the emitting or receiving organism, allelochemicals are classified into different categories (Fig. 10.1, Table 10.1).

PHEROMONES

A dazzling variety of behaviour, from sexual attraction and dispersal to caste determination, is controlled by pheromones. It is thus natural that pheromones have attracted the attention of applied entomologists for exploitation in the control of insect pests. Pheromones may be divided into two categories, viz. *releasers,* which induce an immediate behavioural change, and *primers,* which initiate changes in development, such as sexual maturation, and so do not result in immediate behavioural changes, but predispose to them (Fig. 10.1).

Types of Pheromones

Pheromones are categorized according to the function they perform, viz. sex pheromones, aggregation pheromones, alarm pheromons, trail pheromones and host-marking pheromones.

(*i*) Sex pheromones. Sex pheromones are often produced by the females to attract males for mating, but they may also be produced by males to attract females. They seem to be highly developed in Lepidoptera and are frequently produced by eversible glands at the tip of the abdomen. The release of sex pheromones is a complex physiological process, often associated with sexual maturity and environmental stimuli such as photoperiod and light intensity. Female sex pheromones are usually received by sensory sensillae on male antennae, and males search up wind, following the odour corridor of the female.

The sex pheromone of an insect usually consists of a blend of different components, which are volatile, specific to one species or a small number of related species, and is very potent over considerable distances. This specificity allows targeted application against a specific pest and with minimal influence on the ecosystem. Lepidopteran sex pheromones are usually simple molecules (e.g. long-chained aliphatic, lipophilic, acetates, aldehydes, or alcohols), often with one or two double bonds. Sex pheromones of Diptera, Coleoptera and other groups have usually more complex chemical structures, which are comparatively unstable and, therefore, much more diffcult to synthesize and formulate (Table 10.2).

Table 10.2 Some of the important female sex pheromones

S. No.	Insect	Sex pheromone	Chemical compound	Chemical structure
1.	*Bombyx mori*	Bombykol	10, 12-hexadecadienol	$CH_3(CH_2)_2(CH{=}CH)_2(CH_2)_8CH_2OH$
2.	*Lymantria dispar*	Gyplure	10-acetoxy-cis-7-hexa-decnol	$CH_3(CH_2)_5CHCH_2CH{=}CH(CH_2)_5CH_2OH$
3.	*Pectinophora gossypiella*	Gossyplure	10-propyl-trans-5, 9-tridecadienyl acetate	$[CH_3(CH_2)_2]_2O{=}CH(CH_2)_2CH$ $=CH(CH_2)_3CH_2OCH_3$
4.	*Trichoplusia ni*	Looplure	cis-7-dodecenyl acetate	$CH_3(CH_2)_3CH{=}CH(CH_2)_6OC(O)CH_3$
5.	*Apis mellifera*	Queen	9-OXO-2-decenoic acid	$CH_3(CH_2)_5CH{=}CHCOOH$

(*ii*) Aggregation pheromones. These pheromones cause insects to aggregate or congregate at food sites, reproductive habitats, hibernation sites, etc. and are prominent in some species of beetles. They are particularly well understood in bark beetles, *Ips* spp. and *Dendroctonus* spp., which are involved in tree attacks. They are attractive to both sexes and tend to operate over a long range and have the potential of attracting thousands of individuals. Generally, aggregation pheromones have more complex chemical structures, not very stable or amenable to synthesis and deployment, and elicit a much more complex behaviour that is less open to manipulation.

(*iii*) Alarm pheromones. Alarm pheromones are common in social insects such as ants and bees, and aphids, which are usually found to occur in aggregation. The function of this type of pheromone is to raise alert in conspecifics, to raise a defense response, and/or to initiate avoidance. For instance, the remains of the sting apparatus of a honey bee left in the victim's body releases an alarm pheromone that attracts other bees and stimulates them to sting. A dose response of attractancy and repellency has been demonstrated for several pure volatiles from the venom of common wasp, *Vespa vulgaris* and the German wasp, *V. germanica*. The alarm pheromones are usually highly volatile (low molecular weight) compounds such as hexanal, 1-hexanol, sesquiterpenes [e.g. (E)-β-farnesene for aphids], spiroacetals or ketones.

The applications of (E)-β-farnesene alongwith host plant volatiles caused the aphids to move away from feeding sites and may be utilized to prevent colonization of the host plants by the aphids. It also increased the mobility of aphids, which is useful for increasing the pick up of contact insecticides or microbial pathogens. (E)-β-farnesene is now commercially available for use against a number of aphid species including *Aphis gossypii* and *Lipaphis erysimi*. Farnesol and nerolidol are the alarm pheromones from the two-spotted mite, *Tetranychus urticae*, and are released under natural conditions when the population is threatened or is being attacked by a mite predator. The result is an increase in activity of mites with consequent greater exposure to a co-applied miticide.

***(iv)* Trail pheromones.** Trail pheromones are produced by foraging ants, termites and larvae of some lepidopteran insects. They are essentially used to indicate sources of requisites to other members of the colony. While trail pheromones are frequently associated with walking insects such as ants, they are also known from other insects. Bees use trail pheromones during foraging for making attractive foraging sites as well as for scent marking of unproductive food sources. Trail pheromones are characteristically less volatile than alarm pheromones. The trails are continuously replenished through traffic, otherwise they dissipate. Identification and synthesis of trail pheromone of bumble bees could lead to increased efficiency in their use for pollination. It is also possible to manipulate trail following and recruitment of tent caterpillars, *Malacosoma americanum*.

***(v)* Host-marking pheromones.** Host marking, spacing or epidietic pheromones elicit dispersal away from potentially crowded food sources, thereby reducing numbers. These pheromones reduce intraspecific competition by disrupting landing, feeding or oviposition of pests on their host plants. They are thus one of the few pheromones that serve to repel rather than attract the insects. They are known from a number of insect orders, viz. Coleoptera, Lepidoptera, Diptera, Homoptera, Orthoptera and Hymenoptera. The females of apple maggot, *Rhagoletis pomonella* and cherry fruit fly, *R. cerasi*, ovipositing in fruit, mark the surface to deter other females. Mating deterrent pheromones are known from a number of insects including tsetse flies, house flies and other Diptera. There is also exploitation of prey host marking and sex pheromones by parasitoids, which use signal persistence of these intrasepcific cues to find their hosts. The host-marking pheromones of the bark beetles, *Dendroctonus* spp., such as verbenone for *D. frontalis* and 3,2-methylcyclohexane (MCH) for *D. pseudotsugae*, are well known. The beetles that have successfully colonized a host release these pheromones. These compounds, in combination with aggregation pheromones, tend to keep beetle densities within an optimal range (6-8 per 1000 cm2 of bark surface).

Strategies for Exploitation of Pheromones

The first attempt to utilize pheromones for insect control was made in 1940s when crude extracts of abdominal tips of female gypsy moths were used in monitoring traps in USA. However, it was not until two decades later that the possibility of using pheromones in crop protection was accepted, and the first meaningful field trial on mating disruption of a lepidopteran pest was reported. There was a rapid growth in the identification of insect pheromones during 1970s and by the end of 1980s pheromones and pheromone mimics were known for about 1000 species of insects. To-day, more than 1500 moth sex pheromones and hundreds of other pheromones have been identified, including sex and aggregation pheromones from beetles and other groups of insects. A variety of strategies have been employed to exploit pheromones for pest suppression (Table 10.3).

Table 10.3 Potential uses of pheromones in pest suppression

Monitoring
❒ Detect the presence of a species
❒ Estimate density of population of a species
❒ Measure the seasonal abundance of the pest
❒ Evaluate the effectiveness of mating disruption
❒ Assess levels of insecticide resistance
❒ Provide decision support to undertake control measures
Direct control
❒ Mass deployment of pheromone-baited traps
❒ Application of attract-and-kill formulations or devices
❒ Lure and infect with microbial agents
❒ Pheromone-mediated mating disruption
❒ Alarm pheromones to move pests away from feeding sites
❒ Host-marking pheromones to disrupt landing, feeding or oviposition by pests on their host plants

Mating disruption. The most successful approach using pheromones for pest suppression over the last few decades has been the release of large amounts of synthetic pheromone into a crop. Here, the aim is to prevent or delay mating and hence reduce the incidence of the insect in the next generation. The potential to control insects through mating disruption was first demonstrated for *Trichoplusia ni* about 40 years ago. It has now become an accepted control option for a number of lepidopteran pests of fruits, vegetables and forests.

There has been considerable debate about the mechanisms underlying mating disruption, although there is general agreement now that more than one mechanism may be operational at the same time, and they may vary between species. The most popular explanatory models for disruption of pheromone based communication are: (*i*) sensory adaptation at the peripheral level affecting olfactory receptors, (*ii*) habituation affecting processing of normal responsiveness to olfactory information reaching the central nervous system, (*iii*) camouflage of female produced plumes, and (*iv*) false trail following of synthetic pheromone plumes by male moths. Different combinations of the above mechanisms may be important in practical mating disruption programmes based on crop canopy structure, wind speed, pheromone chemistry, pheromone delivery system and the insect species.

The success of mating disruption depends on achieving an even distribution of sufficient quantities of pheromone. Crop damage in pheromone treated plantings is often greater on the borders than in the interior. Two processes are thought to contribute to the development of border infestations. Mated females emigrate from adjacent plantings that are not treated with pheromone. In addition, pheromone concentrations may be lower on the borders than in the interior, thus increasing the likelihood of males locating females and mating on the borders. Among the tactics used to protect borders is the application of extra pheromone near the edge of the planting or the extension of the pheromone treated adjacent plantings, if possible. The best approach for limiting edge effects is area-wide treatment with pheromone. Hot spots and edge infestations of Oriental fruit moth were eliminated after implementing an area-wide disruption programme in Australia.

Monitoring. The use of sex pheromones as attractants in traps is one of the oldest applications of semiochemicals in pest suppression. Currently, either sex pheromones or aggregation pheromones may be employed to monitor insect activity. Unlike other sampling methods that may be very time consuming and require technical expertise, pheromone based monitoring is efficient and easy to use. In addition, the approach is effective over a range of pest densities and often provides the most practical means of monitoring adult activity. However, the ideal monitoring system must meet certain criteria. In principle, the trap efficiency (number of insects caught per visiting insect) should remain more or less constant. Otherwise the number of insects caught may not reflect the population density in a useful way. In practice, trap efficiency may be influenced by several factors (Table 10.4).

Table 10.4 Considerations for the design of pheromone-based traps

S.No.	Parameter	Ideal feature(s)	Problem(s)
1.	Lure	Constant attraction	Changing release rate, blend, isomers, and active space
2.	Physical shape	Noninhibitory omnidirectional	Visual, physical, and plume structure interference
3.	Colour	Attractive or neutral	Nontarget catch (e.g. bees)
4.	Durability	Long lived	UV, rain
5.	Trapping surface	Constant retention rate	Saturation, glue aging (dust/insect parts), glue viscosity (temperature), evaporation (liquid trapping well)
6.	Service frequency	Relatively infrequent	Labour cost
7.	Cost	Low cost	Manufacturing volume, complex designs, short durability

Traps using sticky surfaces to retain insects may saturate, leading to reduced efficiency at higher catches. The release rate and stability of the attractive components are very important for the efficacy of lures. Many insects respond to pheromones only over a certain concentration range or exposure to a defined blend. The efficacy may be disrupted by the presence of isomers that may appear in the lure over a time due to isomerization, oxidation and polymerization. Trap efficiency may also be affected by insect phenology. For instance, early emergence of male tortricid moths leads to a change in the rate of competition between traps and virgin females, which leads to reduction in the proportion of male moth population after emergence of the females.

***(i)* Detection of pest.** Pheromone-baited traps provide a relatively simple and reliable means of detecting the presence of insects. They are one of the primary tools employed in quarantine surveys, where the aim is to determine the presence of a species and prevent its establishment and spread. Traps are routinely deployed around airports and harbours to detect potential introductions of exotic pests at these high-risk sites. Similarly, large number of traps is used in regional survey programmes to determine the distribution of specific pests and provide the required information for preventing spread to new areas. The use of attractant-baited traps to demonstrate pest-free production and storage zones is assuming significance. The process often requires implementing a defined monitoring programme to allow for the export of various agricultural commodities to specific countries.

***(ii)* Measurement of pest density.** Traps baited with sex pheromones are commonly used to monitor the population density of pests. Pheromone traps have also been used in areawide studies of pest disruption and dispersal. Stored product pests have been successfully monitored from food processing plants and warehouses, using pheromone or food traps. Sex pheromones are used for moths, and beetles usually use aggregation pheromones and/or food baits. Quantitative relationships between adult captures and counts of larval stages or signs of larval feeding, such as feces or damage, have been found for pests of tree fruits, annual crops and forests.

***(iii)* Assessment of density of natural enemies.** Sex pheromones have been employed to trap the insect biological control agents. Pheromone traps have also been used for monitoring the establishement of a biological control agent, *Cydia succedana* (Tortricidae), introduced for the control of a weed, gorse (*Ulex europeaus*) in New Zealand. This new tool would permit monitoring of presence, phenology and relative abundance of the biocontrol agents and could give an indication to the growers whether the population in future might be high enough for successful control of the particular pest.

***(iv)* Assessment of pest phenology.** The combination of pheromone traps and predictive phenology models can provide a reliable method for predicting the timing of flight activity or life stages. The first moth catch (referred to as 'biofix') has been used as a predictor of the beginning of adult emergence. The precision of this method has been well documented for codling moth, a key pest of pome fruits throughout the world. The phenology model for this pest is based on accumulating degree-days (base 10°C) beginning on the day the first moth is captured in a pheromone trap, provided moths are captured on two successive trapping dates. In 6 of the 10 years in the state of Washington, USA, this model predicted the start of egg hatch on the same day that it was observed in the field and there was never a discrepancy of more than two days between the predicted and observed event. Traps have generally been less effective in predicting peak emergence and the emergence of later generations probably because of trap saturation, pesticide use, female moth-trap competition, and the variability associated with the degree of trap and lure maintenance. This approach is likely to be particularly useful for biorationals such as IGRs, which require precise timing as they are primarily active against specific instars or life stages.

***(v)* Assessment of effectiveness of mating disruption.** An increasingly important use of attractant-baited traps is to measure the efficacy of mating disruption formulations. Capture of zero (complete shutdown) or very few moths in a pheromone-baited trap has been used to indicate successful disruption of the target pest. However, it is not uncommon to record low moth catches in traps and still have less than adequate pest control in pheromone-treated plots. In some cases, it is also possible to greatly inhibit catches in pheromone traps but still detect substantial numbers of females mating. Two approaches have been suggested to improve the utility of pheromone-baited traps as monitoring tools in pheromone-treated plots. Firstly, a lure with an emission rate closer to the natural rate would seem to be the most suitable for measuring the efficacy of a disruption treatment. The second approach is to use lures with very high release rates as a means following changes in adult population densities in spite of air permeation with pheromone.

***(vi)* Monitoring of insecticide resistance.** Pheromone-bated traps are one of the more widely adopted methods for monitoring insecticide resistance in several lepidopteran pests. The technique involves collecting large number of males in traps and testing for expression of resistance by topical application of insecticides or through incorporation of the insecticide through glue. The major advantage of pheromone-trap bioassays is the rapid collection and determination of resistance for large samples of the pest without incurring the costs in time and money associated with rearing of large numbers of insects. However, the technique may overestimate the impact of resistance in the field because only males are captured and assayed. Sex-related differences in tolerance to insecticides in insects are known, with females more susceptible than males. Moreover, this approach cannot be used to monitor for resistance to materials whose primary mode of action requires ingestion.

***(vii)* Decision support.** Pheromone-based monitoring systems can be used to assess population trends and determine the need to treat. Thresholds of catch have been developed for a large number of insects and used as the basis for conventional pest management interventions. Basing management decisions on adult catches rather than taking a preventive or calender-based approach is a key step in many efforts to reduce the number of insecticide applications. The approach works on the principle that an intervention with a spray is required only if certain defined sampling threshold is exceeded. The decision may be based on a single weekly catch, consecutive catches or cumulative catches over an extended period, such as a generation. A threshold of apple leafroller, *Epiphyas postvittana*, pheromone trap catch has been determined from a correlation of catch with fruit damage at harvest. Thus catches greater than the threshold led to recommendation for application of a selective insecticide. Treatment thresholds for codling moth, *Cydia pomonella*, based on moth captures in pheromone traps, have been developed for most pome fruit producing regions of the world. A threshold of 1-5 moths per trap per week has been established as the point at which pesticides need to be applied depending upon location. This need-based application has led to 50-75 per cent reduction in pesticide use.

Mass trapping. Mass trapping aims at catching substantial proportion of a pest population before mating, oviposition or feeding and thus preventing damage to the crop. Success with this technique requires the combination of a very attractive lure and a highly efficient trap. The lure should be very attractive, eventually out-competing the naturally occurring attractant. For Lepidoptera, it is essential that males are trapped before mating, and it is most likely to succeed with insects that mate only once. In case of Coleptera, trapping based on aggregation pheromones aims to reduce the number of both sexes before eggs are laid or damage is done by feeding adults. It is most important that there is minimal influx of the pest from outside the protected areas. In addition, mass trapping is rather cost-and labour-intensive because of trap maintenance. As with other traps, there may also be problems with the blend, change of release rate, or trap efficiency over time. The ability to attract and retain very high numbers will be affected by trap design, placement and maintenance.

Mass trapping is considered most effective for pests, which are geographically isolated and/or at low densities. Four year of mass trapping with a sex and floral lure reduced a small pocket of Japanese beetles in a city park by 97 per cent. Male removal using sex pheromone traps was shown to be an effective means of controlling Chinese tortrix, *Cydia trasias*, on street-planted Chinese scholar trees. Success of these efforts in urban or park settings was, in part, due to the isolation of the sites and relatively low population densities. Similarly, food warehouses and other enclosed situations provide a high level of isolation, which should enhance the prospects for mass trapping. Perhaps the most successful use of mass trapping has been for the control of several species of beetles on forest trees. One of the most effective uses has been for the control of ambrosia beetles in timber-processing facilities in British Columbia. In this case, the programme probably benefited from the trapping being somewhat isolated from beetle populations in the forest. Control of some forest beetles may be enhanced by use of deterrents to push the target beetles away from a host, combined with attractant baited traps or trap trees to 'pull' them away. Recently, the potential of using lures containing the aggregation pheromone components in combination with ethyl acetate, cut sugarcane and insecticide (permethrin), was demonstrated for mass trapping of New Guinea sugarcane weevil, *Rhabdoscleus obscurus*,in Guam.

***(i)* Lure and kill.** The lure and kill approach is a modification of mass trapping, where instead of being trapped, the responding insects come in contact with a toxicant and get killed. In many ways, this method also suffers the same constraints as for mass trapping, e.g. population density, attractiveness of the lure and efficiency of the method of killing. However, the problem of trap-saturation may be eliminated and this may improve the effectiveness of control in high-density situations. The problems of trap maintenance and high cost of the control programme may also be mitigated to some extent, especially if the system relies on attracting the insects to a plant surface treated with an insecticide rather than to some kind of target device.

The lure and kill formulations have been developed for the control of various beetles, moths and flies. Some of the earliest applications of attractants in combination with insecticides have been for the control of tephritid fruit flies. The most successful example is the control of olive fly, *Bactrocera oleae* in Greece. Protein/insecticide-bait sprays have been used to control this pest in most Mediterranean olive-growing areas for a number of years. However, due to toxicity to natural enemies, a system was developed based on the use of target traps baited with either a food-attractant or a sex pheromone dispenser. This target-device method of controlling *B. oleae* was effective in reducing fruit infestation, especially when applied on area-wide basis. The most recent development for fruit fly control has been microencapsulated sprayable formulation, comprising of the sex pheromone of this species, 1,7-diozaspiro, and an insecticide (either dimethoate or malathion). Recently, biodegradable or wooden spheres laced with a low dose of imidacloprid have shown promise for the control of *Rhagoletis pomonella* in apple and *R. mendax* in blueberry. In Punjab state of India, scientists at the Punjab Agricultural University (PAU), Ludhiana has has designed a trap , better known as 'PAU Fruit fly Trap' which provides an eco-friendly solution to the fruit fly menace in guava, pear, peach, mango and plum. For effective control, it is recommended to fix the traps @ 16 traps/acre in the second week of April in plum, first week of May in peach, third week of May in mango, first week of June in pear, first week of July in guava and second week of August in kinnow.

***(ii)* Lure and infect.** This innovative and promising approach combines an attractive lure with an entomopathogen. This technique is also called 'autodissemination'. In this case, the insects that arrive at the source are not killed, but are inoculated with the pathogen with the idea to magnify the treatment by spreading the disease to other individuals. Different pathogens could be used with slightly different pathways including viruses, bacteria, fungi and nematodes. This approach can generate disease outbreaks that can multiply in the area and affect the pest populations. Fewer insects may need to be directly attracted to the pathogen stations, which could reduce the cost and labour required. However, the critical requirements for success with pathogens may be difficult to achieve and include biological factors as well as operational factors such as formulation and delivery systems.

The lure and infect approach has been explored with nucleopolyhedrosis virus against tobacco budworm; a granulosis virus against codling moth; a protozoan against stored-product insect, *Trogoderma glabrum;* and fungi against diamondback moth, Japanese beetle and termites. Fungi seem to be the best candidates as they are transferred between adults and larvae, and do not require consumption or copulation to be pathogenic. Once an appropriate pathogen is selected, a formulation must be developed that protects the organism from environmental degradation. A major constraint with these systems, as with mass trapping, is likely to be the ability to make them cost-effective as many bait stations may need to be developed for the approach to be effective.

ALLELOCHEMICALS

Allelochemicals are the chemicals that mediate interactions between different species. These interactions may benefit both the species (synomones), the emitting organism (allomones), or the receiving organism (kairomones). Herbivores and plants have coexisted for nearly 400 million years and during this time many remarkable mutualisms have developed between them. There are also, of necessity, antagonisms in that herbivores eat plants and the plants tend to kill herbivores. Among the most effective weapons developed by plants against phytophagous insects are the noxious phytochemicals, which adversely affect the survival, growth, development and behaviour of these pests. Moreover, the allelochemicals released by phytophagous insects and their natural enemies (parasitoids and predators) are important in some situations. Allelochemicals can be manipulated for use for monitoring, mass trapping, augmentation of natural enemies, and as repellents and deterrents.

Monitoring

A number of volatile plant kairomones have been found to be attractive to several species of insects (Table 10.5). Kairomones have been very important for monitoring and control of fruit flies, Japanese beetle and Diabroticite rootworm beetles. Kairomone-baited traps may be effective for monitoring, but like pheromone traps require similar levels of intensive development of trap design, deployment strategy and lure formulation to overcome the problems of low catches or intensive maintenance. There have been further improvements for monitoring and control of such pests using kairomones. For example, there are equivalent captures of *Bactrocera dorsalis* to coffee juice compared to the standard kairomone lure, which may lead to new attractants.

Kairomone-based monitoring systems can act as useful tools to determine population trends of different categories of pests. Sticky-coated red spheres baited with synthetic apple volatiles can be used to monitor apple maggot activity and alert growers regarding the need to spray. An action threshold of 8 flies per trap allowed for a 70 per cent reduction in sprays and acceptable levels of control. Reducing the threshold to 5 flies per trap resulted in 0.6 fewer sprays, but the conservative threshold was more likely to be adopted by apple growers. Traps baited with isothiocyanates catch the brassica pod midge, *Dasyneura brassicae* and may be used in monitoring programmes. Similarly, a mixture of isothiocyanates has been used for monitoring the phenology of cabbage seed weevil, *Ceutorhynchus assimilis* in oilseed rape. Several attractive constituents from pig manure have been identified that elicit upwind flight to the source in house flies. House flies can also be monitored using multicomponent lures releasing ethanol, skatole, ammonia, fermentation products and other compounds.

Monitoring with kairomones has been applied extensively for bark and timber beetles. The traps or trap trees baited with the gas ethylene have been proposed for monitoring and management of the olive beetle, *Phloetribus scarabaeoides*. The attraction of bark beetles to host trees under natural conditions requires several steps involving the release of kairomones and other semiochemicals. The females of *Dendroctonus ponderosae* are initially attracted to a suitable tree releasing a kairomone, myrcene. These females start releasing a sex pheromone, (+)-exobrevicomin, that attracts males. Males entering the tree release an aggregation pheromone,

Table 10.5 Selected volatile plant kairomones attractive to insects

Insect(s)	Kairomone(s)	Source(s)
Coleoptera		
Striped cucumber beetle	Indole	Cucurbit blossoms
Root worms	Eugenol, isoeugenol, cinnamyl alcohol, cinammaldehyde, indole, estragole, β-ionone	Cucurbit blossoms and synthetics
Colorado potato beetle	Trans-2-hexen-1-o1	Potato
Cabbage and striped flea beetles	Allyl isothiocyanate	Brassicaceae
Sweet clover weevil	Coumarin	Sweet clover
Diptera		
Mediterranean fruit fly	Terpineol acetate, α-copaine, α-ylangene	Various
Onion maggot fly	Dipropyl disulfide	Onion
Cabbage maggot fly	Allyl isothiocyanate	Brassicaceae
Carrot rust fly	Trans-asarone, trans-2-hexenol, hexanal, heptanal	Carrot
Apple maggot fly	Butyl 2-methylbutanoate, propyl hexanoate, butyl hexanoate, hexyl propanoate, hexyl butanoate	Apple
Lepidoptera		
Corn earworm, European corn borer and other noctuid moths	Phenylacetaldehyde	Corn silk
Oriental fruit moth	Terpineol acetate	Peach
Codling moth	α-Farnesene, ethyl-2,4-decadienoate	Various

-(-) frontalin, that attracts both males and females to the attacked tree in a mass attack, in order to rapidly overcome the host defense system.

Mass Trapping

Mass trapping of fruit flies (both sexes) and lepidopteran males, based on kairomone attractants, has been attempted with success. Pesticide-treated wooden spheres rely on a combination of attractants, a feeding stimulant and a toxicant to lure and kill apple maggot, *Rhagoletis pomonella*. Placement of biodegradable spheres baited with an attractive component of host odour, butyl hexanoate, on perimeter trees of commercial apple blocks were nearly as effective as insecticide sprays at intercepting apple maggot flies and preventing fruit injury. A kairomonal attracticide has been developed for the control of *Amyelois transitella* on almonds. Initial control of tsetse flies in Africa used odours released by buffalo or oxen urine to attract flies to cloth doped with insecticides. Subsequently, flies were attracted to electrified nets with these and other odours.

Augmentation of Natural Enemies

Chemical information provided by the arthropod host (kairomones) and the plant (allomones) plays an important role in both the short-range and long-range location of hosts by parasitoids. Successful parasitism involves a series of interactions often mediated by allelochemicals, including host habitat location, host location and host acceptance. Host kairomones may be found in moth scales, host feces, silk, cuticular components, gland secretions and host sex pheromones. Volatiles may also be released by the plant in response to herbivore damage, i.e. herbivore-induced synomones.

Many of the toxic or repellent plant allelochemicals have been found to be attractive or stimulating to parasitoids. For example, allyl isothiocyanates from crucifer plants, which are toxic to a number of herbivores, attract the braconid parasitoid, *Diaeretiella rapae*. Similarly, *Diadromus pulchellus*, an inchneumonid parasitoid of caterpillars that feed on *Allium* spp., becomes excited in the presence of several of the odorus sulphur compounds from this plant. Damaged cotton plants release the terpenoid, β-caryopyllene, which attracts the predatory green lace wing, *Chrysoperla carnea*. The cotton terpenoids, γ-bisabolene, β-caryophyllene oxide and gossonorol attract the ichneumonid parasitoid, *Campoletis sonorensis*. It has been demonstrated that a specialist parasitoid, *Microplitis demolitor* is attracted by the volatile, 3-octanone, found in the host plant, *Glycine max,* of its herbivore host, *Pseudoplusia includens*. However, it was attracted and markedly more arrested by the volatile guaiacol, which was found in its host's frass. Although generalist parasitoids respond to volatiles from the host plant of their host herbivore, volatiles from host feces are more important as kairomones for the specialist parasitoids.

It has been shown that the allelochemicals released following herbivory not only influence specialist and/or generalist natural enemies but can also affect the behaviour of the herbivore and, through plant-plant communication, can make adjacent plants more attractive to natural enemies. Cotton, maize and tobacco plants release distinct blends of volatiles when they are exposed to herbivory by two closely related lepidopteran larvae, *Heliothis virescens* and *Helicoverpa zea*. It has been demonstrated in chemical/behavioural assays that the specialist parasitoid, *Cardiochiles nigriceps* was able to discriminate between these blends, being attracted specifically to its own host, *H. virescens*.

The most commonly used manipulation of allelochemicals in augmenting biological control is through exposing the parasitoids to allelochemicals prior to release. The allelochemicals which are attractive to or which arrest the parasitoid could be sprayed on the crop to maintain or attract the parasitoid to the crop. For example, increased parasitization of California red scale, *Aphytis melinus*, has been obtained by exposing its parasitoid, *Aphelinus mali,* to a synthetic kairomone. It was possible to attract tachinid parasitoid, *Cyzenis albicans* of the winter moth, *Operophthera brumata,* to apple trees by using borneol, but there was no increase in oviposition.

Repellents and Deterrents

Repellents are chemicals that cause insects to orient their movements away from a source. Allied materials that do not cause movement away but do prevent feeding or oviposition by insects are called deterrents. In concept, repellents are conventionally viewed as chemicals applied to surfaces to drive insects away. Deterrents, on the other hand, are usually thought of as natural plant constituents that are most important in host plant resistance. In the early 1900s, repellency of several essential oils, including oil of citronella, was discovered, and these were widely used as mosquito repellents. Pine oil has been found to have repellent or oviposition deterrent properties against some insects. Constituents of pine oil, such as linalool, may reduce feeding and oviposition by house flies. In addition, α-pinene is being developed as an oviposition repellent against cherry bark tortrix, *Enarmonia formosana*.Some of the most common repellents used today for protection of humans are DEET (N, N-diethyl-m-toluamide) (Fig. 10.3A) against biting flies and mosquitoes, and benzyl benzoate (Fig.10.3B) against ticks and chiggers.

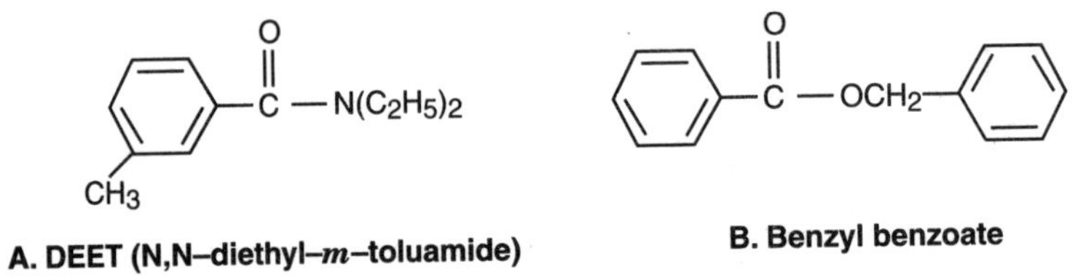

A. DEET (N,N–diethyl–*m*–toluamide)

B. Benzyl benzoate

Fig. 10.3 Structures of common insect repellents

Naturally occurring feeding deterrents exist for many insects and play a major role in host selection and specificity (Table 10.6). In addition, oviposition deterrents have been found in several agricultural and horticultural crops. For example, an allelochemical, pentadecanal, has been isolated from a rice variety TKM6, which has exhibited oviposition deterrent properties

Table 10.6 Feeding deterrents in host plants

Plant	Feeding deterrent(s)	Insect(s)
Cruciferae	Sinigrin	*Pieris brassicae*
Cucumis sativus	Cucurbitacin	*Tetranychus urticae, Phyllotreta nemorum*
Gossypium spp.	Gossypol	*Heliothis virescens, Spodoptera littoralis, Earias insulana*
	Isoquercitrin, quercitrin, quercetin	*Helicoverpa zea, Pectinophora gossypiella*
Hordeum spp.	Gramine	*Schizaphis graminum*
Lycopersicon esculentum	Rutin, chlorogenic acid, α-tomatine	*H. zea*
Lycopersicon hirsutum f. *glabratum*	2-Tridecanone	*H. zea*
Medicago spp.	Coumarin	*Hypera postica, Sitona cylindricollis*
	Dicoumaril	*Acyrthosiphon pisum*
Mililotus spp.	Coumarin	*Listroderes costirustris*
Momordica charantia	Momordicine II	*Aulacophora foveicollis*
Solanaceae (potato, tomato)	Demissine, solacauline, tomatine, leptine I and II	*Leptinotarsa decemlineata Manduca sexta*
Solanum spp.	Tomatine, solanidine, α-chaconine	*Choristoneura fumiferana*
Solanum tuberosum	Tomatine	*Empoasca fabae*
Sorghum bicolor	*p*-Hydroxybenzaldehyde, dhurrin, procyanidin	*S. graminun*
Triticum aestivum	Hydroxamic acid	*Metopolophium dirhodum*
Zea mays	DIMBOA	*Ostrinia nubilalis*

Source: Panda and Khush (1995)

against striped stem borer, *Chilo suppressalis*. The most recent work on plant allomones has been with azadirachtin and related analogues isolated from the fruits of the neem tree, *Azadirachta indica* A. Juss. Azadirachtin has a number of deterrent effects on the behaviour of arthropod species, modifying, for instance, feeding and oviposition. In addition, azadirachtin may cause several types of physiological effects, including disruption of ecdysone biosynthesis, reduced fecundity, and decreased egg hatch.

PUSH-PULL STRATEGY

The push-pull strategy involves behavioural manipulation of insect pests and their natural enemies by integration of stimuli that act to make the protected resource unattractive or unsuitable to the pests (push), while luring them towards an attractive source (pull), from where the pests are subsequently removed. The pests are repelled or deterred away from the resource (a crop or a farm animal) by using stimuli that mask host apparency or are repellent or deterrent. The pests are simultaneously attracted, using highly apparent and attractive stimuli, to other areas such as traps or trap crops, where they are concentrated, facilitating their elimination. The stimuli for push components include visual cues (host colour, shape or size), synthetic repellents, non-host volatiles, host-derived semiochemicals, antiaggregation pheromones, alarm pheromones, antifeedants, oviposition deterrents and oviposition deterring pheromones. The stimuli for pull components include visual stimulants (traps or trap crops), host volatiles, sex and aggregation pheromones, and gustatory and oviposition stimulants.

The principles of the push-pull strategy are to maximize control efficacy, efficiency, sustainability and output, while minimising negative environmental effects. This strategy maximises the efficiency of behaviour-manipulating stimuli through the additive and synergistic effects of integrating their use. The efficacy and efficiency of population reducing methods can also be increased by cocentrating the pests in a predetermined site. Population reduction by biocontrol methods or highly selective botanical pesticides is preferred to broad-spectrum synthetic pesticides. The deployment of renewable sources, particularly plants, for the production of semiochemicals is encouraged. In agricultural systems, the goal is to maximise output from the whole system while minimising cost, and using harvestable trap crops or intercrops, rather than sacrificial crops, wherever feasible. The development of reliable and sustainable push-pull strategy requires a clear understanding of the pest's biology and the behavioural/ chemical ecology of the interactions with its hosts, conspecifics and natural enemies.

The push-pull strategies are under development or used in practice in the major areas of pest control. However, the most successful example currently used in practice, was developed in Africa for the control of lepidoptern stem borers, viz., *Chilo partellus, Eldana saccharina, Busseola fusca,* and *Sesamia calamistis* in maize and sorghum. The strategy involves the combined use of intercrops and trap crops, using plants that are appropriate to the farmers and that also exploit natural enemies. The stem borers are repelled from the crops by repellent non-host intercrops, particularly molasses grass (*Melinis minutiflora*), silverleaf desmodium (*Desmodium uncinatum*) or greenleaf desmodium (*D. intortum*) (push). These are concentrated on attractive trap plants, primarily Napier grass (*Pennisetum purpureum*) or Sudan grass (*Sorghum vulgare sudanense*) (pull). Molasses grass, when intercropped with maize, not only reduced stem borer infestation, but also increased parasitism by *Cotesia sesamiae*. A trap crop of Sudan grass also increased the efficiency of stem borer natural enemies. The push-pull strategy has contributed to increased crop yields and livestock production, resulting in a significant impact on food security in the region.

COMMERCIALIZATION

The first trials that involved assaying pheromones for pest control were carried out in mid-1960s. Since then, hundreds of other pheromones have been identified and there are more than 50 (in over 300 different formulations), that can be used in pest control programmes (Table 10.7). Several reputed international companies are marketing pheromone formulations. Noteables among them are AgriSense-BCS (UK), International Pheromone Systems (UK), Shin-Etsu (Japan), Chemtech BC (The Netherlands), Trace and Mycotech (USA), Bioprax (France), Agrimont (Italy), Flora (Estonia) and Pheronet (Sweden). It is estimated that at present pheromones account for 10-12 per cent of the insecticide market. However, it is expected to touch 20-30 per cent within a decade.

Table 10.7 Commercially available pheromone formulations at global level

Target species 1	Common name 2	Pheromone 3	Mode of action 4
Adoxophyces orana	Leaf roller	Sex pheromone	Mating disruption of male moths
Anarsia lineatella	Peach tree borer	Sex pheromone	Mating disruption of male moths
Anthonomus grandis	Boll weevil	Sex pheromone	Monitoring and mass trapping of both males and females
Bactrocera cucurbitae	Melon fly	Sex pheromone	Lure and kill of female flies
Bactrocera oleae	Olive fly	Sex pheromone	Monitoring, and lure and kill of male flies
Carpsosina niponensis	Peach fruit moth	Sex pheromone	Mating disruption of male moths
Chilo suppressalis	Rice stem borer	Sex pheromone	Mating disruption of male moths
Cosmopolites sordidus	Banana corm weevil	Aggregation pheromone	Mass trapping of males and females
Cydia funebrana	Plum fruit moth	Sex pheromone	Monitoring, mating disruption, and lure and kill of male moths
Cydia molesta	Oriental fruit moth	Sex pheromone	Mating disruption of male moths
Cydia nigricana	Pea moth	Sex pheromone	Monitoring male populations
Cydia pomonella	Codling moth	Sex pheromone	Monitoring, mating disruption, and lure and kill of male moths
Dendroctonus frontalis	Southern pine beetle	Aggregation pheromone	Mass trapping of males and females
Dendroctonus ponderosae	Mountain pine beetle	Aggregation pheromone	Mass trapping of males and females
Dendroctonus rufipennis	Spruce beetle	Aggregation pheromone	Mass trapping of males and females
Dryocoetes confusus	Balsam bark beetle	Aggregation pheromone	Mass trapping of males and females
Eucosma gloriola	Pine shoot borer	Sex pheromone	Mating disruption of male moths
Eupoecillia ambiguella	Grape berry moth	Sex pheromone	Mating disruption of male moths
Heliothis virescens	Tobacco budworm	Sex pheromone	Mating disruption of male moths
Homona magnanima	Tea tortrix moth	Sex pheromone	Mating disruption of male moths
Ips sexdantatus	Six-spined ips beetle	Aggregation pheromone	Mass trapping of males and females

Ips typographus	Spruce bark beetle	Aggregation pheromone	Mass trapping of males and females
Keiferia lycopersicella	Tomato pinworm moth	Sex pheromone	Mating disruption of male moths
Lobesia botrana	Grapevine moth	Sex phermone	Mating disruption of male moths
Lymantria dispar	Gypsy moth	Sex pheromone	Mating disruption of male moths
Musca domestica	House fly	Sex pheromone	Mating disruption of male flies
Oryctes rhinoceros	Rhinoceros beetle	Aggregation pheromone	Mass trapping of males and females
Ostrinia nubilalis	Corn stem borer	Sex pheromone	Monitoring adult males
Pectinophora gossypiella	Pink bollworm	Sex pheromone	Mating disruption of male moths
Pityogenes chalcographus	Spruce bark beetle	Aggregation pheromone	Mass trapping of males and females
Platynota idaeusalis	Tufted apple moth	Sex pheromone	Mating disruption, and lure and kill of male moths
Platyptilia carduidactyla	Artichoke plume moth	Sex pheromone	Mating disruption of male moths
Plutella xylostella	Diamondback moth	Sex pheromone	Mating disruption of male moths
Popillia japonica	Japanese beetle	Sex pheromone	Lure and kill of both males and females
Prays citri	Citrus flower moth	Sex pheromone	Mating disruption of male moths
Prays oleae	Olive moth	Sex pheromone	Mating disruption of male moths
Rhyacionia buoliana	Pine shoot moth	Sex pheromone	Mating disruption of male moths
Rhynchophorus ferrugineus	Red palm weevil	Aggregation pheromone	Mass trapping of males and females
Rhychophorus palmarum	American palm weevil	Aggregation pheromone	Mass trapping of males and females
Sanninoidea exitiosa	Peach twig borer	Sex pheromone	Mating disruption of male moths
Scolytus multistriatus	European elm bark beetle	Sex pheromone	Monitoring, and lure and kill of male beetles
Spodoptera exigua	Beet armyworm	Sex pheromone	Mating disruption of male moths
Spodoptera frugiperda	Fall armyworm	Sex pheromone	Mating disruption of male moths
Synanthedon hector	Cherry tree borer	Sex pheromone	Mating disruption of male moths
Synanthedon myopa-eformis	Apple clearwing moth	Sex pheromone	Mating disruption of male moths
Synanthedon pictipes	Lesser peach tree borer	Sex pheromone	Mating disruption of male moths
Synanthedon tipuliformis	Currant clearwing moth	Sex pheromone	Mating disruption of male moths
Tetranychus urticae	Two-spotted spider mite	Alarm pheromone	Improved pesticide activity
Thaumetopoea pityocampa	Pine processionary moth	Sex pheromone	Monitoring and mass trapping of male moths
Trypodendron lineatum	Ambrosia beetle	Aggregation pheromone	Mass trapping of males and females
Zeuzera pyrina	Leopard moth	Sex pheromone	Mating disruption of male moths

Source :Copping (2001)

Although more than 1500 pheromonal compounds have been identified from Lepidoptera alone, only a small proportion have been developed for pest control. The reasons for this lack of development are many, but certainly include the following:

- Lack of basic knowledge concerning insect communication
- Lack of investment in developing pheromonal products
- Lack of detailed field evaluation
- Difficulty in obtaining enough material to undertake preliminary experiments
- Lack of detailed studies on trap designs
- Lack of studies on blends and release rates
- Lack of studies on significance of isomerism

Like pheromones, parapheromones involve non-toxic modes of action and show relatively low toxicity, with the exception of some co-fluorinated analogues, Moreover, the reduced risks of side effects on non-target organisms due to their species specificity, low doses required, and their high volatility minimize the risks of their utilization in the field. However, extensive research is required before their registration and commercial utilization can take place. Markets for the new compounds are likely to be relatively small, but because of their character of anthropogenic compounds, parapheromones might be better protected by patents than pheromones. Finally, parapheromones will probably be developed for use on major crops only because of the time and cost required for registration.

A global survey of companies offering semiochemical-based monitoring and control systems revealed that 41 suppliers provided products for use against 257 arthropod pests. Of the registered products about 80 per cent are for Lepidoptera, 10 per cent for Coleoptera, and the remaining 10 per cent for Diptera, Orthoptera and Hymenoptera. Cropwise analysis revealed that maximum number of pests for which products are available are from field crops (89), followed by orchards (79), vegetables (63) and forests (55). Out of a total of 302 products, 230 are meant for monitoring and the remaining for mating disruption, mass trapping and other uses (Inscoe *et al.*, 1990). In India, pheromone technology has been developed for 30 insect pests of which more than 20 are commercially available (Table 10.8). More than 30 companies spread over 19 states supply these pheromones. Phermone traps have been included in different IPM programmes throughout the country in cotton, chickpea, pigeonpea, groundnut, rice, vegetables, fruits, etc. at different locations.

Table 10.8 Insect pests for which pheromones are commercially available in India

Insect pest		Source(s) of availability
Latin name	**Common name**	
Field crops		
Aproaerema modicella	Groundnut leaf miner	L
Chilo infuscatellus	Sugarcane early shoot borer	J
Chilo partellus	Sorghum stem borer	A, C
Chilo sacchariphagus indicus	Sugarcane internode borer	B, J
Earias insulana, *E. vittella*	Spotted bollworms	B, C, D, E, G, I, J, K

Helicoverpa armigera	American bollworm	B, C, D, E, F, G, I, J, K
Holotrichia consanguinea	White grub	H
Pectinophora gossypiella	Pink bollworm	B, C, D, E, F, G, I, J, K
Scirpophaga incertulas	Yellow stem borer	B, C, D, G, I, J, K
Spodoptera litura	Tobacco caterpillar	B, C, D, E, F, G, I, J, K
Vegetable crops		
Agrotis spp.	Cutworms	A
Bactrocera cucurbitae	Melon fly	C, I, J
Bactrocera dorsalis	Fruit fly	C, I, J
Cylas formicaricus	Sweet potato weevil	A
Leucinodes orbonalis	Brinjal fruit and shoot borer	B, D, J, K
Phthorimaea operculella	Potato tuber moth	A, C
Plutella xylostella	Diamondback moth	C, D, E, I, J
Fruits		
Aonidiella aurantii	California red scale	A
Cydia pomonella	Codling moth	C
Quadraspidiotus perniciosus	San Jose scale	A
Plantation crops		
Rhynchophorus ferrugineus	Red palm weevil	J

A = AgriSense BCS (Biosys Subsidiary), Mumbai; B = Basarass Biocontrol Research, Eraiyur Pennadam R.S., Cuddalore Distt., Tamil Nadu; C = Bio-Sense Crop Protection (Eco-Max Agro Systems Ltd.), Mumbai; D = Biotech International Ltd., New Delhi; E = Ganesh Bio Control System, Gondal, Gujarat; F = Green Tech Agro Products Pvt. Ltd., Coimbatore; G = Indore Biotech Inputs & Research (Pvt.) Ltd., Indore; H = J.K. Traders, Delhi; I = Margo Biocontrols Pvt. Ltd., Bangalore; J = Pest Control (India) Pvt. Ltd., Udaipur; K = Pheromone Chemicals, Hyderabad; L = SOM-IPM Systems (India) Ltd., Hyderabad.

ROLE IN PEST MANAGEMENT

Chemical ecological methods have currently emerged as viable alternatives to monitor and suppress pest populations. Besides the problems that have occurred in the practical application of semiochemicals, there are a number of examples of large-scale mass trapping and mating disruption efforts with sex pheromones or other lures (Table 10.9). A few selected examples are enumerated here.

Allelochemicals

Although a number of kairomones have been isolated and identified from plants and animals, only a few of them have been exploited for pest suppression.

Corn rootworms. Three species of corn rootworms, viz. the western corn rootworm, *Diabrotica virgifera* the southern corn rootworm, *D. undecimpunctata howardi* and the northern corn rootworm, *D. barberi,* are known to attack corn. Two features of diabroticite chemical ecology are helpful in manipulation of their behaviour. Firstly, the association between these beetles and cucurbitacin, a potent arrestant and feeding stimulant, may be so strong that other behaviours such as sex attraction are masked. Secondly, several plant-derived volatile attractants appear to mediate host selection by *Diabrotica* beetles. Powdered gourd roots and squash fruits have been evaluated for improving the capture of beetles in monitoring programmes. In addition, palatable baits containing cucurbitacins and an insecticide have been employed for

Table 10.9 Selected examples of use of semiochemicals in pest suppression

Insect pest		Crop/Commodity
Common name	Species	
Mass trapping		
Ambrosia beetle	*Gnathotrichus sulcatus*	Forests
Apple maggot fly	*Rhagoletis pomonella*	Apples
Bark beetles	*Dendroctonus* spp.	Forests
Beet armyworm	*Spodoptera exigua*	Onions
Blueberry maggot fly	*Rhagoletis mendax*	Blueberry
Chinese tortrix	*Cydia trasias*	Chinese scholar tree
Cigarette beetle	*Lasioderma serricorne*	Tobacco stores
Cocoa pod borer	*Conopomorpha cramerella*	Cocoa
Codling moth	*Cydia pomonella*	Apples
Conifer bark beetle	*Ips typographus*	Forests
Corn rootworms	*Diabrotica* spp.	Corn
Diamondback moth	*Plutella xylostella*	Crucifers
Indian meal moth	*Plodia interpunctella*	Stored products
Japanese beetle	*Popillia japonica*	City park
Light brown apple moth	*Epiphyas postvittana*	Apples
Mediterranean flour moth	*Ephestia kuehniella*	Flour mills
Mountain pine beetle	*Dendroctonus ponderosae*	Forests
New Guinea sugarcane weevil	*Rhabdoscelus obscurus*	Sugarcane
Olive fruit fly	*Bactrocera oleae*	Olives
Olive moth	*Prays oleae*	Olives
Spruce bark beetle	*Ips typographus*	Forests
Sugarcane wireworm	*Melanotus okinawensis*	Sugarcane
Tropical warehouse moth	*Heliothis virescens*	Tobacco
Tobacco budworm	*Ephestia cautella*	Stored products
Tsetse flies	*Glossina* spp.	Cattle
Mating disruption		
California red scale	*Aonidiella aurantii*	Citrus
Citrus mealy bug	*Planococcus citri*	Citrus
Codling moth	*C. pomonella*	Apples
Diamondback moth	*P. xylostella*	Brassicas
Grape berry moth	*Eupoecilia ambiguella*	Grapes
Gypsy moth	*Lymantria dispar*	Broad leaved/Oak forests
Light brown apple moth	*E. postvittana*	Apples
Long horn beetle	*Migdolus fryanus*	Sugarcane
Mullein bug	*Campylomma verbasci*	Apples
Oriental fruit moth	*Cydia molesta*	Stone fruits
Oriental tea tortrix	*Homona magnanima*	Tea
Pink bollworm	*Pectinophora gossypiella*	Cotton
Rice stem borers	*Chilo suppressalis, Scirpophaga incertulas*	Rice
Smaller tea tortrix	*Adoxophyes* spp.	Tea
Sugarcane beetle	*Migdolus fryanus*	Sugarcane
Sweet potato weevil	*Cylas formicarius*	Sweet potato
Tomato pinworm	*Keiferia lycopersicella*	Tomato

Source **:**Dhaliwal and Koul (2007)

short-term suppression of rootworm populations. The addition of a volatile plant-derived attractant also enhanced the suppression of *D. undecimpunctata howardi.* The first insecticide-laced bait was registered for use against corn rootworms in 1993 and it was applied to 12,000 ha in 1994. This approach reduced the insecticide use in corn by 90-95 per cent. However, three factors may limit further adoption of this approach; (*a*) adult management requires more intensive scouting and better timing than conventional approaches; (*b*) adult management is feasible in only corn-corn rotations; and (*c*) in view of difficulties in extracting cucurbitacin from the buffalo gourd, *Cucurbita foetidissima,* this approach is costly.

Tsetse flies. Traditionally, tsetse flies, *Glossina* spp., have been managed by clearing suitable habitat and by area-wide insecticide applications. Early experimentation with semiochemicals made use of livestock treated with toxicants to attract and kill flies. Specific attractants, such as 1-octen-3-ol, isolated from cattle, when combined with acetone and carbon dioxide, were similar to ox odour in attracting the flies. The addition of cattle urine further enhanced the attraction. The commonly used bait to attract the flies is a combination of acetone, 1-octen-3-ol, 4-methylphenol and 3-propylphenol. Baited traps have been used to monitor the presence of tsetse fly. Baited targets have also been used in combination with insecticides and a setrilant for pest suppression. This approach has resulted in eradication of tsetse fly from a number of areas, but continual reintroductions of flies demand that a yearly trapping programme be maintained. Recently, the introduction of artificial cow that attracted tsetse flies saved thousands of cattle from nagana infection (caused by tsetse flies) in Zimbabwe. The kairomones mimic the smell of real cattle and attract the tsetse flies to fake cow, which is loaded with pesticide.

Pheromones

Pheromones have been extensively employed for monitoring, mass trapping and mating disruption of a number of lepidopteran and coleopteran pests.

Pink bollworm. Pink bollworm, *Pectinophora gossypiella,* a key pest of cotton, has been successfully managed in a number of countries including USA, Egypt and Pakistan by using controlled release formulations of its female sex pheromone, a 1:1 mixture of (Z, E) and (Z, Z)-7, 11-hexadecadienyl acetate known as gossyplure. In Egypt, 1,50,000 ha of cotton (about 36% of the country cotton acreage) were treated with pheromones against *P. gossypiella* in 1994. Mating disruption has been successfully employed in San Joaquin Valley, Imperial Valley of California and Parker Valley of Arizona of USA. Continual immigration of pink bollworms into the Imperial Valley and severe outbreaks of whiteflies, have reduced cotton production and adoption of mating disruption in this region. The growers in Parker Valley formed an informal pest control district in 1990 and adopted the use of mating disruption over 1,20,000 ha of cotton. The programme has been very successful, but problem of whiteflies has increased and a more expensive pheromone-insecticide strategy is required.

Sex pheromones of cotton bollworms have been extremely useful for monitoring, survey and surveillance, and assessing damage to cotton in India. Gossyplure is commonly used for monitoring the pink bollworm throughout the cotton belt. In Punjab, pheromone traps used for monitoring the activity of cotton bollworms on *hirsutum* cotton indicate that the maximum activity of *P. gossypiella, Helicoverpa armigera* and *Earias* spp. was July, September and mid October to the end of season, respectively. Monitoring the population of bollworms can help in their early detection and build up, and a need-based control measure can be adopted depending upon the severity of a particular species of bollworms. The pheromone trap catches of *H. armigera* moths have been successfully used to predict the egg and larval populations of this insect and damage to cotton plant reproductive bodies.

In Pakistan, a single twist-tie formulation containing pheromones of both pink and spotted bollworms has been successfully used to obtain season long control of bollworm complex. A single application of the pheromone either alone or in combination with a conventional insecticide provided effective control, while the conventional spray programme required 4-5 sprays per season to achieve a similar level of control.

Gypsy moth. The identification of a female produced sex pheromone, disparlure, has led to spectacular advances in the management of gypsy moth, *Lymantria dispar*. Mating disruption programmes were established on about 7000 ha from 1979 to 1987 in the eastern United States. In 1993, a federal programme 'Slow the Spread' was launched to slow the rate of gypsy moth expansion by following IPM strategies over an area of 3,000,000 ha spread in four states. About 13,000 ha are treated each year and mating disruption is used on 15 per cent of this area. The greatest use of disparlure has been in surveys to determine the need for management tactics. In the western United States, incipient infestations of gypsy moth were detected in mid 1970s. In Washington state, gypsy moth adults were trapped only in a few sites, but by early ninties, 13-35 new outbreak sites were located each year. The standard protocol for monitoring gypsy moth in Washington state each year is to place about 10,000 traps at a density of one trap per square mile in all high-risk areas. When a moth is captured, a grid of traps is placed within a 3-mile radius around each site. If additional moths are caught and other life stages are also found, three sprays of *Bacillus thuringiensis* are applied. This strategy has prevented the establishment of gypsy moth in western Unites States and British Columbia.

Codling moth. Codlemone, the major sex pheromone component of codling moth, *Cydia pomonella,* has been used extensively for monitoring and timing of pesticide applications. It was also used for mass trapping in some of the earliest evaluations. Mating disruption with codlemone has been tested in several apple-growing regions, including Australia, USA and parts of Europe. The effectiveness of mating disruption in these trials was determined by moth density, moth immigration, amount of pheromone released, and the number and positioning of dispensers used per area. A three-component blend housed in a polyethylene dispenser was registered in USA in 1991 and was applied to treat about 10,000 ha in 1994.

Oriental fruit moth. The Oriental fruit moth, *Cydia molesta* was successfully controlled over 2000 ha of mixed stone fruit area in South Africa in early nineties. The area-wide application of hand-applied pheromone dispensers in the entire Tulbagh Valley was made in 1991-92. Despite recording 85-100 per cent tip damage in the last generation of the previous season, complete control was achieved in a single season, with no supplementing applications of insecticides. The Tulbagh Valley pheromone treatment rates were halved in 1992-93 and populations again did not recover to damaging level.

Tomato pinworm. The tomato pinworm, *Keiferia lycopersicella* has been amenable to control with mating disruption due to several features of the pest: (*a*) the host range of the tomato pinworm is restricted to plants in the family Solanaceae; (*b*) as the pest feeds inside the calyx of the fruit, the insecticides have not proved to be highly effective in its control; and (*c*) the pest has developed high levels of resistance due to the overuse of pesticides. The sex pheromone of the tomato pinworm was identified in 1979 and the first large scale trials (500 ha) were conducted in Culican, Mexico, in 1981. The results of this trial demonstrated that the programme reduced fruit injury with less use of insecticide and was economical as compared to conventional insecticide programmes. These results gave impetus to adoption of an IPM programme for tomatoes using pheromones, biological control, *Bacillus thuringiensis* and cultural control.

Rice stem borers. Two species of rice stem borers, viz. *Chilo suppressalis* and *Scirpophaga incertulas* have been effectively controlled with sex pheromones in large scale field trials. In Spain, *C. suppressalis* has been successfully controlled for upto 100 days in 1500 ha of rice in both the Ebro Delta and Valencia rice-growing areas. Deployed at the rate of 2500 polymer dispensers ha–1 (8 mg active pheromone each) translating into 20 g ha–1, they performed as well as conventional insecticide (fenitrothion) by controlling stem borers down to a damage level of 0.2 per cent. Confusion efficacy rates were approaching 100 per cent. Similarly, high rates and control levels were achieved by reducing the point sources to 500 or 100 ha–1, depending on infestation history and using, respectively 1.6 or 8.0 g pieces of polymer to give a total dosage of 40g ha–1, a system which is now recommended commercially in Spain.

Similarly, a single application of a polymer formulation of the pheromone of yellow stem borer, *S. incertulas* of rice provided effective, season-long control of the pest in Andhra Pradesh, India in large scale field trials. Under normal pest pressure, the control was at least as good as achieved with several applications of conventional insecticides, but under high pest pressure both approaches failed to provide adequate control. Field trials on 20 ha of rice in West Bengal showed pheromone control to be equal to that achieved with insecticide regimes against yellow stem borer, *S. incertulas.* The PVC resin formulation is deployed 1 m above the water level, attached to sticks, at a specific stage in crop development (10-14 days after transplanting) to coincide with moth activity and crop susceptibility. Lengths of PVC resin (20 cm) are tied to stakes at a rate of 625 pieces ha–1, representing a dosage rate of 40 g/ha. This gives a mating disruption effect that lasts for 60-80 days. In Uttarakhand, mass trapping resulted in 5.78 per cent white ears due to *S. incertulas,* 70 days after installation of the pheromone traps, as compared to 17.90 per cent white ears in plots treated with insecticides, suggesting that sex pheromonea mediated male annihilation technique is self-sufficient to keep pest under control. The use of pheromones for mating disruption of rice stem borers has also been made in Indonesia, China, Korea and Thailand.

Bark beetles. A female produced aggregation pheromone of the bark beetles, *Dendroctonus* spp. has been identified as *trans*-verbenol, which is an oxidation product of the host tree compound α-pinene. The attractiveness of *trans*-verbenol to male mountain pine beetle, *D. ponderosae,* is increased when it is combined with the host volatile, myrcene. When a compound, exo-brevicomin, produced by males, is combined with additional volatiles, it functions as an aggregation pheromone at low concentrations and as an antiaggregation pheromone at high concentrations. A blend of these compounds has been marketed for use in monitoring and trapping mountain pine beetles. This programme has four operational components; (*a*) population monitoring, (*b*) containment and concentration of beetle populations, (*c*) port logging mop-up, and (*d*) eradication of isolated infestations.

A multicomponent aggregation pheromone is produced by *D. pseudotsugae,* which plays an important role in host colonization. As the number of colonizing beetles increases, an antiggregation pheromone, 3-methyl-2-cyclohexen-1-one (MCH) is released by the females, which reduces the intraspecific competition. Colonization of trees by *D. pseudotsugae* can be prevented by application of MCH. The application of plastic bead formulation containing MCH by aircraft greatly decreased attacks of *D. pseudotsugae* on susceptible trees. Point source application of MCH for preventing attack on high value trees has also given encouraging results.

In India, in addition to bollworms and yellow stem borer, successful attempts have been made for the control of sweet potato weevil, *Cylas formicarius*; sugarcane early shoot borer, *Chilo infuscatellus*; sugarcane internode borer, *Chilo sacchariphagus indicus*; tobacco caterpillar, *Spodoptera litura*; gram pod borer, *Helicoverpa armigera* and groundnut leaf miner, *Aproaerema modicella.*

Parapheromones

Parapheromones have a high potential as alternative material in integrated pest management programmes, particularly when the natural pheromones are expensive to produce, present longevity problems, or are quickly degraded under field conditions. Three important criteria need to be taken into consideration to include them in synthetic formulations, viz. the efficiency of the blend must be optimized, the specificity must be observed, and the stability must be improved. A number of field experiments have demonstrated that parapheromones meet these prerequisites for their use in insect monitoring or control.

The most extensive application of parapheromones has been the use of lures to attract tephritid fruit flies. Early detection of pest introductions using traps baited with male lures allows quick eradication of incipient populations. New infestations of the Oriental fruit fly, *Bactrocera dorsalis*, in California have been eradicated 12 times since 1966 using methyl eugenol in an insecticide-laced bait. Another parapheromone, trimedlure, has been developed for monitoring the Mediterranean fruit fly, *Ceratis capitata*, and has been used in traps to pinpoint the location and size of infestation sites. The flies can then be eradicated through the use of a sprayable formulation of protein hydrolysate and an insecticide.

The standard monitoring programme for *C. capitata* in California is five traps baited with trimedlure per square mile in urban areas. After flies are detected, additional 1700 traps are baited in a 4.5 mile radius for three generations. In Los Angeles, the release of sterile flies in combination with helicopter spraying of malathion mixed with protein hydrolysate was successful in eradicating infestations of *C. capitata*. However, this programme was not favoured due to perceived environmetal and health risks. The baited traps were first developed in 1970 and are still in use in many countries today. The lure has proven particularly useful for monitoring pest presence within import/export crops at airports and seaports.

Structural modification of the pheromone generally reduces field activity, but a significant increase in catches has sometimes been reported. More males of *Cydia pomonella* were caught in traps baited with (*E,E*)–10, 11–difluro-8, 10-dodecadienol or (*E,E*)–11-chloro-8, 10-undecadienol than in traps containing codlemone. In large scale field trials, pheromone communication was disrupted in the navel orangeworm, *Amyelois transitella*, by air permeation with (Z, Z)-9,11-tetradececadien-1-ol formate, the formate analogue of the main pheromone component (Z,Z) –11-13-hexadecadienal. A novel olefin analogue was also found to disrupt mating communication in this insect. Both compounds are more stable than the natural aldehyde pheromone component.

BEHAVIOURAL RESPONSE OF INSECTS TO INSECTICIDES

Documentation of development of resistance in insects to insecticides and induction of resurgence in response to sublethal doses of the insecticides, is widely reported. However, studies on behavioural changes in insects, manifested as a result of insecticidal applications has received far less attention of entomologists, the world over and even less so in India. Apart from biochemical and physiological mechanisms, the insects may also develop resistance to the applied insecticides through behavioural mechanisms. Behaviour of insects may play a crucial role in resistance development to insecticides. The behavioural mechanisms may be defined as evolved behaviours that tend to reduce an insect's exposure to insecticides or any other toxin that helps an insect to survive, that otherwise would have proved lethal. The role of behaviour, however, is crucial to an understanding of insects' adaptation to toxins. The behavioural mechanisms are usually undetectable and most bioassays are aimed at monitoring resistance. For instance, topical bioassays are unable to detect difference in behaviour. It is difficult to quantify a change in behaviour, potentially requiring novel approaches and bioassays. In fact, comprehensive knowledge and understanding of insect behaviour is important in preventing development of insecticide resistance in various insect pests.

The behavioural resistance to insecticides include changes in activity that alters contact with the insecticide residues. Many insects exhibited changes in their mobility, feeding and/ or reproductive behaviour in response to the insecticidal application; even the behaviour of susceptible and resistant insects differed.

Locomotory behaviour

Locomotory behaviour of insects determines their exposure to insecticides and facilitates insect dispersal. Infact, mobility of insects has played a pivotal role in success of the class insecta and towards attaining pest status by many insects species. Dispersal helps insects to avoid mortality agents, such as predators or inhospitable environments.

There are many reports of behavioural resistance in dipterous insects; especially the adults that are much mobile and against which the selection is directed. DDT and pyrethriods are involved nearly in 60 % cases of behavioural resistance. Further, irritancy due to pyrethroids was greater in resistant horn flies, *Haemotobia irritans* (Linnaeus) than to the susceptible ones. The insecticide-resistant tobacco budworm, *Heliothis virescens* (Fabricius) larvae consistently picked up less permethrin than the susceptible ones. Similarly, DDT-resistant house flies preferred not to rest on the sprayed surfaces and this behaviour may be linked to the physiological resistance. Knowledge of insect behaviour in response to the applied insecticides, holds potential for the management of many insect pests of crops. There are several reports where many coleopterous and lepidopterous insects preferred to feed on foliage not treated with insecticides. Insects are capable of changing their behaviour in response to their sensory perception of insecticides, which may compromise insecticide efficacy.

Some interesting differences between insecticide-susceptible and resistant populations of diamondback moth, *Plutella xylostella* (Linnaeus) were observed. Larvae from the susceptible population of moth have been observed to travel more distance on insecticide-treated or untreated surface and consequently their speed was also more as compared to those taken from the insecticide-resistant population. The resistant larvae travelled significantly less distance on the surfaces treated with endosulfan, quinalphos, fenvalerate and spinosad. Further, susceptible *P. xylostella* larvae travelled significantly more distance as compared to the larvae from insecticide-resistant population, at different temperatures. The resistant larvae starved for 24 h travelled significantly lesser distance as compared to unstarved ones.

It is a known fact that insecticidal applications seldom cover the entire surface of a pest habitat, and hence behavioural responses of target insects to insecticide deposits often plays an important role in determining dose acquisition. If an insect is able to avoid insecticidal deposits wholly or partially, its ability to survive insecticide application greatly enhances. Such responses obviously reduce larval exposure to insecticides under field conditions. Further, the observed tendency to move swiftly out of insecticide-treated areas is likely to reduce the lethal effects of an insecticide.

An amazing behaviour exhibited by insects is the phenomenon of 'Leg Autotomy' to escape *i.e.* entrapment. It is derived from Greek words, *auto-* "self-" and *tome* "severing"; it is a sort of self amputation i.e. a behavioural mechanism whereby an animal sheds or discards one or more of its own appendages. Several insect species are known to autotomize one or both metathoracic legs following tarsal contact with insecticidal deposits.

Autotomy in response to DDT, pyrethriods and several other insecticides have been reported in mosquitoes (*Anopheles maculipennis* Meigen, *Culex pipeus* Linnaeus, *Aedes albopictus*

(Skuse)) and in the moths (*Sitotroga cerealella* (Olivier), *Cheimatobia brumata* (Linnaeus), *Plutella xylostella* (Linnaeus), *Pectinophora gossypiella* (Saunders) It is noteworthy that moths experience little difficulty for walking after they autotomize one or both metathoracic legs. Interestingly, autotomized adult moths could fly, mate and produce viable offspring. *P. xylostella* adults tend to autotomize their metathoracic legs at the trochanter-femur joint after walking on insecticide-treated surface; nearly 74 % moths exposed to fenvalerate residues dropped one or more legs. It was observed that the moths which dropped legs suffered lower mortality and were more likely to recover from knockdown as compared to those who did not drop legs. Thus, the leg autotomy facilitated the moth to avoid the insecticidal poisoning by eliminating the dosage partially before it moves from the legs to the rest of the body.

Feeding behaviour

Feeding is mandatory for the maintenance of all life processes and food consumption rate is primarily an easily quantifiable behavioural end point. On food sources contaminated with sublethal doses of various pesticides, including neonicotinoids, behaviour of many insects may be interfered by the feeding on the insecticide-treated food by repellent, antifeedant, or reduced olfactory capacity effects. Reduced feeding in several phytophagous insects has been demonstrated after exposure to pesticide-treated surfaces. Abnormalities in clean food consumption rate (CFCR) serve as an indicator of physiological stress resulting from exposure to insecticides.

Rrepellency and feeding deterrence are two behavioural effects documented for a number of insecticides including pyrethroids, neonicotinoids, and several plant origin insecticides. Pyrethroids deterred feeding and exhibited repellent effect on several insects and subsequently ingestion of *Bacillus thuringiensis* Berliner could be reduced. Similar effects were also reported on *Leptinotarsa decemlineata* Say. *P. xylostella* populations exposed to permethrin, experienced that irritation and intoxication were responsible for behavioural and physiological response. Both sexes of resistant strain of German cockroach, *Blatella germanica* (Linnaeus.), avoided harbourages treated with cypermethrin and survived the choice-tests but more females than males avoided harbourages treated with chlorpyriphos and survived, but in susceptible strain almost all died. Neither sex avoided harbourages treated with either cypermethrin or chlorpyriphos. A remarkable reduction in feeding in the predatory beetle, *Platynus_assimilis* (Paykull) was recorded with sublethal dose of neonicotinoid insecticide, thiamethoxam. Extracts from *Melia azedarach* Linnaeus. and *Azadirachta indica* A. Juss. demonstrated feeding deterrence towards larvae of *P. xylostella;* the larvae preferred the untreated sides of cabbage leaves for feeding and the food consumption was reduced.

Reproductive behaviour

The ability of female insects for selection of oviposition sites on host plants in response to the chemical stimuli and rejection of the non-host plants, is well documented. Insecticides might also modify their oviposition choice. Insecticides are known to exert a significant impact on mobile adult insects as regards their population dynamics and dispersal behaviour. When the insecticides are applied to control larvae in the field, the adult insects are often exposed to these treatments. However, little is known about the influence of insecticides' residues on oviposition behaviour of the adult insects. Most of the studies are aimed at determining effects of insecticides on larval populations. Through behavioural modifications, these insects often survive toxins in natural and managed systems. Adult avoidance of contact with pyrethroids has been documented in mosquitoes, house flies, cockroaches, and beetles Lepidoptera.

P. xylostella presents a well documented case of behavioural resistance to insecticides through oviposition site selection. Avoidance of treated surfaces by ovipositing females is known to significantly decrease the exposure of their progeny to insecticides. Adults of the moth oviposited to a lesser extent on cabbage leaf-discs and seedlings treated with permethrin. Further, a decrease in the fecundity of *P. xylostella* females was recorded upon treatment with fenvalerate as compared to the females in control treatments. Higher fecundity in resistant females was observed than susceptible ones and further the females from resistant strains laid smaller eggs than susceptible strain. A detailed study conducted at the Punjab Agricultural University, Ludhiana endorsed the earlier observations that the females of *P. xylostella* deposited more eggs on stem near the soil-stem interface than on leaves; obviously a behavioural modification to avoid lethal doses of foliar-applied insecticides in the field. This knowledge of behavioural response by the adult moth to the insecticidal treatments provides ample scope to design strategies for effective and better management of the pest in the field by directing the insecticidal sprays towards the stem bases.

CONCLUSIONS

There has been a rapid progress in the utilisation of semiochemicals in pest management during the last 2-3 decades. Semiochemicals are species specific, non-pollutant and do not cause adverse effect on non-target organisms. Since they are used in minute quantities and kill a large number of insects, they are bound to be economical. This approach is labour saving, since large number of insect pests could be brought from long distances right at the door for being destroyed. They offer an easy means to monitor the building-up of pest populations, and are the only means to keep a surveillance on entry of foreign pests into a country through its ports and airports, with the help of which, development of new pest problems could be checked at the point of entry itself.

Development of semiochemical-based techniques for pest management faces a number of constraints. Quick results cannot be obtained with semiochemicals, so they cannot be employed in short term control measures. Sex pheromones can attract only one sex, the other sex could still be there and continue to inflict the damage. Moreover, semiochemicals for many species of insect pests are still unknown. The wide-scale use of semiochemicals, such as sex pheromones of pink bollworm and tomato pinworm raises the possibility that resistance may develop. Developing long-lived controlled-release dispensers for chemicals that are often highly volatile and susceptible to degradation is difficult. Commercialisation of semiochemical-based products is strongly affected by the size of the potential market, cost of registration and product's price competitiveness. The lack of commercial interest by the major agrochemical firms has clearly hampered the development of semiochemical-based products.

These problems are not insurmountable and could be solved by undertaking further research. There is a need for fundamental research on controlled release systems, which are cheap, non-toxic and biodegradable. Suitable application technology also needs to be developed for these formulations. The relative importance of different communication systems in the life of insects needs investigation. The behavioural responses of insects and effects of various meteorological and physico-chemical factors on these responses need to be elucidated. Registration procedures for these products need to be simplified. Further exploration of all aspects of arthropod chemical ecology should produce new and more elegant tools to manage pest populations in the future.

Work on behavioural physiology of insects and their response to insecticides is meagre. However, comprehensive studies on behavioural modification in response to insecticides amongst insects, need to be undertaken with reference to pest management.

☆☆☆☆☆

CHAPTER 11 HOST PLANT RESISTANCE

INTRODUCTION

Plants with constitutive insect resistance, possess genetically inherited qualities that result in a plant of one cultivar being less damaged than a susceptible plant lacking these qualities. Although insect-resistant plants have been recognised for many years as a sound approach to crop protection, it is only during the last two decades that insect-plant interactions have been extensively investigated from the behavioural, ecological and physiological points of view. Today, there are more than 400 public breeding programmes in 100 countries, which have released more than 8000 modern varieties of major crops. Since the start of the modern breeding programmes, thousands of insect-resistant germplasm have been developed by national research programmes and international research centres. During the last 20 years alone, more than 500 commercial insect-resistant varieties of rice, maize, cotton, sorghum, alfalfa and wheat have been developed and released worldwide. These varieties are grown on million of hectares annually and help the farmers to save billions of dollars in insecticide costs.

The development and use of insect-resistant crop cultivars has led to significant crop improvements in the major food producing areas of the world over the past 50 years. These improvements include increased food production, alleviation of hunger and better human nutrition. One of the most spectacular successes of insect-resistant crops occurred during the green revolution era in tropical Asia during 1960s, when high yielding pest-resistant cultivars of rice were introduced into production agriculture. The cultivation of such cultivars has made significant improvements in the economies of several south and south-east Asian countries, with the result that many countries that were previously food importers, are now food exporters.

HISTORICAL ASPECTS

The first observation on host plant resistance seems to have been made in the third century BC, when Theophrastus recorded differences in susceptibility of plants to fungal pathogens. However, the first documented record of an insect-resistant variety was reported in 1782, when a wheat variety 'Underhill' was found to be resistant to the Hessian fly, *Mayetiola destructor* in New York. Another early instance of an insect-resistant variety is that of the apple variety 'Winter Majetin', found to be resistant to the woolly apple aphid, *Eriosoma lanigerum* in England in the early 1900s (Table 11.1). The scientific investigations into the mechanisms of host plant resistance date back to approximately 100 years, when the first significant economic contribution to host plant resistance in agriculture was made in the late 1800s. The credit for this success goes to the distinguished 10th century entomologist, Charles Valentine Riley, who imported phylloxera-resistant American grape rootstocks to France. The European grape vines were successfully grafted on to the resistant rootstocks to save the French wine industry from destruction by grape phylloxera, *Daktulosphaira(Viteus) vitifoliae.* This insect had destroyed over 1 million ha of vineyards, but the use of resistant rootstocks allowed a quick recovery and is still considered to be the principal method of phylloxera control worldwide.

Table 11.1 Some historical milestones in the development of host plant resistance

Year	Milestone
Third century BC	Theophrastus recorded differences in disease susceptibility among crops.
1782	Wheat variety 'Underhill' reported resistant to Hessian fly, *Mayetiola destructor*.
1817	Sorghum reported to be resistant to grasshoppers, *Melanoplus* spp.
1831	Apple variety 'Winter Majetin' reported resistant to the woolly apple aphid, *Eriosoma lanigerum.*
1885	North American grape rootstocks reported resistant to the grape phylloxera, *Daktulosphaira vitifoliae.*
1935	Cotton reported to be resistant to leafhoppers, *Empoasca* spp.

Source **:** Thacker (2002)

CONCEPT OF HOST PLANT RESISTANCE

Since host plant resistance is the result of interactions between the plant and the insect, it is, therefore, assumed that optimum conditions under which a plant species is grown are also favourable enough for the growth and development of the insect so that the plant species is accepted by the insect. The concept of host plant resistance should, therefore, be viewed by comparing the performance of a variety under optimum conditions for the growth and development of the plant in the absence and presence of insect population capable of causing maximum loss to the host plant.

Painter (1951) described plant resistance as the relative amount of heritable qualities that influence the ultimate degree of damage done by the insect. In practical agriculture, resistance represents the ability of a certain variety to produce a larger crop of good quality than do ordinary varieties at the same level of insect population. Maxwell *et al.* (1972) extended the definition of Painter (1951) by considering level of insect infestation and environmental conditions. According to them, resistance is those heritable characteristics possessed by the plant which influence the ultimate degree of damage done by the insect. From a practical point of view, resistance is the ability of certain variety to produce larger yield of good quality than other varieties at the same initial level of infestation and under similar environmental conditions.

According to Kogan (1994) resistance to insects is the inheritable property that enables a plant to restrain the growth of insect populations or to recover from injury caused by populations that were not restrained. Inhibition of population growth generally derives from the biochemical and morphological characteristics of a plant which affect the behaviour or the metabolism of insects so as to reduce the relative degree of damage these insects can potentially cause.

Most of the attempts to explain the concept of host plant resistance are from farmer's point of view, that too ignoring different heritable potentialities of the host plant in the absence of insect infestation. In order to overcome this limitation host plant resistance has been defined as the heritable qualities of a cultivar to counteract the activities of insects so as to cause minimum per cent reduction in yield as compared to other cultivars of the same species under similar conditions (Dhaliwal *et al.,* 1993). The emphasis here is not on the absolute yield pattern but on the proportional decrease in yield among the cultivars in the presence of insect vis-a-vis the yield obtained in its absence. It means that a cultivar may yield poor but carries the genes for resistance and, on the contrary, a cultivar may yield good without having any genes for resistance. Moreover, it is not always true that resistance is manifested only in the form of greater yields because there can be stage or age specific characteristics imparting resistance.

There are four major characteristics by which resistance can be assessed (Panda and Khush, 1995):

- Resistance is heritable and controlled by one or more major genes.
- Resistance is relative and can be measured only by comparing with a susceptible cultivar of the same species.
- Resistance is measurable and its magnitude can be determined quantitatively (by insect establishment) and qualitatively (by analysis of the standard scoring systems).
- Resistance is variable and can be modified by abiotic and biotic components of the environment.

TYPES OF RESISTANCE

Host plant resistance to insects may be divided into different categories based on several parameters :

(*i*) Intensity of resistance. Interactions between host plants and insects are spread over a wide spectrum of intensity. In terms of the host plant, lesser the population of the insect and/ or lesser the damage they cause to the plant, more resistant the plant is likely to be. On the other hand, from the point of view of the insect, interaction varies from totally unsuitable host to completely suitable for growth and development of the insect. Therefore, intensity of resistance is a relative term and should be discussed in relation to a susceptible cultivar of the same species. Painter (1951) used the following scale to classify degrees of resistance based on intensity :

(*a*) ***Immunity***. An immune variety is one which a specific insect will never consume or injure under any known conditions. There are thus few, if any, cultivars immune to the attack of specific insects which are, otherwise, known to attack cultivars of the same species.

(*b*) ***High resistance.*** A variety with high resistance is one which possesses qualities resulting in small damage by a specific insect under a given set of conditions.

(*c*) ***Low resistance.*** A low level of resistance indicates the possession of qualities which cause a variety to show lesser damage or infestation by an insect than the average for the crop under consideration.

(*d*) ***Susceptibility.*** A susceptible variety is one which shows average or more than average damage caused by an insect.

(*e*) ***High susceptibility.*** A variety shows high susceptibility when much more than average damage is done by the insect under consideration.

These terms are relevant to express resistance vis-a-vis screening of varieties under field conditions and have nothing to do with the mechanism of resistance. An intermediate level of resistance is sometimes referred to as ***moderate resistance***.

(*ii*) Ecological resistance. Sometimes a plant or a variety may be classified as resistant due to unfavourable environmental conditions for the insect and no heritable trait is involved. In this case, there may be differential impact of the environment on the host and on the insect which affects the expression of resistance. Painter (1951) called this type of resistance as ***pseudoresistance***, which refers to apparent resistance resulting from transitory characters in potentially susceptible host plants. Pseudoresistance is generally classified into three broad categories :

(*a*) ***Host evasion.*** Under some circumstances, a host may pass through the most susceptible stage quickly or at a time when number of insects is less. Some varieties evade injury by early maturing. Late planting of an early maturing variety or other special experiments will indicate whether true resistance is present or not.

(*b*) ***Induced resistance.*** This term may be used for increase in resistance temporarily as a result of some changed conditions of plants or environment, such as change in the amount of water or nutrient status of the soil. Such induced resis-tance may be of great significance especially in the field of horticulture, but should not be confused with inherent differenc-es in resistance which exist between varieties or individual plants.

(*c*) ***Escape.*** Escape refers to the absence of infestation or injury to the host plant because of transitory circumstances such as incomplete infestation. Thus, an uninfested plant located in a susceptible population does not necessarily mean that it is resistant. Even under very heavy infestation, susceptible plants will occasionally escape and only studies of their progenies will establish their true expression of resistance or susceptibility.

The terms host evasion and escape seem to be synonyms but critical analysis reveals that host evasion pertains to whole population of the host and insect is absent or insignificant while escape pertains to one or a few individuals in the presence of insects causing damage to other plants.

(*iii*) Evolutionary concept. Resistance to an insect is evolved either due to long host plant and insect association at the gene centers or due to pleiotropic effects of genes which are present as a result of selective forces unrelated to the insect. Based on these factors host plant resistance to insects can be divided into sympatric and allopatric resistance.

(*a*) ***Sympatric resistance.*** Sympatric resistance may be defined as those heritable qualities possessed by an organism which in-fluence the ultimate degree of damage done by a parasitic species having a prior continuous, coevolutionary history with that species of organism. This type of resistance evolves at original home of plants and insects. Association at the gene centres results in natural selection for resistance in plants. The resis-tance is evolved as a result of gene-for-gene nature of coevolu-tion of plants and herbivores.

(*b*) ***Allopatric resistance.***Allopatric resistance may be defined as those heritable qualities possessed by an organism which influence the ultimate degree of damage done by a parasitic species having no prior continuous coevolutionary history with that species of organism. The resistance to insects in plants is evolved in the absence of insects to which the host is resistant. Allopatric resistance is not the result of coevolution, but rather due to fortuitous, pleiotropic effects of genes which are present as a result of selective forces unrelated to the pest insect.

Though not essential, in general, sympatric resistance is governed by major genes and allopatric resistance is polygenic in nature.

(*iv*) Genetic resistance. Genetic resistance may be grouped under various categories:

A. Number of Genes

(*a*) ***Monogenic resistance.***When resistance is controlled by single gene, it is called monogenic resistance.

(*b*) ***Oligogenic resistance.*** When resistance is governed by few genes, it is called oligogenic resistance.

(*c*) ***Polygenic resistance.***When resistance is governed by many genes, it is referred to as polygenic resistance. The term horizontal resistance is also used to denote the resistance governed by polygenes.

B. Major or Minor Genes

(*a*) ***Major gene resistance.*** The resistance controlled by one (monogenic) or a few (oligogenic) major genes is called major gene resistance. This is also called ***vertical resistance***. Major genes have a strong effect and these can be identified easily.

(*b*) ***Minor gene resistance.*** When resistance is controlled by a number of minor genes, each contributing a small effect, it is called minor gene resistance. This is also referred to as ***horizontal resistance***. In certain crops, the cumulative effect of minor genes is expressed when the plants grow older and this phenomenon is termed as ***adult resistance***, ***mature resistance*** or ***field resistance***.

C. Biotype Reaction

(*a*) ***Vertical resistance.***This type of resistance is effective against certain specific biotypes of the insect but not against others. It is also called ***specific resistance.*** Vertical resis-tance is qualitative as the frequency distribution of resis-tance and susceptible plants is discontinuous.

(*b*) ***Horizontal resistance.***This type of resistance is effective against all the known biotypes of the insect. It is also called ***nonspecific resistance***. Horizontal resistance is quantitative as the degree of resistance depends on the number of minor genes each contributing a small effect.

(*v*) Multitrophic interactions. Interaction among host plants, insect pests and their natural enemies (tritrophic interaction) leads to effective defense and attack at each level (Fig. 11.1). On this basis, two types of plant resistance have been recognised.

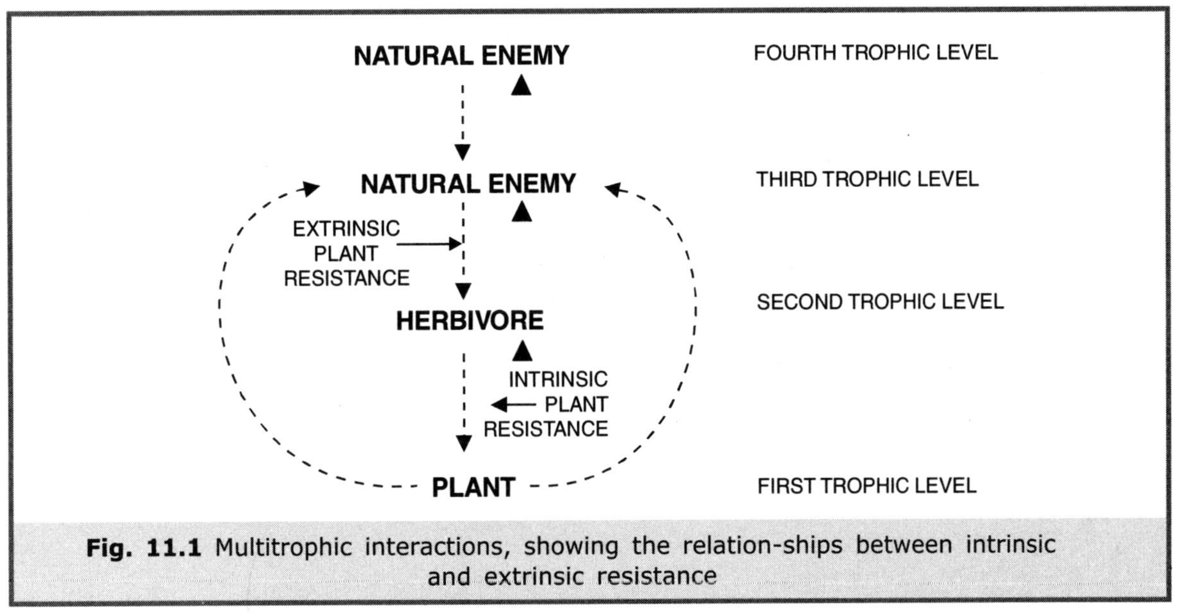

Fig. 11.1 Multitrophic interactions, showing the relation-ships between intrinsic and extrinsic resistance

(*a*) ***Intrinsic resistance.*** Here the plant alone produces defense through physical means (trichomes or toughness) or through production of chemicals (toxins or digestibility reducers) or both (glandular trichomes or resins).

(*b*) ***Extrinsic resistance.*** Here the natural enemies (third trophic level) of insect pests (second trophic level) benefit the host plants (first trophic level) by reducing the pest abundance.

MECHANISMS OF RESISTANCE

Painter (1951) grouped mechanisms of resistance into three main categories, viz. nonpreference, antibiosis and tolerance. As the term ***nonpreference*** pertains to the insect reaction and not to the host plant characteristics, the term ***antixenosis*** was proposed to describe the host plant properties responsible for nonpreference.

Antixenosis

Antixenosis refers to the resistance mechanism employed by host plant to deter or reduce colonization by insects. The plants may deter the insects from feeding, oviposition and/or seeking shelter, and the insects are unable to colonize. Antixenosis signifies that the plant is considered an undesirable or a bad host. Antixenosis may result from certain morphological characteristics or the presence of allelochemicals in the host plant. Antixenosis may represent one or more breaks in the chain of responses leading to oviposition or feeding. These breaks may be due to (*i*) the absence of an arrestant or attractant, (*ii*) the presence of a repellent, or (*iii*) an unfavourable balance between an attractant and a repellent.

Under certain circumstances antixenosis can be quite important, especially when light infestations cause severe damage, *e.g.* infestation by insect vectors of plant diseases or insects which sever growing parts or peduncles of the plants such as stem borer infestation resulting in white heads. In field plantings, antixenotic varieties frequently escape infestation and even when insects are caged on nonpreferred hosts, they lay fewer eggs and thereby develop smaller populations than those caged on susceptible varieties.

Antibiosis

Antibiosis refers to the adverse effect of the host plant on the biology (survival, development or reproduction) of the insects and their progeny infesting it. All these adverse physiological effects of permanent or temporary nature following ingestion of a plant by an insect are attributed to antibiosis. The insects feeding on resistant plants may manifest antibiotic symptoms varying from acute or lethal to subchronic or very mild. A number of secondary plant substances are most often associated with antibiosis.

The most commonly observed symptoms in insects include adverse effects on the nutritional physiology of the insect including consumption, assimilation, utilization and subsequent allocation for reproduction. This is manifested by larval death in first few instars, abnormal growth rates, disruption in conversion of ingested food, decline in size and weight of larvae or nymphs, prolongation of the larval period, failure to pupate, failure of adults to emerge from pupae, abnormal adults, inability to concentrate food reserves followed by failure to hibernate, decreased fecundity, reduction in fertility, restlessness and abnormal behaviour. These symptoms may appear due to various physiological processes, viz. presence of toxic substances, absence or insufficient amount of essential nutrients, nutrient imbalances, presence of antimetabolites and enzymes adversely affecting food digestion and utilization of nutrients.

Tolerance

Tolerance refers to the ability of the host plant to withstand an insect population sufficient to damage severely the susceptible plants. It is generally attributable to plant vigour, regrowth of damaged tissues, resistance to lodging, ability to produce additional branches, utilization of non-vital parts by insects and compensation by growth of neighbouring plants. However, tolerance has no adverse effect on the insect infestation for longer periods without loss in yield or quality than the susceptible varieties and enables them to frequently escape insect damage through compensation by the plants. As tolerance is not likely to provide a high level of resistance, it could be useful in combination with other mechanisms of resistance.

Tolerance is useful in pest management programmes due to certain distinct advantages:

- Tolerant varieties have a higher economic threshold level than the susceptible varieties and hence require less insecticide application and promote biocontrol.
- Tolerant varieties do not depress insect populations nor do they provide any selection pressure on the insect and thus are useful in preventing the development of insect biotypes.
- In varieties with a combination of three mechanisms of resistance, tolerance increases yield stability by providing at least a moderate level of resistance, when vertical genes providing a high level of resistance through antixenosis and antibiosis succumb to the new biotype.

Although the above widely recognised classification of mechanisms appears to provide a generally acceptable breakdown of the phenomenon of host plant resistance, however, under certain circumstances, some overlap may occur between antixenosis and antibiosis, and these may not be clearly separated from each other due to the presence of extreme deterrent chemicals and/or physical factor(s) in the plant cultivar. In other words, the toxins and deterrent chemicals in the plant are sometimes difficult to distinguish. The same may be the case of certain morphological characteristics of the plant such as leaf trichomes or tissue toughness. Moreover, there are often overlaps between the morphological and biochemical bases of resistance.

Sometimes it becomes difficult to separate the two mechanisms unless the insect-plant relationship is fully examined. The exact mechanism of resistance depends upon the particular point in the sequence of insect host finding, location and acceptance Antixenosis functions by altering the olfactory, visual, tactile and gustatory plant cues, used by an insect to successfully locate a host plant, feed on it and/or use it as a habitat for reproduction. Antibiosis works by causing insect mortality or delayed development, after contact with or ingestion of plant tissues, containing the morphological or allelochemical defences. In other words, antixenosis refers to undesirability, *i.e.* avoidance by the insect, whereas antibiosis refers to unsuitability, *i.e.* adverse effects on the insect after feeding on the host plant. For example, *Eruca sativa* (*taramira*) is not a preferred host of mustard aphid, *Lipaphis erysimi*. The growth and development of this insect was observed to be slower on *E. sativa* as compared to that on *Brassica* species in confinement. The mechanism appeared to be antibiosis, but it has been found that the poor development was due to reduced feed uptake because of the presence of certain allelochemicals in *E. sativa*, indicating antixenosis.

BASES OF RESISTANCE

A number of plant characteristics are known to render the cultivars less suitable or unsuitable for feeding, oviposition and development of insect pests. Broadly, these characteristics can be classified into two categories, *i.e.* biophysical and biochemical.

Biophysical Bases

The plant resistance is controlled by several morphological factors like remote factors, *e.g.* colour, shape, size, etc. and close range or contact factors, i.e. thickening of cell walls and rapid proliferation of plant tissues, solidness and other stem characteristics, trichomes, incrustation of minerals in cuticle, surface waxes and anatomical adaptations of organs. The resistance mechanisms related to morphological or structural plant features that impair normal feeding or oviposition by insects or contribute to the action of other mortality factors are together called ***phenetic resistance***. The morphological characteristics of the host plant may also influence the nutrition of the insect by limiting the amount of feeding due to shape, colour or texture which may limit the ingestion of the nutritive material and influence the digestibility and utilization of food by the insect.

A general association between resistance to stem borers and several morphological and anatomical characteristics of the rice plant, viz. tightly wrapped leaf sheaths, closely packed vascular bundles, thick sclerenchyma and high silica content has been recorded. The solid stem of Rescue and other wheat varieties is considered to be the major cause of resistance to the wheat stem saw fly, *Cephus cinctus*. The sawfly eggs tend to be mechanically damaged and desiccated in resistant varieties and the hatching larvae are restricted in their movements. The minimum stem solidness required to obtain field control of sawfly has been established.

A highly significant association between resistance to brown planthopper, *Nilaparvata lugens* and red pericarp in rice has been found. There is a highly significant and positive correlation between leaf colour and percentage of dead hearts caused by shoot fly, *Atherigona soccata* on sorghum, and negative and highly significant correlation with leaf length/breadth ratio, plant height, glossiness of leaves, trichome density and length. The stem tips of cotton varieties tolerant to aphid, *Aphis gossypii* were nearly twice as stiff as those of susceptible cultivars and, therefore, indicated hardness, for piercing the proboscis into the stems of tolerant strains, as one of the main causes for nonpreference by aphids. The resistance in sorghum to the sorghum midge, *Contarinia sorghicola* was positively correlated with the size of floral parts, viz. glume, lemma, palea, lodicule, anther, style and stigma.

Many leafhoppers are unable to establish on plants whose epidermis is covered with a thick layer of long cellulose hairs. Pubescent varieties of soybean are known to be highly resistant to potato leafhopper, *Empoasca fabae*. Trichomes affect the behaviour, oviposition, and growth and development of a number of insect pests. Okra varieties resistant to *Amrasca biguttula* had more and longer hairs on mid rib and lamina of leaves than susceptible varieties. Insect resistance was influenced by the number and length of hairs rather than their density.

The resistance in clones of beach strawberry to black vine weevil, *Otiorhynchus sulcatus* was found to be due to dense covering of simple hairs on the abaxial surface of the leaves. Trichomes on the pods of *Vignavexillata* partly accounted for resistance to pod-sucking bug, *Clavigralla tomentosicollis*. Pubescence in sugarcane adversely affected oviposition and larval movement by the pyralid, *Diatraea saccharalis*. However, tobacco budworm, *Heliothis virescens* moths oviposited twice as many eggs on the hairy lines as on glabrous cottons. Leaf hairs also do not alter attack by the saddle gallmidge, *Haplodiplosis marginata* on wheat. Surface wax is an important mechanism of resistance in rice to *N. lugens*. The increased activity of *N. lugens* on IR46 over IR22 and IR62 was shown to be due to chemical composition of the surface wax. The effect is caused by the hydrocarbon and carbonyl-containing fractions of the wax of IR46.

The frego bract in cotton helps to reduce the number of eggs laid and subsequent damage by boll weevil, *Anthonomus grandis*. The bracts of frego cotton are narrow, elongated, twisted and flaring away from the bud or boll. In field experiments, frego-bract cotton showed 50 per cent less damage from oviposition than normal cottons. Boll weevils showed eight times as much plant-to-plant movement, required twice as much time for feeding and oviposition puncture, and spent much less time on squares of frego-bract cotton. Due to their restless wandering over the plants, weevils are more likely to come in contact with insecticide residues and exposure to natural enemies.

Biochemical Bases

A wide array of chemical substances including inorganic chemicals, primary and intermediary metabolites and secondary substances are known to impart resistance to a wide variety of insect pests. Broadly, the chemicals imparting resistance to insects can be classified into two main categories :

Nutrients. The host plant may be deficient in certain nutritional elements required by the insect and hence prove resistant. The nutritionally deficient plant may cause antibiotic and antixenotic effects on the insect. The antibiosis may result from the absence of certain nutritional substances in the host plant, deficiency of some nutritional materials and/or imbalance of available nutrients. Pea varieties resistant to pea aphid, *Acyrthosiphon pisum* were generally deficient in amino acids and hence were less nutritious than the susceptible varieties. Resistance in bean varieties to Mexican bean beetle, *Epilachna varivestis* has been attributed to low amounts of carbohydrates and reducing sugars. The resistance of Canby raspberry to the aphid, *Amphorophora agathonica* is related to the deficiency of both solids (largely sugars) and nitrogenous compounds in the sap.

The occurrence of asparagine in minute quantities in rice variety Mudgo was considered to be the primary cause of resistance to *N. lugens*. Young females of *N. lugens* caged on Mudgo had underdeveloped ovaries containing few eggs while those caged on susceptible varieties had normal ovaries full of eggs. It has been suggested that the selection for low total free amino acids and high surface wax may lead to increase in resistance to cereal aphids in barley. Most of the resistant lines of oats and barley to *Rhopalosiphum padi* contained less asparagine, but higher amount of glutamic acid. The basis of resistance in maize to larval leaf-feeding of fall armyworm, *Spodoptera frugiperda* has been explained in terms of amino acids. Although ratios of essential amino acids in susceptible and resistant lines were similar, there were differences in non-essential amino acids particularly aspartic acid, which was higher in resistant lines.

Allelochemicals. Allelochemicals are non-nutritional chemicals produced by an organism of one species and affect the growth, health, behaviour or population biology of individuals of another species. The allelochemicals have been broadly classified into two categories, viz. (a) ***Allomones***-tending to confer an adaptive advantage to the producing organism, *i.e.* the host plant, and (b) ***Kairomones***-tending to give an adaptive advantage to the receiving organism, *i.e.* the phytophagous insect. The involvement of allelochemicals in various types of insect-plant relationships can determine the status of a plant either as a host (presence of kairomone) and non-host (absence of kairomone) or as resistant (presence of allomone) and susceptible (absence of allomone). Allomones are considered to be a major factor of insect resistance in plants and these have been exploited to increase levels of resistance in several agricultural crops.

One of the most classical examples of exploitation of allelochemicals in an economic crop is that of resistance in maize to first generation of the European corn borer, *Ostrinia nubilalis*. The chemical compound resistance factor A (RFA), identified as MBOA

(6-methoxy-2- benzoxazolinone), appears to function as a repellent and/or feeding deterrent. MBOA does not exist in uninjured corn tissues, but DIMBOA (2, 4-dihydroxy-7-methoxy-1, 4-benzoxazin- 3-one) in its glucoside form is present in uninjured corn leaves. Injury to the plant tissue due to larval feeding results in the enzymatic conversion of the glucoside to the aglycone DIMBOA (Fig. 11.2). DIMBOA decomposes in a reaction, via intermediates, to yield MBOA and formic acid. The yield of MBOA from the decomposition of DIMBOA increases with increase in pH of the midgut of most lepidopteran larvae. It has been shown that DIMBOA is a resistance factor in maize to first brood borers. A significant correlation existed between the concentration of DIMBOA in the leaf whorl tissue and resistance to first brood borers. The chemical analysis of plant tissue for DIMBOA was employed as a method of screening for resistance to the first brood corn borer larvae. A correlation between the DIMBOA content of maize varieties and resistance to *O. nubilalis* larvae has been established and it has been suggested that it could form the basis of a rapid method for assessing resistance. In fact, a high correlation between leaf damage caused by first generation *O. nubilalis* and MBOA content in midwhorl leaves of maize has been found.

Another factor in corn toxic to the southwestern corn borer, *Diatraea grandiosella* has been identified as 2-dihydroxy-4, 7-dimethoxy-1, 4-benzoxazin-3-one (N-O-ME-DIMBOA). It is present in the corn whorl surface waxes at a higher concentration than DIMBOA or MBOA. This compound may have some role in resistance of corn to this pest because the total surface wax content is higher in resistant than in susceptible lines.

The major allelochemical imparting resistance to several insect pests in cotton has been found to be gossypol (8, 8'- dicarboxyaldehyde-1, 1,' 7, 7'-hexahydroxy -5, 5' diisopropyl-3, 3'-

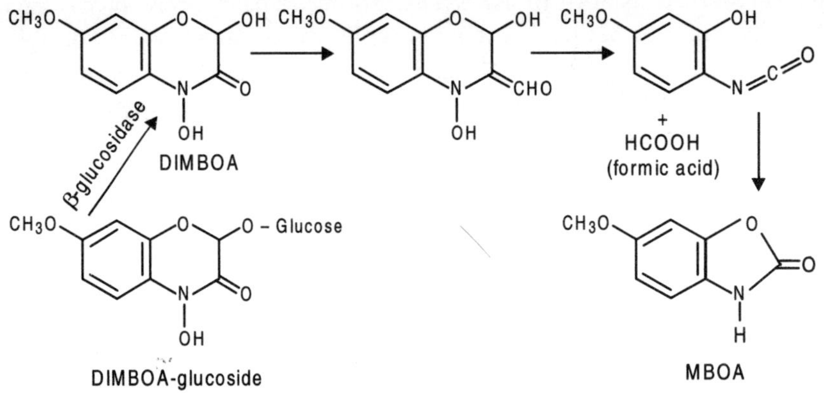

Fig. 11.2 Chemical degradation of DIMBOA glucoside

dimethyl-2, 2'-binaphthalene) (Fig. 11.3A), which occurs in much higher quantities in glanded than in glandless varieties. The survival and development of major insect pests of cotton on high gossypol containing varieties is much less as compared to those containing lower amounts of gossypol. The efforts to transfer high gossypol into good agronomic varieties have met with success and some good agronomic types with high gossypol content have been developed.

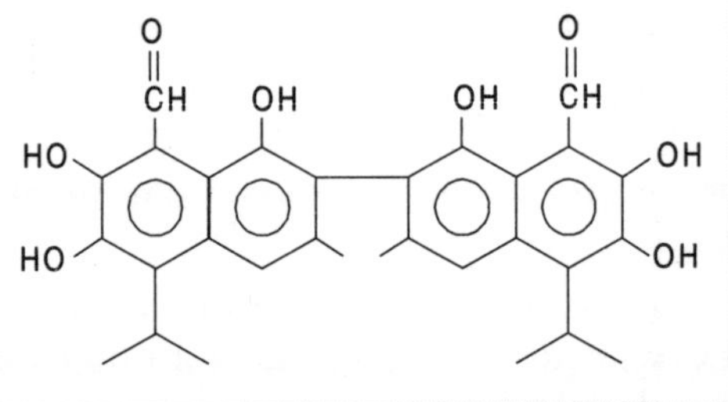

Fig. 11.3 Structure of gossypol and cucurbitacin B

The cucurbitacins are a group of about 20 tetracyclic triterpenoids isolated from the family Cucurbitaceae. These are extremely bitter and are typically found in the roots, stems, cotyledons, leaves and fruits of the plants of the Cucurbitaceae. Cucurbitacin B is the predominant compound (Fig. 11.3B) and is found in about 91 per cent of all the species characterized. Cucurbitacins are feeding deterrents for a number of arthropods including cucumber leaf beetles, *Phyllotreta* spp., *Phaedon* spp. and *Cerotoma trifurcata* ; stem borer, *Margonia hyalinata*; and red spider mites. In contrast, beetles of the tribe Luperini, such as the spotted cucumber beetle, *Diabrotica undecimpunctata howardi* are immune to the toxic effects of dietary cucurbitacins. Cucurbitacin B acts as a powerful host-recognition cue for luperine beetles and stimulates feeding even at very low concentrations.

The resistance of an isogenic strain of barley to greenbug, *Schizaphis graminum*, was reported to be governed by benzyl alcohol which was also found in the resistant parent strain Omugi but absent in the susceptible parent Rogers. Gramine (N, N-dimethyl-3-aminomethylindole) has been suggested to be one of the factors responsible for resistance of barley seedlings to *R. padi*.

The same plant allelochemical may play the dual role of repellent as well as attractant to different insects. For example, glucosinolates and their hydrolysis products are highly toxic to the unadapted lepidopteran, the swallowtail butterfly, *Papilio polyxenes*, but are a feeding stimulant and provide host plant recognition clues for adapted insect, *Pieris brassicae*. Such a phenomenon suggests that a chemical messenger can, therefore, be a 'double agent' (Table 11.2). Hence, classification of a chemical as a repellent, deterrent, feeding suppressant, toxin or digestibility reducer, may be situation and dose-dependent.

Table 11.2 Dual role of allelochemicals in insect-plant interactions

Allelochemical	Insect reaction	
	Stimulant	Deterrent
Cucurbitacin	*Diabrotica undecimpunctata*	*Epilachna tredecimnotata*
Cucurbitacin E and I	Diabroticites	*Phyllotreta nemorum*
Cyanogenic glycoside	*Epilachna varivestris*	Many phytophagous insects
Furanocoumarins	*Papilio polyxenes*	*Spodoptera exempta*, *S. litura*, *S.eridania*
Glucosinolate	*Pieris rapae*	*P. polyxenes*
Gossypol	*Anthonomus grandis*	*Helicoverpa zea*
Iridoid	*Euphydryas editha*	*Locusta migratoria*
Lignin	*Bootettix argentalus*	*Ligurotettix coquilletti*
Lupanin	*Macrosiphon albifons*	*Acyrthosiphon pisum*
Tannin	*Anacridium melanorhodon*	*H. zea*
Tomatine	*Pieris brassicae*	*Leptinotarsa decemlineata*, *Empoasca fabae*

***Source* :** Panda and Khush (1995)

The defensive role of glandular trichomes of certain members of the Solanaceae plants against herbivorous insects has been studied. In certain wild potato species (*Solanum polyadenium*, *S. berthaultii* and *S. tariyense*), an exudate is discharged from the four-lobed head of the glandular hairs when aphids, *Myzus persicae* or *Macrosiphum euphorbiae* mechanically rupture the cell wall. On contact with atmospheric oxygen, the clear, water-soluble exudate is changed into an insoluble black substance that hardens around the aphid's tarsi and seriously impedes its movement. Further accumulation of glandular material sticks the aphid firmly to the plant and starvation leads to death.

The nature and effect of exudates of trichomes against a number of insect pests have been elucidated. The trichomes exude a sticky substance, then sesquiterpenoids are released which disturb the insect and causes agitated movements. Subsequently, polyphenoloxidase and phenolic substrate react to form quinones. These events lead to insect immobilisation, cessation of feeding and ultimately death of the insect. The methyl ketones, 2-tridecanone and 2-undecanone occur in the tips of glandular trichomes of the wild tomato, *Lycopersicon hirsutum* f. *glabaratum*, that is resistant to the tomato pests, *Manduca sexta* and *H. zea*. Incorporation of these compounds into artificial diets fed to the larvae of these species caused mortality and pupal malformations.

Usually, a complex of allelochemicals is involved in imparting resistance to insect pests in agricultural crops. The substances like gallic, vanillic and salicylic acids, besides resorcinol, phloroglucinol and gossypol in cotton cultivars have been known to impart resistance against *Helicoverpa armigera* and *Spodoptera litura*. A number of chemical substances including phenols, alkaloids and methyl ketones have been demonstrated to be involved in host plant resistance in *Lycopersicon* to several insect pests. The growth of tobacco budworm larvae is known to be retarded by several compounds, viz. gossypol and related compounds, several flavonoids, catechin condensed tannins, cyanidin, delphinidin and their glucosides. A profile of components including volatiles, amino acids and *trans*-aconitic acid are involved in host plant resistance in rice to several insect pests. One of these chemicals, pentadecanal, has been isolated from TKM 6, a *Chilo suppressalis* resistant rice variety. This chemical has exhibited semiochemical properties against several agricultural insect pests.

Nutrient-allelochemical interactions. Allelochemicals interact with nutrients in a number of ways that are deleterious to the survival of herbivores. Oak leaf tannins markedly inhibit the growth of the winter moth larvae, *Operophtera brumata* because of the formation of relatively indigestible complexes with the available proteins, thus reducing the rate of assimilation of dietary N. The glucosinolates in the leaf tissues of the Cruciferae interfere with assimilation of biomass and/or N, because glucosinolates are known to be gut irritants in mammals and reduce digestibility in non-adapted insects. The feeding and growth inhibition of *Ostrinia nubilalis* seems to be mediated partly by a mixture of cyclic hydroxamates. It is likely that a combination of nutritional and allelochemical factors has mediated leaf-feeding and stalk-boring resistance to *O. nubilalis*.

GENETICS OF RESISTANCE

Information on the number of genes involved in resistance of plants to a particular insect pest, has great practical significance in identifying diverse sources of resistance and using these for breeding broad-based resistant plants. The inheritance of Hessian fly resistance in wheat has been most thoroughly investigated and there are 19 genes identified that are dominant or partially dominant for resistance. The resistance to first brood European corn borer in corn inbreds has been found to result from one gene pair; two or more gene action controlling resistance has been variously reported as dominant or partially dominant, primarily additive or having a significant epistatic component. The inheritance of resistance in corn to the corn leaf aphid, *Rhopalosiphum maidis*, is determined by many genes with varying degrees of dominance and additivity.

The resistance to brown planthopper and green leafhopper in rice is simply inherited. Four dominant (*Bph-1, Bph-4, Bph-6* and *Bph-9*) and five recessive (*bph-2, bph-4, bph-5, bph-7* and *bph-8*) genes for brown planthopper resistance have been identified from rice varieties. Ten dominant (*Glh-1, Glh-2, Glh-3, Glh-5, Glh-6, Glh-7, Glh-9(t), Glh-11(t), Glh-12(t)* and *Glh-13(t)*), and three recessive (*glh-4, glh-8* and *glh-10*) genes for green leafhopper resistance have also been identified. The resis-tance to whitebacked planthopper, *Sogatella furcifera*, has been found to be governed by four dominant genes designated as *Wbph-1, Wbph-2, Wbph-3* and *Wbph-5*, and one recessive gene *wbph-4*. The resistance to gall midge in rice is attributed to seven dominant genes (*Gm-1, Gm-2, Gm-4, Gm-5, Gm-6, Gm-7(t)* and *Gm-8(t)*, and one recessive gene (*gm*-3). The resistance to Hessian fly in wheat is governed by 32 dominant genes (*H*-1 to *H*-32) and in barley to three dominant genes (*Hf, Hf*-1 and *Hf*-2).

The significance of genetic analysis of resistance is evident from the success of host plant resistance programme in rice for the brown planthopper (BPH). The first BPH-resistant variety with *Bph-1* gene, IR26, was released in 1973. It was widely accepted in Indonesia, Philippines and Vietnam, but becam susceptible in 1976-77 due to the development of biotype 2 of BPH. IR36 with *bph-2* gene replaced IR26 and is still widely grown. Meanwhile, when a biotype capable of damaging IR36 appeared in small pockets in the Philippines and Indonesia, IR56 and IR60 with *Bph-3* gene for resistance were released. IR66 with *bph-4* gene for resistance was released in 1987, while IR68, IR70, IR72 and IR74, all with *Bph-3* gene were released in 1988. These varieties are now extensively grown in tropical and subtropical rice-growing countries.

BREEDING PLANTS FOR INSECT RESISTANCE

Conventional breeding programmes for insect resistance, generally require 10-15 years for developing resistant varieties. Because this method of development is so long, the emphasis on these programmes has been to make the process as efficient as possible. The most conventional plant breeding for insect resistance is carried out by universities and public research institutes. The long-term commitment required has been unattractive to private commercial companies.

The first requirement of a breeding programme is the need and potential for plant resistance to insects within the pest management and cropping system. This will determine the type and level of resistance required, which in turn, will depend upon the pest biology and the production and commercial requirements for the crop. For example, if the insect feeds directly on a cosmetically important part of the plant, either antixenosis or a high level of antibiosis to prevent noticeable damage to the commercial product will be required. If, however, the insect population takes several generations on the crop to build-up to the economic threshold levels, moderate levels of any of the three types of resistance would be sufficient.

Development and standardization of screening techniques is pre-requisite to any effective resistance breeding programme. Information about the periods of greatest insect activity and hot spots is the first step to initiate work on resistance screening. Other effective means of augmenting insect populations, viz. delayed plantings and use of infester rows of a susceptible cultivar may also be employed. These techniques have been effectively used for gall midge, planthoppers and leafhoppers in rice; shoot fly, stem borers, midge and head bugs in sorghum; leafminer and jassids in groundnut; pod borer and pod fly in pigeonpea; pod borer in chickpea; shootfly in pearlmillet, etc.

Screening for insect resistance under natural conditions is a long term process. Because of variations in insect populations in space and time, it is difficult to identify reliable and stable sources of resistance under natural multi-choice field conditions. In order to overcome these problems, it is essential to develop and standardize multi- or no-choice screening techniques where test cultivars can be subjected to uniform insect pressure at the most susceptible stage of the crop. This is done by placing relatively immobile stages, such as eggs, young larvae or apterous adults directly on the plants. These insects may be collected from the field, but more often, they are reared in the laboratory/screenhouse on susceptible host plants or artificial media. The results of the test are then rated in a standard manner, evaluating either the damage done by the insect to the plant or the effects of the plant on the attraction, growth, survival or reproduction of the insect. Such techniques have been developed in India for leafhoppers, gall midge and borers in rice; shoot fly, stem borer, midge and head bugs in sorghum; armyworm in pearlmillet and sorghum; leaf miner, aphids, jassids and *Spodoptera* in groundnut; pod borer in chickpea and pigeonpea; stem borer in maize, etc.

Once source of resistance has been identified, further information is needed to be able to transfer resistance through plant breeding techniques. The development of a resistant variety is based on the breeding system of the crop plant (self-pollinated, cross-pollinated or clonally propagated), and the genetic basis of resistance. Resistance may be based on one, a few or many genes, and these may be linked structurally or may interact functionally, with each other or with genes for other important traits.

The traditional breeding approaches have generally aimed at developing durable major gene resistance to single dominant pest, based on some morphological/phenological/biochemical characteristics of the host plant. This type of resistance is known as vertical resistance in contrast to horizontal resistance which confers resistance against a broad range of genotypes but has low heritability. Horizontal resistance is literally ubiquitous, but due to traditional breeding techniques, it is often reduced to such a degree that it confers only a low level of protection against insect infestation. One of the reasons for this is that most breeding for plant yield and quality is carried out under the protection of insecticide application. In the absence of selection pressure (*i.e.* presence of the pest), horizontal resistance is lost. However, even partial horizontal resistance offers another advantage in the form of reduced selection pressure on a pest so that chances of breaking down of resistance are minimum. This form of resistance is, therefore, the most desirable from the point of view of IPM because of its stability.

Considerable progress has been made in India in identification and utilization of resistance for crop pests (Table 11.3). Resistance breeding programmes are underway only for a few crop pests. Insect resistance should be one of the major components in the development and release of new crop varieties. Insect resistant varieties have been developed for rice (gall midge, stem borers, brown planthopper and green leafhopper), maize (maize stem borer and pink stem borer), sorghum (shoot fly and midge), pigeonpea (*Helicoverpa*), groundnut (*Spodoptera,* leafminer, jassids and thrips), rapeseed and mustard (aphid), cotton (bollworms and jassids), sugarcane (top borer, scale insects, mealy bugs and whitefly), tobacco (stem borer and *Spodoptera*) and pea (pod borer and leafminer), and these are being currently grown by farmers in India (Dhaliwal and Singh, 2005).

Table 11.3 Insect-resistant varieties of different crops released in India

Crop	Insect	Varieties
Rice	Gall midge	Phalguna, Shakti, Surekha, Kakatiya, Kunti
	Stem borer	Ratna, Sasyasree, Saket, Vikas
	Brown planthopper	Co42, Co46, Jyothi, Rasmi, Pratibha
	Green leafhopper	IR20, Vani, Vikram
	Whitebacked planthopper	AR 133, Amelbero, HKR 120, HKR 126
Maize	Maize borer	Ganga 9, Ganga Safed 2
	Pink stem borer	Deccan 101, 103
Sorghum	Shoot fly	M35-1, SPV 491, Swati
	Midge	ICSV 197, ICSV 745
Mung	Galerucid beetle	Jawahar 45, Gujarat 1, PIMS 4
Chickpea	Pod borer	C235, PantG 114, Pusa 261, Vijay, Vishal
Groundnut	Tobacco caterpillar & leaf miner	ICGV 86031, FDRS-10
	Jassids & thrips	M13, ICG5043
Rapeseed and mustard	Aphid	Regent, Laha 101, Pusa Kalyani
Cotton	Bollworms	Sanguineum, Sujata, Adadhita
	Jassids	MCUS, Krishna, Khandwa, Mahalaxmi
Sugarcane	Top borer	Co 67, Co 1158, Co 7224, CoP 9302
	Stalk borer	Co 7302, Co 5767
	Scale insect	Co 5671, Co 8014, Co 611
Tobacco	Stem borer	SBR 1, SBR 2
	Tobacco caterpillar	GT4, DWFC
Pea	Pod borer	Bonville, T 6113, PS 410
	Leaf miner	PS40, PS41-6, KMPR9
Tomato	Fruit borer	T 32, T 27, Punjab Kesri, Pant Bahar
Brinjal	Fruit and shoot borer	Doli 5, Pusa Purple Long, Pusa Purple Round
Okra	Fruit and shoot borer	AE 57, PM 58, Parkins Long Green, Nasnaul Special

Source : Dhaliwal and Koul (2010)

Varieties possessing multiple resistance to a number of insect pests and diseases are ideal in IPM programmes. The progress in breeding for resistance to multiple pest species varies among different crops and depends on a number of factors including the importance of the crop, importance of pests as constraints to production and the availability of resistant donors to use as parents in the breeding programme. Cultivars with multiple resistance to insects, nematodes, pathogens and tolerance to abiotic stresses (drought, soil mineral toxicity, etc.) have been developed in various crops, viz. wheat, alfalfa, cowpeas, maize, pearlmillet, sorghum, soybean and rice.

A spectacular success in development of improved varieties that possess resistance to as many as four insect pests and five diseases has been achieved at the International Rice Research Institute, Manila, Philippines. For example, IR36 is resistant to brown planthopper, green leafhopper, stem borers, gall midge, blast, bacterial blight and tungro (Table 11.4). The yield of IR8 fluctuates widely due to the pressure of insect pests and diseases, whereas the yield of IR36 and IR42, having multiple resistance, shows little variation from year to year. Thus, insect-resistant cultivars have greater yield stability and ensure food security. IR36 is alone planted on about 11 million ha of area in the world and yields an additional income of one

Table 11.4 Insect and disease reactions of IR varieties of rice

Variety	Insect or disease reactions							
	Brown planth-opper	**Green leafh-opper**	**Stem borer**	**Gall midge**	**Blast**	**Bacterial blight**	**Grassy stunt**	**Tungro**
IR5	S	R	MR	S	MR	S	S	S
IR8	S	R	S	S	S	S	S	S
IR20	S	R	MR	S	MR	R	S	S
IR22	S	S	S	S	S	R	S	S
IR24	S	R	S	S	S	S	S	S
IR26	R	R	MR	S	MR	R	S	MR
IR28	R	R	MR	S	R	R	R	R
IR32	R	R	MR	R	MR	R	R	R
IR36	R	R	MR	R	MR	R	R	R
IR38	R	R	MR	R	MR	R	R	R
IR42	R	R	MR	R	MR	R	R	R
IR46	R	R	MR	R	MR	R	R	R
IR50	R	R	S	NK	S	R	R	R
IR54	R	R	MR	NK	MR	R	R	R
IR58	R	R	S	NK	MR	R	R	R
IR60	R	R	MR	NK	MR	R	R	R
IR62	R	R	MR	NK	MR	R	R	R
IR64	R	R	MR	NK	MR	R	R	R
IR66	R	R	MR	NK	MR	R	R	R
IR68	R	R	MR	NK	MR	R	R	R
IR72	R	R	MR	NK	MR	R	R	R

R=Resistant; MR=Moderately resistant; S = Susceptible; NK=Not known

Source : Panda and Khush (1995)

billion dollars annually to rice growers and processors. Rice varieties resistant to brown planthopper and green leafhopper are grown over 20 million ha of riceland in Asia. These resistant varieties can be grown with the minimum use of insecticides and are an important component of integrated pest management programmes. Dr Gurdev S. Khush was awarded the 1996 World Food Prize for developing multiple pest resistant variety IR36 and other high yielding varieties of rice.

Various strategies can be adopted to prolong the useful life of the resistant varieties or to develop varieties with different genes so that the farmers may have access to new varieties when the resistance of the current varieties breaks down.

Major Gene Resistance

Several strategies can be employed to maintain varietal resistance and to prolong the useful life of major genes.

Sequential release of varieties. The sequential release of varieties with major genes involves the incorporation of a single major gene into commercial varieties. This strategy has been successfully followed for controlling the brown planthopper (BPH) of rice in Asia. Widespread outbreaks of BPH occurred in 1973-74 in several rice-growing countries. The rice varieties with *Bph-1* gene for resistance such as 1R26, 1R28 and 1R30 were released in several countries such as Indonesia, Vietnam and the Philippines. By 1977-78, a new biotype capable of attacking these varieties appeared and varieties with *Bph-2* gene such as 1R36, 1R38 and 1R42 were released. These were widely grown for about a decade when a new biotype appeared. Varieties with *Bph-3* were then released and are now widely grown. This strategy has also been followed for resistance to the Hessian fly in wheat.

Gene pyramiding. Pyramiding of major genes aims to combine two or more major genes into the same variety. Varieties with two or more major genes are likely to have a longer useful life as the development of new biotypes will be slower. It has been postulated that a simultaneous release of varieties with two genes for resistance to the Hessian fly of wheat would result in better durability than a sequential release. Pyramiding of two *Bt* genes through genetic engineering has also been proposed to prolong the useful life of transgenic resistance. Similarly, combining genes encoding a toxin and a repellent may offer longer lasting resistance than either approach alone.

Rotation of varieties. The process of adaptation of an insect can be interrupted by growing a resistant variety in one season and another resistant variety with a different gene during the next season. This strategy was followed to protect the rice crop from tungro virus epidemics in South Sulawesi, Indonesia, in 1970s. Varieties with one gene for green leafhopper (vector for virus) resistance were planted in one season and another variety with a different gene for resistance was planted in the next season. This strategy has been very effective in prolonging the useful life of the vector-resistant varieties.

Multiline varieties. The multiline approach envisages the incorporation of several major genes into an isogenic background and the mixing of these lines to form a multiline variety. This strategy was successfully employed for breeding oats with crown rust resistance. However, the effectiveness of this strategy in developing insect-resistant varieties is little known.

Varietal mixtures. This strategy employs the use of varietal mixtures consisting of 80-90 per cent resistant plants and 10-20 per cent susceptible plants of similar varietal background. Such varietal mixtures exert lower selection pressure on the insect as they are able to survive and reproduce on the susceptible plants.

Polygenic Resistance

Polygenic resistance is a quantitative trait that is governed by a large number of genes, each with a small contribution to resistance. The level of resistance is not generally high and it does not exert strong selection pressure on the insect, hence a virulent biotype rarely if ever develops and the resistance is more durable. However, parents with polygenic resistance are generally landraces with poor agronomic traits. In the process of selecting plants with better agronomic traits in crosses involving such parents, not all the polygenes are transferred and the level of resistance is diluted. Alfalfa germplasm resistant to the spotted alfalfa aphid has been developed through mass selection for polygenic variation.

CONCEPT OF BIOTYPES

The continuous growing of insect-resistant varieties may lead to certain physiological and behavioural changes in insect pests so that they are capable of feeding and developing on the resistant varieties. The term biotype is generally used to describe a population capable of damaging and surviving on plants previously known to be resistant to other populations of the same species. More specifically, biotype refers to the populations within a species which can survive on and destroy varieties that have genes for resistance. Broadly speaking, the term biotype is an intraspecific category referring to insect population of similar genetic composition for a biological attribute.

Although the occurrence of biotypes among insects is comparatively less frequent than in plant pathogens, however, biotypes have been recorded in a number of insect species. Biotype selection is, in fact, one of the major constraints encountered in breeding programmes for varietal resistance. Most biotypes do not arise *de novo* due to cultivation of resistant varieties but are present at a very low level in natural populations and increase in frequency as a result of continuous cultivation of resistant varieties. The concept of biotypes involves gene for gene relationship between the genotype for resistance in the host plant and the genotype for virulence in the insect. This phenomenon is well illustrated in case of brown planthopper in which the occurrence of five biotypes has been established. Biotype 1 destroys varieties that do not possess any gene for resistance (TN1). Biotype 2 damages varieties with *Bph-1* resistance gene (Mudgo). Biotype 3 thrives on varieties with *bph-2* gene for resistance (ASD7). Biotype 4 damages varieties with *Bph-3* gene (Rathu Heenati), whereas Biotype 5 destroys varieties with *bph-4* gene for resistance. Biotypes 1 and 2 are widely distributed in Southeast Asia, biotype 3 is a laboratory biotype produced in the Philippines, and biotype 4 is used to represent undefined population spread across the South Asia, including countries like India, Nepal, Bangladesh and Sri Lanka.

The development of insect biotypes has posed a serious threat to the success of plant resistance for management of insect pests. Biotypes are known to occur in more than 40 arthropod species belonging to 17 families of six orders. A list of selected insect pests showing biotype development is given in Table 11.5. Aphids constitute about 50 per cent of the species with known biotypes. Since most of the aphid species are parthenogenic, even one mutant capable of feeding on resistant variety can result into a new biotype. Biotypes are known to develop on varieties where antibiosis is the mechanism of resistance and they rarely develop on varieties where antixenosis/tolerance is the mechanism of resistance. Although biotypes have not yet posed a major threat to breeding for insect resistance in India, however, the occurrence of 6 biotypes in rice gall midge, *Orseolia oryzae* should be viewed with concern.

Table 11.5 Biotypes of selected insect pests of agricultural crops

Insect species	Common name	Number of biotypes	Crop(s)
Acyrthosiphon pisum	Pea aphid	9	Alfalfa
Amphorophora rubi	Raspberry aphid	6	Raspberry
Aphis craccivora	Cowpea aphid	6	Bush sitao
Bomisia tabaci	Whitefly	9	Cotton, okra, cassava, squash, etc.
Diuraphis noxia	Russian wheat aphid	5	Wheat
Eriosoma lanigerum	Woolly apple aphid	3	Apple
Mayetiola destructor	Hessian fly	14	Wheat
Nephotettix virescens	Green leafhopper	3	Rice
Nilaparvata lugens	Brown planthopper	5	Rice
Orseolia oryzae	Gall midge	6	Rice
Ostrinia nubilalis	European corn borer	4	Maize
Rhopalosiphum maidis	Corn leaf aphid	5	Maize
Schizaphis graminum	Greenbug	11	Wheat
Therioaphis trifolii f. *maculata*	Spotted alfalfa aphid	6	Alfalfa

Source **:** Dhaliwal and Singh (2005), Smith (2005)

A systematic surveillance programme for monitoring the shift to new virulent biotypes should be developed. The techniques to develop biotypes in the laboratory should be established so as to predict the stability of resistance in the field. In order to overcome the development of biotypes in monogenic resistant varieties, two breeding strategies are adopted.

(*i*) Sequential release. When a variety with a major gene becomes susceptible due to selection for a new biotype, another variety with a new major gene for resistance is released.

(*ii*) Gene pyramiding. Two or more major genes for vertical resistance are incorporated into a variety to impart resistance to more biotypes and also increase the stability of resistance.

The following additional breeding strategies involving major and minor genes are suggested to prevent or slow down the development of biotypes :

- The level of horizontal resistance and its stability may be enhanced by increasing the number of minor genes in a variety.
- Minor genes may be combined with major genes.
- The major genes may be rotated by seasonally alternating varietal groups having different major genes so that the selection pressure of the resistant varieties on insect population may be reduced.
- Breeding tolerant varieties would not only check yield loss caused by insects, but this character can also be combined with major genes which decrease the insect population and provide a high level of resistance.

FACTORS AFFECTING HOST PLANT RESISTANCE

The most desirable form of insect resistance is one which is stable across locations and seasons. However, the level and nature of insect resistance are influenced by several climatic and edaphic factors. Several environmental factors are known to influence the inherited characters, especially those involving physiological characteristics of crop plants.

Temperature

Temperature is one of the most important physical factors of the environment affecting the behaviour and physiological interactions of insects and plants. Temperature-induced stress can cause changes in plant physiology and affect the expression of genetic resistance, resulting in changes in morphological defenses and/or changes in the levels of biochemicals or nutritional quality of the host plant. Temperature also has pronounced effect on plant growth and indirectly influences the extent of damage. Temperature also affects the biology and behaviour of insects and thus influences insect growth and population build-up. In general, low temperatures cause a negative effect on resistance. Differences between resistant and susceptible genotypes of sorghum to greenbug increase with an increase in temperature. The level of resistance to pea aphid and alfalfa aphid in alfalfa is greater at higher temperatures. On the other hand, progressive loss of resistance to Hessian fly in wheat, has been reported at temperatures higher than 18°C.

Soil Moisture

The level of plant resistance is influenced by water stress. High levels of water stress reduce the damage by sorghum shoot fly, *Atherigona soccata*. The populations of *Aphis fabae* have lower rates of reproduction on water stressed plants. However, water stressed plants suffer greater damage due to aphid feeding. Thus, moisture stress can alter the plant reaction to insect damage leading either to increased or lower susceptibility to insect damage. Atmospheric humidity also influences the insect-plant interaction. High humidity increases the ease of detecting of odours which may influence host finding and antixenosis mechanism of resistance to insects.

Photoperiod

Photoperiod affects the development of both the crop plants and their insect pests. It may also bring about changes in the physico-chemical characteristics of crop plants and thus influence the interaction between insects and plants. Intensity and quality of light have been reported to influence biosynthesis of anthocyanins and phenylpropanoids. Continuous high intensity light is reported to induce susceptibility in resistant PI 227687 soybean plants to cabbage looper, *Trichoplusia ni*. Reduction in light intensity leads to loss in resistance of some wheat cultivars to wheat stem saw fly by decreasing stem solidness and density. Shade-induced loss of resistance has also been reported in sugarbeet genotypes resistant to the green peach aphid. Similarly, shading has been known to reduce resistance in potato genotypes to Colorado potato beetle, which is due to reduced levels of steroidal glycosides, some of which are known to limit growth and development of beetle.

Nutrients

Plant nutrition exerts pronounced effect on resistance of plants to insects. In several cases, high levels of nutrients increase the susceptibility, whereas in others they increase the level of resistance. Application of nitrogenous fertilizers decreases the damage by shootfly and stem borer, *Chilo partellus* in sorghum. Application of phosphatic fertilizers is reported to decrease the damage of shoot fly. Similarly, application of potash decreases the incidence of sugarcane top borer, *Scirpophaga excerptalis*, and several rice insect pests like yellow stem borer, brown planthopper, green leafhopper, leaf folder, whorl maggot and thrips. However, high levels of nitrogen are known to increase the damage by cotton jassid, *Amrasca biguttula*; rice stem borer, *Scirpophaga incertulas* and many other insect pests of agricultural crops. In alfalfa, excess levels of nitrogen and magnesium, and low levels of calcium and potassium, have been associated with loss of resistance to the spotted alfalfa aphid.

Soil pH

Plants can grow in soils over a pH range of 3.0 to 9.0, but extreme conditions stress the plants. Foliar damage to whorl-stage sorghum by the fall armyworm, *Spodoptera frugiperda* was greater in acidic soils (pH 5.4) than in plants grown in soils with a pH higher than 6.0. Salinity induces plant responses that can alter the suitability of a plant as a host for insects. Salinity stress at 1.25 m–1 increased nitrogen, decreased potassium and reduced the production of allelochemicals in rice-plant leaf sheaths. The salinity-stressed rice plants were conducive to the feeding and survival of the whitebacked planthopper, *Sogatella furcifera*. The salinity stress led to increase in insects' growth and development, longevity, fecundity and population build-up.

Air Pollution

Air pollution refers to the presence in the outdoor atmosphere of one or more contaminants such as dust, fumes, gas, mist, odour, smoke or vapour in such quantities and duration as to be injurious to human, plant, or animal life or to property. Air pollution has been demonstrated to influence insect-plant interactions. When Mexican bean beetles were fed on soybean fumigated intermittently with SO2, the mean number of beetle progeny was 1.5 times greater than that of beetles feeding on the control plants. Mexican bean beetles under laboratory conditions preferred to eat soybean leaves pre-fumigated with ozone-enriched ambient air. Substantial modifications in the form and content of plant nitrogen and sugars have been reported following plant exposure to moderate levels of ozone. Such nutritionally enriched plants are better hosts for insect herbivores, especially aphids.

Plant Factors

Insects have often exhibited feeding preferences for particular plant organs or for foliage of certain specific age. Moreover, variations in physical growth conditions such as plant canopy and plant height may influence host selection and subsequent population development. For example, *Myzus persicae* was relatively more successful in feeding on older leaves of Brussels sprouts than *Brevicoryne brassicae* and vice-versa. The early-maturing genotypes of soybean show greater defoliation by velvet bean caterpillar, *Anticarsia gemmatalis*; soybean looper, *Chrysodeixis includens* and beet armyworm, *Spodoptera exigua*. The damage by the sorghum midge, *Contarinia sorghicola* on sorghum hybrid CSH5 was higher in plots with low plant densities. In contrast, infestation by wheat stem saw fly, *Cephus pygmeus* was higher in low plant densities. Wheat plants sown at low densities (40 × 40 cm, 2.5 kg seed ha–1) had a longer interval between plant development stages and had higher stem solidness than those sown at higher densities (10 × 3 cm, 133 kg seed ha–1). Stem solidness was negatively correlated with the percentage of sawfly-infested stems.

Insect Factors

The age, sex and levels of infestation of insects affect the preference for host plants with varying levels of resistance. Young (3-day old) female Mexican bean beetles showed no preference for leaves of susceptible Deane soybean over resistant soybean leaves. In contrast,

14-day old Mexican bean beetle females showed a marked preference for leaves of susceptible plants. In feeding bioassays, the female beetles demonstrated a distinct preference for leaves of susceptible soybean over the resistant soybean leaves, but males did not. The size of sorghum shootfly, *Atherigona varia* population had a pronounced effect on both absolute and relative rates of oviposition in various sorghum genotypes. The resistance was partially dominant when evaluated under low shootfly populations, however, when evaluated under high populations, susceptibility appeared dominant.

ECONOMIC AND ECOLOGICAL BENEFITS

The development and adoption of insect resistant crop cultivars provide numerous economical and ecological advantages. Crop yields may be improved while insect monitoring and management costs are reduced. Insect-resistant crops require fewer insecticide applications leading to reductions in insecticide related costs and pesticide residues. The reduction in pesticide treatments may also benefit non-target organisms, including beneficial insect populations and protect groundwater from pesticide contamination. Thus, insect-resistant varieties provide substantial environmental benefits and contribute to reduce insecticide use and residues, hence improving the food, health and safety to the consumers. Insect resistant varieties provide substantial economic returns on investment in research and development. The returns on resistant cultivar research compared with insecticide range from 100:1 to 10:1, making it a valuable component of crop production and greatly improving the competitiveness of farmers in many countries. It has been estimated that insect resistant cultivars of alfalfa, corn and beet returned about $320 for each $1 invested in research. Wheat cultivars developed for resistance to the Hessian fly, *Mayetiola destructor*, provided a 120-fold greater return on investment than pesticides. The research on resistance in corn to the corn earworm, *Helicoverpa zea* returned $20 to the growers for each $1 invested by the US Department of Agriculture between 1950 and 1970. Hessian fly resistance developed in Moroccan bread wheats provided a 9:1 return on investment in research.

The current value of insect resistant varieties due to reduced insect damage and reduced cost of insecticide application, varies with economic conditions. The annual value of grain sorghum cultivars resistant to the greenbug, *Schizaphis graminum* in Texas is approximately $30 million. It has been estimated by the Prdue USDA Small Grain Improvement Programme that a $3.4 billion increase in farm income is attributable to improved cultivars of wheat with resistance to the Hessian fly. The annual return exceeded $4.6 million per scientific year invested and calculated over a period of 64 years of the programme. The economic benefit of using resistant wheat cultivars in Georgia to control the Hessian fly averaged $104 per ha. The multiple insect resistant rice variety, IR36, has provided $1 billion additional annual income to rice producers and processors in South and South East Asia. The estimated value of Kansas grain sorghum cultivars resistant to greenbug or chinch bug. *Blissus leucopterous*, is about $45 million per year. The economic value of genetic resistance in wheat to all the major global arthropod pests amounts to just over $250 million per year.

In Asia, Africa and Latin America, the value of arthropod resistant cultivars of chickpea, sorghum and pearl millet is estimated to be worth more than $580 million per year. The resistance in *Phaseolus* to the leafhopper, *Empoasca krameri*, in Latin America is providing approximately $500 per ha per year. Based on a survey of US alfalfa production, it has been estimated that the increase in annual income to farmers from the use of multiple arthropod and disease-resistant alfalfa is to the tune of approximately $300 million per year. The current total estimated global value of arthropod resistant crop cultivars is approximately $2.18 billion (Table 11.6).

Table 11.6 Net annual global economic value of arthropod resistant crop cultivars

Crop	Pest(s)	Region	Value (million $)
Oryza sativa	Plant-and leafhoppers	Asia	1,000
Gossypium hirsutum	Lepidopteran larvae	World	570
Medicago sativa	Aphids	USA	300
Sorghum bicolor	*Schizaphis graminum*	USA	113
Triticum aestivum	*Aceria tosichella*	North America	150
	Mayetiola destructor	USA	17
	Diuraphis noxia	USA	13
	Cephus cinctus	USA	12

Source : Smith (2005)

Resistant varieties can facilitate economical production of a crop in a region where it had not been possible earlier because of extreme pest pressure. For example, the production of sweet corn was unprofitable in the southeastern United States before 1951, even with the use of pesticides. However, loana sweet corn, with low to intermediate levels of resistance to the corn earworm, was released in 1951. This single release allowed growers to produce sweet corn with pesiticides and to-day higher levels of resistance in sweet corn are available to growers. Another example of a crop that can now be grown more profitably due to resistance to insects is greenbug resistant hybrid sorghums. The insecticides used on sorghum increased drastically after the greenbug became a pest in 1968. However, the cultivation of greenbug resistant sorghum with insecticides provided the highest returns ($203/ha) followed by greenbug resistant sorghum without insecticides ($200/ha), non-resistant sorghum with insecticides ($199/ha), and lastly nonresistant sorghum without insecticides ($165/ha).

The long term economic and ecological benefits of host plant resistance have been spectacular. Ten-fold reduction in insect pest population and 50 per cent increase in crop yield are not uncommon wherever insect resistant rice varieties have been introduced and maintained in South and Southeast Asia. It had been estimated that production of insect resistant varieties of alfalfa, barley, maize and sorghum eliminated the annual application of over 319,000 tons of insecticides (about 37% of the total insecticides applied during the 1960s) in USA. If this trend has remained constant since then, insect resistant varieties have helped avoid the application of more than 6 million tons of insecticides, largely because of cultivation of insect resistant varieties of corn, cotton, sorghum and vegetables.

PRINCIPAL METHOD OF PEST CONTROL

Host plant resistance to insects has been used as a primary method of pest control long before the advent of synthetic organic insecticides. A few insect pests have been controlled for many years by the use of resistant crop varieties alone (Table 11.7). The first deliberate use of plant resistance to control a major insect pest was the importation in 1873 of American phylloxera-resistant rootstock into France for the control of grape phylloxera, *Dactulosphairavitifoliae.* This insect had destroyed over 1 million ha of vineyards and caused

Table 11.7 Selected examples of deliberate use of varieties with resistance to insect pests as the principal method of control

Crop	Insect pest		Region
	Common name	Scientific name	
Alfalfa	Spotted alfalfa aphid Pea aphid	*Therioaphis maculata* *Acyrthosiphon pisum*	USA
Corn	European corn borer Corn earworm	*Ostrinia nubilalis* *Helicoverpa zea*	USA
Cotton	Cotton jassid	*Jacobiella facialis*	Africa
Grapes	Grape phylloxera	*Daktulosphaira vitifoliae*	Worldwide
Rice	Brown planthopper Green leafhopper	*Nilaparvata lugens* *Nephotettix virescens*	Worldwide
Sorghum	Greenbug	*Schizaphis graminum*	USA
Sorghum	Sorghum midge	*Contarinia sorghicola*	India
Wheat	Hessian fly Wheat stem saw fly	*Mayetiola destructor* *Cephus cinctus*	Worldwide

Source : Stoner (1996)

tremendous loss to the French wine industry, but the use of resistant rootstock allowed a quick recovery, resulting in effective control of phylloxera for more than 100 years. This is still the principal method of phylloxera control worldwide.

The resistant varieties of wheat in USA have provided the principal method of control of the Hessian fly, *M. destructor*. Pawnee, Ponca, Poso 42 and Big Club 43 developed in Kansas and California, were the first Hessian fly resistant varieties released. These were followed by the release of the resistant varieties Dual and Benkur in Indiana. By 1974, 8 million ha of wheat in USA were planted with 42 varieties resistant to Hessian fly and 0.6 million ha included five varieties resistant to wheat stem sawfly, *Cephus cinctus*. As a consequence of the use of resistant varieties, losses inflicted by Hessian fly were reduced to less than 1 per cent and this insect was reduced to the status of a minor pest.

The control of European corn borer, *Ostrinia nubilalis*, a major pest of com in USA also depends on the use of resistant varieties. The control of borer by insecticides and cultural methods generally has not been satisfactory and the insect caused $350 million worth of damage in 1949. A major research effort was directed towards the development of borer resistant varieties. Widespread planting of hybrids with partial, polygenic resistance reduced corn borer survival and damage to the plant over a wide area and reduced annual losses to an average of $100 million annually in the late 1960s. All the field com hybrids grown on 33 million ha in USA are routinely screened to maintain at least a moderate level of resistance.

In India, insect resistant varieties have been developed for the control of a number of insect pests. Several insect pests have been kept under check through the use of insect resistant cultivars, e.g. *Amrasca biguttula* - Krishna, Mahalaxmi, Khandwa2 and MCU5; rice gall midge, *Orseolia oryzae* - IR36, Kakatiya, Surekha and Rajendradhan, and sorghum shoot fly, *Atherigona soccata*-Maldandi, Swati and Phule Yashoda.

INTEGRATION WITH OTHER TACTICS

Host plant resistance can be effectively used in combination with other control tactics of IPM. High levels of resistance are not necessary for a crop variety to be of practical value in IPM. Varieties with low or moderate levels of resistance can be used to good advantage for pest suppression.

Chemical Control

There are many examples of host plant resistance enhancing the efficacy of insecticides. Evaluations of rice insecticides indicate that they cause higher mortality of planthoppers and leafhoppers feeding on resistant than on susceptible rice varieties. Mortality of brown planthopper when reared on either a moderately resistant ASD7 or a highly resistant cultivar Sinna Sivappu was higher than when feeding on a susceptible TN1 cultivar. The LD50 of whitebacked planthopper was 9.4 on the susceptible variety TN1 treated with ethylan, but only 2.8 on moderately resistant N22. The combination of moderate varietal resistance and low dose of pesticide resulted in effective hopper control. The integration of host plant resistance and insecticides has cumulative effect on *Nephotettix virescens,* the vector of rice tungro virus. There was no tungro virus infection on the resistant cultivar IR28 even without the application of the insecticides. On the moderately resistant cultivar, IR36, tungro virus infected plants decreased from 42 per cent in the 0 kg a.i./ha treatment to 10 per cent in the 0.5 kg a.i./ha rate. On the susceptible cultivar, IR22, virus infestation was higher at all insecticide rates decreasing from 92 per cent in the control to 74 per cent in the 1 kg a.i./ha rate. Cotton cultivars exhibiting the frego bract and okra (thin) leaf traits allow more than 30 per cent penetration of insecticides into the cotton foliage canopy, increasing the efficiency and decreasing the amount of insecticide required for control.

Generally, a lower concentration of insecticide is needed to control insects feeding on a resistant variety than those feeding on a susceptible variety. In this regard, nymphs of the wheat grain aphid, *Sitobion avenae,* reared on resistant wheat variety Altar possessing the antibiosis compound DIMBOA were significantly more susceptible to the insecticide deltamethrin than nymphs on the susceptible wheat variety Dollarbird. The LD50 was reduced by 91 per cent for nymphs reared on the cultivar with a high DIMBOA content. Although the population of the aphid, *M. persicae* on the partially resistant variety of Brussels sprouts was about 85 per cent of that on the susceptible variety, the LD50 of malathion was only about 55 per cent, *i.e.* the insecticide requirement was much less on the partially resistant variety.

It has been demonstrated that the insecticide applications for the control of southern corn rootworm, *Diabroticaundecimpunctata howardi,* on a resistant groundnut variety were reduced by 80 per cent of the normally applied amount of insecticide. Similarly, insecticide applications for the control of thrips and *Empoasca fabae* on resistant groundnut cultivars were reduced by approximately 60 per cent. The doses of pirimicarb to a cultivar of cabbage with moderate level of resistance to *Myzus persicae* could be reduced by 85 per cent of the recommended dosage, compared to susceptible cultivars that required a three-fold greater dose. Soil insecticide applications in plantings of resistant carrot cultivar Sytan, require only one-third the amount of insecticide normally used on a susceptible cultivar.

In spite of many positive interactions between plant resistance and insecticides, negative interactions between the two tactics do occur. This is mainly due to the enhanced detoxification of insecticides when pest insects are fed foliage containing high levels of allelochemicals that mediate insect resistance in several agricultural crops.

Biological Control

Pest resistant varieties are usually compatible with biological control but may sometimes have an adverse effect on natural enemies. By reducing pest numbers, resistant varieties help to shift the pest : predator ratios in favour of biological control. In field studies at International Rice Research Institute (IRRI), Philippines, the brown planthopper, *Nilaparvata lugens* : spider, *Lycosa pseudoannulata* ratios increased with the level of susceptibility from ASD7 and IR36, both highly resistant rice cultivars to IR42 and Triveni, moderately resistant cultivars to IR8 and TN1, susceptible cultivars.

The host plant resistance may also enhance the predatory activity. A moderate level of resistance in rice varieties IR46 and Utri Rajapan effectively increased the predation rate of the spiders, *Lycosa* spp., on the brown planthopper. This was attributed to the greater movement of hoppers in search of suitable feeding sites. Predation rate of the mirid bug, *Cyrtorhinus lividipennis,* when feeding on the first instar *Nilaparvata lugens* nymphs, increased on the resistant cultivar, IR36 as compared to the susceptible IR8. Combinations of host plant resistance and predation by the mirid bug, *C. lividipennis* have a cumulative effect on the population increase of the green leafhopper, *Nephotettix virescens.* In cage studies, the number of green leafhopper reached only 6 on IR29 (resistant) with the predator and 31 without the predator, while there were 91 and 220 hoppers, respectively, on susceptible IR22. Partial resistance combined with predation, has been found to be more effective in lessening black bean aphid, *Aphis fabae,* numbers on faba bean than either the predator or the plant resistance alone. Greenhouse experiments indicated that release of a newly hatched larva of *Coccinella septempunctata* onto susceptible and partial resistant variety, reduced aphid denisty to 32.8 and 57.2 per cent, respectively, on 14th day. Laboratory tests showed that the prey, *A. fabae,* raised on susceptible cultivar was more suitable for the predator as food source, enhancing the development rate and fecundity than aphids fed on the partially resistant cultivar.

In case of sugarcane, tightness of leafsheath and increased hardness of stalk tissues conferring resistance to the borer, *Diatraea saccharalis* prolong the time during which the pest remains in an exposed situation, vulnerable to the action of natural control agents. The compatible nature of plant resistance and biological control has been demonstrated in case of interaction between resistant varieties of barley and sorghum, and parasitization of the greenbug, *Schizaphis graminum.* The movement of greenbugs on the resistant sorghum cultivars exposes them to greater parasitization. The parasitoid, *Lysiphlebus testaceipes* was able to keep the biotype C greenbug population nearly static on both susceptible and resistant barley, when the initial population of the aphid was three per plant. But when 12 aphids and one female parasitoid were introduced per plant, the parasitoid could suppress the aphid population only on the resistant barley. Thus, damage to barley was reduced by the combined effect of varietal resistance and parasitoids. There is also synergistic interaction between maize cultivars resistant to the leaf feeding fallworm, *Spodoptera frugiperda* or the corn earworm, *Helicoverpa zea* and nuclear polyhedrosis virus (NPV) disease of fallworm. Insects feeding on resistant inbred lines were more susceptible to infection and mortality from NPV.

There are many ways natural enemies could be adversely affected by plant characteristics, such as pubescence or sticky glandular trichomes that interfere with searching; high levels of allelochemicals that accumulate in the body of the pest and affect natural enemies feeding on the pest, or changes in plant characteristics, such as colour structure or volatile chemicals used for habitat location by the natural enemy. High trichome density in insect-resistant cotton potato and tomato has been shown to be detrimental to predators and parasitoids. The effects of the parasitoid, *Trichogramma pretiosum* and the predator, *Chrysopa rufilabcis* on the larvae of the bollworm, *Heliothis virescens* are reduced with increasing degrees of cotton leaf pubescence. The density of trichomes on the stems of tomato plants affects the ability of the predatory mite, *Phytoseiulus persimilis* to control the phytophagous, two-spotted spider mite, *Tetranychus urticae*. Similarly, densely pubescent genotypes of cucumber impede the movement of *Encarsia formosa* to locate the greenhouse whitefly, *Trialeurodes vaporariorum*.

Suppression of the effects of beneficial arthropod populations may also result from the effects of allelochemicals in resistant plant cultivars being transferred to the predators or parasitoids. Some genotypes of insect-resistant potato, tomato and soybean contain levels of toxic allelochemicals that have negative effects on beneficial insects, entomopathogenic fungi and insect viruses. The first example of negative interaction between host plant resistance and natural enemies was the toxicity of α-tomatine, an alkaloid from resistant tomato cultivars, to *Hyposoter exiguae*, an endoparasitoid of *Helicoverpa zea*. The reduction in parasitism of *H. zea* and *M. sexta* eggs by *Telenomus sphingis* and *T. pretiosum* on accession PI134417 of *Lycopersicon hirsutum* f. *glabratum*, is due to the effects of exposures to methyl ketones (2-tridecanone and 2-undecanone), as well as reduced parasitoid mobility after entrapment in trichome adhesive exudates. Similarly, high levels of isoflavone-based resistance in soybean are detrimental to a number of natural enemies. Thus, a better understanding of the evolution of crop plants, pests and pest biological control agents is required to understand how plant resistance and biological control can be integrated for more durable insect pest management.

Cultural Control

Cultural control practices combined with growing resistant crop cultivars are more effective in controlling arthropod pests than using cultural controls with susceptible cultivars. The use of early plantings in combination with resistant varieties has been recommended to avoid arthropod attacks on rice, wheat, corn, sorghum and cotton. It has been demonstrated that *Nilaparvata lugens* populations and *N. lugens* : predator ratios are significantly lower on very early-and early-maturing rice cultivars than those on mid-season maturing cultivars. Thus, the incorporation of *N. lugens* resistance into early maturing cultivars can enhance the crop protection from this pest. Infestation of the greenbug, *Schizaphis graminum*, has been shown to be effectively reduced by combining the planting of a *S. graminum* resistant sorghum cultivar at a later than a normal planting date, in combination with no tillage cultivation of the preceding crop stubble.

Trap crops that attract insect pest populations (so that they may be destroyed) are synergistic when used in combination with insect resistant cultivars of several agricultural crops. The growing of antixenotic cotton cultivars resistant to boll weevil, *Anthonomus grandis* in combination with early maturing cotton cultivars, is effective in suppressing boll weevil populations. Treatment of boll weevil on the trap crop, causes a 20 per cent reduction in overall insecticide application and increases yield by 14-33 per cent. Rice trap crop planted 20 days earlier than the main crop (a brown planthopper resistant cultivar), attracts more hopper population, preserves more natural enemies and yields significantly more than the fields without trap crop.

POTENTIAL IN IPM

Host plant resistance holds a great promise for exploitation in IPM programmes because of the following unique features :

(*i*) **Specificity.** Host plant resistance is usually specific against a particular insect pest or pest complex and does not possess any adverse effect on non-target or beneficial organisms.

(*ii*) **Cumulative effect.** The effect of host plant resistance does not end with a generation of the insect pest, but lasts against successive generations.

(*iii*) **Ecofriendly.** Host plant resistance does not cause pollution in any component of the environment nor does it have any deleterious effect on man or wildlife.

(*iv*) **Easily adoptable.** An insect resistant variety with high yield potential can easily be adopted by farmers, as it does not require much higher cost and seed is to be procured otherwise also.

(*v*) **Effectiveness.** Resistant varieties increase the susceptibility of insect pests to insecticides and many natural enemies of insect pests are more effective on resistant varieties.

(*vi*) **Compatibility.** When host plant resistance alone cannot maintain the insect population below the economic threshold, it can easily be combined with other tactics of insect pest management.

(*vii*) **Decreased pesticide application.** Resistant varieties usually need less frequent treatment with a pesticide or may require low rates of application or pesticide application may not be necessary at all.

(*viii*) **Persistence.** Some varieties with durable resistance are likely to maintain their resistance for long periods.

(*ix*) **Unique situations.** Host plant resistance may serve as a means of control in unique niches where other controls are not feasible or difficult to use, *e.g.* (*a*) when there is a critical timing in which the insect is exposed for only a brief period of its life cycle, (*b*) crop is of low economic value, and (*c*) pest is continuously present and is a single limiting factor over a large area.

In spite of the above advantages of host plant resistance, the following limitations have usually been recognized.

(*i*) **Time consuming.** Host plant resistance is not favourable for solving sudden or localized pest problems as the time taken for identification of sources of resistance and breeding of resistant varieties is usually longer, and varies from 5 to 10 years. However, this time can be shortened by employing modern biotechnological tools.

(*ii*) **Biotype development.** The use of varieties with vertical resistance may lead to development of insect biotypes. However, this problem may be tackled by employing polygenic resistance or breeding varieties resistant to specific biotypes.

(*iii*) **Complexity of pests.** Most of the crops are attacked by a complex of pests and there is a potential problem of resistance to one pest being linked to susceptibility to another. For example, pubescence in plants may be attractive to some pests and provide resistance to others. Similarly, high levels of allelochemicals may provide protection from one species, but may be attractive to other species.

(*iv*) **Effects on non-target species.** Plants that are resistant to arthropod pests, may have adverse impact on non-target species in two ways. Firstly, elevated toxin levels may be unpalatable, allergenic or even dangerous for consumers. For example, potatoes with higher glycoaldehyde levels that were resistant to the Colorado potato beetle were withdrawn because of customer complaints. Secondly, some secondary plant substances may be toxic to beneficial species such as parasitoids.

(*v*) **Genetic limitations.** The use of host plant resistance may be limited by the absence of preadaptive resistance genes among available germplasm. Moreover, resistant cultivars may lack the potential to produce high yields. Farmers will not accept resistant varieties unless their yield is atleast as good as the susceptible varieties that need chemical protection from pests.

(*vi*) **Interdisciplinary approach.** Dedicated interdisciplinary efforts are required to combine insect resistance with all the desirable traits needed in an elite, commercially competitive variety. Sometimes, the failure of entomologists and plant breeders to proceed systematically after locating or developing an arthropod resistant germplasm becomes a major bottleneck.

CONCLUSIONS

The co-operative efforts of plant breeders, entomologists, molecular biologists and biochemists to identify, quantify and develop insect resistant crop cultivars during past several decades have led to the most significant accomplishment of modern agricultural research in the development of insect resistant varieties of crop plants. The use of resistant varieties provides crop protection that is biologically, ecologically, economically and socially acceptable. Host plant resistance represents the key for opening up major advances in insect pest management. It would have a major impact on the need or rather the lack of need for other control tactics.

Host plant resistance to arthropods has been successfully integrated with allied pest management tactics in many of the world's major food and fibre crops. Plant resistance has been found to be compatible with natural enemies but secondary plant compounds in some cases may adversely affect the natural enemies. In a similar way, use of insecticides has been reduced considerably on insect resistant cultivars, but some time, secondary plant compounds lead to the incompatibility of insecticides with resistant plants. These compounds increase the activity of detoxifying enzymes which enables the insect to tolerate insecticides. Hence, detailed studies on different allelochemicals in plants or secondary plant metabolites and their effect on herbivores and natural enemies must be an integral part of development of insect resistant varieties.

Durable resistance to insects is possible provided varieties are selected for horizontal rather than vertical resistance. Selection for horizontal resistance should not be made purely on the basis of a single mechanism of resistance. Multilocation testing of the identified sources and breeding material needs to be strengthened to identify stable and diverse sources of resistance, and identify the presence and/or emergence of new insect biotypes. Resistance to insects should be given as much weightage as the yield performance to identify new varieties and hybrids for cultivation by the farmers. Insect-resistant varieties with a yield potential comparable to commercial cultivars should be released for areas endemic to a particular pest. These reistant cultivars provide a better control of insect pests, but do not give complete protection to the crops from the pests. Therefore, resistant cultivars should be used in combination with other methods of pest control to achieve sustainable pest management.

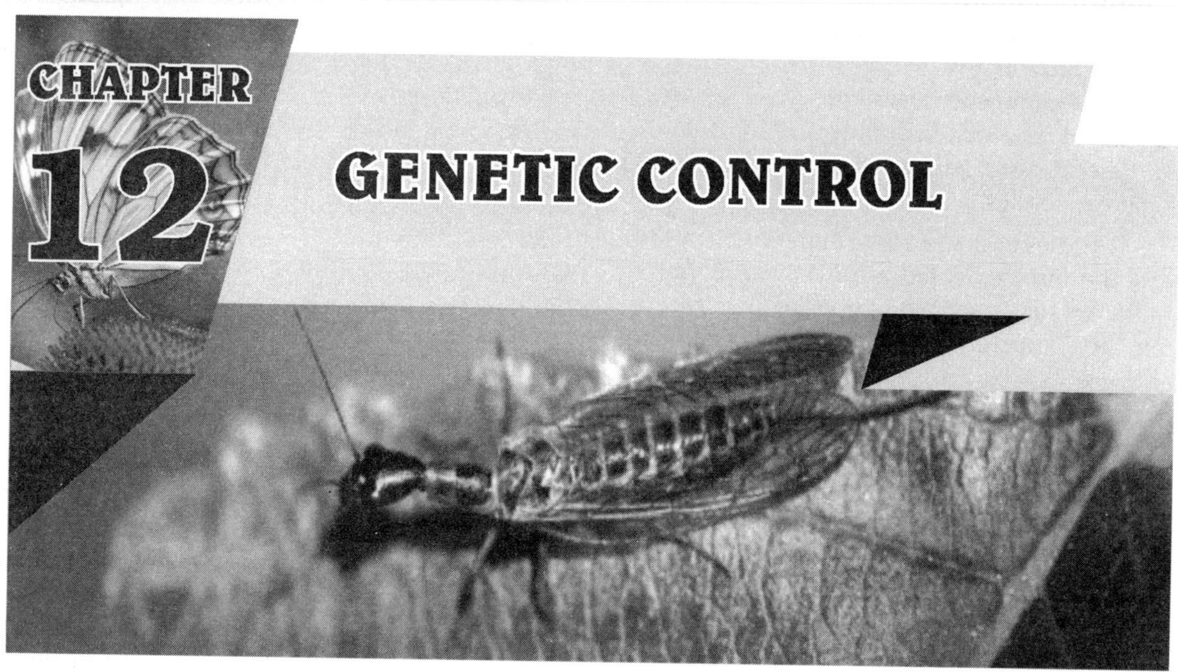

CHAPTER 12 GENETIC CONTROL

INTRODUCTION

Genetic pest control strategies involve alterations of a target pest's ability to reproduce or the insertion of some deleterious character into a pest population. Since the genetic control methods utilise insect pests for their own destruction, these are also known as autocidal methods. Genetic approaches for managing arthropod pests have been considered by scientists for more than half a century. Yet, because of recent and current emerging technologies, genetic approaches are often regarded as novel and uproven. Certainly, current advances and theory in this field of study remain to be implemented, but some applications of these methods, such as the sterile insect technique, are well known in their effectiveness and have great potential for managing arthropod pests. Emerging technologies also hold great promise as future pest control methods. Research and development for genetic autocidal programme demand a long-term commitment before potential benefits can be realised. Therefore, genetic approaches are usually developed only for the most economically important pest species.

STERILE INSECT TECHNIQUE

The idea of controlling insects by sterilising technique, was first conceied by E.F. Knipling as far back as 1937 in a laboratory in Texas, USA. While studying the biology of the screwworm, fly, *Cochliomyia hominivorax,* he observed that the female fly mated only once (monogamous). From this, he argued that if the males of this fly could somehow be sterilised, the females would fail to produce viable eggs and the insect's population could thus be controlled. While entomologists were looking for sterilising agents to test Knipling's idea, geneticists were accidently sterilising insects in their own search for chemical mutagens immediately after World War II.

E.F. Knipling conceived a new approach for insect control in which the pest's natural reproductive processes would be disrupted by physical or chemical means. This concept, as it was applied to the screwworm fly starting in the early 1950s, eventually came to be known as the sterile insect technique (SIT), or the sterile insect release method (SIRM). Interestingly, about the time that Knipling was formulating his concept of insect control, a Russian geneticist, A. Serebrovsky, suggested the use of chromosomal translocations to reduce reproduction in harmful species.

Studies of insect reproduction, from the early 1900s to the present time, have demonstrated that the insects treated with certain mutagenic chemicals (chemosterilands) or X-ray or gamma radiation, are unable to produce a normal number of living progency. Treated insects (which may be competely or only partially sterile) are released in large number into a field environment and are expected to mate with the normal insects, thus interfering with reproduction. If the matings between treated insects and normal insects are successful, reproduction of the field populations will be disrupted, and the population will decline.

A. Chemosterilants

Any chemical that can inhibit the growth of gonads or interfere with the reproductive capacity of an insect in any other way (such as prevent copulation and production of viable eggs, induce dominant lethal mutations, inhibit development of progeny at any stage—egg, larval or pupal) is called a ***chemosterilant.***

Chemicals that are currently employed as chemosterilants can be grouped as alkylating agents, antimetabolites and miscellaneous compounds :

Alkylating Agents

These compounds were discovered by LaBrecque in 1961 in the USA. They contain several groups of aziridinyls (aziridines or ethylenimines) (Fig. 12.1) and can be classified into three categories : apholate, aphomide and aphoxide whose examples will be described below:

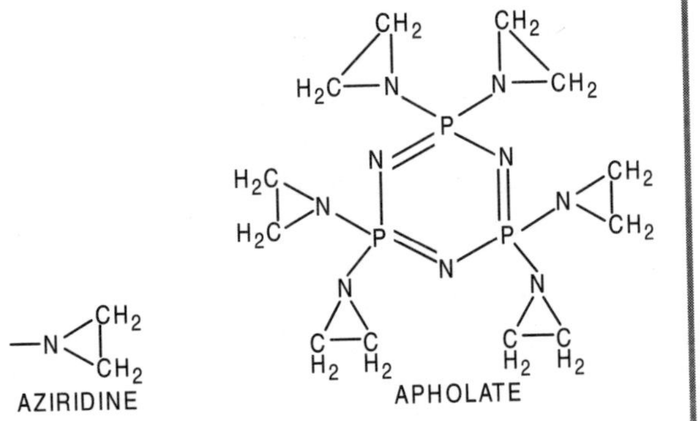

Apholate. Chemically, this compound is 2, 2, 4, 4, 6, 6-hexakis (1-aziridinyl) 2, 2, 4, 4, 6, 6-hexahydro—1, 3, 5, 2, 4, 6-triazatriphosphorine. It is a white odourless and crystalline substance, partially soluble in water and organic solvents (alcohol, chloroform, acetone), stable in cool dry condition and affected by humidity and high temperature.

Fig. 12.1 Chemical structure of chemosterilants (alkylating agents)

Aphomide. Chemically, this compound is N, N′-ethylenebis, [p, p-bis (1-aziridinyl) N″-methylphosphinic amide].

*Aphoxide.*Chemically, this compound is tris (1-aziridinyl) phosphine oxide, also called TEPA. It is a crystalline, colourless and odourless substance, extremely soluble in water, and highly soluble in alcohol, ether and acetone, and hygroscopic and unstable. Its other derivatives are METEPA, phosphine oxide, tris (2-methyl 1-aziridinyl) and thio-TEPA (phosphine sulphide, tris (1-aziridinyl) The former is a straw coloured liquid completely soluble in water and solvents, and the latter, a white crystalline solid relatively less soluble.

Biological properties. The most important biological property of all alkylating agents is that they are highly reactive and readily combine with a variety of chemicals and biochemicals (nucleic acids and proteins) replacing a hydrogen atom by an alkyl or a substituted alkyl group such as aminoalkyl, hydroxyalkyl and thioalkyl. The process of replacement of the H atom is called alkylation which is actually responsible for the sterility in insects. The agents produce permanent sterility in both sexes and are readily absorbed through the skin. This property explains their toxicity to mammals.

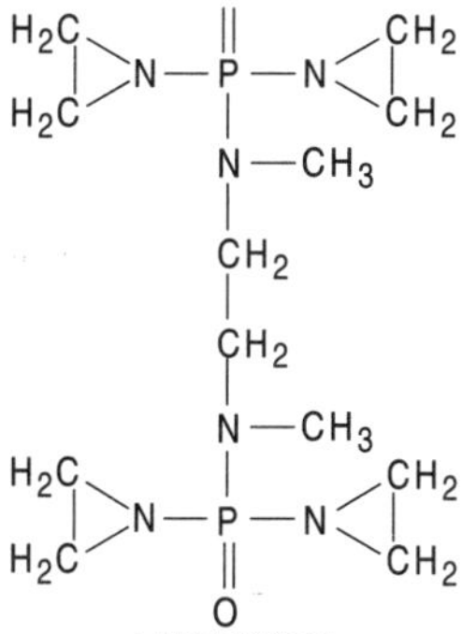

APHOMIDE 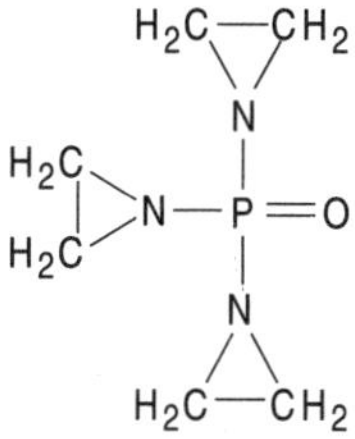 TEPA 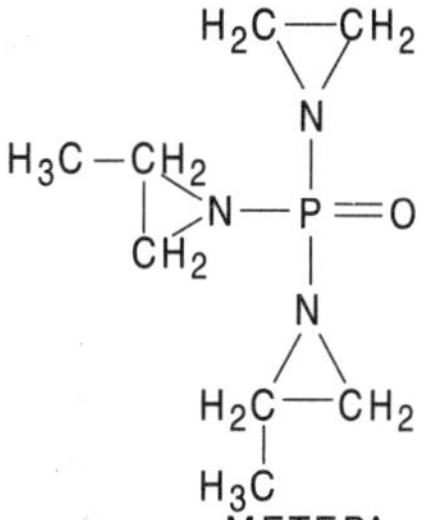 METEPA 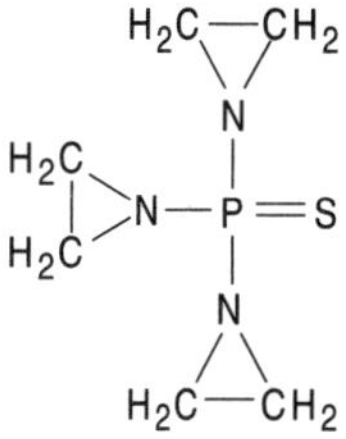 Thio-TEPA

Mechanism of action. The exact mechanism through which, alkylation brings about sterility is not known. Some indirect evidences suggest that alkylating agents probably act in the following way :

(*i*) **Nucleic acid (DNA, RNA) synthesis.** Insects treated with alkylating agents like apholates had their eggs deficient in DNA and RNA leading to complete sterility. It is, however, not known if this effect is direct at the molecular level or indirect through ovarian damage, hormonal imbalance, or any other metabolic abnormality.

(*ii*) **Gonadial development.** Many alkylating agents like TEPA, chloroethylamine or nitrogen mustard when given in high doses, prevent the development of ovaries in houseflies.

(*iii*) **Mutagenic effects.** Many alkylating agents produce effects similar to those produced by ionic radiation such as mutation, chromosomal aberration, cancer and sterility. Some chemicals like thio-TEPA induce mutagenic changes only in oocytes and others like tretamine, both in oocytes and sperms. The effects are called *dominant lethal mutations* which express themselves during the development of zygote or any time thereafter.

Table 12.1 Different groups of antimetabolite chemoesterilants

Purine analogues	Pyrimidine analogues	Folic acid analogues	Others
5-Fluorouracil	2-Amino-4-methyl-	Amithopterin	L—Leucine
(5-FU)	pyrimidine	Aminopterin	DL—Methionine
5-Fluoroorotic acid	1, 2, 3, 6-Tetrahydro-	Methotrexate	DL—Tyrosine
(FO)	2, 6-Dioxi-4-pyrimi-		
	dineacetic acid,	Folic acid	Colchicine
5-Bromouracil,	2-Thiourea		
2-Thiouracil,	Aldrin		
2, 6-Diaminopurine	Carbamic acid esters		

Antimetabolites

Antimetabolites are chemicals which are structurally related to biologically active substances. Due to their structural similarity, the biological system fails to distinguish them from their own natural substances and commits the mistake of utilising them in place of the latter. For example, if bacteria are grown in a medium containing 5-fluorouracil, the latter will replace a large percentage of the normal metabolite, uracil, in the RNA of the former. Three groups of antimetabolites are more important : purine compounds, pyrimidine compounds and folic acid compounds whose examples are given in Table 12.1.

Mechanism of action. Antimetabolites are regarded as antagonistic structural analogues of the natural metabolites interfering with the synthesis of the nucleic acids. They may be doing so in the following three ways : (*i*) they may compete with the normal nucleotides for enzymes and thus, prevent the orderly incorporation of the nucleotides into the nucleic acids; (*ii*) they may exert a feed-back control on the synthesis of the nucleotides themselves, and (*iii*) they may get directly incorporated into the nucleic acids.

The foregoing effects in some way not yet clearly understood, sterilise the insects. If 5-fluorouracil is fed to insects, it replaces the normal uracil from the RNA of the eggs and this may be the cause of the eggs' inviability. This effect may be temporary, for when the chemical is depleted in the body, the eggs become viable again.

Miscellaneous Compounds

Under this are kept the chemosterilants which are structurally unrelated (Fig. 12.2). They are of the following categories :

Non-alkylating analogues of aziridinyl compounds. These chemicals were discovered in an attempt to find safer chemicals. They are HEMPA (hexamethylpho-sphoramide), a dimethylamine of TEPA and HEMEL (hexamethylemelamine), a dimethylamine analogue of tretamine, both being male housefly sterilants.

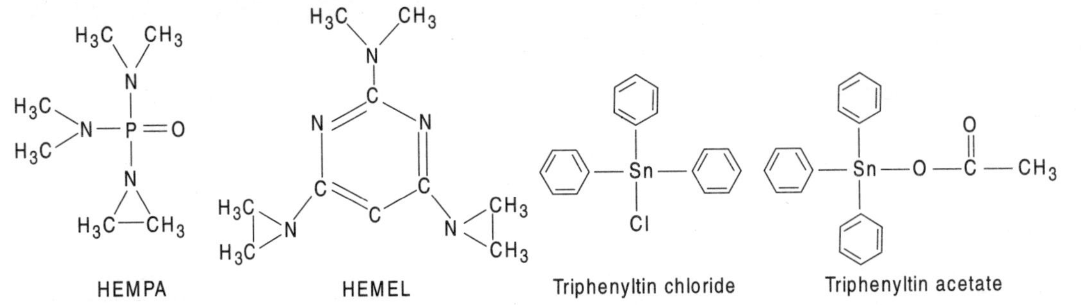

HEMPA HEMEL Triphenyltin chloride Triphenyltin acetate

Fig. 12.2 Chemical structure of chemosterilants (miscellaneous compounds)

Organotin compounds. Numerous triphenyltin derivatives such as tripenyltin hydroxide, triphenyltin chloride (chlorotriphenyltin), triphenyltin acetate (acetoxy triphenyltin), bis (triphenyltin) sulfide, alkyltriphenyltin, etc., have found to be reproduction inhibitors in the house flies. They sterilise both males and females, but the females are more sensitive because they are affected at a much lower concentration than the males.

Mode of Application

Sprays and dusts. Like conventional insecticides, chemosterilants can also be applied as sprays and dusts. This technique will particularly be useful for treating ponds, lakes, reservoirs and open ditches to sterilise aquatic insects. Mosquito larvae, reared in water, containing 10 ppm TEPA were found to develop into sterile adults.

Insecticide-chemosterilant mixture. This method will serve the dual purpose : first, the insect population will be reduced to give quick protection to crops and second, those few pests left, would be sterilised, thereby providing a further reduction in insect numbers. Such an approach will be more acceptable to farmers who are more concerned with immediate results.

Direct contact with residues. Instead of applying chemosterilants to the insects, they are applied to the places where the insects like to rest, congregate or breed such as decaying materials, manure-piles, etc. Also, pre-treated screens of glass plates, mesonite sheets, boards, etc., could be fixed at places where insects might be expected to come in contact with them. Obviously, for such-purposes, quick sterilising chemicals will be needed and there are chemicals available now which can sterilise within 4-48 hours. The method would be more profitable if the insects could be lured to selected and treated areas by the use of baits and sex attractants. An interesting method was devised for sterilising house flies. A small piece of soft leather (chamois) pad impregnated with METEPA was attached to the abdomen of the female insect so that during copulation, the male contacted it and got sterilised.

Oral ingestion. Chemosterilants could also be sprayed on the natural food of insect or mixed with baits and kept in fields—in case of the houselies, in the refuse they breed in. The insects will ingest the chemicals along with their food and get sterilised. In practice, this method has been found particularly useful for the control of house flies.

Field Trials

Agricultural pests. Not much effort has been made to control agricultural pests by chemosterilants. Most of the work that has been carried out, relates to cage experiments performed in various laboratories. Such experiments have been tried with lepidopteran insects like cabbage looper (*Trichoplusia ni*), pink bollworm (*Pectinophora gossypiella*), etc. However, some actual field trials have been attempted in California on Mexican fruit flies (with TEPA) and in Alabama on the cotton boll weevil (with apholate). In spite of the success in the case of the former, chemosterilants were abandoned in favour or irradiation for the sake of safety. The latter could not meet with complete success due to insufficient isolation of the treated areas.

Public health pests. The house flies were the first to be tried with TEPA mixed in food bait and used in 0.6 ha refuse dump in Florida in 1962. Nine weekly treatments brought the insect population down. Measurements were done by counting the number of flies landing per minute on a grid 45" × 45" kept at ten scattered localities. However, the population soon increased because the area was not isolated. Attempts to control houseflies have also been made in Italy (1964), Sicily (1967) and Japan (1968). While some success was achieved, the problem of reinvasion from the nearby untreated areas was always there to annul the effects of the treatment. Evidences that the house flies are getting resistant to chemosterilants are now coming in. Testse flies were chemosterilised in Zimbabwe and 98 per cent control was achieved but complete eradication could not be possible due to reinvasion from the adjoining areas. Mosquitoes (*Aedes, Culex*) were also put to chemosterilant treatments. The first field release of chemosterilised mosquitoes was made in Seahorse Key islands off the coast of Florida in 1968, another, in Kenya (1971) , and then in India at villages Bamnauli (1971), and Dhulsiras (1972), near Delhi. Controls were only partial again due to the lack of isolation of these places.

B. Ionising Radiations

Sterilisation of insects by irradiation can be brought about by exposing them to

γ-radiation (gamma-radiation or alpha and beta particles), X-rays and neutrons. Of these, γ-raidation by 60CO with its half-life of 6 years, is the most common method of sterilisation. Radiation dosesdiffer for different species and even for different developmental stages of the same species. A high dose will provide complete sterilisation (*i.e.* all generations produced by the sterilised insects will be sterile), while lower (substerilisation) dose will provide a partial sterility which may not continue beyond the F1 generation. However, higher doses adversely affect longevity and competitiveness, and, therefore, partial rather than complete sterility is preferred (atleast in the cases of pests affecting costly crops or those of more serious diseases), so that some control (atleast up to F1 generation) could be achieved. Competitiveness being more crucial for males, allowing residual fertility (partial sterility) in males and complete sterility in females, will maximise the impact in a control (not eradication) programme.

In every insect species, a radiation dose that does not adversely affect longevity and competitiveness has to be determined separately by experimentation because such a dose differs for different species. Sterilising doses of some of the more common insects are given in Table 12.2.

Table 12.2 Estimated doses of γ-rays and X-rays for male sterilisation

Scientific name	Common name	Stage	Sterilising dose (rads)
Musca domestica	House fly	2-3 days pupae	3000
Cochliomyia hominivorax	Screwworm	5 days pupae	2500
		1 day adult	5000-7000
Drosophila melanogaster	Fruit fly	Adult males	11000-12000
Culex fatigans	House mosquito	Pupae	7700
Apis mellifera	Honey bee	Adults	7000-11000
Sitophilus oryzae	Rice weevil	7 days adults	7500-10000
Tribolium confusum	Confused flour beetle	Old pupae	4000

Concept of Knipling's Technique

The concept of E.F. Knipling's technique involves two systems, viz. sterile male technique and sterile insect technique. Although both the procedures envisage the common principle of sterility, they greatly differ in the manner in which populations are affected.

Sterile male technique. According to this technique, if fully competitive sterile males are released in the natural (*i.e.* wild) populations, it will reduce the reproductive potential of the natural populations in the same ratio as sterile to fertile. If, for instance, the sterile to fertile (S : F) ratio is 1:1, then according to the law of chances, both sterile and fertile males will have an equal (fifty-fifty) chance of mating with the wild females. The matings with the sterile males will be infructuous (eggs will be non-viable or sterile), which will mean that the reproductive capacity of the natural population is reduced by 50 per cent. In other words, a control of 50 per cent has been achieved. Thus, if the

S : F ratio is increased to 9 : 1, then the control (atleast theoretically) will be 90 per cent. This technique is now synonymous with the sterile insect release method (SIRM), wherein both males and females, mass reared and sterilised in the laboratory, are released at every generation until the pest is eradicated or controlled.

Sterile insect technique. This technique envisages the sterilisation of a portion of the wild population itself (both males and females) by chemosterilants. The effect then will be two-fold : (*i*) the percentage sterilised, cannot reproduce and, in effect, will amount to killing the same proportion of insects (same as in the sterile male technique), and (*ii*) additionally, the sterilised males and females of the wild population will, in turn, nullify the reproductive capacity of a proportionate number of the fertile individuals in the population by competing with them. This method, in a way, combines chemical and biological control methods; the effect of the chemosterilant will be chemical, and that of the sterilised insects, biological. Thus, if 90 per cent of the given population is sterilised, this percentage cannot reproduce, which will amount to 90 per cent killed (first effect). Of the remaining fertile 10 per cent, only 1 per cent be expected to have fertile mating because of the existence of 90 per cent sterilised insects in the population (second or *bonuseffect*, as termed by Knipling). This, a total of 90 + 9 = 99 per cent of the insect population, will fail to have fertile mating, amounting to 99 per cent control. An added effect produced by released insects on the natural population, could be to exert an additional pressure on their struggle for existence by competing with them for food and shelter. Besides, this method does not cause hazards to man and his environment.

Knipling's SIRM Model

The SIRM model of Knipling has been illustrated in Table 12.3. The assumed number of insects in the wild population is 1000, and that of the sterile insects released in each generation, is 2000.

Table 12.3 The SIRM model of Knipling

Generation	Natural population	Sterile insects released	S : F matings	Infertile (%) progeny	No. fertile progeny
1	1000	2000	2 : 1	66.7	333
2	333	2000	6 : 1	85.7	47
3	47	2000	42 : 1	97.7	1
4	1	2000	2000 : 1	99.9	0

If for an assumed natural population of 1000 insects (1000 males and 1000 females), 2000 fully competitive males are released in each generation, the ratio of sterile to fertile (S : F)in the population will be 2:1. This means that only one-third of the natural wild females can be expected to mate with the wild fertile males and two-thirds with the released sterile males resulting in 1000 × 2/3 = 66.7 per cent infertile mating. Thus, only 333 progeny of each sex will be produced instead of 1000. In the next generation, the release of 2000 sterile males will result in a 6:1 sterile to fertile ratio and only one-seventh of the 333 wild fertile females will be expected to mate with the fertile males, producing 47 progeny and six-seventh with the released sterile males resulting in 100 × 6/7 = 85.7 per cent infertile matings. The release of 2000 sterile males in the third generation will raise the S:F ratio to 42:1, resulting in only 1 progeny which, in the fourth generation, will be eliminated because of its having 2000 times greater chance of mating with the sterile than with the fertile males.

The aforestated model, assumes a constant insect population in each generaton, which is not the case in nature. In each generation, the insect population tends to increase. And though the potential rate of increase of most insect populations is very high, casualties due to various factors (such as parasitism, predation, natural hazards), bring the net increase down to a lower rate. According to Knipling's own estimate, an insect population tends to increase five-fold in each generation. Therefore, to offset (neutralise) this increase, a constant number of sterile insects has to be released every generation. Since the control brought about by the sterile insect is more than the annual increase, a time comes when the sterile to fertile ratio becomes so disproportionate that, there may not be any fertile matings, resulting in complete control or eradication.

The significant feature of the SIRM is that, each release of sterile insects achieves an increasingly higher sterile to fertile ratio and thus becomes progressively more efficient, which is an advantage over the insecticides, where the kill in each generation remains constant. The results shown in Tables 12.4 and 12.5 will bear this out.

Table 12.4 Number of generations needed to eradicate a population of 1000 insects by insecticides envisaging a control of 90 per cent and an annual population increase of five-fold

Generation	Natural population treated with insecticides	Survivors	Five-fold increase
1	1000	100.0	500
2	500	50.0	225
3	225	22.8	114
4	114	11.4	56
5	56	5.6	28
6	28	2.8	14
7	14	1.4	6
8	6	0.0	0

Table 12.5 Number of generations needed to eradicate a population of 1000 insects by SIRM envisaging a control of 90 per cent and an annual population increase of five-fold

Generation	Natural population	Sterile insects released	S : F matings	Progeny	Five-fold increase
1	1000	9000	9 : 1	100.0	500.0
2	500	9000	18 : 1	26.0	130.0
3	130	9000	67 : 1	1.9	9.5
4	10	9000	900 : 1	0.0	0.0

When both the Tables are compared, it becomes obvious that while it takes eight generations to eradicate the insects by the insecticide control system, it takes only four by the SIRM, the latter getting progressively more efficient.

Eradication of Screwworm Fly

The screwworm fly, *Cochliomyia hominivorax,*was the first insect pest that was put to this method of control. This is a muscid fly parasitising on warm-blooded animals from the southern parts of the USA to South America and certain West Indian islands. The females of this insect lay eggs in skin lesions where the larvae hatch and feed for 5-6 days before falling off to the ground for pupation in the soil. Due to the severity of infestation, the animals die. Before 1958, the estimated loss due to this pest used to be to the tune of $ 12 million a year.

The monogamous habit of this insect led Knipling in 1937 to develop his sterile male and sterile insect techniques. The first successful attempt to control this insect by the release of irradiated insects was made in 1952 on a small island named Sanibel, 3.2 km off the west coast of Florida (USA). Irradiated flies at the rate of 200 (100 of each sex)/2.59 km^2 (each 2.59 km^2 is estimated to have 10 insects) were released once a week. After two weeks, 80 per cent of the egg masses sampled proved to be sterile and after three months, the fly population was almost zero. However, the fly could not be eradicated completely because of the island's proximity to the uncontrolled mainland.

Subsequently, spectacular success was achieved in the eradication of screwworm on the 440.3 km^2 Island of Curacao during 1954-55. The males sterilised at a dose of 2500r were released at the rate of 400 per 2.59 km^2 per week. By concerted efforts, screwworms were eradicated from Florida (eastern coast) by 1960, from Texas and New Mexico (mid-mainland) by 1964 and from Arizona and California (west mainland) by 1965. To neutralise the effect of invasion from untreated neighbouring areas, barrier releases

(*i.e.* additional releases) between the treated and untreated zones were carried out.

In 1972, the population of the screw worm fly increased beyond the effective management by the sterile fly releases. Some of the reasons could be :

- Unusually favourable conditions for winter survival of screwworms in northern Mexico, south of the sterile-fly release area and in the sterile fly barrier.
- More favourable weather conditions in the spring and summer in the south western United States.
- Relaxation in animal husbandry practices which result in the breeding of animals virtually the year round (Earlier, livestock owners followed breeding practices to assure the birth of most calves, lambs and other livestock when screwworms were absent or scarce).
- Failure of livestock owners to follow other animal management practices such as minimal surgical operations and careful surveillance of animals during the fly season to look for and treat infested animals before larvae can mature.
- A general increase in deer populations throughout the normal range of the screwworm.
- An upsurge in the Gulf Coast tick, *Amblyomma maculatum*, which is one of the principal natural predisposing causes of screwworm cases in livestock.
- Changes in the behaviour and competitiveness of the released sterile flies because of genetic deterioration.
- Changes in the competitiveness of flies due to modifications in the rearing procedures.
- Changes in the behaviour of native population through genetic selection pressure making the adults prone to avoid matings with the released strain.

The situation, however, improved in 1973 to 1975 because the sterile fly production rate was doubled to about 200 million per week. New strains of screwworms were established to release flies that were not maintained as laboratory cultures for long. Other modifications of the programme were also made including better distribution of sterile flies. Dr Edward F. Knipling and Dr Raymond C. Bushland were awarded the 1992 World Food Prize for developing ecofriendly SIT to control or eradicate insect pests that threaten vast sources of food, especially livestock and wildlife populations.

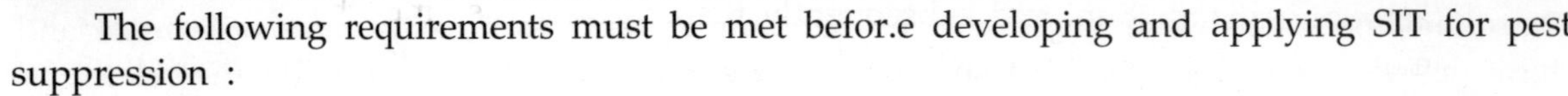

The following requirements must be met befor.e developing and applying SIT for pest suppression :

- Practical procedures must be developed for rearing enough insects to overflood the natural population.
- Methods of inducing sterility or strains possessing appropriate genetic defects must be available.
- Reasonably accurate estimates of absolute numbers of the insects in the natural population are essential to determine how many insects must be reared for release, considering the relative competitiveness of the released and native insects.
- The released insects must be distributed so that they will be in reasonable spatial competition with the natural population for mating.
- Information on the normal rate of increase of the natural population is desirable as a guide to the rate of overflooding required to achieve the necessary results.
- The degree of infiltration of the target pest and its impact on the effectiveness of the technique must be considered.
- The numbers of released insects required for control or elimination must not be unduly hazardous to crops, animals or man.
- A critical analysis of the candidate insect pests, including costs, effectiveness and ecological effects of available alternative control methods, is essential in appraising the value of SIT as a replacement or supplement for other methods of control.

Eradication of Mexican fruit Fly

The Mexican fruit fly, *Anastrepha ludens* (Loew), a native of Mexico, is a major pest of citrus fruits in commercial orchards situated in higher altitudes of Mexico, Belize, Guatemala, and the Lower Rio Grande Valley (LRGV) of Texas (USA). Besides, the fly is a frequent invader in southern California and Arizona. Mexican fruit fly also poses a threat to Florida because of its special affinity for grapefruit, of which Florida is one of the world's leading producers. The female fly attacks ripening fruit, piercing the soft skin and laying eggs in the puncture. Subsequently, the eggs hatch into larvae (maggots), which feed inside the fruit pulp, making the fruit unfit for human consumption.

To prevent damage of fruits caused by the fruit fly, the U.S. Department of Agriculture's (USDA) Animal and Plant Health Inspection Service (APHIS) operates control and eradication programmes in cooperation with State officials. APHIS also cooperates with Mexico in a programme to suppress the pest in northern Mexico. Once a fly is captured in a detection trap, more number of such traps are set in the area to determine if an infestation exists and to determine the limits of the infested area. In case an infestation exists, a quarantine on all kinds of fruits is imposed that can be Mexican fruit fly hosts in the infested area. All potential host material is inspected and treated before if can be transported out of the quarantine zone. Once the pest is contained within an area, a three step eradication programme begins, as given below:

- **Selective Bait Spray**: Using airplanes and ground sprayers, programme workers apply a bait spray approved for use by the Environmental Protection Agency on the affected area by using air planes and ground sprays. The spray containing malathion and a sweet protein nutrient that attracts the flies, is applied to fruit trees.
- **The Sterile Insect Technique (SIT):** This biological control technique involves mass-rearing of the Mexican fruit flies, followed by sterilization by exposing them to a small

amount of irradiation, and subsequently their mass release into the areas where they mate with wild flies. Such matings do not produce offspring and eventually population of the wild flies is eliminated through attrition. The Mexican fruit fly rearing facility at Mission, Texas (USA) is capable of producing about 80 million sterile flies per week. The sterile flies are released on a weekly basis in densities varying from 250,000 to 320,000 flies per mi^2 (400 to 500 flies per acre).

- **Targeted Insecticide Applications**: The insecticides are applied on the soil under host trees to kill the larvae as they enter the soil to pupate and the emerging adults. Insecticides are applied on the soil only when larvae are detected.

To maintain Mexican fruit fly free area, surveillance at 5 traps per mi^2, is conducted at a two week interval. Further, a preventive release programme is recommended for high risk areas at 100,000 sterile males per mi^2 or 200,000 male/female per mi^2.

HYBRID STERILITY

Hybrid sterility refers to sterility that occurs when certain strains, races, or closely related species are crossed and either one or both sexes of F1 progeny are viable but cannot produce viable progeny. In hybrid sterility, mating is induced between closely related species under laboratory conditions. If such mating leads to fertilization, the hybrid individuals may die in the embryonic stage, in one of the pre-adult stages or early in the adult stage. Alternatively, apparently normal adults produced may show partial or complete sterility in one or both the sexes. The various defects in the mating between such insects are either an imperfect copulation due to structural differences in their genitalia or if the copulation is perfect, it may lack insemination and if inseminated, the fertilization may not take place and even if fertilized, the individuals may die before hatching, any time between larval and adult stages or they may even survive, but only as hybrid adults.

The hybrid adults may look quite normal externally or may even show heterosis (*i.e.* hybrid vigour with increased longevity, increased sexual aggressiveness, increased competitiveness, etc.), but one or both sexes will be partially or completely sterile or will have defective gametogenesis resulting in premature death of the progeny at any stage of their development. This phenomenon has been investigated and used in the management of several pest speies, (*e.g.*between species of the tsetse flies, *Glossina morsitans* and *G. swynnertoni*; between races of the gypsy moth, *Lymantria dispar*, and between the moth species *Heliothis virescens* and *H. subflexa*).

The hydridisation of *H. virescens* and *H. subflexa* stimulated interest in reducing field populations of *H. virescens*, using released backcross insects. In an experiment on St. Croix, US Virgin Islands, using both male and female backcross insects, sterility was infused into a field population with release ratios of 20 sterile backcross : 1 feral insect. The frequency of sterile male progeny increased for one generation after release, and the distribution of backcross frequencies became homogeneous througout the population. During a 6-week period, 94 per cent of trapped males were sterile progeny from released or field-reared backcross females the native males. Isolated populations of *H. virescens*, probably can be eradicated, using this method, given a sufficient number of released hybrid individuals.

Many attempts have been made to produce strile hybrids from other pest species. For example, *Helicopverpa zea* has been mated with *H. armigera* from Australia, Russia, and China, and *H. assulta* from Pakistan and Thailand. These hydridisation attempts failed to produce a sterile hybrid. Similarly, no measurable hybrid sterility has been found in crosses between the pink bollworm from areas within the United States, Mexico, Puerto Rico, or St. Croix. There was no incompatibility between a strain of the pink bollworm from southern India and two strains (one long-term laboratory strain, the other a newly colonised strain) from Arizona.

CYTOPLASMIC INCOMPATIBILITY

In this case, a cross between two apparently conspecific populations results in only partial embryonation in some ova. Spermatozoa enter the egg cytoplasm, but no fusion occurs between the nuclei of spermatozoa and ova with the result, that zygote is not formed and the egg remains sterile. This sterility appears to be due to a cytoplasmic factor and not to chromosomal incompatibilities. It has been found that crosses between individuals from certain populations of the same species of mosquito (*Culex pipiens*) sre sterile. Crosses between other populations are somtimes completely fertile or partially sterile. The phenomenon has also been discovered in a number of other mosquito species and has been used as a control measure in experimental releases. The phenomenon is best known in the crosses between the subspecies of *Culex pipiens,* collectively referred to as the *C. pipiens*–complex, viz. *C. pipiens* (temperate region), *C. fatigans* (tropical and subtropical) and *C.p. australicus* (restricted to Australia and nearby regions). The same subspecies existing in a different part of the wild forms a strain reproductively incompatible with a strain of another country. At least 20 reproductive types amongst these three subspecies are known which show three types of incompatibilities :

(*i*) Partial incompatibility, where crossing of two strains produces low hatches of eggs.

(*ii*) Unidirectional incompatibility, where only one of the sexes of a particular strain is capable of producing sterile eggs.

(*iii*) Bidirectional incompatibility, where the reciprocal crosses are incompatible.

Field trials of this method were carried out in a village near Rangoon in Myanmar in 1971 and at Delhi in 1972 under a WHO/ICMR programme. The method involved release of incompatible strains of the mosquito, *C.p. fatigans* from other (temperate) regions. Before actual release, suitable backcrosses in tropical and temperate strains were carried out to produce a variety that would survive tropical conditions without losing its incompatibility. This is possible in backcrosses between unidirectional incompatibilities. The trials at both the places demonstrated the efficacy of the method, but the invasion by mosquitoes from untreated regions was the obstacle preventing a complete eradication of the species.

Cytoplasmic incompatibility has also been observed in the plum curculio, *Conotrachelus nenuphar*; cherry fruit fly, *Rhagoletis cerasi*; and *Ephestia cautella* leading to the hope that it might occur in many economically important insects. The use of sterility induced by cytoplasmic incompatibility has one serious drawback. Released strains of insects must be separated by sex before release, so that they might not interbreed and become established in the field.

CHROMOSOME TRANSLOCATION

Translocation is the breakage of two non-homologous (dissimilar) chromosomes (as in a heterozygote) and the re-attachment of the broken parts to the wrong partners as shown in Fig. 12.3. During meiosis in gamete formation, the translocated chromosome segregates out into six types of gametes as indicated in the figure. Of the six types of gametes, only two are balanced (orthoploid), having a full gene complement and, therefore, viable and four are unbalanced (aneuploid), having more genes of one chromosome and less of the other and, therefore, non-viable or lethal. Eggs produced by gametes having lethal genes will be sterile. This phenomenon can be utilised in the control of insects.

Translocations in insects can be produced by exposure to irradiation and to radiomimetic chemical (such as EMS, MMS, bleomycin, mitomycin-c, nitrogen mustard, etc.). Such translocated insects could be released into wild population. Mating between wild and translocated heterozygote individuals will result in the reduction of population of the wild type by a fall in the viable egg production. By persisting in the release of more and more translocated insects, the wild population (theoretically atleast) can be eliminated.

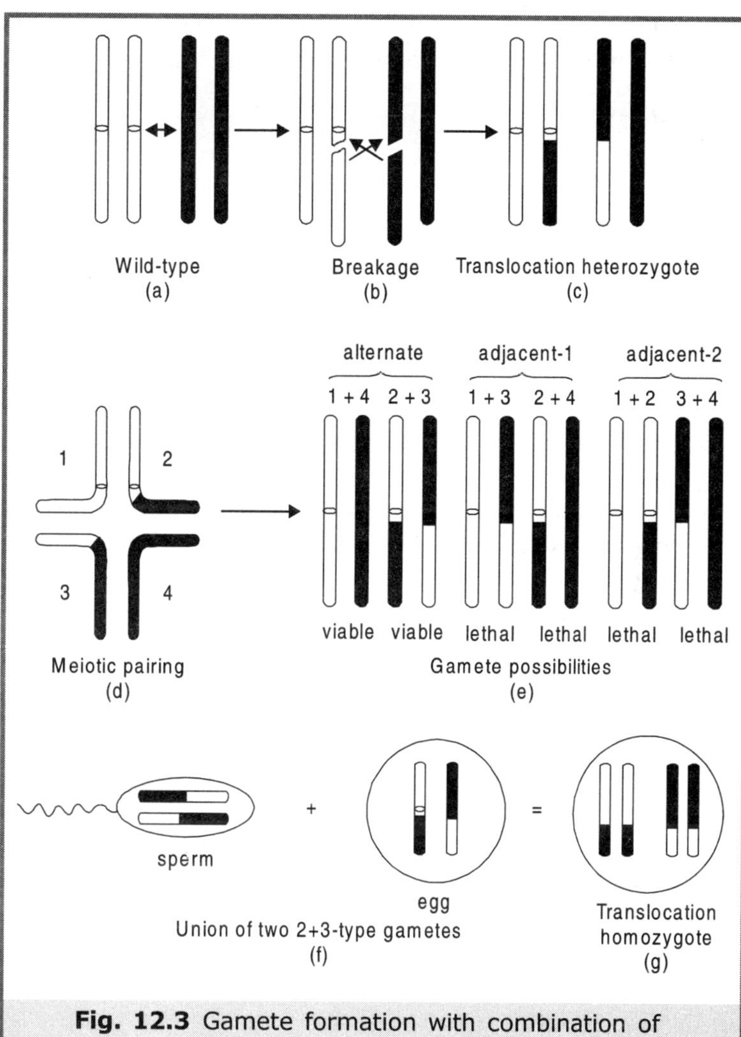

Fig. 12.3 Gamete formation with combination of translocated chromosomes

This method has been tried only in laboratory in cage experiments on mosquitoes (*Culex*, *Aedes* and *Anopheles*), house fly (*M. domestica*), lepidopteran pests (codling moth, cabbage looper, pink bollworm), etc. At first, translocated and wild population is kept in small cages under laboratory conditions. If there is a decline in the wild population, the same experiment is repeated with large population in large-sized cages kept under field conditions.

LETHAL FACTORS

Natural population carries a considerable load of deleterious genes which are detrimental to their survival. Two such types of genes can exsit, *i.e.* straightforward lethal genes and conditional lethal genes. The straightforward lethal genes are recessive, being kept suppressed by suppressor genes, but can be isolated (made dominant) by inbreeding in the laboratory. When released in homozygous or heterozygous conditions, such insects could produce progeny that would soon be eliminated by a normal process of natural selection. The conditional lethal genes are dominant, but have deleterious effects under some conditions, but not under others. For example, there are temperature sensitive (hot or cold) lethal genes. Insects with such genes could be mass reared and released in wild population in conditions favourable to them, so that they could, by mating with wild population, produce a progeny that would not survive a later change in climatic conditions (temperature). For example,where diapause is necessary for the survivial of the pink bollworm during host-free or environmentally unsuitable periods, its inability to enter diapause would be a conditional lethal trait. A non-diapausing strain could be reared readily in the laboratory, but progeny produced by this strain in the field would not diapause, and it would not be able to reproduce during the host-free period. Similarly, a cocoon-producing insect could be made to produce a progeny incapable of producing cocoons. In either case, the progeny will die to the vicissitudes of the climatic changes.

SEX-RATIO DISTORTION

Some insects produce progeny of one sex more than the other—these can be male producing or female producing. Such insects when mass reared in the laboratory and released in nature, compete with wild population to mate and produce offsprings that are predominantly of one sex. In course of time, imbalance in the sex-ratio leads to a reduction in the population and ultimately to the extinction of the species itself. The mechanism by which the above distortion is brought about is called meiotic drive where (*i*) a factor called segregation distorter, present on a chromosome, drives only one of the two chromosomes of the XY (sex chromosome) pair to the poles to form gametes during meiosis, (*ii*) the driven chromosome undergoes supplementary replication with a concomittant loss of its homologue, or (*iii*) only one of the XY pair of chromosomes survives to end up in functional gametes, the other one, degenerating and being reabsorbed (Fig. 12.4).

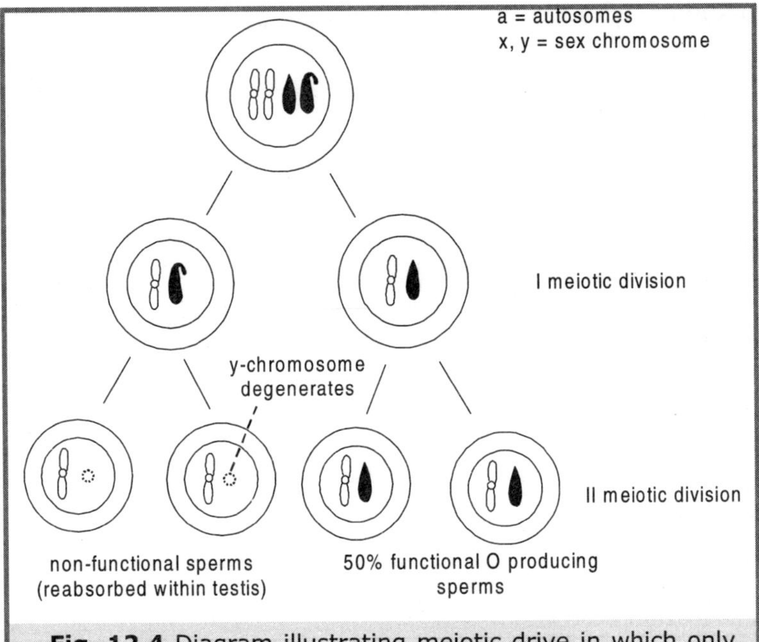

Fig. 12.4 Diagram illustrating meiotic drive in which only one sex (female) producing sperms are formed

The sex-ratio distortion, it is believed, can also be caused by a differential sperm behaviour. Depending upon the genetic constitution, one of the two kinds (X or Y) of sperms may compete better than the other to fertilise the ovum or even by a selective acceptance by the ovum of the two kinds of sperms. In nature, meiotic drive sex-ratio distortion has been found in the mosquito, *Aedes aegypti*. Some strains of this mosquito are predominantly male producing. Such males, when mass reared and released into wild populations, will produce mostly male progeny, which in course of time will not only lead to their extinction but will also have an additional effect in reducing disease transmission, since it is only the female of this species that transmits the disease. If the genetic constitution of an insect is known, it is also possible to produce sex distortion artificially by a selective breeding. A strain of *Musca domestica* has now been produced in the laboratory that is predominantly male producing. Thus, the method of sex-ratio distortion offers a great promise in insect pest control.

SPECIES REPLACEMENT

It has been observed that of the two species or strains of a single species living in the same ecological niche, one is more competitive than the other. The males of the better competitor can be mass reared and released to mate with the female of the other. Such matings result in the production of sterile eggs and ultimately lead to the replacement of the species. An attempt has been made to replace *A.e. polynensiensis*, the natural vector of periodic *Wuchereia bancrofti* (filaria producing nematode) in the South Pacific with the non-vector allopatric species *A.e. albopictus* from Pune, Maharashtra. The males of the latter, readily mate with the female of the former even in presence of their own males. The result of such a mating is sterile eggs.

GENETIC CONTROL : SUCCESSES

The SIT and other genetic methods are species specific and have no negative impact on the environment. But their complexity puts them beyond the reach of individual farmers and the programmes have to be planned, organized and implemented by the government agencies. Perhaps due to this reason, hardly any SIT programmes have been undertaken in Asian countries where farms are very small and large-scale, centralized pest control strategies are difficult to implement. The only exceptions to this are fruit fly, *Dacus cucurbitae* eradication programme undertaken extensively in Japan from 1972 onwards and the *Bactrocera dorsalis* suppression programme in Taiwan from 1975 onwards. On the other hand, Mediterranean fruitfly, *Ceratitis capitata* eradication programme was a huge success in Mexico and other Central American Countries. For a number of other pests including onion fly, *Delia antiqua*; European cockchafer, *Melolontha melolontha*; European cherry fruit fly, *Rhagoletis cerasi*; coding moth, *Cydia pomonella* and grape moth, *Eupoecilia ambiguella*, large scale programmes are in operation in a number of European countries. A list of the more notable trials that have been carried out to date, is given in Table 12.4 and some selected examples are discussed herein.

Screwworm

The first major use of SIT was for the eradication of the primary screwworm from the island of Curacao in 1954. Following this success, the pest was then eradicated from the southeastern United States in 1959 and from Puerto Rico in 1975. Eradication of the screwworm was initiated in the south-western United States in 1962 and completed in 1982. Because of the extensive damage that the screwworm causes in Mexico, and because it was impossible to prevent reinfestation into the United States, a Mexican-American Commission was created in 1972 to eradicate the pest from northern and western Mexico and to establish a "sterile fly barrier" at the Isthmus of Tehuantepec. In 1986, the commission extended its eradication activities to the Yucatan Peninsula and countries of Central America. As a result of this programme, Mexico, Belize, and most of Guatemala are now fee of the screwworm. Operations are in progress to eradicate the screwworm from Honduras and El Salvador. The present goals of the programme are to eradicate the pest from Central America and Panama and to establish a sterile fly barrier at the Darien Gap to prevent its reinfestation. Also, efforts will be made to eradiate the screwworm from Caribbean islands which are still infested.

Table 12.4 Major field trials for control of insect pests using sterile insect release technique

Insect		Trial locations
Common name	**Scientific name**	
Diptera		
Screw worm	*Cochliomyia hominivorax*	North America, Central America, Libya
Mediterranean fruit fly	*Ceratitis capitata*	Central America, Hawaii, Canary islands
Mexican fruit fly	*Anastrepha ludens*	Mexico
Queensland	*Bactrocera tryoni*	Australia
Cherry fruit fly	*Rhagoletis cerasi*	Switzerland
Oriental fruit fly	*Bactrocera dorsalis*	Guam
Melon fly	*Bactrocera cucurbitae*	Various Japanese islands
Onion fly	*Delia antiqua*	Netherlands
Olive fly	*Bactrocera oleae*	Various European countries
House mosquito	*Culex quinquefasciatus*	Florida
Malarial mosquito	*Anopheles ludens*	El Salvador
Stable fly	*Stomoxys calcitrans*	St. Croix (Virgin Islands)
Tsetse fly	*Glossina palpalis*	Nigera, Upper Volta
Lepidoptera		
Grape moth	*Eupoecilia ambiguella*	Various European countries
Codling moth	*Cydia pomonella*	USA, Canada, Switzerland
Coleoptera		
European cockchafer	*Melolontha melolontha*	Switzerland
Pink bollworm	*Pectinophora gossypiella*	California, USA
Boll weevil	*Anthonomus grandis*	Louisiana, USA

Source : Thacker (2002)

The screwworm invaded North Africa in the 1980s and became established in the Libyan Arab Jamahiriya. After detecting the screworm in 1988 and confirming its presence in 1989, a joint decision was made by the Food and Agriculture Organization/International Atomic Energy Agency (FAO/IAEA) and the government of the Libyan Arab Jamahiriya to initiate an eradication campaign using the sterile insect technique. The campaign was implemented late in 1990 and completed in October of 1991. North Africa was declared free of the screwworm in June 1992.

Fruit Flies

Genetic control programmes using the SIT have been successful against several species of fruit flies (Diptera : Tephritidae). Limited field application of the SIT has resulted in population suppression or eradication of the Caribbean fruit fly, *Anastropha suspensa* in Florida; cherry fruit fly, *Rhagoletis cerasi,* in Switzerland; Oriental fruit fly, *Bactrocera dorsalis,* in the Mariana Islands; Queensland fruit fly, *Dacus tyroni*; and Chinese citrus fly, *B. citri,* in China. However, area-wide use of the SIT has been successful in the eradication or control of several species of fruit flies. The most spectacular successes have been with eradication of the Mediterranean fruit fly, *Ceratitis capitata,* from southern Mexico, and of the melon fly, *B. cucurbitae* from Japan, and the prevention of Mexican fruit fly from invading California and Texas.

After the first detection of the Mediterranean fruit fly in Mexico, the Ministries of Agriculture of Mexico and Guatemala, and the United States Department of Agriculture, formed the Moscamed programme to combat this pest. The objectives of the programme were to stop the northern advance of the pest, to eradicate it from southern Mexico and Guatemala, and in the long-term, to eradicate it from Central America and Panama. By combining the discrete use of malathion bait spray with the release of sterile flies, the med fly was eradicated from Mexico in 1982. The programme has also been successful in Guatemala.

The Japanese government initiated a project to eradicate the melon fly in 1972. Using the SIT, following one or more treatments of a lure/toxicant, the eradication effort began on Kume Island and was expanded until the melon fly had been eradicated from all the infested islands of the Kagoshima and Okinawa Prefectures. Japan was declared free of the melon fly in 1992. Although the eradication programme required an investment of about $100 million, the benefits from eradication of the melon fly should be over $100 million per year.

Pink Bollworm

The pink bollworm, *Pectinophora gossypiella,* is a serious pest of cotton in many parts of the world. Although the pink bollworm is occasionally recovered from states east of Texas, this pest is most destructive in Arizona, southern California, and the adjacent northwest Mexican desert. After its introduction and establishment in central Arizona in the mid 1950s and in the Colorado River Basin of western Arizona, southern California, and northwestern Mexico in 1965, a programme was initiated in 1968 to protect the 500,000 ha of cotton in the San Joaquin Valley. This programme has prevented the establishment of the pink bollworm through the use of sterile insect-release technology, minor use of pheromones as a mating disruptant, and adequate cultural control. The California cotton industry considers the 27-year old San Joaquin Valley Exclusion Project to be a major success.

INTEGRATION WITH OTHER APPROACHES

The advantage of combining genetic control methods with other pest control methods has been recognized from the inception of genetic control. All the successful genetic control programme mentioned above have non-genetic components that have served vital roles in the control or eradication of pests, as well as preventing re-infestation of pests. Most often, genetic control methods have been integrated with insecticide applications, cultural controls, and quarantines. However, population models constructed to predict the potential advantages of combining genetic control methods with other methods, such as inundative releases of parasitoids, host plant resistance, pheromones for mating disruption, and insect pathogens, have suggested that these combinations would yield synergistic effects. Because the ratio between irradiated and non-irradiated insects is the most critical factor in regulating the efficacy of SIT or F1 sterility release programmes, any mortality agent (i.e. resistant host plants, insecticides) applied during a continuous release of genetically altered insects, would benefit a release programme. Although the mortality agent would reduce the number of both released and wild insects, it would not change the ratio. Therefore, subsequent to the application of the mortality agents, wild population would be lower and the ratio of released to wild insects would be increased by continual releases of genetically altered insects.

Integration of genetic techniques and inundative releases of parasitoids may be more complementary than most other pest control combinations because their optimal actions are at opposite ends of the host density spectrum and do not interfere with each other. Although the use of parasitoids and sterile insect techniques have different modes of action, the effectiveness of the sterile insect technique increases the ratio of adult parasitoids to adult hosts, and the effectiveness of the parasitoids increases the ratio of sterile to fertile insects. Greater pest suppression could be expected if parasitoid releases were combined with the F1 sterility technique. Not only is F1 sterility in lepidopterans more effective than full sterility in reducing population increases, the F1 sterility technique produces eggs and sterile F1 larvae that would provide an increased number of hosts for the parasitoids.

Several laboratory and field studies have been conducted to determine the compatibility and effectiveness of combining different types of genetic control techniques with other control techniques. The effects of F1 sterility and host plant resistance on *Helicoverpa zea* and *Spodoptera frugiperda* development were investigated. It was found that larvae resulting from irradiated male by non-irradiated female crosses were equally competitive with normal larvae for all measured parameters. Ovipositional acceptance tests and parasitism studies with *Microplitis croceipes* in the laboratory and field using *Heliothis virescens* and *H. virescens–H. subflexa* backcross larvae as hosts were conducted. It was concluded that augmentative releases of *M. croceipes* during or following a sterile backcross release should not adversely affect the backcross release ratio, and that the two control techniques possibly could be used effectively together in an area-wide management programme for controlling *H. virescens*. The effect of concurrent parasitoid and sterile fly releases on wild *Ceratitis capitata* populations in the Kula area of Maui, Hawaii was investigated. It was concluded that concurrent SIT and parasitoid augmentation programme may interact synergistically, producing a greater suppression in targetoid insect population than either method used alone.

CONCLUSIONS

Genetic methods are highly specific to a pest species, safe to pest control workers, non-polluting to the environment, long lasting and area-wide in approach, and compatible with most other pest control strategies. Some obstacles slow the rate of progress in the use of genetic methods for controlling pests. Research and development requirements for genetic approaches often demand a long-term commitment before benefits can be realized. Also, technological constraints, such as the difficulty and high cost of insect rearing, may impede progress. The major factor which has limited the success of genetic methods is the lack of information about the behaviour and quality of sterile insects. The background ecological information, so important to the success of these programmes, is also wanting in many cases.

Perhaps the most formidable obstacle to the successful use of genetic methods for pest control is our historical concept of pest managment. Although evolving for the past 50 years, concepts of pest management have not kept pace with, nor fully used, rapidly developing genetic technologies. Before genetic control methods could be more fully implemented for pest management, the concepts of preventative and area-wide pest management must gain wider acceptance. Future pest management strategies for major pests and pest complexes should be developed with definable, long-term goals. These exercises in strategic planning should consider the long-range economic and ecological advantages that genetic approaches may provide as components of integrated pest management. With the generation of additional information, genetic methods are likely to fit into a broader concept of IPM to achieve a range of control from suppression or eradication on the one hand to preventive quarantine on the other.

☆☆☆☆☆

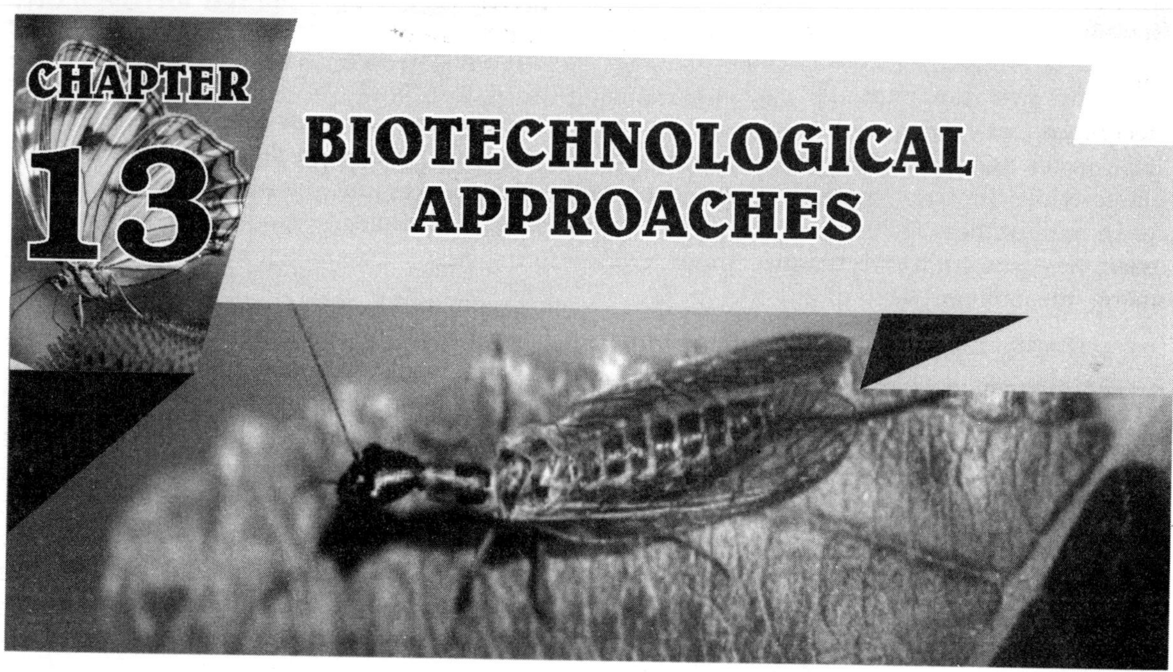

INTRODUCTION

Biotechnology has been defined as any technique that uses living organisms or part of organisms to make or modify products, to improve plants or animals or to develop microorganisms for specific uses. Biotechnology involves the production, isolation, modification and use of substances derived by means of biosynthesis. These substances can be produced from microorganisms and plant cells as well as from the entire plants. Thus, agriculture based on such plants can be looked at as biotechnology. Therefore, biotechnology is not a discipline, rather it depends on advances in biology, genetics, chemistry and engineering and has been redefined as the integrated use of molecular genetics, biochemistry, microbiology and process technology to supply goods and services, employing microorganisms, part of microorganisms, or cells and tissues of higher organisms. Biotechnology includes any process in which organisms, tissues, cells, organelles or isolated enzymes are used to convert biological or other raw materials to products of greater value. In other words, biotechnology involves the utilization of biological agents such as microorganisms, cells of higher plants or animals or their cellular constituents for the isolation of useful products related to human welfare. In pest management, it is the use of genetically modified organisms in the production of crops or animals including the production of insect suppressive agents.

METHODS IN BIOTECHNOLOGY

Biotechnology, as an aid to crop improvement, became scientifically established following developments in our understanding of the genetics that took place in the early 1900s. These developments led to the production of high yielding crop varieties that substantially boosted global agricultural output throughout the twentieth century. However, developments in cell and molecular biology that have taken place since the early 1970s have permitted scientists to shift their attention from yield to pest control. The main biotechnological methods that can be used to produce genetically modified organisms that are of relevance to pest control can be split into two (not mutually exclusive) categories, i.e. (*i*) those that involve tissue culture techniques, and (*ii*) those that involve the use of recombinant DNA technology (Table 13.1). The former techniques have been extensively developed in relation to the production of crop plants while the latter have been employed with plants, pests and natural enemies. In many cases, both of these techniques have been used to produce genetically modified organisms. For example, tissue culture techniques are often used to regenerate plants that have been produced using recombinant technology.

Table 13.1 Biotechnological methods employed in crop improvement

Technique	Application	Example(s)
Tissue culture techniques		
Protoplast fusion	Production of somatic hybrids-novel plants from species that would not cross in the wild	(i) Herbicide-resistant potato plants. (ii) The pomato-cross between potato and tomato plants
Clonal propagation	Culturing protoplasts to produce uniform plants	Disease-free potatoes and strawberries
Somaclonal variation	Culturing protoplasts with useful traits that are normally hidden	Research with a range of crops currently under way
Mutant selection	Culturing protoplasts and stressing them. Surviving cells are selected	Herbicide-resistant maize
Recombinant techniques		
Agrobacterium-based plant transformation	Ti-plasmid (tumour-inducing plasmid) used to carry novel DNA into plants	Bt insect-resistant crop plants (tobacco, corn, cotton)
Particle acceleration	DNA-coated gold particles fired into growing tissue	Used to produce transgenic soybean
Electroporation	Electric current used to alter protoplast membranes permitting DNA uptake	Used to produce transgenic rice
Microinjection	DNA injected into the nucleus or cytoplasm of a protoplast	Used to produce transgenic tomato

Tissue Culture

Tissue culture is a technique of growing plant tissues on synthetic medium under controlled and aseptic conditions. A German plant physiologist, G. Haberlandt, is considered to be the father of plant tissue culture who in 1902 conceived the idea of totipotency, which refers to the capability of a cell to give rise to a complete plant under suitable cultural conditions. Such a property of the cell has far reaching implications to manipulate plant cells for rapid multiplication of plants, to cross plants at the level of somatic cells by overcoming the limit of crossability, and also to regenerate adult plants after modifying the DNA molecule at the cellular level. One of the principle advantages of using tissue culture is that the desirable traits can be selected in the laboratory and the screening process can, therefore, be completed relatively quickly in contrast to consider whole plants in a field-based situation. Plant tissue culture includes several specialized areas, like micropropagation, somaclonal variation, prototoplast and anther culture.

Micropropagation. Micropropagation involves the production of plants from very small (0.2-1.0 mm) plant parts through tissue culture techniques. Micropropagation of selected plant species is one of the best and most successful examples of commercial application of tissue culture technology for mass multiplication of plants that has four distinct advantages, viz. (*i*) It is independent of seasonal constraints and hence ensures year-round rapid propagation. (*ii*) Micropropagated plants are generally true to type. (*iii*) Micropropagated plants are disease free. (*iv*) Micropropagated field grown plants usually exhibit vigorous growth, better quality and higher yields.

Somaclonal variation. Somaclonal variation refers to variation among tissues or plants derived from the *in vitro* somatic cell cultures, i.e. callus and suspension cultures. Historically, it was accepted that all plants arising from tissue culture should be exact copies of the parental plants. However, phenotypic variability was observed among regenerated plants, which was usually ignored. Plants regenerated from stem callus have been referred to as ***calliclones*** and those from protoplasts as ***protoclones***. A general term ***somaclone*** has been proposed for plants derived from any form of cell culture and the variation among such plants termed as somaclonal variation. The somaclonal variation may be genetic or it may result from culture induced epigenetic changes. The epigenetic changes are expressed at cell culture stage but usually disappear when plants are regenerated or they reproduce sexually. Variation arising out of anther/pollen culture is more precisely known as ***gametoclonal variation*** and that through protoplast culture is called ***protoclonal variation***.

The major steps involved in the isolation of somaclones for insect resistance are (*i*) growing calli or cell suspension cultures for several cycles from a high yielding and well-adapted susceptible variety, (*ii*) regeneration of plants from such long-term cell lines, and (*iii*) evaluation of large population of regenerated plants for insect resistance. Using this procedure, somaclonal variants of sugarcane and sorghum have been obtained with good levels of resistance to sugarcane borer, *Diatraea saccharalis* and fall armyworm, *Spodoptera frugiperda*, respectively.

Protoplast culture and somatic hybridization. Somatic hybridization is an effective approach to hybridize the sexually incompatible species. Complete fusion of the nuclei and cytoplasms of somatic cells from both species leads to the formation of somatic hybrid cell and plant. Likewise, the fusion of cytoplasm from two species and nuclear genes from any one leads to the development of cybrid. The plant cells are surrounded by a thick cell wall which does not allow the two cells to fuse to get somatic hybrid cell/plant. However, the protoplast can be easily fused and employed in several experiments aiming at the genetic modification of the plants. Protoplast is a naked cell without cell wall surrounded by plasma membrane and potentially capable of cell wall regeneration, growth and division, The techniques of isolation, culture and regeneration of protoplasts have been established in more than 100 plant species including major field, vegetable and fruit crops.

***In vitro* production of haploids.** In self-pollinated crops, an inordinately long period is required to recombine desirable gene combinations from different sources in homozygous form. Generally, it takes 8-10 years to develop stable, homozygous and ready to use material from a fresh cross of two or more lines. Likewise, due to inbreeding depression in cross-pollinated crops, it is difficult to obtain vigorous inbreds for hybrid seed production programmes. In this regard, haploids possessing gametic chromosome number are very useful for producing instant homozygous true breeding lines. Besides, haploids constitute an important material for induction and selection of mutants particularly for recessive genes. The period required to develop homozygous true breeding line is less through haploid breeding as compared to conventional breeding.

Recombinant DNA Technology

One of the most significant breakthroughs in modern science is the development of techniques to transfer genes from unrelated sources into crop plants. Until recently, scientists could manipulate only the primary and secondary gene pools of the cultivated species for crop improvement. However, recent advances in molecular biology have made it possible to introduce genes from diverse sources such as unrelated plants, bacteria, viruses, fungi, insects, higher animals and even from chemical synthesis in the laboratory. The recombinant DNA technology involves the use of genetic engineering so that the modified plants carry the functional foreign genes. These novel genes either reinforce the existing functions or add new traits to the transformed plants. These developments have provided the opportunity to develop crops with novel genes for insect resistance.

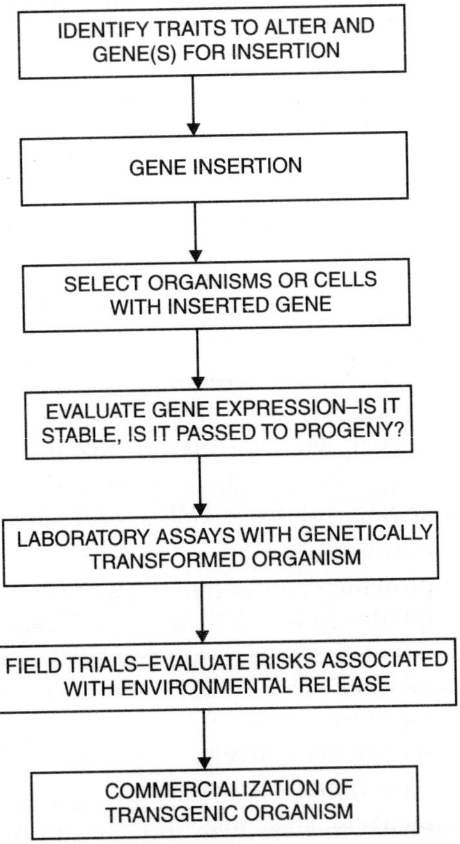

IDENTIFY TRAITS TO ALTER AND GENE(S) FOR INSERTION
↓
GENE INSERTION
↓
SELECT ORGANISMS OR CELLS WITH INSERTED GENE
↓
EVALUATE GENE EXPRESSION–IS IT STABLE, IS IT PASSED TO PROGENY?
↓
LABORATORY ASSAYS WITH GENETICALLY TRANSFORMED ORGANISM
↓
FIELD TRIALS–EVALUATE RISKS ASSOCIATED WITH ENVIRONMENTAL RELEASE
↓
COMMERCIALIZATION OF TRANSGENIC ORGANISM

Fig. 13.1 Steps involved in producing a transgenic organism

The whole process of introduction, integration and expression of the foreign gene(s) in the host is called genetic transfor-mation or transgenesis. In fact, transgenesis has emerged as a novel tool to carry out single gene breeding or transgenic breeding of crop plants. Unlike conventional plant breeding, in this case only the cloned gene(s) of agronomic importance are introduced into the plants without the co-transfer of other undesirable genes from the donor. The recipient genotype is least disturbed thereby setting aside the need for any backcross. This approach has the potential to serve as an effective means to remove certain defects of an otherwise well adapted cultivar, which are not easily manageable through conven-tional breeding approaches. The steps or processes involved in producing a transgenic organism are summarized in Fig. 13.1.

Foreign genes can be transferred through vector-mediated or direct DNA transfer methods using protoplasts or other tissues. In vector-mediated approach, the transgene is combined with a vector, which takes it to the target cells for integration. In direct gene transfer, on the other hand, the gene is physically delivered to the target tissue.

Vector-mediated gene transfer. A vector is a vehicle that transports the foreign genes into the recipient cells, protoplasts or intact plant. It is a DNA molecule, capable of replication in a host organism, into which a gene is inserted to construct a recombinant DNA molecule. This method is also called indirect method of gene transfer. A vector could be either a DNA virus such as caulimovirus or geminivirus or could be plasmids such as tumor inducing (Ti) and root inducing (Ri) plasmids of *Agrobacterium tumefaciens* and *A. rhizogenes,* respectively. A plasmid is usually a circular piece of DNA, primarily independent of host chromosome often found in bacterial cells. The cells to be used for transformation must be replicating DNA, which is available in wounded or dedifferentiated cells or protoplasts.

Direct gene transfer methods. Since the host range of *Agrobacterium* has been largely limited to dicotyledonous plant species, some other methods of transfer of genes to monocotyledonous plants such as cereals have been developed. Many grain legume species and woody plants are also not amenable to *Agrobacterium*-mediated transformation. For genetic transformation of such recalcitrant crops, techniques of direct gene delivery have been attempted. Direct gene transfer methods make use of chemical, physical or electrical methods to introduce DNA into the cells.

(i) Direct uptake of DNA. This method is based on the ability of the protoplasts to uptake the foreign DNA from the surrounding solution. An isolated plasmid DNA (vector) is mixed with the protoplasts in the presence of polyethylene glycol (PEG), polyvinyl alcohol and calcium phosphate, which enhance the uptake of DNA by protoplasts. After 15-20 minutes of incubation, the protoplasts are cultured in the presence of appropriate selective agent. Upon treatment with PEG, the permeability of the plasma-membrane is increased, leading to transient formation of pores, thus facilitating the uptake of DNA by protoplasts. Foreign gene of interest can be as naked DNA such Ti or *E. coli* plasmids or can be encapsulated into liposomes. Although the frequency of integration of DNA into plant genome is relatively low, regeneration of transferred protoplasts selected for the presence of the particular selectable marker, yields transgenic plants. This method, however, depends on the plant regeneration ability of the protoplasts and has been successfully used to produce transgenic plants in brassica, strawberry, lettuce, rice, wheat and maize.

(ii) Electroporation. In this technique, a high voltage current is applied in a pulsed manner, which creates tiny holes in the plant cell membrane. These holes are large enough for DNA molecule to diffuse into the cell. The cells recovered from the electric shock can be regenerated into whole plants. Generally, protoplasts are used since they have exposed plasma membrane. Protoplasts are suspended in buffered saline solution containing plasmid DNA in a cuvette and an electrical impulse is applied across two platinum electrodes in the cuvette. The protoplasts are then cultured to regenerate the plants. Electroporation has been successfully used for obtaining transgenics in tobacco, maize, rice, wheat and sugarcane.

(iii) Microprojectile bombardment. This method is also called *biolistic approach* and has been a major development in direct gene transfer of DNA. It has enabled transformation of many plant species that were not amenable to *Agrobacterium* or protoplast based gene transfer techniques. The method is considered independent of genotype and the tissue. This method consists of delivering DNA into cells of intact plant organs, cultured tissues or cell suspensions via projectile bombardment. High-density particles, usually gold or tungsten (1-2 μm in diameter) coated with plasmid DNA containing the foreign gene are accelerated to high velocity by a particle gun apparatus. These dense particles thus acquire sufficient kinetic energy to penetrate the membranes, and thus to deliver the DNA into the cells. The transgenic plants have been recovered in several important crops including banana, barley, bean, canola, cassava, cotton, maize, papaya, peanut, poplar, rice, soybean, squash, sugarbeet, sugarcane, sunflower and wheat, by using more regenerable tissues/organs such as embryogenic calli, immature embryos and shoot meristems.

(iv) Microinjection. This method involves the injection of DNA directly into the plant cell nucleus or intact plant organ. The foreign DNA is delivered into protoplasts using a glass micropippette having an orifice diameter of less than one μm. It is a useful technique for the precise delivery of DNA into target cell. In this method, the location of DNA delivery can be controlled with micromanipulator and the volume of injection can be controlled by the microinjection apparatus. It is a direct and precise method of delivery of DNA into specific cell compartments. Microinjection of DNA into the nucleus can give high efficiency of transformation. This method raises the possibility of microinjecting a variety of materials such as chromosomes, and even chloroplasts and mitochondria can also be transferred by microinjection. This technique has been successfully used in alfalfa, tobacco and brassica crops.

TRANSGENIC CROP PROTECTION

A transgenic plant is defined as one that has had foreign genetic material purposefully introduced and stably incorporated into the plant genome through means other than those that naturally occur in the environment. In other words, transgenic plants are those which carry additional stably integrated and expressed foreign gene(s), usually transferred from unrelated organisms. The major components for the development of transgenic plants are (*i*) development of reliable tissue culture and regeneration systems, (*ii*) proportion of gene constructs and transformation with suitable vectors, (*iii*) efficient techniques of transformation for introduction of genes into the crop plants, (*iv*) recovery and multiplication of transgenic plants, (*v*) molecular and genetic characterization of transgenic plants for stable and efficient gene expression, (*vi*) transfer of genes into elite cultivars by conventional breeding methods, and (*vii*) evaluation of transgenic plants for their effectiveness in alleviating the biotic and abiotic stresses without being an environmental hazard.

Before taking up any attempt to produce transgenic plants to counter insect attack, the following requirements and priorities need to be identified. (*i*) The factors for resistance should be controlled by single genes. (*ii*) Standardization of methods for transfer of such genes can easily be accomplished. (*iii*) Expression of transferred gene should occur in the desired tissues at the appropriate time. (*iv*) The transgenic plant should be safe for consumption. (*v*) Inheritance of the gene in the successive generations should be very stable. (*vi*) There should be no penalty for yield in terms of other quantitative characters.

Remarkable achievements have been made in the production, characterization and field evaluation of transgenic plants. Both *Agrobacterium*-mediated gene transfer and direct DNA transfer methods have been used to produce transgenic plants with new genetic properties. Genes conferring resistance to insects have been inserted into crop plants such as maize, rice, wheat, sorghum, sugarcane, cotton, potato, tabacco, broccoli, cabbage, chickpea, pigeonpea, cowpea, groundnut, tomato, brinjal and soybean, Development of insect-resistant transgenic crop cultivars has focused on two distinct approaches : (*i*) integration of bacterial genes encoding for production of toxic proteins, especially from *Bacillus thuringiensis* (Bt), and (*ii*) integration of plant genes encoding for production of enzyme inhibitors and sugar-binding lectins. Both the approaches were pioneered in the mid-1980s and thus have developed in parallel. However, the first approach, based in particular on integration of δ-endotoxin genes derived from various subspecies of Bt, has undoubtedly received more attention and thus enjoyed greater progress. To date, all commercially available insect-resistant transgenic cultivars express semi-active Bt toxins, whereas cultivars expressing insecticidal plant proteins are not currently available outside research institutions.

Bt Endotoxins

Bacillus thuringiensis (Bt) is a gram positive entomocidal spore-forming bacterium. Bt synthesizes an insecticidal crystal protein (Cry) which when ingested by insect larvae is solubilized in the alkaline conditions of the midgut and processed by midgut proteases to produce a protease resistance polypeptide toxic to the insect. The crystal proteins are grouped into different classes based on sequence homology and insecticidal specificity. Bt toxins are thus, highly specific, some strains are specific to Lepidoptera, while others are specific to Diptera and Coleoptera. Bt toxins from different strains vary widely in their spectrum of activity. The most important are those produced from a strain *kurstaki* called *Btk,* effective against lepidopteran pests of forest trees, vegetables, cotton and ornamentals. These products have been sold since the early 1960s and account for bulk of Btapplications. In the late 1970s, another strain called *Bti* (*i* for *israelensis*) was identified, the products of which are effective against dipteran insects. It is estimated that more than 2000 tons of these preparations are being applied worldwide every year with no undesirable effects.

Although there have been dozens of Bt foliar products marketed, the total sales of Bt products is less than 2 per cent of the total value of all insecticides. However, the usefulness of Cry proteins in commercial spray applications has been limited due to their relatively high cost, rapid environmental inactivation, poor crop coverage and less than desired level of pest control, especially when compared to other less expensive conventional chemical insecticides. But the compelling reason for using Bt sprays is their safety; safety to applicators, beneficial insects, consumer and the environment. Foliar sprays of Bt can be applied on crops up to the day the crop is harvested and sold to the consumer. We have all consumed this bacterium and its Cry proteins and DNA repeatedly on uncooked vegetables, especially salads, for most of our lives without suffering from any ill effects.

In order to overcome some of the limitations, it was recognized that expression of *B. thuringiensis* toxin genes in transgenic plants might increase their utility in insect control. Bt endotoxins are attractive candidates for insect-resistant crop development using transgenic technology because (*i*) they have an established safety record, (*ii*) they act rapidly and are completely biodegradable and proven safe to humans and non-target organisms, and the environment, and (*iii*) the endotoxins are the products of single genes and are highly effective against the larvae of Lepidoptera, a major group of destructive insect pests. Therefore, the genes encoding the δ-endotoxins were cloned in the early 1980s and expression of modified toxin genes in transgenic tabacco and tomato provided the first examples of genetically engineered insect resistance in plants. Since then, Bt genes have been introduced into and expressed in a wide range of crop species (Table 13.2).

Table 13.2 Transgenic crops carrying Bt genes for insect resistance

Transgenic crop	Transgene(s)	Target insect pest(s)
Alfalfa	*Cry1C*	*Spodoptera littoralis*
Brinjal	*Cry (III)b*	*Leptinotarsa decemlineata*
	Cry1A(c)	*Leucinodes orbonalis*
Broccoli	*Cry1C*	*Plutella xylostella, Trichoplusia ni, Pieris rapae*
Canola	*Cry1A(c)*	*Helicoverpa zea, Spodoptera exigua*
Chickpea	*Cry1A(c)*	*Helicoverpa armigera*

Cotton	*Cry1A(b), Cry1A(c)*	*H. armigera, H. zea, Heliothis virescens, Pectinophora gossypiella, S. exigua, T. ni*
Groundnut	*Cry1A(c)*	*Elasmopalpus lignosellus*
Maize	*Cry1A(b), Cry1A(c),*	*Ostrinia nubilalis, Chilo partellus,*
	Cry9C	*Busseola fusca, H. zea*
Poplar	*Cry1A(a)*	*Lymantria dispar*
Potato	*CryIA(b), Cry1A(b)6*	*Phthorimaea operculella*
	CryIIIA, CryIIIB	*L. decemlineata*
	Cry1Ac9, CryV-Bt	*P. operculella*
Rice	*Cry1A(b), Cry1A(c),*	*Chilo suppressalis, Cnaphalocrocis medinalis,*
	CryII(a)	*Scirpophaga incertulas*
Sorghum	*Cry1A(c)*	*C. partellus*
Soybean	*Cry1A(c)*	*H. virescens, H.zea*
Sugarcane	*Cry1A(b)*	*Diatraea saccharalis*
Tobacco	*Cry1A(b), Cry1A(c)*	*H. virescens, M. sexta*
	CryIIa5	*H. armigera*
	Cry1Aa2	*H. zea*
Tomato	*Cry1A(c)*	*M. sexta*
	Bt(k)	*H.zea, M. sexta, Keifera lycopersicella*

Source : Modified from Dhaliwal and Koul (2007)

Although the early transgenic plants containing Bt genes demonstrated some enhanced resistance to target pests, it was soon apparent that expression levels from the native bacterial genes were too low to provide adequate protection from major pest species in the field. Hence, *cry* genes were modified for plant preferred codon usage, i.e. removal of polyadenylation signals, a higher GC content and removal of secondary structure and mRNA destabilization motifs while keeping the amino acid sequence unaltered. For the expression of *cry* genes in plants, suitable plant expression promoters such as the constitutive promoters, which allow expression in all plant parts at all times, e.g. cauliflower mosaic virus (CaMV), and ubiquitin promoter have been used. On the contrary, for a more controlled expression of the transgene in only certain specified plant parts, a tissue specific promoter, e.g. phosphoenol pyruvate carboxylase (PEPC) promoter, which expresses only in green tissue, and maize pollen-specific promoter have been used. For maternal transmission of the transgene, chloroplast transformation vectors have been developed such that the expression of the transgene is confined and does not spread through pollen. As a result, majority Bt genes now in use for plant genetic engineering have been substantially modified and essentially rebuilt, with expression levels in transgenics much higher (100x) than was obtainable using native Bt genes.

Cotton. Considerable progress has been made in developing cotton cultivars with Btgenes for resistance. The first generation Btcotton varieties were developed by Monsanto and their seed partners to express the CryIAc protein. Worldwide, several different Cry1Ac events are grown commercially. In the USA and some other countries, Bollgard® event MON531 was used by seed company breeding programmes to develop the first commercial Bt cotton varieties. In Australia and other countries, Ingard® event MON757 was used. The tobacco budworm, *Heliothis virescens* and pink bollworm, *Pectinophora gossypiella* are very well controlled by Bollgard® cotton whereas the cotton bollworm, *Helicoverpazea* is controlled satisfactorily except during the bloom stage when feeding on reproductive parts of flowers which tend to have a lower concentration of Cry protein than other plant parts. The introduction of Bt cotton in 1996 and 1997 was very timely since *P. gossypiella* and *H. virescens* in the USA and *H. armigera* in China and Australia had become resistant to many of the conventional insecticides and Bt cotton offered a reasonable solution to the problem.

Cotton cultivar Coker 312, transformed with the *cry1A(c)* gene (having 0.1% toxin protein), has shown high levels of resistance to cabbage looper, *Trichoplusia ni,* tobacco caterpillar, *Spodoptera exigua* and cotton bolloworms, *H. zea* and *H. virescens*. In transgenic cotton, bollworm damage was reduced to 2.3 per cent in flowers and 1.1 per cent in bolls compared to 23 per cent damage in flowers and 12 per cent damage in the commercial cultivar, Coker 312.

The second-generation Bt crops, developed with stacked *cry* genes, have been shown to improve the level of control and broaden the spectrum of caterpiller pests controlled. China has developed the new events, GK (expressing fused Cry1Ab and Cry1Ac proteins) and SGK (expressing the fused Cry1Ac-Cry1Ab and stacked CpTi proteins). Monsanto has created Bollgard® II by inserting a synthetic gene from *B. thuringiensis, cry2Ab,* expressing Cry2Ab protein, into the Bollgard® cotton variety, DP50B, already expressing Cry1Ac through event MON531, creating the new stacked gene event 15985. Bollgard® II is much more effective than Bollgard® at controlling all the caterpiller pests of cotton worldwide, especially *H. armigera, S. exigua, S. frugiperda* and *H. zea*. Laboratory and field studies have shown that Bollgard® II increased mortality of *H. zea* from 84.2 to 92.2 per cent, *S. frugiperda* from 16.1 to 100 per cent, *S. exigua* from 50.1 to 94.9 per cent and *T. ni* from 1.2 to 97.4 per cent. This high level of pest control is due, in part, to the very high concentration of Cry2Ab protein in Bollgard® II.

Maize. The first generation Bt proteins engineered into maize were Cry1Ab (from *B. thuringiensis*) and Cry9c (from *B. thuringiensis* subsp. *tolworthi*) and these were highly effective against European corn borer, *Ostrinia nubilalis*. The dominant Cry1Ab events are Monsanto's YieldGard® maize, event MON810; Syngenta's BT11 sold under the NK-brand as YieldGard®, and Syngenta's event 176, known as Knockout®. The level of expression of Bt proteins tends to be lower in fresh leaves of 176 than MON810 and BT11. Recently, Cry1F, has been introduced in maize (Dow's Herculex I®) and maize with a *cry3Bb* gene or a binary toxin genetic system for control of the maize rootworm (*Diabrotica*) complex is being developed.

Maize plants transformed with Bt genes have also been found to be effective against the spotted stem borer, *Chilo partellus* and the maize stalk borer, *Busseola fusca* in Southern Africa. Maize plants with *cry1Ab* gene are also resistant to the sugarcane borers, *Diatraea grandiosella* and *D. saccharalis*. Transgenic tropical maize inbred lines with *cryIAb* or *cryIAc* genes with resistance to corn earworm, *H. zea;* fall armyworm, *S. frugiperda;* Southwestern corn borer, *Diabrotica undecimpunctata howardi* and Western maize rootworm, *D. virgifera virgifera* have also been developed.

Rice. Various Chinese universities and research institutes, in cooperation with the International Rice Research Institute (IRRI) and universities in many countries have transformed rice by inserting the *cry1Ab* gene alone and a fused *cry1Ab/cry1Ac* into conventional rice varieties and hybrids. Initial field and laboratory tests of these Bt lines against lepidopteran pests have shown good season long control. Rice plants having 0.05 per cent toxin of the total soluble leaf protein have shown high levels of resistance to the striped stem borer, *Chilo suppressalis* and rice leaf folder, *Cnaphalocrocis medinalis*. Field testing of transgenic rice lines showed high protection against *Scirpophaga incertulas* and *C. medinalis*. The percentage of plants with white heads was significantly lower on the Bt Shanyou 63 (11%) as compared to control

Shanyou 63 (44%) plants. Similarly, transgenic plants showed no damage by *C. medinalis* as compared to 47.9 per cent damaged plants in non-transgenic rice. Scented varieties of rice (Basmati 370 and M7) have been transformed with *cryII(a)* and are resistant to *S. incertulas* and *C. medinalis*. Selected Bt-lines of IR64 and Pusa Basmati 1, having Bt-titres of 0.1 per cent (of total soluble protein) showed 100 per cent mortality of *S. incertulas* larvae within 4 days of infection in cut-stems as well as at the vegetative stage in whole plant assays.

Potato. A modified *cry3A* gene has been expressed in potato plants with resistance to Colorado potato beetle, *Leptinotarsa decemlineata*. Transgenic potato plants containing the *cry1A(b)* gene (*Bt 884*) and a truncated gene *cry1A(b)6* resulted in less damage to the leaves by the potato tuber moth, *Phthorimaea operculella*. However, the size of the leaf tunnels increased over time in plants containing only the *Bt 884* gene, while there was no increase in tunnel length in those containing *cry1A(b)6*. The latter also resulted in 100 per cent mortality of the insects in tubers stored up to six months. Several other Bt potato lines showing complete mortality of larvae of *P. operculella* have also been developed. However, the marketing of Bt potatoes was stopped in 2001 due to opposition from several food producers not to use Bt potatoes in their products.

Brinjal. Bt brinjal has been developed by Mahyco in 2000 by inserting *cry*1*Ac* gene and is resistant to the brinjal fruit and shoot borer, *Leucinodes orbonalis*. Mahyco partnered with Sathguru Management Consultants Pvt. Ltd., Hyderabad, and the technology was then made available to several public institutes in South and Southeast Asia. Mahyco has transferred the technology and basic breeding material of Bt brinjal to public sector institutions like Tamil Nadu Agricultural University, Coinbatore; University of Agricultural Sciences, Dharwad; and the Indian Institute of Vegetable Research, Varanasi, to develop, breed and distribute their own Bt brinjal varieties. The Genetic Engineering Approval Committee (GEAC) of the Government of India approved four Bt brinjal hybrids, viz. MHB-4Bt, MHB-9Bt, MHB-80Bt and MHB-99Bt, for environmental release in October 2009. However, in February 2010, Government of India withheld commercial release of Bt brinjal till more scientific data on biosafety are generated.

Plant-derived Genes

The search for insect control proteins alternative to Bt has concentrated, with a few exceptions, on those derived from plants. One major advantage of using plant genes as a source of crop resistance is their broad spectrum of activity across several orders, including sap-sucking insect pests, such as Hemiptera, in addition to Lepidoptera, Coleoptera and Orthoptera. Thus far, a number of economically important crop plants, such as oilseeds, potato, rice, sugarcane, tobacco, among others, have been genetically transformed to express various genes of plant origin (Table 13.3).

Largely, plant transformation involving plant genes has focused on (*i*) protease inhibitors, which disrupt amino acid metabolism; (*ii*) α-amylase inhibitors, which target carbohydrate metabolism; (*iii*) lectins, which cause agglutination and cell aggregation; and (*iv*) enzymes such as chitinase, which target insect exoskeleton. The varied modes of action and levels of specificity of these gene products increase the potential target-pest range of transgenic cultivars and allow the possibility of combining (pyramiding) genes that are active at various target sites within a pest insect or against various pests. However, levels of protection provided by genes of plant origin are typically lower than those provided by genes expressing Bt toxins. Frequently, effects on target insects are sublethal, including reductions in feeding, weight gain, developmental rates and fecundity. Even then, transgenic cultivars with sublethal or chronic effects on target

Table 13.3 Transgenic crops expressing insecticidal plant genes

Transgenic crop 1	Transgene(s) transgene 2	Origin of 3	Target insect pest(s) 4
Alfalfa	*Manduca E-I*	*Manduca sexta*	Thrips
Apple	*CpTi*	Cowpea	*Cydia pomonella*
Adzuki bean	*α-AI*	Bean α-amylase I	*Callosobruchus chinensis, C.maculatus*
Cabbage	Modified *CpTi (sck)*	Cowpea	*Pieris rapae, Helicoverpa armigera*
Cotton	*CpTi* *Manduca serpin*	Cowpea *M. sexta*	*H. armigera*
Lettuce	*Pot PI-II*	Potato	*Teleogryllus commodus*
Maize	*Avidin* *WGA*	Chicken avidin Wheat	Storage insect pests *Ostrinia nubilalis, Diabrotica* spp.
Mustard	*WGA* *OC-1* *C-II*	Wheat Rice Soybean	*Lipaphis erysimi* Coleoptera Lepidoptera, Diptera
Pea	*α-AI*	Bean α-amylase I	*Bruchus pisorum* *Zabrotes subfasciatus*
Poplar	*OC-I* *C-II* *Pot PI-II*	Rice Soybean Potato	*Chrysomela tremulae* Lepidoptera *Plagiodera versicolora*
Potato	*CpTi* *GNA* *BCH* *OC-1* *Kti3, C-II, PI-IV*	Cowpea Snowdrop Bean chitinase Rice Soybean	*Lacanobia oleracea* *L. oleracea, Myzus persicae, Aulacorthum solani* *M. persicae, A. solani* *Leptinotarsa decemlineata* *Spodoptera littoralis*
Rice	*CpTi* *Pot PI-II* *Pin 2* *mwti1b* *GNA* *SBTI* *CC*	Cowpea Potato Potato Synthetic Snowdrop Soybean Corn	*Chilo suppressalis, Sesamia inferens* *C. suppressalis, S. inferens* *C. suppressalis* *C. suppressalis* *Nilaparvata lugens, Nephotettix virescens* *N. lugens* *Sitophilus zeamais*
Strawberry	*CpTi*	Cowpea	*Otiorhynchus sulcatus*
Sugarcane	*GNA* *Pot PI-II*	Snowdrop Potato	*Eoruma loftini, Diatraea saccharalis, Antitrogus consanguineus* *A. consanguineus*
Sweet potato	*CpTi*	Cowpea	*Euscepes postfasciatus*
Tobacco	*CpTi* *Pot PI-II* *Tom PI-II* *α-AI*	Cowpea Potato Tomato Bean α-amylase	*Heliothis virescens, H. armigera, H. zea, M. sexta* *M. sexta, Chrysodeixis eriosoma* *M. sexta* *Agrotis ipsilon, Tenebrio molitor*

	GNA	Snowdrop	*H. virescens, M. persicae*
	p-Lec	Pea	*H. virescens*
	GTPI	Giant taro	*H. armigera*
	NaPI	*Nicotiana alata*	*Helicoverpa punctigera*
	Kti3, C-II, PI-IV	Soybean	*S. littoralis*
	SBTI	Soybean	*H. armigera, H. zea, H. virescens, S. littoralis, M. sexta*
	Manduca serpin	*M. sexta*	*Bemisia tabaci*
	SpTi	Sweet potato	*S. litura*
	Insect chitinase gene	Insect chitinase	*H. virescens*
	AaIT	Scorpion (*Androctonus australis*)	*H. armigera*
Tomato	*CpTi*	Cowpea	*L. oleracea*
	GNA	Snowdrop	*L. oleracea*
	Pot PI-I	Potato	*H. armigera, T. commodus*
	Pot PI-II	Potato	*H. armigera, T. commodus*
Wheat	*CMe*	Barley	*Sitotroga cerealella*
	GNA	Snowdrop	*Sitobion avenae*

α-AI = α-Amylase inhibitor, *BCH* = Bean chitinase, *C-II* = Double headed serine protease inhibitor from soybean, *CC* = Corn cystatin, *CpTi* = Cowpea trypsin inhibitor, *GNA* = Snowdrop lectin, *GTPI* = Giant taro (*Alocasia macrorrhiza*) proteinase inhibitor, *NaPI* = *Nicotiana alata* protease inhibitor,

OC-I = Oryzacystatin I, *p-lec* = Pea lectin, *Pot PI-I* = Potato proteinase inhibitor I, *Pot PI-II* = Potato proteinase inhibitor II, *SBTI* = Soybean Kunitz-type trypsin inhibitor, *SpTi* = Sweet potato trypsin, *Tom PI-II* = Tomato proteinase inhibitor II, *WGA* = Wheat germ agglutinin

Source :Dhaliwal and Koul (2007)

pests may be more attractive components of IPM strategies than cultivars with acute toxic effects because they are more likely to be compatible or act synergistically with other biopesticide strategies.

Protease inhibitors. The presence of antimetabolic proteins, which interfere with the processes of digestion in insects, is a strategy for defence that plants have used extensively. Proteins can occur constitutively in tissues that are particularly vulnerable to attack, such as seeds, or mechanical wounding in tissues attacked by chewing insects can induce them. Analysis of the effects of dietary protease inhibitors has shown that these are detrimental to the growth and development of insects from a variety of genera including *Helicoverpa, Spodoptera, Diabrotica* and *Tribolium.* Plants can now be transformed with protease inhibitor genes with strong promoters to express the inhibitor proteins in relatively high levels at specific times.

Several classes of protease inhibitors corresponding to different types of insect gut proteases have been characterized. Many insects, particularly members of Lepidoptera, depend on serine proteases (trypsin, chymotrypsin and elastase like endoproteases) as their primary protein digestive enzymes and genes encoding members of various serine protease inhibitor families have been cloned and introduced into transgenic plants. Insects also produce their own serine protease inhibitors for the regulation of their digestive proteases. It has been suggested that these could be turned against the insects by expressing them in transgenic plants. Other pests rely on cystein proteases (thiol proteases) as their primary digestive proteases, which act on papain and cathepsin. These have been targeted with cysteine protease inhibitors, which have been shown to exert chronic effects on important pests such as corn root worm, *Diabrotica* spp., against which there are no effective Bts.

Serine protease inhibitors. The first gene of plant origin to be used in transgenic crop protection was that isolated from cowpea encoding a double-headed trypsin inhibitor (CpTi) and transferred in tobacco. A simple construct was prepared in which a full length coding sequence derived from a cDNA clone was placed under the control of the constitutively expressed cauliflower mosaic virus (CaMV) 35S promoter. Transformants were screened for CpTi expression, which showed that many of the resulting plants expressed CpTi at levels greater than 0.1 per cent of total soluble protein. Subsequent experience has shown that this is generally the case for expression of genes of plant origin encoding defensive proteins in transgenic plants, in contrast to the very low level of expression observed for unmodified toxin genes of bacterial origin. CpTi is a small polypeptide of about 80 amino acids, homologous sequences are encoded by a moderately repetitive gene family in the cowpea genome. This protein is considered to be particularly suitable candidate for transfer to other species through genetic engineering because (*i*) it is an effective antimetabolite against a wide range of field and storage pests belonging to Lepidoptera, Coleoptera and Orthoptera, (*ii*) has no deleterious effects on mammals, and (*iii*) also has a small polypeptide of about 80 amino acids.

Biossays against *H. virescens* caterpillars showed that transgenics expressing CpTi at the highest levels (about 1% of total soluble protein) caused increased mortality, reduced growth and reduced plant damage. The antimetabolic effects of CpTi expressed in transgenic tobacco have also been observed with other lepidopteran pests including *H. zea, S. littoralis* and *M. sexta.* Subsequent trials carried out in California showed that expression of CpTi in tobacco afforded significant protection against *H. zea* in the field. Following on from the study using tobacco as a model system, the gene encoding CpTi has been expressed in a range of different crops (Table 13.3). For example, constitutive expression of CpTi in rice conferred significantly enhanced levels of resistance towards two species of rice stem borer, viz. *Chilo suppressalis* and *Sesamia inferens* in the field. Furthermore, the trials with CpTi transgenic strawberry plants suggested that these plants were highly resistant to the vine weevil, *Otiorhynchus sulcatus.*

Cysteine protease inhibitors. Cysteine proteases are used by plants for protein mobilisation and by animals for intracellular lysozomal protein digestion, and protein inhibitors of cysteine proteases (cystatins) are widely distributed throughout all living organisms to regulate these endogenous proteases, even if they are usually present in small amount. The genes encoding cysteine protease inhibitors have been suggested for use in transgenic plants for the control of coleopteran pests. Although there have been several studies carried out demonstrating *in vitro* inhibition of insect digestive proteases by cysteine protease inhibitors, with a few examples of their deleterious effects against insects when incorporated into artificial diets, as yet there are few published reports describing their insecticidal effects *in planta.*

A gene encoding a rice cystein proteinase inhibitor oryzacystatin, has been expressed constitutively in transgenic poplar trees, conferring resistance to the coleopteran pest, *Chrysomela tremulae.* Corn cystatin (CC) has been introduced into protoplasts of rice and cystatin activity of the transgenic rice plants was assayed against a crude midgut proteinase fraction from *Sitophilus zeamais.* The results showed that 50 per cent of the midgut protease activity in *S. zeamais* was inhibited by 2 μg and completely inhibited by 5 μg of transgenic seed protein fraction, whereas untransformed rice seeds had no significant effect.

Alpha-amylase inhibitors. Plants produce inhibitors of insect gut alpha-amylases, which are required for the digestion of starch, a major energy source, particularly for the weevils. The alpha-amylase inhibitors produced by plants have different types of structure and different mode of action and target specificity, and hence can be used for insect control in transgenic plants. Transgenic tobacco plants expressing amylase inhibitors from wheat (wheat alpha-amylase inhibitor, WAAI) increase the mortality of lepidopteran larvae by 30-40 per cent. Similarly, transgenic pea seeds expressing alpha-amylase inhibitor derived from common beans (BAAI) were found to exhibit increased resistance against bruchid beetles, *Callosobruchus* spp. and pea weevil, *Bruchus pisorum*.

Enhanced levels of resistance to the bruchids have been observed in transgenic adzuki beans expressing the alpha-amylase inhibitor of common bean. While even low levels of the amylase inhibitor were sufficient to provide resistance to the adzuki bean weevil, higher levels of the protein make the seeds resistant to the cowpea weevil, *C. maculatus* and pea weevil, *C. chinensis* as well. Two alpha-amylase inhibitors, α-AI-1 and α-AI-2, from the common bean inserted into pea, are effective in protecting peas against the pea weevil, *B pisorum* under field conditions. α-AI-1 provided complete protection from *B. pisorum,* by inhibiting alpha-amylase by 80 per cent, while α-AI-2 inhibits the enzyme by 40 per cent. α-AI-1 results in larval mortality, whereas α-AI-2 delays the maturation of the larvae.

Lectins. Lectins are plant-derived proteins that bind to oligo-and polysaccharides, and cause agglutination and cell aggregation. Lectins have been isolated and characterized from a wide variety of plants such as pea, rice, wheat, snowdrop, castor, soybean, mungbean, garlic, sweet potato, tobacco, chickpea and groundnut. A number of plant lectins exhibiting insecticidal characteristics are being evaluated as alternatives to Bt δ-endotoxins. The precise mode of action of insecticidal lectins is unknown. However, binding to specific carbohydrates and agglutination (fusion by adhesive substances) in the insect midgut has been clearly demonstrated. Specifically, lectins may interfere with development and structural integrity of the midgut peritrophic membrane; bind to glycosated targets in the insect midgut, thereby inhibiting nutrient absorption or cell disruption in the midgut; or bind or block the peritrophic membrane protecting the insect midgut surface.

Lectins from wheat (wheat germ agglutinin, WGA) and the snowdrop plant (*Galanthus nivalis* agglutinin, GNA) are inhibitory to the sap-sucking homopteran pests such as aphids, leafhoppers and planthoppers, which feed on the phloem exudates and against which there are no known Cry proteins. In addition, lectins have also exhibited inhibitory activity against several lepidopteran and coleopteran pests. A gene encoding the pea lectin (*p-lec*) has been expressed in transgenic tobacco and the plants expressing pea lectin upto 1 per cent of total protein reduced the larval biomass of *Heliothis virescens* and leaf damage. Transgenic tobacco plants containing both CpTi and and P-Lec were obtained through hybridization of two primary transformed lines. The plants expressing two insecticidal proteins reduced the insect biomass by 90 per cent as compared to 50 per cent reduction in plants expressing either CpTi or P-Lec. This study demonstrated that not only the products of lectin genes could enhance resistance to insect attack in transgenic plants, but also showed that additive protective effects could be obtained from different plant-derived insect-resistant genes.

Survival of the brown planthopper, *Nilaparvata lugens* decreased to 60 per cent in transgenic rice expressing GNA protein (2% of total protein), under the control of phloem tissue-specific sucrose synthase promoter which directs the expression of the gene in the phloem of leaves, stems, petioles and roots for protection from the phloem feeding pests. Wheat germ agglutinin (WGA) is antimetabolic, antifeedant and insecticidal to the mustard aphid, *Lipaphis erysimi.* Bioassays using leaf discs showed that feeding on transgenics induced high mortality and significantly reduced fecundity of aphids. Thus, plant lectins have shown biological activity against a wide range of insects. However, consideration should be given with regard to their deployment in transgenic plants because of their known toxicity to mammals and humans.

Enzymes. Transgenic expression of various enzymes has been proposed as a crop protection strategy. The most obvious candidate is chitinase, which is an important structural component of insects. Expression of an insect chitinase in transgenic tobacco enhances resistance to some lepidopterans. Similar marginal protective effects have been observed from expression of bean chitinase (BCH) in transgenic tobacco. Transgenic potato plants expressing a gene encoding BCH were found to reduce fecundity of the glasshouse potato aphid, *Aulacorthum solani,* though this reduction was not statistically significant. However, nymphs produced on these BCH expressing plants were significantly smaller compared to those on control, non-transformed plants.

Other novel genes. The genes derived from other sources such as chicken, scorpion and spider are also being screened for their insecticidal potential. Avidin, a glycoprotein found in chicken egg white, sequesters the vitamin biotin. Transgenic maize containing *avidin* gene has been produced. The avidin at ≥ 100 ppm is toxic to and prevents development of insects that damage grains during storage. Insect-specific neurotoxin AaIT from the venom of the scorpion, *Androctonus australis,* in tobacco has shown insecticidal activity against *H. armigera* larvae (up to 100% mortality after 6 days). Transgenic plants of tobacco have been obtained containing an insecticidal spider peptide gene, and some of these plants have exhibited resistance to *H. armigera.* The role of neurotoxins from insects and spiders need to be studied in greater detail before they are deployed in other organisms and plants because of their possible toxicity to mammals.

RESISTANCE IN PESTS TO TRANSGENICS

The insects are exposed to the toxin proteins in transgenic crops throughout the feeding cycle and season, and as a result, the insect populations are under continuous selection pressure. As the toxins are expressed in all parts of the plant, there is a serious threat of rapid development of resistance in insect pests. Toxin production may also decrease over the crop-growing season. Low doses of the toxins eliminate the most sensitive individuals of a population, leaving a population in which resistance can develop much faster. The first documented case of development of resistance to a Bt crop in the field has been reported from USA, where *Helicoverpa zea* has shown resistance in Arkansas and Mississippi cotton fields. There are also occasional reports of survival of *Helicoverpa armigera* on Bt cotton in Australia, China and India.

By far the biggest problem that is likely to occur following the use of transgenic crop plants for pest control is the development of resistance in pest species. This phenomenon, of course, occurs with conventional insecticides. However, the critical difference is that a pesticide application represents a selective force that is time-limited, i.e. to the time the application is made. The current transgenic crops express toxins throughout their tissues continuously and selective pressure on the target population to adapt will thus be substantial. The strategies for managing insect resistance to toxins expressed in transgenic plants are comparable to those used for managing resistance to conventional insecticides, with only a few exceptions.

High Expression Level

High expression level of toxins in transgenic crops is comparable to the high dose strategy in case of resistance to conventional pesticides. The premise in this case is that toxin concentration is so high that all individuals of the target species are killed. This approach seems to be very effective in theory and practice provided the toxin expression is consistently high and stable over a period of time or among different plant issues. The high dose strategy assumes that resistance to transgenic plants is recessive and is conferred by a single locus with two alleles, resulting in three insect genotypes, viz. susceptible homozygotes (SS), heterozygotes (RS) and resistant homozygotes (RR). It also assumes that there will be random mating between resistant and susceptible adults. Under ideal circumstances, only rare RR individuals will survive a high dose produced by the transgenic crop and both SS and RS individuals will be susceptible to the toxin.

The production of toxin is generally expected to decrease over time due to plant senescence. If the level of production of Bt toxin decreases toward the reproductive phase, heterozygous individuals, which may often be slightly more resistant than susceptible homozygotes, might be able to survive and transmit resistance alleles to the offspring. As Bt transgenic cotton plants matured Bt toxin concentrations decreased, increasing the chances that pests such as *Heliothis virescens* will encounter sublethal or low doses of Bt toxins, leading to development of resistance more rapidly. Moreover, different levels of toxins were found in various plant parts, thus increasing the chances that target pests will receive a lower dose.

Similarly, if wild host plants of herbivorous pests or non-transgenic host plants of the same or different species are located in close proximity to the transgenic plants, then pests can move to these non-toxic plants before they receive a lethal dose. Also, an insect displaying a high frequency of movement may feed alternatively on toxic and non-toxic plants thus diluting the dose of the toxin. In fact, such cases would actually increase the rate of resistance by allowing the survival of partially-resistant genotypes. For protease inhibitors, amylase inhibitors and lectins, the doses that can be engineered into plants are generally insufficient to control a target pest and for these compounds, high dose strategy cannot be implemented. Although some of these substances may be engineered at high doses in the future, many of these are harmful to man, other mammals and birds, particularly at high doses.

Refuge Strategy

Refuges or refugia are areas of crops or host plants free of insecticidal toxins that allow part of the pest population to survive and to act as a reservoir of wild-type susceptible alleles. By maintaining a refuge area close to the transgenic field, surviving individuals (RR) that have been exposed to insecticidal toxins will mate with unselected individuals (SS) coming from the refuge and produce RS heterozygotes that will be killed by the transgenic crop. This strategy would dilute resistant (R) alleles, reduce the intensity of selection and delay the evolution of resistance. Spatial organization of refuges has been considered in various ways. One type of spatial refuge includes mixtures of transgenic and non-transgenic plants; the mixture may be obtained by mixing seeds before planting or by planting a smaller proportion of the field with the non-transgenic strain. Another type of spatial refuge results from the expression of toxins only in critical areas of the plant. A third type of spatial refuge, plantings of Bt-transgenic crops with non-Bt transgenic crops, such as Bt-transgenic corn with non-transgenic cotton, could be applied for resistance management with polyphagous pests such as *Helicoverpa zea*. Temporal refuges involve alternating transgenic plants with non-transgenic plants over growing seasons.

Another aspect of resistance management with refuges is that there must be random mating between individuals from the refuge and the transgenic plants, which means that the refuge must be located close to the transgenic planting. At the same time, for individual pests that tend to feed on several plants rather than just one, the refuge and toxic plant plots must be located far enough apart so that susceptible individuals do not move from non-toxic to toxic plants. Similarly, if refuge fields are less attractive than transgenic plantings to female insects for oviposition, the effective size would be decreased.

According to the recent refuge requirements approved by Environmental Protection Agency (EPA) of USA for Bt corn grown outside cotton-growing areas, growers have to have a minimum of 20 per cent non-Bt corn refuge (treatable with other pest control products). In cotton-growing regions, a minimum of 50 per cent non-Bt corn refuge has to be planted. Refuges planted as external blocks should either be adjacent or in proximity to the Bt corn field. The current requirement for corn is that the refuges should be within approximately 800 meters of the Bt field, although within approximately 400 meters is the preferred distance.

Tissue and Temporal Expression of Toxins

The tissue and temporal expression of toxins is based on the principle that specific gene promoters could be used to express genes only in (*i*) the most important tissue (tissue or structure specific expression) or (*ii*) critical growth periods (temporal specific expression) or (*iii*) be environmentally benign chemical. Thus the production of toxins is limited to the most economically sensitive or most vulnerable parts of plant or to specific time. This strategy does not require external refugia as the plant itself acts as such. However, efficient tissue or time-specific promoters are not yet available. This strategy is dependent on the feeding behaviour of the pests and can be influenced by the feeding deterrent effect of Bt transgenic plants. Also, an *in planta* refugia may be relevant for protection against a given member of a group of pests but may fail to provide protection against a secondary pest attacking the plant at the same time but feeding on a different part. Moreover, several potential economical and sociological problems are related to the use of chemical-inducible promoters. The chemicals to be used for induction might be costly and negatively perceived with respect to environmental protection due to potential pollution hazards.

Tissue-or structure-specific expression could perhaps leave refuges within each plant. This has been suggested for a maize genotype where the Cry toxin is under the control of a phosphoenolpyruvate carboxylase (PEPC) promoter, which provided high levels of expression in green tissue and much lower expression in kernels. However, the level of expression in the kernel is still 4-6 times the LC50 for *Ostrinia nubilalis*. Damage to corn kernels is tolerable for corn grown for feed, but this level of expression suggests that the ear will not prove to be a very hospitable site for susceptible corn borers. A slight variation of this idea is to deter insects from feeding on the most economically important plant structures without being killed, thereby lowering selection pressure while protecting the crop. For example, in case of cotton, considerable damage can be tolerated to leaves but not flower buds and bolls. However, to be fully effective, expression in the transgenic structures may have to be higher than in current constitutive varieties, and will have to provide sufficiently high expression in all important tissues without affecting the tissues that can be sacrificed. In cotton, for example, both bolls and terminal meristems must be protected.

Rotations

In case of transgenic crops, rotations refer to the alteration over time of two or more varieties containing different toxins. Rotation is based on the assumption that the frequency of resistance alleles will decrease when the selection pressure is reduced. However, many reports indicate that resistance could remain stable or decrease slowly after removal of selection pressure, making the use of rotation inefficient. The resistance of individuals to one toxin must decline during the use of second toxin for rotations to be effective. However, assuming no occurrence of cross-resistance between toxins and that resistance does not increase in the absence of toxins, then alternating two toxins over a period of time would actually at least double (if the increase were linear) the time to resistance. Similarly, alternating three toxins would at least triple the time to resistance, and so on. However, if a fitness cost to resistance or negative cross-resistance exists, rotations can be particularly effective. For insect-resistant transgenic plants, there are limited possibilities for the use of rotations. Bt toxins have similar modes of action and hence there is a problem of cross resistance, thus rotating between different toxins from year to year is unlikely to slow down resistance. Other insect toxins such as enzyme inhibitors and lectins have not so far given adequate protection when used alone and hence would not be useful in rotations.

Gene Pyramiding

Gene pyramiding or gene stacking relies on the simultaneous delivery of toxins recognising different binding sites. This strategy assumes that resistance to each toxin is monogenic, there is no cross-resistance among toxins used, resistant pest individuals are rare so that no one individual is resistant to both toxins and the toxins have equal persistence. If this is achieved, then the other toxin will kill pests that survive one of the toxins. In contrast to chemical insecticides, at least two features of transgenic plants suggest that mixtures of two or more factors pyramided into the same variety will greatly delay resistance. Transgenic plants offer a way to get consistently high control of SS homozygotes, and Cry toxins provide at least one good candidate gene with consistently fairly recessive inheritance of resistance. It has been observed that Cry1Aa has overcome a 500-fold resistance to Cry3Aa already established in cotton wood leaf beetle, *Chrysomela scripta.*

Pyramids also have several advantages over single gene strategies :

- Fitness costs should have a greater impact on delaying resistance to mixtures than single toxins.
- Pyramids are less sensitive to initial resistance allele frequency; even resistance frequencies of 10–3 could allow significant benefits.
- Pyramids can be greatly improved by manipulating the mortality of susceptible homozygotes, which can be measured.
- Pyramids are more robust to survival of heterozygotes, which cannot be measured with certainty until resistance has evolved.
- Pyramids can be very effective with a smaller refuge.

Ideally, the two toxins to be used in a pyramided variety should be very different to avoid cross-resistance. It is believed that mixtures of plant protease inhibitors may be the best way to prevent insect resistance to these compounds. Plants naturally improve the efficacy of protease inhibitors by exhibiting multidomain or multimeric variants. Feeding studies have confirmed that inhibitor combinations act synergistically to reduce insect herbivore growth. Since genes for different proteases have been found in nature and engineered into crop plants, the success rates for use of protease and amylase inhibitors in plant resistance to insects can be greatly improved, especially through pyramiding genes that produce a variety of these compounds. The activity of Bt genes in transgenic plants is enhanced by serine protease inhibitors and tannic acid. Similarly, protease inhibitors engineered into cotton with high gossypol and/or tannic content may achieve greater protection against *H. armigera.*

Mosaics

Mosaics are a spatial patchwork of two or more varieties of the same crop species expressing different toxins at the same time. For mosaics to delay resistance, it is assumed that there is no cross-resistance among the different toxins, so that the individuals resistant to one toxin are susceptible to other toxins. Thus, susceptible individuals are maintained and are able to move among different patches. The mosaic theory is not considered appropriate to deploy two toxin genes. It is assumed that each of the varieties can serve as a refuge for the other, however, they cannot since neither is producing many susceptible insects. Even with an untreated refuge, the mosaic system essentially selects for resistance to each of the toxins simultaneously.

Trap Plant Strategy

This approach is closely related to the refuge system. In this approach, the transgenic crop is considered as a trap crop and not as the main source of protection. The Bt-transgenic plants are planted earlier than the non-transgenic plants and owing to their advanced maturation attract the pests that are killed after feeding, thus leaving the non-transgenic varieties relatively unharmed. There is, however, no evidence that the basic key assumptions on movement and absence of ovipositing preference will be verified in the field for the target species or for another one. However, a computer model designed on slightly different assumptions about feeding preference and movements demonstrated that this strategy was not successful. Indeed, avoidance of transgenic plants and ovipositing preferences were demonstrated. Even if an insect species may be suitable for the trap plant strategy owing to its feeding preferences, the presence of Bt toxins may adversely alter its feeding behaviour.

Integration of Tactics

The most important approach to manage resistance to transgenic plants is to diversify pest management techniques as well as resistance management techniques. This is particularly so in case of multiple crops and multiple pests prevalent in tropical and sub-tropical countries like India. A toxin may be highly active against a given pest but be moderately active against another pest also present in the same crop or in the same area, and for which the dose delivered by the transgenic plant does not correspond to a high dose. In that case, the second pest will be exposed to a moderate dose and may develop resistance. As there is no single answer or strategy to delay resistance, only a logical combination of various tactics will provide sustainability.

The multiple tactics for Bt resistance management in transgenic crops are as follows : (*i*) provide refuge for susceptibles, (*ii*) do not use pesticides that kill susceptibles, (*iii*) do not use pesticides that kill natural enemies, (*iv*) enhance natural control through crop rotation or tillage, and rotate between susceptible and resistant crop genotypes over large areas. The high-dose refuge strategy, and especially the association of this approach with combinations of toxins is advocated by scientists, seed companies and administrators as the best approach of controlling evolution of resistance. This composite strategy allows flexibility in terms of spatial organization of refuge areas and choice of toxins that will help adaptation and implementation in various agronomic systems.

COMMERCIALIZATION OF TRANSGENIC CROPS

The People's Republic of China was the first country to commercialize transgenic crops in the early 1990s, with the introduction of a virus resistant tobacco, followed by virus resistant tomato. In 1994, the USA followed when the Calgene Company got the first approval to commercialize a genetically modified tomato 'Flavr Saver TM', the delayed ripening tomato. From then onwards, the development and use of transgenic crops gained momentum.

First Decade of Commercialization (1996-2005)

The global area under transgenic crops increased more than fifty-fold, from 1.7 million ha in 1996 to 90.0 million ha in 2005 (Table 13.4). The transgenic crops were grown in 21 countries by 8.5 million farmers in 2005, 90 per cent of the beneficiary farmers were resource poor farmers from developing countries. The largest area under transgenic crops was in USA,

Table 13.4 Global area (million ha) of transgenic crops during first decade of commercialization, 1996-2005

Country	1996	1997	1998	1999	2000	2001	2002	2003	2004	2005
USA	1.5	8.1	20.5	28.7	30.3	35.7	39.0	42.8	47.6	49.8
Argentina	0.1	1.4	4.3	6.7	10.0	11.8	13.5	13.9	16.2	17.1
Brazil	0.0	0.0	0.0	0.0	0.0	0.0	0.0	3.0	5.0	9.4
Canada	0.1	1.3	2.8	4.0	3.0	3.2	3.5	4.4	5.4	5.8
China	<0.1	<0.1	<0.1	0.3	0.5	1.5	2.1	2.8	3.7	3.3
Paraguay	0.0	0.0	0.0	0.0	0.0	0.0	0.0	0.0	1.2	1.8
India	0.0	0.0	0.0	0.0	0.0	0.0	<0.1	0.1	0.5	1.3
South Africa	0.0	0.0	<0.1	0.1	0.2	0.2	0.3	0.4	0.5	0.5
Uruguay	0.0	0.0	0.0	0.0	<0.1	<0.1	<0.1	0.1	0.3	0.3
Australia	<0.1	0.1	0.1	0.1	0.2	0.2	0.1	0.1	0.2	0.3
Mexico	<0.1	<0.1	<0.1	<0.1	<0.1	<0.1	<0.1	<0.1	0.1	0.1
Romania	0.0	0.0	0.0	<0.1	<0.1	<0.1	<0.1	<0.1	0.1	0.1
Philippines	0.0	0.0	0.0	0.0	0.0	0.0	0.0	<0.1	<0.1	0.1
Spain	0.0	0.0	<0.1	<0.1	<0.1	<0.1	<0.1	<0.1	<0.1	0.1
Colombia	0.0	0.0	0.0	0.0	0.0	0.0	<0.1	<0.1	<0.1	<0.1
Iran	0.0	0.0	0.0	0.0	0.0	0.0	0.0	0.0	0.0	<0.1
Honduras	0.0	0.0	0.0	0.0	0.0	0.0	<0.1	<0.1	<0.1	<0.1
Portugal	0.0	0.0	0.0	0.0	0.0	0.0	0.0	0.0	0.0	<0.1
Germany	0.0	0.0	0.0	0.0	<0.1	<0.1	<0.1	<0.1	<0.1	<0.1
France	0.0	0.0	<0.1	<0.1	<0.1	0.0	0.0	0.0	0.0	<0.1
Czech Republic	0.0	0.0	0.0	0.0	0.0	0.0	0.0	0.0	0.0	<0.1
Total	**1.7**	**11.0**	**27.8**	**39.9**	**44.2**	**52.6**	**58.7**	**67.7**	**81.0**	**90.0**

Source : Dhaliwal and Koul (2010)

followed by Argentina, Brazil, Canada and China-the principal adopters of transgenic crops globally. In 2005, the 21 countries growing transgenic crops included 11 developing countries and 10 industrial countries. More than one–third (33.9 million ha, 38%) of the global transgenic area was grown in developing countries. In 2005, Bt rice was grown commercially for the first time on approximately 4,000 ha in Iran by several hundred farmers. In the first decade, the accumulated biotech crop area was 475 million ha, equivalent to almost half of the total land area of the USA or China.

The Government of India's Genetic Engineering Approval Committee (GEAC) approved the commercial cultivation of Bt transgenic cotton in the country in 2002. Two Bt cotton varieties, viz. MECH-162 and MECH-184 were recommended for the Central Zone and MECH-12 for the South Zone. Six Bt cotton varieties, viz. RCH-134, RCH-317, Ankur-651, Ankur-2534, MRC-6301 and MRC-6304 were approved in March 2005 for commercial cultivation under north Indian conditions. Bt cotton was planted in an area of 50,000 ha in 2002, which went upto about, 1,00,000 ha in 2003, 0.5 million ha in 2004 and 1.3 million ha in 2005. India had by far the largest year-on-year proportional increase, with almost three-fold increase from 2004. A total of 20 Bt cotton hybrids were approved for cultivation in 2005. The largest hectarage under Bt cotton was in Maharashtra (0.607 millon ha), followed by Andhra Pradesh (0.283 million ha), Gujarat (0.164 million ha), Madhya Pradesh (0.148 million ha), Northern states (0.064 million ha), Karnataka (0.040 million ha) and Tamil Nadu (0.029 million ha). The number of farmers growing Bt cotton hybrids in India increased from 300,000 small farmers in 2004 to 1 million in 2005. According to a survey conducted by Indian Market Research Bureau in 2004, cultivation of Bt cotton resulted in five-fold decrease in insecticides, an average of 58 per cent increase in yield and an average of 163 per cent increase in profit for Bt cotton farmers. India is estimated to have enhanced farm income from Bt cotton by $124 million between 2002-2004.

Second Decade of Commercialization (2006-2015)

In the first year (2006) of the second decade of commercialization, the area under transgenic crops increased to 102 million ha. In 2007, 12 million farmers from 23 countries planted these crops on an area of 114.3 million ha. In 2008, the area under transgenic crops increased to 125 million ha in 25 countries and the total number of farmers growing these crops increased to 13.3 million. The highest area was in USA (62.5 million ha) followed by Argentina (21.0), Brazil (15.8), India (7.6), Canada (7.6) and China (3.8). Transgenic soybean occupied the highest area (65.8 million ha), followed by maize (37.3), cotton (15.5) and canola (5.9). Till the year 2015, the number of countries had increased to 28 where transgenic crops were grown and the area under cultivation was recorded at 179.7 million hectares (Table 13.5), that accounts for more than 10% of the world's arable land. The USA, Brazil and Argentina are the major producers.The area under soybean was maximum (92.1 MHa), followed by maize (53.6 Mha), cotton (24 Mha) and oilseed rape (canola) (8.5 Mha). On the whole, about 83% of the world production of soybean, 75% of production of cotton, 29% of the world's maize production and almost a quarter of the world's oilseed rape was made up by transgenic (GM) crops.

In India, the area under Bt cotton in 2006 was 3.8 million ha, which increased to 6.2 million ha in 2007. In 2008, 5 million small and marginal farmers in India benefited from planting 7.6 million ha of Bt cotton. The conservative estimates for small farmers indicate that the yield increased by 31 per cent, insecticide decreased by 39 per cent and profitability increased by 88 per cent equivalent to US$ 250 per ha. In 2008, Bt Bikaneri Narma, the first public sector transgenic crop was released for commercial cultivation in India. This variety has been developed by the Central Institute of Cotton Research, Nagpur; University of Agricultural Services, Dharwad and the Indian Agricultural Research Institute, New Delhi. Currently, total cultivated area under Bt cotton in India is 11.6 million ha.

The global net economic benefits to transgenic crop farmers in 2007 alone were US$ 10 billion ($6 billion for developing countries and $4 billion for industrial countries). The accumulated benefits during the period 1996-2007 were US$ 44 billion with $ 22 billion each for developing and industrial countries. The accumulative reduction in pesticides for 1996-2007 has been estimated to be 3,59,000 metric tonnes of active ingredient.

Table 13.5. Area of Commercial GM Crops by Country (2015)

Country	Cultivation area (Million Hectares)	Crops and traits
USA	70.9	Maize, soybean, cotton, canola, sugarbeet, alfalfa, Papaya, squash, potato
Brazil	44.2	Soybean, maize, cotton
Argentina	24.5	Soybean, maize, cotton
India	11.6	Cotton
Canada	11.0	Canola, maize, soybean, sugarbeet
China	3.7	Cotton, papaya, poplar
Paraguay	3.6	Soybean, maize, cotton
Pakistan	2.9	Cotton
South Africa	2.3	Maize, soybean, cotton
Uruguay	1.4	Soybean, maize
Bolivia	1.1	Soybean
Philippines	0.7	Maize
Australia	0.7	Cotton, canola
Burkina Faso	0.4	Cotton
Mynamar	0.3	Cotton
Mexico	0.1	Cotton, soybean
Spain	0.1	Maize
Columbia	0.1	Cotton, maize
Sudan	0.1	Cotton
Honduras	<0.1	Maize
Chile	<0.1	Maize, soybean, canola
Portugal	<0.1	Maize
Vietnam	<0.1	Maize
Czech Republic	<0.1	Maize
Slovakia	<0.1	Maize
Costa Rica	<0.1	Cotton, soybean
Bangladesh	<0.1	Brinjal (aubergine)
Romania	<0.1	Maize

Total cultivated area under GM crops: 179.7 million hectares

(**Source:** http://www.genewatch.org/sub-532326)

The outlook for the second decade of commercialization points to continued growth in the global hectarage of transgenic crops, up to 200 million ha, with at least 20 million farmers growing these crops in up to 40 countries or more by 2015.

The second decade of commercialization is likely to feature significantly more growth in Asia compared with the first decade, which was the decade of the Americas' (Dhaliwal and Koul, 2010).

CONCLUSIONS

Biotechnology has provided new avenues for management of insect pests and it holds great potential to be included in IPM system. If this technology leads to improved control of pests and vectors of diseases, then the benefits will be enormous.

- The low toxicity of proteinase inhibitors and Bt-δ endotoxin as compared to conventional insecticides would reduce the selection pressure and may slow down the development of resistance.
- Since all plant parts including growing points would remain covered with toxins, dependence on weather for efficacy of the sprays would be eliminated.
- Since toxins will always be there, so there will be no need of continuous monitoring of pests.
- Transgenic plants would also provide protection to those plant parts, which are difficult to be treated with pesticides. Thus, transgenics may prove useful for controlling bollworms and borers, which are difficult to control by means of insecticides.
- The cost of application in the form of equipment and labour will be nil or negative.
- The development cost is only a fraction of the cost of development of a conventional pesticide.
- There would be no problem of contamination in the form of drift and ground water contamination or risk to the field workers. By using transgenic technology, the toxin is delivered directly to the target organism. The fact that the plant delivers the toxin and not a person also serves as a means to reduce operator exposure to pesticides.
- Insecticidal activity would be restricted to those insects which actually attack the plants. Transgenic plants would be safe to non-target species and human beings. The earlier reports of toxicity of Bt maize pollen to the larvae of monarch butterfly, *Danais plexippus*, have been proven wrong
- Transgenic plants eliminate the problems of shelf life and field stability faced by pesticide formulations as they provide on site biosynthesis of the toxins. Such crops are easy to adopt because no new practices need to be learned for the basic use of technology. The whole technology is 'all in the seed' and the only challenge is to get the seed into the hands of the farmers.
- Transgenic plants will have inbuilt resistance to various insects replacing some of the current pesticide usage with protection which is intrinsically biodegradable, thus reducing the use of chemical insecticides and minimizing the problem of environmental pollution.

In spite of all these advantages, biotechnology does face uncertainties.

- Gene manipulation is a gray area and needs to be addressed systematically with pragmatic approach, especially in developing countries, where most of the farmers are either poor or marginal.
- The resistance against δ-endotoxin is not ruled out, though it may be slow as compared to insecticides because of continuous exposure of the insect to the toxin. Transgenic plants that are resistant to pests have a selective advantage that may lead them to become weeds.
- Some weeds may introgress an insect resistance gene from related transgenic plants and make them less susceptible to their usual herbivores, thus exhibiting greater reproductive success and may create a weed problem.
- If lepidopteran herbivores were removed from plant species, other insects might experience competitive release and become more common.

- The use of transgenic plants possessing resistance factor in one locality may affect the insect population dynamics in other areas.
- It has been claimed that there are a number of risks to humans associated with eating transgenic food crops. These risks include novel proteins acting as allergens or toxins, altered host metabolism producing new or unknown allergens or toxins, and reduced nutritional quality leading to dietary deficiencies or health problems, e.g. by reduction of antioxidants in plants.

In spite of the potential risks, the transgenic crops are likely to play a dominant role in pest control in the twenty-first century. However, it is necessary to adopt a rational approach with respect to transgenics and follow certain criteria.

- The existence of new transgenic crops and the possible consequences of their use should be converted into a documented information for regional policy makers, regulators, law makers, private industry, extension services, NGOs and consumers. Special attention should be given to food safety, resistance management and gene flow. Local systems, their constraints and socio-economic implications should be strictly considered before adoption of any transgenic material.
- Regional policies should be developed towards transgenic crop use. Specific attention is required to the agroecology of the cropping systems in the region. Policies, laws and regulations should be harmonized.
- The risks of gene flow and its effects need to be studied carefully.
- Given the difficulties of enforcement of regulations, the best option might be to regulate seed distribution. This will help in resistance management as well.
- Cost/benefit analysis is necessary for the introduction of transgenic crops.
- It is necessary to undertake a proactive approach to stimulate the use of the right gene for the right season and in the right way. Regional research institutions can play an important role in developing, testing and recommending management practices appropriate to the transgenic crop technology, local production systems and pests.

Biotechnology has the potential to move farming closer to ecologically sustainable practices, both in developed and developing countries and thus could make a considerable impact on agricultural systems in the future. The strategy to maximize the utility of this approach should involve the use of gene combinations whose products are targeted to different biochemical and physiological processes within the insect. In this way, it is expected to provide a multimechanistic form of resistance, which can be tailored to different crops and prevailing insect pests. However, the sustainability of transgenic crops from the point of view of pest control remains to be seen. There is a potential danger that, just as farmers became trapped in 'pesticide treadmills' during the 1950s and 1960s, so farmers in the twenty-first century may be trapped in 'biotechnology treadmills'.

☆☆☆☆☆

CHAPTER 14 INTEGRATED PEST MANAGEMENT : CONCEPTS AND PRINCIPLES

INTRODUCTION

Integrated pest management (IPM) is based on ecological principles and involves the integration and synthesis of different components/control tactics into a pest management system. Many components of IPM were developed in late 19th and 20th century. By early 1920s, a highly complex and sophisticated system involving the use of multiple component suppression techniques, viz. resistant varieties, sanitation practices and chemical treatments with calcium arsenate at fixed population levels, was clearly developed for the control of boll weevil on cotton in USA. However, during the period from 1920s to 1940s, the emphasis on crop protection shifted from cultural and biological control techniques to inorganic chemical pesticides.

The discovery of insecticidal properties of DDT rapidly followed by the manufacture of other broad spectrum synthetic organic pesticides during 1940s and 1950s virtually eclipsed all other techniques. These insecticides were easy to apply and produced an almost immediate kill. Therefore, they became our first and only line of defence or attack against all insects. However, even at that time, many scientists had warned regarding the consequences of exclusive reliance on chemical insecticides ignoring ecological principles. Unfortunately, their sane voices were drowned in the euphoria generated by the initial success of synthetic insecticides.

The use of toxic chemicals for the control of pests increased tremendously during the green revolution era. It was later realized that many of these chemicals were not biologically degradable and they not only persisted in the environment but also became concentrated through the food chains. With the consciousness of using the chemicals judiciously to minimize the pollution hazards, the scientists recommended that pests should be controlled by integrating the use of biological agents with the use of insecticides.

CONCEPT OF PEST MANAGEMENT

Basic tactics of IPM were proposed and used to protect crop plants against the ravages of insect pests long before the term was coined. In the absence of modern synthetic pesticides, crop protection specialists during the late nineteenth and early twentieth centuries, relied on pest biology and cultural practices to propose multitactical approaches, that could be considered as precursors of modern IPM systems. Stern *et al.* (1959) propounded the concept of 'Integrated Pest Control' which was defined as the blending of biological control agents with chemical control measures. Later on this concept was called as 'protective population management' which was subsequently shortened to 'pest management'. Thus, pest management may be considered -an intelligent selection and use of pest control actions, that will ensure optimal economic, ecological and sociological benefits. Pest management includes all approaches ranging from single component control method to the most sophisticated and complex control method. A number of definitions have been proposed for the twin terms of integrated pest control (IPC) and integrated pest management (IPM).

- According to the expert panel of the Food and Agriculture Organization, integrated pest control may be defined as a system that in the context of the associated environment and the population dynamics of pest species, utilizes all suitable techniques and methods in as compatible a manner as possible and maintains the pest populations at level below those causing economic injury (FAO, 1967).
- According to the National Academy of Sciences, IPM refers to an ecological approach in pest management in which all available necessary techniques are consolidated in a unified programme, so that population can be managed in such a manner that economic damage is avoided and adverse side effects are minimized (NAS, 1969).
- Smith (1978) defined IPM as a multidisciplinary ecological approach to the management of pest populations, which utilizes a variety of control tactics compatibly in a single coordinated pest management system. Dr Ray F. Smith and Dr Perry Adkisson have been awarded the 1997 World Food Prize for their pioneering work on development and implementation of IPM concept.
- Pedigo (2002) expanded the FAO definition to lay stress on the importance of socio-economics, and defined IPM as a pest management strategy that, in the socio-economic context of farming systems, the associated environment and the population dynamics of the pest species, utilizes all suitable techniques and methods in as compatible a manner as possible, and maintains the pest population levels below those causing economic injury.
- Based on an analysis of 64 definitions spanning the past 35 years, Kogan (1998) defined IPM as a decision support system for the selection and use of pest control tactics, singly or harmoniously co-ordinated into a management strategy, based on cost/benefit analyses that take into account the interests of and impacts on producers, society and the environment.

All the definitions share a common theme that IPM is a sustainable, environmentally friendly approach to managing pests by combining biological, cultural, physical and chemical tools in a way that minimises economic, health and environmental risks.

There are a series of phases in the evolution of an IPM programme:

(*i*) *Single tactic phase.* Emphasis is generally placed on a single pest utilizing a single tactic. This phase does not represent IPM, but the limitations in this approach may lead to its development.

(*ii*) *Multiple tactic phase.* This phase embraces a variety of tactics (cultural, mechanical, physical, chemical, biological, host resistance, regulatory, etc.) in manipulating pest populations.

(*iii*) *Biological monitoring phase.* This phase introduces monitoring of pest, natural enemies and host plant (phenology) populations as the basis for timing the application of various control tactics.

(*iv*) *Modelling phase.* This involves the conceptualization of the processes involved in pest management systems through mental, pictorial, flowchart and mathematical models. As the volume and complexity of data increase, more sophisticated modelling techniques become necessary.

(*v*) *Management or optimization phase.* This process involves the construction of a functional IPM system utilizing compatible subsystems in optimizing the integration of this IPM system with the overall crop production system.

(*vi*) *Systems implementation phase.* This is the ultimate phase through which the optimal systems are unified for delivery to and utilization by the farmer.

The ultimate aim of scientific pest management is to maintain a low level of pest population which would not only maintain the damage lower than the economic injury level but will also support the growth and survival of its natural enemies. The concept is to suppress the pest but not to annihilate it. For that very reason, the broad spectrum insecticides should not be used because they often have the effect of eliminating the pest as well as its natural enemies, thus upsetting the balancing of natural system of insect parasitoid relationship.

NEW CONCEPTS IN IPM

Although the success of IPM has been accepted worldwide, some alternative terms have been proposed to lay emphasis on particular strategies. The term 'biologically intensive IPM' or 'biointensive IPM' has been proposed, which would rely upon host plant resistance, biological control and cultural control. In fact, the utilisation of biological control and other non-chemical methods has been amply stressed in all IPM programmes. A special committee of the National Research Council's Board of Agriculture in 1996 proposed 'ecologically based pest management' (EBPM), emphasising that it was (*i*) safe for farmers and consumers, (*ii*) cost-effective and easy to adopt and integrate with other crop protection practices, (*iii*) durable and without adverse environmental and safety consequences, and (*iv*) used with ecosystems as the ecological focus. All these goals have been well taken care of by the concept of IPM. The emphasis on deployment of ecologically based integrated pest management (EBIPM) systems has increased greatly in recent years and some key issues that need to be highlighted are as follows (Koul and Cuperus, 2007).

- In EBIPM, programmes should emphasize on an understanding of the ecological relationships between the host plant and the management practices like cultural control, biological control and host plant resistance.
- Integration of management practices involves biological (*e.g.* parasitoids, predators and fungi), chemical (*e.g.* selective pesticides and pheromones), cultural (*e.g.* crop rotation, planting date and aeration). These ecological factors regulate the system.
- Sustainability implies durability over time. This is the true test for a management system.
- EBIPM programmes should minimize economic, environment and health risks.

The idea behind EBIPM is to shift the IBM paradigm from focusing on pest management strategies relying on pesticide management to a system approach relying primarily on biological knowledge of pests and on their interaction with the crops. This suggests that EBIPM programmes should represent a sustainable approach to manage pests combining biological, chemical, physical and cultural tools to ensure favourable economic, ecological and sociological consequences.

In EBIPM, programmes should emphasize on an understanding of the ecological relationships between the host plant and the management practices such as cultural control, biological control, host plant resistance and gene technology. The goal of EBIPM is to develop sustainable, environmentally sound, economically viable and socially acceptable systems (Table 14.1). EBIPM should have a focused road map based on the ecological concepts with specific priorities and strategic plans, which are designed with consumer needs and implementation aspects in mind (Koul and Cuperus, 2007).

Table 14.1 Approaches to pest management : Retrospect and prospect

S. No.	Parameter	Pest management system			
		Traditional	**Industrial**	**IPM**	**Ecologically based IPM**
1.	Goal	Reduce losses due to pests	Eliminate or reduce pest species	Reduce costs of production	Multiple-ecological, economic and social
2.	Diversity	High	Low	Low to medium	High
3.	Ecosystem stability	Uncertain	Highly unstable	Unstable	Striving towards stability and equilibrium
4.	Spatial scale	Single farm	Single farm	Single farm or small region defined by pests	Biogeographic regions
5.	Time scale	Long term	Immediate	Single season	Long term steady state oscillatory dynamics
6.	Target	Single pest or closely related groups of pests	Single pest	Several pests around a crop and their natural enemies	Fauna and flora of a cultivated area and linkages with non-cultivated ecologies
7.	Criteria for intervention	Past experience	Calendar date or presence of pest	Economic threshold	Multiple criteria
8.	Principal method	Cultural and mechanical measures	Pesticides	Resistant varieties, cultural practices, monitoring, product substitution, insecticide resistance management and multiple interventions	Agroecosystem design to minimize pest outbreaks and mixed strategies including group action on an area-wide basis to complement pest controls aimed at individual fields
9.	Research goal	Nil due to absence of organized effort	Improved pesticides	More kinds of interventions	Minimize need for intervention

10.	Extension technique	Nil	Transfer of technology (TOT)	TOT	Complimentarity between TOT and Farmer First (FF) mode
11.	Effect on environ-mental quality	Usually negligible	Highly detrimental	Moderately detrimental	Neglible

Source : Dhaliwal and Koul (2010)

The EBIPM programmes should be implemented on area-wide basis- what is commonly known as area wide pest management (AWPM). AWPM has been defined as the systematic reduction of a target pest(s), to predetermined levels by uniformly applied mandatory pest mitigation measures over geographical areas clearly defined by biologically based criteria, *e.g.* pest colonisation, dispersal potential, etc. E.F. Knipling and G.G. Rohwer presented a proposal to the North American Plant Protection Organization, entitiled 'Area-wide Pest Management' in September 1992. They argued that AWPM programmes (*i*) must be conducted on large geographical areas; (*ii*) should be coordinated by organizations rather than by individual farmers; (*iii*) should focus on reducing and maintaining key pest population at acceptable low densities, although eradication may be involved if considered practical and advantageous; and (*iv*) must involve a mandatory component to ensure project success within the entire geographical area, because voluntary programmes have historically not provided the desired level of pest management. On the other hand, IPM is generally applied to individual farms or cropping systems and is often voluntary in nature. The major advantage of managing pests on area-wide basis is that AWPM can offer a long-term solution to agricultural pest problems as opposed to quick-fix solutions on individual crops or small acreage. If properly implemented, this approach could prevent major pest outbreaks and provide a more permanent control of the pests (Koul *et al.*, 2008).

CONCEPTS OF INJURY LEVELS

The critical factor which determines the damaging capacity or otherwise of an insect is its population level. The concept of injury level was propounded to enable us to identify the population level at which an insect would cause damage to a crop.

Economic Injury Level (EIL)

According to Stern *et al.* (1959), it is the lowest pest population density that will cause economic damage. It is the level at which damage can no longer be tolerated and, therefore, at that point or before reaching that level, it is desirable to initiate deliberate control operations.

Although expressed as number of insects per unit area, the EIL, in reality, is a level of injury. Because injury is difficult to measure in a field situation, however, numbers of insects are used as an index of that injury. It may, therefore, be more useful to express EIL in standard units of injury. The standard units of injury are the injury equivalent, i.e. the amount of injury that could be produced by one pest through its complete life cycle, and equivalency, i.e. total injury equivalents (for a population) at a point of time. If management action (insect suppression) can be taken quickly and loss averted completely, EIL may be expressed as follows:

$$EIL = \frac{C}{VID} \quad ...(1)$$

Where:

EIL = No. of injury equivalents per production unit (insects/ha)

C = Cost of management activity per unit of production (Rs/ha)

V = Market value per unit of product (Rs/kg)

I = Crop injury per pest density

D = Damage per unit injury (kg reduction/ha)

These primary variables are affected by a number of complex variables.

In instances, where some loss from the insect is unavoidable, the relationship becomes:

$$EIL = \frac{C}{V \times I \times D \times K} \quad ...(2)$$

where K represents proportionate reduction in injury (e.g. 0.6 for 60%)

Economic Threshold Level (ETL)

It is the pest density at which control measures should be applied to prevent an increasing pest population from reaching the economic injury level. Control measures are taken at this stage so that the pest does not exceed the economic injury level. ETL is the best known and most widely used index in making pest management decisions. Although expressed in insect numbers, ETL is, in fact, a time parameter, with pest numbers being used as index for when to implement management strategies. Just as with EILs, ETLs can also be expressed in insect equivalents.

ETL is a complex value based on EIL, population dynamics of the pest, weather forecasting, and pest's potential for injury. The relationship between ETL and EIL is shown in Fig. 14.1. When no action is taken at ETL, population exceeds EIL, while when management steps for pest suppression are taken as the population crosses ETL, the population is forced down before it could reach EIL. ETL is a direct function of EIL and as such is subject to changes in EIL variables. In addition, ETL varies with logistical considerations associated with time delays that may vary from one situation to another.

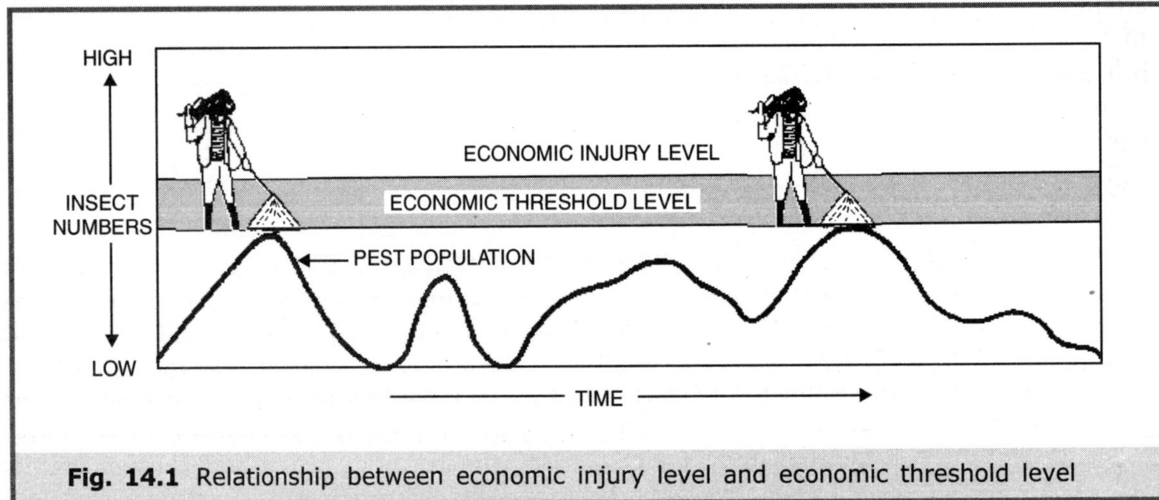

Fig. 14.1 Relationship between economic injury level and economic threshold level

The concept of EIL and ETL gained wide acceptability from the time it was presented. However, implementation of the concept in practice has been very slow. This is due to a number of serious limitations in the concept. Some of these limitations are given below:

- The terms EIL and ETL are themselves misleading because both are defined in terms of population densities, while former represents an injury level and the latter the time for taking control measures. This limitation may be overcome by defining these levels in terms of injury equivalents. Moreover, it would then be possible to describe the same type of injury for many pest species.
- There is a lack of rigorous definition of economic damage, i.e. the amount of injury that will justify the cost of control.
- The EIL concept overlooks the influence of other production factors that can affect the crop/pest systems. The externalities left out include interseasonal dynamics, biological relationships with other pests and natural enemies, environmental contamination by pesticides, resistance to pesticides, effect of control in neighbouring fields and health problems relating to pesticides.
- Decision levels for management of some types of pests cannot be determined with EILs. Besides medical and veterinary pests, it includes most vectors. It is very difficult to place a monetary value on the reduction in aesthetic value associated with a given type of injury. A similar problem exists with respect to forest pests. Almost all components of EILs are difficult to estimate for forest pests; accurate market values are a problem, management costs may vary greatly and frequently include mere environmental and social costs, and the injury/crop response relationships may be difficult to determine because the growth of the crop spans many years.
- The concept is unsuitable in case of attack of multiple pests on a single crop at the same stage.

However, inspite of these limitations, EIL concept continues to offer a practical approach to pest related decision making in a broad sense.

Environmental Economic Injury Levels (EEIL)

The challenge of attempting to decrease pesticide inputs further can be met by developing environmentally based EILs and their concomitant ETLs. An environmental EIL is an EIL that evaluates a management tactic based on not only its direct costs and benefits to the user but also its effects on the environment. The EIL equation (equation 2) integrates many management elements, each of which may have a role in making pest management environmentally most sustainable.

(*i*) ***Assigning realistic management costs* (*C*).** Component C of the EIL equation represents costs associated with taking management action against a pest population, and increased costs cause EIL to increase proportionally. Generally, C does not take into account the environmental costs associated with environmental risks; it is possible to include these costs in variable C of EIL. One approach for estimating environmental costs of pesticides through economic techniques of contingent valuation has been presented by scientists. The level of risk posed by 32 field crop insecticides to different environmental elements (surface water, ground water, aquatic organisms, birds, mammals, beneficial insects, etc) and to human health (acute and chronic toxicity) was estimated. The relative importance of avoiding risk to each of these elements was also estimated from the survey data. Additionally, survey respondents (producers) indicated how much they would be willing to pay, in either higher pesticide costs (for safer pesticides), or yield losses, to avoid different levels of risk (high, moderate, low) from a single application of a pesticide. With these data, the individual environmental costs for each insecticide were calculated as below:

$$\text{Environmental EIL} = \frac{\text{PC} + \text{KC}}{\text{VDIK}}$$

(*ii*) ***Manipulating crop market value*** **(*V*).** This could be achieved by putting a higher market value for a pesticide-free produce. The extent of increase would depend on the consumer's willingness to pay for a safer product.

(*iii*) ***Reducing damage per pest*** **(*D*).** Reducing D implies that less loss of yield occurs for a given amount of injury. This is possible if plant is able to tolerate and compensate for injury. Plants that can tolerate or compensate for injury do not place selection pressures on pest populations. Therefore, the benefits of tolerance and compensation in plant are sustainable and permanent. Even partial tolerance will increase EILs (by decreasing D). The need for pesticides and the risks to environment will be reduced correspondingly.

(*iv*) ***Developing environmentally responsible K value.*** Modified K is the proportion of total pest injury averted by timely application of a management tactic. Increasing the EIL to improve environmental quality implies that we are willing to tolerate more pests. But this is not always the case. By reducing D or K, EIL can be increased even without causing increased losses or costs.

General Equilibrium Position (GEP)

It is the average population density of a pest over a long period of time unaffected by the temporary interventions of pest control. The population fluctuates around a mean level as an outcome of the influence of density dependent factors such as parasitoids, predators, diseases, etc. It may be understood that EIL may be at any level from well below to well above the GEP. In certain insects, GEP is well below the EIL or even ETL and never reaches the latter two parameters. Such insects are rarely noticed physically but the damage caused by them through the introduction of a virus or any other disease can be most significant.

GEP touches EIL and ETL, approximately 2 to 5 years for many insect pest species. Such insects are called 'occasional pests'. The increase in population may be due to the injurious effect of pesticides or due to favourable weather conditions. For example, in Punjab outbreaks of the armyworm, *Mythimna separata*, on wheat are recorded every

2 to 5 years. Sometimes, the control measures are required frequently to bring down the GEP well below the EIL and ETL. Such a situation has been observed in the tobacco caterpillar, *Spodoptera litura*, which is a 'regular pest' of cruciferous vegetables.

The known severe pests form another category altogether and in their case, EIL and ETL are below the GEP level. The maize borer, *Chilo partellus*, is a severe pest of maize and its severity increases in some Himalayan valleys where the climate is mild. Moreover, it is much more severe on the hybrid corn varieties than on the local, comparatively low yielding maize.

Cost/Benefit and Benefit/Risk

As we improve the capability for predicting pest appearance, we can determine precisely the ETLs, and know exactly when to apply control measures. There is a need to emphasize costs and benefits. The preparation of crop life tables provides a solid foundation for analysis of pest damage and, cost/benefit ratio in pest management. If a crop is grown more than once in a year in the same field we should work out the crop season life tables. In most pest control activities, the benefits are usually not known, because those cannot be measured, hence the cost of prevention becomes the cost of production. In other words, the use of pesticides can rarely contribute to increase in yield and, at best, it can prevent the loss of yield, making the benefit both indirect and incalculable.

Benefit/risk analysis provides the means for assessing relevant economics versus risks in pest control. The judicious use of insecticides should be the philosophy of pest management. It is estimated that, generally, 1 per cent of the insecticide applied, reaches the target pest and the rest merely contaminates the environment as residue or causes mortality of the non-target or even useful species. Some non-degradable insecticides, such as the chlorinated hydrocarbons, attain biological magnification in the environment through food chains. Thus, a grower while ensuring safety in handling and applying a higher toxic pesticide, should also consider its injurious effects in the environment.

INTEGRATION OF TACTICS

The pest management tactics are either preventive or therapeutic. Preventive practice utilizes tactics to lower environmental carrying capacity (reduce the general equilibrium position) or increase tolerance of the host to pest injury. Prevention relies on an intimate understanding of the pest life cycle, behaviour and ecology. The preventive tactics involve natural enemies, host resistance and cultural practices. In addition, quarantines are also an important component of preventive tactics. Therapeutic tactics are applied as a correction to the system when necessary. The objective of therapy is to dampen pest population below EIL. The only widely used therapeutic tactic is the use of conventional insecticides but other approaches like microbial agents, augmentation of natural enemies, use of insect growth regulators, etc. also play a vital role.

Actual integration involves proper choice of compatible tactics and blending them so that each component potentiates or complements the other. Probably, the earliest example of integration of techniques was the use of a combination of resistant varieties and sanitation practices as prophylactic measures combined with application of calcium arsenate at high population level in case of boll weevil on cotton in USA in early 1920s. Similar programmes were being developed for other pests also but the advent of synthetic organic insecticides intervened and these techniques were relegated to the background. The misuses and abuses of insecticides have again focused our attention on integrated control measures.

It has been found that the rate of parasitism by *Bracon mellitor*, the most important native parasite of boll weevil, *Anthonomus grandis* was higher on frego bract (resistant) than on normal bract (susceptible cotton). The mortality of *Nephotettix virescens* has been found to be highest and population lowest when resistant varieties IR26 and IR56 were combined with predators, myrid bug, *Cyrtorhinus lividipennis* and spider, *Lycosa pseudoannulata*. The feeding of *Helicoverpa zea* on ED 73-371, a soybean genotype resistant to the Mexican bean beetle, *Epilachna varivestis* increased its susceptibility to *Bacillus thuringiensis*. Thus, Btwhich is normally ineffective against *H. zea* might be effective on resistant soybean.

Natural control by parasitoids and predators can be greatly strengthened by use of a large number of cultural practices like intercropping, trap cropping, strip harvesting, etc. Modification of the crop environment by manipulation of irrigation, fertilizer, row spacing, seed rate and tillage operations, etc. may also lead to substantial improvement in benefits of biological control. A combination of moderate resistance to carrot fly, *Psila rosae,* with specific sowing and harvesting dates, has enabled satisfactory yield of marketable carrots in heavily infested fields. The effect of plant resistance, planting dates and tillage practices was complementary in reducing greenbug, *Schizaphis graminum* population on sorghum; the resistant hybrids coupled with late planting dates and no tillage have been consistently effective for controlling the pest.

Combining plant resistance with well timed lower dosages of insecticides can sometimes achieve adequate pest suppression while reducing otherwise high insecticide inputs. Sweet corn hybrids resistant to corn earworm require less insecticide than susceptible hybrids to obtain an equivalent reduction in pest incidence. The insecticide rates on an insect-resistant groundnut cultivar (NC 6) can be reduced by 75-80per cent against *Diabrotica undecimpunctata howardi* and 60 per cent against *Frankliniella fusca.*

Insect pest management in cotton in Texas is a good example of integration of different tactics. The foundation of the programme begins with preventive tactics aimed at boll weevils. The basic tactic in prevention is a return to early planting of short season cotton cultivars, moderate fertilizer use and well timed irrigation. Plant thinning is delayed or not implemented, which suppresses vegetative growth and stimulates early fruiting. These practices shorten the production season and period of vulnerability to insects. Early harvesting, stalk destruction and use of defoliants late in the season prevent further weevil production and weaken or starve weevils going into hibernation. Pest surveillance and therapeutic treatments with organophosphates against boll weevil and flea hopper, *Psallus seriatus* are used at ETLs. Pyrethroids are applied in case of *Heliothis* outbreaks.

The Indian Institute of Horticultural Research has developed IPM in cabbage and tomato by employing trap cropping and biopesticides. Growing of Indian mustard in paired rows at the beginning and after every 25 rows of cabbage attracted more than 80 per cent of diamondback moth infestation besides almost entire population of leafwebber, stem borer, bugs and aphids. To control the remaining attack of diamondback moth, a 4 per cent neem seed kernel extract (NSKE) is applied at primordial or head initiation stage of the crop. Similarly, trap cropping of marigold after every 8 rows of tomato attracts most of the ovipositing moths of *Helicoverpa armigera* to the former crop. The use of conventional insecticides on the trap crop reduces their attractiveness to the pest. Therefore, the pest on the trap crop has to be removed mechanically. The residual pest population on both the crops is controlled by sprays of *H. armigera* NPV @ 500 larval equivalents per ha.

PRE-REQUISITES FOR DECISION MAKING

There are certain essential pre-requisites which must be followed before deciding to employ the pest management options.

1. Correct identification of pest. The correct identification of the pest is the first most important step on which the next course of action depends. Mis-identification of a pest can lead to complication of the problem rather than solving it. Efforts should be made to identify a pest up to species level as closely related species differ with respect to several biological parameters.

2. Life cycle. The knowledge of the sequence of developmental stages (egg to adult), their duration, number of generations and method of overwintering is essential to know the 'weakest link' in the life cycle. This would help to aim control measures effectively at the most vulnerable stage of the pest.

3. Habits. The important features of habits of pests which have a bearing on their control include the developmental stages responsible for plant injury, mode of feeding, parts of the plants attacked and whether the pest feeds externally or bores into the plant. Moreover, it is essential to know whether the pest transmits any disease in addition to causing direct injury to the plant.

4. Host range. It is essential to know whether the pest is monophagous (feeds only on one host plant), oligophagous (feeds on several plant species) or polyphagous (feeds on many plant species). Moreover, the non-cultivated plants which may act as reservoir of infestation should also be known. Plant host range can help to decide the proper crop rotation to be followed to keep the pest under check.

5. Natural regulating factors. Some pests can be kept under check by the activity of natural controlling factors like parasitoids, predators and disease organisms. Their precise role in specific circumstances should be understood to make the best use of natural mortality factors and their integration with other control measures.

6. Reinfestation. It is important to know the capacity of a pest to re-infest an area following its elimination. Some pests are highly mobile and quick fliers, and capable of rapidly re-invading the area. In contrast, some pests have very limited capacity to move and are very slow to reinfest.

7. Crop value. Expenditure on control measures can only be justified when increase in marketable yield of the crop produced is worth more than the cost of the control. Control measures should, therefore, only be initiated when they are economically justifiable. Usually, costly controls can be applied more logically to florist and fruit crops than to field crops.

8. Consumer pressure. Consumer demands have an important bearing on pest control. Certain fruits and vegetables may be rejected by the processor by mere presence of one or more insects in the samples of the produce. Similarly, even slight blemishes may not be tolerated on certain top-grade fruits.

9. Survey and detection. It is essential to carry out regular monitoring surveys to detect low-level pest infestations before they become damaging. It would help in devising strategies to prevent the pests to reach damaging levels. If the pest population tends to grow beyond damage threshold, appropriate control measures can be undertaken.

10. Selection ofmanagement options. The choice of appropriate option is very critical for the successful management of the pest. Before resorting to chemical control, the possibility of employing natural control agents, cultural practices and resistant varieties should be explored. If insecticides are to be used, information on their toxicity, cost, effectiveness, formulation, method and time of application, and their impact on beneficial arthropods in agroecosystem must be known.

DECISION MAKING

Decision making in pest management, like all other economic problems, involves allocating scarce resources to meet human needs. Initially, there is the choice of whether, when and how to attempt to manage insects and other pests with scarce capital or labour. Other resources may be scarce, however, such as pesticide-susceptible insect strains, an uncontaminated environment or information on the extent of pest infestation may also affect the desirability ofparticular choices.

Decision makers in IPM exist at many levels, from farmers, managers and contractors, each ofwhom are concerned with single fields, to industry and government personnel who are concerned with regional or national policies. Decision making at any ofthese levels would require generation ofinformation on the following aspects:

(*i*) *Fundamental information,* concerned with basic technical, biological and ecological processes that affect the damage caused by pests and the effectiveness of control measures.

(*ii*) *Historical information,* in the form ofrecords ofprevious pest incidence and damage, used to indicate trends in pest development and to assess the probability of future attacks.

(*iii*) *Real-time information,* collected by on-farm monitoring schemes or by regional surveillance and concerns on current pest status. Real time information on pest attack and damage can be obtained by direct assessment or indirectly through meteorological measurements.

(*iv*) *Forecast information,* involving estimates of future levels of attack and damage. This can be obtained by combining the previous categories of information often by means of a regression or more complex model.

The information so generated is analysed for the purpose of decision-making. This requires the use of decision making techniques like linear programming, goal programming, simulation modeling, decision trees and dynamic programming. As the information based on various aspects of pest management increased dramatically, computers were used first to process data and information followed by knowledge processing and decision making. Computer based systems could be used to provide access to information by serving as a cache, integrate and synchronize the information for use, interpret the information and serve as implementation coach.

DEVELOPMENT OF IPM PROGRAMME

The development of an integrated pest management programme involves three distinct phases, viz. the problem definition phase, the research phase and the implementation phase (Fig. 14.2).

Problem Definition Phase

The successful integration and use of control options in an integrated pest management programme depends to a vary large extent on the time and effort apportioned to the definition phase of the programme. This is a critical phase that is rarely given the amount of consideration needed for the subsequent development of an appropriate management programme. It is essential that the true dimensions of a pest problem be understood, not just in terms of perceived damage or yield losses caused by a pest, but in terms of actual yield losses and the socio-economic context of the farming system, in which these losses are known to occur. An understanding of the impact of a pest attack in this wider context, will point the way to an appropriate selection of control measures. To take this approach, however, would involve a significant effort, since yield loss evaluations and a socio-economic exploratory survey would be required, with the former possibly taking a number of years to carry out properly.

Such long-term approaches to simply defining a problem are clearly ideal, but rarely practical, especially where pest outbreaks are haivng a major impact on crop production and immediate control action is required. It will rarely be possible for all of the information required to be obtained, but it is becoming increasingly obvious that the least that is required in these initial stages is a socio-economic evaluation of the situation. This should take the form of an exploratory survey. While other information may have to be obtained from the literature, this information and that obtained from an exploratory survey, will need to be carefully analysed in order that the best possible representation of the pest problem can be produced. This problem framing part of the procedure should aim to define the limits of the problem, *i.e.* it needs to identify the key processes and variables, provide a synthesis of what is already known, and determine exactly what needs to be known if a pest management programme is to be developed. It is at this stage of the definition phase that modelling can play an important role, with the construction of a conceptual model of the problem. The model may or may not be developed as a mathematical model as the programme progresses.

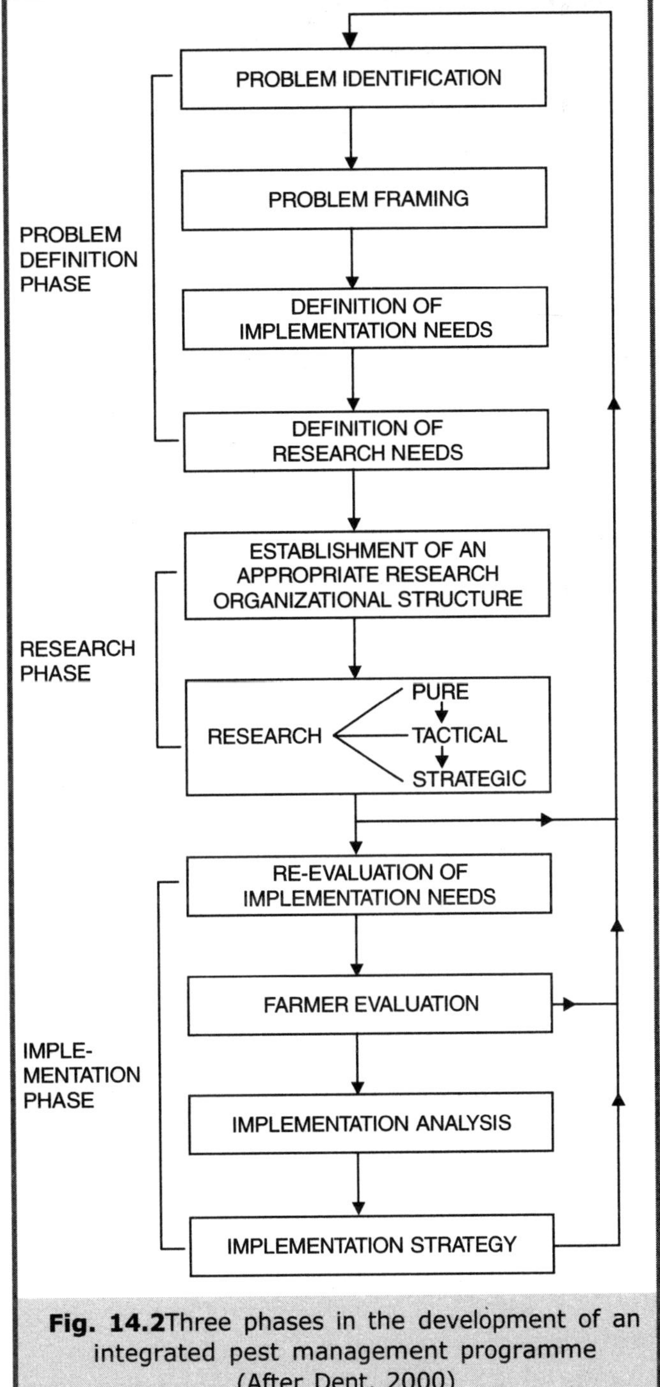

Fig. 14.2 Three phases in the development of an integrated pest management programme (After Dent, 2000)

Research Phase

The emphasis on specialisation in research has meant that research projects are considered for funding on a piecemeal basis and on individual merit. There is little or no co-ordination between projects and in some cases, different institutes working on similar projects do not know of the other's work. While this approach to funding research may be highly appropriate for promoting innovative, specialist projects within a single discipline, it is much less suitable for promoting the objectives of a co-ordinated multidisciplinary research effort such as that required for a research programme in IPM. Even if the separate components needed for an integrated approach were funded, there would still be little hope for integration because no organizational structure exists to co-ordinate the efforts and direct them towards a common goal. This lack of an appropriate organizational structure for management of research projects has important implications during both the definition and the research phases of a programme. During the definition phase, it is important that a common paradigm of the problem be developed to integrate the individual goals of each research group and to provide a common objective. In the absence of this, each group will carry out their own research in isolation from every other group. This will result in a number of separate solutions to a number of unrelated problems, because each group will perceive their objectives differently according to their own perceptions and expertise. Thus, organizational structures have an important role to play in pest management research to provide an appropriate institutional framework within which integration can take place.

Implementation Phase

The development of an implementation strategy should not be left to the final phases of any IPM programme. It should initially be considered during problem formulation and then continually readdressed throughout the research phase of the programme. The two factors essential for the implementation of most IPM programmes, *i.e.* farmer's participation and the legislative measures are discussed below.

Farmers' participation. To be effective and economically feasible, implementation of IPM at the farm level requires a degree of training, experience and attention to individual field conditions beyond the capabilities of most farmers, who must devote most of their time and energy to other aspects of crop production. On the other hand, top-down extension perpetuates an ideology of elitism, paternalism/passivity and social control. There is, thus, a need for a relationship of equality and dialogue between extension agent and farmer such that the partial knowledge of each is combined to solve problems and bring about positive change more effectively.

Since it is relatively complex, location specific and management-intensive, IPM is an educational challenge. The farmer must learn the principles and acquire the knowledge and skills necessary to make autonomous decisions based on specific farm conditions. There is a need for farmers' participation at every step of the R & D process in order to draw on farmers' intimate understanding of local conditions and constraints, their innovativeness and their skill at making the best possible living using limited resources.

Agricultural specialists should not dominate but instead should act as consultants, facilitators and collaborators, simulating and empowering farmers to analyse their own situation, to experiment and to make constructive choices. Extension agents should teach them analysis and decision making process. Placing the farmer at the centre of the technology development process is wholly consistent with the IPM goal of making the farmer a confident manager and decision maker, free from dependence on a constant stream of pest control instructions from outside.

An innovative approach recently applied for the implementation of IPM programmes is the 'Farmer First' approach which is being used for IPM on rice in Indonesia. In this method, farmers are divided into small groups to monitor the crop and then each group analyses the field situation by identifying the key factors. Group members then decide, whether any action is required. At a combined meeting, each group presents and defends its summary to other trainees. The trainer facilitates by asking leading questions or adding technical information if necessary. This process allows farmers to integrate and practise their skills and knowledge, and gives trainers an opportunity to evaluate the trainees' ability. Thousands of farmers have been trained utilizing this approach and it is being tried on a pilot scale. A survey among these farmers during the first post-training season revealed that they really decreased their frequency of pesticide sprays to a level consistently lower than that of non-IPM farmers. The percentage of farmers not applying pesticides was also significantly higher among the trained ones. Inspite of lower pest control expenditures, these farmers obtained higher yield than the non-IPM farmers. Other viable and easily implementable approaches need to be developed locally taking into account small holding size, low income and general literacy level of the average farmer in the area.

Legislative measures. IPM is an information system and its adoption reduces pest control costs. The alternative to IPM is the indiscriminate use of broad spectrum synthetic organic pesticides. Unfortunately, while pesticide manufacturers and users (farmers) derive the full benefits from the use of these chemicals, they pass on the environmental and ecological costs of their use to the society as a whole. If they are made to bear the full cost of the use of these toxicants, they may find IPM a more economical and attractive alternative. This could be achieved by enforcing suitable legislative measures.

Secondly, in order for an IPM programme to be successful, it must be followed by most, if not all, farmers in a geographical area. Ideally, all farmers may adopt an IPM programme voluntarily but some farmers may hold out. Such farmers called 'spoiler holdouts' may impair the success of a programme by failing to adopt a necessary practice. Legislative measures are required to impose the programmes upon an unwilling minority.

Thirdly, the importance and benefits of pesticides are being overemphasized by a multibillion dollar industry, utilizing the services of not only their salesmen but also agricultural scientists, administrators and planners. There is not yet a strong market in IPM information. Much important information which might induce a farmer to adopt IPM is not immediately observable and is, therefore, not sought by him. A manufacturer has no incentive to recommend a programme that uses less pesticides or even selective pesticides that kill a limited range of pests. This distortion could only be corrected by legislative action.

FRAMEWORK OF IPM PROGRAMME

There has been a widespread tendency to work within specialized subject areas of IPM and this movement towards specialization among researchers has now reached its peak of ascendancy. The need now is to place this specialist knowledge, abilities and skills within a broader scientific framework. There ought to be better coordination and exploitation of this valuable resource. This means that work of specialist groups dealing with different aspects of a common problem of insect pest control needs to be coordinated and placed in the context of the framework of an integrated pest management programme. This integration needs to be started at the top, in funding policy, and reach up to the lowest level, in implementation.

- The funding authorities need to develop a coherent policy and ensure that all individual research groups working on similar cropping systems coordinate their approaches. There is a need to allocate funds for development of complete pest management programmes.
- Secondly, there is an urgent need to develop conceptual and theoretical framework for IPM. The present situation is that IPM is made up of a great many isolated parts, each

of which can be developed internally but which is not clearly connected to anything else, *e.g.* farming systems, host plant resistance, natural enemies and decision-making behaviour. These pieces ought to be combined in an integrated programme. This requires a theoretical framework that will provide guidelines for pest managers. The framework will incorporate pest outbreak theory, a classification of pest types, their hosts and farming systems, and to identify options most appropriate for management strategies.

- Thirdly, integrative level of research in the form of field trials to test combination of control options for their compatibility and effectiveness is essential. This integrative research will require the combined input of all relevant disciplines to design, carry out and analyze the data from suitable factorial or multifactorial experiments. These experimental designs will be necessary to assess the interaction between the various treatments under test and arrive at a combination of options that produce higher yields.
- Fourthly, integration is required at the level of organizational behaviour. It is important that appropriate organizational structures are developed because they are fundamental to good management. Without them, integration of research will be less likely to occur and at a different level it may be found to affect motivation, innovation, morale and decision-making, and exacerbate conflict and poor coordination.
- Ideally, IPM should involve integration of control options for the management of all types of pests and not just insects. Insect pest management will then just be a subsystem of integrated pest management (IPM). This will require multidisciplinary research encompassing insects, pathogens, weeds and other pests. The importance of integrating the control of insects and pathogens is illustrated by an early story involving control of grape phylloxera on grapes in Europe. This example is often cited to illustrate the importance of plant resistance. The other part of the story is not so well known. Ironically, plants introduced from North America carried the pathogen of *Plasmopara viticola,* the causal agent of downy mildew to which European grapes were highly susceptible. The American root stock saved French vineyards from grape phylloxera but exposed them to an even more dangerous risk. The devastating epidemic of downy mildew that followed threatened wine production throughout Europe. Ultimately, the development of Bordeaux mixture, an early fungicide against the pathogen, saved European vineyards. This example underlines the need to consider the whole pest complex and the implications of any management strategy.
- Lastly, the development of an implementation strategy should not be left to the final phases of a research programme. It should initially be considered during problem formulation and then continually readdressed througout the research phase of the programme because it is often at the point of implementation that many pest management programmes fail.

CONCLUSIONS

The strategy of exclusive reliance on insecticides for all pest problems created a number of ecological and environmental problems. We now know that insects possess a remarkable ability to survive in the face of selection pressure exerted by insecticides and other forms of pest control. To overcome these problems, integrated pest management based on ecological principles was developed as a viable and attractive alternative. Though the concept of IPM has been universally accepted, there are as yet few IPM programmes functioning at the farmers' level.

A major limitation is the lack of a theoretical framework into which various components of IPM can be fitted to develop a viable IPM system. There is an urgent need to develop IPM systems for different crops, which are environmentally benign, conserve our plant and animal genetic resources and are economically viable. This requires intensified research efforts in formulation, research and implementation phases of the IPM programmes.

The insecticides will continue to be essential components in most of the IPM programmes but their use must be based on the concept of ETLs. With rapid development of insecticide resistance and widespread occurrence of multiple and cross resistance, insecticide resistance management (IRM) should also form an integral part of all IPM programmes. Methodology for monitoring of insect pests and natural enemies needs to be refined to obtain more accurate information. Development of mathematical models will help in predicting outbreaks of important pests. Newer approaches based on biotechnological tools must be exploited for the development of insect-resistant varieties and biopesticides. The role of allelochemicals and other substances in insect-plant interactions needs to be studied in case of different insect pests. Tritrophic interaction involving natural enemies, phytophagous insects and host plants should also be utilized for increasing the effectiveness of natural enemies. Development of technology for mass production of promising parasitoids, predators and pathogens is essential for their large scale utilization. Lastly, the farmers need to be convinced of the benefits of IPM programmes so that these are implemented in true letter and spirit. Innovations in farmers' participation and training can help to overcome many of the implementation problems.

PART–III

PERSPECTIVE

- **Integrated Pest Management : Progress and Perspectives**

INTRODUCTION

In the history of the world, no century can match the population growth of the one that has just come to a close. We entered the 20th century with less than 2 billion people and left it with more than 6 billion. The global population reached 7.7 billion in October-2019 and is likely to reach 9.35 billion towards the middle of the 21st century. It has been estimated that the population may grow even more in the 21st century, but in a different manner. The developed countries, which almost doubled their population size in the 20th century, will grow slowly or not at all. The new century's growth will occur almost exclusively in the developing countries. India would overtake China by 2050 to occupy the first position with a population of 1.75 billion followed by China with 1.44 billion people. The population growth will tax food supplies and outstrip countries' efforts in many areas. It is thus clear that the world's farmers will need to produce enough food to feed the expanding population. The efforts to increase food production in the 20th century have caused many environmental, economic and social problems. Therefore, we face a gigantic task of ensuring environmental and food security in the twenty-first century.

Remarkable progress has been made to increase the yield of food crops during the later half of the twentieth century. Major yield increases between 1962 and 2002 were achieved in case of wheat (200%), rice (117%), maize (150%), sorghum (57%), potato (77%) and cassava (43%). Despite these gains, 800 million still consume less than 2000 calories per day, 127 million pre-school children suffer from vitamin deficiencies, 400 million child-bearing women have iron deficiencies, 24,000 people (75% are children) die of hunger each day, 75 per cent of one billion people live in rural poverty, earning less than $1 per day. Today, the rate of production gains in developing countries from conventional breeding for staple food crops has slowed from 2.9 per cent (green revolution era) to 1.9 per cent, with gains frequently being offset by environmental stresses. The integrated pest management approach can play a pivotal role to further increase food production and protect the environment, as it is primarily based on ecological principles.

PEST MANAGEMENT : FROM TRADITIONAL TO SUSTAINABLE APPROACH

Though it is not generally recognized, evolution of the concept of pest management spans a period of more than a century (Table 15.1). Many components of integrated pest management (IPM) were developed in the late 19th and early 20th century. The rapidly developing technologies and changing societal values had their impact on the pest control tactics also. The modern concept of pest management is based on ecological principles and involves the integration and synthesis of different components/control tactics into a pest management system. IPM, in turn, is a component of the agroecosystem management technology for sustainable crop production.

During ancient times, humans had to live with and tolerate the ravages of insects and other pests, but gradually learned to improve their condition through trial and error experiences. Over the centuries, farmers developed a number of mechanical, cultural, physical and biological control measures to minimize the damage caused by phytophagous insects. Synthetic organic insecticides developed during the mid-twentieth century initially provided spectacular control of these insects and resulted in the abandonment of traditional pest control practices. This was followed by the development of high yielding varieties of important crop plants. The intensive cultivation of these varieties, together with the application of increasing amounts of fertilizers and pesticides, has resulted in a manyfold increase in productivity. However, this technology package has also resulted in aggravation of pest problems in agricultural crops. The importance of achieving sustainable food production through the use of ecofriendly sustainable pest management techniques is being realized more and more in the recent past. Hence the increasing problems encountered with insecticide use resulted in the origin of the integrated pest management (IPM) concept. The history of agricultural pest control, thus, has three distinct phases, viz. the era of traditional approaches, the era of pesticides and the era of IPM.

Era of Traditional Approaches (Ancient-1938)

Cultural and mechanical practices like crop rotation, field sanitation, deep ploughing, flooding, collection and destruction of damaging insects/insect infested plants, etc. developed by farmers through experience were among the oldest methods developed by humans to minimize the damage caused by insect pests. This was followed by the use of plant products from neem, chrysanthemum, rotenone, tobacco and several other lesser known plants in different parts of the world. The Chinese were probably the pioneers in the use of botanical pesticides as well as biological control methods for the management of insect pests of stored grains and field crops. However, systematized work on many important tactics of pest control including the use of resistant varieties, biological control agents and botanical and inorganic insecticides was done in the USA from the end of the 18th to the end of the 19th century. Remarkable success was achieved in the management of grape phylloxera caused by *Daktulosphaira vitifoliae* by grafting of European grape vine scions to resistant North American rootstocks during the 1880s. At around the same time, cottony cushion scale, *Icerya purchasi,* which was causing havoc to the citrus industry in California, USA was successfully controlled by release of the Vedalia beetle, *Rodolia cardinalis,* imported from Australia.

Table 15.1 Landmarks in the history of agricultural insect pest management

Period	Landmark(s)
(1)	(2)
	Era of Traditional Approaches
Ancient	The Chinese used chalk and woodash for the control of insect pests in enclosed spaces and botanical insecticides for seed treatment. They also used ants for biological control of stored grain as well as foliage feeding insects. In India, neem leaves were placed in grain bins to keep away troublesome pests. In Middle and Near East, powder of chrysanthemum flowers was used as an insecticide.
900 AD	The Chinese used arsenic to control garden pests.
1690	The tobacco extract was used as a plant spray in parts of Europe.
1762	*Mynah* (a bird) from India was imported for the control of locusts in Mauritius.
1782	"Underhill" variety of wheat reported resistant to Hessian fly in USA.
1831	"Winter Majetin" variety of apple reported resistant to woolly apple in USA.
1848	Derris (Rotenone) reported to be used in insect control in Asia.
1855	A. Fitch reported the role of lady bird beetles, green lacewings and other predaceous insects in the control of insect pests of crops.
1858	Pyrethrum first used for insect control in the USA.
1887	Balfour published his book *The Agricultural Pests of India and of Eastern and Southern Asia*. It was the first publication dealing with agricultural insect pest control in this region.
1889	Biological control of cottony cushion scale on citrus in the USA by use of Vedalia beetle imported from Australia.
1890	Control of grape phylloxera in Europe by grafting of European grapevine scions to resistant North American rootstocks.
1892	Lead arsenate used for the control of gypsy moth in the USA.
1898	The coccinellid, *Cryptolaemus montrouzieri* from Australia was released against coffee green scale, *Coccus viridis*, in India. It established but failed to control the scale.
1911	Cotton Pest Act was enforced in the erstwhile Madras State. Under the Act cotton stalks had to be removed by 1st August every year to minimise the incidence of pink bollworm.
1923	Multiple component suppression techniques involving the use of resistant varieties, sanitation practices and need-based application of insecticides developed for the control of bollweevil in the USA.
1931	The cottony cushion scale attacking wattle of commerce, *Acacia decurrens* was controlled in India by release of predatory beetle, *Rodolia cardinalis*, from California.
	Era of Pesticides
1939	• Insecticidal properties of DDT reported by Paul Muller in Switzerland. • *Bacillus thuringiensis* first used as a microbial insecticide.
1940	Work on the development of jassid-resistant varieties was undertaken in India resulting in the release of varieties like LSS, 4F, 289F, etc., during 1940s.
1941	Insecticidal activity of Hexachlorocyclohexane (HCH) discovered in France.
1946	Parathion, the first organo-phosphatic insecticide developed.
1948	• Use of DDT and HCH on agricultural crops in India.

	• "Doom" based on *Bacillus popilliae* and *B.lentimorbus* registered in USA for the control of Japanese beetle larvae on turf.
1951	• R.H. Painter published his classic book *Insect Resistance in Crop Plants.*
	• Introduction of first carbamate insecticide, Isolan
1952	First plant to produce HCH established at Rishra (India).
1959	• Concept of integrated control involving integration of chemical and biological control introduced.
	• Concept of economic injury level and economic threshold developed by V.M. Stern and coworkers.
1962	Publication of the book *Silent Spring* by Rachel Carson which dramatized the impact of misuse and overuse of pesticides on the environment.
1964	Publication of the book *Biological Control of Insect Pests and Weeds* by Paul DeBach, which established biological control as a separate discipline in Entomology.
	Green Revolution Era
1970	Establishment of US. Environmental Protection Agency (EPA), armed with responsibility for registration of pesticides.
1972	The first major IPM project, commonly called the Huffaker Project (1972-1978), was launched in USA, and covered six crops (alfalfa, citrus, cotton, pines, pome and stone fruits, and soybean).
1973	Development of first photo-stable pyrethroid, permethrin.
1975	• Elcar (*Helicoverpa* NPV) registered for the control of bollworm and tobacco budworm on cotton.
	• First insect growth regulator (Methoprene) registered for commercial use in USA.
	• Publication of the book *Introduction to Insect Pest Management* by R.L. Metcalf and W.H. Luckmann, which was the first comprehensive treatise on IPM and established the concept on a firm footing.
	• Another large scale IPM project, called the consortium for Integrated Pest Management (CIPM) (1979-1985) with a focus on four major crops (alfalfa, apple, cotton and soybean), was launched in USA.
1980	The interest in botanical pesticides revived and the First International Conference on Neem was held at Rottach-Egern, Germany.
1985	Structure of azadirachtin determined.
	Post-Green Revolution Era
1987	Development of first transgenic plant, reported by M. Vaeck and coworkers of Belgian Biotechnology Company, Plant Genetic Systems by transferring *B. thuringiensis*d-endotoxin gene to tobacco for the control of *Manduca sexta*.
1989	An IPM Task Force was established to garner international support for development and implementation of IPM programmes. A team of consultants appointed by the Task Force reviewed the status of IPM and made recommendations. The Task Force was later reconstituted as the Integrated Pest Management Working Group (IPWG) in 1990.
1992	• Concept of Environmental Economic Injury Levels proposed by L.P. Pedigo and L.G. Higley.
	• Dr Edward F. Knipling and Dr Raymond C. Bushland were awarded the World Food Prize for developing sterile insect technique.

	• United Nations Conference on Environment and Development (Rio de Janeiro, Argentina) assigned a pivotal role to IPM in the agricultural programmes and policies envisaged as part of its Agenda 21
1994	A Task Force consisting of FAO, the World Bank, UNDP and UNEP co-sponsored the establishment of the Global IPM Facility with the secretariat located at FAO, Rome.
1995	Dr Hans R. Herren was awarded the World Food Prize for developing and implementing the world's largest biological control project for cassava mealybug which had almost destroyed the entire cassava crop of Africa.
1997	Dr Ray F. Smith and Dr Perry L. Adkisson were awarded the World Food Prize for their pioneering work in development and implementation of integrated pest management (IPM) concept.
	Gene Revolution Era
2002	Bt cotton approved for commercialisation in India by the Genetic Engineering Approval Committee (GEAC) with the release of three hybrids, viz. MECH 12 Bt, MECH 162 Bt and MECH 184 Bt.
2004	One Bt cotton hybrid (RCH 2 Bt) released for commercial cultivation in India.
2005	• The first decade (1996-2005) of commercialisation of transgenic crops completed. The transgenic crops were grown on an area of 90 million ha in 2005.
	• Sixteen Bt cotton hybrids were released for commercial cultivation in India.
2006	• The area under transgenic crops crossed 100 million ha. These crops were grown by 10.3 million farmers in 22 countries on an area of 102 million ha.
	• Bt brinjal was approved for large-scale field trials in India by GEAC.
	• A total of 42 Bt coton hybrids were released for commercial cultivation in India.
2007	• Transgenic crops were grown on an area of 114.3 million ha by 12 million farmers in 23 countries.
	• A total 69 Bt cotton hydrids were released for commercial cultivation in India.
	• Azadirachtin was synthesized in the laboratory by Dr Steven V. Ley and colleagues, University of Cambridge, Cambridge (UK).
2008	• A team of scientists led by Dr B.E. Tabashnik, University of Arizona, reported the first documented case of development of resistance to Bt cotton in *Helicoverpa zea* in the field in Arkansas and Mississippi states.
	• The increase in resistance allele frequency to Bt cotton in field populations of *Helicoverpa armigera* was reported for the first time in China.
	• GEAC approved 84 new Bt cotton hybrids, 45 for Central zone, 35 for North zone and 18 for South zone.
	• GEAC approved Bt cotton variety developed by using an indigenous variety Bikaneri Narma. This is the first public sector transgenic crop in India and has been approved for North, Central and South zones of the country.
	• Transgenic crops were grown on an area of 125 million ha by 13.3 million farmers in 25 countries. Bt cotton in India was grown on 7.6 million ha by 5 million farmers.
2009	• GEAC approved Bt brinjal for environmental release in India.
	• Bt chickpea developed by CCS Haryana Agricultural University, Hisar.
	• Transgenic rice, tomato, maize, cabbage, cauliflower, castor and okra are at various stages of development in India.
2010	• Government of India withholds commercial release of Bt brinjal till more scientific data on biosafety are available.

Source **:** Modified from Dhaliwal and Koul (2010)

A number of synthetic inorganic insecticides containing arsenic, mercury, tin and copper were also developed towards the end of the nineteenth and the beginning of the twentieth century. With the development of these insecticides, the focus of research in entomology slowly shifted from ecological and cultural control to chemical control, even before the development of synthetic organic insecticides.

Era of Pesticides (1939-1975)

The synthetic inorganic insecticides were broad spectrum biocides and were highly toxic to all living organisms. These were followed in due course by the synthetic organic insecticides like alkyl thiocyanates, lethane, etc. The era of pesticides, however, began with the discovery of the insecticidal properties of DDT [2, 2-(*p*-chlorophenyl) –1, 1, 1-trichloroethane] by Paul Muller in 1939. The impact of DDT on pest control is perhaps unmatched by any other synthetic substance and Muller was awarded Nobel Prize for this work in 1948. DDT was soon followed by a number of other insecticides like HCH, chlordane, aldrin, dieldrin, heptachlor (organochlorine group); parathion, toxaphene, schradan, EPN (organophosphorus group) and allethrin (synthetic pyrethroid) during the 1950s and a large number of other popularly used organophosphates and carbamates in the ensuing decade.

Due to their efficacy, convenience, flexibility and economy, these pesticides played a major role in increasing crop production. The success of high yielding varieties of wheat and rice that ushered in the 'green revolution' was partially due to the protection umbrella of pesticides. The spectacular success of these pesticides masked their limitations. The intensive and extensive use, misuse and abuse of pesticides during the ensuing decades caused widespread damage to the environment. In addition, insect pest problems in some crops increased following the continuous application of pesticides. This, in turn, further increased the consumption of pesticides resulting in the phenomenon of the pesticide treadmill. The combined impact of all these problems together with the rising cost of pesticides provided the necessary feedback for limiting the use of chemical control strategy and led to the development of the IPM concept.

Era of IPM (1976 onwards)

Although many IPM programmes were initiated in late 1960s and early 1970s in several parts of the world, it was only in late 1970s that IPM gained momentum. The first major IPM project in USA, commonly called the Huffaker Project, spanned 1972-78 and covered six crops, *i.e.* alfalfa, citrus, cotton, pines, pome and stone fruits, and soybean. This was followed by another large scale IPM project called CIPM, the Consortium for Integrated Pest Management (1979-85), which focused on alfalfa, apple, cotton and soybean.

The national IPM programmes were launched in late 1980s and early 1990s in several developing countries. The most outstanding success has been the FAO-IPM programme for rice in Southeast Asia. Several other programmes were launched to promote IPM, some of which are outlined below.

Global IPM Facility. The Global IPM Facility has been established at FAO, Rome, and is co-sponsored by FAO, UNDP, UNEP and the World Bank. The concept is in response to the UN Conference on Environment and Development, held at Rio de Janerio, Brazil in 1992, which assigned a central role for IPM in agriculture as part of "Agenda 21". The Facility will serve as a coordinating, consulting, advising and promoting agency for the advancement of IPM worldwide.

CGIAR SP-IPM. The systemwide programme on IPM (SP-IPM) is an inter-centre initiative of the Consultative Group on International Agricultural Research (CGIAR).The programme was launched in 1995 in recognition of the need for a radically different approach if IPM research is to be more responsive to sustainable agricultural development. The SP-IPM is a global network of CG and other International Agricultural Research Centres. The SP-IPM targeted zones are in Africa, Asia and Latin America. The beneficiaries of the programme are farmers, national and international agricultural research organizations, extension programmes and NGOs who benefit from exchange of expertise, information as well as genetic and other resources to increase their capacity to manage pest problems, stabilize productivity and income, and foster a pesticide-safe environment.

USAID IPM Collaborative Research Support Progamme (CRSP). The United States Agency for International Development (USAID) has established a Collaborative Research Support Programme (CRSP) on IPM. The programme includes a consortium of several public and private institutions, NGOs, and national progammes of selected countries in Asia, Africa and Latin America. This is a research, education/training and information exchange collaborative partnership among USA and developing country institutions.

IPM Europe/IPM Forum. IPM Forum is an initiative of the Natural Research Institute (NRI) in UK. The aim of the IPM Forum is to help poor farmers in developing countries by strengthening the capacity of NGOs to promote and implement appropriate IPM approaches and techniques, as a component of sustainable agricultural development at the farm level.

Consortium for International Crop Protection (CICP). The CICP is a non-profiteering organization, which was formed in 1978 by a group of US universities. Its main purpose was to assist developing nations to reduce food crop losses caused by pests, while also safeguarding the environment. CICP's basic goal is to advance economically efficient and environmentally sound protection practices in developing countries and to ensure the health of rural and urban communities.

ICIPE and Africa IPM Forum. The International Centre of Insect Physiology and Ecology (ICIPE) located in Kenya coordinates the Africa IPM Forum. The primary mandate of ICIPE is research, capacity and institution building in integrated arthropod management. The Africa IPM Forum is a web-based forum for online IPM information sharing and discussion.

PROGRESS IN IPM

IPM has emerged as a science-based approach to minimize the risks associated with the use of pesticides. Both the developed and developing countries have taken major initiatives to promote IPM in principal agricultural crops.

A. IPM in Developed Countries

Many developed countries took a lead in developing IPM systems in major agricultural crops and achieved varying levels of success. The pioneering efforts were made in USA for the development and implementation of IPM in economically important crops.

Huffaker Project

The first major IPM project in the USA, commonly called the Huffaker Project, spanned 1972-1978 and covered six crops, viz. alfalfa, citrus, cotton, pines, pome and stone fruits, and soybean. The crops were selected on the basis of three criteria, *i.e.* (*i*) current level of insecticide use (very high in cotton and citrus, and very low in soybean), (*ii*) potential for successful biological control (alfalfa, citrus, pome and stone fruits), and (*iii*) representation of a non-agricultural system (pines). An anticipated outcome of the programme was 40-45 per cent reduction in the use of more environmentally polluting insecticides within a 5 year period and 70-80 per cent in 10 years. Advances were made in many aspects implementing improved IPM strategies for all systems. The project improved integrated insect control programmes that lessen the dependence on chemical insecticides especially on cotton and apples.

Consortium for IPM

After the success of the Huffaker Project, a group of scientists under the leadership of P.L. Adkisson secured funding for the second large scale IPM project in the United States, called the Consortium for Integrated Pest Management (CIPM) (1979-1985). The project focused on four major crops, viz. alfalfa, apple, cotton and soybean. It was claimed that the average adoption of IPM for four crops was 66 per cent over 5·76 million ha. The main indicators of adoption were the use of economic thresholds and economic injury levels for spray decisions, use of selective pesticides or application of lower dosages of broad spectrum insecticides. A significant achievement of the programme was the genuine attempt to integrate weed science and plant pathology, and the emphasis on economic assessment of IPM adoption.

National IPM Initiative

The U.S. Department of Agriculture (USDA) launched National IPM Initiative in 1993, the goal of which was to implement IPM practices on 75 per cent of the nation's crop area by 2000. To measure the level of adoption, USDA put forth the PAMS concept, the acronym for prevention, avoidance, monitoring and suppression. To qualify as an IPM practitioner, a farmer was required to utilize at least three of the four PAMS components. It has been estimated that some level of IPM has been implemented on about 70 per cent of the US crop acreage. The highest percentage of cropland under IPM was in case of cotton (86) and vegetables (86), followed by soybeans (78), maize (76), barley (71), wheat (65), other crops and pasture (63), fruits and nuts (62), and lucrene hay (40).

Integrated Fruit Production System

The pome fruit growers in Australia are funding a national system for integrated fruit production (IFP). This system incorporates whole-farm planning, site-specific selection of scion/rootstock combinations, IPM, irrigation and nutrition, crop management, quality assurance, food safety and occupational health and safety. IFP takes a broad approach to pest management decision making by encouraging integration and understanding of the interactions occurring in the orchard and their impacts on crop quality. On the basis of a survey conducted in all production areas, it has been found that slightly more growers selected pesticides on the basis of compatibility with predators (86%) than efficacy against the target pest (84%), suggesting that they are prepared to balance pest control with the value of maintaining a predator population. Nearly all (92%) based spraying decisions on the basis of monitoring. Overall, 45 per cent had their own staff trained to monitor pest populations, while 57 per cent used a consultant for their pest management.

The search for apple IPM system in New Zealand gained momentum in the 1980s and 1990s with a focus to minimize environmental and human health impact. Solutions that have been adopted for individual pests include a decision support model for European red mite, biological control, chemical control and pheromone traps to reduce insecticide applications against leafrollers. Recently, the introduction of insect growth regulators for leafroller and codling moth has enabled the development of selective pest management and increased the focus on integrating natural enemies within the apple IPM programme. This development has been an integral part of the apple industry's IFP programme that requires pest monitoring and justification of all pesticide use, backed up by auditing and certification systems. There has been very significant reductions in the use of broad-spectrum insecticides after several years of development and implementation of IFP. For example, from 1997 to 2000, there was a 72 per cent reduction in organophospate use in New Zealand apple orchards, with a 90 per cent reduction in the use of azinophos methyl. By 2000-01 season, this was equivalent to an overall 90 per cent reduction in organophosphate use, wide application of the IFP programme by growers occuring in the 2001 season.

IPM in Greenhouses

The greenhouse crops are grown over an area of 300,000 ha worldwide. Vegetables are produced in two-third of these greenhouses and ornamentals in one-third. Although this represents a tiny fraction (0.02%) of the 1.5 billion ha under crops worldwide, greenhouses offer the opportunity to grow larger quantities of high-quality crops on a very small area. For example, in the Netherlands 30 per cent (by value) of agricultural output is produced in greenhouses that occupy only 0.5 per cent of the total agricultural land. IPM is used on a large scale in all the main vegetable crops grown in greenhouses in Europe. In the Netherlands, for example, more than 90 per cent of all tomatoes, cucumbers and sweet peppers are produced under IPM. Worldwide 5 per cent of the greenhouse area is under IPM and there is a potential for increase to about 20 per cent of the area in the next decade (Thacker, 2002).

A good example of an IPM programme is the one used for tomato in Europe. It involves more than 10 natural enemies and several other methods like host plant resistance, climate control and cultural control. When tomatoes are grown in soil, soil sterilization by steaming is used shortly before planting the main crop to eliminate the soil-borne diseases such as tomato mosaic virus (TMV), *Fusarium* and *Verticillium*, and insect pests such as tomato moth, *Lacanobia oleracea* and three species of leaf-miners, *Liriomyza* spp. Therefore, only foliage pests and *Botrytis cinerea* require direct control measures.

B. IPM in Developing Countries

The developing countries are characterized by tropical and sub-tropical climates. The integrated pest management strategy appears to be more feasible in these regions because of the following factors :

- Climate and physical environment in tropical and sub-tropical areas generally allow populations of both pests and natural enemies to proliferate throughout the year. Regulation of numbers by natural biotic mechanisms thus can function optimally and in relative abundance.
- Agroecosystems, which have not yet been subjected to rigorous economic development generally have been only little disturbed by pesticide applications. They offer a relatively sound base for the development of an IPM system and farmers do not have to be re-educated.
- If the agricultural production is destined for home consumption, farmers usually pay little attention to light infestation and they would hardly spray for cosmetic reasons. However, transformation to market-oriented production leads to excessive use of pesticides, particularly on vegetables, fruits and flowers.

- Where new areas are opened up for agricultural production, as may be the case in sparsely inhabited parts of Africa, Asia and South America, there would be an opportunity to introduce IPM from the beginning and to ban unwanted chemical control practices.

Growing concern among the general public for environmental issues, particularly pesticide misuse, has prompted many developing countries to formally and explicitly advocate the use of IPM as an environmentally friendly form of crop protection. For example, the Governments of India and Malaysia adopted IPM as official policy in 1985 by Ministerial Declaration. Similarly, Governments of Indonesia and Philippines promulgated Presidential Decree/ Declaration to adopt IPM as official policy. China introduced the Green Certificate programme and banned highly toxic pesticides on vegetable crops. Biological control is a national priority for Cuba; the new policy is intended to make IPM biointensive, with 80 per cent of pests managed through biological control. Iran formed the High Council of Policy and Planning for Reduction of Agricultural Pesticides. Nepal and Sri Lanka have adopted national IPM policies. Under such conditions, the cases for funding IPM programmes will be heard more sympathetically and the agencies empowered by government to allocate resources will give proper attention to the needs of IPM (Koul *et al.*, 2004).

The philosophy of IPM did not percolate down to the farmers for quite a long time after its presentation and prescription for solving pest problems in modern agriculture. It was also suggested that the illiterate farmers of the developing countries were unable to grasp the concept of IPM and, therefore, could not implement it. However, the pessimists have been proven wrong and the same farmers have now demonstrated that they are quite capable of understanding the intricacies of IPM. The success of *Farmer Field Schools* (FFSs) in the implementation of IPM in many Asian counties proves that farmers are quite responsive to appropriate technologies which give due weightage to their traditional wisdom, local conditions and socioeconomic constraints (Bergvinson, 2004).

Participatory IPM led by farmers is now practised in over 50,000 communities found mostly in Indonesia, Vietnam, Philippines, Bangladesh, China, Sri Lanka, India, Cambodia, Laos, Republic of Korea, Ghana, Kenya, Cote d'Ivoire, Burkina Faso, Mali, Egypt, Sudan, Honduras, Nicaragua, Senegal and Zimbabwe. This is over 2 per cent of all rural villages in all developing countries. There are over 30,000 competent IPM trainers any of whom can facilitate a Farmer Field School through an entire crop season, and then the resulting farmers' IPM group through the remainder of their year-round production agroecosystem. Farmers practicing IPM have increased yields per hectare from 1 to over 10 per cent, reduced pesticide use by 30 to over 95 per cent (and often eliminating insecticide use) and substantially lowered occupational health risks. Most of the communities practicing IPM grow rice, but IPM is also practiced by farmers of maize, soybean and other field beans, cabbage, tomato, groundnut, coconut, cacao, coffee, peppers, sweet potato, cotton, mango and cucumber (Dhaliwal and Arora, 2006).

The Government of India adopted IPM as the official guiding principle of plant protection strategies in 1985. The notable initiatives taken by the Government of India for promotion of IPM include :

Policy Support:

- Phasing out pesticide subsidies and diverting the savings to promotion of IPM programmes.

- Emphasis on production and release of biological control agents.
- Phasing out, banning, or restricting the use of hazardous pesticides.

Human Resource Development:

- Organizing season-long training programmes for IPM trainers.
- Establishing FFS to train agricultural extension officers and farmers.

Infrastructure Development:

- Enhanced budgetary provisions for promotion of IPM.
- Assistance to states for establishing biocontrol laboratories.

The IPM programme has been strengthened in India since 1994 and 10562 Farmer Field Schools have been conducted in rice, cotton, vegetables, pulses and oilseeds, where 43,301 Agriculture/Horticulture Extension Officers and 3,18,246 farmers have been trained up to 2007. The yield increase in rice and cotton in IPM-areas, varied from 7 to 40 per cent and 23 to 27 per cent, respectively, as compaired to non-IPM areas. There was a reduction in pesticide consumption to the tune of 50-100 per cent and 30-50 per cent in rice and cotton respectively, in IPM-areas. The use of Bt-based and neem-based pesticides increased from 123 metric tonnes during 1994-95 to 1920 metric tonnes during 2005-06. Overall consumption of chemical pesticides in the country decreased from 75033 metric tonnes (technical grade) during 1990-91 to 39773 metric tonnes during 2005-06.

Rice

Major efforts in implementing IPM in irrigated rice have been carried out in Asia by the United Nations Food and Agriculture Organization (FAO) through the Inter Country Programme for the Development and Application of Integrated Pest Control in Rice in South and South-east Asia. This programme remains one of the best examples of IPM implementation in the tropical region. It involves purposeful, direct efforts to change farmers' practices in contrast to some more indirect routes of IPM technology diffusion in many industrialized, temperate environments. The programme itself has evolved into its present transnational form from a relatively small project supported by Australia in the late 1970s, following the large-scale pest outbreaks in several Southeast Asian countries.

The first phase of the FAO programme (1980-86) focused on developing and testing the technical aspects of the IPM concept in its seven participating countries, viz. Bangladesh, India, Indonesia, Malaysia, Philippines, Sri Lanka and Thailand. More recently, the project has been directed towards enhancing farmers' adoption of IPM. The programme is supported by Australia, the Netherlands and the Arab Gulf Fund. One significant accomplishment of the programme has been to cause policy changes within several governments, in the form of official support of IPM as the means for national plant protection in the Philippines, Indonesia, India, Sri Lanka and Malaysia.

A case study of the National IPM Programme in Indonesia as a part of the regional programme during 1989-1991 provides an interesting scenario. Indonesia subsidised up to 85 per cent of the cost of pesticides during the early 1980s. Following research findings showing the relation between brown planthopper outbreaks and high pesticide use, the Indonesian government banned the use of 57 of the 66 broad-spectrum pesticides used on rice. By 1989, pesticide subsidies were no longer offered and IPM was declared as the national pest control strategy. These measures, created a favourable climate for the large scale implementation of IPM. Consequently, there was dramatic increase in Indonesian rice production; production rose from 38 to 45 million tonnes, while Indonesia went from a net importer of pesticides (US$ 47 million) to a net exporter (US$ 15 million). It has been estimated that FAO training of 200,000 farmers in IPM techniques has resulted into a saving of $160 million in pesticide subsidies. By 2002, rice production reached 51 million tonnes, providing a good example of what progressive policies combined with massive farmer training can accomplish.

China, which had been experimenting with IPM for the control of rice pests since early 1980s, was also invited to join the FAO project in 1989. During 1989-90 alone, nearly 1,60,000 farmers from over 2000 villages received IPM training. Compared with untrained farmers, IPM-trained farmers saved roughly a third of the pesticides in rice cultivation and still obtained 7 per cent higher yield. It was estimated that the investment in IPM training generated a return of more than 400 per cent. Encouraged by these results, the Ministry of Agriculture has set up a National Steering Committee for the comprehensive prevention and control of diseases and insect pests to protect the nation's rice crop and increase profits. The Committee conducts IPM tests, gives demonstrations and makes appraisals.

In Philippines, National IPM Programme was launched in 1993 and a total of 40,024 farmers have been trained during 1993-95, among whom 36, 024 are rice farmers. Among 1,632 FFSs, 1470 were devoted to rice farmers. The increase in rice yield obtained by IPM farmers varied from 4.7 to 62 per cent. The expenditure on pesticide use

(15% of total cost) was almost eliminated in case of IPM farmers. In Vietnam, during 1992-95, 5941 FFSs have been organized in 3095 villages (out of 9274 villages of the country), with a total of 1,73,650 farmers trained. The number of insecticide applications by IPM farmers were reduced by 80-90 per cent and in some agroecological regions, there was almost no use of insecticides. IPM fields produced 150-460 kg/ha more rice than non-IPM fields. One study of over 1300 villages in Vietnam showed a 4 per cent yield increase in rice and over 20 per cent increase in profits.

In Bangladesh, Cooperative for American Relief Everywhere (CARE) began introducing IPM activities into an ongoing rice irrigation project in the late 1980s. Most of the farmers that CARE worked with were very small, owning less than half hectare of land. The farmers were trained in rice-fish culture and IPM. A survey among the farmers trained in rice-fish culture and IPM revealed that during 1992-93, virtually all of them stopped using pesticides and satisfactory control of insect pests was being provided by fish and naturally occurring parasitoids and predators. Farmers cultivating fish in their rice fields totally eliminated the use of pesticides even without training in IPM. However, only 20 per cent of the farmers could cultivate fish, mainly due to lack of adequate water, poor water holdingcapacity of the soil and risk of flooding. These farmers who could not cultivate fish still reduced their pesticide use by 76 per cent with IPM training. By the harvest time, some of the farmers were able to harvest quantities of fish worth as much as their rice. These results underline the need for undertaking IPM programmes as part of overall rural development programmes.

During 1995, farmers at IPM schools applied an average of 0.19 spray/season as compared to 1.65 sprays/season during the pre-training period. The average yield increased by 17 per cent from 3.76 tonnes/ha during the pre-training period to 4.4 tonnes/ha after IPM training. The average number of pests per 10 rice hills decreased from 20 to 11 and the number of natural enemies increased from 18 to 31.

In India, the first IPM programme in rice was started at Cuttack in 1975 covering an area of about 1000 ha in 10 villages. As a result of implementation of a number of cultural practices and ETL based applications of insecticides, the number of applications was reduced from 3-4 to usually single one. Subsequently, an Operational Research Project (ORP) was instituted on integrated control of rice pests at six locations in five provinces. This resulted in a reduction in the number of sprays and increased yield of the crop. Successful implementation of the IPM programme in Warangal district in Andhra Pradesh resulted in reducing the gall midge to a status of minor pest, managing the population of other pests at below economic damage and consequent avoidance of yield losses. Intensity of insecticide use was also brought down to some extent (1.78 to 1.24-1.33 per spray per ha). Average yield in the adopted village was established at 4.1 t/ha as compared to 3.1 t/ha yield of bench mark level in 1977. High level of awareness was created among farming community regarding the identity of the insect pests and diseases, and IPM. On the basis of 5 years of ORP at Kuttanad in Kerala, it has been observed that, on an average, one-third of expenditure on plant protection operations can be saved by practising pest management methods. Prophylactic sprays and spray schedules have been abandoned by the cultivators and plant protection measures were taken only when the pest population exceeded economic threshold.

The validation of IPM in Basmati rice (Pusa Basmati 1) was demonstrated in village Shikohpur in Distt Baghpat (UP) during 1999. This village had the history of indiscriminate use of pesticides on this crop and some farmers had applied 10-12 rounds of highly toxic chemicals. The success of IPM approach during 1999 led entire village to follow and adopt this technology in an area of 120 ha in 2000 and 160 ha during kharif 2001 and 2002. By following the IPM tactics, the pesticide use was drastically cut, other input costs like fertilizers, number of irrigations, etc. reduced and farmers could secure residue free higher produce. The cost : benefit ratios were 1:3.18 (IPM) and 1:2.28 (non-IPM) in 2000, 1:3.16 (IPM) and 1:2.12 (non-IPM) in 2001, and 1:2.21 (IPM) and 1:1.64 (non-IPM) in 2002.

After the success of IPM in Pusa Basmati-1, this approach was evaluated on another Basmati variety (Taraori) at village Chhajpur Khurd, near Panipat in Haryana. A total area of 28 and 80 ha was earmarked for IPM in 2002 and 2003, respectively. The economic analysis indicated the average cost : benefit ratios over a two year period were higher in IPM (1:2.88) than in non-IPM (1:1.77). IPM technology was also more effective and sustainable in organic basmati rice (Taraori) fields in comparison to indigenous traditional knowledge (ITK)-based and conventional chemical (CC)-based strategies. The yield in IPM, ITK and CC was 3.23, 2.95 and 3.11 tonnes per ha, whereas the corresponding C:B ratios were 1:5.11, 1:4.24 and 1:4.19.

However, judging from the current low percentage adoption, it would appear that there is much scope for increased IPM in almost all the rice growing areas. This may also result in substantial savings to national treasuries as a result of elimination of pesticide subsidies. The savings to the Goverment of Indonesia by eliminating the subsidies have exceeded US$ 1 billion. India eliminated a US$ 30 million annual subsidy by the central government for insecticides, and instead imposed a 10 per cent excise tax on them. This has meant US$ 60 million annual new income to the government, which spends over US$ 10 million per year on IPM field training.

Cotton

The cotton production systems of the world illustrate well the ecological and environmental problems associated with intensive insecticide use. Cotton growing in the Canete Valley, Peru is a well documented case that has become a classical example of integrated control. Even prior to the advent of synthetic organic insecticides, the increasing use of inorganic insecticides resulted in serious outbreaks of *Heliothis virescens* and *Aphis gossypii*. The advent of synthetic organic insecticides resulted in extensive use of these chemicals. Both *H. virescens* and *A. gossypii* soon became resistant to these insecticides. A number of other pests like leafrollers, mealy bugs, leaf perforator, etc. also became serious. The frequency of treatments decreased from 8-15 days to every

3 days. The average number of insecticide applications were increased to 16 but still lint yields touched the lowest levels of 332 kg/ha. A set of integrated control measures involving the use of natural enemies (*Trichogramma* spp., lady beetles and carabid beetles), cultural practices (early maturing varieties, crop rotation, fixed sowing dates and clean up campaigns) and selective use of inorganic insecticides were implemented from 1956 onwards and by 1959 productivity reached a level of 800 kg/ha. The number of insecticide applications declined to 2-3 per season and increase in cotton yields was sustained for the following two decades. However, during the last decade, the area planted to cotton has been reduced to half, following the break-up of large estates and pesticide use has begun to increase again. IPM is still practised on a small area of organic cotton, but a large proportion of the cotton crop is now treated intensively with pesticides.

The adoption of IPM system in Columbia led to considerable decrease in insecticide use and increase in cotton yield. In 1977, 22-28 insecticide treatments were carried out in cotton, most of them to combat *H. virescens*. This pest had developed resistance to methyl parathion and all other available insecticides. With the introduction of pyrethroids, it again became possible to control the pests effectively, with a much smaller quantity of active ingredient per hectare than had been needed before. At the same time, an IPM programme was set up–the pest populations were carefully monitored and measures to control them only implemented if relevant threshold values were exceeded. Massive numbers of beneficial arthropods were then released. Rigid calender based treatments were replaced with crop monitoring, which allowed pest attacks to be detected at an early stage. This in turn, allowed insecticides to be employed in a targeted manner. Insecticide use was optimized in this IPM system, and developed as a complement to biological control measures.

The success of Farmer Field School programme on rice in Asia has encouraged the testing and adoption of this approach in cotton. The major recent cotton FFS programme is the EC's 2000-2004 programme 'IPM Programme for Cotton in Asia'. This US$ 12 million programme, implemented by the FAO Global IPM Facility, covered Bangladesh, China, India, Pakistan, the Philippines and Vietnam; the countries which together produce over 40 per cent of the world's cotton. In 2002 cotton season,some 800 Farmer Field Schools were run across the region by about 500 trained facilitators, with 20,000 farmers passing through 3,800 FFS programmes; well on the way to the target of 90,000 farmers at the end of the programme. In 2002, FFS IPM farmers in China made a net profit of $ 1150 per ha as against $ 520 per ha for normal farmers practice areas. However, the average net profit for Bt cotton farmers using IPM was $ 1600 per ha.

In India, the Indian Council of Agricultural Research, sponsored a village level IPM project to test and demonstrate the efficacy, practicability and economics of IPM in cotton. The IPM programme called the Operational Research Project (ORP), was initiated in Punjab and Tamil Nadu in 1975 and 1980, respectively. In Punjab, 15 villages during different years were covered up in ORP to test and demonstrate the efficacy, practicability and economics of IPM strategy. Farmers were educated by ORP staff about different insect pest problems, side effects of excessive use of insecticides and cultivation of susceptible long duration varieties and concept of ETL/IPM strategy. The first main achievement of the project was change in the cultivation of varietal pattern. Prior to start of project, long duration varieties, mainly LSS(*Gossypiumhirsutum*) covered majority (88.8%) of cotton area, while the area under short duration and insect-tolerant variety Bikaneri Narma (BN) /F 414 was only 9.9 per cent. By 1978, LSS variety was completely replaced by BN/F 414. Induction of BN/F 414 made possible the cotton-wheat rotation. The adoption of IPM technology resulted in 73.7 and 12.4 per cent reduction in the number of insecticide sprays for control of sucking pests and bollworms, respectively. The reduction of bollworm incidence in ORP villages was 38.55 per cent higher than non-ORP villages leading to 23.1 per cent higher yield and 31.1 per cent higher net income per unit area. The yield of seed cotton obtained in demonstration fields was 20.45 q/ha as against 10.17 q/ ha on other fields.

ORP project on IPM has also been successful at Coimbatore in Tamil Nadu in reducing the use of insecticides without affecting the yield of seed cotton, at the same time encouraging the natural enemies and reducing the environmental pollution. The mean quantity of insecticides used in the project villages was 3.82 kg a.i./ha in 6 applications at spray interval of 15-18 days, which was 58.6 per cent less than the amount (9.23 kg a.i./ha) used in non-project villages with 11 sprays at an interval of 7-8 days. The IPM system increased the abundance of native natural enemies by three fold, reduced the cost of insecticide and environmental pollution by 50.3 and 53.4 per cent, respectively. The officials of Department of Agriculture, Tamil Nadu demonstrated IPM technology in 48 villages in three districts covering 2650 ha cotton area during 1984. The farmers in IPM villages harvested, on an average, yield of 26.70 q/ha as against 22.25 q/ha in control villages. These studies have demonstrated the efficacy and economics of IPM on cotton, which need to be conducted still on large scale to educate the farmers about the long range utility of IPM.

To overcome the downward trend in the productivity of cotton in India, many new IPM programmes were launched. These include the regional programme on cotton IPM by the Commonwealth Agricultural Bureaux International (CABI) in 1993, FAO-European Union IPM programme for cotton in 2000, National Agricultural Technology Project (NATP) in 2000 and the Insecticide Resistance Management (IRM) Programme in 2002. The focus of these IPM programmes was to reduce and rationalise pesticide use by encourgaging farmers to adopt other pest management practices.

The Insecticide Resistance Management programme was launched in 26 cotton-growing districts in 10 states, which consume 80 per cent of India's insecticide use on coton. The basic objectives of the IRM strategy are to disseminate available technology related to IPM, to monitor the level of resistance to commonly used insecticides, to assess the impact of IRM strategy on economic status of the farmers and to validate the IRM technology. In Punjab, three districts (Bathinda, Ferozepur and Mansa) have been covered, which account for more than 70 per cent of the total area under cotton cultivation. Three more districts, *viz.* Muktsar, Faridkot and Barnala were adopted in 2006. The district Bathinda is considered to be the hot -spot for pesticide consumption, where 50 per cent of the cost of cultivation is on pesticides. From about 2-3 insecticide applications in cotton in 1970s, farmers have been reported to resort to more than 30 insecticide applications towards the beginning of the twenty-first century.

The impact of IRM based IPM strategy, has been summarised in Table 8.3. In general, there was less damage by the bollworm complex, lower incidence of sucking pests, higher number of natural enemies, less number of insecticidal sprays, lowest cost of production and increase in net income.

The total number of sprays carried out for the control of insect pests was 9.6 and 9.5 in IRM villages as compared to 12.7 and 16.2 in non-IRM villages during 2002 and 2003, respectively. The total number of sprays in IRM villages was 4.3 and 3.4 as compared to 8.1 and 5.2 in non-IRM villages in 2004 and 2005, respectively. The implementation of IRM strategy resulted in 46.9 and 34.6 per cent reduction in insecticidal applications during 2004 and 2005, respectively. The validation of IRM strategies during 2002-06 revealed that the number of sprays was less in IRM plots (6.4) as compared to non-IRM plots (10.0), thus, resulting in 36 per cent reduction in the number of sprays. The reduction in cost of sprays and increase in seed cotton yield in IRM plots was 36.7 and 12.9 per cent, respectively. During 2008, reduction in cost of sprays and increase in yield in IRM villages were 62.2 and 19.3 per cent, respectively. The decrease in pesticide load, led to increase in the population of natural enemies during early season which helped in reducing the pest population and ultimately the damage caused to the crop.

A landmark in cotton IPM has been the validation of the cropping system based holistic community approach of IPM at village Ashta (1998-2001) in Nanded district (Mahrashtra). The baseline information indicated less than a quintal average seed cotton yield per ha in the *H. armigera* epidemic year of 1997 when the farmers had applied more than 12-13 chemical pesticide spray rounds. All the farmers of the village were involved and the IPM approach covered 180 ha cotton area. The off-season practices included management of *H. armigera* on pigeonpea and chickpea through use of neem seed kernel extract (NSKE) and HaNPV, field sanitation and deep ploughing. In the

pre-sowing practices, multiplicity of cultivars was avoided by selecting only two sucking pest moderately resistant cultivars and treating the seed with imidacloprid. The sowing of the entire village was completed within a week to avoid vulnerability of crop over a long period. The IPM interventions included use of *Trichogramma chilonis*, HaNPV and NSKE. Lastly, chemical pesticides were used when needed and these included spray of endosulfan/bavistin for the management of bollworms or grey mildew in certain pockets. The cost of plant protection was reduced by 31.3 per cent, chemical pesticide consumption reduced by 94.3 per cent and seed cotton yield increased by 56.9 per cent. The system has become self-sustainable as the farmers of Ashta have themselves become decision-makers and have started adopting many IPM practices on their own. The average cost: benefit ratio over the four year period was 1:1.473 (IPM) and 1:1.018 (non-IPM).

Vegetable Crops

The practical application of IPM in vegetable cultivation is generally still limited, although simple packages do exist for some key pests. China is the only country in the region where IPM in major vegetable crops has been carried out through an exclusive technical body since late 1970s. In 1987, more than 1,07,000 ha of non-polluted vegetables were cultivated in 200 cities of 22 provinces, producing more than 6.4 million tonnes of vegetables. The Chinese have used the cultural control method as the foundation, while giving priority to biocontrol agents followed by judicious use of safer insecticides. During the past decade, efforts have been made to develop IPM technology in situations where chemical insecticides have failed to provide effective control in other countries of Asia.

The diamondback moth (DBM) has emerged as the most serious pest on cabbage, cauliflower and Chinese cabbage throughout South and Southeast Asia. The research conducted at the Asian Vegetable Research and Development Centre (AVRDC) on the control of DBM without pesticides has resulted in the development of an IPM programme. A collaborative Vegetable

Research Network for Southeast Asia (AVNET) was jointly established by Indonesia, Malaysia, the Philippines and Thailand in 1989. Another network, the South Asian Research Network (SAVERNET) has linked Bangladesh, Bhutan, India, Nepal, Pakistan and Sri Lanka since 1992. Both networks are supported by the Asian Development Bank with AVRDC as the executive agency and both have IPM of DBM as one of their sub-networks.

On the basis of decisions arrived at joint meetings of two networks, a master plan is developed for implementation in all the participating countries. It involves releases of a parasitoid, *Diadegma semiclausum*; a bacterial insecticide *Bacillus thuringiensis* or neem kernel extract sprays, pheromone traps and growing mustard as a trap crop. To date, parasitoid rearing facilities have been established in all Southeast Asian countries. Introduction and release of *D. semiclausum* has reduced the use of chemical insecticides by up to 86 per cent in the highlands of Malaysia. In Philippines, when cabbages were contaminated by over use of pesticides, IPM training resulted in farmers reducing from over 20 applications per season to three, including one treatment with an insect pathogen. It is estimated that in the Philippines highland area of Cordillera, extension and adoption of the IPM technology by all farmers in the 7000 ha cabbage area would result in a cost reduction of US$ 10.5 million over three cropping seasons. In Thailand, adoption of IPM technology resulted in a more than 145 per cent increase in net profits in IPM fields over non-IPM fields in crucifers. In Vietnam, the number of pesticide applications in cabbage have been reduced from 6 of chemical pesticides to 1 of Bt in IPM areas, in tomato from 14 (3 insecticides, 10 fungicides, 1 of 2, 4-D as growth stimulator) to no application in IPM.

Researchers at the Indian Institute of Horticultural Research (IIHR), Bangalore have developed an IPM combination to control DBM and it is becoming increasingly popular among the farmers. It involves growing of paired rows of bold-seeded Indian mustard as a trap crop at the beginning and after every 25 cabbage rows. Among the paired rows, the first is sown 15 days prior to cabbage planting while the second is sown 25 days after planting. This attracts upto 80-93 per cent of DBM for colonization. Depending upon the severity of infestation some attack of DBM and other pests is recorded on cabbage. To control these, 4 per cent neem seed kernel extract (NSKE) or neem soap (1%) or pongamia soap (1%) is applied at primordial or head initiation stage; 2-3 post-heading sprays may be applied at 10-15 days interval depending on population pressure. NSKE is safe to *Apanteles plutellae*, which is the dominant parasitoid of DBM found in the cabbage ecosystem. The insects colonizing Indian mustard may defoliate the entire plant and move on to cabbage. To control these, 0.1 per cent dichlorvos is applied at 9-15 days interval after first mustard sowing. This technology has been validated at three locations near Bangalore (50ha), Varanasi (15.6 ha) and Ranchi (6.3 ha) during 2001-2004. The overall cost : benefit ratios were 1:3.13 (IPM) and 1:2.11 (non-IPM).

Tomato is another vegetable crop in which successful IPM technology has been developed for the management of fruit borer, *Helicoverpa armigera* at IIHR. It involves growing of African tall marigold cv. Golden Age as a trap crop. Marigold nursery is raised 15 days earlier to tomato and 40-day old marigold and 25-day old tomato seedlings are simultaneously planted in the field. One row of marigold is alternated after every 16 tomato rows. Fruit borer moths lay eggs predominantly on the buds and flowers of marigold. It has also been observed that marigold has an added attraction potential for the serpentine leafminer, *Liriomyza trifolii*, which infests tomato. The tomato fruits may suffer about 10 per cent infestation in the trap crop fields. This infestation may be controlled by sprays of NPV at 250 larval equivalents (LE)/ha or by use of conventional insecticides on tomato crop. The marigold crop is not sprayed to maintain its attraction of fruit borer moths for oviposition and colonization. It also helps in conserving the natural enemies. The grown up *H. armigera* may be hand collected from the marigold flowers and put in a pail of water containing any insecticide solution. The above technology has been validated at three locations near Bangalore (40 ha), Varanasi (25.4 ha) and Ranchi (8.9 ha) during 2001-2004. The overall cost : benefit ratios were 1:1.41 (IPM) and 1:1.32 (non-IPM).

Plantation Crops

IPM considerations are especially important in tropical plantation crops, where, unlike annual crops, biological interactions have a chance to reach equilibrium or near equilibrium conditions. Adoption of IPM is feasible for the effective management of rhinoceros beetle, *Oryctesrhinoceros*, one of the major pests of coconut palm. The beetle suffers from natural epizootics produced by a fungus, *Metarhizium anisopliae* and a baculovirus of *Oryctes* (OBU). Release of baculovrius infested beetles has been successfully used for the biosuppression of the beetle in several countries including South Pacific Islands, Fiji, Mauritius, Seychelles, Papua New Guinea and Mauritius. In India, the damage by *O. rhinoceros* was substantially checked when the OBV infected beetles were released in Minicoy and Androth islands of Lakshadweep, Chhittilappilly in Trichur and Sipighat of Andaman islands. The release of *O. rhinoceros* beetles infected with Kerala isolate of the virus resulted in over 99 per cent reduction in palm damage within three years of augmentation in Andaman islands.

There have been reports of resurgence of the beetle in some other regions including Kerala and Western Samoa. There is also the possibility of development of resistance to baculovirus in Indonesia, East Java and South Sulawese. To over come these problems, an IPM has been proposed for the management of the beetle which includes planting legumes as cover crops to conceal the potential breeding sites of the beetle; extracting the adult beetles by means of a metal rod (about 0.5m long) with a hook at one end during peak period of pest abundance (June-September) from the infested sites; treatment of breeding places of the beetle with the entomopathogen, *M. anisopliae*; promoting the spread of the virus by leaving some dead standing palms; increasing the prevalence of the virus by releasing virus-infected beetles (10-15 per ha), preferably during dusk; and treating the breeding sites with carbaryl (0.01%) where biological control is not possible.

CONCLUSIONS

The burgeoning human population requires increased amount of food and fibre from a shrinking agricultural land base. During the next two decades, it is estimated that the world will have to feed approximately 2.5 billion more people, with most of the growth occurring in developing countries, resulting in a shortfall of 197 million tonnes of cereals. Much of this production will need to come from developing countries, which are showing stagnation in yield gains, dropping from 2.9 per cent during the green revolution to a predicted 1.2 per cent during the next 20 years. Asia is considered to be the home of green revolution, and will probably be the major player in the evergreen revolution. Increasing the rate of yield gain will rely heavily on integrated crop management (ICM), which is the economical production of high quality crops, giving priority to ecologicially safe methods of crop cultivation, minimising the undesirable side effects and use of crop protection products to enhance the safeguards to environment and human health. A central component of ICM is integrated pest management (IPM), which has moved from a peripheral position to the centre stage of agricultural insect pest control programmes during the last two decades.

Pest management practices may not be sustainable for a variety of reasons : (*i*) The control tactic may no longer be effective over time due to selection against pests that are susceptible to the tactic. (*ii*) The control tactic leads to disruption in the ecosystem that may result in further outbreak of the targete pest or outbreaks of new pests. (*iii*) The cost of the practice may be too expensive to maintain indefinitely. (*iv*) The practice may degrade the quality of human health, environment or agronomic resources over time. (*v*) New pest problems may arise due to introduction of pests or natural enemies that attack existing biological control agents and thereby, increase pest populations. (*vi*) As the types and the abundance of pests change due to crop intensification, the previous management tactics may not adequately control pest population. Therefore, pest management decisions will have to be taken, keeping in view the dynamics of pest population, sustainability of the management tactics, compatibility of the tactics and stability of the agroecosystem. As control measures are generally disruptive to the eocsystems, preventing the pest problem from arising in the first place, is preferable to control and promote sustainability. If pesticides are part of the IPM system, a pesticide resistance management strategy is essential, so that the target pest's susceptibility to pesticide does not decline over time. Other management tactics like pest-resistant cultivars, biological control agents and cultural practices are not necessarily sustaintable over time, which may require periodical monitoring. Farmers' own management practices need to be incorporated in IPM systems to make them more acceptable and sustainable.

According to a recent survey, only less than 5 per cent of the farmers follow IPM packages despite huge networks and efforts in various cropping systems. Virtually, there has been little effort to integrate the locally available and compatible management measures to develop economically viable IPM practices. India should formulate a National Pest and Pesticide Management Policy in order to achieve systematic reduction in the usage of pesticides over time, leading towards the larger goal of agricultural and environmental sustainability. Strict adoption of IPM in at least 75 per cent of the gross cropped area in every state of India, along with declaration of some sensitive ecological zones as pesticide free zones, where no pesticide marketing or use is allowed, should be one of the main policy components. The policy should take into consideration all aspects of pest management, including environmental and human health risks, and hazards to applicators and other associated social and economic issues of agricultural sustainability.

The gene revolution has added a new dimension to the pest management. The transgenic Bt crops have found wide acceptance among the farmers and the area under them has shown a dramatic increase every year. There were reports of reduction in pesticide load in agroecosystem in view of the in-built resistance of Bt crops to lepidopteran pests. However, recent reports indicate the emergence of sucking pests in serious proportions on cotton, which need to be controlled with applications of insecticides. Thus, the initial gains achieved from the introduction of gene technology in the form of reduction in pesticide use, seem to be offset.

Moreover, warning signals have come from USA where *Helicoverpa zea* has developed resistance to Bt cotton in Arkansas and Mississippi fields. There are also indications of development of resistance in *H. armigera* in parts of China. There are also occasional reports of survival of *H. armigera* on Bt cotton in Australia, particularly during flowering. In China, transgenic Bt rice has been reported to provide only a low level of control of *Sesamia inferens* during the late growing season, which may accelerate the evolution of resistance. It is, therefore, essential to take corrective measures, so that the farmers may not be trapped in 'gene treadmill' in the 21st century as had happened in case of 'pesticide treadmill' during the green revolution era.

The green revolution, which addressed the food-security crisis of the 1960s and 1970s, involved scientific innovation and active promotion of high-yielding varieties that could transform fertilizer inputs into grain production, but it created many ecological problems. The future IPM programmes should be so designed that they minimise the risks associated with the green revolution technology and maximise the benefits of the gene technology. The pest management system should blend the traditional ecological principles and frontier technologies. This implies that the IPM programmes should represent a sustainable approach to manage pests combining biological, chemical, cultural and biotechnological tools to ensure favourable economic, ecological and sociological consequences. For the evergreen revolution to succeed in feeding the world through sustainable cropping systems, a concerted and integrated effort on the part of scientists, farmers and policy makers will be required to create awareness and a political and regulatory environment in which sustainable technologies like IPM are embraced to meet the food and fibre needs of the 21st century.

SELECTED BIBLIOGRAPHY

Altieri M.A. and Nicholls, C.J. (2004) *Biodiversity and Pest Management in Agroecosystems.* Food Products Press, Binghamton, New York.

Anonymous (2019). *Package of Practices for cultivation of fruits.* Punjab Agric. Univ., Ludhiana, India

Atwal, A.S. and Dhaliwal, G.S. (2009) *Agricultural Pests of South Asia and Their Management.* Kalyani Publishers, New Delhi.

Bonning, B.C., Boughton, A.J., Jin, H. and Harrison, R.L. (2003) Genetic enhancement of baculovirus insecticides. In : R.K. Upadhyay (ed.) *Advances in Microbial Control of Insect Pests.* Kluwer Academic/Plenum Publishers, New York, pp. 109-125.

Chandi, A.K. and Singh, G. (2013) Behavioural physiology of susceptible and insecticide resistant populations of diamondback moth, *Plutella xylostella* (Linnaeus). *J. Insect Sci.***26** (1): 1-23.

Ciancio, A. and Mukherji, K.G. (eds) (2007) *General Concepts in Integrated Pest and Disease Management.* Springer, Dordrecht, The Netherlands.

Copping, L.G. (2001) *Biopesticide Manual.* British Crop Protection Council, Farnham, Surrey, U.K.

Culliney T. (2014) Crop Losses to Arthropods. In: Pimentel D., Peshin R. (eds) *Integrated Pest Management.* Springer, Dordrecht

David, B.V. (2002) *Elements of Economic Entomology,* Popular Book Depot, Chennai, India.

Dent, D. (2000) *Insect Pest Management.* CAB International, Wallingford, U.K.

Dhaliwal, G.S. and Arora, R. (2006) *Integrated Pest Management : Concepts and Approaches.* Kalyani Publishers, New Delhi.

Dhaliwal G.S. and Heinrichs, E.A. (eds) (1998) *Critical Issues in Insect Pest Management.* Commonwealth Publishers, New Delhi.

Dhaliwal, G.S. and Koul, O. (2007) *Biopesticides and Pest Management : Conventional and Biotechnological Approaches.* Kalyani Publishers, New Delhi.

Dhaliwal, G.S. and Koul, O. (2010) *Quest for Pest Management : From Green Revolution to Gene Revolution.* Kalyani Publishers, New Delhi.

Dhaliwal G.S. and Singh, B. (eds) (2000) *Pesticides and Environment.* Commonwealth Publishers, New Delhi.

Dhaliwal, G.S. and Singh, R. (eds) (2005) *Host Plant Resistance to Insects : Conventional and Biotechnological Approaches.* Panima Publishing Corporation, New Delhi.

Dhaliwal, G.S., Dhawan, A.K. and Singh, R. (2007) Biodiversity and ecological agriculture.: Issues and perspectives. *Indian J. Ecol.* **34**(2) : 100-109

Dhaliwal, G.S., Dilawari, V.K. and Saini, R.S. (1993) Host plant resistance to insects : Basic concepts. In : G.S. Dhaliwar and V.K. Dilawari (eds) *Advances in Host Plant Resistance to Insects*. Kalyani Publishers, New Delhi, pp. 1-30.

Dhaliwal, G.S., Singh, R. and Chhillar, B.S. (2006) *Essentials of Agricultural Entomology*. Kalyani Publishers, New Delhi.

Dhawan, A.K., Dhaliwal, G.S. and Chelliah, S. (2000) Insecticide-induced resurgence of insect pests in crop plants. In : G.S. Dhaliwal and B. Singh (eds) *Pesticides and Environment*. Commonwealth Publishers, New Delhi, pp. 86-127.

FAO (1967) *Report of the First Session of the FAO Panel of Experts on Integrated Pest Control*. Food and Agriculture Organization of the United Nations, Rome

Flexner, J.L. and Belnavis, D.L. (2000) Microbial insecticides. In : J.E. Recheigl and N.A. Recheigl (eds) *Biological and Biotechnological Control of Insect Pests*. Lewis Publisers, Boca Raton, Florida, pp. 35-61.

Grainge, M. and Ahmed, S. (1988) *Hand Book of Plants with Pest Control Properties*. John Wiley & Sons, New York.

Groombridge, R. (ed.) (1992) *Global Biodiversity Status of Earth's Living Resources*. Chapman & Hall, London.

Gupta, H.C.L., Kumar, A., Ameta, O.P. and Jain, S. (eds) (2005) *Alternatives to Chemical Pesticides in Pest Management*. Agrotech Publishing Academy, Udaipur.

Hagler, J.R. (2000) Biological control of insects. In : J.E. Recheigl and N.A. Recheigl (eds) *Insect Pest Management : Techniques for EnvironmentalProtection*. Lewis Publishers, Boca Raton, Florida, pp. 207-241.

Howse, P.E., Stevens, L.D.R. and Jones, O.T. (1998) *Insect Pheromones and Their Use in Pest Management*. Chapman & Hall, London.

Josan, A. and Singh, G. (2000) Sublethal effects of lufenuron on the diamondback moth, *Plutella xylostella* (Linnaeus). *Insect Sci. Applic.* **20** : 303-308.

Kalmakoff, J. and Ward, V.K. (2004) *Baculoviruses*. University of Otago, Dunedin, New Zealand (www.micro.msb.le.ac.uk/3035/kalmakoff/baculo/baculo.html)

Kogan, M. (1994) Plant resistance in pest management. In : R.L. Metcalf and W.H. Luckmann (eds) *Introduction to Insect Pest Management*.John Wiley & Sons, New York, pp. 73-127.

Kogan, M. (1998) Integrated pest management : Historical perspectives and contemporary developments. *Annu. Rev. Entomol.* **43** : 243-270.

Koppenhofer, A.M. and Kaya, H.K. (2002) Etomopathogenic nematodes and insect pest management. In : O. Koul and G.S. Dhaliwal (eds) *Microbial Biopesticides*. Taylor & Francis, London, pp. 277-305.

Koul, O. and Cuperus, G.W. (eds) (2007) *Ecologically Based Integrated Pest Management*. CAB International, Wallingford, U.K.

Koul, O. and Dhaliwal, G.S. (eds) (2001) *Phytochemical Biopesticides*. Harwood Academic Publishers, Amsterdam, The Netherlands.

Koul, O. and Dhaliwal, G.S. (eds) (2002) *Microbial Biopesticides*. Taylor & Francis, London.

Koul, O. and Dhaliwal, G.S. (eds) (2003) *Predators and Parasitoids*. Taylor & Francis, London.

Koul, O. and Dhaliwal, G.S. (eds) (2004) *Transgenic Crop Protection : Concepts and Strategies*. Science Publishers, Enfield (NH), USA.

Koul, O., Cuperus, G. and Elliott, N. (eds) (2008) *Areawide Pest Management : Theory and Implementation.* CAB International, Wallingford, UK.

Koul, O., Dhaliwal, G.S. and Cuperus, G.W. (eds) *Integrated Pest Management : Potential, Constraints and Challenges.* CAB International, Wallingford, UK.

Koul, O., Dhaliwal, G.S. and Kaul, V.K. (eds) (2009) *Sustainable Crop Protection : Biopesticide Strategies.* Kalyani Publishers, New Delhi.

Lewis, J.C. (2007) Ecological considerations for the use of entomopathogens in integrated pest management. In : O. Koul and G.W. Cuperus (eds) *Ecologically Based Integrated Pest Management.* CAB International, Wallingford, UK, pp. 37-54.

Luttrell, R.G. (2007) Ecological effects of chemical control practices : The environmental perspective. In : O. Koul and G.W. Cuperus (eds) *Ecologically Based Integrated Pest Management.* CAB International, Wallingford, pp. 111-153.

Maredia, K.M., Dakouo, D. and Mota-Sanchez, D. (eds) (2003) *Integrated Pest Management in the Global Arena.* CAB International, Wallingford, UK.

Maxwell, F.G., Jenkins, J.N. and Parrot, W.L. (1972) Resistance of plants to insects. *Adv. Agron.* **24** : 187-265.

Mehrotra, K.N. and Phokela, A. (2000) Insecticide resistance in insect pests : Current status and future strategies. In : G.S. Dhaliwal and B. Singh (eds) *Pesticides and Environment..* Commonwealth Publishers, New Delhi, pp. 39-85.

NAS (1969) *Principles of Plant and Animal Pest Control.* Vol. 3. *Insect Management and Control.* National Academy of Sciences, Washingtron, DC, USA.

Norris, R.F., CasWell-Chen, E.P. and Kogan, M. (2002) *Concepts in Integrated Pest Management.* Prentice-Hall of India Pvt. Ltd., New Delhi.

Oerke, E-C. (2006) Crop losses to pests. *J. Agric. Sci.* **144** : 31-43.

Onstad, D.W. (ed.) (2008) *Insect Resistance Management : Biology, Economics and Prediction.* Elsevier, London.

Painter, R.H. (1951) *Insect Resistance in Crop Plants.* The MacMillan Co., New York, USA.

Panda, N. and Khush, G.S. (1995) *Host Plant Resistance to Insects.* CAB International, Wallingford, UK.

Pedigo, P. (2002) *Entomology and Pest Management.* Prentice-Hall of India Pvt. Ltd., New Delhi.

Peshin, R. and Dhawan, A.K. (eds) (2009) *Integrated Pest Management : Innovation-Development.* Vol. 1. Springer, Dordrecht, The Netherlands.

Ramani, S., Bhumannavar, B.S. and Rabindra, R.J. (eds) (2004) *Quarantine Procedures and Facilities for Biological Control Agents.* Project Directorate of Biological Control, Bangalore.

Resilva, S. S., Hernandez, E. and Obra, G. B. (2019) Rediation sterilization of Mexican fruit fly, *Anastepha ludens* (Leow) based on pupal eye color. *Philippine Journal of Science,* **148** (1): 45-50.

Roy, N.K. (2002) *Chemistry of Pesticides.* CBS Publishers & Distributors, New Delhi.

Schoonhoven, L.M., van Loon, J.L.A. and Dicke, M. (2006) *Insect-Plant Biology.* Oxford University Press, New Delhi.

Sharma, H.C. (2009) *Biotechnological Approaches for Pest Management and Ecological Sustainability.* CRC Press, Boca Raton, Florida, USA.

Singh, A., Sharma, O.P. and Garg, D.K. (eds) (2005) *Integrated Pest Management : Principles and Applications.* Vol. 1. *Principles.* CBS Publishers & Distributors, New Delhi.

Singh, G. and Sidhu, H. S. (1992) Morphogenetic abnormalities of alatiform mustard aphid, *Lipaphis erysimi* following topical application of juvenile hormone analogues. *Insect Sci. Applic.* **11**: 69-72.

Singh, R.P. (2000) Botanicals in pest management : An ecological perspective. In : G.S. Dhaliwal and B. Singh (eds) *Pesticides and Environment*. Commonwealth Publishers, New Delhi, pp. 279-443.

Singh, S.P., Murphy, S.T. and Ballal, C.R. (eds) (2001) *Augmentative Biocontrol,* CABI Bioscience, UK and Project Directorate of Biological Control, Bangalore.

Smith, C.M. (2005) *Plant Resistance to Arthropods : Molecular and Conventional Approaches.* Springer, Dordrecht, The Netherlands.

Smith, R.F. (1978) History and complexity of integrated pest management. In : E.H. Smith and D. Pimentel (eds) *Pest Control Strategies*. Acdemic Press, New York, pp. 41-53.

Stern, V.M., Smith, R.F., van den Bosch, R. and Hagen, K.S. (1959) The integration of chemical and biological control of the spotted alfalfa aphid-I. The integrated control concept. *Hilgardia***29** : 81-101.

Stoner, K.A. (1996) Plant resistance to insects : A resource available for sustainable agriculture. *Biol. Agric. Hort.* **13** : 7-38.

Strong, D.R., Lawton, J.H and Southwood, T.R.E. (1984) *Insects on Plants : Community Patterns and Mechanisms*. Blackwell Scientific Publications, Oxford.

Thacker, J.R.M. (2002) *An Introduction to Arthropod Pest Control*. Cambridge University Press, Cambridge.

Tomlin C. (2000) *The Pesticide Manual*. British Crop Protection Council, Farnham,

Surrey, UK.

van Lenteren, J.C. (2000) Success in biological control of arthropods by augmentation of natural enemies. In : G. Gurr and S. Wratten (eds) *Biological Control : Measures of Success*. Kluwer Academic Publishers, Dordrecht, The Netherlands, pp. 77-103.

van Lenteren, J.C. (2012) BioControl, 57: 1. https://doi.org/10.1007/s10526-011-9395-1

Vincent, C., Goettel, M.S. and Lazarovits (eds) (2007) *Biological Control : A Global Perspective*. CAB International, Wallingford.

Vreysen, M.J.B., Robinson, A.S. and Hendrichs, J. (eds) (2007) *Area-Wide Control of Insect Pests: From Research to Field Implementation.* Springer, Dordrecht, The Netherlands.

☆☆☆☆☆

INDEX

C

D

E

F

G

H

I

J

K

L

M

N

O

P

Q

R

S

T

U

V

W

X

☆☆☆☆☆